From the Nation's Leading Social Studies Educator

Adventures

ENHANCE YOUR TEACHING AND HAVE MORE FUN HELPING

in

GRADE 2

GRADE 1

GRADE 3

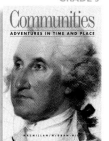

YOUR STUDENTS TO BECOME

Time

GRADE 4

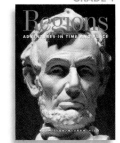

GRADE K

21ST CENTURY CITIZENS &

and

GRADE 6

GEOGRAPHY-LITERATE EXPLORERS

Place

GRADE 5

& HISTORY-SMART ADVENTURERS

MACMILLAN / McGRAW-HILL

Program Philosophy

Each and every one of the educators, authors, editors, and designers who created Macmillan/McGraw-Hill's *Adventures in Time and Place* share a deep commitment to provide

- rich, relevant content in all areas of social studies, at every grade level.
- geographic literacy skills for all students, created in partnership with the National Geographic Society.
- easy-to-use teaching materials with choices to suit different student learning styles and diversity in teaching styles.

Program Authorship

National Geographic Society, the world's premier authority on

NATIONAL GEOGRAPHIC SOCIETY geography and geography education, joins the same team that created the best-selling Macmillan/McGraw-Hill Social Studies Program **THE WORLD AROUND US** to bring you a brand new program... *Adventures in Time and Place.*

DR. BARRY BEYER
George Mason University
Fairfax, VA

DR. JAMES BANKS
University of Washington
Seattle, WA

JEAN CRAVEN
Albuquerque Public Schools
Albuquerque, NM

DR. GLORIA CONTRERAS
University of North Texas
Denton, TX

DR. MARY MCFARLAND
Parkway Public Schools
Creve Coeur, MO

DR. WALTER PARKER
University of Washington
Seattle, WA

DR. GLORIA LADSON-BILLINGS
University of Wisconsin-Madison
Madison, WI

Adventures in Rich, Relevant Content

1 **Active Citizenship is taught through skill lessons, interactive activities and concrete examples.**

- **Citizenship and Thinking Skills lessons help form the ideas, and thought processes needed by citizens of the 21st century.**

- **"Making a Difference" introduces everyday people who practice good citizenship in their communities.**

FROM GRADE 4 PUPIL EDITION

- **"Viewpoints" in grades 3–6 provide chances for students to discover and appreciate many different points of view — and to learn to handle differences.**

2 **Geographic Literacy for all students is assured through the co-authorship of the National Geographic Society.**

FROM GRADE 6 PUPIL EDITION

- **Geography's impact on history is emphasized to teach students the connection between them.**

- **Geography's five fundamental themes are the focus of skill lessons and features that support the ties among past and present people, places and events.**

- **Map skills are developed systematically for use in real life situations and for standardized test-taking.**

3 **History lessons link past and present in ways that make sense for all students — at all grade levels.**

- **More solid content at grades 1 and 2, with a narrative style that puts the "story" back in history, and lets you teach real history at primary grade levels.**

- **"Many Voices" from meaningful primary sources and literature are integrated in text features to bring history alive in words and pictures.**

- **Historical figures of many backgrounds, both famous and ordinary, provide reflections on our past from diverse perspectives.**

FROM GRADE 3 PUPIL EDITION

Designed for teacher-friendly classroom management

COMPONENTS CHART

	K HERE I AM	1 MY WORLD	2 PEOPLE TOGETHER	3 COMMUNITIES	4 REGIONS	5 UNITED STATES	6 WORLD
PUPIL EDITION		✔	✔	✔	✔	✔	✔
PUPIL EDITION ON CASSETTE		✔	✔	✔	✔	✔	✔
TEACHER'S MULTIMEDIA EDITION	✔	✔	✔	✔	✔	✔	✔
COLOR MAP TRANSPARENCIES		✔	✔	✔	✔	✔	✔
GRAPHIC ORGANIZERS				✔	✔	✔	✔
THEME BIG BOOKS	✔	✔	✔				
STICKERS FOR THEME BIG BOOKS	✔	✔	✔				
LITERATURE BIG BOOKS	✔	✔	✔				
GEO BIG BOOK	✔	✔	✔	✔			
PRACTICE BOOK		✔	✔	✔	✔	✔	✔
PROJECT BOOK	✔	✔	✔	✔			
GEOADVENTURES/ DAILY GEOGRAPHY ACTIVITIES		✔	✔	✔	✔	✔	✔
FLOOR MAP	✔	✔	✔	✔			
DESK MAPS	✔	✔	✔	✔	✔	✔	✔
OUTLINE MAPS		✔	✔	✔	✔	✔	✔
INFLATABLE GLOBE	✔	✔	✔	✔	✔	✔	✔
STUDENT ATLAS		✔	✔	✔	✔	✔	✔
SOURCES, STORIES AND SONGS/ READ ALOUD ANTHOLOGY	✔	✔	✔	✔	✔	✔	✔
SOURCES, STORIES AND SONGS CASSETTE	✔	✔	✔	✔	✔	✔	✔
CLASSROOM LIBRARY TRADE BOOKS	✔	✔	✔	✔	✔	✔	✔
CLASSROOM LIBRARY TEACHER'S GUIDES	✔	✔	✔	✔	✔	✔	✔
POSTERS	✔	✔	✔	✔	✔	✔	✔
UNIT TESTS		✔	✔	✔	✔	✔	✔
CHAPTER TESTS				✔	✔	✔	✔
PERFORMANCE ASSESSMENT	✔	✔	✔	✔	✔	✔	✔
VIDEODISCS	✔	✔	✔	✔	✔	✔	✔
VIDEOTAPES	✔	✔	✔	✔	✔	✔	✔
CD-ROM		✔	✔	✔	✔	✔	✔
INTERNET PROJECT HANDBOOK				✔	✔	✔	✔

Adventures in Time and Place...

COME ALONG AND BRING YOUR STUDENTS TO JOIN IN ON THE ADVENTURE!

Macmillan
McGraw-Hill

TEACHER'S *MULTIMEDIA* EDITION

Communities

ADVENTURES IN TIME AND PLACE

James A. Banks

Barry K. Beyer

Gloria Contreras

Jean Craven

Gloria Ladson-Billings

Mary A. McFarland

Walter C. Parker

NATIONAL GEOGRAPHIC SOCIETY

GEORGE WASHINGTON WAS OUR COUNTRY'S FIRST PRESIDENT. THIS PAINTING OF HIM BY THE ARTIST JOHN TRUMBULL IS IN THE WINTERTHUR MUSEUM IN DELAWARE. IS THERE A PLACE NAMED FOR GEORGE WASHINGTON NEAR YOUR COMMUNITY?

Macmillan McGraw-Hill

New York   Farmington

PROGRAM AUTHORS

Dr. James A. Banks
Professor of Education and Director of the Center for Multicultural Education
University of Washington
Seattle, Washington

Dr. Barry K. Beyer
Professor Emeritus, Graduate School of Education
George Mason University
Fairfax, Virginia

Dr. Gloria Contreras
Professor of Education
University of North Texas
Denton, Texas

Jean Craven
District Coordinator of Curriculum Development
Albuquerque Public Schools
Albuquerque, New Mexico

Dr. Gloria Ladson-Billings
Professor of Education
University of Wisconsin
Madison, Wisconsin

Dr. Mary A. McFarland
Instructional Coordinator of Social Studies, K–12, and Director of Staff Development
Parkway School District
Chesterfield, Missouri

Dr. Walter C. Parker
Professor and Program Chair for Social Studies Education
University of Washington
Seattle, Washington

NATIONAL
GEOGRAPHIC
SOCIETY
Washington, D.C.

PROGRAM CONSULTANTS

Daniel Berman
Asian Studies Specialist
Coordinator of Social Studies
Bedford Central Schools
Bedford, New York

Dr. Khalid Y. Blankinship
Affiliated Scholar, Council on Islamic Education
Fountain Valley, California
Assistant Professor of Religion
Temple University
Philadelphia, Pennsylvania

Dr. John Bodnar
Professor of History
Indiana University
Bloomington, Indiana

Dr. Roberto R. Calderón
Department of Ethnic Studies
University of California at Riverside
Riverside, California

Dr. Sheilah Clarke-Ekong
Asst. Professor, Department of Anthropology and Research Associate, Center for International Studies
University of Missouri, St. Louis
St. Louis, Missouri

Dr. John L. Esposito
Professor of Religion and International Affairs
Georgetown University
Washington, D.C.

Dr. Darlene Clark Hine
John A. Hannah Professor of History
Michigan State University
East Lansing, Michigan

Paulla Dove Jennings
Project Director
The Rhode Island Indian Council, Inc.
Providence, Rhode Island

Dr. Henrietta Mann
Professor of Native American Studies
University of Montana, Missoula
Missoula, Montana

Dr. Gary Manson
Professor, Department of Geography
Michigan State University
East Lansing, Michigan

Dr. Juan Mora-Torrés
Professor of Latin American History
University of Texas at San Antonio
San Antonio, Texas

Dr. Valerie Ooka Pang
Professor, School of Teacher Education
San Diego State University
San Diego, California

Dr. Joseph R. Rosenbloom
Professor, Classics Department
Washington University
St. Louis, Missouri

Dr. Joseph B. Rubin
Director of Reading
Fort Worth Independent School District
Fort Worth, Texas

Dr. Robert M. Seltzer
Professor of Jewish History
Hunter College of The City University of New York
New York, New York

Dr. Peter N. Stearns
Dean, College of Humanities and Social Studies
Carnegie Mellon University
Pittsburgh, Pennsylvania

GRADE-LEVEL CONSULTANTS

Rob Allen
Elementary School Teacher
Two Mile Prairie Elementary School
Columbia, Missouri

Elaine Culton Braucher
Third Grade Teacher
North Side Elementary School
Harrisburg, Pennsylvania

Glenda S. LaFavers
Third Grade Teacher
Windsor Elementary School
Amarillo, Texas

Mary Ann McGrath, Ph.D.
Third Grade Teacher
Lyman Elementary School
Lyman, South Carolina

Vicki Mirabal
Elementary School Teacher
Chelwood Elementary School
Albuquerque, New Mexico

Donna Yamada
Elementary School Teacher
Booksin Elementary School
San Jose, California

CONTRIBUTING WRITERS

Karen C. Baicker
New York, New York

Linda Scher
Raleigh, North Carolina

Acknowledgments

The publisher gratefully acknowledges permission to reprint the following copyrighted material:

From "The Channel Tunnel" by Adam Westgarth from **Connexions** by Adam Westgarth and others. Reprinted by permission.
From "Coyote Gets Turkey Up a Tree" from **And it is Still That Way** by Tina Naiche-collected by Byrd Baylor. Reprinted by permission.
From "The Express Train" **More Sounds We Found** by Barbara Mariconda and Denise Puccio. Copyright 1988 by Wide World Music, Inc. (ASCAP), a division of Shawnee Press, Inc. International Copyright Secured. All rights reserved. Reprinted by permission. From "The Light at the End of the Chunnel" reprinted by permission of National Geographic Society. From **Uncle Jed's Barbershop.** Text copyright 1993 by Margaree King Mitchell. Illustrations copyright 1993 by James Ransome. Simon and Schuster. "Open Range" (Poem) from **Cowboys and Indians** by Kathryn and Bryon Jackson. Copyright 1948 by Simon & Schuster, Inc. and Artists and Writers Guild.

(continued on page R40)

Macmillan/McGraw-Hill

*A Division of The **McGraw·Hill** Companies*

CONTENTS

UNIT TWO

64

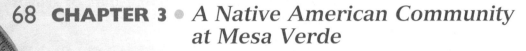

Looking Back to the Past

v

REFERENCE SECTION

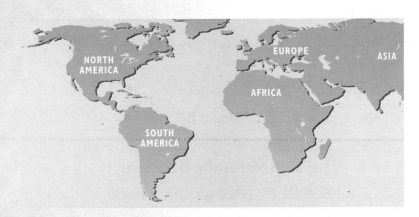

FEATURES

SKILLS

Geography Skills

Thinking Skills

Study Skills

CITIZENSHIP

Making a Difference

Viewpoints

LEGACIES

CHARTS, GRAPHS, & DIAGRAMS

TIME LINES

MAPS

INTRODUCING THE TEXT

PAGES XII–XIII

Point out that the Table of Contents lists all the different parts of the textbook in page order.

Look at Your World On pages G2–G3 students are introduced to the five themes of geography: *Region, Place, Movement, Human/Environment Interaction, Location.*

Suggested Question

● **What do the pictures on the sample page show?** *(They show an airplane and a desert in the Southwest. Point out that the pictures illustrate Movement and Region, two of the five themes of geography.)*

A Typical Lesson Have students examine the excerpt from *Chapter 6, Lesson 1: Ben Franklin and Philadelphia.*

Suggested Question

● **How does Lesson 1 begin?** *(with a Read Aloud)*

Discussing Special Features Within Lessons Recurring features within lessons expand on the text and relate it to other content areas. *Many Voices* features excerpts from primary sources as well as literature, art, and music. *Links* engages students in cross-curriculum activities. *Did You Know?* offers relevant facts of interest.

Suggested Question

● **What is the Many Voices selection shown in the picture?** *("America")*

Discussing Infographics Point out that *Infographics* combine pictures and words.

Suggested Question

● **What does the sample Infographic show?** *(A Day with the Anasazi)*

YOUR TEXTBOOK at a glance

Your book is *Communities: Adventures in Time and Place.* It has twelve chapters and a special section, as well as many other parts to study and enjoy.

Special pages from National Geographic bring you ideas and Adventures in geography.

◀ **Some lessons have Links or Did You Know—activities and facts to share. You will also see Many Voices—songs, writing, and art by many people.**

Additional Features of the Textbook

UNIT OPENER Have students turn to the *Unit Opener* on pp. 2–3. Point out how the visuals illustrate the Unit's theme.

CHAPTER OPENER Have students examine the *Chapter 1* and *5 Openers* on pp. 6–7 and 116–117. Ask students to distinguish the information shown in *Chapter 1* from the information shown in *Chapter 5.*

VISUAL AIDS Have students identify visual aids included throughout the text such as: illustrations, charts, graphs, diagrams, time lines, and maps. (Note that with the exception of illustrations, all the visual aids are listed in the Table of Contents.)

ook at the special lessons
nd features shown at
ght. They build your
kills and bring you
teresting subjects from
he past and present.

eet Ben Franklin

e in Philadelphia was talking
person—Benjamin Franklin.
d to be everywhere, doing just
rything.
anklin grew up in Boston,
setts, in a family of 17 children. When
, his father sent him to live and work
lder brother James, a printer. Ben
arned a lot about printing. But he did
ong with his brother. When he was
for Philadelphia.
e arrived in Philadelphia in 1723, Ben
exciting city. He talked to everyone
made many friends. He loved his new
e set out to make it even better.

young man, Ben
klin learned to use
printing press.

147

▲
Each lesson begins with a **Read Aloud**
selection. A **Read to Learn** question and
a list of important words, people, and places
will guide your reading.

Your book has a **Reference
Section** at the end. Use it to
look up words, people, and
places as you study them.
▼

xiii

Additional Features of the Textbook

ADVENTURES WITH NATIONAL GEOGRAPHIC Following each unit opener is this two-page spread, which describes and illustrates adventures young people have had. Have students examine these features, such as the one on pp. 4–5.

CHAPTER SUMMARIES AND REVIEWS Have students examine a typical *Chapter Review,* such as the one on pp. 94–95. Ask students to identify the types of information (for example, vocabulary and facts) and skills (thinking and writing) they are asked to review.

UNIT REVIEWS Have students examine a typical Unit Review, such as the one on pp. 138–139. Explain to students that a Unit Review will help them refresh their memories about information covered in the unit.

REFERENCE SECTION Have students examine the sections not covered above: Atlas (R4–R11), Gazetteer (R14–R18), Glossary (R23–R31), Index (R32–R39).

Discussing Skills Lessons Tell students that their textbook includes *Thinking Skills, Geography Skills,* and *Study Skills* lessons.

Suggested Question
● *What kind of sample Skills Lesson is shown?* (a Geography Skills lesson)

Discussing Legacy Use the subhead on the sample page to help students understand the concept of a legacy.

Suggested Question
● *What legacy does the picture show?* (our country's flag)

Discussing Citizenship Have students examine the *Citizenship* features in the Table of Contents. Point out that *Citizenship* features are of two types: *Viewpoints* and *Making a Difference.*

Suggested Question
● *What type of Citizenship feature is shown on this page?* (a Viewpoints feature)

Exploring the Reference Section Have students examine the reference section, which begins on p. R2.

Suggested Question
● *What parts are in the reference section?* (Atlas, Dictionary of Geographic Terms, Gazetteer, Biographical Dictionary, Glossary, Index)

Explain that the *Biographical Dictionary* alphabetically lists the names of some of the people discussed in the textbook. The dictionary also provides a brief description and an illustration of each person. The *Dictionary of Geographic Terms* lists different types of land and bodies of water along with corresponding definitions.

Sum up by noting that all these features will help students better understand the history and geography of the United States.

Suggested Questions
● *Where would you look for information and illustrations of people discussed in your textbook?* (in the Biographical Dictionary)

● *Where would you look for definitions and illustrations of geographic words?* (in the Dictionary of Geographic Terms)

LOOK AT YOUR WORLD

PAGES G2–G3

Lesson Overview
Geographers divide the study of geography into five basic themes.

Lesson Objective
★ Describe the five themes of geography.

1 PREPARE

MOTIVATE Initiate a general discussion of geography by writing the word on the chalkboard and asking students what it brings to mind. Elicit responses that culminate in a definition of geography as the study of Earth's land, water, weather, plants, and animals.

SET PURPOSE Tell students that geographers divide the study of geography into five categories, or themes: *Region, Place, Location, Movement, People and Their Environment*. Define any words that may be unfamiliar, such as *environment*. Then write the five themes in a geography word web on the board. Have students copy the web so they can refer to it as they proceed through this book.

2 TEACH

Discussing the Five Themes Add the definitions of the five themes to the word web.

Region: an area with common features that set it apart from other areas;

People and Their Environment: the relationship between people and their surroundings;

Place: a description of an area based on its natural and/or human-made features;

Location: the exact or relative location of a place;

Movement: the movement of people, goods, and ideas around the world.

Resource **REMINDER**

Desk Maps
Poster

How do people travel from one place to another?

What are some things that help make the Southwest special?

G2

THE FIVE THEMES AND THE NATIONAL GEOGRAPHY STANDARDS

Geography encompasses all the places and people in the world, and all the interconnections among them. To help organize and convey geographic knowledge, the five themes of geography were introduced in 1984. The popularity of the themes set the stage for a more comprehensive framework—the National Geography Standards.

How do the themes and the standards relate to each other? The themes are content organizers; they provide a framework for structuring and focusing lessons. The standards identify the specific subject matter that students should master. The themes can be used in teaching any of the material in the standards.

For more information about the standards or to order a copy of the document *Geography for Life: National Geography Standards 1994*, contact: National Geographic Society, P.O. Box 98171, Washington, D.C. 20013–8171.

What makes this place different from other places?

How does mail get to exactly the right place?

What foods do people get from trees?

The following questions can help students understand the five themes of geography and relate them to the local community.

Suggested Questions

● ***In what part of the United States do we live? What are some things that make it special?*** *(Help students identify the region in which they live and its distinguishing characteristics.)* Region

● ***What is one way our surroundings affect us? What is one way we affect our surroundings?*** *(Students can mention the interaction between people and local weather, land, water, and/or natural resources.)* People and Their Environment

● ***How would you describe the place where you live?*** *(As students answer the question, guide them to distinguish between natural and human-made features.)* Place

● ***How could you help a visitor find your home?*** *(You could provide your address; you could explain where your home is in relation to other places.)* Location

● ***Think of a place you want to visit. How could you get there?*** *(On the board, list the forms of transportation mentioned.)* Movement

Examining the Pictures Have students look at the pictures, read the questions, and try to predict the answers. Tell them that they will be able to check their predictions as they work through the book. Then have students use what they learned about the five themes of geography to decide which theme belongs with each picture. *(p. G2 top:* Movement, *bottom:* Region; *p. G3 top:* Place, *Center:* Location; *bottom:* People and Their Environment)

3 CLOSE

SUM IT UP
Have students use their own words to define the five themes of geography. Then suggest that they add the definitions to their word webs.

Write About It Have students use the five themes of geography to write a paragraph describing their community.

Background INFORMATION

DEVELOPING GEOGRAPHY SKILLS
The following activity is designed to help students become familiar with different aspects of geography.

● Have each student list three places anywhere in the world that they would like to visit.

● Have students locate the three places they list on their *Desk Maps.* Provide assistance, if necessary.

● Then begin a discussion with students about each of the places they chose. Topics for discussion may include: which two places look farthest from each other; what the climate of each place may be like; and how the student might travel to each place.

Part I: Using Globes

INTRODUCE

Discuss the words in the *Vocabulary* list that students may already know. Then write the definitions of the other words on the chalkboard.

DISCUSS

Invite students to examine a globe, such as the *Inflatable Globe*. Help them identify the continents and the oceans. Encourage students to use the globe to quiz each other. (Example: "Are we closer to the North Pole or the South Pole?")

EXTEND

Have students compare and contrast globes and maps. Ask them to suggest situations where reading one or another might be preferable. (Students may note that because a globe is a three-dimensional model of Earth, it shows more accurately the sizes and shapes of the continents and the oceans.)

Resource REMINDER
Practice Book: *pp.1–5*
Geo Adventures *Daily Geography Activities*
Inflatable Globe
Geo Big Book

Reviewing
GEOGRAPHY SKILLS

PART 1
Using Globes

VOCABULARY
North Pole
South Pole
equator

What are globes?
- A globe is a small model, or copy, of Earth.
- Find the North Pole and the South Pole on the globe. The North Pole is the farthest place north on Earth. The South Pole is the farthest place south on Earth.
- Find the equator on the globe. The equator is an imaginary line circling Earth, halfway between the North Pole and the South Pole. On a globe the equator is shown as a real line. The equator divides Earth in half. At the top is the northern half. What half is at the bottom? southern half

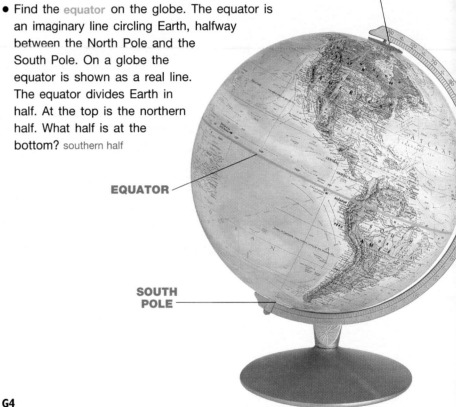

NORTH POLE

EQUATOR

SOUTH POLE

G4

Background INFORMATION

SUGGESTIONS FOR USING THE SECTION
The following section is in three parts:

- Using Globes, p. G4
- Using Maps, pp. G5–G9
- Different Kinds of Maps, pp. G10–G11

This section contains geography skills that students should be familiar with from previous years of study. Use the section to assess students' knowledge of basic map and geography skills. Encourage students to reread this section or specific parts of it throughout the year in order to explore and reinforce key concepts related to basic geography skills.

Background INFORMATION

HOW TO USE THE GLOBE
After students have examined the globe, ask them a series of questions to help hone map reading skills. You may want to ask:

- Is Canada closer to the North Pole or the South Pole? *(North Pole)*
- Is Canada is the northern or southern half of Earth? *(northern)*
- What are the names of two continents located on the southern half of Earth? *(Australia, South America, Africa, or Antarctica)*

PART 2
Using Maps

VOCABULARY

continent   map key   locator
ocean   cardinal directions
symbol   compass rose

What are maps?

- A map is a flat drawing of a place. This map shows Earth's seven continents. A continent is a very large body of land. Find the continents on the map. What are they called? North America, South America, Europe, Africa, Asia, Australia, Antarctica

- The map also shows Earth's four oceans. An ocean is a very large body of salt water. Find and name the oceans. Pacific Ocean, Atlantic Ocean, Arctic Ocean, Indian Ocean

More Practice

There are other maps that show continents and oceans in this book. For examples, see pages 58, 59, and R10-R11.

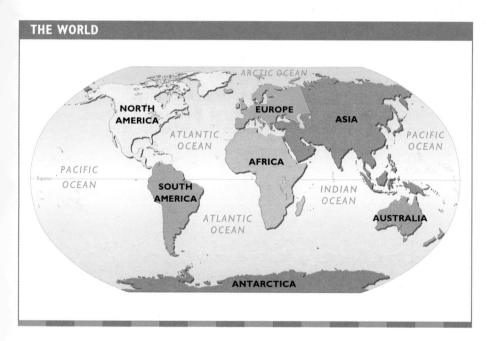

THE WORLD

G5

Part II: Using Maps

INTRODUCE

Introduce each of the *Vocabulary* words at the top of the page. Tell students that these concepts will be explained more clearly on the following pages.

Ask students to copy the *Vocabulary* words on a sheet of paper. Have them write the definition of each word as they learn it in this lesson.

Then have students look through the *Atlas* or the *Geo Big Book* to examine different kinds of maps. Although students may not be familiar with the name of every kind of map, they can point out differences and similarities between them.

DISCUSS

Be sure students understand that the map on this page represents the same places on Earth as those that are represented by the globe. Ask them to compare the map to the globe to note how three-dimensional space is shown on a flat page. Then invite them to discuss any questions they may have about the continents and oceans.

Background INFORMATION

UNDERSTANDING THE MAPS

Reinforce the text by inviting students to quiz each other about the information on this page. You may wish to provide starter questions such as the following:

- What is a map? *(a flat drawing of a place)*
- What does the map on this page represent? *(Earth)*
- What is a continent? *(a very large body of land)*
- How many continents are there? *(seven)*
- On which continent do we live? *(North America)*
- Which continents does the equator cross? *(South America, Africa)*

- What is an ocean? *(a very large body of salt water)*
- How many oceans are there? *(four)*
- Which oceans surround South America and North America? *(Pacific and Atlantic oceans)*
- Which ocean is at the North Pole? *(Arctic Ocean)*
- Which ocean separates Africa and Australia? *(Indian Ocean)*

Tell students that many maps are based on aerial photographs—photos taken from the air that show what an area looks like when seen from above. Then explain that the map on p. G7 was based on the aerial photograph shown on this page.

Have students examine the photograph and compare it to the map. Help them link the symbols on the map with real objects in the photo.

Be sure students understand that although symbols may represent different things on different maps, a color or picture is usually closely related to the real thing it represents. Point out that on most maps, the symbol for water is blue and the symbol for land is brown and/or green. Explain that the symbols on this map are picture symbols. They are small pictures of the things they represent.

Why do maps use symbols?

- Look at the map at the top of the next page. It is a map of the real place shown in the photo above. How are the map and the photo alike? How are they different? Answers may vary.

- Many maps have symbols. A symbol is something that stands for something else. The symbols on a map stand for real things and places. What symbols do you see on the map? pool, house, tree, sidewalk, road

- Symbols can be lines, shapes, colors, or pictures. The same kind of symbol sometimes stands for different things on other maps. The color green, for example, could stand for parks on one map and farmland on another. What might a picture of a cow stand for? Answers may vary, possibly including cows, a farm, or a dairy.

G6

Background INFORMATION

HOW TO USE THE MAPS

Invite students to examine the above photograph and the map on the facing page. Help them compare and contrast the map and the neighborhood it represents. Then ask students the following questions:

- What does the picture above show? *(a neighborhood with houses, trees, sidewalks, streets, and pools)*

- What does the map on the following page show? *(the same neighborhood)*

- How is the map different from the picture? *(The map shows symbols of the real things.)*

- What is a symbol? *(something that stands for something else)*

- What are some common symbols used on maps? *(lines, shapes, colors, pictures)*

- What is an example of a color symbol on a map? *(blue might stand for water)*

- What might green stand for on a map? *(It might stand for farmland, parks, or forests.)*

Neighborhood Map

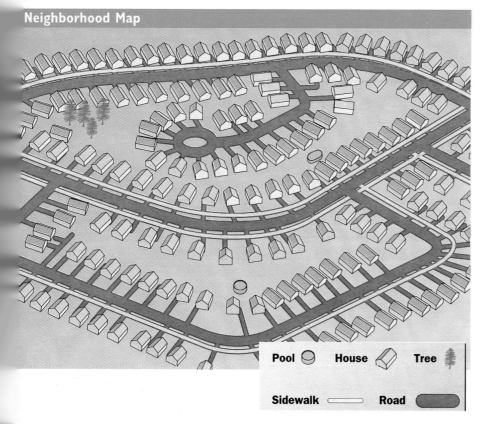

Pool ⬭	House ◿	Tree 🌲
Sidewalk ▭	Road ▬	

Why read a map title and map key?

- A map title tells you what the map shows. What is the title of this map? Neighborhood Map

- To find out what symbols on a map mean, you can look at a map key. A map key tells what the symbols on a map stand for. Look at the map on this page. What does the blue circle stand for? What symbol means tree? pool; a tree

More Practice

You can practice working with symbols and map keys on many maps in this book. For examples, see pages 25, 249, and 302.

Background INFORMATION

HOW TO USE THE MAPS

Have students use the information on this page to answer the following questions.

- What information does a map title give us? *(The title tells us the area the map shows and the kind of information the map includes.)*
- What does the title of this map tell us? *(This is a map of a neighborhood.)*
- What is a map key? *(a box on a map that shows the map symbols and explains what they mean)*
- How is a map key helpful? *(It helps us recognize symbols on a map so that we can locate different items and places.)*

- What symbols can you see in the map key? *(pool, house, tree, sidewalk, road)*
- What symbol on the map represents a pool? *(a round blue shape)*
- How many pools are in this neighborhood? *(one)*
- How many trees are in this neighborhood? *(four)*
- If you wanted to know why an area of a map had stripes, where would you look? *(on the map key)*

Explain that a map key can usually be found in a box in or near a corner of a map. In the map key, we find symbols used on the map and an explanation of what they mean. Be sure students understand that map keys are not interchangeable and that every map will have its own special key.

Have students examine the map and the map key. Invite them to suggest other places that might be included on a neighborhood map. (Examples: community center, school, train track, fire hydrant, playgound.) Ask students what symbols they would use to represent those places.

This review of cardinal directions will help students prepare for a lesson on intermediate directions in *Chapter 2,* pp. 50–51. Invite students to read the text and examine the compass rose at the bottom of the page.

When students are locating their home state on the map on the next page, explain that a compass rose can be used with any map. On some maps, an arrow pointing north is used instead of a compass rose. Help students understand how the three other cardinal directions can be determined once north is established.

Invite students to hold their texts so that north on the compass rose faces magnetic north. Then have them use cardinal directions to describe the locations of various objects in the classroom.

What are cardinal directions?

- There are four cardinal directions. These directions are north, south, east, and west.

- North is the direction toward the North Pole. When you face the North Pole, you are facing north. South is directly behind you. East is to your right. Which direction is to your left? west

What is a compass rose?

- How do you find directions if a map does not show the North Pole? You can use a small drawing on a map, called a compass rose, to help you find directions.

- Look at the picture of the compass rose below. The compass rose shows cardinal directions. North is shown by **N**. What letters stand for east, south, and west? Find your home state on the map of the United States at the bottom of the next page. What lies to the north of your state? What lies east, south, and west? E, S, W; answers will vary depending on state

More Practice

You can practice finding directions and using a compass rose on most maps in this book. For examples, see pages 126, 243, and 257.

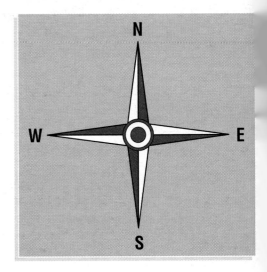

Background INFORMATION

HOW TO USE THE COMPASS ROSE

After students have read the text and examined the compass rose on this page, you may wish to use the following questions to facilitate class discussion:

- How many cardinal directions are there? *(four)*

- What are the names of the cardinal directions? *(north, south, east, west)*

- In which direction are you facing when you face the North Pole? *(north)*

- Which direction is to your right when you face the North Pole? to your left? *(east; west)*

- Which direction is behind you when you are facing north? *(south)*

- When would it be helpful to know the four cardinal directions? *(when you are traveling someplace unfamiliar, when you want to locate a place on a map or in the real world)*

- What is a compass rose? *(a small drawing on a map that shows the four cardinal directions)*

- Look at the map on the following page. In what direction is Mexico from your state? *(south)*

- In what direction is Canada from Texas? *(north)*

- What country is east of Mexico? *(Cuba)*

- What body of water is west of the Atlantic Ocean? *(Pacific Ocean)*

What is a locator?

A locator is a small map included on a bigger, or main, map. A locator shows where the area in the main map is located. The area of the main map is shown in red on the locator. Find the locator on the map below.

Study the locator. What does it show? Find the red area on the locator. On which continent is the red area? What country does the red area show? Now look at the main map. What does it show? Earth; North America; United States; United States

More Practice

There are other maps with locators in this book. For examples, see pages 53, 79, and 293.

Have students read the text and study the locator map in the upper right-hand corner. Be sure students understand that this locator map helps us understand where the United States is on Earth. The locator also helps us understand where Alaska is in relation to the rest of the United States.

EXTEND

As a class project, have students create a map of your classroom. Explain that they will include the map elements they have reviewed in this lesson.

Before beginning, ask four groups to prepare sketches and research information. Have one group create symbols for classroom objects, doors, and windows and sketch them in a map key. Ask another group to sketch a classroom map to approximate scale. A third group can use a compass to determine magnetic north, sketch a compass rose showing the cardinal directions, and show the class how the map must be placed on the page. A fourth group can sketch a locator map that shows the school and your classroom within it.

When the sketches are complete, provide students with posterboard, pencils, and markers. Invite them to work together to draw the map, map key, compass rose, and locator.

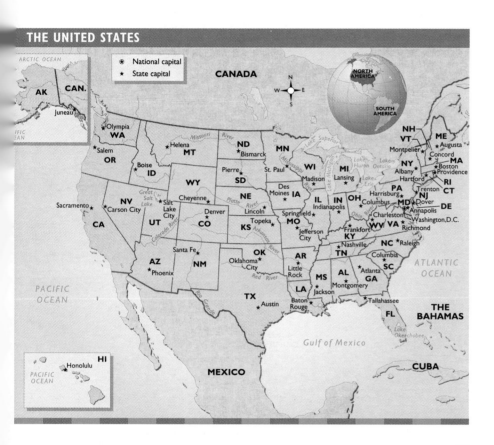

THE UNITED STATES

G9

Background Information

HOW TO USE THE MAP

Students can review the information in this section by making up a quiz based on the map, map key, compass rose, and locator shown on this page. You may wish to provide the following questions to help students get started:

- What area does the map show? How do you know this? *(We can read the title, The United States, and we can see the area on the locator map.)*
- What continent is south of the United States? How do you know? *(South America; by looking at the locator map)*
- What direction would you travel if you wanted to go from Washington State to Alaska? *(north)*

- What is the capital of our country? How do you know? *(We know from looking at the map key that the capital of our country is Washington, D.C.)*
- What is the capital of our state? How do you know? *(Answers will vary; from looking at the map key.)*
- In what direction would we travel to get from our state to Washington, D.C.? *(Answers will vary depending upon the location of your state.)*

Part III: Different Kinds of Maps

INTRODUCE

Tell students that there are many different kinds of maps. For example, the *Atlas* and *Geo Big Book* include political maps, which show boundaries, and physical maps, which show Earth's physical features.

Challenge students to think of other kinds of maps and what they show. (Examples: road and transportation maps show routes, product maps show where things are grown or made, weather maps show weather patterns.)

Then point out the *Vocabulary* words and encourage students to share what they know about each kind of map.

DISCUSS

Have students explain what we can learn from the map key (what the colors on the map mean and what the capital of North Carolina is) and the locator map (where North Carolina is in relation to the rest of the United States).

Then have students use the map key to write three questions about the landform map. Students can exchange questions with a partner and then check each other's answers.

PART 3
Different Kinds of Maps

VOCABULARY
landform map
grid map

What is a landform map?
- The map below is a landform map. This kind of map shows the different landforms on Earth. Many landform maps use different colors to show the different kinds of land. Look at the map key. What color shows mountains? What other landforms are shown? dark orange; hills and plains

More Practice
There is another landform map in this book. See pages 40-41.

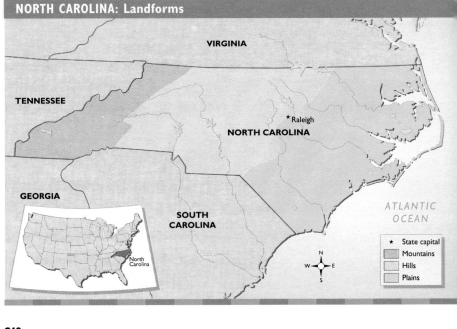

NORTH CAROLINA: Landforms

G10

Background INFORMATION

HOW TO USE THE MAPS
Use the following questions to review the material on this page:

- What is a landform map? *(a map that shows different landforms on Earth)*
- What does this map show? *(landforms in North Carolina)*
- What symbols are used on this landform map? *(colors and a star for the state capital)*
- What is the capital of North Carolina? *(Raleigh)*
- What is the land like in the eastern part of the state? *(There are plains in the eastern part.)*
- What is the land like in the western part of the state? *(There are mountains in the west.)*
- What is the land like in the central part of the state? *(There are hills in the center.)*
- If you were in Raleigh, in which direction would you travel to get to the mountains? *(west)*

What is a grid map?

When you visit a new place, a grid map can help you find your way around. A grid map uses a set of boxes, or grid, to locate places.

Look at the grid map below. The boxes on a grid map have letters and numbers. All the boxes in the first row across are As. All the boxes in the first row down are 1s. So the first box to the left in the top row is A1. What is the second box in the second row? What place is located in C3? B2; zoo

More Practice

There are other grid maps shown in this book. For examples, see pages 176–177 and 179.

Encourage students to use their fingers as guides when reading the grid map. Suggest that students use one finger to trace the number column down or up and one finger on the other hand to trace the letter column across.

Have students work with partners to practice reading the grid map. They can take turns finding landmarks and naming their grid locations.

EXTEND

Have students work on the following map projects and share their completed work with the class.

One group of students can create a landform map of your schoolyard or playground. Remind them to choose three or four symbols to represent landforms and to include them in a map key. Remind them also to include a locator map and compass rose.

A second group can carefully draw grid lines over the classroom map that students made as an extension activity at the end of Part II of this section (Extend, p. G9). Students can number and letter the rows and columns and practice locating items on the grid map.

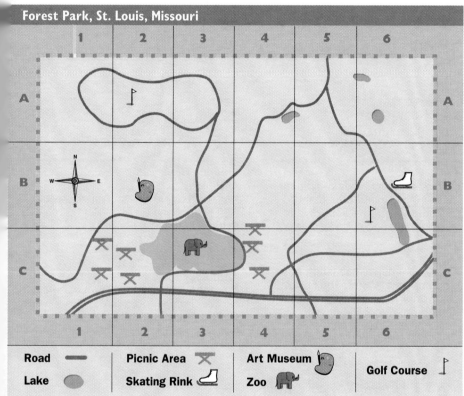

Forest Park, St. Louis, Missouri

| Road | — | Picnic Area | Art Museum | Golf Course |
| Lake | | Skating Rink | Zoo | |

G11

Background INFORMATION

HOW TO USE THE MAPS

Use the following questions to help students complete their review of grid maps:

- What is a grid map? (a map that has numbered and lettered lines to help find things and places)
- When might you use a grid map? (when you visit a new city or park and want to find your way around)
- What area does the grid map show? (Forest Park, St. Louis, Missouri)
- In what box is the skating rink? (B6)
- In what boxes are there picnic areas? (C1, C2, C4, and B4)
- In what two directions would you walk to travel from the zoo to the art museum? (north and west)

WHERE TO ORDER MAPS

Many kinds of maps, including contour maps of any area of the United States, can be ordered at nominal prices by calling the U.S. Geological Survey (USGS) at (800) USA-MAPS. You can also write to them at 12201 Sunrise Valley Drive, Mail Stop 119-X, Reston, VA 22092.

Living in Communities

PAGES 2–63

UNIT OVERVIEW

There are many types of communities in the United States and around the world. They vary from rural and small town to suburban and urban. Each community has beautiful landforms and bodies of water that provide us with food, jobs, and fun. People work together to protect their environment so that they can continue to enjoy where they live.

Adventures with National Geographic pp. 4–5

UNIT PLANNING GUIDE

CHAPTER	SUGGESTED PACING	CHAPTER OVERVIEW	CHAPTER RESOURCES
1 **Understanding Communities** pp. 6–33	16–18 days	There are many types of communities in the United States and around the world. People live in rural, urban, and suburban areas.	*Practice Book* pp. 6–9 *Anthology* pp. 2–14 *Project Book* pp. 3–5 ● *Transparency:* 6 *Technology:* Videodisc/Video Tape, CD-ROM *Outline Maps* pp. 4–5, 7, 9 *Geo Big Book* pp. 4–5
2 **Communities and Geography** pp. 34–61	16–18 days	Every community has landforms and bodies of water. The land and water provide food, jobs, and fun. People work together to protect their environment.	*Practice Book* pp. 11–15 *Anthology* pp. 15–24 *Project Book* pp. 6–7 ● *Transparency:* 7–8 *Technology:* Videodisc/Video Tape, CD-ROM *Outline Maps* pp. 2–3, 6 *Geo Big Book* pp. 8–9 ● *Inflatable Globe*

ASSESSMENT OPPORTUNITIES

Internet CONNECTION

The **Internet Project Handbook** and the Home Page at **http://www.mmh-school.com** contain on-line student activities related to this unit.

UNIT ASSESSMENT
Unit Review pp. 62–63
 Unit Projects pp. 62–63

Assessment Book
 Unit Test Unit 1 Test
 Performance Assessment Unit 1

DAILY ASSESSMENT
Geo Adventures Daily Geography Activities

CHAPTER ASSESSMENT
Meeting Individual Needs pp. 7, 13, 15, 21, 23, 29, 35, 43, 45, 49, 51, 56, 59
Write About It pp. 13, 15, 21, 29, 43, 45, 49, 56
Chapter Reviews pp. 32–33, 60–61

Assessment Book
 Chapter Tests Ch. 1 Test, Ch. 2 Test
 Performance Assessments Ch. 1, Ch. 2

ANNOTATED BIBLIOGRAPHY

Classroom Library

■ Garza, Carmen Lomas. *Family Pictures*. San Francisco, CA: Children's Book Press, 1990. This illustrated book describes daily life and traditions of a Mexican family living in Texas.

Student Books

Gibbons, Gail. *Surrounded by Sea: Life on a New England Fishing Island*. Boston, MA: Little, Brown and Co., 1991. Contemporary everyday life in a New England fishing village is described and illustrated. **(Easy)**

Griffith, Helen. *Granddaddy's Place*. New York: Greenwillow Books, 1987. Janetta has difficulty adjusting to her grandfather's farm since she has only known life in the city. **(Average)**

Ikuhara, Yoshiyuki. *Mexico*. Milwaukee, WI: Gareth Stevens Publishing Co., 1987. This book describes a young girl's life with her family in Mexico. **(Challenging)**

■ Jakobsen, Kathy. *My New York*. Boston, MA: Little, Brown and Co., 1993. This tour of New York City is done with detailed, beautiful illustrations. **(Average)**

■ Locker, Thomas. *Where the River Begins*. New York: Dial Books, 1984. Two young boys and their grandfather go on a camping trip to find the source of a river. **(Average)**

■ MacLachlan, Patricia. *All the Places to Love*. New York: HarperCollins, 1994. A young boy describes his favorite places and memories on his grandparent's farm. **(Average)**

Martel, Cruz. *Yagua Days*. New York: Dial Press, 1972. A young boy visits Puerto Rico for the first time and learns about the community where his family came from. **(Average)**

■ Provensen, Alice, and Martin Provensen. *Town and Country*. New York: Crown Publishing, 1985. The differences in city and country life are explained and colorfully illustrated in great detail. **(Challenging)**

Shulevitz, Uri. *Toddlecreek Post Office*. New York: Farrar, Straus and Giroux, 1990. The residents of Toddlecreek discover they will lose more than a post office if it closes. **(Challenging)**

Teacher Books

■ The Earthworks Group. *50 Simple Things Kids Can Do to Recycle*. Berkeley, CA: Earthworks Press, 1994. Hands-on ideas for ways in which students can learn about helping the environment.

Jungreis, Abigail. *Know Your Hometown History*. New York: Franklin Watts, 1992. Projects and activities accompany text on how to research the history of your town.

Read Aloud Books

Lord, John Vernon. *The Great Jam Sandwich*. Boston, MA: Houghton Mifflin, 1972. The people of Itching Down have to find a way to get rid of the wasps that flew into their town.

Pryor, Bonnie. *The House on Maple Street*. New York: William Morrow, 1987. Many changes occur over three hundred years around this house.

Technology Multimedia

Communities and How They Work. Video. No. 4182-106. This is a discussion of what communities provide to their residents and how services work. Britannica Videos. (800) 554-9862.

How the Rhinoceros Got His Skin and *How the Camel Got His Hump*. Video. Two tales about how animals acquired their physical characteristics. *Paul Bunyan*. Video. This gigantic logger and his blue ox, Babe, clear the Dakotas for new settlers. Story Lane Theater, Macmillan/McGraw-Hill. (800) 442-9685.

Neighborhoods and Communities. 8 sound filmstrips. The similarities, differences, and interrelationships of communities are presented. Society For Visual Education. (800) 829-1900.

Free or Inexpensive Materials

For a brochure on why trees are so important in our world and how we can conserve them, send to: National Arbor Day Foundation; 100 Arbor Avenue; Nebraska City, NE 68410.

■ *Book excerpted in the Anthology*

■ *Book featured in the student bibliography of the Unit Review*

National Geographic technology

2B

Ideas for Active Learning

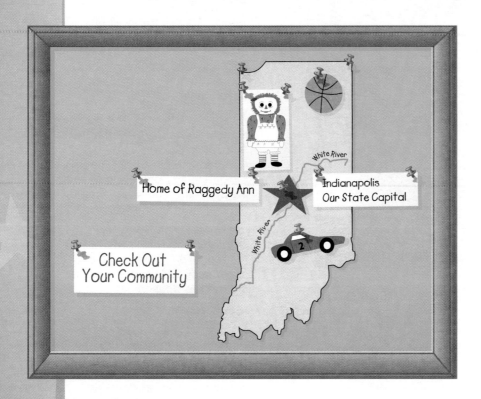

Living in Communities

Help students to create a multimedia display titled "Check Out Your Community." Ask volunteers to contribute visual and written information about their own community.

- Students may choose to draw landforms, contribute maps or brochures, create visuals about their environment, cut out pictures of local wildlife, find information about the history of their community, or contribute their own photographs that show an aspect of their community.

- For each item, ask students to use an index card to write a caption telling how the visual represents the idea of community. Help children organize the material they have collected by making subtitles for the bulletin board such as "Our Geography" or "Our Cultures."

Thanks to: Mrs. Lindy Thomas, Southampton School #1, Vincentown, New Jersey

"Bread Box" Communities

GROUP · 30 MINUTES OR LONGER

Materials: large bread boxes (for school bread delivery); construction paper; crayons; paint; scissors; aluminum foil; soil, grass, straw; shoe boxes, jewelry boxes, milk cartons; toy people, cars, animals, trees; large and small cardboard tubes.

1. After reading the unit, students form groups and do library research to become "experts" on one type of U.S. community. They should focus on where the citizens live, work and play.
2. Next they meet to plan their "bread box" communities. Tell them to sketch what they want to show and make a list of materials. Some members may bring items from home.
3. Help students with suggestions to create community elements. For example, foil-covered drinking straws can become pipelines.
4. When the communities are completed, groups can give their "expert" reports to an audience of their peers or invited guests, using their model villages to illustrate the main points. If possible, have the presentation videotaped.

Enriching with Multimedia

RESOURCE: *Internet Project Handbook*

- Look at the ***Internet Project Handbook*** for student projects related to this unit or have students go online at http://www.mmhschool.com, Macmillan/McGraw-Hill School's home page on the World Wide Web.

RESOURCE: *Videodisc/Video Tape 1*

- Enrich Unit 1 with the Videodisc *glossary* segments.

Search Frame 53777

Understanding the Environment

- Throughout the unit, students have opportunities to learn about how communities can protect their natural resources. Talk with students about environmental problems in the communities they read about and the efforts made to solve them. Generate a list for students to take home.

- Encourage students to make a circle chart at home of environmental issues in their community and ways in which their families can help protect the environment. Families can work together to list products they use and processes they take part in—for example, cans and recycling—that affect the environment. In class, have students tell how the choices they make can help conserve their community's natural resources.

Community Chart

CURRICULUM CONNECTION **Art/Language Arts**

RESOURCE: Project Book p. 2.

For this unit, students will work individually and in groups to create a chart that demonstrates their understanding of communities.

1. After each chapter, students should use information from the lessons to note features of different types of communities. They can store this information in a folder.
2. Once notes are complete, students can work in small groups to create a group chart incorporating the information each member compiled. Construction paper can be used for the chart.
3. When the chart is complete, group members can use it to discuss similarities and differences among communities.

 Assessment suggestions for this activity appear on p. 62.

Introducing the Unit

Give students a few moments to look at the pictures and to read the *Why Does It Matter?* passage on the facing page.

Exploring Prior Knowledge Discuss with students the architecture and landforms in your community. Ask them to talk about how your community is special.

Suggested Questions

● *What kinds of things do people do in most communities?* (Possible answers: They go to school and work; they have fun; they help each other.)

● *What do you know about big cities?* (Students will probably mention crowds, tall buildings, and traffic, as well as museums, theaters, and restaurants.)

● *What do you know about suburban communities?* (Students may mention that they are located near cities and have shopping centers such as malls.)

● *What do you know about life in the country?* (Students can share what they know about farming, mountain, and seaside communities.)

Looking Ahead Students will learn how people live, work, and play together in communities and how landforms and climate affect their lives. They will investigate the differences and similarities between rural, urban, and suburban communities.

Background INFORMATION

ABOUT THE PHOTOGRAPHS

● **GRAND CANYON** For about two million years, the Colorado River has steadily worn away a rock plateau in northern Arizona. Today the Grand Canyon is a magnificent natural gorge, 1 mile deep and 4–18 miles wide. The Grand Canyon draws more tourists than any other natural landform. Visitors walk trails from the rim to the valley floor.

● **IN-LINE SKATING** This type of skate was developed as a hybrid or combination of the ice skate and the roller skate. The wheels have been put "in-line" and down the center in place of the metal runner on ice skates.

● **SINGLE-FAMILY HOMES** Families throughout rural America live in wood-frame houses. The house in the picture is built in the "gingerbread" style, with fancy shapes and lavish ornaments, which was popular during the Victorian period.

UNIT ONE

Living in Communities

WHY DOES IT MATTER?

How would you describe where you live to someone who has never been there?

You could describe your family, your friends, your street, and the land and water nearby. In doing so, you are describing your community.

Your community is special. In this unit you will find out about communities across the country and around the world. Some may be like your community, and some may be very different. All are shaped by where they are located. And in their own ways, all communities are special.

SunBank

Discussing the Photographs
Encourage students to study the photographs for clues about different kinds of communities.

Suggested Questions

● **In what kind of community do you think the skaters live?** *(Students will probably describe a suburban community with quiet streets.)*

● **What kinds of things probably happen inside the tall city buildings?** *(Students should mention that people live in apartment buildings and work in office buildings.)*

● **In what kind of community might you see a flamingo?** *(in a quiet country community near the water)*

Discussing WHY DOES IT MATTER?
After students have read the text, make a list on the chalkboard of people and places that make your community special.

Suggested Questions

● **Look at the pictures in this unit. Which remind you of your community? Why?** *(Answers will vary.)*

★**THINKING FURTHER:** *Making Conclusions* **Why do you think people live in different kinds of communities?** *(Possible answers: Their families have always lived there; they have to find work in a specific place; they like the way a place looks.)*

Background INFORMATION

● **MIAMI, FLORIDA** The view of the skyscrapers was taken in Miami, a busy modern city with a major international airport. It is valued as a resort and a port for cruise ships, a processing and shipping center for crops grown in the southern states, and a major center of trade with Latin America.

● **THE FLAMINGO** This three- to five-foot bird with long legs and a long neck is related to the heron and the stork. Flamingos are known for their rosy-white plumage and pink-to-scarlet wings. They live in the tropics, wading into bays and wetlands, where they fish for food. In Paracas, Peru, people are working to protect the flamingo and other wild animals.

3

Introducing
Circus School

Exploring Prior Knowledge Have students close their eyes. Ask them what comes to mind when they hear the word "circus." Then invite students to talk about circuses they have seen or read about.

Links to the Unit In Unit 1, students will learn about communities in many different locations. The Circus School is an example of a community—a community on the move.

Circus School Ask students to read the text. Then have them invent brief stories about what is happening in each of the pictures on the page. As students look at the map of the United States, explain that the small dots represent the route followed by the circus train.

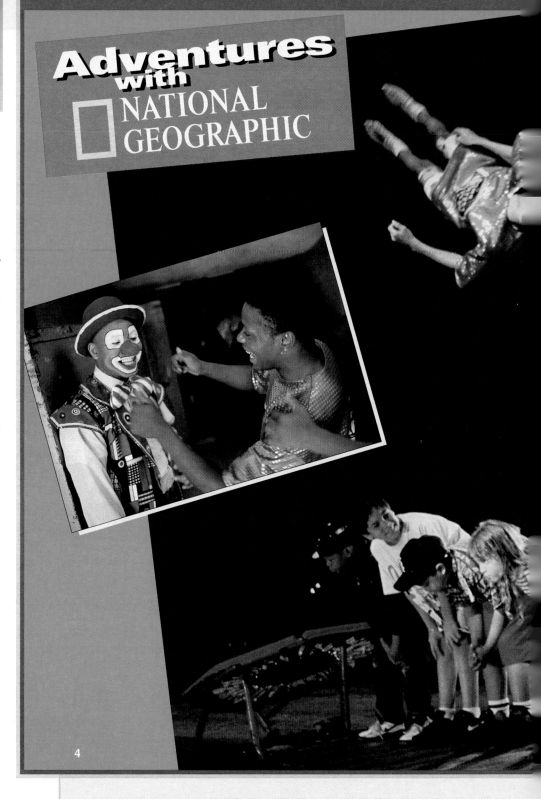

Resource **REMINDER**

National Geographic Poster

Geo Adventures *Daily Geography Activities*

Technology: *Adventures CD-ROM*

Background INFORMATION

MORE ABOUT CIRCUS SCHOOL

• The kids shown in these photographs are part of a tumbling troupe called Chicago Kidz. Many of them got their start with the Jesse White Tumbling Troupe in Chicago. Ringling Bros. and Barnum & Bailey Circus auditioned kids from other cities as well. They brought all of the kids together and a Russian coach trained them for seven months in Florida.

• For two years Chicago Kidz live on the road in a circus train. They have a regular schedule of eight performances a week. In two years, the train traveled 30,000 miles!

• These children have found a second family with their new circus friends. Members of the circus community eat, work, and play together. The Chicago Kidz keep in touch with their real families by phone.

CIRCUS SCHOOL

You'd flip for a chance to go to this school! It's for kids who perform with the Ringling Bros. and Barnum & Bailey Circus. These kids are part of a tumbling troupe that travels all over our country with the circus. Since they can't go to a regular school, they study in a trailer called the "Little Red Schoolhouse." And yes—even circus performers have to do homework.

GEO JOURNAL

The circus school is part of a community. Write about a special place in your own community.

Be sure students understand that working in a circus is both fun and hard work. Point out the picture of the students who are studying. Explain that they are sitting inside "The Little Red Schoolhouse, " which can be seen at the top of the page. Young tumblers spend at least three hours a day studying. They study the same subjects as children in communities across the United States. In addition to schoolwork, the Chicago Kidz have a busy schedule of practice and performance.

You may also want to talk about the large picture in the center. Tell students that it is important in any community for people to work together. Ask students to explain why working as a team is important in circus tumbling.

Draw students' attention to the picture of the laughing clown on p. 4. Explain that this clown is a man named Huel Speight. He is one of the guardians who helps supervise the kids. Because the Chicago Kidz are away from their families, they are assigned guardians while on the road. Guardians help the kids remember their responsibilities. They are there when a kid needs help or advice.

Using the Geo Journal Remind students to illustrate their Geo Journal writing.

Technology CONNECTION

ADVENTURES CD-ROM
Enrich this feature with the *Discoveries* section of the CD-ROM.

Curriculum CONNECTION

LANGUAGE ARTS Invite students to visit the library to find out more about life in the circus. There are many picture books about the circus available for third-grade readers. Suggest that students share the books they check out.

Have students write one-page reports about life in the circus community. Students can tell how people live and work together. Suggest that they write about how people work together on a specific circus performance or project. Ask students to tell why it important for circus communities to work together, and how sharing skills and energy can be satisfying and rewarding.

Understanding Communities

PAGES 6–33

CHAPTER OVERVIEW

There are many types of communites in the United States and around the world. People live in rural areas in country houses, farms, and small towns. People also live in urban areas in and around cities whose homes are in skyscraper apartments and suburban housing developments.

CHAPTER PLANNING GUIDE
Suggested pacing: 16–18 days

LESSON	LESSON FOCUS	LESSON RESOURCES
1 LOOKING AT A COMMUNITY pages 8–13	A Community in Texas	*Practice Book* p. 6 *Anthology* pp. 2–5 *Outline Maps* p. 5 *Geo Big Book* pp. 4-5
LEGACY pages 14–15	Main Street, U.S.A.: Linking Past and Present	
2 COMMUNITIES ACROSS THE UNITED STATES pages 16–21	A Land of Different Communities	*Practice Book* p. 7 ▤ *Anthology* pp. 6-14 ▤ *Anthology Cassette:* The Express Train ◉ *Technology:* Adventures CD-ROM *Outline Map* p. 5
GEOGRAPHY SKILLS pages 22–23	Using Map Scales	*Practice Book* p. 8 *Transparency:* 6 ◉ *Technology:* Videodisc/Video Tape, CD-ROM
GLOBAL CONNECTIONS pages 24–29	A Community in Mexico	*Practice Book* p. 9 ◉ *Technology:* Adventures CD-ROM *Outline Maps* pp. 4, 9
CITIZENSHIP Viewpoints pages 30–31	What Do People Say About Zoos?	
CHAPTER REVIEW pages 32–33	Students' understanding of vocabulary, content, and skills is assessed.	*Assessment:* Ch. 1 Test, Performance Assessment Ch. 1 *Transparency:* Graphic Organizer

OPTIONS FOR STUDENT ACTIVITIES

Citizenship pp. 11, 14, 19, 31

Curriculum Connection pp. 11, 12, 14, 15, 17, 20, 25, 27, 28

Using the Anthology pp. 12, 20

ASSESSMENT OPPORTUNITIES

Meeting Individual Needs pp. 7, 13, 15, 21, 23, 29

Write About It pp. 13, 15, 21, 29

Chapter Review pp. 32–33

Assessment Book

Chapter Test Ch. 1 Test

Performance Assessment Ch. 1

Using the Floor Map Use the Floor Map and the Project Book to enhance Lesson 2 by inviting students to build several different kinds of communities.

Using Geo Adventures Use **Geo Adventures** Daily Geography Activities to assess students' understanding of geography skills.

Using the Vocabulary Cards The vocabulary words for each lesson are available on *Vocabulary Cards* for review and practice.

GETTING READY FOR THE CHAPTER

Make a Welcome Brochure
GROUP · 30 MINUTES OR LONGER

Objective: To raise awareness of how people work and have fun together in your school community.

Materials: *Project Book* pp. 3–5, crayons, construction paper, glue

1. Have students work in small groups. Let the groups know that their job is to plan and make a brochure that will welcome new students as well as visitors to your school.

2. Encourage group members to discuss important people in the school and places newcomers would need to know about.

3. After students have talked about information they might include, have each member choose part of the brochure to produce. One group member will draw a picture for the cover using Project Book p. 3. Another will write a letter welcoming others to your school. The remaining students can complete Project Book pp. 4 and 5 by each choosing a particular person or place to draw and write about.

4. Have groups assemble their brochures by cutting out their work and gluing it onto construction paper. Let each group share its brochure with the class and talk about the role each member had.

> **SECOND-LANGUAGE SUPPORT**
> Second-language learners may benefit from working with an English-proficient peer during part or all of this activity.
>
> Additional Second-Language Support Tips: pp. 9, 18, 24

Introducing the Chapter

To initiate a discussion about geography and culture, have students describe geographical settings which are very different from the one you live in. Ask them how your community would change if the land around it were completely different.

THINKING ABOUT GEOGRAPHY AND CULTURE

Help students link locations on the map with the communities shown in the photographs. Ask volunteers to tell what they see in each picture.

RURAL COMMUNITIES

Suggested Questions

● **Would you classify Big Hole, Montana, as the country, a big town, or a city?** *(the country)*

● **Do more people live in Chicago, Illinois, or Big Hole, Montana? How do you know?** *(More people live in Chicago. Chicago is a big city with many buildings and Big Hole has just a few houses.)*

● **What would you like to learn about living in the country?** *(Invite students to list questions and refer to them as they read the chapter.)*

SUBURBAN COMMUNITIES

Suggested Questions

● **In what kind of homes do people live in this community?** *(mostly one house to each family with a yard)*

● **Look at the pictures on the Unit Opener pages 2–3. Which picture might belong in this community?** *(the one of children skating)*

Resource REMINDER

Technology: *Videodisc/Video Tape 1*

Understanding Communities

THINKING ABOUT GEOGRAPHY AND CULTURE

What is special about your community's people? Perhaps they live on farms or maybe they work in tall skyscrapers. To find the locations of the communities shown, match the colored triangles on the map with the triangles by the pictures.

In Chapter 1 you will see several different types of communities. One of them might even be like yours.

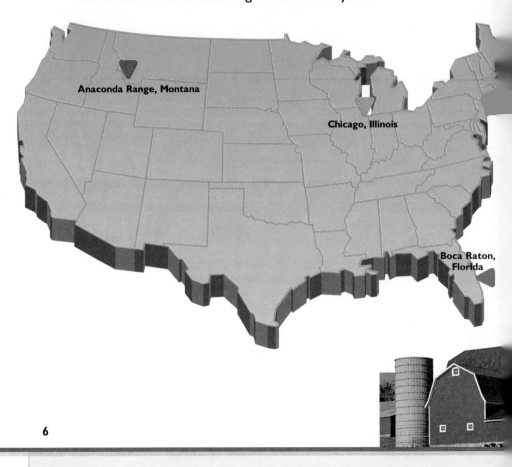

6

Background INFORMATION

LINKING THE MAP TO THE PHOTOGRAPHS

● Rural living in America is often centered around agriculture. Large tracts of farmland separate houses. Small towns provide services—such as stores, schools, post offices, churches, and movie houses—for community members living within a wide area.

● Boca Raton, Florida, is a suburban community situated between two large cities—West Palm Beach and Ft. Lauderdale. About 165,000 people live in Boca Raton. Suburban cities like this one provide quiet neighborhoods and parks for people who work in cities.

● In big cities like Chicago, people live in crowded conditions. Skyscrapers serve as office buildings and apartment complexes. Public buses and trains carry thousands of people to work every day. Cities are also exciting centers of culture and art.

This rural community is located in Montana.

Chicago, Illinois, is an urban community.

Boca Raton, Florida, is a suburban community.

7

- **What would you like to learn about suburban living?** *(Invite students to list questions about the word suburban and elements of the photograph.)*

URBAN COMMUNITIES

Suggested Questions

- **Chicago is an urban community. What do you think the word urban means?** *(Most students will understand from the photograph that urban refers to the city.)*

- **What are three things you might see in a big city?** *(Students may mention tall buildings, buses, cars, traffic lights, and businesspeople.)*

- **What do you know about city living? What more would you like to know?** *(Encourage students to share their knowledge and questions.)*

★**THINKING FURTHER:** *Compare and Contrast* **Which of these three pictures looks most like your community? Why?** *(Students can describe the geographic and constructed features in their community.)*

★**THINKING FURTHER:** *Making Decisions* **Which of these three communities would you most like to live in? Which would you enjoy visiting?** *(Invite students to say what they like about different communities.)*

Technology CONNECTION

VIDEODISC/VIDEO TAPE 1
Enrich Chapter 1 with the Videodisc *map* and *glossary* segments.

Search Frame 53777

Meeting *Individual* Needs

EXTENSION (Easy) Invite students to make drawings of houses in which people live in each of the communities present.

RETEACHING (Average) Have students list communities near you that look like those in the photographs.

ENRICHMENT (Challenging) Ask students to consider what it would be like to live in a community much smaller or larger than yours. Have them write descriptions of what daily life would be like. Ask them to give a few examples of major differences and similarities. Explain that they will be learning more facts about different communities as they read the chapter.

LESSON 1
PAGES 8–13

Lesson Overview
A community is a place where people live, work, and play together.

Lesson Objectives
★ Define the term *community*.

★ Identify characteristics that communities have in common.

★ Compare and contrast the local community with a community in Texas.

1 PREPARE

MOTIVATE Tell students that the picture shows a street in Galveston, Texas. The star in the picture appears on the flag of Texas, which is nicknamed the Lone Star State. Then have a volunteer read the *Read Aloud*. Ask students what questions they might ask if they were visiting Mrs. Roy's class in Galveston.

SET PURPOSE Have students read the *Read to Learn* question. Invite speculation about the answer. Then explain that in this lesson, students will discuss their own community as well as Galveston. Finally, point out the *Vocabulary* words and tell students to watch for them as they read.

2 TEACH

Thinking About People and Places Call students' attention to the picture on page 9. Have them refer to the information on Mrs. Roy's chalkboard as they discuss what a community is.

Suggested Questions

● *What do people in a community do together?* (live, work, have fun)

★THINKING FURTHER: *Making Conclusions* **Is a community usually bigger or smaller than a neighborhood? How do you know?** (Bigger; it usually includes several neighborhoods.)

Resource REMINDER
Practice Book: *p. 6*

Anthology: *The Town that Moved, pp. 2–5*

Outline Maps: *p. 7*

Geo Big Book: *pp. 4–5*

Focus Activity

READ TO LEARN
What is a community?

VOCABULARY
community
island
port
hurricane
citizen
pollution

PLACES
Galveston, Texas

8

Looking at a Community

READ ALOUD
It's the start of the school year for Mrs. Roy's third-grade class in Galveston, Texas. Students want to write to other third-grade classes around the United States and the world. Today they are writing postcards describing Galveston.

People and Places

Before writing the postcards, Mrs. Roy's class discussed life in their community. "What *is* a community, anyway?" asked Mrs. Roy.

Max said a community is a special place. It is made up of many neighborhoods where people live. Karen said it is a place where friends and family have fun. And Marcus said a community is libraries, schools, and businesses.

"In a way each of you is right," said Mrs. Roy. "A community is usually made up of several neighborhoods. It is a place where different people live. It's also where people work and have fun together. People make communities special."

Reading STRATEGIES *and* Language DEVELOPMENT

MAKING AND SUPPORTING GENERALIZATIONS Read the following aloud: *Our school has teachers. The school in Galveston has teachers. Every school I know of has teachers. All schools have teachers.* Point out that the last sentence is a general statement, or *generalization*, about schools that is supported by facts. Then tell students that by the end of the lesson they will be able to answer the *Read to Learn* question with a generalization about communities that is supported by facts.

ADJECTIVES Write the following questions on the chalkboard: *How* big *is our community? Is it* bigger *than Galveston? Is it the* biggest *community you have ever seen?* Explain that when we compare two things, we add *er* to most adjectives. When we compare more than two things, we add *est*. Encourage students to practice using the comparative and superlative forms as they discuss the text.

Living Together

"We have a lot of people living here in our community," said Karen. "I think that our community is big."

"That depends," Mrs. Roy said. "What community are you comparing it to? Say you lived in a big city. Galveston would then seem very small. If you lived in a small town, it might appear very big."

Galveston, Texas, has about 60,000 people. But no matter what its size, every community is special. Think about your own community. What is special about it?

Mrs. Roy's class learns about communities.

Discussing Living Together Help students understand that communities vary in size and that size is relative. To make this concept tangible, give children an opportunity to compare their class to smaller and larger classes in your school.

Suggested Questions

● *What would you like about living in a large community? What would you like about living in a small one?* (Guide students to see the relationship between the size of a community and the lifestyle of its residents. For example, a large community might offer more cultural and recreational activities than a small community, but the latter might be a friendlier, more relaxing place to live.)

● *What makes your community special to you?* (Students may refer to specific people and places, as well as to the size of their community.)

★THINKING FURTHER: *Compare and Contrast* **Do you think your community is big or small compared to Galveston? How could you find out?** (Students can speculate about the answer and then use the library to find out how the population of their community compares to Galveston's.)

9

Background INFORMATION

ABOUT GALVESTON

● The city of Galveston is on Galveston Island, about two miles off the Texas mainland. Situated on the Gulf of Mexico, the island is linked to the mainland by three highways.

● In addition to being a major seaport, Galveston is a resort community, attracting 7 million visitors annually.

● The earliest inhabitants of the island were the Karankawa people. The first American colonists arrived in 1827, and the city of Galveston was founded nine years later.

● According to local legend, there is buried treasure somewhere on the island, leftover from the days when Jean Lafitte and his band of pirates had headquarters there (1817–1821).

Second-Language Support

MAKING CONNECTIONS To help second-language learners better grasp the concept of community, encourage them to discuss the community they lived in when they were in their native country. If appropriate, ask them to compare and contrast their former community with the one they live in now.

More MAP WORK

Suggested Questions

- **Does the seawall reach the northern or southern tip of Galveston?** *(northern)*

- **In which direction would you travel to get from the port of Galveston to Galveston Island State Park?** *(south)*

Discussing Working Together

Point out that jobs may vary from one community to another, but all jobs require cooperation.

Suggested Questions

- **Why do many people in Galveston work in shipping?** *(Galveston is on an island surrounded by water.)*

- **How do boat captains and dockworkers help make Galveston one of the "fastest" ports in the country?** *(They work together to load and unload cargo quickly.)*

- **What kinds of jobs do people in your community have? Which do they do in your community? Which do they do someplace else?** *(Help students see why some jobs can be done locally, while others cannot.)*

- **Why is it important for workers to help each other?** *(People do better work when they cooperate.)*

- ★**THINKING FURTHER:** *Making Conclusions* **How are workers at Galveston's port helping their community? How are they helping other communities?** *(They are bringing in goods that Galveston needs and shipping out goods that other communities need.)*

GALVESTON, TEXAS — MAP WORK

Central business district
Seawall

Port of Galveston

Galveston Island

Gulf of Mexico

Galveston Island State Park

0 3 6 Miles
0 3 6 Kilometers

TEXAS
Galveston

Galveston is on an **island**.

1. Along what body of water is the seawall located?

2. Is the port of Galveston east or west of the seawall?

3. Why do you think the central business district is located near the port?

Ships from around the world load and unload goods at the port of Galveston.

Working Together

One thing that makes each community special is the way people can make a living there. Look at the map on this page. Since Galveston is on an **island**, many people have jobs in shipping. An island is land that is surrounded on all sides by water.

The **port** of Galveston is a busy place. A port is a place where ships load and unload goods. At the port you may see dockworkers unload bananas. They will be sold in stores in Galveston. Other boats are loaded with cotton, rice, and wheat. They will be shipped to countries far away.

Galveston has one of the "fastest" ports in the country. Boats can dock quickly. Boat captains and dockworkers work together. They load and unload goods so that boats are out in record time.

People in Galveston work at the port and many other places. What jobs do people have in your community?

10

Global CONNECTIONS

GATEWAY TO THE WORLD Display a map of the U.S. in the *Atlas* or the *Geo Big Book,* and explain that farmers from every state ship their crops to Galveston. The port's location on the Gulf of Mexico makes it an ideal base for transporting those crops to cities along the Atlantic Coast as well as overseas. In addition to carrying goods out of Galveston, ships also bring them in.

Students may wish to research one of the following imports or exports to find out how it gets from its place of origin through the port of Galveston to its final destination: *Imports:* raw sugar, automobiles, bananas; *Exports:* cotton, rice, wheat.

Field Trip

Give the class an opportunity to see people in your community at work together. Make arrangements to visit a local place of business such as a grocery store, newspaper office, or radio station. Before the trip, provide students with background information about the place they are going to see. During the visit, have them note how the workers cooperate with each other to get the job done.

As an alternative, invite a member of the Chamber of Commerce to talk to the class about how people in the community make a living.

Helping Each Other

Communities need people to solve problems. Here's what one woman said about people helping each other during the great Galveston hurricane of 1900. A hurricane is a storm with very strong winds and heavy rain.

I grew up on stories about 1900. Everything about who we are today was shaped by that hurricane. We worked together to rebuild Galveston. People wanted to help each other.

The great hurricane almost destroyed Galveston. There were almost no homes or businesses left. But the citizens of Galveston refused to give up. A citizen is a member of a community or a country. The citizens of Galveston rebuilt their community. To make sure Galveston would be safe, they built a 17-foot seawall that still stands today.

Today some citizens are working together again. They are helping to fight air pollution in Galveston. Pollution is anything that spoils land, water, and air. Cars can cause a lot of pollution. To help, some citizens in Galveston are driving together in car pools. In the years ahead Galveston will be an even cleaner place to live.

Building the seawall required hard work and cooperation.

Thinking About Helping Each Other Use the picture and the text to help students understand why it is important for *citizens* in a community to help one another.

Suggested Questions

● **How did the hurricane of 1900 hurt Galveston?** *(It destroyed almost all the homes and businesses.)*

● **Why was it important for the people of Galveston to work together after the hurricane?** *(By working together, they were able to rebuild the town and build the seawall. They could not have achieved the same results working alone.)*

● **What problem does Galveston have today? How are people in the community trying to solve it?** *(They are trying to reduce air pollution by working together to form car pools.)*

● **Think of a problem your community has. What is one step people could take to try to solve it?** *(They could form a group to work together on the problem.)*

★**THINKING FURTHER:** *Cause and Effect* **How is the work the citizens of Galveston did 100 years ago still helping the community today? How will the work people do today help citizens in the future?** *(The seawall still helps protect Galveston from the sea. Efforts to reduce pollution through car pools will make Galveston a cleaner place to live.)*

Curriculum CONNECTION

LINKS TO MATHEMATICS After the hurricane the citizens of Galveston raised their city an average of six feet to protect it from the sea. Work with students to create a chalkboard diagram that illustrates how the town was raised.

● Draw a wavy line to represent the island's hills and valleys; a house on each hill and in each valley; a circle off to the side to represent the surrounding lowlands; pipelines from the lowland area to the valleys.

● Explain that workers jacked up all the houses and made them the same height. On your diagram, make the highest house a bit higher, then raise the other houses to the same height. Draw stilts under the houses to represent the jacks.

● Explain that workers pumped mud from the lowlands through the pipes to fill the spaces under the houses. When the mud dried, they lowered the houses. On your diagram, erase the "jacks" and fill in the spaces.

★ CITIZENSHIP

USING CURRENT EVENTS Initiate a discussion about social, environmental, and/or economic problems in the community. Then have students work in groups to research one problem and the efforts local residents are making to solve it. Students can get information from local newspapers, news broadcasts, and community groups.

Encourage groups to publish their findings in a magazine called *Helping Each Other,* which can be circulated in school.

Having Fun

Look at the picture of the seawall below. You can see what it has become. It is now more than a wall to protect Galveston from the sea. Along the seawall is a sidewalk. People stroll there and ride bicycles. They also roller-skate and jog. Below on the beach, people come to relax in the sand and swim. These are just some of the things that people in Galveston do for fun.

Galveston Island State Park is nearby. Many people go camping there. They also enjoy birdwatching, swimming, and fishing.

In many communities the land and water shape how people have fun. This is also true of Galveston.

For people in Galveston and other communities, having fun also means just being with friends and family. What are some ways you and your family have fun in your community?

Along the seawall and at Galveston Island State Park there is much to see and do.

12

WHY IT MATTERS

By learning about Galveston with Mrs. Roy's class, you now know what a community is. As you read this book, you will explore how people in different communities live and work together.

One way to see how people live and work together is to visit the main street of a community. Around the United States the main street is often the center of community life. Turn the page and you too can visit "Main Street."

Having fun in Galveston means sharing good times with people.

✓ Reviewing Facts and Ideas

SUM IT UP

- A community is a place where different people live, work, and have fun together. There are usually several neighborhoods in a community.

- Galveston, Texas, is a place where people live and work together to take care of their community.

- A community needs people who care about it and each other.

THINK ABOUT IT

1. Describe Galveston's location. What are two ways location is important?

2. **FOCUS** What is a community?

3. **THINKING SKILL** How is your community _different_ from Galveston? How are they _alike_?

4. **WRITE** Suppose Mrs. Roy's students had written to your class. Write a postcard to them describing your community.

13

Understanding WHY IT MATTERS

Be sure students have grasped the main idea of the lesson: Communities have certain characteristics in common as well as unique characteristics of their own.

Suggested Questions

- **What do we learn when we compare and contrast our community with Galveston?** (Communities are alike in some ways and different in others.)

⭐ 3 CLOSE

SUM IT UP

Have students answer these questions.

Suggested Questions

- **How is a community like a neighborhood? How is it different?** (People live, work, and play in both places, but a community usually consists of several neighborhoods.)

- **How can you tell that the citizens cared about Galveston in the past and still care about it today?** (They rebuilt Galveston after the hurricane and are now trying to reduce air pollution.)

- **Why does a community need people who care about it and each other?** (Answers should reflect such concepts as the sum is the whole of its parts; in unity there is strength.)

EVALUATE
✓ Answers to Think About It

1. Galveston is an ocean island. This location affects how citizens live, work, and play.

2. A community is a place where people live, work, and play together.

3. Students can compare and contrast Galveston and the local community in terms of size, location, jobs, recreation, problems, and efforts to deal with them.

4. Students can expand on aspects of the local community that they cited in their answer to question 3.

Write About It Ask students to write a paragraph explaining why it is important to learn about other communities besides their own.

Meeting Individual Needs

RETEACHING (Easy) Have students review the illustrations and section titles in the lesson. Then have individuals choose one title, think about how it relates to their community, draw a picture illustrating their ideas, and write a caption.

EXTENSION (Average) Draw a Venn diagram on the chalkboard and have students copy it. Show them how to use the diagram to compare and contrast their community with Galveston. Then have students complete the diagram on their own.

ENRICHMENT (Challenging) Have students work in groups to plan a model community. Their plans should include characteristics that all communities share as well as features that make their model community special. Groups can adapt _Outline Map_ p. 7 to illustrate their plans.

Lesson Overview
Main Street is a community legacy.

Lesson Objective
★Understand how a community's past can live on in the present.

1 PREPARE

MOTIVATE Tell students that many communities started out with just one street. People from miles around came to that street to shop, meet friends, and conduct business. Over time, people built towns around that street, and they gave it a name. They called it Main Street because of its central location and importance to the community.

SET PURPOSE Read aloud the text on this page as students follow in their books. Then review the pronunciation and meaning of the word *legacy.* Tell students that they are going to discover how this word applies to themselves as well as to their community.

2 TEACH

Understanding the Concept of a Legacy Use the *Curriculum Connection* activity at the bottom of the page to help students understand the concept of a legacy.

Examining the Pictures Have students look at the pictures while volunteers read the captions aloud.

Legacy
LINKING PAST AND PRESENT

Main Street, U.S.A.

Where do you go to get a library book or to meet a friend? You might go to the main street of your community.

Many communities have a main street. In the past Main Street was often the center of a community. Today people still go there to shop and to meet each other.

Because the main street is part of a community's past and present, you can call it a **legacy** (LEG uh see). A legacy is something that we value in our lives today and that is also a valued part of our past.

A main street in Madison, New Jersey, 1913

14

Curriculum CONNECTION

LINKS TO LANGUAGE ARTS To help students understand the concept of legacies, invite them to bring in a possession that they valued in the past; for example, a favorite toy or the first book they ever read. Then have children explain the significance of the object—why it was important to them in the past and why they have kept it. Finally, suggest that they might want to give their possession to a younger friend or sibling someday. Explain that the object would then be considered a legacy-something that is passed on from one person to the next.

★ CITIZENSHIP

LINKING PAST AND PRESENT The following activities can help students appreciate their hometown history.

● Display a community map that shows streets, parks, and important buildings. Have students locate places that are named after people and then do research to learn what those people contributed to the community.

● Show the class pictures of the local community as it was in the past. Have students talk about how it has changed and then speculate about how it might change even more during their lifetime.

● Invite a senior citizen to talk to the class about life in the local community yesterday and today. Allow time for a question-and-answer period after the talk.

A dogsled race down a main street in Anchorage, Alaska

Main Street in Marshall, North Carolina

A community event along a main street in Galveston, Texas

15

Suggested Questions

- **People gather on the main streets of their communities for many reasons. Why are people gathered on the main street in Anchorage, Alaska?** *(They are watching a dogsled race.)*

- **Why do you think the people on Galveston's main street are holding flags?** *(They are attending a patriotic event.)*

- **What evidence shows that Main Street in Marshall, North Carolina, is a busy place?** *(There are many cars and buildings on the street.)*

★THINKING FURTHER: *Compare and Contrast* **Look at the picture of a main street in Madison, New Jersey. What would be different about the street today? What might be the same?** *(There would be cars instead of the horse and buggy. The houses and trees might still be there.)*

3 CLOSE

SUM IT UP
Be sure students understand that no matter how much communities change over time, they all have legacies that link the past with the present.

EVALUATE
Write About It Have students write a paragraph explaining why the main street of a community is a good example of a legacy.

Curriculum CONNECTION

LINKS TO ART Have students work in small groups to make dioramas of the community main street, mall, or any other place that brings people together. Suggest that group members meet to decide on the contents of their dioramas and to divide up their tasks. When the projects are completed, ask each group to explain why the place it "built" is an important part of the community.

Field Trip

Take students for a walk around a historic neighborhood and have them contrast architectural styles of the past and present. Point out that in time, the contemporary buildings may become legacies, too.

Meeting *Individual* Needs

RETEACHING (Easy) Have students draw a picture of a place in their community where people gather together.

EXTENSION (Average) Have students do research to find out about the origin of their community.

ENRICHMENT (Challenging) Have students write about a place in the community that they consider a legacy and explain the significance of that place in the past and present.

LESSON 2

PAGES 16–21

Lesson Overview

People in the United States live in urban, suburban, and rural communities.

Lesson Objectives

★ Analyze urban, suburban and rural communities.

★ Compare and contrast different types of communities in the U.S.

★ Describe the relationship between people and their environment in various communities.

1 PREPARE

MOTIVATE Have students read the *Read Aloud*. Then ask them how they would answer the questions on the postcard.

SET PURPOSE Explain that the pictures show scenes from three types of communities in our country. Challenge students to use the pictures plus the *Vocabulary* words to speculate about the answer to the *Read to Learn* question.

As you proceed with the lesson, refer to *Using the Anthology* on p. 20 for information about topic-specific selections.

2 TEACH

Discussing Hello from Around Our Country Display an oversized map of the U.S., such as the one in the *Geo Big Book,* so students can see their community in relation to those they are studying. Point out the places they have discussed so far: the local community and Galveston, Texas.

Suggested Questions

★**THINKING FURTHER:** *Making Decisions* **What questions would you add to the postcard Mrs. Roy's class wrote?** *(Students might ask about homes, schools, transportation)*

Resource REMINDER

Practice Book: *p. 7*

Anthology: *All the Places to Love, pp.6–9; City Poems, p. 10; The House on Hillside La, pp. 11–13; The City Blues, p. 14*

Anthology Cassette: *The Express Train*

Technology: *Adventures CD-ROM*

Outline Maps: *p. 5*

Communities Across the United States

READ ALOUD

Focus Activity

READ TO LEARN
What types of communities does our country have?

VOCABULARY
urban
suburb
rural
transportation

PLACES
New Orleans, Louisiana
Bothell, Washington
Rochester, Indiana

> Hello. We are a third-grade class in Galveston, Texas. We want to know about your community. What is it like? What do you do for fun? Where do people work in your community?

Hello from Around Our Country

This postcard was written by Mrs. Roy's class. They sent it to different schools around the United States. A few weeks later they received responses from all over the country. The students were very excited. Let's see what they found out about communities around our country.

16

Reading STRATEGIES *and* Language DEVELOPMENT

MAKING CONCLUSIONS Tell students that they can use the knowledge they have plus new information to make conclusions about what they are reading. As students read the lesson, ask them what conclusions they can make about urban, suburban, and rural communities.

ABBREVIATIONS You might use this opportunity to familiarize students with postal abbreviations for state names. On the chalkboard, write the names and abbreviations of the states that are mentioned in the lesson: *Louisiana/LA; Washington/WA; Indiana/IN.* Explain that these abbreviations do not have periods, but most others do. Illustrate by writing the following on the chalkboard: *Street/St.; Avenue/Ave.; Route/Rte.* For practice with both types of abbreviations, have students write their addresses. For practice with postal abbreviations, have them label the states on p. 5 of their *Outline Maps.* Provide a list of state names and abbreviations for reference.

A Letter from New Orleans

The following letter and photos came from a third-grade class in New Orleans. It is a city located in the state of Louisiana. New Orleans is an urban community. An urban community includes the city and its surrounding areas. What does this letter tell you about urban life?

The French Quarter is a neighborhood in New Orleans known for its music.

New Orleans is a big city. People come from all over the world to hear our jazz music. We even have a park named for one of our famous musicians, Louis Armstrong.

Our sidewalks are full of people. We walk or take streetcars to get around the city. Sometimes it gets crowded. Over 500,000 people live here!

Some of us live in big buildings. Others live in houses that are close together. There are many tall office buildings here. But we have many beautiful old buildings, too.

P.S. What kind of music do you like?

Thinking About A Letter from New Orleans On the map, point out and put a marker on New Orleans. Call attention to the city's location on the Mississippi River and near the Gulf of Mexico. Explain that many big cities are near water because the opportunities for trade spur community growth.

Suggested Questions

● ***What is an urban community?*** *(one that includes a city and its surrounding areas)*

● ***What do the pictures show? What is special about that place?*** *(the French Quarter; its music)*

● ***Why do people from all over the world visit New Orleans?*** *(Possible answers: to hear the music; to see the city's beautiful old buildings; to see Louis Armstrong's hometown)*

● ***Based on the letter from New Orleans, what conclusions can you make about urban communities?*** *(They are crowded; people live close to each other; there are different kinds of buildings and ways to have fun.)*

★**THINKING FURTHER:** *Using Prior Knowledge* ***How do you suppose the location of New Orleans affects the people who live there?*** *(Based on what they learned about Galveston, students should realize that being near the water means that many people work in shipping and related industries. Also, the water provides different opportunities for fun.)*

17

Background INFORMATION

CULTURAL PERSPECTIVES New Orleans was founded by the French in the early 18th century, ruled by the Spanish at the end of that century, and made famous as the birthplace of jazz by African American musicians in the early 20th century.

● The descendants of New Orleans' French and Spanish settlers are known as Creoles. The name comes from the Spanish *criollo,* meaning "native to the place."

● The French introduced Mardi Gras to America when they settled New Orleans. Today, tourists come from all over the world to enjoy the music, the parades, and the costumes that have made the 10-day festival famous.

● The oldest and most picturesque section of New Orleans is the French Quarter, where the architecture reflects French and Spanish colonial influences.

● It was in the French Quarter that musicians like Jelly Roll Morton, King Oliver, and Louis Armstrong came together to produce a uniquely American form of music—jazz. Today jazz is popular around the world.

Curriculum CONNECTION

LINKS TO ART Have students make urban collages, using old magazines and newspapers. Tell them to cut out pictures and words that relate to city life and paste them on tagboard. Invite children to display their collages and talk about the urban characteristics that are shown.

Discussing Hello from Bothell

Point out Seattle on the map; then use a marker to show students that Bothell is about 12 miles north of the city. Explain that many people who live in the suburbs like being close to a big city but do not want to live in one.

Suggested Questions

● **What is a suburb?** *(a community located near a city)*

● **What are some reasons that people might decide to live in a suburb?** *(They can take advantage of a city's cultural, recreational, and employment opportunities, and still enjoy some semblance of small-town life.)*

● **What kinds of jobs do people in Bothell have?** *(They have jobs making airplanes and video games.)*

● **Look at the business park in the picture. Do you think you would find a place like that in New Orleans? Why or why not?** *(No; there wouldn't be enough space.)*

● **How is Bothell changing?** *(It is growing: there is less open space and there are more cars and houses.)*

★**THINKING FURTHER:** *Predicting*
What might happen if Bothell keeps growing? *(Possible answers: It might become more like a city than a suburb. It might become so crowded that some people would move away.)*

Hello from Bothell

Another letter came from the community of Bothell (BAHTH ul), Washington. Bothell is near the city of Seattle. Communities like Bothell are called suburbs. A suburb is a community located near a city. What does this letter tell you about living in a suburb?

In suburbs like Bothell, many people work in large business parks (top), and relax at places like Bothell Landing (bottom).

Hello! Things change quickly here in Bothell. There used to be a lot of open spaces for playing. But now our suburb is growing. Houses are closer and closer together. Even our roads are more crowded with cars. It sure is a problem!

Bothell has many business areas, like the one in the picture above. People work together and live near each other. We make things like airplanes. We even make video games!

For fun we also like to go with our families to walk and relax at Bothell Landing.

P.S. Our teacher helped us write this!

18

Background INFORMATION

MORE ABOUT BOTHELL Like many suburban communities in the United States, Bothell is in danger of outgrowing itself.

● If it continues to grow at its present rate of 5 percent per year, Bothell may soon become one of the biggest cities in the state of Washington.

● Many people move to Bothell because of job opportunities. The suburb is 12 miles from downtown Seattle, an easy commute by bus or car. It is also near a planned business park known as "The Technology Corridor," where workers can enjoy athletic facilities, jogging trails, and miniparks during their breaks.

● Town planners are excited about Bothell's growth, but concerned about losing the community's small-town feeling. They are working together to protect nearby lakes and forests from development.

Second-Language Support

TAKING NOTES Point out that pictures can make languages easier to understand. Encourage second-language learners to keep a journal of new words and phrases in social studies and illustrate their meanings with sketches.

Regards from Rochester

Have you ever seen a round barn? Well, near Rochester, Indiana, we have them.

Rochester is a farming community. Some of our families have farmed here for a long time. We still raise corn and cows. But it's getting harder to make a living. Land and farm equipment are becoming more expensive.

Our houses are far apart here. There are not many stores nearby. But these things are changing as urban areas grow our way.

Maybe one day you'll come and see us and our neat barns!

Bye-bye.

You can see from this letter that Rochester, Indiana, is a rural community. A rural community is a place of farms or open country. Distances between places are far in rural communities. Can you think of other types of rural communities? A small town in the mountains and a fishing village on the ocean are two other examples of rural communities.

In Rochester cars and trucks are the main form of transportation. Transportation is the moving of people and products from place to place. On the next page you will find a song about another type of transportation.

No matter what shape the barn is, farming requires hard work and long days.

19

Discussing Regards from Rochester On the map, point out Indianapolis, the largest urban area near Rochester. Then use a marker to show the class where Rochester is (about 50 miles north of Indianapolis). Have students notice that unlike suburbs, rural communities are far from urban areas.

Suggested Questions

● ***What kind of place is a rural community?*** *(Guide students to see that a rural community is a place far from urban areas, where there is open country and the houses are far apart. Examples: farming communities, small mountain towns, fishing villages.)*

● ***What kind of work do most of the people in Rochester do?*** *(farm work)*

● ***What are some of the problems that people in Rochester have today?*** *(It's hard to make a living in farming; land and equipment are expensive.)*

● ***Why do you suppose the houses in Rochester are farther apart than the houses in Bothell and New Orleans?*** *(They are separated by farmland.)*

● ***How do you know the pictures on this page were taken in a rural community, not in a city or suburb?*** *(The barn is characteristic of a farm, as is the work that the woman is doing.)*

★**THINKING FURTHER:** *Compare and Contrast* ***Which type of community would you like to live in: rural, suburban, or urban? Why?*** *(Guide students to explain their answers by comparing and contrasting the three types of communities.)*

Background INFORMATION

ROUND BARNS
● Round barns were first built in Rochester in the early 1900s. Farmers found them useful because cows could be fed from a central silo inside the barn.
● Although round barns were only used in Rochester for about 60 years, the community shows pride in its past by holding a Round Barn Festival each year.
● In addition to a circus, the festival features demonstrations that show old-fashioned methods of chair-caning, weaving, and hay-baling.

CITIZENSHIP

4-H CLUBS Sponsored by federal, state, and county governments, 4-H clubs instill pride in self and the community.

● Originally a program for farm children, the clubs now offer community service and recreational activities for young people in all types of communities. Club members learn many useful skills, including decision-making and leadership.
● The club's slogan is "Learn by Doing." Its name comes from the four key words in the club's pledge: Head, Heart, Hands, and Health.

Learning from Music Have students think about the relationship between where we live and how we get around.

Suggested Questions

- *In what kind of community does the person on the train probably live? In what kind of community do you think that person works?* (The person probably lives in a suburb and works in a city.)

- *What kinds of transportation do people use in your community? Why are those good ways to get around?* (Possible answers: public transportation in urban areas, where crowded streets make automobile use difficult; cars in suburban areas, where public transportation is not always available; trucks in rural areas, where people often need to transport goods from place to place.)

★**THINKING FURTHER:** *Classifying*
Make a list of different kinds of transportation. Then group the items on your list according to how people get around in urban, suburban, and rural communities. (urban: buses, subways, streetcars, taxis, walking; suburban: buses, trains, cars, taxis, walking; rural: cars, trucks, trains)

Technology CONNECTION

ADVENTURES CD-ROM
Enrich the lesson with the CD-ROM activity *X Marks the Spot.*

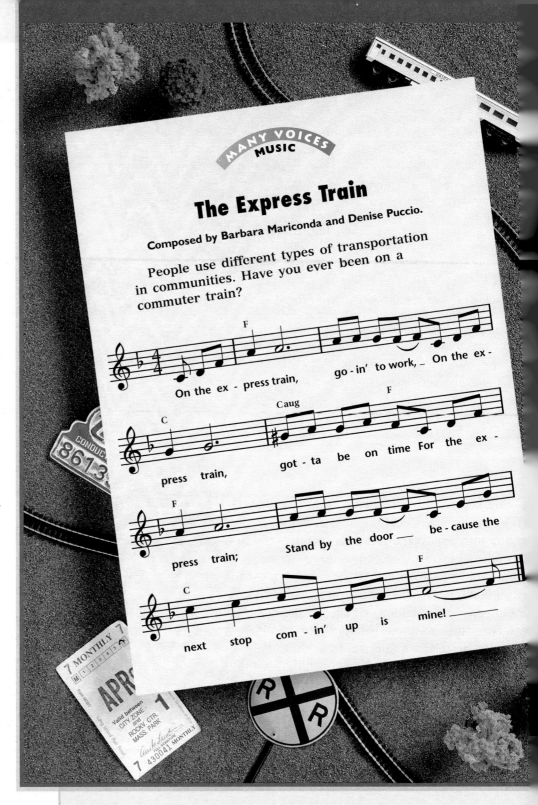

Curriculum CONNECTION

LINKS TO MUSIC Have students work with partners to make up new verses to the song. Help them generate ideas for verses about different forms of transportation by asking them how they get to school, a friend or relative's house, the supermarket, and so on. Remind students that walking is a form of transportation, too. When they have had time to compose and practice their verses, invite students to sing them for the class.

Using the ANTHOLOGY 🖥

CITY POEMS, page 10 In these poems, Langston Hughes paints a picture of San Francisco—the city that some people call the prettiest in the United States.

THE CITY BLUES, page 14 Students will enjoy this song, with verses about some of our country's most well-known cities.

THE HOUSE ON HILLSIDE La, pages 11–13 This selection about a family that moves from the city to the suburbs can help students see the relationship between where we live and how we live.

ALL THE PLACES TO LOVE, pages 6–9 The title of this poem refers to the many places that can make a rural community special.

WHY IT MATTERS

The way we live depends on where we live. In the United States we live in different types of communities. We also have different types of houses, jobs, and transportation. We have different ways of having fun as well.

Some communities are near each other and some are far apart. As communities grow closer together, contact between people increases. To get along with each other, it is important for us to understand neighbors and communities other than our own.

Freight trains carry goods to and from communities across the United States.

✓// Reviewing Facts and Ideas

SUM IT UP

- The United States has different kinds of communities.
- New Orleans, Louisiana, is an urban community.
- Bothell, Washington, is a suburban community.
- Rochester, Indiana, is a rural community.
- Transportation is the moving of people and products from place to place.

THINK ABOUT IT

1. What is a rural community? How is it different from an urban community?

2. **FOCUS** What types of communities does our country have?

3. **THINKING SKILL** In which _group_ would you place your community: urban, suburban, or rural? Why?

4. **GEOGRAPHY** Draw a map showing the route from your community to another one.

21

Understanding WHY IT MATTERS
Review the lesson concept: The United States has different types of communities and lifestyles vary accordingly.

Suggested Questions

- **Why is it important to recognize that the United States is made up of different kinds of communities?** (Guide students to see that the diversity of our country is one of its greatest strengths.)

- **Why is it important to understand how people in different communities live?** (so we can get along together)

⭐ 3 CLOSE

SUM IT UP
Have students work in pairs to answer the questions below and then review the lesson to verify their answers.

Suggested Questions

- **What kinds of communities does our country have?** (urban, rural, suburban)

- **In which kind of community do you find the most people?** (urban)

- **Where are suburban communities located?** (near cities)

- **In which kind of community could you walk for miles and see no one?** (rural)

EVALUATE
✓ **Answers to Think About It**

1. A rural community is a place that is far from urban areas. It is different from a city in that there is plenty of open land, the houses are far apart, the population is relatively small, cars or trucks are a necessity.

2. urban, rural, and suburban

3. To back up their answers, students should cite the distinguishing features of a rural, urban, or suburban community.

4. Have students identify each type of community on their map. _Location_

Write About It Have students write a paragraph describing the type of community they live in without using the words _urban, suburban,_ or _rural._

SKILLS LESSON

Lesson Overview
We use map scales to determine distances between places.

Lesson Objective
★ Use map scales to measure real distance between places.

★ 1 PREPARE

MOTIVATE Briefly review the places students located on the map during *Lesson 2.* Then invite them to speculate about how they could find the distances between those places.

SET PURPOSE Remind students that a map is much smaller than the places it shows. But we can still use maps to find out how far apart places really are. We do this by using a map scale. Point out the map scale on the bottom of the page. Explain that students will learn how to read it in this lesson.

DISCUSSING HELPING YOURSELF
Direct students to the *Helping Yourself* box on the facing page, and ask volunteers to read the steps aloud. Then have students look at the maps on that page to see what differences they can find.

★ 2 TEACH

Why the Skill Matters Have volunteers read the text aloud. Then review the definition of scale.

Using a Map Scale Have students follow the directions and make map scales for use with Map A.

Suggested Questions

● *How far is it from Chicago to Indianapolis?* (100 miles)

● *How far apart are Indianapolis and Cincinnati?* (50 miles)

Resource REMINDER

Practice Book: *p. 8*

Technology: *Videodisc/Video Tape 1;* Adventures *CD-ROM*

Transparency: *6*

GEOGRAPHYSKILLS

Using Map Scales

VOCABULARY
scale

WHY THE SKILL MATTERS

Say you want to visit Rochester, Indiana, and other communities in the state. You start in Rochester, and you want to learn how far it is to Indianapolis. One way to do this is to read the scale of a map. The scale helps to measure the real distance between places. It shows that a certain distance on the map stands for a certain distance on Earth.

USING A MAP SCALE

Look at Map A. The scale is the line with marks that stand for miles. It shows that one inch on Map A stands for 100 miles.

One way to use map scales is to make a scale out of a paper strip. Look at the scale below. Place the long edge of your strip along the top of the scale. Mark every 1/2 inch to show 50 miles. You have just made your own scale. Use it to measure distances on Map A. How far is it from Rochester to Indianapolis? To find out, place the strip so that the **0** is at the dot for Rochester. Now read the number closest to Indianapolis. The distance from Rochester to Indianapolis is about 50 miles.

USING DIFFERENT SCALES

Not all maps have the same scale. Maps have different scales because they show larger or smaller parts of Earth. Even though the scales are different, the real distances remain the same. The scale on Map B is different from the scale on Map A. How many miles are shown by one inch on Map B?*

Make a new strip to match the scale on Map B. Now measure the distance from Rochester to Indianapolis on Map B. Once again, the distance is about 50 miles.

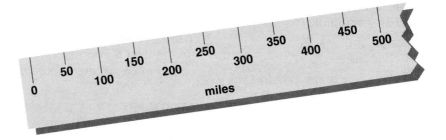

0   50   100   150   200   250   300   350   400   450   500
miles

22   *50 miles

Background INFORMATION

MORE ABOUT MAP SCALES Use an atlas to familiarize students with different kinds of map scales.

● Map scales may be expressed in numbers, as a ratio. On a map of the classroom, for example, the ratio 1:12 means that every inch on the map represents 12 inches, or 1 foot, of floor space.

● Map scales may use the metric system of measurement. Explain that in the United States we measure distance in miles. In most other countries, however, distance is measured in kilometers. One kilometer equals 0.6 of a mile.

TRYING THE SKILL

As you continue to use map scales, look at the Helping Yourself box for reminders. Try measuring some other distances. Use your scale for Map A. Measure the distance from Uniontown to Indianapolis. Place the **0** on your strip at the dot for Uniontown. Line it up so that your strip reaches Indianapolis. How far apart are these two places? Now use your scale for Map B. About how far is it from Louisville to Cincinnati?*

HELPING Yourself

- A **scale** is used to measure distances on a map.
- A map showing fewer miles per inch will show less area.
- A map showing more miles per inch will show more area.

REVIEWING THE SKILL

Use Maps A and B to answer these questions.

1. What are map scales? How are they useful?

2. How many miles is it from Scotland to Indianapolis? How do you know?

3. Which map shows a larger area of Earth? Which scale shows more miles per inch?

4. Other than a paper strip, what could you use for a scale?

MAP A

MAP B

*100 miles; 50 miles

Using Different Scales Have students make map scales for use with Map B. Use the questions below to reinforce the idea that real distances remain the same even when maps have different scales.

Suggested Questions

- **Why do maps have different scales?** (because they show larger or smaller parts of Earth)

- **On Map B, how far apart are Chicago and Indianapolis? Indianapolis and Cincinnati?** (100 miles; 50 miles)

Trying the Skill Have students review the information in the Helping Yourself box.

Suggested Questions

- **You are planning a two-day trip from Springfield, Illinois, to Cincinnati, Ohio. On the way, you will stop in Indianapolis. About how many miles will you travel each day? Which map did you use to find out?** (about 100 miles on the first day and 50 miles on the second; Map A)

3 CLOSE

SUM IT UP
Have students explain why it is important to know how to use map scales.

EVALUATE
√ **Answers to Reviewing the Skill**

1. Measuring lines; they indicate the relationship between distances on maps and real distances.

2. 50 miles; by using the scale on Map A or Map B

3. Map A; Map A

4. Possible answers: ruler, string

Technology CONNECTION

VIDEODISC/VIDEO TAPE 1
Enrich this lesson with the Chapter 1 map segments.

Search Frame 08844

Meeting *Individual* Needs

RETEACHING (Easy) On a map of the United States, have students find the distance from the local community to each community they have studied: Galveston, Texas; New Orleans, Louisiana; Bothell, Washington; Rochester, Indiana.

EXTENSION (Average) Ask students to plan a three-day bus trip from Louisville, Kentucky, to Milwaukee, Wisconsin. On the first day, they will stop in Indianapolis, Indiana. On the second day, they will stop in Rochester, Indiana. On the third day, they will arrive in Milwaukee. Have students use the scale on Map A to find out how many miles they will travel each day.

ENRICHMENT (Challenging) Have students make scale maps of the classroom, using the CD-ROM if possible. They will need a tape measure to measure the room and the distances between doors, furniture, and windows. Suggest a scale of one inch for every foot of floor space.

GLOBAL CONNECTIONS

Lesson Overview
Communities in Mexico and the United States have similarities and differences.

Lesson Objectives
★ Learn about Mexican culture.
★ Compare urban, suburban, and rural communities in Mexico and the U.S.
★ Describe how communities change over time.

1 PREPARE

MOTIVATE Direct students' attention to the *Read Aloud.* If you have a Spanish-speaking student in your class, invite him or her to read the quote in Spanish before you read the English translation. Then have students turn to their Outline Map of North America. Help them find and label Mexico and the border it shares with the United States.

SET PURPOSE Write the *Read to Learn* question on the chalkboard. Then ask students what they would like to learn about communities in Mexico and write their questions on the board. Finally, review the *Vocabulary* words and remind children to watch for them as they read.

2 TEACH

Understanding A World of Communities Tell students that the picture shows Ana Laura Flores, the girl who is identified in the text.

Suggested Questions
★THINKING FURTHER: *Making Conclusions* **Based on what you know so far, would you conclude that Ana's community is urban, suburban, or rural? Explain.** *(Suburban; it's near a city, not in one or far away.)*

Resource REMINDER

Practice Book: *p. 9*
Technology: *Adventures CD-ROM*
Outline Maps: *p. 4; p. 9*

A Community in Mexico

Focus Activity

READ TO LEARN
What are communities like in Mexico?

VOCABULARY
culture
national park

PLACES
Cuajimalpa, Mexico
Mexico City, Mexico

24

READ ALOUD
"I like living near Mexico City. There is so much to do and see here. There is a mixture o the very old and the very new. It's a special community to me."

"A mí me gusta vivir cerca de la Ciudad de México. Hay mucho que hacer y ver aquí. Hay una mezcla de lo viejo y de lo nuevo. Es una comunidad muy especial."

A World of Communities

These are the words of Ana Laura Flores, a ten-year-old girl who lives in Mexico. She wrote a letter to Mrs. Roy's class in Galveston.

As you know, there are urban, rural, and suburban communities in our country. The same types of communities can also be found in other countries.

A big city in the United States has a lot in common with big cities in other countries. The same is true of farming communities as well. But there are also a lot of differences.

In this lesson you will read about some communities in Mexico. As you read, think about how they are the same and different from communities near you.

Reading STRATEGIES *and* Language DEVELOPMENT

COMPARE AND CONTRAST Have students watch for the following signal words as they compare and contrast communities in the United States and Mexico: *same, in common, like; different, but, more than.*

LANGUAGE HISTORY Write the words *community* and *comunidad* on the board and have students note the similarity between the English and Spanish. Explain that both words come from the Latin word *communis,* meaning "common." A *community* is a group of people who share common interests or live in a common region.

Second-Language Support

DIALOGS Second-language learners often have more confidence in their English skills when discussing their native country. Invite them to talk about their country's culture with an English-proficient partner. If appropriate, have partners summarize the discussion for the class.

Living in Mexico City

Ana lives with her family in Cuajimalpa (kwah hee MAHL pah). It is a suburban community near Mexico City. Mexico City is the largest city in Mexico. In fact more people live in or near Mexico City than any other city in the world.

Mexico City has a lot in common with big cities in the United States. It is an exciting place. It has a rich past. Mexico City is the oldest city in North America.

Mexico City is also different from our cities. It has its own special culture. Culture is the way of life of a group of people.

Look at the map of Mexico City below. El Zócalo (el SOH kah loh) is the main square. What can you tell about the names on the map? Most of them are in Spanish. It is the main language of Mexico. Language is an important part of culture. In Mexico you may also hear people speaking many different native languages.

Built in the 1500s, La Catedral still is a popular place on El Zócalo.

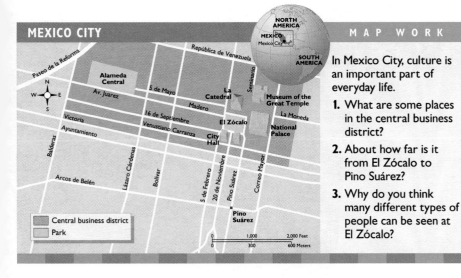

MEXICO CITY

NORTH AMERICA
MEXICO
Mexico City
SOUTH AMERICA

Central business district
Park

República de Venezuela
Paseo de la Reforma
Alameda Central
Av. Juárez
5 de Mayo
La Catedral
Seminario
Museum of the Great Temple
Madero
16 de Septiembre
El Zócalo
La Moneda
Venustiano Carranza
National Palace
Victoria
Ayuntamiento
City Hall
Balderas
Lázaro Cárdenas
Bolívar
5 de Febrero
20 de Noviembre
Pino Suárez
Correo Mayor
Arcos de Belén
Pino Suárez

0   1,000   2,000 Feet
0   300   600 Meters

MAP WORK

In Mexico City, culture is an important part of everyday life.

1. What are some places in the central business district?

2. About how far is it from El Zócalo to Pino Suárez?

3. Why do you think many different types of people can be seen at El Zócalo?

MAP WORK: **1.** Museum of the Great Temple, National Palace, and City Hall **2.** 2,000 feet
3. Its many different places attract people with many different interests.

25

Thinking About Living in Mexico City Help students recognize similarities and differences between Mexico City and U.S. cities.

Suggested Questions

- **Where does Ana live?** *(in Cuajimalpa, a suburb of Mexico City)*

- **What is culture? What is an important part of culture in any community?** *(the way of life of a group of people; language)*

- **What language would you hear most often if you went to Mexico City? What other languages might you hear?** *(Spanish; native languages)*

★**THINKING FURTHER:** *Compare and Contrast* **How is Mexico City like U.S. cities? How is it different?** *(It is like U.S. cities in that it is an exciting place with a rich past. It is different in that it is older and has a larger population; it has its own special culture; its main language is Spanish.)*

More MAP WORK

After students answer the questions, have them turn to their Outline Map of Mexico City. Work with children to label the central business district and to add information to the map key.

Suggested Questions

- **About how far is it from Pino Suárez to City Hall?** *(about 2,000 feet)*

- **Which park is on the western half of the central business district? The eastern half?** *(Alameda Central; El Zócalo)*

Background INFORMATION

MORE ABOUT MEXICO CITY

- Mexico City is the capital of Mexico and its political, economic, and cultural center. About 19 million people live in the metropolitan area, and roughly half a million more move there each year.

- The city stands on the site of Tenochtitlán, the capital of the Aztec empire in the 1400s. The Spanish explorer Cortés conquered the empire and destroyed the capital in 1521. Over the ruins, he built Mexico City.

- The Spanish brought their culture to Mexico, including their language and architecture. Mexico City and other communities were patterned after cities in Spain, with a public square surrounded by government buildings.

Curriculum CONNECTION

LINKS TO ART Introduce students to another aspect of Mexican culture: art. Traditional Mexican folk art has influenced some of the country's foremost artists, among them Diego Rivera, whose murals show Mexican history from pre-Columbian to modern times.

Rivera painted his murals on public buildings, including the presidential palace in Mexico City, because he believed that art should be accessible to everyone. Students can read about the artist and see pictures of his work in *A Weekend with Diego Rivera* by Barbara Braun (Rizzoli, 1994).

Discussing Many Faces of Mexico City The pictures on this page will help students understand how past and present combine to make up the "many faces" of Mexico City. You may wish to have students examine the pictures before discussing the questions below.

Suggested Questions

● *What discovery was made while the Pino Suárez subway station was being built?* (the remains of an Aztec temple)

● *What does that discovery tell us about the history of Mexico City?* (The city has a multicultural heritage; the early inhabitants had religious ceremonies.)

● *What is on display at the station today? Why was that object important to the Aztecs who lived in Mexico City long ago?* (An ancient Aztec stone is on display. It was important because it was used in religious ceremonies.)

● *How is Mexico City changing today?* (Its population is increasing.)

● *What problems does Mexico City have in common with many U.S. cities?* (poverty, overcrowding, unemployment, homelessness)

★THINKING FURTHER: *Making Conclusions Why is the Pino Suárez subway station a good place to learn about the culture of Mexico City?* (Guide students to see that the blend of past and present is an important part of the city's culture. Both elements are present in the modern subway station, where the ancient Aztec stone is on display.)

Many Faces of Mexico City

What can a ride on the subway teach you? In Mexico City a trip on the subway will tell you a lot about Mexicans!

The city once built a subway station called Pino Suárez (PEE noh SWAH res). The remains of a very old Aztec Indian temple were discovered there. Today the station includes a display of an ancient stone. It was once used for religious ceremonies by the Aztecs.

What does this tell us about the people of Mexico City? It says they have a long, rich past of many different peoples and cultures.

Many people move to Mexico City every day. They come from different parts of Mexico. Like many cities in the United States and around the world, there are not enough jobs and homes for everyone. Some people in Mexico City live very well. Many are poor. People will have to work hard as they try to solve these problems.

Remains of an old Aztec temple were found while building the subway in Mexico City.

26

A Suburb Grows

Cuajimalpa is about 14 miles from downtown Mexico City. It used to be a rural village. Farmers, coal miners, and woodcutters lived there. Families like Ana's have lived and worked there for many years. But just as Mexico City has grown, new people have also moved to Cuajimalpa.

Slowly the community of Cuajimalpa is changing. New homes and buildings are being built on what used to be farms. People like Ana's father must find jobs in the city. Cuajimalpa is changing from a rural to a suburban community.

Mr. Flores works in Mexico City. He takes a bus to get there. The bus trip used to take him only 15 minutes. Now, because of increased traffic, the trip takes almost an hour.

Ana's mother takes care of her four children. She also works for a different family in another home nearby. Ana and her three sisters take a bus to school. During their free time they like to go to the town square to meet their friends.

As Cuajimalpa grows, Mr. Flores's bus ride to work takes longer and longer.

Learning How A Suburb Grows
Have students review what they learned about suburbs in the United States and then read about a suburb in Mexico.

Suggested Questions
- **Of all the communities we have studied, which is most like Cuajimalpa? Why?** *(Bothell, Washington; both communities are growing suburbs, where open land is being replaced by buildings and traffic is a problem.)*

- **How did people in Cuajimalpa earn a living in the past? Why do many of the people need jobs in Mexico City today?** *(They worked as farmers, coal miners, and woodcutters; opportunities for such work diminish as the community changes from rural to suburban.)*

- **Why is Mr. Flores's bus trip longer than it used to be?** *(Traffic has increased.)*

- **What does the Flores family have in common with families in your community?** *(Possible answers: Both parents work; the father commutes to work; the mother has two jobs; the children take a bus to school and spend free time with friends.)*

★**THINKING FURTHER:** *Classifying*
What kind of community was Cuajimalpa in the past? What kind of community is it today? What might it become if it keeps growing? *(rural, suburban, urban)*

27

Curriculum CONNECTION

LINKS TO MATHEMATICS Use the following arithmetic problem to help students determine how much Mr. Flores's commute has changed:

- Mr. Flores's bus trip to Mexico City used to take 15 minutes. Now it takes almost 60 minutes. About how much more time is Mr. Flores spending on the bus than he did in the past?

- Guide students to see that there are two ways to answer the question: They can divide 15 into 60 to find that the bus trip takes about 4 times longer than it used to take. Or, they can subtract 15 from 60 to find that the trip is now about 45 minutes longer.

LINKS TO LANGUAGE ARTS This lesson should arouse students' curiosity about changes in their community.

- Divide the class into three groups to make a book called *Our Community: Past, Present, and Future.* Chapter 1 should focus on changes in the community during the last century; Chapter 2 on changes in the community today; Chapter 3 on changes that would make the community a better place to live in the future.

- Help students decide how to allocate tasks such as research, writing, and illustrating. Refer researchers to the school librarian for information.

- Have a contest to decide on a cover illustration. Help students bind the completed book. Then donate it to the school library.

Discussing Communities Change

Guide students to see that all communities change over time.

Suggested Questions

- ● **Where could Mr. Flores take a visitor to show that Cuajimalpa is a blend of the old and new?** *(an old marketplace and a new supermarket)*

- ● **Why did the government make the forest near Cuajimalpa a national park?** *(so everyone could enjoy it; so it wouldn't be "eaten up" by the growth of Mexico City)*

- ● **What is one problem that Cuajimalpa, Mexico City, and Galveston, Texas, share?** *(air pollution)*

- ● **How are people in all three communities trying to solve the problem?** *(by using their cars less often)*

- ★THINKING FURTHER: *Cause and Effect* **What is the main reason for the changes in Cuajimalpa?** *(the growth of Mexico City)*

Technology CONNECTION

ADVENTURES CD-ROM
Enrich this lesson with *Mexico*.

Links to SCIENCE

Easy Breathing

Does your community have a pollution problem?

To find out, build a pollution collector. Make a frame from four equal-sized strips of cardboard. Then place strips of clear tape across the frame with the sticky side up. You now have a pollution collector! Place it outdoors. Check it each day to see how much dirt is on the tape.

Communities Change

"What makes Cuajimalpa special," says Mr. Flores, "is the blend of the old and the new."

In the center of Cuajimalpa is an old marketplace. But the town also has modern supermarkets. While many new people now live in Cuajimalpa, most people have lived there for a long time.

Many people want to move to areas similar to Cuajimalpa. They like the beauty of the land. Near Cuajimalpa there is a large pine-tree forest. It is a national park. A national park is land that is set aside by a government for all people to enjoy. Making the pine forest a national park will protect it. The forest won't be "eaten up" by the growth of Mexico City.

As Cuajimalpa and Mexico City grow, people worry about air pollution. They are using their cars less often to help solve this problem. By working together, the people of Mexico are making their communities better places to live.

People can enjoy hiking in a national park near Cuajimalpa.

28

Curriculum CONNECTION

LINKS TO SCIENCE: EASY BREATHING To help students see how air quality varies from place to place, have them put their pollution collectors in different locations and compare the results.

Background INFORMATION

A SERIOUS PROBLEM Air pollution is Mexico City's most serious environmental problem. The city is in a valley surrounded by mountains, which keep the wind from blowing away polluted air. Over time, pollutants such as car exhaust and factory smoke build up to a dangerous degree. In an attempt to improve the situation, the government has passed laws regulating automobile use and is working on even stricter controls.

Background INFORMATION

WORRIED ABOUT WATER The history of Mexico City can help children understand why it is important to protect natural resources.

- ● When it was the capital of the Aztec empire, the city stood on an island in a huge lake fed by mountain streams. Surrounding the city were canals and raised beds of vegetation.

- ● Over the years, flooding became a problem, and the Spanish drained the lake in the early 1600s.

- ● In Mexico City today, there is serious concern about having enough water! Millions of people use water from the underground reservoir, and the water level is sinking at the rate of one foot a year.

WHY IT MATTERS

Like communities in the United States, communities in Mexico are changing. Many urban and suburban areas are growing out toward rural areas. With this growth old ways of life change and cultures change.

All communities face problems as they grow and change. To solve these problems people must work together.

Outdoor markets are popular places in Mexico to buy food and other products.

✔️ Reviewing Facts and Ideas

SUM IT UP

- Communities in other countries have a lot in common with communities in the United States. They also have differences.
- Culture is an important part of what makes each community different. Mexico has a special culture.
- Cuajimalpa is a suburb of Mexico City. It used to be rural, but it has grown as Mexico City has spread out. Communities change.

THINK ABOUT IT

1. What are some special parts of Mexican culture?

2. **FOCUS** What are communities like in Mexico?

3. **THINKING SKILL** What do you _predict_ will happen as urban areas continue to grow?

4. **GEOGRAPHY** Use the map on page 25 to measure the distance from Pino Suárez to the National Palace.

29

Understanding WHY IT MATTERS

Use the questions students generated at the beginning of the lesson to help them review what they have learned about communities in Mexico.

Suggested Questions

- **Why is it important to learn about communities in Mexico?** (Mexico is our neighbor; we need to understand our neighbors to get along with them.)

- **How does the picture show that the past is alive in Mexico today?** (The people are selling goods in an outdoor market, as people did long ago.)

⭐ 3 CLOSE

SUM IT UP

Divide the class into small groups to discuss the questions below.

Suggested Questions

- **Do you think Mexico City has more in common with New Orleans or with Cuajimalpa? Explain.** (Students should back up their answers by citing similarities between urban areas or between communities in the same country.)

- **What is the main difference between communities in the United States and communities in Mexico?** (culture)

- **What's one problem that the people of Mexico City and Cuajimalpa are working together to solve?** (air pollution)

EVALUATE
✔ **Answers to Think About It**

1. the Spanish language, the blend of old and new

2. urban, rural, and suburban; a mixture of modern and traditional

3. Urban areas will keep expanding into suburbs; suburbs will keep expanding into rural areas.

4. 2,000 feet _Description of Place_

Write About It Ask students to write letters to Ana, describing the similarities and differences between their community and hers.

Meeting _Individual_ Needs

RETEACHING (Easy) Tape butcher paper to the wall and have students draw a mural showing life in Mexico City. Tell children to label the features that can be found in other communities they have studied.

EXTENSION (Average) Have students read the following books about communities that change over time: _Since 1920_ by Alexandra Wallner (Doubleday, 1992) and _New Providence: A Changing Cityscape_ by Renata von Tscharner and Ronald Fleming (Harcourt, Brace & Jovanovich, 1987). Afterward have students create calendars showing the most important changes in each community.

ENRICHMENT (Challenging) Have students work in groups to learn more about Mexico City in the past and present. In addition to library research, students can use the _Adventures_ CD-ROM.

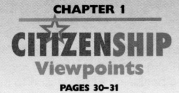

CITIZENSHIP
Viewpoints
PAGES 30–31

Lesson Objective
★ Compare and analyze contrasting points of view about zoos.

Identifying the Issue Have students read the text on this page. Then help them understand why it is important to be open to different viewpoints about the same subject; in this case, zoos.

Suggested Questions

● **What can we learn from listening to different viewpoints about zoos?** *(Guide students to see that we can learn about the negative and positive aspects of zoos. Also, we might learn something that would make us change our own viewpoint.)*

Discussing Three Different Viewpoints Invite volunteers to read aloud the viewpoints on page 31. Then have students discuss the *Suggested Questions.*

ELIJAH KEMP

Suggested Questions

● **Why does Elijah Kemp think zoos are educational?** *(They give people a chance to see live animals first-hand.)*

● **What is another reason why he is in favor of zoos?** *(Endangered species can be raised and protected in zoos.)*

NED MARSEN

Suggested Questions

● **What point is Ned Marsen making when he says "there aren't zoos for people"?** *(Animals don't belong in zoos anymore than people do.)*

● **What are the other reasons for his viewpoint about zoos?** *(Animals in zoos don't have enough space; they are better off in their natural habitats.)*

CITIZENSHIP
VIEWPOINTS

In Kenya, Africa, people can see animals in a type of zoo called a game park.

WHAT DO PEOPLE SAY ABOUT ZOOS?

In communities around the world, many people visit zoos to learn about animals. Many scientists who work with animals believe zoos are important. One person who agrees with this viewpoint is Elijah Kemp. You will read his words on the next page. He says that zoos protect endangered animals. Endangered animals are animals that are in danger of dying out.

Other people do not like zoos. They believe animals should be free in their natural environment. Ned Marsen's words explain this viewpoint.

Some people are not against all zoos. The best zoos, says Elisabeth Turbow, give animals room in a place similar to the animals' natural environment.

Read and think about the three different viewpoints on the next page. A viewpoint is what a person thinks about something. Then answer the questions that follow.

30

Background INFORMATION

A ZOO WITHOUT CAGES Tell students about the San Diego Wildlife Park, where wild animals roam free. Charles Shroeder conceived the idea for such a park in 1961, when he was the director of the San Diego Zoo. With community help, he was able to open the park by 1972.

The park has five sections, each replicating a different natural habitat and hosting a variety of animals. In the "East Africa" habitat, for example, herds of rhinoceros, wildebeest, giraffe, waterbuck, and impala mingle with flocks of flamingos and storks. Animals native to North and South Africa have separate habitats, as do animals from the Asian plains and the Asian swamps. Visitors ride on a silent monorail train above the fields, observing the animals from a safe distance.

The park also has walk-through exhibits, including Lorikeet's Landing, a giant aviary. There, visitors can hold out cups of nectar and colorful Australian parrots will perch on their hands.

Three DIFFERENT Viewpoints

1 ELIJAH KEMP
Third Grader, Cerritos, California
Excerpt from Interview, 1994

I think zoos are very educational because kids get to see animals firsthand. You're looking at them. But they are safe and you're safe. Watching animals in the zoo is not like anything you see on television. It's real! Zoos are also good because they raise endangered species. They protect these animals. That's how they grow!

"... zoos are very educational ..."

2 NED MARSEN
Fourth Grader, Teaneck, New Jersey
Excerpt from Interview, 1994

There aren't zoos for people, so why should there be zoos for animals? We have lots of space, but animals in zoos don't. They should be able to live wherever they want. The best place for them is where they have always lived.

"There aren't zoos for people ..."

3 ELISABETH TURBOW
Fourth Grader, Rochester Hills, Michigan
Excerpt from Interview, 1994

The way I feel about zoos is mixed. Having animals in cages is bad because they can't move a lot. But in many zoos animals are healthy. They get exercise and care. We enjoy seeing them. We're happy and the animals are happy. You also get to see animals like zebras that you wouldn't see if zoos weren't here.

"The way I feel ... is mixed."

BUILDING CITIZENSHIP

1. What is the viewpoint of each person? How does each person support his or her view?
2. How are these viewpoints alike? How are they different?
3. What other viewpoints might people have on this issue?

SHARING VIEWPOINTS

Discuss how you agree or disagree with these and other viewpoints. Make sure you give reasons to support your opinion. Then as a class write one statement about the purpose of zoos that everyone in the class can agree on.

31

CITIZENSHIP

RECOGNIZING PERSPECTIVES Divide the class into Group A, Group B, and Group C. Then present the following hypothetical situation: *You live in a community that has no zoo. Group A wants a zoo. Group B does not want a zoo. Group C wants a zoo but only if enough money can be raised for a very good one. How will you work out the problem?*

Have group members discuss their ideas and appoint a spokesperson to represent them. Then invite the representatives to debate the issue. Ask each one to state their group's viewpoint and the reasons for it. Then have all three respond with questions and alternative proposals.

To keep the entire class involved, have the representatives consult their groups periodically. If children seem unable to reach any common ground, remind them that they all want what is best for the community. How much will they compromise to attain that goal?

Suggested Questions

● **How would you describe Elisabeth Turbow's viewpoint?** (mixed)

● **What does she like and dislike about zoos?** (She likes to see the animals and thinks they are well cared for. She dislikes the fact that they are caged and can't move around much.)

✓ **Answers to Building Citizenship**

1. **Elijah Kemp**—Is in favor of zoos because they are educational and protect endangered species;
   Ned Marsen—Opposes zoos because the animals don't have adequate space and are away from their natural homes;
   Elisabeth Turbow—Has mixed feelings about zoos. She doesn't think it's right to keep animals in cages, where they can't move around much, but she likes to see the animals and thinks they are happy, healthy, and well cared for.

2. Elijah and Elisabeth both like to see the animals and think they are protected in zoos; Elisabeth and Ned are both concerned about inadequate space for animals in zoos. Unlike Elijah and Elisabeth, Ned sees no good reason for zoos.

3. Some people might oppose zoos now but be willing to change their viewpoint under certain conditions; for example, if the animal/space ratio were regulated by law. Others might say that we shouldn't spend time thinking about zoos when so many people in our society have problems that need attention.

Sharing Viewpoints Encourage students to identify the merits and drawbacks of the viewpoints they heard and assess them carefully. Then help them formulate a statement they can all support. Example: *A good reason for a zoo is to protect endangered species and educate people about them.*

Debating Viewpoints The *Citizenship* activity at left will give students an opportunity to debate the issue they have been discussing. Explain that a debate is one way for a community to arrive at a consensus on an issue.

Answers to
THINKING ABOUT VOCABULARY

1. culture
2. citizen
3. suburb
4. transportation
5. community
6. island
7. rural
8. national park
9. pollution
10. urban

Answers to
THINKING ABOUT FACTS

1. homes, parks, and businesses

2. They worked together to build a seawall and raise the whole town.

3. It now has many more people and businesses. More and more people are moving there to live and work.

4. They live in a rural community where places are far apart.

5. Both communities are suburbs. Both have problems with over-crowding and pollution. The people of Cuajimalpa speak Spanish and in Bothell people speak English. Many people in Cuajimalpa commute to the city for work. Many people in Bothell work near their homes.

Resource REMINDER

Project Book: *pp. 3–5*
Assessment Book: *Chapter 1 Test*

CHAPTER 1 REVIEW

THINKING ABOUT VOCABULARY

Number a sheet of paper from 1 to 10. Beside each number write the word or term from the list below that matches the description.

citizen	national park
community	pollution
culture	suburb
rural	transportation
island	urban

1. The way of life of a group of people
2. A member of a community or a country
3. A community located near a city
4. The moving of people and products from place to place
5. A place where different people live, work, and have fun together
6. Land that is surrounded on all sides by water
7. A type of community with farms or open country
8. Land that is set aside by a government for all people to enjoy
9. Anything that spoils land, water, or air
10. A type of community that includes a city and its surrounding areas

THINKING ABOUT FACTS

1. Name three things that make up communities in our country.
2. How did the people of Galveston, Texas, help each other in 1900?
3. How has the community of Bothell, Washington, changed in the past few years? Why are these changes taking place?
4. Why do people in Rochester, Indiana, need cars to get from one place to another?
5. How are the communities of Cuajimalpa, Mexico, and Bothell, Washington, alike? How are they different?

THINK AND WRITE

WRITING A PARAGRAPH
Write a short paragraph describing how people in your community have come together to solve a problem.

WRITING ABOUT CHANGE
Think about a rural community where the drinking water makes everyone look young. Write a paragraph describing how this community might change if people from other communities learned of its water.

MAKING A LIST
In communities across the United States, Main Street is changing. Make a list of three stores or places in your community that were not around long ago. Write a sentence telling why you picked these places.

Suggestions for Think and Write
SIGNS OF SUCCESS

WRITING A PARAGRAPH Students' paragraphs should describe an actual experience in your community—community members working together in an emergency or in an everyday situation.

WRITING ABOUT CHANGE Be sure students' paragraphs describe the process of a rural community growing into an urban one. As more people move in, they will build more homes and businesses on farms and open land, and they will require more forms of transportation.

MAKING A LIST Students' lists should reflect an understanding of changes due to technology and growth of the community. Long ago, there were no service stations or fast food restaurants; tall buildings were built as the population grew.

For performance assessment, see Assessment Book, Chapter 1.

APPLYING GEOGRAPHY SKILLS

USING MAP SCALES

Answer the following questions to practice your skill of using map scales.

1. On the map scale at the right, one inch equals how many miles?

2. How many miles is Cincinnati from Uniontown?

3. What is the distance from St. Louis to Detroit?

4. Is Indianapolis closer to Louisville or to Rochester?

5. Why is it important to be able to read map scales?

INDIANA AND NEIGHBORING STATES

WISCONSIN
Lake Michigan
Lake Huron
MICHIGAN
Milwaukee
Detroit
Lake Erie
Chicago
Rochester
ILLINOIS
INDIANA
OHIO
Springfield
Indianapolis
Cincinnati
St. Louis
Scotland
Louisville
Uniontown
MISSOURI
KENTUCKY

0   50   100 Miles
0   50   100 Kilometers

Answers to APPLYING GEOGRAPHY SKILLS

1. 100 miles
2. about 100 miles
3. about 250 miles
4. Rochester
5. Map scales help us read distances on a map.

Summing Up the Chapter

Review the chapter before making a copy of the main idea pyramid below. The chapter theme is at the top of the pyramid. The main ideas are in the middle. Fill in the bottom with information that supports each main idea. Then describe how communities in both the United States and Mexico have changed in the past few years.

Communities are places where people live, work, and have fun together.

Communities are similar to each other.	Communities are different from each other.
people care about their homes and neighbors people work together to solve problems communities grow and change	rural, suburban, urban, different languages, cultures, different types of homes, different sizes

Suggestions for Summing Up the Chapter

Prepare copies of the diagram for students to fill in, or have students draw diagrams similar to the one in their texts. Suggest students frame each statement as a question. For example, students can ask themselves, "How are communities similar?" Then they can review the chapter to find answers to their questions. Explain that there may be many choices for supporting ideas and invite students to share their completed diagrams before writing their sentences. Suggested answers are written in red at the bottom.

2 CHAPTER ORGANIZER

Communities and Geography

PAGES 34–61

CHAPTER OVERVIEW

Every community has landforms and bodies of water. The land and water provide food, jobs, and fun. People use the land for farming and hiking. The water can be used for fishing or swimming. People work together to protect their environment so they can continue to enjoy where they live.

CHAPTER PLANNING GUIDE

Suggested pacing: 16–18 days

LESSON	LESSON FOCUS	LESSON RESOURCES
1 OUR COUNTRY'S GEOGRAPHY pages 36–43	Landforms and Water of the U.S.A.	*Practice Book* p. 11 *Anthology* pp. 15–18 *Technology:* Adventures CD-ROM *Outline Map* p. 6
Infographic pages 40–41	Our Country's Landforms	*Technology:* Adventures CD-ROM
LEGACY pages 44–45	Fun with the Wind: Linking Past and Present	
2 CARING FOR OUR NATURAL RESOURCES pages 46–49	Protecting Our Environment	*Practice Book* p. 12 *Anthology* pp. 19–24 *Technology:* Videodisc/Video Tape
GEOGRAPHY SKILLS pages 50–51	Using Intermediate Directions	*Practice Book* p. 13 *Transparency:* 7 *Technology:* Videodisc/Video Tape
GLOBAL CONNECTIONS pages 52–56	A Fishing Community in Peru	*Practice Book* p. 14 *Geo Big Book* pp. 8–9
Infographic page 55	Endangered Animals Around the World	*Technology:* Adventures CD-ROM
CITIZENSHIP Making a Difference page 57	Keep Eustace Lake Clean!	
GEOGRAPHY SKILLS pages 58–59	Understanding Hemispheres	*Practice Book* p. 15 *Transparency:* 8 *Technology:* Adventures CD-ROM *Outline Maps* pp. 2–3 *Inflatable Globe*
CHAPTER REVIEW pages 60–61	Students' understanding of vocabulary, content, and skills is assessed.	*Assessment:* Ch. 2 Test, Performance Assessment Ch. 2 *Transparency:* Graphic Organizer

OPTIONS FOR STUDENT ACTIVITIES

Citizenship pp. 40, 48, 57

Curriculum Connection pp. 38, 39, 42, 45, 47, 48, 54

Expanding the *Infographic* pp. 40, 55

Using the Anthology pp. 42, 49

ASSESSMENT OPPORTUNITIES

Meeting Individual Needs pp. 35, 43, 45, 49, 51, 56, 59

Write About It pp. 43, 45, 49, 56

Chapter Review pp. 60–61

Assessment Book

Chapter Test Ch. 2 Test

Performance Assessment Ch. 2

Using the Floor Map Use the Floor Map and the Project Book to enhance Lesson 1 by having students build one community near water and another far from a water source.

Using Geo Adventures Use **Geo Adventures** Daily Geography Activities to assess students' understanding of geography skills.

Using the Vocabulary Cards The vocabulary words for each lesson are available on *Vocabulary Cards* for review and practice.

GETTING READY FOR THE CHAPTER

Plan a Field Trip

Objective: To arouse interest in the great outdoors.

Materials: *Project Book* pp. 6–7, glue

1. Give each student a copy of Project Book p. 6. Encourage students to use their own words to describe the seashore, forest, and mountain scenes.
2. Now ask students to think about spending a day in one of these places. To which place would they like to take a field trip? Invite students to color the picture of the scene they chose.
3. Then pass out copies of Project Book p. 7 and invite students to write about their place.
4. Encourage students to include as many details as they can when writing about their plans. For example, they might mention plants, animals, and people they hope to see.
5. Have students glue their scenes and descriptions on separate pieces of paper.
6. Students may wish to share their choices and ideas with the class.

SECOND-LANGUAGE SUPPORT

As second-language learners work through this activity, they may feel more comfortable sharing thoughts and information with small groups or with a partner before they speak to the whole class.

Additional Second-Language Support Tips: pp. 40, 46, 54

Introducing the Chapter

Ask students to close their eyes and visualize different kinds of land and water in America. Have them share stories about areas of natural beauty and outdoor fun.

THINKING ABOUT GEOGRAPHY AND CITIZENSHIP

As students link the places in the photographs to the points on the map, show additional areas that have similar landforms and bodies of water.

ENJOYING OUR LAND

Suggested Questions

● *Where is the girl in the photograph? How close is this to your community?* (She is underwater in the Atlantic Ocean; answers will vary.)

● *What is she doing?* (She is snorkeling.)

● *What do you enjoy doing outdoors?* (Invite students to share favorite outdoor activities with the class.)

● *What more would you like to learn about outdoor sports?* (Invite students to list their questions and refer to them as they read the chapter.)

★THINKING FURTHER: *Classifying*
What are three different ways people use the ocean? (They fish for food, travel by ship, play on it or in it.)

USING OUR LAND

Suggested Questions

● *Where are the Grand Tetons in relation to the Atlantic Ocean?* (The Grand Tetons are in the northern center of the country, far from the Atlantic Ocean.)

 Resource **REMINDER**

Technology: *Videodisc/Video Tape 1*

Communities and Geography

THINKING ABOUT GEOGRAPHY AND CITIZENSHIP

In Chapter 2, you will see scenes of our country's natural beauty. You will also see the many ways people use the land and water around them.

Land and water are important to all communities. By working together to protect the environment, people will always be able to enjoy the natural wonders of our planet.

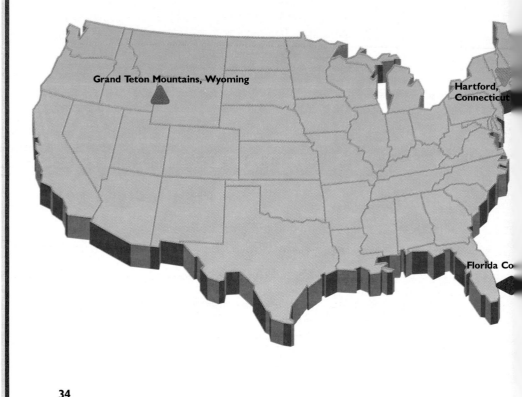

Grand Teton Mountains, Wyoming

Hartford, Connecticut

Florida Co

34

Background INFORMATION

LINKING THE MAP TO THE PHOTOGRAPHS

● Help students locate the Atlantic and Pacific oceans in relation to the United States on the map. Students will study bodies of water such as rivers, lakes, and oceans. They will be introduced also to landforms such as plains, mountains, plateaus, and hills. In the second photograph, students can contrast the plains to a mountain range.

● The United States is a land of abundant resources. Natural resources such as soil, water, and sunlight help us grow the food we eat. Scientists have observed that many of our resources will not last forever. Across the country, people are working together to protect the land from pollution and overuse. Materials such as metals, minerals, and paper pulp (from trees) are used again when communities recycle paper, cans, and bottles.

eople and animals
enjoy the Atlantic
Ocean along the coast
of Florida.

In Hartford, Connecticut, and other communities, people recycle to help protect the environment.

The plains near the Grand Teton Mountains in Wyoming provide food for cows.

35

- **What does the land look like in the second photograph?** *(You can see high mountains and a flat grassy area.)*

- **What more would you like to find out about plains and mountains?** *(Invite students to find answers to their questions as they read.)*

★THINKING FURTHER: *Making Conclusions* **How do the Plains provide food for cows? How do they provide food for humans?** *(Grass grows naturally on the Plains. Cows eat the grass, and we eat the cows.)*

PROTECTING OUR LAND

Suggested Questions

- **What is the boy in the picture doing?** *(He is recycling newspapers.)*

- **Why is he doing this?** *(So people can reuse the paper and save trees.)*

- **What kinds of communities recycle?** *(Any community can recycle.)*

- **What do you know about recycling? What more do you want to know about protecting the environment?** *(Invite students to share their knowledge. You may want to list class questions on the board to spark interest in Chapter 2.)*

★THINKING FURTHER: *Cause and Effect* **What is the effect of one student helping to protect the environment? Of a classroom of children?** *(Even one person can make a difference. If one student can help save one tree, several classrooms over a lifetime might save a forest.)*

Technology CONNECTION

VIDEODISC/VIDEO TAPE 1
Enrich Chapter 2 with the Videodisc *map* and *glossary* segments.

Search Frame 53777

Meeting *Individual* Needs

RETEACHING (Easy) Invite students to draw two pictures like the ones on this page. One picture can show someone having fun outdoors. One picture can show people using natural resources from the land or water for food, clothing, or shelter.

EXTENSION (Average) Have students write descriptions of their favorite places outdoors. Have them tell what each place looks like, what kinds of animals and plants are found there, and how people can enjoy and also take care of the area.

ENRICHMENT (Challenging) Ask students to write an interview with the boy in the picture. Have them ask the boy what he is doing and why, how he does it, and how he found out about it.

LESSON 1

PAGES 36–43

Lesson Overview

When we study *geography*, we learn how Earth's *landforms*, bodies of water, and *climate* affect people and communities.

Lesson Objectives

★ Recognize the diversity of geographical features in the U.S.

★ Distinguish between weather and climate.

★ Evaluate the impact of geography on individuals and communities.

1 PREPARE

MOTIVATE Invite three volunteers to act out the *Read Aloud*. Have one narrate the passage while another pantomimes the woman's actions and the third makes appropriate sound effects. Then use the *Thinking Further* question below to help students recognize how the woman is affected by her environment and how she affects it.

SET PURPOSE Point out the picture at the top of the page. Challenge students to explain how it relates to the *Read to Learn* question. Help them understand that we learn about Earth when we study geography. Then preview the *Vocabulary* words with students.

2 TEACH

Thinking About Geography Every Day Help students understand how geography is a part of daily life.

Suggested Questions

★**THINKING FURTHER:** *Making Conclusions* **How does geography affect the woman in the** Read Aloud? **How does she affect her surroundings?** *(Guide students to see that geography affects her choice of clothes, her activities, even her thoughts. She affects her surroundings by picking up branches, walking on leaves, and disturbing the squirrel.)*

Resource REMINDER

Practice Book: *p. 11*

 Anthology: *Where the River Begins, pp. 15–17; Field, p. 18*

Technology: *Adventures CD-ROM*

Outline Maps: *p. 6*

Focus Activity

READ TO LEARN
What is geography?

VOCABULARY
geography
plain
landform
plateau
climate

PLACES
Atlantic Ocean
Pacific Ocean
Mississippi River
Rocky Mountains

Our Country's Geography

READ ALOUD

It's a clear fall day. The mountain air is chilly. Inside her house, a woman puts on a jacket. She walks into the woods and hikes up the mountain. Along the way she picks up fallen branches. The leaves crunch under her feet. A squirrel runs away. The woman is cold and she thinks, "When I get home, I'll build a fire."

Geography Every Day

In this lesson you will see everyday events like the ones above in a new way. Events like these are part of the story of geography. Geography is the study of Earth's surface and the bodies of water that cover it. Geography is about how Earth is important to people's daily lives. It is also about how people change the land around them.

Take a look at the Infographic on pages 40–41. It shows some important features of our country's geography. You may find it helpful. You can refer to the Infographic as you read this lesson.

Reading STRATEGIES *and* Language DEVELOPMENT

USING VISUALS Help students recognize that visuals are an important source of information by having them examine the pictures in the lesson and predict what they will be learning about. When they get to the *Infographic* (pp. 40–41), challenge students to explain how it relates to the pictures they have discussed so far. Then tell them that they will be referring to the *Infographic* for further information as they read the lesson.

ANTONYMS Explain that *antonyms* are words that have opposite meanings. Direct students to p. 39 and have them identify the antonyms in the heading. Point out that the words help us see just how different climates in our country can be. As students read the lesson, have them note other antonyms that reflect the diverse nature of U.S. geography.

Splish, Splash, and Fish

What covers more of Earth than all the deserts, mountains, forests, cities, towns, and farms combined? The answer is water! How important is water? All plants, animals, and people need water to live.

Oceans are the largest bodies of water. The Atlantic Ocean and the Pacific Ocean are very large. They border the east and west sides of the United States. Oceans are made of salt water.

Rivers and lakes are also bodies of water. They are mostly made of fresh water. Sometimes they are very large. Use the infographic to see which are the largest lakes in our country. Bodies of water can also be very small. A quiet pond or a wandering stream are smaller bodies of water.

People relate to bodies of water in many ways. Francis Akinsulie (ah kihn ZOO lee) is a student who lives in St. Louis, Missouri. Here's what he says about living along the mighty Mississippi River: "I like going to the river to see the boats going past carrying different things. I once saw someone catch a fish there and take it home in a bucket."

Compare the stream (above) with the Mississippi River at St. Louis (below), where Francis Akinsulie lives.

37

Discussing Splish, Splash, and Fish Have students look at the map on pp. R8–R9 to see the Atlantic and Pacific oceans in relation to the United States.

Suggested Questions

● *Which covers more of Earth—land or water?* (water)

● *What are the largest bodies of water? What are some smaller bodies of water?* (oceans; rivers, lakes, ponds, streams)

● *In addition to size, what is another difference between oceans and most other bodies of water?* (Oceans are salt water; most other bodies of water are fresh water.)

● *Why do people need water?* (to drink, to bathe, to make plants grow)

● *Why does Francis Akinsulie like living near the Mississippi River?* (He can watch boats going by and people fishing.)

★**THINKING FURTHER:** *Using Prior Knowledge* **What body of water is closest to where you live? How do people in your community use it?** (Students should be able to name the body of water and/or identify it as a lake, river, ocean, and so on. Guide them to think about how people use the water for fun, work, and/or travel.)

Background INFORMATION

WATER, WATER, EVERYWHERE

● More than 70 percent of Earth is covered by oceans. Although we give them different names (Atlantic, Pacific, Arctic, Indian), all the oceans are connected.

● Life on Earth would not exist without oceans. They regulate air temperature and supply moisture for rain.

● The ocean floor has a variety of landforms, including mountain ranges, hills, valleys, and plains.

● Only 3 percent of Earth's water is fresh, and only 1 percent of that is usable. We see some of our fresh water in rivers, lakes, and streams. But there is 30 times more fresh water in underground reservoirs than on Earth's surface. These reservoirs are everywhere—even under the Sahara Desert.

Background INFORMATION

ABOUT THE MISSISSIPPI Flowing from northwestern Minnesota to the Gulf of Mexico—a span of 2,350 miles—the Mississippi is the longest river in the United States. Its name means "Father of Waters" in the language of the Native Americans who lived near the river long ago.

● With the development of steamboats in the early 1800s, the Mississippi became a major trade and transportation route. Such big cities as St. Paul, Minneapolis, St. Louis, Memphis, and New Orleans sprang up along its banks.

● Today the Mississippi carries more cargo than any other inland waterway in the country, most of it on barges pushed by tugboats.

Discussing Look at Those Land-forms! Students can see examples of the landforms under discussion by looking at the photos on p. 41 of the *Infographic.*

Suggested Questions

● **How are plains and plateaus alike? How are they different?** (*Both are large areas of flat land; plains are mostly flat, while plateaus are raised above the surrounding land.*)

● **What is the difference between hills and mountains?** (*Hills are lower. Technically, the difference is a matter of elevation: hills are lower than 1,000 feet; mountains are higher.*)

● **What can you do on a hill that you can't do on a mountain? What can you do on a mountain that you can't do on a plain?** (*go sledding; go skiing*)

● **What does Luis Garcia like about living in the Rocky Mountains? What are some other things people might like about living in the mountains?** (*skiing and sledding; possible answers: other kinds of outdoor activities such as hiking and rock climbing, mountain scenery*)

● **What are three jobs that people who live in the mountains might have?** (*Possible answers include tourist-related jobs such as ski instructors, tour guides, and hotel workers.*)

★THINKING FURTHER: *Classifying*
Look at the landforms on the Infographic. Which are like landforms in or near your community? (*Students should be able to identify local landforms.*)

Skiing is one way people like Luis Garcia enjoy the Rocky Mountains.

Look at Those Landforms!

Did you ever notice that the land near your community may have different shapes? It can stretch out flat the way a plain does. A plain i a large area of flat land. Or land can also form a mountain, rising steeply to a point.

Mountains and plains are two kinds of landforms. A landform is the shape of the surface of the land. Two other landforms are hills and plateaus (pla TOHZ). A plateau is lan that is raised above surrounding land. Plateaus are usually high and flat. Look at the Infographic. It shows a few of our country's many landforms. What kinds of landforms are near your community?

Luis Garcia lives in the community of Avon, Colorado. You can see from the Infographic that he lives in the Rocky Mountains. Luis says, "In the part of Mexico where I was born, it never snows. But here, with all the mountains, I get to go skiing and sledding. My whole class learned to ski together. Many people here have jobs that help people who come to ski."

38

Curriculum CONNECTION

LINKS TO SCIENCE Have students turn to the *Infographic* (pp. 40–41) and find the Appalachian Mountains. Explain that they are the oldest mountains in North America—more than 150 million years older than the Rockies.

Tell the class that new (or relatively new) mountains like the Rockies are characterized by high, sharp peaks. Older mountains like the Appalachians are characterized by low, rounded slopes.

Challenge students to find out the reason for this phenomenon. They will be able to do so by looking up *erosion* in the encyclopedia.

Background INFORMATION

THE ROCKY MOUNTAINS The largest mountain chain in North America, the Rockies span more than 3,000 miles, from Alaska, through Canada, to New Mexico.

● The Rocky Mountain region covers one-quarter of the United States, but only about five percent of the country's population lives there. Ironically, the inaccessibility that has kept populations low in the mountainous areas is now starting to attract people from overcrowded cities.

● Tourism is a major industry in the Rockies. Visitors enjoy the scenery, outdoor sports, and parks like Yellowstone, the oldest national park in the country.

● The Rockies' highest peaks reach more than 14,000 feet and are snow covered, even in summer. On lower peaks, melting snows trickle down the slopes and turn into streams, which sometimes join to form rivers.

Hot and Cold, Wet and Dry

Like the landforms in our country, the weather is also different in different communities. When we talk about the weather a place has over a long period of time, we are talking about climate.

How hot can it get? Take a July afternoon in Death Valley, California. Some people say you can cook an egg on the ground here before you can say "sunny side up." The climate here is hot and dry most of the year.

How cold can it get? Take a January day in Prospect Creek, Alaska. It's said that tears freeze here before they leave your eyes. Winters here are very cold.

How wet can it get? Take the island of Kauai (KOW i), Hawaii. It rains here about 460 inches every year. That's more rain than Death Valley gets in 400 years!

As you can see, our country has different kinds of climates. How would you describe the climate of your community?

Links to SCIENCE

Rain or Shine?

You can measure rainfall or snowfall the same way scientists do. Take a container with straight sides, such as a jar. Put a piece of masking tape straight up the outside of it. Using a ruler, mark off every 1/4 inch. Leave your container outside. Each day note the amount of rain or snow that falls.

In Death Valley (left) the climate is hot and dry. In Alaska (below) it is often very cold.

Thinking About Hot and Cold, Wet and Dry Encourage students to think about how climate affects daily life.

Suggested Questions

● **What is the difference between weather and climate?** *(Guide students to see that although weather may change from day to day, it follows a predictable pattern over long periods of time. The weather pattern of a particular place is its climate.)*

● **One of the three places mentioned in this section is also known as the Garden Island. Which place do you think it is? Why?** *(Kauai, Hawaii. Students should realize that a wet climate promotes plant growth.)*

● **What kind of clothes would you need if you lived near Death Valley? Prospect Creek? Kauai?** *(lightweight clothes like shorts and sandals; warm clothes like woolen coats and hats; rain clothes like boots and umbrellas)*

● **What is the climate like in your community?** *(Students should be able to describe the local climate.)*

★ **THINKING FURTHER:** *Cause and Effect* **How does climate affect the way people work and play in your community?** *(Students should cite climate-related jobs and recreational activities.)*

Background INFORMATION

CLIMATE Scientists divide Earth into climatic regions, depending upon the amount of precipitation and the temperature range.

● A region's climate is dictated mainly by its location on Earth. This determines how much of the sun's warmth is received throughout the year.

● Areas nearest the poles have the coldest climates with little or no precipitation; those nearest the equator have the warmest, wettest weather.

IT'S COLD OUT What is it like to live in the coldest state in the U.S.? In northern Alaska, winter temperatures range from 10 to 20 degrees below 0. Near the city of Nome, it's so cold that the ocean freezes. But weather doesn't stop Alaskans from having fun. The citizens of Nome hold the Bering Sea Classic, a golf game, on the frozen sea.

Curriculum CONNECTIONS

LINKS TO SCIENCE: RAIN OR SHINE? Have students use their precipitation gauges plus daily weather reports to make a classroom weather chart. Divide the class into groups of weather watchers and have them take turns keeping weekly records of temperature and precipitation. As they track weather patterns over time, students will understand how to describe the local climate.

LINKS TO MATHEMATICS Students may have trouble grasping just how much it rains in Kauai. Help them figure out the island's weekly rainfall (460 inches divided by 52 weeks equals 8.8 inches per week). Then have them check their precipitation gauges to estimate how long it would take for their community to get almost 9 inches of rain or snow.

Infographic

Explain that the *Infographic* is a recurring feature, which appears in every unit of this book. As its name suggests, it presents information graphically, combining text with illustration. In this instance, the *Infographic* provides practice with using a landform map while expanding students' awareness of U.S. geography.

Discussing Our Country's Landforms Have students use the map key to answer the questions in the text. (Plains are shaded green; mountains are shaded brown.)

Suggested Questions

• **What are the names of our country's five largest lakes?** (*Lake Superior, Michigan, Huron, Erie, Ontario. At this point, you may wish to tell students that the five lakes are known collectively as the Great Lakes.*)

• **Which part of our country is covered mostly by plains?** (*the central part*)

• **Which part of our country has the most mountains?** (*the western part*)

• **What type of landform is the Great Basin?** (*plateau*)

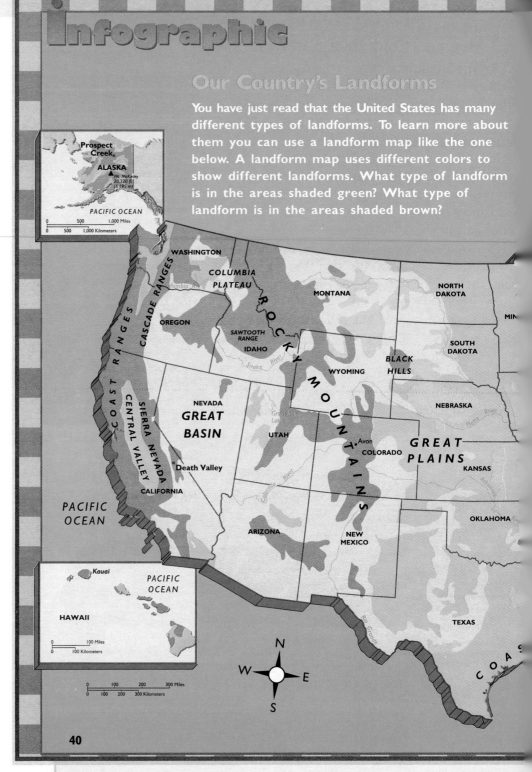

Infographic

Our Country's Landforms

You have just read that the United States has many different types of landforms. To learn more about them you can use a landform map like the one below. A landform map uses different colors to show different landforms. What type of landform is in the areas shaded green? What type of landform is in the areas shaded brown?

40

Expanding the Infographic

ART Have groups of students use the *Infographic* to make a relief map of the United States.

• Draw an outline map of the United States on mural paper. Cut it out, tape it to oaktag, and put it on a desk.

• Have students use nonhardening clay to make models of the landforms and bodies of water on the *Infographic.* Assign one major geographic feature to each group.

• When the models are finished, have students put them on the map, referring to the *Infographic* for position.

• When all the models are in place, have the class find their counterparts on the *Infographic;* adjust shapes, sizes, and positions, if necessary; and then label each feature.

★ CITIZENSHIP

APPRECIATING OUR COUNTRY'S GEOGRAPHY "This Land Is Your Land" by Woody Guthrie celebrates the geographic diversity of the United States. Play the song for the class and teach children the words. Then invite them to make up verses about some of the natural features on the *Infographic.*

Second-Language Support

USING PROPS Second-language students may benefit from increased use of transparencies and atlas maps in order to become familiar with different landforms. If possible, you might also have them use a relief globe as a tactile prop.

THE UNITED STATES: LANDFORMS

■ Mountains	□ Plateaus
□ Hills	■ Plains
● Cities	■ Points of Interest

Sawtooth Mountains in Idaho

Hills in Virginia

Columbia Plateau in Oregon

Great Plains in Kansas

MAINE
VERMONT
NEW HAMPSHIRE
MASSACHUSETTS
NEW YORK
RHODE ISLAND
CONNECTICUT
NEW JERSEY
DELAWARE
MARYLAND
PENNSYLVANIA
MICHIGAN
OHIO
INDIANA
WEST VIRGINIA
VIRGINIA
KENTUCKY
NORTH CAROLINA
TENNESSEE
SOUTH CAROLINA
ALABAMA
GEORGIA
FLORIDA

APPALACHIAN MOUNTAINS
PIEDMONT
COASTAL PLAIN

Lake Huron
Lake Ontario
Lake Erie
Lake St. Clair
Ohio River

ATLANTIC OCEAN
f of Mexico

41

- *Find the Central Valley in California. What type of landform is it? In what type of landform is it located?* (plain; mountain)

- *What type of landform covers most of Prospect Creek, Alaska, and Kauai, Hawaii?* (mountains)

- *What landforms are found in Missouri?* (mountains, hills, plateaus, plains)

★ **THINKING FURTHER:** *Making Conclusions* **Find the Black Hills of South Dakota. Then explain why the name might be confusing.** (The Black Hills are mountains, not hills.)

Technology CONNECTION

ADVENTURES CD-ROM
Enrich the *Infographic* with *Our Country's Geography.*

Background INFORMATION

MORE ABOUT THE LANDFORMS

- **SAWTOOTH MOUNTAINS** Part of the Northern Rocky Mountains, the Sawtooths have peaks of up to 12,000 feet. High mountain passes make parts of this range inaccessible to humans, providing safe havens for bears, deer, and other animals.

- **VIRGINIA HILLS** The hills in the inset are characteristic of Virginia's Piedmont Region, which covers almost half the state. Primarily agricultural, this region produces a variety of crops including tobacco, apples, peaches, and cotton.

- **COLUMBIA PLATEAU** The Columbia Plateau formed thousands of years ago, from lava that flowed out of the earth. Rivers, canyons, and mountains cross the plateau. The Columbia River is a major source of water power, with 14 dams that generate one-third of our country's hydroelectric power. Damming a river is one way people change geography to meet their needs.

- **GREAT PLAINS** The Great Plains cover the western half of Kansas, the state known as the Breadbasket of America because it produces so much wheat. Today, the flat prairies look like golden seas of grain. But back in the frontier days, before the land was cleared for farming, it was covered with grass that was taller than the men who plowed it.

Understanding That A Poem Describes Geography Review the types of natural features discussed in this lesson. Have students notice how some of those features are described in "Open Range."

Learning from Literature Encourage students to think about how the person in the poem is relating to the environment.

Suggested Questions

- **What is the person in the poem doing on the open range?** (camping out)

- **What is the weather like in this place? How can you tell?** (Hot and dry; the grass is sunburnt.)

- **Why does the mountain seem to go to the sky?** (because it's so high)

- **Why does the mountain "go black on the sky"?** (because it's nighttime)

★**THINKING FURTHER:** *Making Conclusions* **What do you think the poem is saying about the geography of our country?** (Possible answers: it's varied; it's magnificent.)

A Poem Describes Geography

People live with landforms around them every day. Read the following poem. How many landforms can you find?

MANY VOICES LITERATURE

OPEN RANGE

Prairie goes to the mountain,
  Mountain goes to the sky.
The sky sweeps across to the distant hills
And here, in the middle,
  Am I.

Hills crowd down to the river,
  River runs by the tree.
Tree throws its shadow on sunburnt grass
And here, in the shadow,
  Is me.

Shadows creep up the mountain,
  Mountain goes black on the sky,
The sky bursts out with a million stars
And here, by the campfire,
  Am I.

by Kathryn and Byron Jackson

range: open area of land
prairie: flat or rolling land covered with tall grasses

42

Curriculum CONNECTION

LINKS TO ART Invite students to interpret the poem visually by drawing pictures that show what it means to them. As an alternative, students can write and illustrate their own poems about geographic features of the U.S.

LINKS TO READING Students who wish to work on their own poems may be inspired by the books of Diane Siebert and Wendell Minor, which combine verse with illustration to convey the grandeur of our country's geography. The following titles are appropriate for advanced readers:

- *Heartland* (Crowell, 1989). This book takes readers through the fertile plains of the Midwest.

- *Sierra* (HarperCollins, 1991). This book reveals the wonders of the Sierra Nevada Mountains.

Using the ANTHOLOGY 🖻

WHERE THE RIVER BEGINS, pages 15–17 In this story, two boys set out to find the source of a river that flows near their house. As students read the selection, have them notice the different landforms the boys come upon during the course of their journey.

FIELD, page 18 This poem paints a vivid picture of a once-wild field that is now a suburban lawn. Use the Anthology Cassette to play the poem for the class. Encourage students to visualize the field during the different seasons the poet describes. Then invite students to describe the suburban lawn during those seasons.

WHY IT MATTERS

What if someone told you that you would be studying geography this year? You might think you would be finding places on maps. But using maps is just one part of geography.

You have seen how geography is important to Francis Akinsulie, who lives near the Mississippi River. How else do you think geography makes a difference in people's lives? Luis Garcia's community is in the Rocky Mountains. Many people there rely on jobs that support skiing.

The location of a community has a lot to do with the jobs people do there. In forest areas many people work with wood from the trees. Where the climate is warm, people may work by providing help to sun-seeking visitors.

Geography makes a difference in people's lives. This difference can be seen every day in many communities throughout the world.

Geography is **important to the kinds of activities people enjoy in communities.**

✓ Reviewing Facts and Ideas

SUM IT UP

- Recognizing landforms is an important part of geography.
- Plains, mountains, hills, and plateaus are important landforms in our country.
- The climate in our country is very different in different areas.
- Geography is important to people's lives every day in different ways. It influences where people work and what they do for fun.

THINK ABOUT IT

1. What is a landform? Give three examples.
2. **FOCUS** What is geography?
3. **THINKING SKILL** If you lived near the water, what do you _predict_ you would do for fun?
4. **GEOGRAPHY** Look at the Infographic on pages 40–41. What plains are around the Arkansas River?

43

Lesson Overview
People have been using the wind to fly kites for over 3,000 years.

Lesson Objective
★ Understand that kite flying is a weather-related legacy.

1 PREPARE

MOTIVATE Draw a word web on the chalkboard with the word *wind* in the center. Then have students think of activities that are commonly associated with wind (for example: flying airplanes, sailing boats, playing Frisbee, flying kites). Use their responses to complete the word web. Guide them to conclude that like all aspects of weather, wind can affect how we work and play. Explain that this feature focuses on kites—a legacy that lets us have fun with the wind today.

SET PURPOSE Invite children who have flown kites to share their experiences with the class. Then call on volunteers to read this page aloud.

2 TEACH

Understanding the Concept of a Legacy To help students understand why kites are a legacy, explain that when we fly them today we have something in common with people who flew them thousands of years ago.

Legacy
LINKING PAST AND PRESENT

Fun with the Wind

People all over the world use the wind to fly kites. The first kites may have been flown in China more than 3,000 years ago.

Long ago kites were not only for fun. In some Asian countries they were used for fishing. More recently box kites have been used to carry weather instruments.

Today kites are used in many ways to explore the air and enjoy the wind.

Wherever you live, kites can be fun for you!

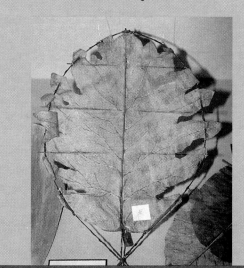

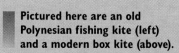
Pictured here are an old Polynesian fishing kite (left) and a modern box kite (above).

Background INFORMATION

MORE ABOUT KITES IN THE PAST

- Kites made of leaves were used by many different cultures. One example is the Polynesian fishing kite, which was used to snare fish swimming near the water's surface.

- The flat kite is the oldest kind of kite. It needs a tail to keep it pointed toward the sky. It was a flat kite that Benjamin Franklin used in his electricity experiment.

- The box kite was invented in 1893. The U.S. Weather Bureau used box kites in the early 1900s to record weather conditions. The Wright brothers used them in tests that led to their invention of the airplane.

MORE ABOUT KITES TODAY

- The Malaysian kite shown on page 45 is the traditional *wau bulan,* used for competitions in Malaysia today.

- On Kite's Day in China, people fly kites shaped like butterflies, dragons, birds, fishes, and flowers. Chinese kites often have whistles, pipes, or harp-like instruments that make music in the wind.

- In a 400-year-old kite-flying festival, the people of Hamamatsu, Japan, fly huge kites that may be three times the size of an adult.

- Scientists use kites to fly cameras into a volcano or near a bird's nest. But most people who make and fly kites today do it just for fun. They like to see how high they can fly their kites and what kinds of loops and turns they can make.

In 1752 Benjamin Franklin used a kite to show that lightning is one form of electricity.

Kites shaped like this come from the Asian country of Malaysia.

A boy in Egypt enjoys his kite. People all over the world have fun making and flying kites.

45

Examining the Pictures Have students look at the pictures while volunteers read the captions aloud.

Suggested Questions

● **What material is the Polynesian fishing kite made from? Why is that a good material for a kite?** (It is made from a leaf, a good material for a kite because it is lightweight.)

● **The "tail" on the Malaysian kite is called a hummer. Can you figure out why?** (Hummers make a buzzing sound as the kites fly.)

● **Where is the Egyptian boy flying his kite? Why is that a good place for kite flying?** (He is in the desert, a good place for kite flying because there is plenty of open space.)

★**THINKING FURTHER:** *Using Prior Knowledge* **Why was Benjamin Franklin's experiment dangerous?** (Students who know about the experiment can explain that he could have been killed by lightning. For additional information, see Curriculum Connection, Links to Science, below.)

3 CLOSE

SUM IT UP
Help students recognize that kites are a legacy that is shared by people all over the world.

EVALUATE
Write About It Have students write a paragraph explaining why they do or do not think kites will continue to be a legacy for people in the future.

Curriculum CONNECTION

LINKS TO SCIENCE In 1752, Benjamin Franklin set out to prove that lightning is electricity. To do so, he attached a brass key to a kite string and flew the kite during a thunderstorm. Lightning traveled down the wet string to the key, causing a spark, and proving Franklin's theory.

It is history's most famous kite experiment and perhaps the most dangerous. Franklin could have been killed by the lightning.

LINKS TO ART Have students make a Safety First poster, itemizing and illustrating safety rules for kite flying. They can find this information in books and encyclopedia articles about kites.

Meeting *Individual* Needs

RETEACHING (Easy) On a large kite-shaped piece of paper, have students draw pictures showing how kites have been used throughout history. Paste the paper to a balsa-wood frame, have children make a tissue-paper tail, and then let them take turns flying their kite.

EXTENSION (Average) Have students do library research to learn more about how kites have been used throughout history. Ask them to make a poster that illustrates their findings.

ENRICHMENT (Challenging) Ask the following question: *How can a kite be heavier than air and still fly?* Have students do research to find the answer and then share their findings with the class.

LESSON 2
PAGES 46–49

Lesson Overview
We need to appreciate and protect our natural resources.

Lesson Objectives
★ Identify and classify our country's *natural resources.*
★ Understand the importance of conserving natural resources.
★ Explain how people can protect the *environment.*

⭐ 1 PREPARE

MOTIVATE Ask a volunteer to recite the *Read Aloud.* Then tell the class that trees are the oldest living things on Earth. If you wish, use this opportunity to share with students the *Background Information* about trees on page 47.

SET PURPOSE Read the *Read to Learn* question aloud. Then direct attention to the picture and explain that trees are a natural resource. Ask students to identify the *Vocabulary* word that names another natural resource. Tell students that in this lesson they will find out why trees, *minerals,* and other natural resources are important.

⭐ 2 TEACH

Discussing A Wealth of Resources Help students understand what a natural resource is.

Suggested Questions
● **What natural resources could you find in a park? How could you use them?** *(Possible answers: trees for shade, water to drink, rocks to sit on.)*

★**THINKING FURTHER:** *Using Prior Knowledge* **What are some ways we use trees?** *(Students should be able to name a variety of wood products just by looking around the room. Point out that that we also use trees for fuel, construction, and so on.)*

Resource REMINDER

Practice Book: *p. 12*

Anthology: *Dear World, pp. 19–20; 50 Simple Things Kids Can Do to Recycle, pp. 21–24*

🔘 **Technology:** *Videodisc/Video Tape 1*

Caring for Our Natural Resources

Focus Activity

READ TO LEARN
Why are natural resources important?

VOCABULARY
natural resource
mineral
environment
recycling

READ ALOUD

The Oak is called the king of trees,
The Aspen quivers in the breeze,
The Poplar grows up straight and tall,
The Peach tree spreads along the wall,
The Sycamore gives pleasant shade,
The Willow droops in watery glade,
The Fir tree useful timber gives,
The Beech amid the forest lives.

A Wealth of Resources

This poem is called "Trees." It was written over 100 years ago by a poet named Sara Coleridge. She describes many different trees that grow on Earth. Do you have any of these trees in your community today?

Look around your classroom. Is there anything made from a tree? Perhaps your pencil or the paper in your book is made from trees. Trees are just one example of a natural resource. A natural resource is something found in nature that people use. In this lesson you will learn about other natural resources and why it is important to respect and care for them.

46

Reading STRATEGIES *and* Language DEVELOPMENT

PROBLEM AND SOLUTION After students read p. 48, have them identify the problem that the girls in El Segundo faced. Then have students itemize the steps taken to solve the problem.

WORDS WITH MULTIPLE MEANINGS Tell students that many words have more than one meaning. To illustrate, write the word *shade* on the chalkboard. Ask students what it means, and write their definitions on the board. Then point out the word *shade* in the *Read Aloud* (line 5). Ask students which definition is correct in this case. Guide them to use the other words in the passage as clues to the answer.

Second-Language Support

DRAMATIZATION Invite students to act out the *Read Aloud.* Before they begin their dramatization, help them think of motions, gestures, and props that can represent each tree.

Land of Plenty

Look at the pictures on this page. They show some of our country's many natural resources. The United States is one of the richest countries in the world in natural resources.

Water is one of our most important natural resources. As you read in the previous lesson, the United States has many bodies of water, large and small. Plants need fresh water to grow. People and animals need fresh water to live. Boats travel on our oceans, rivers, and lakes. They carry people and goods.

Have you ever picked up a handful of soil? Did you know that you were holding another valuable resource? Soil is full of minerals to help plants grow. Minerals are things found in the earth that are not plants or animals. Iron, salt, and diamonds are all minerals.

You may live in the mountains, in the woods, near the ocean, or in the desert. But wherever you live, your community has many natural resources. Even the air you are breathing right now is a natural resource!

Natural resources include water and soil. People also use oil and metals from inside Earth.

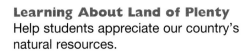

Learning About Land of Plenty
Help students appreciate our country's natural resources.

Suggested Questions

- **What are three natural resources that plants need?** *(air, water, soil)*

- **How do people use plants?** *(We use plants for food; for wood products, since trees are plants; and for cloth, which we make from the fruit of the cotton plant.)*

- **What mineral do we use in cooking? In building? In jewelry-making?** *(salt; iron; diamonds)*

- **We use oil to make gasoline. How do we use gasoline?** *(as fuel for cars, trucks, and buses)*

- **What natural resource is always around us?** *(air)*

- **What natural resources do we have in our community?** *(Students should mention air, water, and soil as well as specific local resources.)*

★**THINKING FURTHER:** *Cause and Effect* **Why is fresh water one of our most important natural resources?** *(Plants cannot survive without water, and people cannot survive without plants.)*

Technology CONNECTION

VIDEODISC/VIDEO TAPE 1
Enrich this lesson with the natural resources segment.

Search Frame 08881

Background INFORMATION

EARTH'S OLDEST LIVING LEGACY

- Some of the world's oldest trees are the sequoias in California's Sequoia National Park. The General Sherman Tree, for example, dates from before 200 B.C. In addition to its age, this tree has the distinction of being the largest living thing in the world.

- Most trees grow a new layer of wood each year. When a tree is cut down, the layers can be seen as rings in the trunk. These annual rings tell us the age of a tree.

- Trees help us conserve soil and water. Their roots help store water in the ground. They also keep soil from being washed away during rainstorms.

- Trees are most valuable to us when they are alive. Their leaves absorb carbon dioxide from the air and change it into the oxygen we breathe.

Curriculum CONNECTION

LINKS TO SCIENCE Point out the picture of the water wheel at the top of the page. Explain that water wheels were an early source of water power. Suggest that students do research to find out how water wheels were used as a source of energy in the past and how dams are used as a source of energy today.

LINKS TO MATHEMATICS All living things need water to survive. In fact, all living things consist mostly of water. For example, humans are about 2/3 water; chickens, 3/4; elephants, 7/10; pineapples, 4/5; watermelons, 9/10. Invite students to draw outlines of these items and color the percent that is water blue. Help them with the proportions by dividing their drawings into equal sections and indicating how many should be blue.

Thinking About Protecting the Environment After students discuss this section, invite them to read the following *Anthology* selection: "50 Simple Things Kids Can Do to Recycle" (pp. 21–24).

Suggested Questions

- **What is the environment?** *(the air, water, land, and living things around us)*

- **What can we learn from the pictures on this page?** *(different ways to protect the environment)*

- **What is recycling?** *(using something over again)*

- **What things in our classroom could we recycle?** *(items made of paper, plastic, metal, or glass)*

- **How did the "Tree Musketeers" improve the environment?** *(They improved the air by planting trees and other plants.)*

- **What is something you could do on your own to protect the environment?** *(Save appropriate items for recycling, put litter in trash cans, turn off leaky faucets, and so on.)*

- **What is something you and your classmates could do together?** *(Possible answers include a school cleanup campaign or recycling drive. Guide students to understand that a group can tackle a bigger task than an individual.)*

★**THINKING FURTHER:** *Making Conclusions* **How do you suppose recycling helps the environment?** *(Guide students to see that recycling helps us conserve natural resources by using fewer of them.)*

Protecting the Environment

"Save the Whales." "Give a hoot . . . Don't pollute!" Have you ever noticed bumper sticker like these on a car? They show that people want to protect the environment. The environment is air, water, land, and the living things around us.

Protecting the environment and its resources takes a lot of work. Just putting a bumper sticker on a car is not enough. Every day you can take personal action to help protect the environment. Every time you use a bottle, can, or piece of paper, you can save it for recycling. Recycling is using something over again. Factories take used plastic, metal, and paper and recycle them.

There are other ways you can help protect the environment. A few years ago some eight-year-old girls in El Segundo, California, wanted to help their community fight air pollution. They knew that plants and trees improve the air. So they formed a group called the "Tree Musketeers." They then decided to plant trees and other plants around their community. Today their community is a more beautiful place to live. According to one Musketeer, Tara Church, "The trees help us keep the air in our community clean."

Tara Church, middle, and others plant trees (right). Recycling (above) helps protect the environment.

48

★ CITIZENSHIP

THE 3 R'S Tell students that they can help protect the environment by practicing the three R's of conservation:

- *Reuse.* Instead of throwing things away, use them again. Reuse paper bags until they wear out. Save wrapping paper, ribbons, and boxes for art projects. Trade old magazines with your friends.

- *Recycle.* Think about what you put in the trash each day. If it's glass, plastic, metal, or paper, save it for recycling. Ask your neighbors to do the same. Make "Recycle It!" posters to display in your neighborhood.

- *Reduce.* Watch for ways to save resources. Don't leave water running while you're washing dishes. Turn off lights when they're not in use. Save a tree—bring your own bag to the store instead of taking one away.

Field Trip

Take students to the school or town recycling center. Have them note that the trash is separated into different categories: newspapers, cardboard, plastic, cans, glass. Invite speculation about the natural resources used to make each item (newspapers and cardboard/trees; plastic/oil; cans/metal; glass/sand).

Curriculum CONNECTION

LINKS TO SCIENCE Make recycled paper with your class. Soak newspaper strips in a pail of water for several hours. Then stir the disintegrated paper to make a sludge-like mixture. Pour the mixture over wire-mesh screening and let the water drain. When the mixture is dry, peel off the new paper.

WHY IT MATTERS

Look around your classroom again. Now you may notice more natural resources than you did before. There is one more resource you may not have noticed: people! You, your teacher, your classmates, and everyone in your community are important resources. It is people who take the other resources around them and make them useful. It is people who will protect our natural resources for years to come.

A garden needs both natural and human resources.

✓ Reviewing Facts and Ideas

SUM IT UP

- Our country is rich in natural resources including water, trees, soil, and the air we breathe.

- It is important to protect our environment. Everyone can take action to help make a difference.

- Recycling is one way to protect our environment.

- People are one of our most important resources.

THINK ABOUT IT

1. What are three examples of natural resources?

2. **FOCUS** Why are natural resources important?

3. **THINKING SKILL** How would you _sort_ materials from your home for recycling?

4. **WRITE** Write and design your own poster telling people to protect the environment. What will it say?

49

Discussing WHY IT MATTERS Help students understand that by protecting our environment today, we are preserving it for the future.

Suggested Questions

- *How does the picture show the importance of natural and human resources?* (People are taking care of the plants. The plants help people by improving the air.)

- *Suppose we stopped taking care of our natural resources. What might happen?* (Have students discuss how our lives would change if we no longer had certain natural resources.)

⭐ 3 CLOSE

SUM IT UP
Ask students to listen to these questions and to answer as many as they can.

Suggested Questions

- *Why is it important not to waste natural resources?* (They might run out.)

- *What is one thing you can do every day to protect the environment?* (Possible answers: Turn off lights and water, save things for recycling.)

- *Why are people one of our most important resources?* (People can make use of natural resources and protect them.)

EVALUATE
✓ **Answers to Think About It**

1. soil, water, trees and other plants, air, people, minerals

2. Everything we eat or make comes from natural resources.

3. glass, newspapers, cardboard, cans, plastic

4. Encourage students to focus on one environmental issue such as recycling or controlling pollution.

Write About It Have students think of one natural resource, including people, and write a paragraph explaining why it is valuable.

Using the ANTHOLOGY

DEAR WORLD, pages 19–20 In this excerpt from *Dear World: How Children Around the World Feel About Our Environment,* children express their thoughts about nature and their hopes for the future.

Meeting *Individual* Needs

RETEACHING (Easy) Have students make posters showing two ways people use the following resources: water, soil, plants, minerals.

EXTENSION (Average) Have students write a report about one natural resource in their community. Ask them to explain why it is important and how it is being protected.

ENRICHMENT (Challenging) Have students work in groups to identify one environmental problem in their community, propose a solution to it, and make a plan for implementing that solution.

SKILLS LESSON

Lesson Overview
Intermediate directions are halfway between cardinal directions.

Lesson Objective
★ Name the *intermediate directions* and use them to describe locations.

1 PREPARE

MOTIVATE Have volunteers use familiar words such as *under, above,* and *behind* to describe the location of different objects in the classroom. Point out that each location is described in relation to something else. For example, *The shelf is* above *the desk.* Explain that we use directions in a similar way—to describe the location of one place in relation to another. Example: *The chalkboard is* north *of the desk.*

SET PURPOSE Have volunteers name the four cardinal directions: North, South, East, West. Then have students look at the intermediate directions on the picture of the compass rose. Explain that in this lesson, they will learn how to use those directions.

DISCUSSING HELPING YOURSELF Point out the *Helping Yourself* box on page 51. Suggest that students refer to it as they work on this lesson.

2 TEACH

Why the Skill Matters Ask students how they would describe the location of a place that was in between two cardinal directions. Guide them to understand that they would need a new set of directions—intermediate directions.

Using the Skill Invite students to take turns reading the text aloud. Call on volunteers to answer the questions as they come up.

Resource REMINDER
Practice Book: *p. 13*
Technology: *Videodisc/Video Tape 1*
Transparency: *7*

GEOGRAPHYSKILLS

Using Intermediate Directions

VOCABULARY
intermediate directions

WHY THE SKILL MATTERS

El Segundo, the hometown of the "Tree Musketeers," is located near Los Angeles. To find where Los Angeles is located, you can look at a map of California. What if you wanted to travel from Los Angeles to Sacramento? Could you use the map to explain which direction to go?

You could if you knew how to use intermediate directions. An intermediate direction is halfway between two cardinal directions.

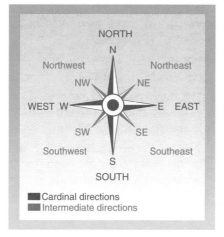

■ Cardinal directions
■ Intermediate directions

50

USING THE SKILL

You have already used a compass rose to find cardinal directions on a map. Look at the compass rose below. The cardinal directions are north, south, east, and west. North is shown by the letter **N**. What letters are used for east, south, and west?*

Now look at the map on the next page. In which direction is Sacramento from Los Angeles? It is neither *exactly* north nor *exactly* west. Instead, it is northwest, which is between north and west. Northwest is an intermediate direction. Look again at the compass rose below and find northwest. It is shown by the letters **NW**. The other intermediate directions are northeast, southeast, and southwest. What letters does the compass rose show for them?**

When you use intermediate directions, start by finding one place on the map. Then find the second place and describe the direction from the first place to the second. You may want to refer to the compass rose. If you start with Sacramento and go to Los Angeles, the direction is southeast.

---

* The letters *E, S,* and *W* are used.
** Other letters for intermediate directions are *NE, SE,* and *SW.*

Background INFORMATION

ABOUT THE COMPASS ROSE If possible, bring in a real compass so students can see how directions on a compass rose relate to real directions on Earth. Explain that when we read a compass, we follow an imaginary line that extends from each direction point. Show students how to line up the compass needle with magnetic North. Then let them find cardinal and intermediate directions in the classroom.

HELPING Yourself

- **Intermediate directions** are northeast, southeast, southwest, and northwest.

- **Find two places on the map. Use the compass rose to describe the direction from the first to the second.**

TRYING THE SKILL

Now try describing directions between other places. Use the Helping Yourself box as you answer these questions.

Look at the map again. In which direction would you travel to go from Los Angeles to Denver, Colorado? In which direction would you go to get from Las Vegas, Nevada, to Los Angeles? How about Colorado Springs, Colorado, to Provo, Utah?*

REVIEWING THE SKILL

1. What are intermediate directions?

2. If you were in Carson City, Nevada, in which direction would you travel to Tucson, Arizona? How can you tell?

3. In which direction is Salt Lake City, Utah, from Sacramento?

4. When is it helpful to know intermediate directions?

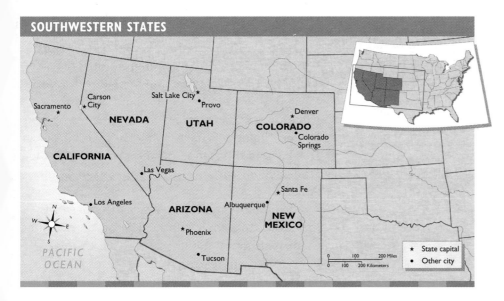

SOUTHWESTERN STATES

Sacramento · Carson City · Salt Lake City · Provo · Denver · Colorado Springs

NEVADA · UTAH · COLORADO

CALIFORNIA · Las Vegas

Los Angeles · ARIZONA · Albuquerque · Santa Fe

NEW MEXICO

Phoenix · Tucson

PACIFIC OCEAN

★ State capital
· Other city

0 100 200 Miles
0 100 200 Kilometers

*To travel from Los Angeles to Denver, you would travel NE; to travel from Las Vegas to Los Angeles, you would travel SW; to travel from Colorado Springs to Provo, you would travel NW. **51**

Suggested Questions

- *Between which cardinal directions is southwest?* (south and west)

- *In which direction would you travel to go from Utah to New Mexico?* (southeast)

Trying the Skill Remind students to use the *Helping Yourself* box as they work.

Suggested Questions

- *In which directions would you travel on a trip from Phoenix, Arizona, through Los Angeles, California, to Las Vegas, Nevada?* (northwest from Phoenix to Los Angeles and northeast from Los Angeles to Las Vegas)

- *You are planning a trip from Santa Fe, New Mexico, to Tucson, Arizona. Along the way, you will stop in Albuquerque, New Mexico, and Phoenix, Arizona. In which directions will you be traveling as you move from one city to the next?* (southwest from Santa Fe to Albuquerque, southwest from Albuquerque to Phoenix, southeast from Phoenix to Tucson)

3 CLOSE

SUM IT UP

Have students sum up what they have learned about intermediate directions.

EVALUATE

✓ **Answers to Reviewing the Skill**

1. directions that are halfway between the cardinal directions

2. southeast; by using the compass rose

3. northeast

4. when you want to describe a direction that is in between two cardinal directions

Technology CONNECTION

VIDEODISC/VIDEO TAPE 1
Enrich this lesson with *Intermediate Directions.*

Search Frame 53917

Meeting *Individual* Needs

RETEACHING (Easy) Have students draw a compass rose and label the cardinal and intermediate directions.

EXTENSION (Average) Have students turn to the *Infographic* on pp. 40–41. Ask them to plan a trip from their community to the four states mentioned on p. 41. Direct students to use cardinal and intermediate directions to describe the route they would follow from one place to the next.

ENRICHMENT (Challenging) Help students to use signs to label the classroom walls with the cardinal directions. Then have them use cardinal and intermediate directions to describe how to get from the room to the following places in your school: the cafeteria, gym, library, assembly hall, and principal's office.

GLOBAL CONNECTIONS

Lesson Overview

Natural resources are important to people in Paracas, Peru, and communities all over the world.

Lesson Objectives

★ Describe natural resources in Paracas, Peru.

★ Explain how people in Paracas are affected by their environment.

★ Recognize that people are responsible for protecting natural resources.

1 PREPARE

MOTIVATE Explain that the community described in the *Read Aloud* is thousands of miles away in the country of Peru. Then use the world map in the *Atlas* or *Geo Big Book* to show students Peru in relation to the United States. Tell them that three U.S. states—Washington, Oregon, and California—are on the same coast as Peru.

SET PURPOSE Have students identify the *Vocabulary* word that names a natural resource. Then direct the class to the *Read to Learn* question. Elicit responses by using the *Making Predictions* exercise at the bottom of this page.

2 TEACH

Discussing A Community by the Ocean Call attention to the picture, which shows fishing boats in Paracas. Then discuss the text.

Suggested Questions

● *In what country is Paracas? On what continent is that country?* (Peru; South America)

● *What is a coast? On what coast is Paracas?* (land next to an ocean; Pacific Coast)

★**THINKING FURTHER:** *Making Conclusions* **Why is the ocean the most important natural resource in Paracas?** (It is the source of other resources, jobs, and so on.)

Resource REMINDER

Practice Book: *p. 14*

Technology: Adventures *CD-ROM*

Geo Big Book: *pp. 8–9*

A Fishing Community in Peru

Focus Activity

READ TO LEARN

How are natural resources important to people in Paracas, Peru?

VOCABULARY

coast
peninsula
wildlife

PLACES

Paracas, Peru

READ ALOUD

"I live by the sea. My community is filled with beautiful beaches. There are hundreds of fish and other sea animals. I am lucky to live here. My family has been here for almost 100 years. I want to live here forever. The land and water provide us with so many things for life."

A Community by the Ocean

These are the words of a young boy. He lives with his family in the community of Paracas (puh RAH kus) in the country of Peru. Peru is located along the Pacific Ocean. That's the same ocean that borders the west coast of the United States. A coast is land next to an ocean. But Peru is thousands of miles away from the United States. It is on the continent of South America.

For communities like Paracas the ocean is important to people's lives. The ocean provides them with many natural resources. In this lesson you will learn about these resources. You will also see that people are concerned about protecting them.

52

Reading STRATEGIES *and* Language DEVELOPMENT

MAKING PREDICTIONS Have students respond to the *Read to Learn* question by making predictions about how natural resources are important to people in Paracas. Explain that when we make a prediction, we are making a guess based on what we know. Guide students to use what they know about natural resources in general, and the ocean in particular, to make their predictions. Encourage them to check their predictions as they read the lesson.

QUOTATION MARKS Direct students to the *Read Aloud.* Ask them how we can be sure that these are the exact words of the person who said them. Guide students to point out the quotation marks that frame the passage. Explain that these punctuation marks let us know we are reading a *quotation*—the exact words that someone has said. Students can practice identifying quotations and quotation marks when they read *Making a Difference,* which follows this lesson.

*An island is completely surrounded by water, but a peninsula has water on all sides but one.

CHAPTER 2 • GLOBAL CONNECTIONS

Living in Paracas

Do you know all the people in your community? Well, most people know each other in Paracas. There are only about 100 houses in this community. Many families have lived there for many years.

Fishing is important to many ocean communities around the world. Fishing is also a very important part of the culture of Paracas. Almost everyone in the community makes a living from fishing.

Look at the map below to locate Paracas. Paracas is a peninsula. A peninsula is land that has water on all sides but one. An island also has water around it. How is a peninsula different from an island?*

For people in Paracas, being near the water is a lot of fun. Many children in Paracas play soccer. But they play on the beach instead of on grass. They watch sea lions. But instead of going to a zoo, they go to a nearby beach. There they can see hundreds of sea lions!

The sea lion is one of many animals that live along the coast of Peru.

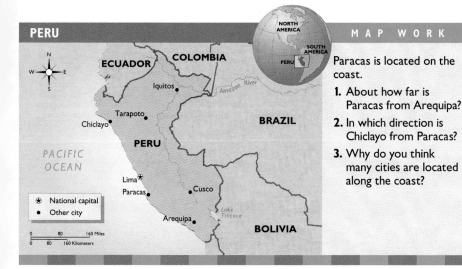

PERU

ECUADOR COLOMBIA

Iquitos

Tarapoto

Chiclayo

PERU

BRAZIL

PACIFIC OCEAN

Lima

Paracas   Cusco

⊛ National capital
• Other city

0   80   160 Miles
0   80   160 Kilometers

Arequipa

Lake Titicaca

BOLIVIA

NORTH AMERICA

SOUTH AMERICA

PERU

MAP WORK

Paracas is located on the coast.

1. About how far is Paracas from Arequipa?

2. In which direction is Chiclayo from Paracas?

3. Why do you think many cities are located along the coast?

MAP WORK: 1. about 160 miles **2.** northwest **3.** People make use of the ocean's natural resources for food, and living on the coast makes ports for shipping available.

53

53

Discussing A Rich Peninsula

Guide students to see that *wildlife* is an important natural resource in Paracas.

Suggested Questions

- **What are the people in the picture doing? What will they probably catch?** *(fishing; anchovies)*

- **What are two examples of wildlife in Paracas? What are two examples of wildlife in your community?** *(Fish, birds, whales, turtles, crabs; possible answers include birds, squirrels, raccoons, insects.)*

- **Why don't we call animals in a zoo wildlife?** *(They aren't in their natural environment.)*

- **Why do many birds from the north spend the winter in Paracas?** *(It's warm there.)*

- **Why do people from all over the world visit Paracas?** *(to see the wild birds and sea creatures)*

- ★**THINKING FURTHER:** *Compare and Contrast* **Think back to what you learned about Avon, Colorado. What is one way Avon and Paracas are alike? What is one way they are different?** *(Both communities attract visitors and offer tourist-related jobs. Avon is in the mountains with a generally cold climate; Paracas is at sea level with a warm climate.)*

Extending Did You Know? Have students work with partners to design a community flag that represents an important local natural resource.

What do flamingos have to do with the flag of Peru?

A long time ago people came to Peru by sailing to Paracas. They were amazed by all the flamingos they saw. The flag of Peru is red and white. The people of Peru chose these colors because of the color of flamingos found near Paracas.

A Rich Peninsula

An important natural resource in Paracas is its wildlife. Wildlife are animals that live naturally in an area. Fish are a kind of wildlife.

In Paracas anchovies (AN choh veez) are the most important fish. That's because many fishers make their living from anchovies. Every year millions of small fish are caught and shipped all over the world. The ocean here also has many whales, turtles, and crabs.

Paracas is one of the most important stopping points for birds. Birds are also wildlife. Many birds migrate, or travel, south to Paracas. During the winter they come from faraway places in the north. Some birds fly all the way to Paracas from Canada! The sanderling is one of these long-distance fliers.

These natural resources are important to Paracas for another reason. Visitors come from all over the world to see the wildlife. Some people in Paracas have jobs helping these visitors.

Anchovies are an important resource for fishers in Paracas.

54

Curriculum CONNECTIONS

LINKS TO SCIENCE Use a map to show students the distance sanderlings travel from their breeding grounds in Canada to their winter homes in Paracas Bay. Then tell students that the Arctic tern flies even farther than that each year. With a round-trip migration route of 22,000 miles, it is the champion of all long-distance fliers.

Invite students to do research to find out more fascinating facts about bird migration—one of nature's most amazing and mystifying events.

LINKS TO READING Students can compare Paracas with a New England fishing village by reading *Surrounded by Sea,* a picture book by Gail Gibbons (Little Brown, 1991). Ask volunteers to tell the class how life in the two communities is alike and different.

Background INFORMATION

WILDLIFE IN PARACAS Paracas has the largest nationally protected coastal wildlife area in Peru. Visitors can watch sanderlings chasing the waves, pelicans catching fish, penguins diving, and sea lions sleeping on the beach. Flamingos can also be seen, although their numbers have dwindled in recent years.

Second-Language Support

USING VISUALS As you read the text aloud, have second-language students draw pictures of the peninsula of Paracas and some of its natural resources. After the lesson, have students use their drawings to tell what they learned about resources in Paracas.

54

Infographic

Endangered Animals Around the World

In Paracas and other communities, wildlife is a valuable natural resource. But sometimes people don't take care to protect resources. Look at the Infographic on this page. Which endangered species have you heard of?

The California condor is the largest flying bird in the United States. Hunting, pollution, and the destruction of open land areas have threatened their existence.

The black rhinoceros lives in Africa. Their horns are used for medicines.

Saltwater crocodiles live in places such as Australia and Asia. Their skins are used to make shoes, wallets, and other products.

Giant pandas come from China. The bamboo trees they need for food are being destroyed.

The sperm whale was hunted for food, oil, and bone around the world. Other types of whales are also endangered.

Infographic

Explain that an endangered species is one that is in danger of dying out, or becoming extinct.

Discussing Endangered Animals Around the World Guide students to recognize that overhunting, habitat destruction, and pollution are the main threats to animal populations.

Suggested Questions

- *Why is the sperm whale endangered?* (It's been overhunted for its food, oil, and bone.)

- *How can shoppers and storekeepers help save crocodiles?* (by refusing to buy and sell products made from crocodile skin)

- *Why is the black rhinoceros hunted?* (Its horns are used for medicine)

- *Why is the California condor endangered?* (hunting, pollution, habitat destruction)

★THINKING FURTHER: *Making Conclusions* **Why do you think people are destroying the bamboo trees giant pandas need?** (Forests are being cut down to make way for housing, agriculture, and so on.)

Technology CONNECTION

ADVENTURES CD-ROM
Enrich the *Infographic* with the *Creature Feature* activity.

Expanding the Infographic

RESEARCHING Have students work in groups to "adopt" one of the endangered species discussed in the text. Direct groups to research the following questions:

- *Why is it important to save their adopted species?*
- *What efforts are being made to do so?*
- *How can children help?*

Have students present their findings in *Infographics* of their own. Sources of information include the CD-ROM, nature magazines like *Ranger Rick,* environmental groups such as the Sierra Club, and the following books: *Children's Atlas of Wildlife,* Elizabeth Fagan (Rand McNally, 1990); *Kids Can Save the Animals! 101 Easy Things to Do,* Ingrid Newkirk (Warner, 1991).

Background INFORMATION

SAVING THE CONDOR Students will find it interesting to learn that scientists have used puppets in a captive-breeding program for condors at the San Diego Wildlife Park. These birds generally lay only one egg every two years. But if something happens to the egg, the female will lay another to replace it.

To increase the breeding rate, park scientists removed the condor eggs from the nests and incubated them artificially. When the chicks hatched, they were raised by surrogate parents—humans using condor puppets. Meanwhile, the real parents were busy making and laying new eggs.

Suggested Questions

★THINKING FURTHER: *Making Conclusions* **Why should people all over the world be concerned about ocean pollution?** *(It contaminates and kills ocean wildlife; it makes the water unsafe for swimming and other activities. Also, pollution travels; even if we wanted to, we could not restrict it to one part of the ocean.)*

Discussing WHY IT MATTERS Be sure students understand why people need to work together to protect natural resources.

Suggested Questions

● **Why is it important for people to work together to protect the environment?** *(What happens in one part of the world affects people all over the world.)*

★ **3 CLOSE**

SUM IT UP
Have students answer the questions.

Suggested Questions

● **What is the most important natural resource in Paracas? How do people use it to earn a living?** *(ocean; by fishing)*

● **What has caused pollution in Paracas?** *(industrial waste)*

● **What are people in Paracas doing about pollution?** *(reducing ocean waste; keeping beaches clean)*

EVALUATE
✓ **Answers to Think About It**
1. Possible answers include: the ocean and wildlife.

2. They are a source of jobs and enjoyment.

3. Answers will vary.

4. Jobs and recreation revolve around the ocean, which surrounds Paracas on three sides. *Human-Environment Interaction*

Write About It Have students write a paragraph explaining why it is important to protect natural resources in Paracas.

Caring for Resources

People in Peru care about their natural resources. Like many communities in the United States, Paracas is becoming polluted. Waste from nearby businesses is dumped into the ocean. Some fish are unsafe to eat.

But the pollution problem in Paracas is improving. People are keeping their beaches clean. Businesses are being more careful not to dump dangerous wastes into the ocean.

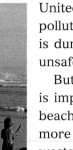

By taking care of natural resources, people will be able to enjoy the beaches around Paracas for years to come.

WHY IT MATTERS

You have seen how important natural resources are to people in Paracas. You have also seen one way that people in communities all over the world are alike. They are all concerned about protecting these resources.

By working together, people will be able to protect Earth's natural resources for many years to come.

✓ Reviewing Facts and Ideas

SUM IT UP

● Paracas is an ocean community in the country of Peru.

● There are many natural resources in Paracas.

● Pollution is dangerous to people and wildlife in Paracas.

● People are working together to help fight pollution in Paracas and other places.

THINK ABOUT IT

1. What do people like about living in Paracas?

2. **FOCUS** How are natural resources important to people in Paracas, Peru?

3. **THINKING SKILL** How are the resources in your community *like* the wildlife in Paracas?

4. **GEOGRAPHY** Paracas is a peninsula. How is this important to life in the community of Paracas?

56

Background INFORMATION

A WORLDWIDE PROBLEM The pollution in Paracas is largely the result of industrial waste from fishmeal factories in the area. The problem has been reduced in recent years, but ocean pollution remains a concern in Paracas as well as in communities all over the world.

Meeting *Individual* Needs

RETEACHING (Easy) Have students make posters illustrating natural resources in Paracas. Direct students to label each resource.

EXTENSION (Average) Have students make a chart comparing and contrasting Paracas with one of the communities they studied in this unit.

ENRICHMENT (Challenging) Students can use an encyclopedia and/or *Adventures* CD-ROM to find out how natural resources are important to other communities in South America. Have them write *Did You Know?* columns based on their findings.

CITIZENSHIP
MAKING A DIFFERENCE

Keep Eustace Lake Clean!

ZUNI, NEW MEXICO— If you visit Eustace Lake in Zuni, New Mexico, you might see a sign that says, "Keep Eustace Lake Clean." It was made by sixth graders who took action to protect their environment.

It all started in the classroom of Jim Bizell, a teacher at Zuni Middle School. One of his students' favorite spots was Eustace Lake. The lake was once a great place to swim, boat, and fish. But it became unsafe to use. Kelton Kallestewa, one of Mr. Bizell's students, described the lake this way: "It was filled with tires, garbage, and bottles. The picnic tables were broken, and the bathroom walls were knocked down."

Mr. Bizell decided that the students could make a difference by cleaning the lake. Here's Kelton's description of what they did: "We began hauling weeds and removing glass. Four kids went out on a boat and took trash out of the lake. Other kids repaired the bathrooms and picnic tables."

Soon other members of the community were helping too. Some gave pipes to make swing sets. Others helped make pathways and put fish back in the lake.

Making a difference is "up to the kids," said Kelton. "We have the ability to do it. It makes me feel proud to have other people proud of me. When I see the lake now, I'm happy. I'll be able to fish!"

"It makes me feel proud . . ."

Kelton Kallestewa

57

CITIZENSHIP

WORKING TOGETHER Give students an opportunity to make a difference in their community by enlisting the aid of government agencies.

- Have the class write to the state Fish and Wildlife Service to inquire about the water quality of a local body of water. If the water is clean, students should find out what they can do to help keep it that way. If it is polluted, they should find out how they can help clean it up.

- Poll students to find out what local environmental issue concerns them the most. Then tell them that one way to get help with the problem is by writing to the Environmental Protection Agency. Explain that the EPA is a federal agency that enforces laws protecting the air, land, and water. The agency answers letters from children all over the United States. Mail should be sent to the U.S. Environmental Protection Agency; Public Information Center, 3404; 401 M St., SW, Washington, DC 20460.

Lesson Objective
★ Recognize that people can work together to improve the environment.

IDENTIFYING THE FOCUS Be sure students understand why cleaning up a lake benefits the environment.

Suggested Questions

- **Why is a polluted lake bad for the environment?** *(It's not safe to go swimming, fishing, or boating in polluted waters. Pollution can harm or kill fish. It is also unsightly.)*

WHY IT MATTERS The class should recognize that children can work together to make a difference in their community.

Suggested Questions

- **How did Eustace Lake become polluted?** *(People dumped trash in it and vandalized the picnic grounds.)*

- **How did Kelton and his classmates save Eustace Lake?** *(They cleaned the lake and the picnic area. Because of their efforts other people in the community began helping too.)*

- **Why did it take a group effort to clean the lake?** *(It was too big a job for one person alone.)*

- **Why do you think Kelton says that making a difference is "up to the kids"?** *(Answers should reflect the idea that like all people, children are responsible for protecting the environment.)*

★**THINKING FURTHER:** *Making Decisions* **What is one way your class could make a difference in your community?** *(Encourage students to think of things they could do as a group to benefit the local environment. At this point, you may wish to refer to the Citizenship activity at the left.)*

SKILLS LESSON
PAGES 58–59

Lesson Overview
Mapmakers divide Earth into four hemispheres.

Lesson Objectives
★ Identify Earth's four *hemispheres*.
★ Define the *equator*.

1 PREPARE

MOTIVATE Display a globe, such as the *Inflatable Globe.* Have students compare it to the maps in this lesson. Guide them to recognize that the globe is round and three-dimensional; the maps are flat and two-dimensional. Challenge students to explain why a globe gives us a more accurate picture of Earth than a map.

SET PURPOSE Invite volunteers to turn the globe. Have them note that no matter how they turn it, they can only see half of it at a time. Explain that mapmakers divide Earth into halves. Students will learn more about those halves as they read the lesson.

DISCUSSING HELPING YOURSELF Direct students to the *Helping Yourself* box on page 59. Have volunteers read each statement aloud.

2 TEACH

Why the Skill Matters After students read the text, review the names of the seven continents.

Using the Skill Have students answer these questions.

Suggested Questions
● *Which hemisphere is opposite the Northern Hemisphere?* (Southern)

● *What is the equator?* (an imaginary line that divides the Northern and Southern hemispheres)

● *Which two continents does the equator cross?* (South America and Africa)

Resource REMINDER

Practice Book: *p. 15*
Technology: *Adventures CD-ROM*
Transparency: *8*
Outline Maps: *pp. 2–3*
Inflatable Globe

GEOGRAPHYSKILLS

Understanding Hemispheres

VOCABULARY
hemisphere
equator

WHY THE SKILL MATTERS

You have read about the community of Paracas in Peru. To describe where Peru is, you can say it is on the continent of South America. By learning about hemispheres, you will also know another way to locate Peru. Use the Helping Yourself box on the next page as you study hemispheres.

USING THE SKILL

Earth is a sphere. A sphere is round like a ball or a globe. Look at Maps A and B. They show Earth divided into hemispheres. *Hemi* means "half," so a hemisphere is half of a sphere.

The Western and Eastern hemispheres are opposite halves of Earth. Peru is in South America, in the Western Hemisphere. Is Asia in the Eastern or Western Hemisphere?*

Maps C and D on the next page show the Northern and Southern hemispheres. The equator, an imaginary line around the middle of Earth, divides these two hemispheres.

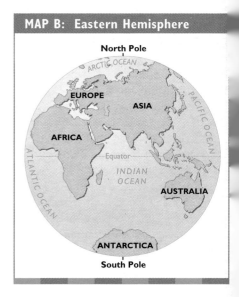

MAP A: Western Hemisphere

North Pole
ARCTIC OCEAN
NORTH AMERICA
ATLANTIC OCEAN
PACIFIC OCEAN
Equator
PERU
Paracas
SOUTH AMERICA
ANTARCTICA
South Pole

MAP B: Eastern Hemisphere

North Pole
ARCTIC OCEAN
EUROPE
ASIA
AFRICA
PACIFIC OCEAN
ATLANTIC OCEAN
Equator
INDIAN OCEAN
AUSTRALIA
ANTARCTICA
South Pole

58

*Asia is in the Eastern Hemisphere.

Background INFORMATION

Use two oranges to help students visualize Earth's hemispheres.

● Display one orange and tell students that it represents Earth. Cut the orange in half horizontally. Explain that the halves represent two of Earth's hemispheres: the northern and the southern. Put the orange together, and point out the cut line that represents the equator—the imaginary line that divides Earth into the northern and southern hemispheres.

● Display the other orange and cut it in half vertically. Explain that these halves represent two other hemispheres of Earth: the eastern and the western.

As you can see on Maps C and D, North America is in the Northern Hemisphere. What other hemisphere includes North America?*

TRYING THE SKILL

Now try locating Europe and Africa on the hemisphere maps. Europe is in the Northern Hemisphere and what other hemisphere? Are Europe and North America in the same hemispheres? In which three hemispheres are parts of Africa?**

HELPING Yourself

- The **equator divides Earth into Northern and Southern hemispheres.**
- **Earth can also be divided into Eastern and Western hemispheres.**

REVIEWING THE SKILL

1. Name the four hemispheres into which we divide Earth.

2. Which three hemispheres contain parts of South America? Which one contains all of South America? How did you find out?

3. Name all the continents found in the Northern Hemisphere.

4. What could you do to help a friend understand hemispheres?

Trying the Skill Remind students to use the *Helping Yourself* box.

Suggested Questions

- *In which two hemispheres is Australia?* (Eastern and Southern)

★**THINKING FURTHER:** *Making Conclusions* **If you could look down on Earth from an airplane flying over the North Pole, which hemisphere would you see?** (Northern)

3 CLOSE

SUM IT UP

Have students use *Outline Maps* pp. 2–3 to label the continents and oceans in the Eastern and Western hemispheres. Then have them draw and label maps of the Northern and Southern hemispheres.

EVALUATE

✓ **Answers to Reviewing the Skill**

1. Northern, Southern, Eastern, Western

2. Western, Northern, Southern; Western; by looking at the four maps

3. North America, Asia, Europe, parts of Africa and South America

4. Answers should reflect the idea that a sphere can be divided vertically and horizontally.

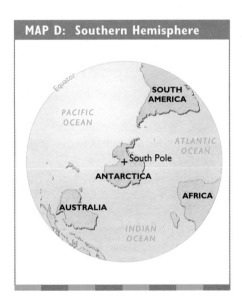

MAP C: Northern Hemisphere

MAP D: Southern Hemisphere

Technology CONNECTION

ADVENTURES CD-ROM
Enrich the skills lesson with the hemisphere maps on the *Adventures* CD-ROM.

** The Eastern Hemisphere; both are in the Northern Hemisphere, but Europe is also in the Eastern Hemisphere while North America is in the Western Hemisphere; Eastern, Northern, and Southern hemispheres.

Curriculum CONNECTION

LINKS TO SCIENCE Earth rotates on its axis, completing one turn every 24 hours. Only half of Earth faces the sun at any given time. That is why daytime in the Western Hemisphere is nighttime in the Eastern Hemisphere. Use a globe and a flashlight to illustrate this concept.

- Have students locate North America in the Western Hemisphere and Asia in the Eastern Hemisphere.

- Shine the flashlight on North America and have students note that Asia is in shadow. Then turn the globe halfway, so Asia faces the light and North America is in shadow. Explain that it would take Earth 12 hours to make the turn you just demonstrated. In another 12 hours, Earth would complete its rotation. By that time, North America would be experiencing daylight once again, while Asia would be in darkness.

Meeting *Individual* Needs

RETEACHING (Easy) Invite students to trace the path of the equator around a globe. Have them tell which countries and cities the equator passes through.

EXTENSION (Average) Invite students to name the countries from which their families or ancestors came. Then have them locate the countries in two or more hemispheres.

ENRICHMENT (Challenging) Have students make two clay models of Earth, divide one in half horizontally and the other vertically, label the four hemispheres they have created, and then list the continents and oceans in each one.

Answers to
THINKING ABOUT VOCABULARY

1. recycling
2. coast
3. wildlife
4. natural resources
5. minerals

Answers to
THINKING ABOUT FACTS

1. water; the oceans
2. A plain is a flat area of land. A plateau is a flat area of land that is higher than the land surrounding it.
3. For example: Our class can recycle classroom paper; we can take public transportation or carpools to school; we can recycle at home; use less electricity or heat; and buy products which are environmentally friendly.
4. They know how valuable the resources are. Many visitors come every year to see the wildlife. It is also important that local fishermen can always find fish in the ocean.
5. For example: In places where it snows in the winter, people ski and sled, or play indoors. In warmer climates, people can swim, ride bicycles, or rollerskate in the wintertime.

Resource REMINDER
Project Book: *pp.6–7*
Assessment Book: *Chapter 2 Test*

CHAPTER 2 REVIEW

THINKING ABOUT VOCABULARY

Number a sheet of paper from 1 to 5. Beside each number write the word or term from the list below that best completes each sentence.

coast   recycling
minerals   wildlife
natural resources

1. Every Saturday my father and I bring bottles and newspapers to our community _____ center.
2. When I visit the _____, I love to walk along the sandy beach.
3. Today people are finding new ways to protect endangered _____ around the world.
4. Trees, water, and soil are three examples of our country's _____ .
5. Things found in the earth that are not plants or animals are known as _____ .

THINKING ABOUT FACTS

1. What covers most of Earth's surface?
2. How does a plain differ from a plateau? How are the two landforms similar?
3. Describe two ways in which your class can help save our country's natural resources.
4. Why are some people in Paracas protecting its natural resources?
5. How does climate influence the things that people do for fun in communities?

THINK AND WRITE

WRITING A JOURNAL ENTRY
Suppose that you are backpacking around the United States. Write an entry in your journal describing three kinds of natural resources that you observed on your trip.

WRITING A SPEECH
Write a speech explaining the importance of protecting endangered species around the world.

WRITING A LETTER
Suppose you were invited to spend a week in Paracas, Peru. Write a letter to your family describing everything you saw there. Remember to include a description of the kinds of natural resources found in Paracas as well as the kinds of things people do there for work and for play.

Suggestion for Think and Write
SIGNS OF SUCCESS

WRITING A JOURNAL ENTRY In students' journal entries they should identify each natural resource they "observe" and tell how it is used.

WRITING A SPEECH Be sure students indicate in their speeches that all species of animals are valuable. They should mention that animals that live in the sea and sky migrate between countries, and that the lives of all animals are interconnected. Students can also suggest how Americans can help protect animals in other countries.

WRITING A LETTER Students' letters—in standard letter form—should describe the coastal town of Paracas where people fish, captain boats, and play soccer. They should mention pelicans, flamingos, and fish as important natural resources.

For performance assessment, see Assessment Book, Chapter 2.

APPLYING GEOGRAPHY SKILLS

USING INTERMEDIATE DIRECTIONS

Answer the following questions about the map at the right to practice your skill at using intermediate directions.

1. What are the four intermediate directions?

2. Which city is southwest of Louisville?

3. Which community is southeast of Scotland?

4. In which direction is Cincinnati from Indianapolis?

5. Why is it important to understand intermediate directions?

Answers to APPLYING GEOGRAPHY SKILLS

1. northeast, northwest, southeast, southwest

2. Uniontown

3. Louisville

4. southeast

5. If you want to travel between towns or cities, you often can't reach them by going directly north, south, east, or west. The intermediate directions explain more clearly directions that are between the cardinal directions.

Summing Up the Chapter

Look at the word map below. Then review the chapter to find at least three items to list under the four headings. When you have filled in a copy of the map, use it to discuss how we depend on Earth and its natural resources.

mountains   plateaus   oceans   rivers

Landforms   **Bodies of Water**

hills   plains   lakes

Geography

cold winters   rainy much of the time   plants   soil

Climate   **Natural Resources**

warm and   hot   wildlife   water
dry

61

Suggestions for Summing Up the Chapter

- Prepare copies of the diagram for the class or help students create their own diagrams.

- Have students complete their webs.

- Then help them create a web on the chalkboard that incorporates everyone's ideas. Lead a discussion about land and natural resources. Have students discuss the topics in each category, comparing landforms, bodies of water, climate, and natural resources in your community with those of other communities they have read about. Have them summarize the effects of the natural world on people's lives.

Answers to
THINKING ABOUT VOCABULARY

1. F
2. T
3. F
4. F
5. T
6. F
7. T
8. T
9. F
10. F

Suggestions for
THINK AND WRITE

Writing About Communities Students' paragraphs should describe how landforms and bodies of water make your community special. They should also describe what citizens do for work and play.

Writing A Poem Students' poems should contain details about landforms, and at least basic use of figurative language.

Writing About Perspectives Students' letters should explain how life in Mexico is different because of the language and culture. They should also show awareness of whether your community is rural, suburban, or urban, and how its size compares with that of the suburban city of Cuajimalpa.

UNIT 1 REVIEW

THINKING ABOUT VOCABULARY

Number a sheet of paper from 1 to 10. Read the definition of each underlined word. Beside each number write **T** if the definition is true and **F** if it is false.

1. A <u>plain</u> is land that is raised above surrounding land.

2. A <u>rural</u> community is a place of farms or open country.

3. <u>Geography</u> is the study of the various plants and animals that live on Earth.

4. A <u>port</u> is a place where trains and buses pick up passengers.

5. A member of a community or a country is known as a <u>citizen</u>.

6. Land that stretches out flat is called a <u>plateau</u>.

7. A <u>peninsula</u> is land surrounded by water on all sides but one.

8. The animals that live naturally in an area are called <u>wildlife</u>.

9. <u>Climate</u> is the way it is outdoors each day.

10. The study of Earth's surface and the bodies of water that cover it is called <u>environment</u>.

THINK AND WRITE

WRITING ABOUT COMMUNITIES
Write a paragraph to convince someone to move to your community. In your writing include those qualities that make your hometown special.

WRITING A POEM
The United States has many different landforms. Read the poem on page 42. Then write a poem describing our country's landforms.

WRITING ABOUT PERSPECTIVES
What if you had just moved to Cuajimalpa, Mexico? Write a letter to a friend in the United States describing how life in Mexico might be different from life back home.

BUILDING SKILLS

1. **Map Scales** Why are map scales included on most maps in this book?

2. **Map Scales** Look at the map of Indiana on page 23. How many miles is it from Rochester to Uniontown?

3. **Hemispheres** Which two hemispheres are divided by the equator?

4. **Intermediate Directions** Look at the map on page 51. In which direction is Las Vegas from Los Angeles?

5. **Intermediate Directions** Why are intermediate directions useful?

Ongoing Unit Project

OPTIONS FOR ASSESSMENT
This ongoing project, begun on page 2D, can be part of your assessment program, along with other forms of evaluation.

PLANNING Let students know that they will draw on information from the unit and that the chart should clearly present similarities and differences among communities studied. Charts should also reflect an understanding of the ways size and geography affect communities.

SIGNS OF SUCCESS
• Students understand the characteristics of different types of communities and the influence of geography.

• Students work together and agree on information to include on the chart.

• Groups can compare communities using their charts.

 FOR THE PORTFOLIO Students can include their individual note sheets in their portfolios.

YESTERDAY, TODAY & *TOMORROW*

In this unit you have read about the importance of natural resources. But in the past people were wasteful. Today, they are learning to care for resources. In the future, do you think people will continue to respect their environment?

READING ON YOUR OWN

Here are some books you might find at the library to help you learn more.

FAMILY PICTURES
by Carmen Lomas Garza
Learn what life is like for a Hispanic family living in Texas.

MY NEW YORK
by Kathy Jakobsen
Take a tour of New York City. See the sights. Wave to the Statue of Liberty.

TOWN AND COUNTRY
by Alice and Martin Provensen
Here's a look at life in the United States, on a farm and in a city.

UNIT PROJECT

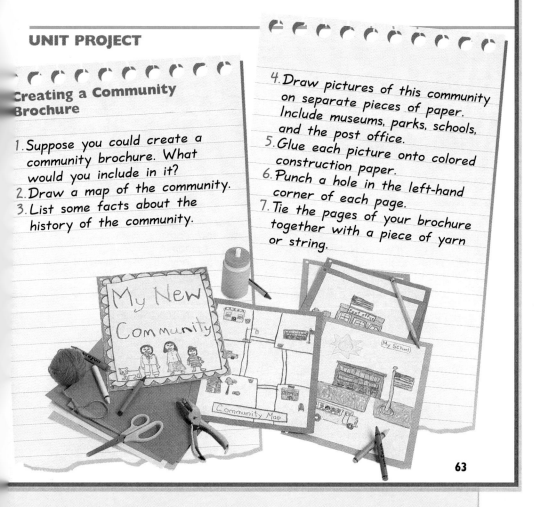

Creating a Community Brochure

1. Suppose you could create a community brochure. What would you include in it?
2. Draw a map of the community.
3. List some facts about the history of the community.
4. Draw pictures of this community on separate pieces of paper. Include museums, parks, schools, and the post office.
5. Glue each picture onto colored construction paper.
6. Punch a hole in the left-hand corner of each page.
7. Tie the pages of your brochure together with a piece of yarn or string.

63

Answers to BUILDING SKILLS

1. Map scales tell us the distances or areas on earth represented by distances or sections of a map. Maps in this book are drawn to different scales.

2. about 150 miles

3. northern hemisphere and southern hemisphere

4. southwest

5. We use intermediate directions when describing directions that lie between the four cardinal directions. It would be difficult to give directions using only north, south, east, and west.

Suggestions for YESTERDAY, TODAY, AND TOMORROW

Explain to students that the importance of recycling and energy conservation is now taught in schools to young people. Point out that although many more people are aware of environmental concerns today, people in America also own many more electric appliances and vehicles then they did many years ago. Many more people today live in big cities and do not spend much time in the earth's natural environment. Encourage students to think how people can conserve resources and protect the environment even though technology is becoming more a part of our daily lives.

Suggestions for READING ON YOUR OWN

Help students locate the library books listed under Reading On Your Own. Additional books can be found in the Unit Bibliography in the Unit Organizer on page 2B. Encourage students to read and report on one of the recommended books. Written book reports can be posted on the bulletin board.

Unit Project: *Creating a Brochure for a Community*

OBJECTIVE: To reinforce the definition of a community.

MATERIALS: crayons or markers, colored paper, drawing paper, hole puncher, yarn

- In group discussions, help students brainstorm ideas for their communities.

- Make different types of maps available so that students can use them to get ideas for their community maps. Then have students draw a map for their brochure.

- Next encourage students to list facts about the history of their community. Encourage them to draw pictures of their community on separate pieces of paper.

- Then have students glue each piece of paper onto colored paper, punch a hole in the left-hand corner of each page and finally tie the pages together with a piece of yarn.

OPTIONS FOR ASSESSMENT

This project can be part of your assessment program.

PLANNING Let students know they may base their communities on the ones in which they live or create new communities. The students should be aware that their brochures should include a map, facts, and descriptions of their community.

SIGNS OF SUCCESS

- Each student's brochure should include a map, facts about the community's history, and drawings and descriptions of interesting places to visit.

- Brochures should show careful planning and organization.

 FOR THE PORTFOLIO Students' brochures can be included in their portfolios.

Looking Back to the Past

PAGES 64–139

UNIT OVERVIEW

The story of a country's earliest communities reveals its history. The first American communities were started by Native Americans who made their clothing, homes, and food from the local natural resources. The English and the Spanish arrived in these lands later and their communities changed the local Native American way of life.

Adventures with National Geographic pp. 66–67

UNIT PLANNING GUIDE

CHAPTER	SUGGESTED PACING	CHAPTER OVERVIEW	CHAPTER RESOURCES
3 **A Native American Community at Mesa Verde** pp. 68–95	15–17 days	The first American communities were started by Native Americans. Mesa Verde was a Native American community built long ago high on the side of a cliff.	*Practice Book* pp. 17–21 *Anthology* pp. 26–35 *Project Book* p. 9 *Transparency:* Graphic Organizer ● *Desk Map* *Technology:* Videodisc/Video Tape, CD-ROM
4 **An English Colony at Jamestown** pp. 96–115	10–12 days	Almost four hundred years ago, people from England sailed to America and built a village called Jamestown in what is today Virginia.	*Practice Book* pp. 23–26 *Anthology* pp. 36–44 *Project Book* pp. 10–11 *Technology:* Videodisc/Video Tape, CD-ROM *Outline Map* p. 13
5 **A Spanish Mission in San Antonio** pp. 116–137	12–14 days	Long ago the Spanish built a mission called San Antonio in what is today Texas. Their priests and soldiers changed the lives of the Native Americans there.	*Practice Book* pp. 28–31 *Anthology* pp. 45–52 *Project Book* p. 12 *Technology:* Videodisc/Video Tape, CD-ROM *Desk Map* World

ASSESSMENT OPPORTUNITIES

Internet CONNECTION

The **Internet Project Handbook** and the Home Page at **http://www.mmh-school.com** contain on-line student activities related to this unit.

UNIT ASSESSMENT

Unit Review pp. 138–139
Unit Projects pp. 138–139

Assessment Book
Unit Test Unit 2 Test
Performance Assessment Unit 2

DAILY ASSESSMENT

Geo Adventures Daily Geography Activities

CHAPTER ASSESSMENT

Meeting Individual Needs pp. 69, 75, 77, 81, 87, 91, 97, 101, 107, 111, 113, 117, 121, 127, 132, 135
Write About It pp. 75, 77, 81, 87, 91, 101, 107, 111, 121, 127, 132
Chapter Reviews pp. 94–95, 114–115, 136–137

Assessment Book
Chapter Tests Ch. 3 Test, Ch. 4 Test, Ch. 5 Test
Performance Assessments Ch. 3, Ch. 4, Ch. 5

ANNOTATED BIBLIOGRAPHY

Classroom Library

- Waters, Kate. *Sarah Morton's Day: A Day in the Life of a Pilgrim Girl.* New York: Scholastic, Inc., 1989. This book describes of how a nine-year-old girl worked and played in a colonial village in 1627.

Student Books

Anderson, Peter. *Maria Martinez: Pueblo Potter.* Chicago, IL: Childrens Press, 1992. This book describes the life and accomplishments of the Pueblo Indian woman who made pottery in the traditional way of her people. **(Challenging)**

Bulla, Clyde Robert. *A Lion to Guard Us.* New York: Thomas Y. Crowell, 1981. Amanda Freebold and her younger brother and sister leave London to rejoin their father in Jamestown. **(Average)**

- Crum, Robert. *Eagle Drum on the Powwow Trail with a Young Grass Dancer.* New York: Macmillan Publishing Co., 1994. A young boy and his family describe their experiences at powwow ceremonies in Montana. **(Challenging)**

Hoyt-Goldsmith, Diane. *Cherokee Summer.* New York: Holiday House, 1993. With great pride, a ten-year-old Cherokee Indian girl describes her life today and the culture of her tribe. **(Challenging)**

- James, Betsy. *The Mud Family.* New York: G. P. Putnam's, 1994. A young girl brings rain to her people by making mud people out of the sand. **(Easy)**

- Knight, James E. *Jamestown: New World Adventure.* Mahwah, NJ: Troll Associates, 1982. This book is the fictional diary of a master carpenter's experience as one of the original Jamestown colonists in 1607. **(Challenging)**

- Lee, Sally. *San Antonio.* New York: Dillon Press, 1992. This book describes the neighborhoods, history, and culture of San Antonio. **(Challenging)**

- McGovern, Ann. *. . . If You Lived in Colonial Times.* New York: Scholastic, Inc., 1992. This book provides information about curious topics from colonial times in question and answer format. **(Average)**

Teacher Books

Ayer, Eleanor H. *The Anasazi.* New York: Walker and Co., 1993. Good background information is provided on the rise and fall of the Anasazi society.

Caney, Stephen. *Kid's America.* New York: Workman Publishing Co., 1978. This book gives suggestions for projects and activities based on life in America long ago.

Read-Alouds

- Baylor, Byrd. *And It's Still That Way: Legends Told by Arizona Indian Children.* Santa Fe, NM: Trails West Press, 1976. A collection of original stories by children about how things came to be.

Hausman, Gerald. *Coyote Walks on Two Legs: A Book of Navajo Myths and Legends.* New York: Philomel, 1995. This is a retelling of five Navajo stories about the trickster, Coyote.

Technology Multimedia

As It Was in Colonial America. Video. S95440-HAVT. Daily life is presented, as it was in Jamestown, Plymouth, and Williamsburg. Society For Visual Education. (800) 829-1900.

Mesa Verde: Mystery of the Silent Cities. Video. No. 3476-106. This is an examination of the Pueblo culture. Britannica Videos. (800) 554-9862.

Free or Inexpensive Materials

For a Jamestown Settlement Teacher's Kit, send to: Jamestown-Yorktown Foundation; Education Dept., P. O. Drawer JF; Williamsburg, VA 23187.

- *Book excerpted in the Anthology*

- *Book featured in the student bibliography of the Unit Review*

National Geographic technology

Ideas for Active Learning

BULLETIN BOARD

Native American Cultures

Ojibwa

Totem poles can show family symbols.

Anasazi

Coahultecan

Caddo

Powhatan

The Powhatan fished and farmed.

Looking Back to the Past

Help students create a bulletin board titled "Native American Cultures." Ask volunteers to label the appropriate areas of a U.S. map with the names of the Native American groups that lived there.

- Have students add pictures showing how the different groups of Native Americans lived in pre-Colonial times. Students might show their dwellings, for example, or the natural resources on which each group relied.

- Have students use index cards to record information about the traditions and lifestyles of the different Native American groups. Help students find information about the Native Americans who lived in your area and add it to the display.

TEACHER EXCHANGE

Thanks to: Mrs. Doris Rankin, Sweetwater School, Glendale, Arizona

Build a Model Pueblo Village

GROUP

CURRICULUM CONNECTION   Art

Materials: shoe boxes, brown tempera paint, black construction paper, modeling clay, craft sticks, art sand, butcher paper

30 MINUTES OR LONGER

1. Talk with students about some of the different types of communities they have studied. Then tell them that they will build a model Pueblo village.
2. Have students paint the shoe boxes and lids with brown tempera paint. When dry, students should tape on rectangles cut from black construction paper to represent windows and doors.
3. Tell each group to use butcher paper as a base and arrange their boxes on two levels in a "U" shape, with doors facing inward.
4. They can sprinkle sand on the paper to represent the desert terrain. If available, they can add small stones and bits of grass also.
5. Then have students use clay to make some miniature pots and an outdoor oven.
6. Students may use craft sticks to construct ladders that reach the second level of homes.

Enriching with Multimedia

RESOURCE: *Internet Project Handbook*

- Look at the ***Internet Project Handbook*** for student projects related to this unit or have students go online at http://www.mmhschool.com, Macmillan/McGraw-Hill School's home page on the World Wide Web.

RESOURCE: *Adventures CD-ROM*

- Enrich Unit 2 with the Unit Activities on the *Adventures* CD-ROM.

Many Cultures

- Throughout the unit, students will have opportunities to learn about a variety of early communities in the United States—Native American communities, British colonies, and Spanish missions. Talk with students about how Native American cultures differed from those of European colonial people. In class, begin a list of all the different ethnic and cultural groups that may now exist in your community, including Native Americans.

- Have students share their list with their families, and work together to identify the groups on the list with whom they share cultural ties. For each entry, students and their families should list the foods, traditions, music, or dances that each group might contribute if there were to be a multicultural gathering in their community.

Artifact Time Line

CURRICULUM CONNECTION Language Arts/Art

RESOURCE: Project Book p. 8.

For this unit, students will work individually and in groups to create time lines of artifacts from the communities they study.

1. After each chapter, have students describe and depict, through drawings or collages, artifacts from the community highlighted. Students can store this work in a folder.

2. When students finish the unit, they can work in small groups to choose a series of artifacts from one chapter. To make their time lines, groups can arrange their artifacts in chronological order and use lengths of string to connect them.

3. Each group member can then describe an artifact, its importance to the community, and any similarities to present-day objects.

Assessment ideas for this activity appear on p. 138.

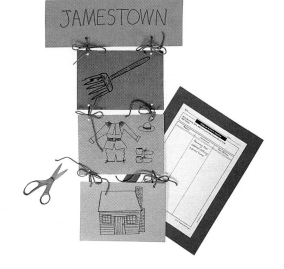

Introducing the Unit

Give students a few minutes to look at the pictures on this spread and to read the *Why Does It Matter?* passage on the facing page.

Exploring Prior Knowledge Help students review what they have learned about living in communities. Also help them review information about Spanish culture.

Suggested Questions

- *What do you know about why people live in communities?* (Students will know that people help each other to build homes, grow food, and work together to help improve their communities.)

- *What do you know about Spanish culture in Mexico?* (Students may know that the Spanish conquered Native Americans in what is today Mexico and Central America, and that most Mexicans today speak Spanish. Their culture reflects both the Native American and Spanish heritages.)

Looking Ahead This chapter introduces three communities from long ago. Students will read about the Native American Anasazi community at Mesa Verde. They will read about the first permanent North American English settlement at Jamestown. They will also investigate the growth of the community of San Antonio, Texas, which began with the Spanish missions.

Background INFORMATION

ABOUT THE PHOTOGRAPHS

- **CLIFF DWELLING AT MESA VERDE** Native Americans called the Anasazi, or Ancient Ones, built stone apartments in the cliffs at Mesa Verde, in what is now Colorado. Ladders were used to climb between building stories in this once-thriving community.

- **ANASAZI POTTERY** The Anasazi dug colored clay from the riverbed and made decorated pots. Pots were used for eating, food storage, and cooking. When the Anasazi deserted their cliff dwellings, hundreds of these beautiful pots were left behind. Today visitors to the Mesa Verde museum can see them.

- **THE ALAMO** This Roman Catholic church—along with many other missions—was built in the 1800s by Spanish missionaries near the San Antonio River in Texas. A community of Spanish priests and Native Americans lived in a walled compound connected to the church.

UNIT TWO

Looking Back to the Past

WHY DOES IT MATTER?

Who first lived in your community? Why do you think they decided to live there?

In this unit you will learn about three very different communities where people lived long ago. These communities were built in different places by different groups of people. Learning about them helps us to discover our country's past and to understand the story of our earliest communities.

As you explore these communities, think about how the past is still part of our lives today.

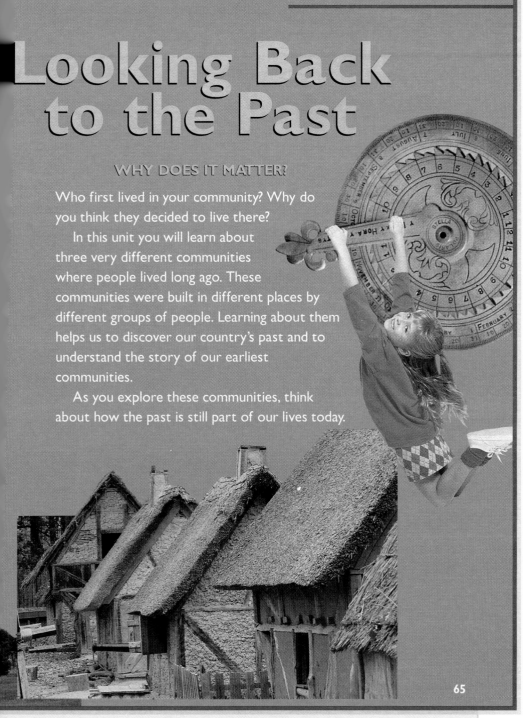

65

Discussing the Photographs Tell students that studying old buildings, tools, and artifacts helps us understand how people used to live.

Suggested Questions

• **People who lived here long ago made these buildings and objects. What natural resources were used to make them?** *(Students may recognize the straw and wood of the homes on the left, the stone from the cliffs in the upper left photograph, and the clay for the pot.)*

★**THINKING FURTHER:** *Compare and Contrast* **Look at each of the buildings on these pages. How are they alike? How are they different?** *(The mission is big and it looks like a church. The thatched houses are small and there are many of them close together. The cliff houses are also clustered together. All of the buildings have small windows.)*

Discussing WHY DOES IT MATTER? Encourage speculation about the answers to the questions raised in the text.

Suggested Questions

• **How could we find out who first lived in our community?** *(Answers will vary. Students should know that we can obtain historical information from libraries, museums, and similar resources.)*

• **Why do you think it is important to learn about our country's early communities?** *(The past is still part of our lives today.)*

Background INFORMATION

ABOUT THE PHOTOGRAPHS

• **HOUSES AT JAMESTOWN SETTLEMENT** The first English settlers built homes in the traditional English style. Using raw materials from the land around them—broken shells, grasses, and wood—they built a new community at Jamestown that looked like an English town.

• **EUROPEAN NAVIGATION INSTRUMENT** Early European explorers relied on the sun and the stars of the night sky to navigate their ships. At night, sailors lined up their navigational instruments with the North Star called Polaris. In this way they would know the four cardinal directions.

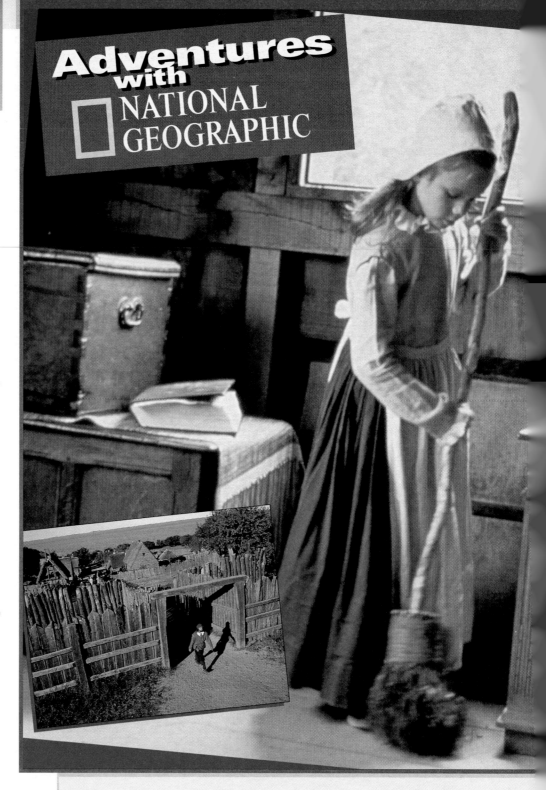

Adventures
with
NATIONAL GEOGRAPHIC

Introducing
Living History

Exploring Prior Knowledge Have students share their knowledge of Pilgrims. Many students will remember that the Pilgrims celebrated the first Thanksgiving feast. Explain that Pilgrims is a name given to only one small group of English people who sailed to America to make new homes.

Links to the Unit As students continue through Unit 2, they will learn how Europeans lived and worked together in early colonial settlements. They will also learn about Native American communities that were North America's first settlements.

Living History Point out the unusual spelling of the word *Plimoth.* Explain that in the early days of the settlement, the name was spelled in many different ways. Most of the records from the Pilgrims come from the first governor of the settlement, William Bradford. In his journals, Bradford spelled the name *Plymouth,* but more frequently, *Plimoth.*

Background INFORMATION

MORE ABOUT PLIMOTH PLANTATION

- In 1620, a ship called the *Mayflower* landed on the shores of North America, bringing 102 Pilgrims from England. The travelers stepped ashore onto Plymouth Rock in what is now Massachusetts. At that time, the land was forested and undeveloped, sparsely settled by Native American communities. Winter was approaching, and the Pilgrims rushed to build shelters. They survived that first winter partly by eating hidden stores of Indian corn. By the year 1627, the Pilgrims had built a primitive but thriving settlement known as Plimoth Plantation. It was at Plimoth Plantation that early settlers celebrated the first Thanksgiving feast. They were grateful for the abundance they found in their new home.

- Today, visitors to the Living History Museum at Plimoth Plantation can experience the settlement as it was in 1627. Houses were rebuilt using the traditional methods and materials. Actors in Pilgrim attire perform daily tasks. Visitors are often surprised at the rugged life of early colonists.

- Explain to students that they will be learning about a community of settlers that arrived on the shores of America a little earlier than the Pilgrims. When students study Jamestown Settlement in Chapter 4, they will also have further opportunity to study a living history museum.

LIVING HISTORY

It's morning at Plimoth Plantation, in Massachusetts. Time to gather firewood and feed the chickens. Later, the floor needs to be swept. It's hard work—especially when you're wearing Pilgrim-style clothes. Young people sometimes work at Plimoth Plantation. This village was built to look just like the one the Pilgrims built after they sailed across the Atlantic Ocean from England. These kids find out for themselves what daily life was like in the 1620s.

GEOJOURNAL

Write a letter to a friend telling about a job you'd like to have at Plimoth Plantation.

67

Point out that each photograph shows children hard at work. Explain that life in Plimoth Plantation was very rough. Everyone in the family had to work hard to build a new home. The photographs show children sweeping the home, gathering firewood, and feeding farm animals. Help students list several other jobs that children might have done. For example, older children might take care of younger ones, carry water from the well, help cook meals, make clothing, plant vegetables, or pull weeds.

The photograph on the lower left side of the spread shows a man leaving the settlement. Be sure students notice the sturdy wooden fence. Explain that the fence protected the settlement from wild animals. Pilgrims had to clear the area of trees before building. They also cut each fence post and wooden beam by hand.

Using the Geo Journal If students are not familiar with the kinds of work colonial children did, have them look again at the pictures. Have them also think about small jobs that would need to be done everyday. Remind them that this community relied completely on nearby natural resources.

Technology CONNECTION

ADVENTURES CD-ROM
Enrich the discussion with *Living History* on the CD-ROM.

Curriculum CONNECTION

LANGUAGE ARTS AND ART Give partners or small groups research topics that relate to Plimoth Plantation. Invite them to look in library books and encyclopedias to research topics such as the following:

- the *Mayflower* arriving on the Massachusetts shore
- the clothing that Pilgrims wore
- the first Thanksgiving
- the work of a colonial community, such as building houses out of cut logs, planting vegetables, gathering firewood
- the weather at Plimoth Plantation
- John and Priscilla Alden

- William Bradford
- William Brewster

Have students read about their topic and look at pictures. Then ask them to draw pictures showing scenes from colonial history or portraits of important Pilgrims or Native Americans. Have them write paragraphs to accompany their drawings, and then exhibit the work on a Plimoth Plantation bulletin board.

A Native American Community at Mesa Verde
PAGES 68-95

CHAPTER OVERVIEW

The first American communities were started by Native Americans. They lived all across the land now called the United States. They made their clothing, homes, and food from the local natural resources. Mesa Verde was a Native American community built long ago high on the side of a cliff.

CHAPTER PLANNING GUIDE
Suggested pacing: 15–17 days

LESSON	LESSON FOCUS	LESSON RESOURCES
1 NATIVE AMERICAN COMMUNITIES pages 70–75	A History of Many Cultures	*Practice Book* p. 17 *Anthology* pp. 26–31 *Technology:* Videodisc/Video Tape
LEGACY pages 76–77	Coming Together at a Powwow: Linking Past and Present	*Anthology* pp. 29–31 *Technology:* Adventures CD-ROM
2 THE GEOGRAPHY OF MESA VERDE pages 78–81	Land of Canyons and Mesas	*Practice Book* p. 18 *Technology:* Videodisc/Video Tape *Desk Map*
3 MESA VERDE LONG AGO pages 82–87	Anasazi Life at Mesa Verde	*Practice Book* p. 19
Infographic pages 84–85	A Day with the Anasazi	*Technology:* Adventures CD-ROM
4 MESA VERDE TODAY pages 88–91	A Visit to Mesa Verde National Park	*Practice Book* p. 20 *Anthology* pp. 32–35
THINKING SKILLS pages 92–93	Making Decisions	*Practice Book* p. 21 *Transparency:* Graphic Organizer
CHAPTER REVIEW pages 94–95	Students' understanding of vocabulary, content, and skills is assessed.	*Assessment:* Ch. 3 Test, Performance Assessment Ch. 3 *Transparency:* Graphic Organizer

OPTIONS FOR STUDENT ACTIVITIES

Citizenship pp. 73, 74, 83, 90

Curriculum Connection pp. 71, 76, 83, 85

Expanding the *Infographic* p. 84

Using the Anthology p. 90

ASSESSMENT OPPORTUNITIES

Meeting Individual Needs pp. 69, 75, 77, 81, 87, 91

Write About It pp. 75, 77, 81, 87, 91

Chapter Review pp. 94–95

Assessment Book

Chapter Test Ch. 3 Test

Performance Assessment Ch. 3

Using the Vocabulary Cards The vocabulary words for each lesson are available on *Vocabulary Cards* for review and practice.

Using Geo Adventures Use **Geo Adventures** Daily Geography Activities to assess students' understanding of geography skills.

GETTING READY FOR THE CHAPTER

Make a Native American Words Booklet

Objective: To see Native American influences in everyday language.

Materials: *Project Book* p. 9, scissors, glue, construction paper, staplers, dictionary

1. Write the following words on the chalkboard: *condor, cougar, raccoon, skunk.* Ask students to tell what all the words have in common. (They are names of animals.) Then let them describe each animal.
2. Explain that the words have one more important thing in common: they all come from Native American language. In fact, many of the words we use to name animals, foods, places, and other things come from the hundreds of languages spoken by different groups of Native Americans.
3. Hand out copies of Project Book p. 9. Let students know these words also come from Native American languages. Have students define each of the words shown there, using a dictionary for help.
4. Invite students to complete their booklets by cutting the word entries apart and gluing each one onto a piece of construction paper. They can then make a cover, alphabetize, and staple the pages together.

> **SECOND-LANGUAGE SUPPORT**
>
> As second-language learners prepare the elements for this activity, encourage them to take notes that they can refer to throughout the process.
>
> Additional Second-Language Support Tips: pp. 72, 85, 90

Introducing the Chapter

To give students a sense of how things change over time, ask students to think about the changes that happen in your community.

THINKING ABOUT GEOGRAPHY AND HISTORY

Have students read the text on this page and locate the site of Mesa Verde on their maps.

1100s-1300s

Suggested Questions

● **What does the name Native American mean?** *(It describes the groups of peoples who have been living in the Americas before and since the Europeans arrived.)*

● **Where did Native Americans live?** *(all across the land we call the United States)*

● **What is Mesa Verde?** *(a Native American community built long ago)*

● **Where is Mesa Verde?** *(in the southwestern United States, where southwest Colorado is today)*

● **On what landform did the Anasazi build their communities?** *(on cliffs)*

★**THINKING FURTHER: Making Conclusions How do you think the Anasazi lived in this hot dry climate?** *(Students might say that the Anasazi built homes that were cool, that they had to build with mud or stone instead of trees, that they had to grow food instead of hunting large animals.)*

Resource **REMINDER**

 Technology: *Videodisc/Video Tape 2*

CHAPTER 3

A Native American Community at Mesa Verde

THINKING ABOUT GEOGRAPHY AND HISTORY

The first American communities were started by Native Americans. They lived all across the land we now call the United States. People in these communities made their clothing, homes, and food from the natural resources they found where they lived.

In Chapter 3 you will learn about the Native Americans. You will also visit Mesa Verde, a Native American community built long ago high on the side of a cliff. The map shows you where Mesa Verde is located. The time line shows you when important events ocurred.

1100s-1300s	**1300s-1450s**
The Anasazi build communities in cliffs	The Anasazi leave Mesa Verde

68

Background INFORMATION

LINKING THE MAP TO THE TIME LINE

● The first box on the time line shows the Mesa Verde community at daily work and play. Using the limited resources in the dry region, they built complex apartments into the cliffs. People farmed together, hunted small desert animals, played games, and met for religious ceremonies.

● No one knows exactly why the Anasazi left Mesa Verde. Some scientists think that drought may have forced them to abandon their cliff dwellings.

● The Southwest has a dry climate. For this reason the cliff dwellings, tools, and pottery of the Anasazi have been remarkably preserved for over 500 years. Rangers at Mesa Verde National Park help people to learn about the Anasazi.

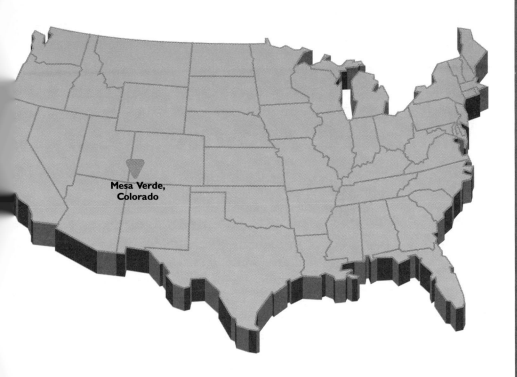

Mesa Verde, Colorado

TODAY

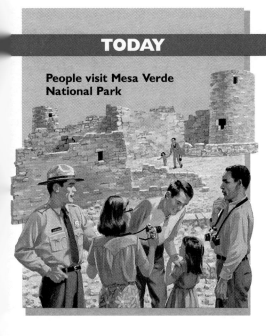

People visit Mesa Verde National Park

69

Suggested Questions

● **What event took place in the years 1300–1450?** *(The Anasazi left Mesa Verde.)*

● **How does the second picture on the time line differ from the first one?** *(The buildings are empty and the people have left.)*

★**THINKING FURTHER:** *Making Conclusions* **Scientists don't know why the Anasazi left. How might knowing about landforms and bodies of water help people solve this puzzle?** *(A natural disaster may have happened such as the river running dry. Maybe studying the land might tell of possible climate changes.)*

Suggested Questions

● **How many years have passed since the Ansazi left Mesa Verde?** *(about 550 to 700 years)*

● **What change has happened to Mesa Verde since that time?** *(It has become a national park.)*

● **What do people do at Mesa Verde today?** *(They visit Mesa Verde National Park. They talk to rangers or historians.)*

● **What period in the past can we learn about at Mesa Verde today?** *(the period from 1100 to 1300 when the Anasazi lived there)*

★**THINKING FURTHER:** *Predicting* **What do you predict visitors to Mesa Verde would see today?** *(Students may predict that visitors would see tools, household items, or the ruins of the cliff dwellings.)*

Technology CONNECTION

VIDEODISC/VIDEO TAPE 2
Enrich Chapter 3 with the Videodisc *glossary* segments.

Search Frame 53777

Meeting *Individual* Needs

EXTENSION (Easy) Ask students to note the location of your community in relation to Mesa Verde and determine in which direction Mesa Verde is from your community.

RETEACHING (Average) Invite groups to draw the pictures from the time line to create a class bulletin board. When recreating the time line, leave room for student descriptions and additional illustrations. Encourage students to add to the display as they read the chapter.

ENRICHMENT (Challenging) Ask partners to research an additional world event for each time frame on the time line. Have students draw their own time lines, showing events at Mesa Verde on the bottom half of the page and parallel world events on the top half.

LESSON 1

Lesson Overview

Native Americans were the first people who lived in North America. Landforms and resources shaped native cultures and communities across the continent.

Lesson Objectives

★ Identify Native Americans as the first inhabitants of North America.

★ Understand how natural resources shaped Native American communities.

1 PREPARE

MOTIVATE Tell students that the picture shows Stormi Welch, a Cherokee Indian who lives in North Carolina. Explain that Native Americans were first called "Indians" by Columbus because he thought he had landed in the East Indies. Then have a volunteer read the *Read Aloud.*

SET PURPOSE Review the *Vocabulary* word with students. Then direct them to the *Read to Learn* question and invite them to discuss possible answers.

2 TEACH

Discussing the First Communities
On the board, draw a two-part time line showing the general periods when Native Americans and Europeans inhabited America. (Native Americans: beginning about 50,000 years ago; Europeans: beginning about 500 years ago.)

Suggested Questions

● **What is history?** *(the story of what happened in the past)*

● **From which Native American group is Stormi Welch?** *(Cherokee)*

● **What is Stormi Welch proud of?** *(being Native American, having ancestors who lived in America long ago)*

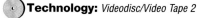

Resource REMINDER

Practice Book: *p. 17*

Anthology: *Why We Have Dogs, pp. 26–28; Eagle Drum, pp. 29–31*

Technology: *Videodisc/Video Tape 2*

Native American Communities

READ ALOUD

"All the time I learn things about my Cherokee culture. Sometimes when I'm doing chores for my mom like pulling up weeds in the backyard, I make little woven baskets out of grass like our people used to make long ago. I am happy to be Cherokee. I am proud of it."

Focus Activity

READ TO LEARN
Who lived in the first American communities?

VOCABULARY
history

The First Communities

These are the words of Stormi Welch. She is a nine-year-old Cherokee who lives in the state of North Carolina. She is very proud of her Cherokee culture and her past. The Cherokee are just one of many Native American groups who live in the United States today.

"Native American" or "Indian" are names for the first people to live in the land that became the United States of America. It is important to understand how Native Americans lived long ago. Native Americans are part of our country's history. History is the story of the past. In this lesson we'll look back at our country's first communities.

70

Reading STRATEGIES *and* Vocabulary DEVELOPMENT

FACT/NONFACT Help students identify the difference between fact and nonfact in this lesson. Explain that facts provide information that can be proved, and that nonfacts tell about something that cannot be proved. Be sure they understand that although the Coyote story (p. 71) tells us something about life and how people sometimes behave, it is fiction, not fact. Students can give some examples of facts from the lesson.

LANGUAGE HISTORY Have students look at the *Atlas* map on p. R6 and locate the states that were honored with the following Native American names:

Alabama *(plant gatherers);* Arkansas (the name is a combination of the Sioux word *ansas* meaning "people of the south wind" and the French word *arc* for *bow);* Iowa *(sleepy ones);* Missouri *(people with the dugout canoes,* now translated as "Big Muddy")

Native American Storytelling

Many different groups of Native Americans lived in this land long ago. Each group had its own culture. But one thing most Native Americans shared is a love of storytelling. They still do today. The following story was written by Tina Naiche (NAH chee), a young Apache. The Apache are a group of Native Americans who live in the southwest part of our country.

MANY VOICES
LITERATURE

Story by Tina Naiche, written in 1976.

Coyote Gets Turkey Up a Tree

Coyote is a great figure for the Apaches. He is good at tricking other animals but he is always getting fooled himself. Coyote stories show our pleasure in outwitting our enemies— and they also show how easy it is to be fooled.

Here's one way Coyote was fooled.

Coyote found Turkey up in a tree.

He knew it would be easy to catch him. All he had to do was chop down the tree.

Coyote chopped and chopped. Just as the tree was about to fall, Turkey flew to another tree.

Coyote knew what to do. He got busy chopping that tree down too. He chopped and chopped. Then just as the tree was falling, Turkey flew again.

That went on all day. By evening Coyote was lying on the ground panting. Turkey just flew away home.

71

Discussing Native American Storytelling Explain that many Native Americans learned stories from their elders, and then told them to their children. The Coyote character appears in many Native American stories.

Suggested Questions
- ***What did Native Americans have in common?*** *(love for storytelling)*

- ***In what area of our country do the Apache live?*** *(Southwest)*

★THINKING FURTHER: *Compare and Contrast* ***How might telling a story be different from writing it down?*** *(Stories that are told are more likely to change than stories that are written down.)*

MANY VOICES

Learning from Literature Have students look at the picture of Coyote to see what kind of animal he is. Discuss how Coyote is fooled in Tina Naiche's story.

Suggested Questions
- ***Who is Coyote?*** *(He is an animal like a wild dog.)*

- ***What does Coyote want?*** *(He wants to eat Turkey.)*

- ***What happens to Coyote in the end?*** *(He works hard, but is fooled by Turkey.)*

★THINKING FURTHER: *Sequencing* ***Tell what happened to Coyote in your own words.*** *(Answers should help students remember the sequence of events in the story.)*

Background INFORMATION

MORE ABOUT NATIVE AMERICAN STORYTELLING Stories were shared and held sacred by both adults and children. They taught about nature, religion, history, law, and other aspects of Native American life. Some stories were sung, others were recited chorally.

Coyote was a favorite Native American character. Coyote stories showed that all living creatures had the potential for both good and bad. Children learned values by listening to the stories and were entertained in the process. Part of the fun was to be able to laugh at Coyote's foolish mistakes as well as to be delighted by his cleverness.

Because the stories were passed down orally, details changed through the years. But Coyote's basic behavior always remained the same.

Curriculum CONNECTION

LINKS TO READING Many cultures have folktales about Tricksters like Coyote. Two examples are Raven, from the Indians of the Pacific Northwest, and Anansi the Spider, from the Ashanti in Africa. Students can read about these characters in the following books:

- *Coyote Stories for Children* adapted by Susan Strauss (Beyond Words Publishing, 1991);
- *Raven's Light* by Susan Hand Shetterly (Atheneum, 1991);
- *Brother Anansi and the Cattle Ranch* told by James de Sauza (Children's Book Press, 1989).

LINKS TO LANGUAGE ARTS Have students use one of the three Tricksters to write an original story. They can practice telling their stories to a partner and then share them with the class.

Discuss with students the diversity of Native American life. Then encourage them to discuss ways that the Plains Indians used their greatest natural resource—the buffalo.

Suggested Questions

- **What is one belief that Native Americans shared?** *(that we can learn from animals)*

- **What was special about each Native American group?** *(Each had its own language, religion, and way of meeting its needs.)*

- **Where are the Great Plains?** *(in the center of the United States)*

- **What natural resource was very important to the Plains Indians?** *(the great herds of buffalo)*

- ★THINKING FURTHER: *Cause/Effect*
  What effect did the buffalo have on the Plains Indians? *(The buffalo provided food and materials for clothes and shelters.)*

Technology CONNECTION

VIDEODISC/VIDEO TAPE 2
Enrich Lesson 1 with the *locator map* for Native American groups.

Search Frame 53756

Many Cultures

What does the story tell you about the Apache? Like most Native American groups, they believed people could learn from animals.

Long ago, Native Americans shared some beliefs, such as learning from animals. But they also had many differences. Some groups were as unlike each other as people from different countries are today. Each group of people had its own special culture. Each had its own language and its own religion.

Native American cultures were partly shaped by the natural resources around them. Look at the map on the next page. You can see that buffalo roamed the Great Plains in the middle of what is now the United States. The Plains Indians skillfully used the buffalo for food, clothing, and shelter. Look at the map again. What can you tell about the cultures of other Native American groups?*

The Plains Indians decorated buffalo hide and used it to make robes and moccasins.

* Native Americans used the natural resources around them for food and shelter.

National Museum of the American Indian

72

Second-Language Support

DIALOGS Accessing prior knowledge of second-language learners will help them feel more confident. Invite dialogs between them and English-proficient partners about Native Americans. Then have partners share their thoughts with you or with the class. Help them clarify information and any factual misunderstandings.

Background INFORMATION

MORE ABOUT THE BUFFALO
Remind students that the Plains Indians used every part of the buffalo.

- *Buffalo meat* and organs were eaten raw or roasted, or dried for carrying on the trail.

- Women stretched *buffalo hides* on frames or pegs in the ground, then scraped and rubbed the hide to soften it. Softened skins were used for shields, sleds, and blankets, as well as for clothing and tepees.

- Native Americans used *bones* for tools; *rib bones* for sled runners; and *hooves, horns,* and *skulls* for ceremonial objects and rattles. *Sinews* and *buffalo hair* were used for thread and rope. *Buffalo chips* (dried manure) were collected and burned for fuel.

MAP WORK: **1.** California-Intermountain; baskets **2.** Menominee **3.** They both farmed for food; they were in different cultural areas so their languages probably differed.

NATIVE AMERICAN CULTURAL AREAS

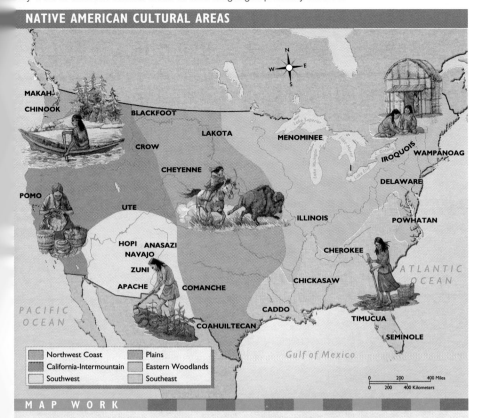

Northwest Coast
California-Intermountain
Southwest
Plains
Eastern Woodlands
Southeast

MAP WORK

Native American groups living in the same area shared similar cultures.

1. In which area did the Pomo live? What did people of that area make?

2. Which Native American group lived by Lake Michigan?

3. How might the Timucua and the Zuni have been alike and different?

From this map you can see where different groups of Native Americans lived long ago. Each color stands for a different cultural area. Groups in the same area shared a similar culture. Find the Native American group called the Anasazi (ah nuh SAH zee) on the map. How did they probably get food? How can you tell?*

*They farmed for food; look at the drawing in the map.

73

More MAP WORK

As students look at the map, talk about the area it covers and explain what each color indicates. Remind students that when we talk about culture, we mean the ideas, skills, tools, arts, and way of life of a certain people at a certain time.

Suggested Questions

● **What are the names of the six Native American cultural groups?** *(Northwest Coast, California-Intermountain, Southwest, Plains, Eastern Woodlands, Southeast)*

★**THINKING FURTHER:** *Classifying*
What are the names of Indian groups that lived in the Southwest? that lived in the Plains? *(Southwest: Navajo, Hopi, Zuni, Anasazi, Apache; Plains: Blackfoot, Lakota, Cheyenne, Comanche, Coahuiltecan, Crow)*

Using Pictures Encourage students to discuss how the natural resources of each region shaped Native American life.

Suggested Questions

● **How did the Pomo Indians use natural resources?** *(They used grasses for baskets.)*

● **How did the Chinook Indians use natural resources?** *(They used rivers for transportation and logs for canoes.)*

★**THINKING FURTHER:** *Compare and Contrast* **How was life on the Plains different from life in the Southwest for Native Americans?** *(Plains Indians hunted buffalo; Indians in the Southwest farmed.)*

Background INFORMATION

MORE ABOUT THE MAP

Point out to students that the culture map shows where Native American groups were when the Europeans came to the Americas. Before this time, native people lived here for some 50,000 years, traveling all over the continent.

As groups came together, they formed new groups and developed common cultures based on how they lived on the land. Several Native American groups migrated from other areas onto the plains and these different ways of life merged into one. As tribes with different languages met while hunting buffalo on the plains they developed a sign language to be able to communicate.

CITIZENSHIP

LINKING PAST AND PRESENT Have student teams find out about Native American groups who live in your community or state. Using resources such as a local historical society or museum, chamber of commerce, or the Museum of the American Indian, teams should prepare a booklet detailing the history of that particular group.

Suggested Questions

- **What culture group did the Iroquois belong to?** *(the Eastern Woodland group)*

- **Where did the Iroquois live?** *(in what is now New York State)*

★**THINKING FURTHER:** *Cause and Effect* **How did natural resources shape the lives of the Iroquois?** *(They farmed on the rich land, used water from the lakes and rivers, and built shelters from the trees in the forests.)*

Living Off the Land

Natural resources helped shape the way Native Americans lived in communities. Look again at the map on page 73. In the Eastern Woodland culture group, find the Iroquois. The land they once lived on is now part of New York State. It was mostly forests. On the rich land they grew corn, beans, and squash. The Iroquois lived in shelters covered with bark called longhouses. These houses held many families. Water came from the lakes and rivers in the Northeast. Today many Iroquois still live in this area.

Dr. Oren Lyons is a leader of the Iroquois people today (left). Long ago Iroquois families shared a longhouse made of wood and bark (below).

74

Background INFORMATION

MORE ABOUT THE IROQUOIS
The Iroquois language was spoken by six nations—Mohawk, Oneida, Onondaga, Cayuga, Seneca, and Tuscarora. Today the Iroquois call themselves *Haudenosaunee,* or *People of the Longhouse.*

- They trapped forest animals for food and clothing and made shirts, leggings, breechcloths, and moccasins from animal skins. They used porcupine quills for decoration and for recording information.

- The community was centered around farming. Iroquois made stone, bone, antler, and wood farming tools. Family names were passed on through the mother, and Iroquois leaders were chosen by the women.

CITIZENSHIP

Understanding Government Two great leaders formed the Iroquois League.

- In about 1570, *Deganawida,* an Iroquois prophet, had a vision: he saw the Iroquois nations gathered under the branches of a Tree of Great Peace. *Hiawatha,* a Mohawk medicine man, traveled the rivers, showing people a wampum belt symbolizing the Great Law of Peace.

- These two men brought together the Iroquois League.

- Iroquois women chose 50 chiefs—sachems—as representatives of the people, and a smaller group—the Pine Tree Sachem—as decision makers.

- Washington, Jefferson, and Franklin admired the Iroquois system and used it as a reference when establishing the government of the United States.

From the map on page 73, locate the Makah (mah KAH). How do you think their environment influenced the way they lived? They lived along the West Coast. The Pacific Ocean and the rivers were valuable resources. The Makah were skilled fishers. Today some Makah still live and fish in this area.

WHY IT MATTERS

Native Americans are an important part of our country today. Stormi Welch's Cherokee people live in North Carolina and Oklahoma. As with many Native American groups, their culture continues to be an important part of Cherokee life today.

In learning about the history of the United States, it is important to study how Native Americans lived long ago. In the next lesson we will read about the Anasazi. We will learn about their land, resources, and culture. We will also see how part of their culture lives on today.

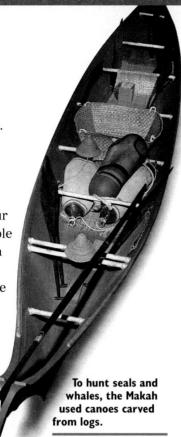

To hunt seals and whales, the Makah used canoes carved from logs.

✓ Reviewing Facts and Ideas

SUM IT UP

- History is the story of the past.
- Native Americans were the first people to live in the land that is now the United States.
- There are many different Native American groups in our country today. Each has its own special culture.

THINK ABOUT IT

1. What is history?
2. **FOCUS** Who lived in the first American communities?
3. **THINKING SKILL** How was the Iroquois community *like* your community? How was it *different*? How can you tell?
4. **GEOGRAPHY** Look at the map on page 73. How do you think geography influenced the Seminole?

75

Discussing WHY IT MATTERS Ask students to share what they have learned about Native Americans. Have them tell why the history of people from long ago is important.

Suggested Questions

- **Why do we study Native American history?** (Native Americans were the first people in America. They are an important part of our country today.)

- **What do you think you could learn about natural resources by studying Native American cultures?** (different ways to use them, how valuable they are to everyone)

★ 3 CLOSE

SUM IT UP
Have students write their answers to the questions below.

Suggested Questions

- **Why do people study history?** (to learn about important ideas, arts, skills, and beliefs of the past)

- **What is one reason that Native American groups in the same area shared similar cultures?** (They were influenced by the same geographic features.)

EVALUATE
✓ **Answers to Think About It**

1. the story of people who lived in the past
2. Native Americans
3. Answers will vary.
4. Water was plentiful; the climate was warm. *Human-Environment Interaction*

Write About It Have students write a paragraph that compares and contrasts two Native American groups.

MEETING *Individual* NEEDS

RETEACHING (Easy) Provide the names of several Indian groups and have students tell what cultural area each group lived in according to the map on p. 73, what the geography of the area was like, and how the people lived.

EXTENSION (Average) Invite groups to create posters or displays showing one aspect of Native American culture. For example, using library books as a guide, a group can draw pictures of several types of Native American clothing. Another group can make models of different kinds of shelters.

ENRICHMENT (Challenging) Ask students to research more information about one Native American group. Ask them to talk to the class in detail about how people in the group dressed, obtained food, cooked, built shelter, and created stories and art.

LEGACY

Lesson Overview

Native Americans share the legacy of music and dance when gathering at a powwow.

Lesson Objectives

★ Recognize the Native American legacy of music and dance, past and present.

1 PREPARE

MOTIVATE Ask students to look at the pictures and talk about what they see. Explain that powwows are an important part of Native American culture today.

SET PURPOSE Ask a volunteer to read aloud the first paragraph. Have students discuss how music and dance can bring people together.

2 TEACH

Understanding the Concept of a Legacy Help students understand that a powwow is a Native American legacy. With its roots in past Native American celebrations, the powwow of today brings people together to sing and dance and visit.

Discussing Coming Together at a Powwow Explain that in the past, groups held powwows within their own communities. Today, many different groups come from many areas to celebrate in a powwow.

Legacy
LINKING PAST AND PRESENT

COMING TOGETHER AT A POWWOW

Native Americans of yesterday and today have many different cultures. Yet one thing most share is a legacy of music and dance.

Today the powwow is one way Native Americans celebrate their culture and their past. Long ago, powwows were used to give good luck to hunters and farmers.

If you were part of a powwow today, you would watch and perform dances and songs from long ago. You might also make new friends. Let's see what it's like to join in at a powwow.

The players and singers around the drum are part of a group called "The Drum" (above). It provides the "heartbeat" for singing and dancing. Young people often make their own costumes (right).

76

Background Information

MORE ABOUT POWWOWS

• There are several theories about the origin of the term *powwow*. Some historians believe that the words *pau wau* once meant "spiritual leader" in the Algonkian language. Europeans watching the dances performed by Native American "medicine men" thought the words referred to the dance rather than the dancers.

• Dancing clothes are an important part of the powwow celebration. Typical clothes include deerskin leggings, beaded vests, moccasins, bells, and feathers. Clothes are often passed down from one generation to another.

• Powwows are on the rise. More than 1,000 are held each year, and they are attended by about 90 percent of American Indians.

Curriculum CONNECTION

LINKS TO READING *Powwow* by George Ancona (Harcourt, 1993) is a photo-essay that documents the largest powwow held in the United States—the summer Crow Fair in Montana. You may wish to read this book with your class.

LINKS TO MUSIC AND DANCE Invite students to research folk dances and music of other cultures, including their own. Students can bring the music to class and demonstrate or describe the dances.

Native Americans in the past also enjoyed visiting with each other. The woman and girls are doing beadwork.

Powwows bring together old and young, boys and girls, and men and women. Some people dress in everyday clothing. Others wear traditional Native American clothing.

77

MEETING *Individual* NEEDS

RETEACHING (Easy) Invite students to draw pictures of the dancers and musicians at a powwow. Ask them to write captions describing each performer's part.

EXTENSION (Average) Have students do library research to find out about the different types of clothing worn by the dancers and musicians.

ENRICHMENT (Challenging) Ask students to write paragraphs that compare and contrast what they have learned about powwow celebrations to the kinds of music and dancing they enjoy.

Suggested Questions
- **Why did Native Americans hold powwows in the past?** *(to give good luck to hunters and farmers)*
- **Why do they hold powwows today?** *(to celebrate their culture and their past)*

★**THINKING FURTHER:** *Compare and Contrast* **Think about dances or ceremonies you have seen. How were they like a powwow? different?** *(Encourage students to describe and compare various cultural or family events they have experienced.)*

Examining the Pictures Have students study the pictures to learn how powwows help Native Americans celebrate their culture and keep their traditions alive.

Suggested Questions
- **Who dances at a powwow?** *(both young and old)*
- **What do people do at a powwow besides dance?** *(make music and visit with each other)*

★**THINKING FURTHER:** *Making conclusions* **Why might the clothing worn at a powwow be very important?** *(It represents traditional dress; it helps people link the past and the present.)*

⭐ 3 CLOSE

SUM IT UP
Be sure students understand how powwows preserve the traditions and values of the past.

EVALUATE
Write About It Have students write a poem or song lyric about something important in their lives. They might accompany their recitation with an improvised dance or movement.

Technology CONNECTION

ADVENTURES CD-ROM
Enrich the lesson with the movie of the powwow on the CD-ROM.

LESSON 2

PAGES 78–81

Lesson Overview
In the high desert mesas of the Southwest, the Anasazi Indians developed a thriving culture.

Lesson Objectives
★ Explore the geography of the Southwest.

★ Analyze how geography shaped the culture of the Anasazi.

⭐ 1 PREPARE

MOTIVATE Explain that the picture shows the remains of cliff dwellings where a group of Native Americans called the Anasazi once lived. Then have students look at the map on p. 73, find the area where the Anasazi lived, and discuss what they know about that region.

SET PURPOSE Direct attention to the *Read to Learn* question. Tell students that in this lesson they will learn about the geography of Mesa Verde and how it affected the Anasazi who lived there. Then preview the *Vocabulary* words.

⭐ 2 TEACH

Discussing Life in The Desert
Have students review what they know about deserts and the plants and animals that live there.

Suggested Questions

● **What is a desert?** *(a very dry environment where little rain falls)*

● **How did Four Corners get its name?** *(It is where four states—Colorado, New Mexico, Utah, and Arizona—meet.)*

● **Where did the Anasazi live?** *(in the southwestern part of the U.S.)*

Resource REMINDER

Practice Book: *p. 18*

Anthology: *Why We Have Dogs in Hopi Villages, pp. 26–28*

Technology: *Videodisc/Video Tape 2*

Desk Map

The Geography of Mesa Verde

Focus Activity

READ TO LEARN
What is the geography of Mesa Verde like?

VOCABULARY
desert
canyon
cliff
mesa
technology

PLACE
Four Corners
Mesa Verde

78

READ ALOUD
Here the land is dotted with table-flat landforms that rise to the hot sun.

Here dramatic cliffs drop suddenly into deep canyons.

Life in the Desert
Have you ever seen a place like the one just described? It is an area in the southwestern part of our country called a desert. A desert is a very dry environment where little rain falls. On a summer's day, the temperature in the desert can get extremely hot. But at night, the temperature drops and it's much cooler.

Look at the map on the next page. It shows part of the states of Colorado, New Mexico, Utah, and Arizona. This desert area is often called the Four Corners. Can you see why? The four states all meet in one place. Long ago no states were there. But there were communities. And the people who lived in these communities were called the Anasazi.

Reading STRATEGIES *and* Vocabulary DEVELOPMENT

REREADING Tell students that good readers often reread passages to be sure they understand information. Have students look again at the word *desert* on p. 78. Ask them to reread the paragraph for clues about the word's meaning. Students can also reread passages to answer questions that come up in class discussion.

HOMOGRAPHS Explain that homographs are words that are spelled the same but have different meanings and different pronunciations. Write these definitions on the chalkboard: *desert—a dry land; desert—to leave someone or something.* Have students notice the spelling and pronunciation of each word. Then direct them to the word *desert* in the first paragraph on p. 78. Ask them to tell which definition is used there and what clues helped them figure this out.

A Difficult Environment

As you learned in the last lesson, Native Americans made good use of natural resources. The Iroquois lived in the northeastern part of our country. They used trees to make houses. The Plains Indians of the West hunted buffalo to use the skins for clothing and shelter. You read that the Makah lived in the northwestern part of the United States. They skillfully used trees to build their homes and boats.

The Anasazi also made the best of their very dry environment. The Anasazi were mostly farmers. They grew corn, beans, and squash. They also raised turkeys, which need little water.

The Anasazi used the resources of the desert to meet their other needs too. They used plants to make shoes and clothes. They also made pottery from the clay of the dry ground.

The Anasazi made sandals from the yucca (YUK uh) plant of the desert.

THE FOUR CORNERS

UTAH

COLORADO

Colorado River

Rio Grande

Mesa Verde

ARIZONA

NEW MEXICO

0 50 100 Miles
0 50 100 Kilometers

MAP WORK

The Four Corners area is in the southwestern part of our country.

1. What four states meet at the Four Corners?
2. In what state is Mesa Verde located?
3. In what direction is Mesa Verde from New Mexico?
4. Do any other four states meet in one place?

MAP WORK: 1. Colorado, New Mexico, Utah, Arizona 2. Colorado 3. north 4. No other four states meet at one place like the Four Corners.

79

● **What is the land like where they lived?** (It is a desert.)

★THINKING FURTHER: *Predicting*
Think about the desert cliffs and canyons in Four Corners. What kinds of houses do you predict the Anasazi would make? Why? (Students might predict mud or clay or stone, as there are no trees and very few animals for other building materials.)

Discussing A Difficult Environment Direct attention to the pictures. Then have students answer the questions.

Suggested Questions
● **What crops did the Anasazi grow?** (corn, beans, squash)

● **What kinds of things did the Anasazi make from plants?** (sandals, clothes, and baskets)

● **What is another natural resource the Anasazi used?** (clay for pottery)

● **Which animal did the Anasazi raise? Why?** (Turkeys; they only need a little water.)

More MAP WORK

Have students use the locator insert to see the area in relation to the 48 contiguous states.

Suggested Questions
● **How does the map tell you that the area is probably very dry?** (few rivers or other bodies of water are shown)

● **About how far is Mesa Verde from the beginning of the Rio Grande?** (about 100 miles)

Background INFORMATION

MORE ABOUT NATURAL RESOURCES
● *Trees:* Pine trees provided piñon nuts and sap to mend pottery and waterproof baskets.
● *Soil* and *water:* The Anasazi collected rain water in reservoirs and canals to irrigate fields. Farmers grew beans, squash, and corn.
● *Stone:* The Anasazi cut stone into blocks to build walls and houses.

Global CONNECTION

ANASAZI TRADERS Chaco Canyon in northwestern New Mexico was an Anasazi center of trade, connecting to Native Americans in Central America and northern regions. Goods were carried over roads that radiated from the city. Historians think the Anasazi may have learned how to farm corn, beans, and squash from Central American farmers.

Discussing Mesas, Cliffs, and Canyons Have students study the photographs of the landforms. You may want to illustrate on the chalkboard how canyons and cliffs divide higher land into mesas.

Suggested Questions

- **What is a canyon?** *(a deep valley with steep sides)*

- **What is a cliff?** *(a steep face of rock)*

- **What is a mesa?** *(a landform that looks like a high flat table)*

★**THINKING FURTHER:** *Cause and Effect* **Why were mesas, cliffs, and canyons good places for building communities?** *(because they provided protection from enemies and the environment)*

Technology CONNECTION

VIDEODISC/VIDEO TAPE 2
Enrich the lesson with the *Mesa Verde* segment.

Search Frame 17486

Mesas, Cliffs, and Canyons

The land of the Southwest is not all flat. As you can see in these pictures, there are many different landforms. To the Anasazi these shapes were not just beautiful. They were also great natural resources.

Deep canyons were carved into the land by mighty rivers. A canyon is a deep river valley with steep sides. Many communities were built along the walls of these canyons. Some Anasazi even made buildings and homes in the cliffs! A cliff is the steep face of a rock.

From the pictures here, find the landform that looks like a high, flat table. The name for that landform is mesa (MAY suh). In fact, *mesa* is the Spanish word for "table." Sometimes the Anasazi built their homes in the steep sides of mesas. Like canyons and cliffs, mesas protected them from enemies and the environment.

One Anasazi community in this area was Mesa Verde (VUR dee). The Spanish word for "green" is *verde*. You already know what *mesa* means. Can you guess why this area is called Mesa Verde?*

* The mesa tops were often green with plants.

Mesas and cliffs are two southwestern landforms. Desert wildlife includes lizards.

80

Background INFORMATION

ANASAZI HOMES

- The first homes the Anasazi built (about 100 B.C.) were rounded and domed pithouses. They were built of mud bricks—adobe—around a central pit dug in the earth.

- Around A.D. 900 the Anasazi began to build pueblos as a protection against the elements and enemies. They cut square pieces of limestone and stacked the blocks to make walls of houses. Then they carried heavy wooden beams, laid them across the roofs, and covered them with sticks, grass, and mud.

- Soon the Anasazi began to construct rooms with shared walls and to stack them one above the other. In Chaco Canyon, people lived in a huge pueblo shaped like a crescent moon. It was five stories high, with 800 apartments. The stacked homes looked like steps; the roof of one house could be used as the front yard of the home above it. The Anasazi used ladders to climb to the upper stories. They also carved toe holds into the rocks.

- Early pueblos were built on the tops of the mesas. Later—around 1000–1300—the Anasazi moved. They built new pueblos, complete with streets and plazas, under the protective overhang of huge rock cliffs.

Using Technology

The Anasazi made use of technology (tek NAHL uh jee) to help them in different ways. Technology is the use of tools and materials to serve people's needs. Pointed sticks were made to dig ditches for collecting the little rain that fell at Mesa Verde. The water was then used to grow crops.

WHY IT MATTERS

Suppose it is a time long ago, before your community was built. There were no highways or telephones. The Native Americans have already built many communities. Like people today, they used the land around them for all of their resources.

In the next lesson you will learn how the Anasazi worked with the land around them. You will see how they lived in a special community in the land of mesas and canyons.

The Anasazi made stone axes to clear fields for farming.

✔// Reviewing Facts and Ideas

SUM IT UP

- The environment of a desert is very dry.
- The landforms of the area now called the Four Corners include canyons, cliffs, and mesas.
- The Anasazi were one group who lived in this desert area. They worked as farmers to meet their needs.
- Technology improved the life of the Anasazi.

THINK ABOUT IT

1. What is the climate of Mesa Verde?

2. **FOCUS** What is the geography of Mesa Verde like?

3. **THINKING SKILL** What do you _predict_ would happen to the plants at Mesa Verde if it did not rain there for a long time? Explain your answer.

4. **WRITE** Look again at the pictures in this lesson. In your own words, describe the landforms you see.

81

Thinking About Using Technology
Have students answer the questions.

Suggested Questions

- **What is technology?** (the use of tools and materials to serve people's needs.)

- **What are two examples of tools the Anasazi used? What natural resources were the tools made from?** (digging tools made from pointed sticks; axes made from stone)

Discussing WHY IT MATTERS Be sure students understand how geography influenced the Anasazi.

Suggested Questions

- **What three landforms can be found at the area called the Four Corners?** (canyons, cliffs, mesas)

- **How did the Anasazi make use of those landforms?** (They built communities in or on them.)

★ 3 CLOSE

SUM IT UP
Encourage students to discuss these questions with a partner.

Suggested Questions

- **What problems does a desert create for people who live there?** (It is hard to find water to drink and to grow things.)

- **How would you describe a mesa?** (It is a high, flat table-shaped landform.)

- **How did the Anasazi clear their land for farming?** (They used axes.)

EVALUATE
✔ **Answers To Think About It**

1. It is hot and dry.

2. Mesa Verde is a landform that looks like a high, flat table. The top of the mesa is green with plants.

3. The plants would die. All plants need water to survive.

4. Be sure students identify the landforms correctly.

Write About It Have students write a haiku or other poem that describes Mesa Verde and its climate.

MEETING _Individual_ NEEDS

RETEACHING (Easy) Have students draw pictures of a mesa and the tools that the Anasazi used. They can look at the pictures and drawings in this lesson to guide their illustrations.

EXTENSION (Average) Ask students to write paragraphs that compare the geography, resources, and culture of the Plains Indians with that of the Anasazi. Have students use their desk maps to highlight the areas they write about.

ENRICHMENT (Challenging) Have students choose one natural resource that the Anasazi used—animals, yucca, soil and water, bone, or stone. Ask them to create an illustrated report that shows how Anasazi and other Native Americans used the same resource. Tell students to visit the library and to look through illustrated books on Native American culture for information.

LESSON 3

PAGES 82–87

Lesson Overview
By studying ancient artifacts, we have learned how members of the Anasazi community at Mesa Verde lived and worked together.

Lesson Objectives
★ Investigate the Anasazi at Mesa Verde.

★ Understand how artifacts help us learn about the past.

1 PREPARE

MOTIVATE Direct attention to the picture and the *Read Aloud.* Then have students use what they have already learned about the Anasazi to speculate about the answer to the *Read to Learn* question.

SET PURPOSE Introduce the *Vocabulary* words as you introduce the lesson. Explain that scientists have learned about the Anasazi by studying *artifacts*—ancient tools and other items found in the ruins of Anasazi communities.

2 TEACH

Discussing Morning at Mesa Verde Help students visualize Little Rabbit's home and understand how his daily life was similar to and different from theirs.

Suggested Questions
● **Where does Little Rabbit live?** *(in a cliff house on the side of the mesa)*

● **What are Little Rabbit's bed and blanket made from?** *(yucca leaves and turkey feathers)*

Resource REMINDER
Practice Book: *p. 19*
Technology: Adventures *CD-ROM*

Mesa Verde Long Ago

Focus Activity

READ TO LEARN
How did the Anasazi live?

VOCABULARY
kiva
artifact

READ ALOUD
A chickadee chirps in the distance. It is early morning, and an eight-year-old boy stirs in his bed. He has a busy day ahead of him.

Morning at Mesa Verde

The description you have just read does not sound very unusual. does it? But let's take a closer look. The boy's bed is actually a mat made from the leaves of the yucca plant. His blanket is made from turkey feathers. His "pajamas" are woven from plants.

He lives with his family in a house with many rooms. It is built into the side of a mesa. It is called a cliff house. As he starts his day, the people in his community are already busy. Some men and women are making pots out of clay. Others are sharpening stones to use as knives. The young boy is eager to join them.

The boy's name is Little Rabbit. He is an eight-year-old Anasazi who lives at Mesa Verde. The time is 1,000 years ago. Let's see what Little Rabbit's day is like.

82

Reading STRATEGIES *and* Language DEVELOPMENT

PROBLEM AND SOLUTION Help students recognize that the lesson identifies problems the Anasazi faced and lists how they solved those problems. For example, students can recognize the general problem of living in a dry, hot environment. Help them note that the Anasazi solved this problem by building houses from stone instead of trees (making them with thick walls so they would stay cool) and working together to survive as a community.

LANGUAGE HISTORY Point out that Little Rabbit's name means something special. Explain that in all cultures, names have meanings. For example, among the Yoruba in Africa, people are given "praise names," like Marvelous, or Friend. These names tell about something special the person has done. Encourage students to find out what their names mean by looking in the dictionary, a name book, or by talking to family members.

Community Life

To start the day, Little Rabbit finds his father, Strong Deer. He is outside sharpening an arrow. The Anasazi men sometimes hunt with spears and bows and arrows. They also farm and weave blankets. Little Rabbit is eager for the day he will be old enough to hunt and weave. "Not today," says his father. "Today you will help your mother."

Little Rabbit's mother is Swift Raven. Like many women, she takes care of the children and the home. She also cooks, makes pottery, and weaves baskets. Little Rabbit's new little sister, Bright Owl, is strapped to a board on her mother's back. "Good morning, Little Rabbit," his mother says. "Will you get me some water for the turkeys?" Little Rabbit takes a basket to the well. The baskets are woven so tightly that no water can spill. That is a good thing. Little Rabbit knows that water can be hard to find.

Soon all the women and children will go to the nearby field to gather beans and corn. All of the families work together and share their food. From the Infographic on the next pages, you can see different ways the Anasazi worked together.

DID YOU KNOW?

How were sandals made?

Anasazi children were helpful in making sandals. They were taught this skill not only by their parents but also by the older people in their community. Sandals were made from yucca. Children who made the best ones could trade them for blankets, arrowheads, and other things.

FOR TRADE

★THINKING FURTHER: *Predicting*
What do you think the rest of Little Rabbit's day will be like? *(Maybe he will hunt, or maybe he will make a pot or help with the farming.)*

Looking at Community Life Focus on the ways men, women, and children work together as you discuss life in the Anasazi community. Discuss this community in relation to your own, focusing on how communities throughout history have shared tasks and community responsibilities.

Suggested Questions

● ***How does Little Rabbit help his family?*** *(He collects water in a basket.)*

● ***How do the children help with the farming?*** *(They help gather beans and corn.)*

● ***What are some of the jobs that Anasazi women do?*** *(take care of the children, cook, make pottery, weave baskets)*

● ***What are some of the jobs the men do?*** *(weave cloth and hunt)*

★THINKING FURTHER: *Compare and Contrast* ***How does the Anasazi community compare to your community? How do people work together in both communities?*** *(Students can compare how people divide work and how they work together to help everyone in both communities.)*

Extending Did You Know? Tell students that the Anasazi boiled the yucca leaves and peeled them to use the soft fibers inside for sandals. Have students look carefully at the picture and share ideas about how the sandals were made. Encourage students to brainstorm a list of things they have that are made from plants, such as cotton clothing, paper, or straw hats.

CITIZENSHIP

LIVING TOGETHER The Anasazi had a well-developed community. They lived together in harmony, working and sharing responsibilities. Encourage students to make a class poster listing some of the things they could learn from the Anasazi about living together in a community.

Curriculum CONNECTION

LINKS TO SCIENCE When a tool, basket, bowl, or ornament is found at Mesa Verde, it is photographed and taken to a museum to be studied. Scientists record where each object was found and its condition. They make maps showing every discovery at a site. By fitting all of the information together, they can recreate how the Anasazi lived.

Have students brainstorm a list of present-day objects that would help scientists of the future understand how we live.

Infographic

Help students appreciate the daily co-operation and hard work of the Anasazi community.

Discussing A Day with the Anasazi Use the Infographic to expand students' awareness of daily life in Anasazi culture. Encourage them to suppose they are visiting Little Rabbit in his home.

Suggested Questions

● **How would you describe the Anasazi community?** *(organized and hardworking)*

★THINKING FURTHER: *Making Generalizations* **Would you have liked living in the Anasazi community? Why or why not?** *(Be sure students support their answers with information.)*

Infographic

A Day with the Anasazi

Pretend you are standing across from the cliff house where Little Rabbit and his family lived long ago. What might you see?

Older women help care for the young children.

Older men are sitting in the sun, telling stories.

The hole in the ground is the entrance to a special room used for religious purposes called a kiva.

Little Rabbit is carrying basket filled with water.

Expanding the Infographic

LINKS TO RESEARCH Invite students to learn more about the Anasazi by doing library research. Relevant books and encyclopedia articles may be listed under the following headings:

● Anasazi

● Cliff Dwellers

● Mesa Verde

Students can share their findings with the class in a picture-essay modeled on the *Infographic.*

LINKS TO READING More advanced students can read and report on *The Village of Blue Stone* by Stephen Trimble (Macmillan, 1990), which recreates a year in the life of an Anasazi community at Mesa Verde.

Background INFORMATION

MORE ABOUT A DAY WITH THE ANASAZI

● The Anasazi had one of the largest and most organized societies in the Southwest. This group had wandered from place to place, possibly for 10,000 years, looking for wild plants and animals to hunt. Because the Southwest had very few animals or wild plants, the Anasazi settled in one place to farm.

● In the Anasazi culture, the fields were owned by everyone, and the harvest was shared by the community.

● Women and men built the houses and women owned them. When a man married, he went to live in his wife's house.

Many storage rooms are used to hold crops and grain.

Women and children are grinding corn.

Swift Raven is making clay pots for cooking and storage.

Strong Deer is sharpening an arrow for hunting.

85

Discuss each group of people and ask students to tell how each person's work helped everyone in the community.

Suggested Questions

● **In what ways do you see children helping?** (grinding corn and carrying water)

● **What kinds of jobs can you see women doing?** (older women care for young children; younger women farm, make pottery, and grind corn)

● **What are the older men doing? Why is this important to the Anasazi?** (Telling stories; the Anasazi didn't have writing, so history and ideas were passed on through stories.)

★**THINKING FURTHER:** *Making Decisions* **What job would you have enjoyed doing if you had lived at Mesa Verde? Why?** (Answers should reflect information about a specific job.)

Technology CONNECTION

ADVENTURES CD-ROM
Enrich the *Infographic* with *Time Machine: Meet the Anasazi.*

Curriculum CONNECTION

LINKS TO ART: ANASAZI POTS Teach students to make clay pots following the coil method used by the Anasazi.

● Have students take a large ball of clay.

● Roll clay into long thin ropes.

● Build a bowl by coiling the clay rope in a spiral. Gently press the coils together.

● To make an "eating" pot, smooth the inside and outside carefully.

● To make a "cooking pot," make pinch marks where the coils meet around the outside of the pot. The pot will be less slippery and have more surface area to heat up in a fire.

● If possible, fire students' pots in a kiln.

Second-Language Support

USING VISUALS Help second-language learners focus on the *Infographic* pictures to increase understanding. Have students talk about the pictures as you model questions. Then ask students to create questions about the visuals to ask and answer with classmates.

Discussing the Anasazi Culture

Explain that the Anasazi religion was based on a respect for nature and on daily appreciation for the natural resources that helped them stay alive.

Suggested Questions

● **What is a kiva?** *(a round pithouse)*

● **What was the kiva used for?** *(religious ceremonies, as a workplace)*

● **Why did the kiva have a hole?** *(The Anasazi believed that people came to Earth from special holes in the ground.)*

★**THINKING FURTHER:** *Cause and Effect* **What is the cause of the outdoor dance?** *(the ripe crops)*

DISCUSSING WHY IT MATTERS Help students understand that the story of the Anasazi is like a puzzle. Pieces of the puzzle include artifacts and ruins, knowledge of the geography and climate, and what modern Pueblo Indians tell us about their culture. The Pueblo are descendants of the Anasazi.

Suggested Questions

● **What are artifacts?** *(objects left behind by people)*

● **How do artifacts tell us about the Anasazi?** *(We can see the kinds of tools they used and crafts they made and guess what they were used for. We can see what clothing they wore.)*

The Anasazi Culture

Religion was an important part of Anasazi culture. In the Infographic you learned that the kiva was used for religious purposes. Sometimes it was also used as a workplace.

The drawing below gives you a close-up view of a kiva in Little Rabbit's community. It was used mostly by men. At times women used the kivas as well. The Anasazi believed that people came to Earth from special holes in the ground. A kiva had a hole for this reason.

The walls of the kiva have colorful paintings. Stone benches are built into the walls. A fire in the center of the floor provides warmth.

Not all religious ceremonies take place in the kiva. For Little Rabbit tomorrow will be an exciting day. There will be a dance held in a field. Dancers will give thanks for the ripe food from the fields. They will wear colorful outfits and masks. One day Little Rabbit will take part in the dance. It too is a part of Anasazi culture.

The Anasazi used a ladder to enter a kiva.

Background INFORMATION

MORE ABOUT ANASAZI RELIGION

● Kivas were used by men as a place for storytelling, blanket weaving, and religious ceremonies. Families may have lived in them during the coldest months.

● Religious ceremonies may have asked for rain or good luck. Wall paintings of animals may have been attempts to gain power before a hunt. Like modern Pueblo Indians, the Anasazi had a deep respect for nature. To a captured animal, one Pueblo group (the Hopi) said, "We grieve that we had to take your life so our people could live."

● The Anasazi believed in an afterlife. They buried their dead with jewelry, combs, weapons, and a new pair of sandals to wear on their journey to the next world.

WHAT HAPPENED TO THE ANASAZI?

● The Anasazi permanently abandoned their cliff houses in about 1300. No signs of fighting or disease were evident. Families left behind valuable belongings as though they planned to return, but they never came back.

● Some archaeologists think they may have been afraid of invaders—the Utes and Apaches. But most believe they left because no rain fell for nearly 15 years—from 1276 to 1299. Without rain, crops and game died, and the Anasazi were probably forced to look elsewhere for food.

WHY IT MATTERS

How do we know what Little Rabbit's day might have been like 1,000 years ago? We do not know for sure. People did not write or take photographs back then. Scientists have tried to piece together the clues by looking at artifacts. Artifacts are objects left behind by a group of people. Pottery, tools, pieces of clothing, and buildings are all artifacts.

The Anasazi left Mesa Verde and other communities about 700 years ago. Scientists are not sure why. Some say that perhaps there was no rain for a long time. Or perhaps they were forced out by another Native American group.

Although the Anasazi have disappeared, parts of their culture remain. Today Pueblo (PWEB loh) villages have kivas. The kivas are just like the ones the Anasazi had long ago. In the next lesson you will learn another way the culture of the Anasazi continues today.

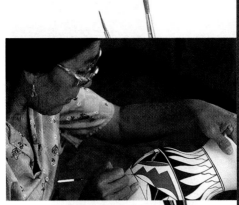

Today, Native Americans like this Pueblo woman still make pottery similar to the Anasazi pottery of long ago.

✓ Reviewing Facts and Ideas

SUM IT UP

- The Anasazi lived in communities built into the sides of mesas.
- Children helped with many tasks.
- Men hunted, farmed, and weaved.
- Women worked in the fields, made pottery, and took care of the younger children.
- Religion was an important part of Anasazi culture.

THINK ABOUT IT

1. What are two ways the Anasazi worked together in their community?

2. **FOCUS** How did the Anasazi live?

3. **THINKING SKILL** _Sort_ activities people did at Mesa Verde into fun activities and work activities.

4. **GEOGRAPHY** What landforms are in Little Rabbit's community?

87

---

3 CLOSE

SUM IT UP

Ask students to answer the following questions to help them sum up the lesson.

Suggested Questions

- **What were the Anasazi houses made of? What did they look like?** (Stone and clay; they looked like an apartment building with many rooms built close together.)

- **What task did Little Rabbit help his mother with?** (carrying water in a basket)

- **What tools did the Anasazi make for hunting?** (spears and arrows)

- **How did the women get clay for making pots?** (They dug it from the ground.)

- **What ceremony did the dancers hold in the fields?** (a dance of gratitude for the crops)

EVALUATE
✓ Answers to Think About It

1. They farmed and built houses together; the women made baskets and pottery; the men hunted and wove cloth.

2. They lived in an organized community that shared many tasks; they raised and ate corn; they worked hard to use the natural resources around them; they held ceremonial dances.

3. Fun: listening to stories. Work: hunting, farming, weaving, cooking, making pottery, grinding corn, making sandals.

4. mesa, desert, mountains _Description of Place_

Write About It Have students write a poem about the life of the Anasazi at Mesa Verde.

MEETING *Individual* NEEDS

RETEACHING (Easy) Have partners make drawings of one Anasazi community member involved in a daily activity. Students can write captions for their drawings and bind them together in a class book about the Anasazi.

EXTENSION (Average) As students look at the Infographic, help them chart comparisons between the Anasazi community and yours. For example, how do children help their families today? How do people in your community get food, plan ceremonies, cook food, and make houses?

ENRICHMENT (Challenging) Challenge students to research information on Pueblo Indians today. When sharing their reports with the class, help them compare Pueblo culture today with ancient Anasazi culture. Ask students to discuss what they think happened to the Anasazi.

LESSON 4

PAGES 88-91

Lesson Overview

Learn about the history of the Anasazi from the ruins of their cliff homes and ancient artifacts at Mesa Verde National Park.

Lesson Objectives

★ Understand the importance of national parks.

★ Understand why it is important to study the past.

1 PREPARE

MOTIVATE Have students talk about what it might be like to visit the ancient home of the Anasazi. Then have a volunteer read the *Read Aloud* and describe the picture.

SET PURPOSE Introduce the lesson Vocabulary word. At the museum, visitors can see many ancient Anasazi artifacts and learn how they were used. Then direct students to the *Read to Learn* question and invite them to speculate about the answer.

2 TEACH

Discussing Mesa Verde National Park Ask students to talk about National Parks they have visited and to share what they learned about geography and American history.

Suggested Questions

● **What is a national park?** *(a protected place for nature)*

● **Why was it important to protect Mesa Verde?** *(because the ancient cliff dwellings tell us much about the past; we wouldn't want them to be destroyed)*

Resource REMINDER

Practice Book: *p. 20*

Anthology: *Before You Came This Way, pp. 32–35*

Mesa Verde Today

READ ALOUD

"Welcome to Mesa Verde National Park. My name is Maxwell Rudolph. Only people who work for the park can live here. My father is a Park Ranger."

Focus Activity

READ TO LEARN

What can be learned by visiting Mesa Verde National Park today?

VOCABULARY

museum

PLACE

Mesa Verde National Park

Mesa Verde National Park

You have just been welcomed to Mesa Verde National Park by Maxwell Rudolph. Maxwell is a nine-year-old boy who lives in the park with his family. Only a few people live in the park today. But long ago many Anasazi lived here in a big community.

As you have read, the Anasazi mysteriously left Mesa Verde long ago. No group of people has lived in the cliff houses since. Today visitors can see the place much as it used to be.

Over many years much of the land in our country has changed. Paved highways have been laid down. Skyscrapers and shopping malls have been built. But as a national park, Mesa Verde has been protected from change. Let's join Maxwell and his father for a tour to see how the Anasazi lived over 700 years ago.

88

Reading STRATEGIES *and* Language DEVELOPMENT

COMPOUNDS Explain that compound words are made of two complete words. Open compounds are written as two words, closed compounds are written as one. Ask students to find examples of compound words— cliff house, shopping mall, highways, and skyscrapers—on p. 88. Have them tell what each word part means and how they work together to create meaning.

MAIN IDEA AND DETAILS The main idea of a paragraph tells what the paragraph is about. The details in the paragraph support, or tell more about, the main idea. For example, in the last paragraph on p. 88, the main idea is expressed in the first sentence: "Over many years much of the land in our country has changed." Ask students to find the supporting details in the paragraph.

Welcome to Mesa Verde!

From the entrance to the park, it takes a half-hour drive just to reach the Far View Visitor Center. That gives you an idea of how big the park is! At the Visitor Center, Maxwell's father greets thousands of visitors every year. Look at the map of Mesa Verde National Park below. It shows you where places to visit are located.

"The best place to start our tour is at the museum," says Mr. Rudolph. A museum is a place where people can look at objects of art, science, or history.

"From here, there are many places to go," says Mr. Rudolph. "Of these places, you can walk by homes from about 1,000 years ago."

By visiting Mesa Verde or looking at jewelry and other objects, people can learn about the Anasazi culture.

MESA VERDE NATIONAL PARK

COLORADO

* Cortez

- Place of Interest
☐ Road
— Park Boundary
// Park Entrance

Far View Visitor Center

Spruce Tree House
Long House ■ ■ Museum
Cliff Palace ■ ■ Balcony House

0   2   4 Miles
0   2   4 Kilometers

MAP WORK

Mesa Verde National Park was created in 1906.

1. What are some places of interest in the park?
2. How far is the museum from the Visitor Center?
3. What happens to the road before it reaches the Visitor Center?

MAP WORK: **1.** Visitor Center, museum, Long House, Spruce Tree House, Cliff Palace, Balcony House **2.** about 4½ miles **3.** The road breaks off, going in two different directions.

89

Discussing Welcome to Mesa Verde! Ask student to imagine that they are on a tour of Mesa Verde. Mr. Rudolph will guide them around many interesting sights.

Suggested Questions

- **What is a museum?** *(It is a place where people can look at objects of art, science, or history.)*

- **What kinds of things can you see in the Mesa Verde museum?** *(artifacts and models of scenes from Native American life)*

★THINKING FURTHER: *Sequence* **Why do you think Mr. Rudolph tells visitors to start their tour at the museum?** *(because then the visitor can make informed choices about what to see)*

More MAP WORK

As students look at the map, help them visualize the sites and the geography of the park. Explain that each site is an ancient cliff dwelling.

★THINKING FURTHER: *Making Decisions* **Look at the boundaries of the park. If you had been planning the park, would you have preserved the same piece of land? Why or why not?** *(Probably yes, because it includes the three home sites and the land of the mesa; different answers should include logical reasons.)*

Background INFORMATION

NATIONAL PARKS AND MESA VERDE The cliff dwellings at Mesa Verde lay abandoned for nearly 600 years. In 1888, a rancher named Richard Wetherill saw the pueblos while looking for lost cattle on a Ute reservation. The Native Americans had always known about the ruins, but left them alone out of respect for their ancestors.

Wetherill felt that he had discovered the ruins and charged visitors to see the site. People began to understand that Mesa Verde needed protecting, and worked together to make this happen.

A Colorado woman named Virginia McClurg gave speeches urging people to protect Mesa Verde. In 1906, President Theodore Roosevelt signed papers to make Mesa Verde a National Park. Native Americans could continue grazing their animals there and the land would be protected for future generations.

Thinking About Respecting the Past Be sure that students understand that the cliff dwellings are the homes of someone's ancestors. The artifacts and kivas represent a heritage that is still very important to Native Americans today.

Suggested Questions

● **How do visitors reach the cliff house sites?** *(They are taken on a tour by the ranger. They climb ladders.)*

● **What are two reasons people should respect the past at Mesa Verde?** *(They are walking through someone's home. There are Native Americans alive today with similar traditions and beliefs.)*

★**THINKING FURTHER:** *Compare and Contrast* **How is Mesa Verde the same as it was 1000 years ago? How is it different?** *(Same: there is still yucca; the land is the same; the ladders, steps, and buildings are still there; different: the buildings are in ruins; there are no people living there anymore.)*

Discussing WHY IT MATTERS Ask a volunteer to read Mr. Rudolph's reminder aloud. Explain the term *long-term effects.* Students can share what they have learned about conserving natural resources from the Anasazi. Then they can tell how we can use resources wisely today to preserve them for people 1000 years from now.

Suggested Questions

● **How do we know that the Anasazi knew how to use and value natural resources?** *(They used every part of plants and animals; they were careful with water.)*

Respecting the Past

Mr. Rudolph takes visitors to sites where the Anasazi lived long ago. On the paths, they hike past yucca plants like the ones used every day by the Anasazi. Visitors climb ladders to reach the old rooms. They also climb down ladders to see the kivas. There are many different things Mr. Rudolph hopes the visitors will learn.

"Of course, I want people to learn what life might have been like long ago," he says. "But that is not the most important thing. I want them to respect the past. I tell them to act as if they are walking through someone's home—because they are!"

Mr. Rudolph also tells visitors to Mesa Verde not to touch or remove any artifacts. He then reminds them that the kivas are still very important to some Native Americans today. Pueblo, Zuni, and Hopi people still live in nearby areas. Many of their beliefs and customs are similar to those of the Anasazi long ago.

Visitors climb a ladder to reach rooms at Long House (left) and see Anasazi homes at Cliff Palace (right).

90

As the tour ends Mr. Rudolph leaves visitors with an important reminder: "We study the past to learn something we can use today. One of the most important things we can learn from the Anasazi is to work well together in our communities. Another important lesson is to respect nature and think about the long-term effects of our actions."

WHY IT MATTERS

By studying the past we learn how people lived in communities. One way to study and learn about the past is to visit a museum or a place like Mesa Verde National Park.

Look around your own community. Ancient artifacts may not be in your backyard. But your community does have a history that goes back a long time. And chances are, if you study that history, you'll learn something about your community today.

Mr. Rudolph teaches children about the Anasazi at Mesa Verde.

Reviewing Facts and Ideas

SUM IT UP

- Visitors to Mesa Verde National Park can learn about the past by seeing artifacts.
- Visitors can see what life was like long ago.
- Visitors must be respectful of the sites they see.
- By learning about the past, we can learn about our communities today.

THINK ABOUT IT

1. Why is the museum a good place to start the park tour?

2. **FOCUS** What can be learned by visiting Mesa Verde National Park today?

3. **THINKING SKILL** What do you _predict_ might happen to Mesa Verde if it were not a national park?

4. **GEOGRAPHY** Look at the map on page 89. Use the scale to find the distance from the Balcony House to the museum.

- **What can we learn about cooperation from the Anasazi community?** (When people work together, they can help their community succeed.)

- **What might you learn from studying the past of your community or early inhabitants?** (how Native Americans used the natural resources there, how they lived and worked together, how we can use our environment more carefully)

3 CLOSE

SUM IT UP

Encourage students to sum up what they have learned in this lesson by answering the questions below.

Suggested Questions

- **What artifacts can visitors see at Mesa Verde National Park?** (ancient kivas, baskets, clay pots, tools, and the ruins of ancient cliff dwellings)

- **How can park visitors show respect for the Anasazi and Pueblo Indians?** (They can treat the cliff dwellings with care and act as though they are in someone's home. They can also be respectful of Native American beliefs and traditions.)

- **How is the Anasazi community like your community?** (Answers should reflect how people work together to improve life.)

EVALUATE

✓ **Answers to Think About It**

1. You can learn about the different sites before you make a decision about where you want to go.

2. You can visit the actual place where the Anasazi lived, look at artifacts, and learn about the life of their community.

3. The buildings might have been ruined or torn down; the artifacts might have been stolen or destroyed.

4. 2 miles _Description of place._

Write About It Have students think of three questions they would like to ask about the history of their community. Have them write to a local historical society to obtain the answers.

SKILLS LESSON
PAGES 92-93

Lesson Overview
Making a decision involves choosing a course of action to achieve a set goal.

Lesson Objective
★ Understand and practice the steps in the decision-making process.

1 PREPARE

MOTIVATE Have volunteers talk about how they made a recent decision or choice. Ask them to tell the possibilities they had to choose from and whether it was easy or difficult to make the decision.

SET PURPOSE Remind students that decision-making is a skill they will use frequently in school and in life. Point out that they will learn a decision-making process in this lesson. Invite them to glance at the *Helping Yourself* box.

2 TEACH

Why the Skill Matters Have students discuss why setting a goal is important to good decision-making. Point out that a goal—the result aimed for—should guide their choice.

Using the Skill Help students move through each step of the decision-making process by creating a flow chart that lists the steps. The chart might have a box labeled "Goal" at the top, with several boxes below it labeled "Choice 1," "Choice 2."

Resource REMINDER
Practice Book: *p. 21*
Transparency: *Graphic Organizer*

THINKINGSKILLS

Making Decisions

VOCABULARY
decision

WHY THE SKILL MATTERS

Every day in your life you make decisions. A decision is a choice that is made. When you choose what clothes to wear in the morning, you are making a decision.

Sometimes making a decision is very easy. You might know that one choice would be a big mistake and the other would be exactly right. But sometimes, making decisions can be hard. Use the Helping Yourself box on the next page to guide you in making decisions.

USING THE SKILL

Suppose that you and your family are visiting Mesa Verde National Park. You have only one day to spend there. After you have visited the museum, your mother says it's up to you to decide where to go next. How would you decide what sites to see?

In making a decision, it is important to set a goal. Your goal could be to see and learn as much as possible at Mesa Verde in only one day.

You could then gather information to learn what your choices are. Pictured above is a visitor's guide to Mesa Verde National Park. It provides important facts about different sites.

Each choice from the guide has advantages and disadvantages. Cliff Palace is the biggest place. Spruce Tree House is not quite as large. Both are near each other.

Long House is the second largest place. It has a beautiful view. But it is far from both Spruce Tree House and Cliff Palace.

You decide that too much time would be spent traveling to Long House. Your decision could be to visit Cliff Palace. Then, if there were time, you could also visit Spruce Tree House. After all, you have only one day to spend at the park!

92

Background INFORMATION

- Cliff Palace contains 23 kivas and more than 200 rooms. It may have housed as many as 400 people. Parts of Cliff Palace are four stories high. Few of the walls still reach their original height, and the rooms no longer have their roofs. Visitors can see Cliff House from the opposite canyon rim.

- Spruce Tree House, named for a large tree that grows in front, has eight kivas and 114 rooms. It was probably the home of 100 to 125 people. Several of the rooms still have their roofs. This is the only cliff dwelling at Mesa Verde that is open to the public all year.

- Long House was almost as large as Cliff Palace, but much of it was destroyed by early explorers looking for pottery, baskets, tools, and other treasures left behind by the Anasazi. Long House contains 15 kivas and has a large plaza in the center that was probably used for ceremonies and dances. It is not known how many rooms it once had.

*Set a goal; you could choose to buy a tour guide booklet.

TRYING THE SKILL

Now suppose you are at the gift shop near the museum. Your mother has given you $5 to spend. From the picture below, you can see what things you can buy for $5. What will you decide to buy? What should you do first to make your decision? If your goal is to learn what Mesa Verde is like today, what would you choose to buy?*

HELPING Yourself

- To make a **decision** is to make a choice.
- Set a goal.
- Identify as many possible choices as you can.
- Think about the possible results of each choice.
- Select the best choice.

REVIEWING THE SKILL

1. What does it mean to make a decision?

2. What is one decision you made today?

3. How did you make your decision?

4. Why is it important to learn how to make good decisions?

PRICE LIST

History Book	$5.00	Photo Book	$5.00
Hat	$5.00	Patch and Pin	$5.00
Tour Guide	$5.00	Key Chains	2 for $5.00
Coloring Book	$5.00		

93

Background INFORMATION

USING THE GRAPHIC ORGANIZER You may want to have students work with this Graphic Organizer transparency to help them organize their information.

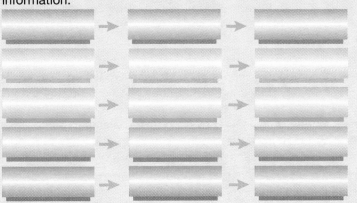

Discussing Major Events Use the following questions to help students practice reading a time line.

Suggested Questions

- *In what year did the Anasazi establish a community at Mesa Verde?* (1100)

- *After how many years did the last Anasazi leave Mesa Verde?* (350)

- *How many centuries does the time line cover?* (10)

Answers to
THINKING ABOUT VOCABULARY

1. T
2. F
3. F
4. F
5. T
6. T
7. T
8. F
9. F
10. T

Resource **REMINDER**

Assessment Book: *Chapter 3 Test*

CHAPTER 3 REVIEW

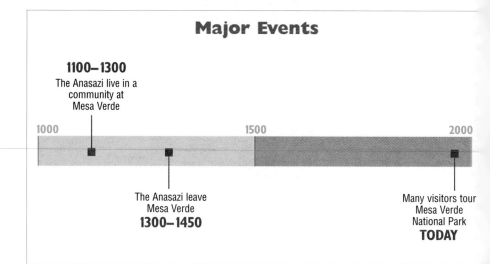

Major Events

1100–1300
The Anasazi live in a community at Mesa Verde

1000   1500   2000

The Anasazi leave Mesa Verde
1300–1450

Many visitors tour Mesa Verde National Park
TODAY

THINKING ABOUT VOCABULARY

Number a piece of paper from 1 to 10. Read the definition of each underlined word. Write **T** if the definition is true and **F** if it is false. If it is false, write a sentence correctly defining the word.

1. A <u>desert</u> is a very dry environment with little rainfall.
2. <u>Technology</u> is the study of how animals live on a farm.
3. <u>Artifacts</u> are tools used to dig up objects left by a group of people.
4. The landform that looks like a high, flat table is a <u>cliff</u>.
5. A <u>canyon</u> is a deep river valley with steep sides.
6. The story of our past is our <u>history</u>.
7. A <u>museum</u> is a place where people can look at objects of art, science, or history.
8. A <u>mesa</u> is a steep face of a rock.
9. A <u>kiva</u> is a large farming tool.
10. A <u>decision</u> is making a choice.

THINKING ABOUT FACTS

1. How did the natural resources in an area matter to the people living there? Give an example.
2. In what area of our country did the Anasazi live long ago?
3. Why did the Anasazi build their homes in cliffs and in the sides of mesas?
4. How do we know what life was probably like for Native Americans long ago?
5. Why do we study the past?

94

Suggestions for **Think and Write**
SIGNS OF SUCCESS

WRITING A JOURNAL ENTRY Journal entries should reflect an understanding of how the Anasazi made use of natural resources to meet their needs and how children and adults worked together for the good of the community.

WRITING A COMPARISON *Alike:* Both groups used natural resources to meet their needs. *Different:* The Makah were fishers who lived along the West Coast. They used trees to build homes and boats and relied on the Pacific Ocean for fish and other resources. The Anasazi were farmers in the Southwest. They used desert plants to make shoes and clothes and clay from the ground to make pots. They built homes in the steep sides of mesas and along the walls of canyons.

WRITING A POSTER Posters should mention important park features such as the cliff dwellings and the museum.

For performance assessment, see Assessment Book, Chapter 3.

THINK AND WRITE

WRITING A JOURNAL ENTRY

Suppose you lived at Mesa Verde long ago. Write a journal entry about a day in your life. Describe what you eat, what you wear, and what you do during the day.

WRITING A COMPARISON

Write a paragraph comparing the life of the Anasazi and the Makah. You may want to compare the area they lived in and what they ate.

WRITING A POSTER

Write a poster encouraging people to visit Mesa Verde National Park. What would you describe about the park? What places would you want to tell people about?

APPLYING THINKING SKILLS

MAKING DECISIONS

Answer the following questions to practice the skill of decision making.

1. What are the steps to follow in making a decision?

2. How do you decide what homework to do first? What do you think about before deciding?

3. Suppose you are invited to play by two different friends. One you play with often. The other you have wanted to play with for a long time. Identify the steps you would take in deciding. What are the possible results of each choice?

4. How do you decide what to do for fun on a rainy day?

5. Why is it important to consider all choices when making a decision?

Answers to THINKING ABOUT FACTS

1. Example: The Anasazi used the soil for farming, clay dug from the ground to make pots, plants to weave baskets, stone and clay to build homes.

2. the southwest

3. for protection from enemies and the elements

4. We study artifacts such as baskets, pottery, and tools.

5. We study the past to learn how people lived in communities.

Answers to APPLYING THINKING SKILLS

1. set a goal, list your choices, think about the possible results of each choice, make the choice that helps you best fulfill your goal

2. Answers will vary depending on students' skill and interest levels.

3. Accept responses that reflect supported thought processes.

4. Answers will vary depending on community resources.

5. Well-thought out decisions reflect the consideration of all choices.

Summing Up the Chapter

Review the chapter and complete a copy of the main idea table below. In the table legs, list how the Anasazi met the basic needs shown in the table feet. Then write an answer to the question: In what ways did the natural resources of the area help shape the way the Anasazi lived?

Main Idea The culture of the Anasazi is partly shaped by the natural resources around them.

FOOD	CLOTHING	SHELTER
corn beans squash turkey	clothes from plants sandals from yucca leaves	cliff houses houses in sides of mesas

---

Suggestions for Summing Up the Chapter

Help students copy the main-idea table or distribute copies for them to work on. Have students complete the table before answering the question.

- To complete the table, students can list kinds of food, clothing, and shelter found in the Anasazi community. You may want to use the annotations to give students one or two examples.

- To answer the question, students can describe the Anasazi's reasons for growing corn and raising turkeys, wearing yucca clothing, and building cliff houses. Students should understand that the Anasazi were farmers because there was little game in the dry region.

CHAPTER ORGANIZER 4

An English Colony at Jamestown

CHAPTER OVERVIEW

Almost four hundred years ago, people from England sailed to America and built a village called Jamestown in what is today Virginia. The land where they settled was first home to the Powhatan. Both groups of people lived off the land, forest, and rivers.

CHAPTER PLANNING GUIDE
Suggested pacing: 10–12 days

LESSON	LESSON FOCUS	LESSON RESOURCES
1 THE GEOGRAPHY OF JAMESTOWN pages 98–101	A River Meets the Bay	*Practice Book* p. 23 *Technology:* Videodisc/Video Tape, CD-ROM *Outline Map* p. 13
2 JAMESTOWN LONG AGO pages 102–107	The Powhatan and the English	*Practice Book* p. 24 *Anthology* pp. 36–44 *Outline Map* p. 13
Infographic page 106	The 13 Colonies	*Technology:* Adventures CD-ROM
3 JAMESTOWN TODAY pages 108–111	Visiting Jamestown Settlement	*Practice Book* p. 25
STUDY SKILLS pages 112–113	Reading Time Lines	*Practice Book* p. 26 *Technology:* Adventures CD-ROM
CHAPTER REVIEW pages 114–115	Students' understanding of vocabulary, content, and skills is assessed.	*Assessment:* Ch. 4 Test, Performance Assessment Ch. 4 *Transparency:* Graphic Organizer

OPTIONS FOR STUDENT ACTIVITIES

Citizenship pp. 105, 106, 109

Curriculum Connection pp. 100, 109, 110, 112

Expanding the *Infographic* p. 106

Using the Anthology p. 105

ASSESSMENT OPPORTUNITIES

Meeting Individual Needs pp. 97, 101, 107, 111, 113

Write About It pp. 101, 107, 111

Chapter Review pp. 114–115

Assessment Book

Chapter Test Ch. 4 Test

Performance Assessment Ch. 4

Using the Floor Map Use the Floor Map and the Project Book with Lesson 2 by inviting students to suppose they are explorers who have "landed" on the floor map. All areas are occupied, except for the island and the mountains to the north.

Using Geo Adventures Use **Geo Adventures** Daily Geography Activities to assess students' understanding of geography skills.

Using the Vocabulary Cards The vocabulary words for each lesson are available on *Vocabulary Cards* for review and practice.

GETTING READY FOR THE CHAPTER

Make a "Time Box" PARTNER 30 MINUTES OR LONGER

Objective: To share prior knowledge of the past.

Materials: *Project Book* pp. 10–11, shoeboxes, paper fasteners, crayons

1. Ask the class if they have ever read stories or seen movies about people who lived in the past. Encourage them to discuss what they know.
2. Pair students with partners and explain that they will make a "time box" that will help them think and find out about the past.
3. Let each pair of students cut out the question wheel, arrow, and designs on Project Book p. 10. Help students attach the wheel and pointer to the shoebox lid, using the paper fastener, and then put the lid on the box. They can then glue on the designs provided, as well as draw some of their own.
4. Now have partners turn the pointer on the wheel. As they do, have them write their responses in the correct space on Project Book p. 11. Have partners share their answers.

> **SECOND-LANGUAGE SUPPORT**
> Second-language learners may benefit from working with an English-proficient peer during this activity.
>
> Additional Second-Language Support Tips: pp. 99, 106

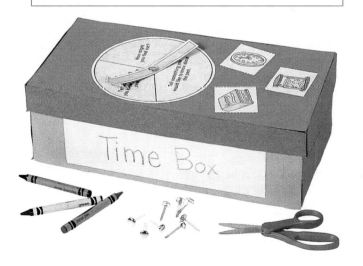

Explain that the Jamestown settlers were the first European settlers to build a community on Powhatan land. Help students understand that, like the Native Americans, the Jamestown settlers had to survive using the resources around them.

THINKING ABOUT GEOGRAPHY AND HISTORY

Ask students to read the page and note the location of Jamestown on the map. Have them note also the direction of the Atlantic Ocean and England.

1607

Suggested Questions

● **When was Jamestown built?** *(in 1607)*

● **Where was Jamestown built? Is Jamestown close to your community?** *(It is on the east coast of North America; answers will vary.)*

● **What more would you like to know about Jamestown?** *(Invite students to list questions about Jamestown. Explain that these questions will be answered in this chapter.)*

★**THINKING FURTHER:** *Making Conclusions* **What materials do you think the Powhatan and the Jamestown settlers used to build their homes?** *(probably wood, logs, bark, mud, brush)*

1614

Suggested Questions

● **What event took place in 1614?** *(John Rolfe and Pocahontas were married.)*

 Resource REMINDER

Technology: *Videodisc/Video Tape 2*

CHAPTER 4

An English Colony at Jamestown

THINKING ABOUT GEOGRAPHY AND HISTORY

About four hundred years ago, a group of people set sail from England to North America. They built a village called Jamestown.

The land where the English settled was home to a group of Native Americans called the Powhatan. It was a place rich in forests and rivers. As you read Chapter 4, see how both groups of people used the land's resources. Start by studying the map and time line here.

1607

Colonists arrive at Jamestown

1614

Marriage of Pocahontas and John Rolfe

96

Background INFORMATION

LINKING THE MAP AND THE TIME LINE

● In 1607, English settlers built the first permanent European settlement in North America. The location was chosen on a protected bay. The settlers, unfamiliar with the land around them, suffered devastating famine and disease.

● The marriage of Pocahontas and John Rolfe was an important event. The marriage united two important families. It gave both communities a reason to live peacefully together for several years. John Rolfe introduced tobacco farming to the settlement and finally assured its financial security.

Jamestown, Virginia

TODAY

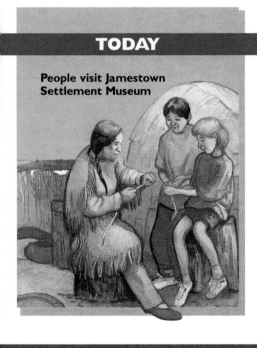

People visit Jamestown Settlement Museum

97

- **What do you already know about Pocahontas?** *(Students may have read stories or seen films about Pocahontas. Invite students to share their knowledge with the class.)*

★**THINKING FURTHER:** *Sequencing* **What picture might you add to the beginning of the time line?** *(Answers could reflect either the Powhatan living in their community, or the English landing in ships.)*

TODAY

Suggested Questions

- **What kinds of things do you think visitors might learn at the Jamestown Settlement Museum?** *(Visitors would learn about the people who lived in and around Jamestown.)*

- **What questions would you want to ask someone at the museum?** *(Students can list questions they have about how the English settlers lived.)*

- **About how much time has passed since Jamestown was built?** *(almost 400 years)*

 Technology CONNECTION

VIDEODISC/VIDEO TAPE 2
Enrich Chapter 4 with the Videodisc *glossary* segments.

Search Frame 53777

Meeting *Individual* Needs

RETEACHING (Easy) Invite students to make lists of questions they have about the Powhatan, the English settlers, and events in the photographs or the geography of this coastal area. As students read the chapter, they can write the answers to their questions.

EXTENSION (Average) Have students write brief news reports telling what is happening in each picture. Remind them to include the dates, names of people, and location.

ENRICHMENT (Challenging) Have students note that seven years passed between the building of Jamestown and the marriage of John Rolfe and Pocahontas. Have students write paragraphs about what kinds of things may have happened to bring the settlers closer to the Native Americans over this seven year period.

LESSON 1

PAGES 98–101

Lesson Overview
The geography of Jamestown was an important factor in the decision to build an English settlement there.

Lesson Objectives
★ Describe the geography of Jamestown.
★ Examine how the Powhatan and the English were affected by their environment.

1 PREPARE

MOTIVATE Explain that the *Read Aloud* quotation was spoken almost 400 years ago by an Englishman who came to North America to help start a new community. Tell students that in this lesson, they will learn why the English came to this country and what they found here.

SET PURPOSE Have students read the *Read to Learn* question. Then explain that the map on p. 99 will help them answer the question. Have students look at the map and find the *Vocabulary* word that appears there.

2 TEACH

Discussing Land of Many Resources Point out the picture, which shows a replica of one of the ships that brought the settlers to Jamestown. Then discuss the text.

Suggested Questions

● **Why did George Percy come to America?** *(He hoped to find riches; he wanted to build a community there.)*

● **For whom did the colonists name their community?** *(King James, the King of England at the time)*

● **What state is Jamestown in today?** *(Virginia)*

Resource REMINDER

Practice Book: *p. 23*
Technology: *Videodisc/Video Tape 2;* Adventures *CD-ROM*
Outline Maps: *p. 13*

The Geography of Jamestown

Focus Activity

READ TO LEARN
What is the geography of Jamestown like?

VOCABULARY
bay
coastal plain

PLACES
Jamestown
Virginia
Chesapeake Bay

READ ALOUD
"There are fair meadows and goodly tall trees . . . beautiful strawberries and excellent good timber."

Land of Many Resources

These words were written a long time ago by George Percy. He was a passenger on a small ship that sailed from England to North America in 1607. Percy and other Englishmen on the ship dreamed of gold and other riches in the land that is now the United States.

Look at the map on the next page. The area where the Englishmen started their community is called Jamestown. It was named for the King of England, James I. Today it is in the state of Virginia.

As you can tell from George Percy's words, the environment of Jamestown seemed good. There were trees for building houses and food to eat. It looked like a fine place to build a community. In this lesson let's take a closer look at the geography of Jamestown.

98

Reading STRATEGIES *and* Language DEVELOPMENT

MAIN IDEA AND DETAILS Explain that a paragraph usually has one main idea and several details that tell more about that idea. Recognizing each main idea and its supporting details will help readers understand and remember information. Ask a volunteer to state the main idea of the first paragraph on p. 99. Write the sentence beginning "Native Americans had lived . . ." on the chalkboard. Then ask volunteers to list the supporting details as you write them on the board.

PROPER NOUNS Remind students that the names of people are *proper nouns*. Help them see that Jamestown is a place named after a person. Have students brainstorm a list of other place names they know that are named for people. Have them add to the list as they continue through the unit.

Using Natural Resources

The English were not the first people to build communities in Virginia. Native Americans had lived in the area for thousands of years. They had learned over time how to make good use of natural resources. Tall pine trees were used for building houses and for making bows and arrows. They also carved out trees and used them as canoes.

Look at the map shown below. In 1607 a Native American people called the Powhatan (pow uh TAN) lived in what is now eastern Virginia. They fished in the James River and Chesapeake Bay. A bay is a body of water partly surrounded by land. Can you find where Chesapeake Bay meets the James River?

Native Americans used resources like trees to build canoes and other important items.

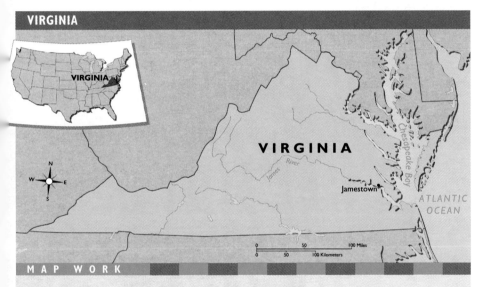

VIRGINIA

MAP WORK

English colonists built a community at Jamestown in 1607.

1. How far is Jamestown from the Atlantic Ocean?
2. What body of water is between the Atlantic Ocean and the James River?
3. Why do you think canoes were important to the Powhatan people?

MAP WORK: 1. about 50 miles 2. Chesapeake Bay 3. Because so many bodies of water were in the area, canoes were important to fish for food and to travel by water.

Thinking About Using Natural Resources Have students look at the Native American culture map on p. 73 to see the cultural area in which the Powhatan lived.

Suggested Questions

● *Who were the first people to build communities in the area we now call Virginia?* (Native Americans)

● *How did they use natural resources?* (They made houses, bows and arrows, and canoes from trees; they fished in and traveled on the James River and Chesapeake Bay.)

● *What is a bay?* (a body of water partly surrounded by land)

● *What group of Native Americans lived in the Chesapeake Bay area when the English arrived?* (the Powhatan)

More **MAP WORK**

Have students use the map to answer the questions.

Suggested Questions

● *Into what body of water does the Chesapeake Bay flow?* (Atlantic Ocean)

● *If you followed the James River to Jamestown, in what direction would you travel?* (east)

★**THINKING FURTHER:** *Using Prior Knowledge* **On what type of landform was Jamestown built? Of the communities we have studied so far, which is on the same type of landform?** (a peninsula; Paracas, Peru)

Second-Language **Support**

READING STRATEGIES Purpose-setting questions can help second-language learners focus attention as they read. You may wish to use questions such as the following with each section of this lesson:

● What resources did the English find in Jamestown? (p. 98)

● How did the Powhatan make use of natural resources? (p. 99)

● How was the environment around Jamestown different from the environment around Mesa Verde? (p. 100)

Background Information

ABOUT THE POWHATAN The Powhatan occupied the Chesapeake Bay area for at least 300 years before the English arrived. Like other peoples of the Eastern Woodlands, the Powhatan were mainly farmers. They supplemented their vegetarian diet with fish and game.

● Powhatan women worked the fields with tools made from deer antlers. They also collected nuts, berries, and roots, with the help of children and the elderly.

● Powhatan men fished from dugout canoes, using nets made of animal sinews and plant fibers, lines with bone hooks, and arrows tied to cords. They also made dams with stones or wooden stakes to trap fish.

● The Powhatan preserved food for times when food was scarce by drying fish and meat and by storing nuts in covered holes.

Links to
CURRENT EVENTS

Catch of the Day!

What are new ways people use natural resources?

Virginia's waters have long provided people with food. Today fish and shellfish are not only found in the water, but also on land! They are now raised in tanks on fish farms in Virginia.

Where do the foods you eat come from? Keep a list. Then compare your list with others from your class.

This artwork from the 1800s shows the English using resources of the forest to build Jamestown.

Living with the Environment

In the last chapter you read about how the Anasazi used natural resources to survive in the dry environment of Mesa Verde. But the Powhatan's environment around Jamestown was different. There was plenty of rain for plants and trees. The area around Jamestown is a coastal plain. A coastal plain is flat land along the coast. It was good for farming. The Powhatan grew corn, beans, and squash. They also hunted deer and other animals.

The English also liked Jamestown's environment. They saw the location as a good place to build a community. Their boats had a good port in the deep waters of Chesapeake Bay. The waters, which surrounded the English on three sides, helped to protect the English against attack. The Native Americans and the Spanish often used land routes for attack.

The Granger Co

WHY IT MATTERS

Environment makes a difference to communities. People need resources from the environment to live. This fact was true in our country's past too.

For the Powhatan long ago, the environment provided resources for farming and fishing. For the English, Jamestown provided a good port for ships. The port was also useful in protecting against attacks by their enemies. The land around Jamestown also provided wood for building houses.

For both the Powhatan and the English, survival meant living with the environment around them.

Corn, squash, and beans were among the foods that the Powhatan grew.

✓✓ Reviewing Facts and Ideas

SUM IT UP

- Hundreds of years ago, people sailed from England to build a community in the area they named Jamestown.
- Native Americans were already living in communities in the area around Jamestown.
- Jamestown's environment was good for farming.
- The land around Jamestown was called a coastal plain.
- Chesapeake Bay provided a good port for the English ships. It also provided food for the Powhatan.

THINK ABOUT IT

1. How did the English and the Powhatan use the natural resources at Jamestown?
2. **FOCUS** What is the geography of Jamestown like?
3. **THINKING SKILL** Suppose you wanted to build a community. How would you _decide_ on a place? State your goals.
4. **GEOGRAPHY** Name two bodies of water near Jamestown. You can use the map on page 99.

101

LESSON 2

PAGES 102–107

Lesson Overview
The English colony at Jamestown struggled hard to survive in their new environment.

Lesson Objectives
★ Understand what a colony is.

★ Investigate colonial life in Jamestown.

★ Learn about the original 13 colonies that became our first states.

1 PREPARE

MOTIVATE Explain that the picture shows an advertisement from colonial times that was used to attract settlers to North America. Then have students read the *Read Aloud* and speculate about the reactions the English and Powhatan might have had toward each other.

SET PURPOSE Review the *Vocabulary* words with students. Then direct attention to the *Read to Learn* question and invite speculation about the answer.

2 TEACH

Thinking About Powhatan and the English Meet Have students answer the questions.

Suggested Questions

● **Who was the leader of the Powhatan people in 1607? Who was the English leader?** (Powhatan; John Smith)

★ THINKING FURTHER: *Making Conclusions* **Why did Powhatan insist that the English get rid of their weapons?** (to keep the peace)

Resource REMINDER

Practice Book: *p. 24*

Anthology: *Jamestown: New World Adventure, pp. 36–40; ...If you LIved in Colonial Times, pp. 41–43; In Good Old Colony Times, p. 44*

Technology: *Adventures CD-ROM*

Outline Maps: *p. 13*

NOVA BRITANNIA.
OFFERING MOST
Excellent fruites by Planting in
VIRGINIA.
Exciting all such as be well affected
to further the same.

LONDON
Printed for SAMVEL MACHAM, and are to be sold at
his Shop in Pauls Church-yard, at the
Signe of the Bul-head.
1609.

Bettmann

Focus Activity

READ TO LEARN
What was life like for the colonists?

VOCABULARY
colony
colonist
slavery

PEOPLE
Powhatan
John Smith
John Rolfe
Pocahontas

102

Jamestown Long Ago

READ ALOUD
"I insist that the guns and swords, the cause of all our jealousy and uneasiness, be removed and sent away."

Powhatan and the English Meet

These words were said by Powhatan, the leader of the Powhatan people in 1609. He was speaking to John Smith, the leader of the English at Jamestown. Powhatan was hoping for peace between his people and the English.

The Powhatan and the English met in 1607. That was the year the English first arrived at Jamestown. It was a very long time ago— almost 400 years!

The meeting between the Powhatan and the English is one of the early stories in the history of our country. It is a story of good times. It is also the story of hard times. The English struggled to build a community at Jamestown. The Powhatan struggled to find a way to live peacefully with the English. In this lesson you will meet some of the important people who helped the new community survive.

Reading STRATEGIES *and* Language DEVELOPMENT

CONTEXT CLUES Have students practice finding context clues by rereading the words of George Percy in the *Primary Source* on p. 104. Ask volunteers to share the clues in the quote that help explain the word *misery*. Encourage students to continue using this strategy as they read.

SYNONYMS AND ANTONYMS Explain to students that *synonyms* are words that mean the same thing and that *antonyms* are words that mean the opposite of one another. Ask students to think of synonyms and antonyms for some of the words in the *Primary Source: misery, departed, famine,* for example. Help students understand that finding synonyms and antonyms helps readers expand their vocabularies.

The English at Jamestown

Men like John Smith were sent by England to start a colony at Jamestown. A colony is a place that is ruled by another country. The English hoped that the colony would provide resources and riches like gold for people back in England.

The people sent to Jamestown were called colonists. A colonist is someone who lives in a colony. Colonists did not only want to build a new community. They also hoped that they, too, would get rich from Jamestown's resources.

Powhatan (below left) and his people were already living around Jamestown when John Smith (in frame) and other English colonists arrived.

The Granger Collection

104

Discussing Difficult Times Help students understand how hard life was for the English, even with Powhatan's help.

Suggested Questions

● **What kinds of problems did the colonists have?** *(They couldn't or wouldn't farm; they became sick and were starving.)*

● **What rule did John Smith make? Why did he make it?** *(Those who did not work would not get food. Smith knew that the colony would survive only if everyone did their share of the work.)*

● **How did the Powhatan help the English?** *(by teaching them how to grow corn and other food)*

★**THINKING FURTHER:** *Making Decisions* **If you were John Smith, would you have asked the Powhatan for help? Why or why not?** *(Possible answer: Yes, because the Powhatan had been living there for so long and knew so much more about the environment.)*

Discussing the Primary Source
Before reading the excerpt aloud to the class, explain that George Percy was the governor of Jamestown during the "starving time" and that this historic document contains his actual words.

Suggested Questions

● **Why did so many people die during the winter of 1609?** *(They died from disease and famine.)*

● **Why is Percy's writing a reliable source of information about life in Jamestown?** *(It is an eyewitness account.)*

Difficult Times

Soon after arriving at Jamestown, the colonists found life hard. They had problems growing food. Many of them were not farmers. They did not realize how hard they needed to work. Some colonists even refused to work.

A strong leader was needed to help the English. They found one in John Smith. He made a new rule. He said, "He that will not work, shall not eat."

Smith made another important decision. He asked the Powhatan for help. The colonists learned how to grow corn and other food from the Powhatan.

Even with the help of Powhatan and his people, the colonists struggled. The winter of 1609 was called a "starving time." There was little food. Colonists were dying from diseases. Read once again the words of colonist George Percy. What does he say about life in Jamestown?

The Trenching Spade Cutting it's trench & the Water Following

Colonists had to learn how to farm for food in order to survive.

MANY VOICES
PRIMARY SOURCE

Written by George Percy, about 1609.

Our men were destroyed with cruel diseases and swellings and burning fevers and by wars. Some **departed** suddenly, but for the most part they died of **famine**. There were never Englishmen left in such misery as we were. The settlers began to feel the sharp hunger which no man can truly describe.

departed: died
famine: starving, hunger

104

Background INFORMATION

ABOUT JOHN SMITH The Virginia Company had selected seven men to lead the colony, but only John Smith had the necessary leadership skills. Under his direction, the settlers built houses, dug a well, and planted crops.

● In the fall of 1609, Smith sailed to England for treatment of an injury. Angered by his strict rule, a number of colonists were glad to see him go.

● Smith returned to America in 1614 to explore the coast in the Massachusetts Bay area. He drew the first accurate map of the area, which he named New England.

● Smith wrote several books promoting American colonization. He stressed the value of such resources as fur and timber, criticized the fruitless searches for precious metals, and urged that future colonists be chosen for their willingness to work.

Background INFORMATION

MORE ABOUT THE STARVING TIME A number of factors resulted in the period known as the "starving time."

● New colonists had arrived in the summer of 1609, bringing the population to 500 and straining Jamestown's meager resources.

● After Smith left, some settlers stopped farming and resumed the search for gold. The colonists lost the good will of the Powhatan and trading for corn stopped.

● The colonists were so desperate they ate shoe leather and rats. Those who did not die of starvation died of disease. The drinking water was unsanitary and the swamps infested with malaria-bearing mosquitoes.

● Three out of four colonists died during this starving time. In Jamestown today, a cross marks 300 of their graves.

The Colony Survives

Life continued to be hard for the colonists. Their dreams of finding gold never came true. But in 1612 some changes turned the colony around. A colonist named John Rolfe began growing a new kind of tobacco and sending it back to England. The tobacco was sold for a lot of money. It helped make the colony and England richer.

Until this time the English sometimes fought with the Powhatan. But in 1614 John Rolfe married Pocahontas. She was the daughter of Powhatan. Their marriage led to a long time of peace between the Powhatan and the English. The colony began to grow.

By 1624 other English colonies were also growing along the coast of the Atlantic Ocean. To learn more about the early years of these colonies turn the page.

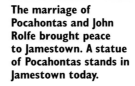

The marriage of Pocahontas and John Rolfe brought peace to Jamestown. A statue of Pocahontas stands in Jamestown today.

Discussing The Colony Survives
Have students focus on how the Jamestown community worked together to solve their problems.

Suggested Questions
- **Who was John Rolfe?** (He was a farmer in the Jamestown colony.)
- **How did John Rolfe help the entire Jamestown community?** (He grew a new kind of expensive tobacco.)
- **Who was Pocahantas?** (She was Powhatan's daughter.)

★**THINKING FURTHER:** *Cause and Effect* **What caused the long period of peace between the Powhatan and the English? What effect did that peaceful period have on the colony?** (Cause: John Rolfe and Pocahontas got married. Effect: the colony began to grow.)

105

Using the ANTHOLOGY

JAMESTOWN: NEW WORLD ADVENTURE, pages 36–40 This selection offers excerpts from a fictitious but fact-based journal of an English carpenter who travels to America to help begin the colony of "James Towne."

...IF YOU LIVED IN COLONIAL TIMES, pages 41–43 These questions and answers about colonial life provide an opportunity for students to compare and contrast their lifestyle with that of a colonial child.

IN GOOD OLD COLONY TIMES, page 44 Children will enjoy this famous colonial ballad. Invite students to sing along as you play the song on the *Anthology Cassette.* If possible, make arrangements for them to perform the song at a school assembly.

CITIZENSHIP

UNDERSTANDING GOVERNMENT Help students understand how self-government began in the colonies.

- As Jamestown expanded, the colonists began to resent laws decreed from England. In 1619 the wealthiest men formed the House of Burgesses (villagers), and met to discuss recommendations for the king. This council was a representative assembly but did not represent everyone. However, it was the colonists' first step toward governing themselves.
- Students will learn more about the development of our democratic form of government in *Unit 3.*

Infographic

Have students look at the pictures as volunteers read the text aloud.

Discussing The Thirteen Colonies
If students wonder why Vermont is not shown, explain that in colonial times that area was claimed by both New York and New Hampshire.

Suggested Questions

- ***Why did the Pilgrims come to America? What state did the Pilgrim colony become?*** *(to be free to practice their religion; Massachusetts)*

- ***What state is Philadelphia in?*** *(Pennsylvania)*

- ***Who started the community in Philadelphia and why?*** *(William Penn; to be free to be a Quaker)*

- ***Why did some English people come to Savannah?*** *(to make money to repay debts)*

Technology CONNECTION

ADVENTURES CD-ROM
Enrich the *Infographic* with the *Key Places* segment on the U.S. map.

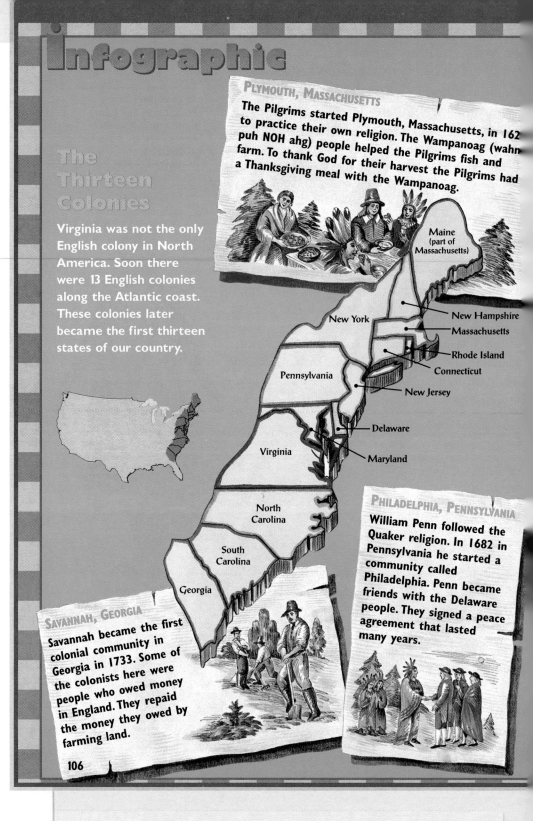

Infographic

The Thirteen Colonies

Virginia was not the only English colony in North America. Soon there were 13 English colonies along the Atlantic coast. These colonies later became the first thirteen states of our country.

PLYMOUTH, MASSACHUSETTS

The Pilgrims started Plymouth, Massachusetts, in 162 to practice their own religion. The Wampanoag (wahn puh NOH ahg) people helped the Pilgrims fish and farm. To thank God for their harvest the Pilgrims had a Thanksgiving meal with the Wampanoag.

Maine (part of Massachusetts)

New York · New Hampshire · Massachusetts · Rhode Island · Connecticut · New Jersey

Pennsylvania

Delaware

Virginia · Maryland

North Carolina

South Carolina

Georgia

PHILADELPHIA, PENNSYLVANIA

William Penn followed the Quaker religion. In 1682 in Pennsylvania he started a community called Philadelphia. Penn became friends with the Delaware people. They signed a peace agreement that lasted many years.

SAVANNAH, GEORGIA

Savannah became the first colonial community in Georgia in 1733. Some of the colonists here were people who owed money in England. They repaid the money they owed by farming land.

106

Expanding the Infographic

RESEARCH Divide the class into groups and have each group research one of the 13 colonies, using library resources and/or *Adventures* CD-ROM. Pose the following questions to help students focus their research:

- When was the colony founded? By whom?
- Where did the first settlers come from?
- Why did they leave their homes?
- What natural resources did they find in North America?

Second-Language Support

USING PROPS To reinforce the names and locations of the 13 colonies, have students draw outlines of each one, cut them out, add labels, and tape them together in the correct position.

Background Information

MORE ABOUT AFRICANS ARRIVE The first Africans in the North American colonies arrived in Virginia in 1619. They were treated as indentured servants with the same status as their English counterparts.

In exchange for their passage to North America, indentured servants worked for Virginia planters for a set number of years—ususally five to ten. At the end of that time, they were free to start their own lives.

As the colonies grew, the need for cheap labor increased. The indenture system could not meet that need. The colonists began to bring Africans to North America to work as slaves. By the early 1700s, enslaved Africans were the main source of labor in the southern colonies.

Africans Arrive

Many different people came to the colonies. Some came to build new lives. Some came to seek riches. Others were looking for religious freedom. Some who came had been forced into slavery. Slavery is the practice of one person owning another.

People forced into slavery in the colonies came from Africa. They were captured and taken across the Atlantic Ocean in slave ships. They were then sold into slavery.

WHY IT MATTERS

Starting a community was hard for the colonists. But after years of struggle, the little community of Jamestown grew larger. It was joined by other colonies. Later, these colonies—13 in all—came together as a new country, the United States of America.

Bettmann

African people were sold into slavery in the colonies.

✓// Reviewing Facts and Ideas

SUM IT UP

- The English colonists began Jamestown in 1607.
- The winter of 1609 was called a "starving time." Many colonists died.
- In 1612 John Rolfe introduced a new kind of tobacco. It made the colony richer.
- There were 13 English colonies, which later became the United States of America.

THINK ABOUT IT

1. Why did the English set sail for Jamestown?

2. **FOCUS** What was life like for the colonists?

3. **THINKING SKILL** Look at the Infographic on page 106. Put Plymouth, Philadelphia, and Savannah in *order* by the dates they were started.

4. **WRITE** Imagine you are a colonist living in Jamestown. Write a letter describing your new life to your family back in England.

107

LESSON 3

Lesson Overview
Jamestown Settlement is a living history museum that depicts daily life in the English and Powhatan communities.

Lesson Objectives
★ Understand the concept of a living history museum.

★ Compare and contrast the lifestyles of the Powhatan and the colonists.

1 PREPARE

MOTIVATE Point out that Jamestown exists today as a living history museum. Then have a volunteer read the *Read Aloud*. Ask students what questions they might like to ask the Jamestown guide pictured here.

SET PURPOSE Review the *Vocabulary* words with students. Then direct them to the *Read to Learn* question and invite speculation about the answer.

2 TEACH

Thinking About A Step Back in Time Explain that historians have carefully studied artifacts and historical writing to make Jamestown Settlement an authentic representation of life in the past.

Suggested Questions

● **What is a living history museum?** *(It is a place where people act out life as it was in the past.)*

● **How are guides dressed at Jamestown Settlement?** *(like people of the 1600s, English or Native American)*

● **Why is Jamestown Settlement an important place for Americans?** *(It teaches us about the history of our first colony.)*

Resource REMINDER
Practice Book: *p. 25*

Jamestown Today

READ ALOUD
"We do many of the things that the Powhatan and the English did long ago. We have cooking fires burning. We tan deer hides. We even show kids making rope."

A Step Back in Time

These are the words of Erik Holland. He is a guide at Jamestown Settlement. The settlement is a living history museum. A living history museum takes you back in time. It is a place where people dress, talk, and do things as they did long ago. Erik's job is to show people how English colonists and the Powhatan lived here in the 1600s.

Let's visit Jamestown Settlement. The first thing you notice is people's clothing. Guides like Erik are dressed in clothes like those worn by Native Americans or colonists hundreds of years ago. While they may look different at first, Erik tells visitors: "My moccasins are almost like the tennis shoes kids wear today. Tennis shoes are made from animal skins. So are my moccasins."

Focus Activity

READ TO LEARN
What do visitors see at Jamestown Settlement?

VOCABULARY
living history museum

PLACES
Jamestown Settlement

108

Reading STRATEGIES *and* Language DEVELOPMENT

COMPARE AND CONTRAST This lesson provides many opportunities for students to compare and contrast the Powhatan and colonial English lifestyles. You may want to create a class chart to list differences and similarities between the clothing, shelter, religion, food, tools, and histories of the two communities.

MULTIPLE MEANINGS Explain to students that some words have more than one meaning. Explain that the way the words are used in a sentence tells us which meaning of the word the writer intends. Point out the words *hides* and *tan* in the opening quotation and write two definitions of each word on the chalkboard. Have volunteers tell which meaning of each word is intended and explain how they know. Then ask students to use other meanings of the words in new sentences.

English Village

Like Erik's moccasins, most of the things you see at Jamestown Settlement are not the actual artifacts from long ago. Instead, they are copies. People have studied Jamestown's history very carefully to create copies that look real.

Look at the pictures on this page. The English houses are built from plaster and grass. The clothes people are wearing are made from wool and cotton. The ship instruments they are using are made from iron and wood.

Near the houses are three ships docked in the James River. They are named *Susan Constant, Godspeed,* and *Discovery.* They are copies of the original boats colonists like Captain John Smith sailed on many years ago. Climb aboard! You will see how small the spaces are. You can imagine how crowded it must have been. After all, the colonists also had to bring pigs, chickens, goats, and lots of supplies.

Jamestown/Yorktown Foundation

Fun at Jamestown Settlement includes visiting ships and seeing how people lived in the 1600s.

Jamestown Virginia

Thinking About An English Village Have students look at the pictures as they discuss the questions. Refer to the *Background Information* on p. 110 for *More About an English Village.*

Suggested Questions

- *What natural resources did the colonists use?* (soil/mud, water, branches, grass, wool, cotton, iron)

- *How did the people who built Jamestown Settlement make it look so realistic?* (They studied Jamestown's history very carefully.)

- *What were the names of the ships the colonists sailed on?* (Susan Constant, Godspeed, Discovery)

★**THINKING FURTHER:** *Compare and Contrast* **How is the settlement at Jamestown different from your community? How is it the same?** (Answers should reflect differences and similarities in houses, clothing, and kinds of work.)

Background INFORMATION

MORE ABOUT JAMESTOWN SETTLEMENT

- The living history museum was built next to—not on—the original site of Jamestown Colony.

- The location has been preserved since 1893, when the Association for the Preservation of Virginia Antiquities acquired the site of the original colony.

- Archaeologists first unearthed colonial buildings and homes in the 1930s and continued excavations into the 1950s.

- In 1994, scientists found a helmet, armor, sword and musket parts, glass and copper beads, brass tokens, and pottery. They also found an Indian spear point that is about 11,000 years old.

- For more information about Jamestown Settlement, a *Jamestown Teacher's Kit* can be obtained without charge by writing to Jamestown-Yorktown, PO Drawer JF, Williamsburg, VA 23187.

Curriculum CONNECTION

LINKS TO MATH Help students visualize the crowded ships. Ask them to pace out the length of the *Discovery*—49 feet. Have 21 students—12 passengers, 9 crew—stand in the space and have them discuss spending four months on the ocean in such close quarters.

LINKS TO READING Students can experience another living history museum—Plimouth Plantation—by reading the classroom library selection for this unit, *Sarah Morton's Day: A Day in the Life of a Pilgram Girl* by Kate Waters (Scholastic, 1989).

Suggested Questions

- *What kinds of work did the Powhatan do in their village?* (ground corn, cooked, made rope)

- *What are some kinds of food the Powhatan ate?* (corn, fish, meat)

- *How did the Powhatan cook their meals?* (over an open fire)

★THINKING FURTHER: *Classifying In what ways did the Powhatan use fire? In what ways did they use plants and animals? (They used fire for warmth and cooking; plants for food, rope, homes, toys, clothing; animals for food and clothing.)*

At the Powhatan village visitors learn to make rope the way people did long ago.

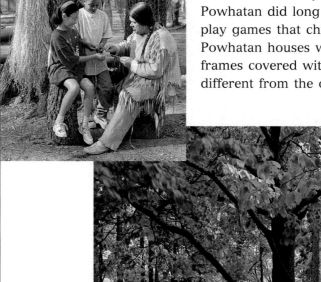

Powhatan Village

In talking about visiting Jamestown Settlement today, Erik tells visitors, "It's fun to see different cultures from the past. You have seen how the English lived. Now let's see how the Powhatan lived."

In the Powhatan village you can see Native Americans grinding corn. You can see how they cooked their meals. You can even smell fish and meat cooking. But stand back. The fire is hot!

You can actually make rope like the Powhatan did long ago. You will even get to play games that children played long ago. The Powhatan houses were made from wood frames covered with grass. How are they different from the ones the colonists lived in?*

110

*They were different shapes. English houses were square. They were made from grass and plaster. Powhatan houses were round. They were made from wood frames covered with grass.

Background INFORMATION

MORE ABOUT AN ENGLISH VILLAGE The first buildings erected at Jamestown were a church, which served as a meeting place; a storehouse, which held all the colony's food, tools, and weapons; and a guardhouse, which served as sleeping quarters for the soldiers. In addition to these public buildings, the early settlers built houses, which were shared by six to eight men.

More About a Powhatan Village The Powhatan lived in longhouses, or yehakin, which were built by the women. They bent saplings for a frame and covered the frame with tree bark or grass mats. Inside the yehakin, the fire was always kept burning to keep the house warm and dry. As many as 20 family members lived in one house. Villages ranged in size from 30 to 2,000 people.

Curriculum CONNECTION

LINKS TO PHYSICAL EDUCATION Explain that Powhatan children played games to improve hunting skills. Students can play this Powhatan game:

- You will need several dried corncobs, feathers, and about 20 feet of rope or clothesline.

- Stick the feathers into one end of each corncob.

- Tie the rope between two trees, posts, or doorknobs. From this rope, hang several circles of rope.

- Players can throw the corncob "darts" through the rope circles. Swing the rope to make a toss more difficult.

Learning History

When you visit Jamestown Settlement, something may occur to you. In some ways the lives of these two groups were so different. But in other ways their lives were similar. They both needed to make homes, clothes, and food. They both took care of their communities. As he closes his tour, Erik tells visitors, "By visiting us here you see and do things that people in the past did every day. It's a great way to learn history."

WHY IT MATTERS

Visiting a place like Jamestown Settlement is a fun and interesting way to learn about the history of people and their communities. Reading books, watching movies, and talking to people can also teach you about history.

In our country today, we live with our history all around us. In the next chapter you will learn about another community with a history that is important to its people today.

The Powhatan made needles from bone and used them to sew clothing made from animal skins.

✔ Reviewing Facts and Ideas

SUM IT UP

- Jamestown Settlement was created to show people what life was like long ago.

- Visitors can see and do many things. They can climb aboard ships, smell food cooking, and visit a Powhatan village and an English village. They can even make things like people did long ago!

THINK ABOUT IT

1. What is a living history museum?

2. **FOCUS** What do visitors see at Jamestown Settlement?

3. **THINKING SKILL** How was life in the Powhatan village *like* life for the colonists? How was it *different*?

4. **WRITE** Write a brief travel guide for Jamestown Settlement. Describe what people can visit.

111

MEETING *Individual* NEEDS

RETEACHING (Easy) Invite students to illustrate some aspect of daily life in a colonial English or Powhatan community.

EXTENSION (Average) Invite small groups to write and perform skits about events that might have taken place in the Jamestown settlement. Encourage students to use desks, brooms, and other classroom objects for props and to rehearse their skits before they act them out.

ENRICHMENT (Challenging) Challenge students to write a collection of stories about Jamestown Settlement. Individuals or partners can write—from the colonist or Native American perspective—how their day began, how they dressed, and how they worked to help the community. Encourage students to share these stories with a younger class.

Thinking About Learning History

Have students focus on the value of living history museums.

Suggested Questions

★**THINKING FURTHER:** *Compare and Contrast* **How are the Powhatan village and the colony at Jamestown alike and different?** *(Answers should compare and contrast houses, clothing and work.)*

Discussing WHY IT MATTERS You may wish to review what students have learned about various communities in this and previous chapters.

Suggested Questions

- **What was the most interesting thing you learned in this chapter about a historical community?** *(Answers should include pertinent details from the lessons.)*

- **What communities have you learned about through reading, watching movies, or talking with people?** *(Answers should reflect students' experiences.)*

⭐ 3 CLOSE

SUM IT UP

Have students answer these questions.

Suggested Questions

- **Why was Jamestown Settlement created?** *(to show what life was like long ago)*

- **What would you like to see there?** *(Answers will vary.)*

EVALUATE
✓ **Answers to Think About It**

1. a place where scenes from the past are acted out with realistic costumes and artifacts

2. what daily life was like for the English and the Powhatan

3. They both had to work hard, cook, make shelters, and use natural resources. The Powhatan had experience living in the area, and the English brought new technology.

4. Answers should describe both the English and the Powhatan communities.

Write About It Ask students to write a letter to Eric, asking questions about Jamestown Settlement.

SKILLS LESSON
PAGES 112-113

Lesson Overview
A time line shows the order in which historical events took place.

Lesson Objective
★ Read a time line to understand the order of historical events.

1 PREPARE

MOTIVATE Have students discuss the order of events in the school day yesterday. As students talk, draw a time line on the chalkboard that illustrates the school day.

SET PURPOSE Explain the *Vocabulary* word to students, using your chalkboard illustration. Help them relate the points on the line to dates, and explain that a time line of historical events can give us a clearer picture of the order in which events occurred long ago.

2 TEACH

Why the Skill Matters Have students read the statements in the *Helping Yourself* box. Then discuss why a time line might help them understand and remember important events from history.

Using the Skill Have students read through the time line on the history of Newtown. Explain that the time line lets them know what events have happened there and when they happened.

Suggested Questions

● **Do you read a time line from the right or the left?** *(from the left, just like reading a sentence)*

● **What kinds of information do you see on the time line?** *(the date and a description of what happened on that date)*

Resource REMINDER

Practice Book: *p. 26*

Technology: Adventures *CD-ROM*

STUDYSKILLS

Reading Time Lines

VOCABULARY
time line

WHY THE SKILL MATTERS

The events you have read about in Jamestown happened hundreds of years ago. Sometimes reading about the past can be confusing. What happened first? What happened next? A time line can tell you the order in which events happened. Reading time lines will help you to understand history.

USING THE SKILL

You have read about how Jamestown grew as a community. How do you think a new community would grow today? Suppose that a group of people call their community "Newtown." Look at the time line below to see how this community might grow.

Read the time line from left to right. The dates tell you that the earliest event is the building of roads and houses. The last event is the opening of the shopping center. What happened the year before the Fire Department started?*

Newtown's Early History

1990	**1991**	**1992**	**1993**	**1994**
Roads are paved and first houses are built	People move into houses	Community leaders are chosen	Fire department is started and hospital opens	Main Street shopping center opens

*In 1992, community leaders are chosen.

Curriculum CONNECTION

LINKS TO READING Have students use the reference section of the school library to find books that use time lines. Encourage them to list the books in chronological order according to the publication year. As an extension, have students plot the years on a Reference Book Time Line.

TRYING THE SKILL

When you read about Jamestown, you saw words such as "long ago" and "starving time." These words told you something about time and let you know when things happened at Jamestown.

There were many important events in Jamestown's early history. The time line below will help you understand the order in which some of these events happened.

This time line shows events between 1600–1615. How many events does it show? Read the time

HELPING Yourself

● **Time lines** show the order in which things happen.

● **Read time lines** from left to right.

● **Note the date** of each event.

line. What is first on the time line? In what year did the next event happen? What was it?*

REVIEWING THE SKILL

1. What do time lines show?

2. Which did the people of Newtown build first—a shopping center or a hospital? How do you know?

3. In what year did John Rolfe and Pocahontas get married?

4. How do time lines help you to understand history?

Jamestown's Early History

1600
Native Americans are living in an area later called Virginia

1607
Colonists arrive at James River to start the colony of Jamestown

1609
Many colonists die during a "starving time"

1614
Pocahontas marries John Rolfe

1600   1605   1610   1615

* The time line shows 4 events; Native Americans are living in area later called Virginia; the next event happened in 1607; the colonists arrive at James River to start Jamestown.

113

● **What happened in Newtown just after roads were paved and houses were built?** (People moved into houses.)

● **In what year did the hospital open?** (1993)

Trying the Skill Remind students that the time line should be read from left to right. Earlier events are to the left, later events are to the right. Point out that the *Helping Yourself* box is a good reference aid.

Suggested Questions

● **Who lived in the area of Virginia before the colonists arrived at the James River?** (Native Americans)

● **In what year did many colonists die of starvation?** (1609)

★**THINKING FURTHER:** *Sequencing* **The first two women arrived in the colony in 1608. Between which events would you put that on the time line?** (between the first colonists arriving and the starving time)

3 CLOSE

SUM IT UP
Have students explain how to read a time line.

EVALUATE
✓ **Answers to Reviewing the Skill**

1. the order in which historical events happened

2. hospital; from the time line

3. 1614

4. by visually presenting when important events happened

Technology CONNECTION

ADVENTURES CD-ROM
Enrich the lesson with the U.S. historical *Time Lines* segment on the CD-ROM.

Meeting *Individual* Needs

RETEACHING (Easy) Have students make a time line showing the date each of the original 13 colonies was founded.

EXTENSION (Average) Have students make cartoon strips showing the Jamestown events in sequence. Give students papers with empty horizontal cartoon strips and ask them to write a date over each box. They can fill in the boxes with illustrations and write captions to describe the consecutive events.

ENRICHMENT (Challenging) Invite students to create a time line for their own lives. Ask them to include four or five important events that have happened during their lives. Suggest that they make the day they were born the first event on their time line, and include, for example, vacations, the birth of siblings, or other special events.

Discussing Major Events Use the following questions to help students practice reading a time line.

Suggested Questions

- ***In what year did the colonists first land at Jamestown, Virginia?*** *(1607)*

- ***When did the colonists at Jamestown suffer through the "starving time"?*** *(1609)*

- ***What year did John Rolfe begin growing a new kind of tobacco to sell in England?*** *(1612)*

Resource REMINDER

Project Book: *pp. 10–11*
Assessment Book: *Chapter 4 Test*

CHAPTER 4 REVIEW

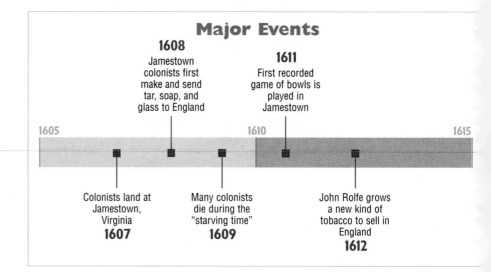

Major Events

1608
Jamestown colonists first make and send tar, soap, and glass to England

1611
First recorded game of bowls is played in Jamestown

1605   1610   1615

Colonists land at Jamestown, Virginia
1607

Many colonists die during the "starving time"
1609

John Rolfe grows a new kind of tobacco to sell in England
1612

THINKING ABOUT VOCABULARY

Number a piece of paper from 1 to 5. Beside each number write the word or term from the list below that matches the statement.

bay   colony
coastal plain   slavery
living history museum

1. A place that is ruled by another country
2. A body of water that is partly surrounded by land
3. The practice of one person owning another
4. A place where people dress, talk, and do things as they did long ago
5. An area of flat land along the coast

THINKING ABOUT FACTS

1. Why was Jamestown a good spot to start a colony?
2. Why did England begin colonies in North America? Why did people come to the colonies?
3. What problems did the first colonists of Jamestown have?
4. Why do people visit Jamestown Settlement today?
5. In what ways were the Powhatan houses similar to the English ones? How were they different?

114

Suggestions for Think and Write
SIGNS OF SUCCESS

WRITING A COMPARISON Students should understand that the geography of Mesa Verde includes tall mesas and deep river canyons. The geography of Jamestown includes a river that runs through a forest and a coastal plain. The flat and sandy land is on the edge of a bay.

WRITING A LETTER Following standard letter form, students' letters can describe events such as the starving time or building a home by erecting a framework of sticks and covering it with plaster. Letters should convey the understanding that neither English or Powhatan understood each other's language, beliefs, or customs.

WRITING A CONVERSATION Conversations can convey how each community lived on the land and how they might have shared their skills and tools.

For performance assessment, see Assessment Book, Chapter 4.

THINK AND WRITE

WRITING A COMPARISON

Write a paragraph comparing the geography of Mesa Verde with that of Jamestown.

WRITING A LETTER

Suppose you are a colonist at Jamestown in 1607. Write a letter to somebody in England about your life in North America. Include experiences such as meeting a Native American, building a home, and surviving a hard winter.

WRITING A CONVERSATION

Write a made-up dialogue between a Native American and a colonist at Jamestown.

APPLYING STUDY SKILLS

READING TIME LINES

Answer the following questions to practice the skill of reading time lines. Use the Major Events time line shown on the previous page.

1. What is a time line?
2. What happened in 1609?
3. Which event happened first, the first shipment of goods to England or the development of a new kind of tobacco? In what year did each take place?
4. What is one thing colonists did for fun at Jamestown?
5. When are time lines useful?

Summing Up the Chapter

First review the chapter. Then copy the main idea diagram and fill it in with information that supports each main idea. Then answer the following question: Why were natural resources and human resources important to the success of Jamestown?

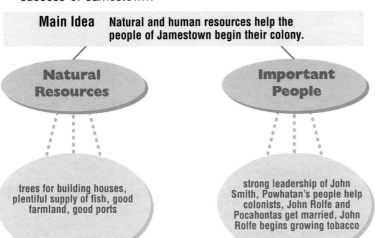

Main Idea Natural and human resources help the people of Jamestown begin their colony.

Natural Resources

trees for building houses, plentiful supply of fish, good farmland, good ports

Important People

strong leadership of John Smith, Powhatan's people help colonists, John Rolfe and Pocahontas get married, John Rolfe begins growing tobacco

115

Suggestions for Summing Up the Chapter

- Prepare copies of the main-idea diagram for the class. As an alternative, students can draw their own diagrams.
- Ask students to complete their diagrams. Invite them to share their ideas with partners or small groups before answering the question.
- Possible answers for the diagram are written in red. Students answers to the question should indicate the complete reliance of the Jamestown settlers on the land, resources, and people around them, and on each other. Students should understand that settlers could not obtain goods or help from other sources. They should give specific examples of the resources people used and how they struggled together to survive.

Answers to THINKING ABOUT VOCABULARY

1. colony
2. bay
3. slavery
4. living history museum
5. coastal plain

Answers to THINKING ABOUT FACTS

1. It was on a peninsula in a bay. The settlers' enemies could only arrive by sea, and Jamestown was well hidden from passing boats.

2. They had heard the Spanish stories of gold and riches in the Americas. They were looking for new opportunities and natural resources. Eventually people came to find religious freedom and settle on fertile farmland.

3. They didn't realize how much hard work it would take to survive and their farms did not grow enough food. Some of the Native Americans shared with them, but others made life difficult for them. The land the English settled was near a swamp, and many settlers came down with malaria.

4. The living history museum shows visitors what life was like in the 1600s. Learning about history helps us understand our country today.

5. They both used natural resources from the forests and beaches around them. The Powhatan homes were made of wood. The English homes were made of wood and plaster made from sand, mud, and shells. Many families lived in a Powhatan house. Several men lived in an English house.

Answers to APPLYING STUDY SKILLS

1. A line showing important events in time order.

2. Many colonists died during the "starving time."

3. the first shipment of goods to England. The first shipment happened in 1608. The new tobacco was grown in 1612.

4. They played a game called "bowls."

5. When you want to clearly see the order of events in history.

5 CHAPTER ORGANIZER

A Spanish Mission in San Antonio

PAGES 116–137

CHAPTER OVERVIEW

Long ago the Spanish built a mission called San Antonio in what is today Texas. Their priests and soldiers changed the lives of the Native Americans who had lived in this area before them. This started a new kind of community, which continues to grow and celebrate Spanish culture today.

CHAPTER PLANNING GUIDE
Suggested pacing: 12–14 days

LESSON	LESSON FOCUS	LESSON RESOURCES
1 THE GEOGRAPHY OF SAN ANTONIO pages 118–121	A Community Along the River	*Practice Book* p. 28 **Technology:** Videodisc/Video Tape, CD-ROM **Desk Map** World
2 SAN ANTONIO LONG AGO pages 122–127	Spanish and Native American Life	*Practice Book* p. 29 **Anthology** pp. 45–51
Infographic pages 124–125	Living at a Mission	**Technology:** Adventures CD-ROM
3 SAN ANTONIO TODAY pages 128–132	San Antonio Celebrates Its Culture	*Practice Book* p. 30 **Anthology** p. 52 **Technology:** Adventures CD-ROM
CITIZENSHIP Making a Difference page 133	From the Community Garden	
STUDY SKILLS pages 134–135	Reading Bar and Line Graphs	*Practice Book* p. 31
CHAPTER REVIEW pages 136–137	Students' understanding of vocabulary, content, and skills is assessed.	*Assessment:* Ch. 5 Test, Performance Assessment Ch. 5 *Transparency:* Graphic Organizer

OPTIONS FOR STUDENT ACTIVITIES

Citizenship pp. 119, 133

Curriculum Connection pp. 126, 131, 134

Expanding the *Infographic* p. 124

Using the Anthology pp. 125, 131

ASSESSMENT OPPORTUNITIES

Meeting Individual Needs pp. 117, 121, 127, 132, 135

Write About It pp. 121, 127, 132,

Chapter Review pp. 136–137

Assessment Book

Chapter Test Ch. 5 Test

Performance Assessment Ch. 5

Using Geo Adventures Use **Geo Adventures** Daily Geography Activities to assess students' understanding of geography skills.

Using the Vocabulary Cards The vocabulary words for each lesson are available on *Vocabulary Cards* for review and practice.

GETTING READY FOR THE CHAPTER

Make "Something Special" Banners
GROUP · 30 MINUTES OR LONGER

Objective: To learn how different traditions enrich the classroom community.

Materials: *Project Book* p. 12, construction paper, streamer-type crepe paper, tape

1. Have students work in small groups. Share with groups that they will make a banner and that each member will contribute something of special meaning to it.
2. Ask students to fill in information about a favorite book, story, or poem in the labels provided on Project Book p. 12. Then have them cut out their labels.
3. Have each student fold a piece of construction paper in half. Students can then glue their completed labels on the front and use the inside to write about why their choices are meaningful to them.
4. To assemble the banners, have the groups tape their labels onto the crepe paper.
5. Display the banners around the classroom. If possible, make one class banner.

> **SECOND-LANGUAGE SUPPORT**
> As second-language learners work through this activity, they may feel more comfortable sharing thoughts and information with small groups or with a partner before they speak to the whole class.
>
> Additional Second-Language Support Tips: pp. 120, 123, 129

Invite students to connect this time line with the time line in the Introduction for Chapter 4, pp. 96–97. Have them note how many years passed between the English arrival in Jamestown and the Spanish settlement in what is now Texas.

THINKING ABOUT GEOGRAPHY AND HISTORY

Ask students to read the paragraphs on this page and answer any questions they may have. Discuss the following questions with the class.

1700s

Suggested Questions

- **What event happened in the 1700s?** *(The Spanish missions were built.)*

- **What more would you like to know about the missions?** *(Invite students to list questions about San Antonio and explain that these questions will be answered in this chapter.)*

- ★**THINKING FURTHER:** *Cause and Effect* **What effect did the early Spanish settlers have on San Antonio today?** *(They built the community and they brought the Spanish language and culture to Texas.)*

1836

Suggested Questions

- **What happened in 1836?** *(Texas won independence from Mexico.)*

Resource REMINDER

 Technology: *Videodisc/Video Tape 2*

A Spanish Mission in San Antonio

THINKING ABOUT GEOGRAPHY AND HISTORY

Today San Antonio is a busy city on a river in Texas. Long ago Native Americans lived along the same river. Their lives changed when Spanish people came and started a new kind of community.

In Chapter 5 you will learn about these new communities and the growth of San Antonio. You will also see how Spanish culture is still a celebrated part of life in San Antonio today.

1700s
Missions are built

1836
Texas wins freedom from Mexico

Background INFORMATION

LINKING THE MAP AND THE TIME LINE

- Spanish missionaries built missions along the San Antonio River. These communities grew into the busy city of present-day San Antonio in south central Texas, with a metropolitan-area population of over a million people.

- Since Texas became independent in 1836, it has retained much of its Spanish and Mexican cultural heritage. Texas shares a border with Mexico along the Rio Grande.

- The San Antonio River plays a major role in the history of Texas. The river attracted Spanish settlers but it ruined early Texan communities in a series of floods. Today it winds peacefully through San Antonio in a canal.

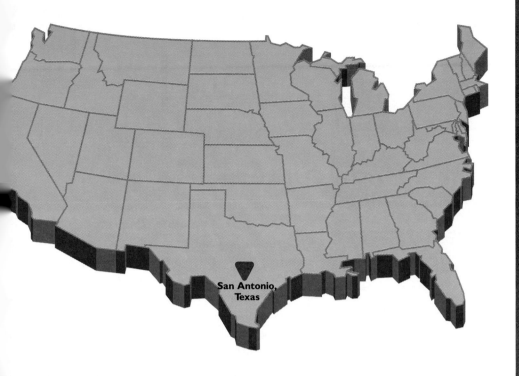

San Antonio,
Texas

TODAY

People enjoy the River Walk in San Antonio

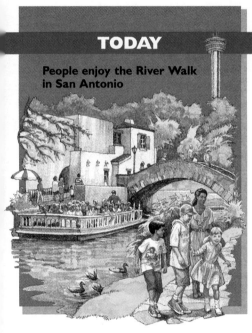

- **What does it mean to win independence?** *(to no longer be ruled by another country; to be free)*

- **Describe the men in the picture. What more would you like to find out about them?** *(Answers will vary. The soldier is carrying the Texas flag. They are equipped with rifles, sabers, and a cannon.)*

★**THINKING FURTHER:** *Sequencing*
How many years passed between the Spanish missions and the independence of Texas? Between independence from Mexico and today? *(136; about 161)*

TODAY

Suggested Questions

- **Which body of water flows through San Antonio?** *(the San Antonio River)*

- **What are the children in the picture doing?** *(walking and playing by the river)*

- **What more would you like to learn about San Antonio?** *(Students can keep their lists of questions and refer to them while reading the chapter.)*

Technology CONNECTION

VIDEODISC/VIDEO TAPE 2
Enrich Chapter 5 with the Videodisc *map* and *glossary* segments.

Search Frame 53777

Meeting *Individual* Needs

RETEACHING (Easy) Ask students to think about other cities and towns that were built on rivers. Have them discuss how rivers affect the way people live in general and about life in San Antonio specifically.

EXTENSION (Average) Ask students to review what they learned about the Powhatan and the English settlers. Then have them write comparisons to Texas with the following questions in mind: What might Spanish settlers hope to do by settling in Texas? What effect might this have on the Native American culture?

ENRICHMENT (Challenging) Ask students to write about an event in the history of Texas that happened between 1836 and today. Invite them to find out the date on which Texas became a state and create a captioned illustration that would fit in the time line.

LESSON 1

PAGES 118–121

Lesson Overview

Throughout history, the San Antonio River has provided water, shade, timber, and beauty for many communities.

Lesson Objectives

★ Describe the geography of San Antonio, Texas.

★ Understand the relationship between the San Antonio River and life in that city.

⭐ 1 PREPARE

MOTIVATE Direct attention to the *Read Aloud* and then the *Read to Learn* question. Invite speculation about the importance of the San Antonio River to people in the past and present.

SET PURPOSE Point out that the picture shows people enjoying the San Antonio River. Tell students that they will learn more about the river in this lesson.

⭐ 2 TEACH

Discussing The River Walk Have students answer these questions.

Suggested Questions

● **What is the River Walk?** *(an area by the river with sidewalks, trees, and shops)*

● **Whose idea was it to build the River Walk?** *(Robert Hugman's)*

★**THINKING FURTHER:** *Cause and Effect* **What did Hugman hope to accomplish with the River Walk? How does the River Walk make a difference in San Antonio today?** *(Hugman hoped to help business and protect the beauty of the river. Today, the River Walk is a place where people can enjoy the river. It also provides many people with jobs.)*

Resource REMINDER

Practice Book: *p. 28*

Technology: *Videodisc/Video Tape; Adventures CD-ROM*

Desk Maps: *World*

The Geography of San Antonio

Focus Activity

READ TO LEARN

How is the San Antonio River important?

PLACES

San Antonio, Texas
River Walk
San Antonio River

READ ALOUD

Thousands of years ago a Native American group called the Payaya (PĬ yah yah) Indians lived along the San Antonio River. They called it Yanaguana (YAH nah GWAH nah), which means "refreshing waters" in their language. Let's take a walk along the river to see how it is important to people today.

The River Walk

Pretend it is a hot summer day in San Antonio, Texas. The thermometer reads 93°F. You decide to head for the River Walk.

What is the River Walk? In the 1920s citizens of San Antonio had different ideas about what to build along the San Antonio River. But one idea by a man named Robert Hugman drew a lot of attention. He came up with a plan to build the River Walk. He hoped it would help business and protect the beauty of the river. Today it is an area with sidewalks, trees, restaurants, and shops. It also provides jobs for many people.

118

Reading STRATEGIES *and* Language DEVELOPMENT

USING VISUALS Remind students that authors include illustrations to help readers learn more about a topic. Ask volunteers to tell what they see in each picture in the lesson, and why they think each picture was included.

SPELLING STRATEGIES Focus on the words *attention* and *mission* to help students recognize confusing spelling patterns. Point out how the sound *shun* is spelled in each word and invite students to list other words that contain this sound. Write their suggestions on the chalkboard in categories according to how they are spelled. Explain that because different spellings create an identical sound, the spellings of words such as *attention, mission, creation, expression, lotion,* and *relation* must be memorized.

The San Antonio River

On days like today it may seem that half the people in San Antonio can be found along the San Antonio River. The breeze off the river cools the air.

The sounds of people and music lead you right to the heart of the River Walk. People are speaking English and Spanish. Other languages can be heard, too. People from all over the world come to visit this community. They can learn a lot about the geography and culture of San Antonio.

You're not here just to see people, though. You want to see the San Antonio River. You enjoy watching the water flow by. You also like seeing the many trees and flowers.

From restaurants to riverboats to music, there are many ways people have fun at the River Walk.

Discussing The San Antonio River Help students understand that the river is an exciting cultural and commercial center of the San Antonio community.

Suggested Questions

- **Why do people like to visit the River Walk?** (to enjoy the river and to shop, hear music, talk to people, stay cool)

- **What are two languages you might hear along the River Walk?** (Spanish and English)

★**THINKING FURTHER: Making Decisions Look at the pictures. What would you like to do if you visited the River Walk? Why?** (Accept answers that the students support with reasons.)

Technology CONNECTION

VIDEODISC/VIDEO TAPE
Enrich the lesson with the Texas maps.

Search Frame 53680

Background INFORMATION

MORE ABOUT RIVER WALK

- In 1921, when floods killed 50 people and ruined many buildings along the river, the people of San Antonio considered draining it, but in 1924 the San Antonio Conservation Society successfully fought to save the river's natural state. A new flood control plan was devised to hold the river in its banks. The plan also included a canal upstream that would direct extra water around the city when it rained enough to flood.

- In the 1960s, many old buildings along the River Walk were rebuilt to prepare for San Antonio's world exposition in 1968. Today, year-round cultural events bring visitors to the River Walk. Summer visitors enjoy outdoor theater, musicians, art exhibitions, and canoe races.

CITIZENSHIP

LINKING PAST AND PRESENT Help students research local community projects similar to the River Walk such as a community park, playground, or library. For a short project, help students research the history of the name of your school or the street where it is located. They can ask adults in the school to tell them the story or they can visit the library to look up information. Encourage students to focus on the kind of community effort required to plan and complete projects—even ones as seemingly simple as naming streets and schools.

Thinking About Babbling Waters

Have students notice the descriptive details in this section.

Suggested Questions

★**THINKING FURTHER:** *Compare and Contrast* **Compare two different parts of the River Walk: the part described on this page and the part described on p. 119.** *(This page: This part of the River Walk is secluded; instead of shops and sidewalks there are trees and flowers and instead of music and laughter there are the sounds of the river and rustling leaves. P. 119: This is the heart of the River Walk, filled with people enjoying restaurants and shops as well as the river.)*

More **MAP WORK**

Have students use the map to answer these questions.

Suggested Questions

● **In what part of Texas is San Antonio?** *(southern)*

● **Which two points of interest are near the beginning of the river?** *(San Antonio Zoo, San Pedro Playhouse)*

● **Which mission is closest to the River Walk?** *(The Alamo)*

★**THINKING FURTHER:** *Making Conclusions* **Find the other missions. Why do you think they were all built along the San Antonio River?** *(The river provided a source of water and means of travel.)*

Babbling Waters

You stroll along the River Walk for a while. Then you come to your favorite spot by the river. There are no more shops and sidewalks, no more music and laughing. You see beautiful flowers and tall cypress and pecan trees.

You sit down on the grass along the river. You can hear leaves rustling in the trees. You can also hear the babbling waters of the river.

You may wonder where the river begins. Look carefully at the map below. About where does the river start?*

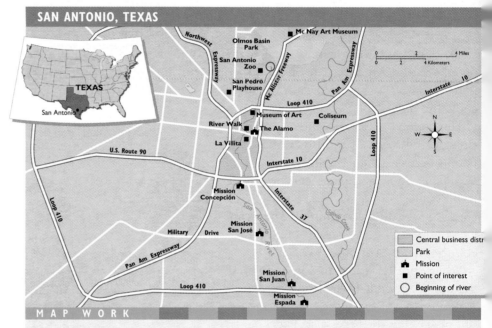

SAN ANTONIO, TEXAS

TEXAS

San Antonio

Northwest Expressway

Mc Nay Art Museum
Olmos Basin Park
San Antonio Zoo
San Pedro Playhouse
Mc Allister Freeway
Pan Am Expressway
Interstate 10
Loop 410
Museum of Art
Coliseum
River Walk
The Alamo
La Villita
U.S. Route 90
Interstate 10
Loop 410
N W E S
Mission Concepción
San Antonio River
Salado Creek
Interstate 37
Mission San José
Military Drive
Pan Am Expressway
Loop 410
Mission San Juan
Mission Espada

0   2   4 Miles
0   2   4 Kilometers

▢ Central business distr
▢ Park
⚓ Mission
■ Point of interest
○ Beginning of river

MAP WORK

San Antonio is a growing city in Texas.

1. What points of interest are located within the central business district?

2. In which direction does the river run below the business district?

3. How does the map show that the river is important to San Antonio?

120 MAP WORK: **1.** River Walk, La Villita, Museum of Art **2.** southeast **3.** The location of the city's central business district and the points of interest on the river show the river's importance.

Second-Language Support

CREATING VISUALS Second-language learners may benefit from drawing pictures of what they read. Invite students to create their own picture postcards of the San Antonio River Walk. Have students talk about their pictures with partners and then write messages to friends about their pictures. Encourage students to describe the River Walk and the San Antonio River.

Global CONNECTION

FROM THE NEAR EAST TO THE FAR WEST Have students use their desk maps to locate the regions mentioned as you present the information below.

● Moslems from the Near East once invaded Spain. While living in Spain, the Moslems taught the Spanish how to use irrigation ditches to farm in dry regions.

● They dammed water at a high elevation, and built ditches and aqueducts all tilted slightly downhill. Water leaving the dam flowed smoothly to the fields.

● When the Spanish arrived in the dry San Antonio region, they used the same design to bring water to over 3,000 acres of farmland. Today, farms still use this ancient form of protecting and using the precious resource of the San Antonio River.

Living with the River

You hear some noises from the busy shops at the River Walk. You smile at the sound of people enjoying the river. The city of San Antonio grew because of the river.

Until the 1950s much of the land around the San Antonio River was used for growing crops. Water from the river made the soil moist and full of minerals. The climate was good for farming.

But today most of the land is used in a different way. Buildings and roads are being built on the land once used for farming.

Long ago the land near the San Antonio River was used mostly for farming.

WHY IT MATTERS

The San Antonio River is just one part of the geography of San Antonio. It is important to the growth of the city. But San Antonio has grown for other reasons as well. In the next lesson you will learn more about the history of this city.

✔// Reviewing Facts and Ideas

SUM IT UP

- The San Antonio River has been important to life in the area for thousands of years.
- The River Walk is an area of shops and restaurants along the San Antonio River today. It provides jobs for many people.
- The river made it possible to farm for food.

THINK ABOUT IT

1. What is the River Walk?
2. **FOCUS** How is the San Antonio River important?
3. **THINKING SKILL** What would you *decide* to do if you visited the San Antonio River?
4. **GEOGRAPHY** Look at the map on page 120. How far is the River Walk from the beginning of the San Antonio River?

121

MEETING *Individual* NEEDS

RETEACHING (Easy) Ask students to write original poetry about a river or their favorite body of water.

EXTENSION (Average) Ask students to suppose they are senior citizens in San Antonio. Have them write paragraphs describing how their city has changed over the years. Students can use the library and/or *Adventures* CD-ROM to obtain information.

ENRICHMENT (Challenging) Ask students to draw their own plans to use a river in a city. Encourage them to design canals, river walks, bridges, bypasses or other interesting solutions. Tell them to remember to include places for relaxing and having fun along the river.

Thinking About Living with the River Have students look at the picture and then discuss these questions.

Suggested Questions

- *What kind of community was San Antonio before the 1950s?* (rural)
- *What natural resources did the community depend upon?* (good soil, water, warm climate)

★**THINKING FURTHER:** *Making Conclusions* *What kind of community is San Antonio today? How do you know?* (It is urban; buildings and roads have replaced farmland.)

Discussing WHY IT MATTERS Help students sum up what they learned about the San Antonio River.

Suggested Questions

★**THINKING FURTHER:** *Making Conclusions* *Based on what evidence can we conclude that the San Antonio River has been important to people for thousands of years?* (Native Americans lived near the river for thousands of years; missionaries and farmers settled near it; the River Walk was built along the river.)

⭐ 3 CLOSE

SUM IT UP

Have students answer these questions.

Suggested Questions

- *Why was the River Walk built?* (to help business and protect the river)
- *What natural resources did the river provide?* (water and good soil for crops)

EVALUATE
✔ **Answers to Think About It**

1. a place along the San Antonio River where there are sidewalks, shops, and restaurants
2. It is a cool place in the summer; people gather there for fun and relaxation; it is a center for commercial and community life.
3. Answers should reflect the information in the text.
4. four miles. *Description of place*

Write About It Ask students to write a letter to a friend, describing an afternoon at the River Walk.

LESSON 2

Lesson Overview
Throughout history, the San Antonio area has been the home of Native Americans, Spanish missionaries, and Mexican and United States citizens.

Lesson Objectives
★ Learn about the history of San Antonio.
★ Describe how San Antonio has changed over time.

1 PREPARE

MOTIVATE Read or have a volunteer read the *Read Aloud*. Then preview the *Vocabulary* words and have students identify the one that applies to the picture.

SET PURPOSE Direct students to the *Read to Learn* question and invite them to speculate about the answers. Then tell students that they will learn about mission life in this lesson.

2 TEACH

Thinking About Early People in Texas Have students answer these questions.

Suggested Questions

● *What Native American groups lived on the land that is now Texas?*
(Caddo; Payaya or Coahuiltecan)

● *What natural resources did the Coahuiltecan use for their homes?*
(grass and branches)

● *What did the Coahuiltecan eat?*
(roots, nuts, cactus, sometimes lizards and deer)

★THINKING FURTHER: *Cause and Effect* **What was the effect of the hot, dry climate on the animal life of the area?** *(The desert land did not grow enough food to support many large animals.)*

Resource REMINDER

Practice Book: *p. 29*

Anthology: *Juan Seguin: A Hero of Texas, pp. 45–49; The Alamo, pp. 50–51*

Technology: *Adventures CD-ROM*

Focus Activity

READ TO LEARN
What was life like in a mission in San Antonio?

VOCABULARY
cactus
mission
missionary
independence

122

San Antonio Long Ago

READ ALOUD
Do you know where the name Texas comes from? One Native American people, the Caddo, called each other Tejas (TAY hahs). That meant "friends." When the Spanish people arrived, they called the area Texas.

Early People in Texas

Long ago there were many groups of Native Americans, such as the Caddo, living in what is now the state of Texas. In the last lesson you read about the Payaya. They were part of another group of Native Americans called the Coahuiltecan (kwah weel TEH kan). The Coahuiltecan lived for many years throughout a large part of what is now Texas and Mexico.

Like the Anasazi, the Coahuiltecan used the natural resources around them. Their homes were made from grass and branches. They ate roots, nuts, and fruit. In hot, dry areas the Coahuiltecan ate the fruit of cactus plants. A cactus is a type of plant with sharp spines. It grows in dry environments. In some areas there were few large animals. As a result, the Coahuiltecan had to hunt for smaller animals like lizards and deer.

Reading STRATEGIES and Language DEVELOPMENT

COMPARE AND CONTRAST Help the class chart the differences and similarities between the Coahuiltecan way of life before and after entering the missions.

PREFIXES: Write the *Vocabulary* word *independent* on the chalkboard. Underline the prefix *in-* and circle *dependent*. Explain that *dependent* describes someone who relies on someone else for support. *In-* is a prefix meaning *not*. Ask students to combine the two meanings and explain what *independent* means. Ask a volunteer to repeat this process with the word *disappeared* (p. 126), explaining that *dis-* also means *not*. Then ask students to list and discuss other words beginning with *in-* or *dis-*.

The Spanish Begin Missions

In the 1700s life changed for the Coahuiltecan. Spanish-speaking people came north from Mexico and set up missions. Missions were communities set up by Roman Catholic priests to teach their religion to others. The priests who set up the missions were called missionaries.

Missions offered Native Americans food and a safe place to live. The Native Americans were expected to work for their food. They also had to learn more about the Catholic religion.

In the 1700s there were five missions in what is now the city of San Antonio. To learn about life in a mission, turn the page.

The Coahuiltecan used natural resources like the cactus for food. They used trees and stones to build missions.

123

Discussing **The Spanish Begin Missions** Help students view the events of the 1700s from both the Spanish and Native American point of view.

Suggested Questions

- **What is a mission?** *(a community set up by the Spanish to teach the Catholic religion)*

- **Who were the missionaries?** *(Spanish priests who set up the missions)*

- **When did the missionaries come to the area in which the Coahuiltecan lived?** *(in the 1700s)*

- **Where did the missionaries come from?** *(Mexico)*

- **Why did some Native Americans want to live in the missions?** *(for safety and food)*

★**THINKING FURTHER:** *Making Decisions **If you had been a Coahuiltecan, do you think you would have decided to live in a mission? Why or why not?** (Possible answers: Yes, because the missions offered safety and food; no, because they wanted to retain their culture and freedom.)*

Background INFORMATION

THE COAHUILTECAN

- Traditionally, small bands of Coahuiltecan traveled from place to place following food sources. The women and children gathered fruit, seeds, nuts, beans, and roots. The men hunted lizards, birds, and small mammals like rabbits and deer.

- When the Spanish arrived, many Coahuiltecan communities were suffering hard times. Their food and supplies were often stolen when they were attacked by groups of northern Native Americans. The communities were getting smaller as people died of hunger and disease. They accepted Spanish security and food in exchange for labor and religious conversion.

Second-Language Support

TAKING NOTES Second-language learners may have difficulty using the pronunciation guides in parentheses that appear in the text. Use the guide for the word *Tejas (TAY has)* in the *Read Aloud* (p. 122) to show students that the syllables are separated by a space and that the capitalized syllable is the one that should be stressed. Then have students follow your example to sound out the word *Coahuiltecan,* which appears in the first paragraph of the text.

Infographic

Help students visualize daily life in the missions for the Spanish and Native Americans.

Discussing Living at a Mission
Use the *Infographic to* provide students with a more detailed picture of mission life. Point out how the mission walls provided the community with safety and how daily life was structured by the missionaries.

Suggested Questions
- **Who lived inside the mission?** *(Native Americans and Spanish priests)*

- **What buildings were inside the mission walls?** *(the church, homes, workshops, school)*

- **What were the Native Americans expected to do besides work?** *(attend church, pray, and learn Spanish)*

★**THINKING FURTHER:** *Sequencing*
Beginning at sunrise, what was the daily schedule like at the mission? *(The bell rang, people prayed, people worked, people prayed at noon, people worked, people prayed again.)*

Infographic

Living at a Mission

This Infographic shows mission life long ago. What were some of the tasks people did to support their community?

Men make wood and metal tools and other things needed at the mission.

The church is the center of th community. Missionaries live rooms behind the church.

Women spin cotton, weave, and make pottery and baskets. They also fish, care for the children, and prepare food. Corn is an important crop.

124

Expanding the Infographic

LINKS TO ART To help students focus on the specific details of mission life, engage them in a cooperative class project: painting a mural of mission life.

- **DECISION MAKING** On the chalkboard, help students list topics they want to include in a mural of the entire mission with its buildings, farms, and people. Help students form groups according to topics. Be sure they choose simple topics that they can easily paint. For example, you may want to suggest that separate groups paint the outer walls of the mission; buildings inside the mission; one Native American at work; the bell; some pots or baskets; fields of corn, beans, fruit, cotton, or sugarcane; one Spanish missionary at work, the San Antonio River.

- **RESEARCH** Have research groups find additional pictures of their topics to use as guides when painting. Students will find general examples under these entries in encyclopedias and nonfiction library books: missions, Texas history, The Alamo, or San Antonio Mission.

- **PAINTING THE MURAL** Ask each group to make sketches from the *Infographic* and other books. Provide all groups with mural paper and art supplies. After they finish their artwork, students may want to write captions under their pictures.

- **EXHIBITION** Exhibit the mural in a school hallway, if possible.

Native Americans live in rooms built within the thick stone mission walls.

Missionaries teach Native American children to read and write in Spanish.

Every day starts with prayer. At noon and in the evening the whole community gathers to pray again.

125

Ask students to describe the details of the inset pictures as they read the captions.

Suggested Questions

● ***What kinds of work did the Native American women do?*** *(They did spinning and weaving, made pottery and baskets, fished, and cared for the children.)*

● ***What kind of work did the men do?*** *(They made furniture and tools and did farmwork.)*

● ***What kind of work did the mission-aries do?*** *(They worked as teachers and religious leaders.)*

Technology CONNECTION

***ADVENTURES* CD-ROM**
Enrich the *Infographic* with the CD-ROM activity, *Missions at Work*.

Background INFORMATION

MORE ABOUT LIVING AT A MISSION

● Most missions were built on the fertile lands along the San Antonio River. Fruit trees and delicate crops such as melons and grapes were cultivated in small, fenced-in plots just outside the mission walls. Larger crops like corn and beans were grown in fields farther out.

● Cotton was grown in mission fields, and sheep were raised for wool. Fabrics woven at the missions were used for clothes, blankets, mattresses, and rugs.

● Although their goal was to be self-sufficient, most missions engaged in some trade with each other as well as with local townspeople. They also earned income by selling fruit and cattle to San Antonio's military.

Using the ANTHOLOGY 🖥

JUAN SEGUIN: A HERO OF TEXAS, pages 45–49 Juan Seguin is remembered for his heroism during the war between Texas and Mexico. In this biographical excerpt about Seguin's twelfth birthday, students will learn about some of the Spanish and Mexican traditions that are still part of life in the Southwest today.

THE ALAMO, pages 50–51 Use the *Anthology Cassette* to play this song for students. Then have students read the lyrics and discuss any new information they learned about The Alamo.

125

Suggested Questions

- **How did mission life change the Coahuiltecan?** *(They learned the Spanish language and became Catholic. Eventually, their own culture disappeared.)*

- **What happened in 1821?** *(Mexico won independence from Spain.)*

- **Why was this event important for Texas?** *(Texas was part of Mexico.)*

- **Why were the Mexicans and Texans fighting in 1836?** *(Texas wanted independence from Mexico.)*

- **Who won the battle of The Alamo and who lost?** *(The Mexicans won, and the Texans lost.)*

- **When did Texas become part of the United States?** *(1845)*

MAP WORK

Have students use the map to answer these questions.

Suggested Questions

- **In what direction is San Antonio from San Francisco? In what direction is San Antonio from St. Augustine?** *(east; west)*

- **Which settlement is closest to the Mexican border?** *(Laredo)*

Texas Joins the United States

Mission life continued over one hundred years. Over that time some Native American groups kept their culture. But many groups like the Coahuiltecan lost their old way of life. They began to speak Spanish. They became Catholic. Over time the Coahuiltecan's own culture disappeared.

In 1821 another important change came to Texas. The people of Mexico won their independence from Spain. Independence is freedom from others. The new country of Mexico now included Texas. But many people in Texas did not want to be part of Mexico.

A war began in 1836 between Texas and Mexico. One battle took place at the mission called The Alamo. During this battle a large Mexican army defeated a small group of Texans. But after more battles that same year, Texas finally defeated Mexico and won its independence. Several years later, in 1845, Texas joined the United States of America.

Today people in Texas are proud of their state flag.

SPANISH COLONIAL SETTLEMENTS

Settlement started by Spanish colonists
Present-day state boundaries are shown.

CANADA

San Francisco
Los Angeles
San Diego
Tucson
Santa Fe
Albuquerque
San Antonio
Laredo
St. Augustine

PACIFIC OCEAN
MEXICO
Gulf of Mexico
ATLANTIC OCEAN

MAP WORK

Many Spanish missionaries and colonists came north from Mexico to settle in Texas and other places.

1. Which settlements are located on an ocean?

2. About how many miles is it from San Antonio to San Diego?

3. What could you predict about the culture of the communities shown?

MAP WORK: 1. Pacific: San Francisco, Los Angeles, San Diego; Atlantic: St. Augustine **2.** between 1175 and 1250 **3.** Because these communities were started by Spanish people and many are close to Mexico, some people there today probably speak Spanish.

126

Curriculum CONNECTION

LINKS TO READING Students may be familiar with tall tales about Davy Crockett, the legendary frontiersman who was said to "run faster, jump higher, squat lower, dive deeper and stay under longer and come out drier than any man in the whole country." Explain that the tales are fiction, but the man was not.

Davy Crockett was a hunter, scout, politician, and soldier who was killed at the Battle of The Alamo. For information about him, students can read *Davy Crockett: Young Pioneer* by Laurence Santrey (Troll Assocs., 1983). For folk tales about him, students can read *The Narrow Escapes of Davy Crockett* by Ariane Dewey (Morrow, 1993) and *Sally Ann Thunder Ann Whirlwind Crockett* by Caron Cohen (Morrow, 1993).

Each year many people visit The Alamo. It is now a museum.

WHY IT MATTERS

Look at the map on the previous page. As you can see, there were many settlements started by Spanish colonists in what are now cities in the United States. Today Spanish culture is still an important part of life in San Antonio as well as other cities in our country.

✓ Reviewing Facts and Ideas

SUM IT UP

- The Coahuiltecan lived in what is now Texas and Mexico.
- Spanish missionaries set up missions to teach Native Americans the Catholic religion.
- Many Native Americans lost their own culture because of mission life.
- In 1821 Mexico won its freedom from Spain.
- Texas joined the United States of America in 1845.

THINK ABOUT IT

1. How did the Coahuiltecan use their resources?
2. What did the missionaries offer the Native Americans?
3. **FOCUS** What was life like in a mission in San Antonio?
4. **THINKING SKILL** How was life for men in the mission *different* from life for women? How was it *alike*?
5. **GEOGRAPHY** Look at the map on page 126. In what direction is Laredo from Santa Fe?

127

Discussing WHY IT MATTERS Help students understand that Spanish culture has been alive in many parts of the southwestern United States for over 300 years.

Suggested Questions

★**THINKING FURTHER:** *Making Conclusions* **Why are many of the cities with Spanish names in the southwestern United States?** *(Spanish-speaking people settled in much of that area.)*

⭐ 3 CLOSE

SUM IT UP

Have students answer the questions below.

Suggested Questions

- **Why did many Native Americans lose their own culture?** *(because of mission life)*
- **Why was Mexico's independence from Spain important to Texas?** *(Texas was part of Mexico.)*
- **How did Texas become independent from Mexico?** *(Texas fought and won a war against Mexico.)*

EVALUATE
✓ **Answers to Think About It**

1. They ate cactus, nuts, fruits and berries, and built grass huts.
2. safety and food
3. The Spanish religion, language, and way of life predominated.
4. Men did farmwork and building. Women fished, cared for children, cooked, spun, and wove. Both men and women were expected to work hard and to pray.
5. Southeast *Location*

Write About It Invite students to write a diary entry from the Coahuiltecan point of view. Have them tell about life before and after entering a mission.

MEETING *Individual* NEEDS

RETEACHING (Easy) Ask students to review the *Infographic* and tell stories aloud about the people who lived at the missions.

EXTENSION (Average) Invite the class to create an illustrated book on the history of Texas. Groups can use the information in the text as a source of information for pictures and captions about the following topics: the Coahuiltecan, the missions, the battle of The Alamo, Texas statehood. Photocopy the pages and bind them together to make a take-home Texas history coloring book.

ENRICHMENT (Challenging) Encourage students to research one of the following topics and prepare an oral report for the class: Davy Crockett; Jim Bowie; the Battle of The Alamo; Padre Junípero Serra.

LESSON 3

PAGES 128–132

Lesson Overview

San Antonio today is a thriving city whose culture reflects its Spanish heritage.

Lesson Objectives

★ Link San Antonio's past communities to its present one.

★ Analyze how communities are shaped by people and events in their past.

⭐ 1 PREPARE

MOTIVATE Have a volunteer read the *Read Aloud*. Encourage students to think about what kinds of questions they might like to ask Barbara Shupp about San Antonio.

SET PURPOSE Preview the *Vocabulary* words with students. Then direct their attention to the *Read to Learn* question and invite speculation about the answer.

⭐ 2 TEACH

Discussing A Growing City Direct attention to the picture, which illustrates the blend of old and new that is characteristic of San Antonio.

Suggested Questions

● **How has San Antonio changed since Mrs. Shupp was young?** *(When Mrs. Shupp was young, San Antonio was like a small town. There were small shops instead of malls, River Walk was not built up, and there were few cars.)*

● **How has San Antonio changed since the days of the missions?** *(It has grown into the tenth-largest city in the U.S.)*

Resource REMINDER

Practice Book: *p. 30*
Anthology: *San Antonio Mission Trail, p. 52*
◉ **Technology:** *Adventures CD-ROM*

San Antonio Today

Focus Activity

READ TO LEARN
How do people celebrate San Antonio's culture?

VOCABULARY
Fiesta
volunteer

READ ALOUD

Barbara Shupp has lived in San Antonio for over 60 years. "I went to many famous cities," Mrs. Shupp said. "But do you know what? When I came back to San Antonio, I decided it was the prettiest city in the world. No other city compares!" In this lesson you will see why many people proudly call San Antonio home.

A Growing City

You just read about mission life in San Antonio. Today San Antonio is very different. It has grown from the days of the missions. San Antonio is the tenth largest city in the United States. It was also the first major city to have a mayor of Hispanic descent, Henry Cisneros.

Mrs. Shupp has seen a lot of changes take place in San Antonio. She likes to watch her nine-year-old granddaughter, Susann Speer, grow up in the same city she did. "But in some ways," Mrs. Shupp laughs, "San Antonio is not the same city at all! When I was a young girl like my granddaughter, San Antonio was like a small town. River Walk was not built up. There were no shopping malls. Instead, there were many small shops. We could even rollerskate in the streets because there were very few cars!"

128

Reading STRATEGIES *and* Language DEVELOPMENT

MAIN IDEA AND DETAILS Review with students how main ideas and supporting details supply information. As they work through this lesson, have them keep track of the main ideas and details they find in each section.

LANGUAGE HISTORY Explain that it was on the Catholic holy day of Saint Anthony of Padua that the Spanish explorers first sighted what is now the San Antonio River. They named the river in his honor—*San Antonio*. English speakers adopted many other words from their Spanish neighbors. Two that appear in the lesson are *fiesta* and *piñata*.

The Past Lives On

San Antonio is a city that combines its history with its life today. Every year thousands of people visit the missions. They learn about how the Spanish and Native Americans lived long ago. Some of the missions are still used as churches. The Alamo is now a museum honoring Texas's past.

The past continues in other ways as well. San Antonio's Spanish and Mexican roots can be seen and heard everywhere. Many people are Mexican American. They speak Spanish as well as English. Susann likes the mix of people. "Sometimes my friends and I sing Christmas carols for people in a nursing home," she says. "We sing the songs in Spanish and English. I'd like to learn more Spanish."

Susann Speer (above) likes the mixture of the past and present in San Antonio. Mission San José is still an active church (below). People celebrate their culture in festive costumes (below right).

Discussing The Past Lives On Explain that more than half of San Antonio's population is of Spanish heritage.

Suggested Questions

● **Why do people visit the missions?** *(to learn how the Spanish and Native Americans lived)*

● **How are some of the missions used today?** *(Some are churches, one is a museum.)*

● **If you visited San Antonio, how would you know that the Spanish had once settled there?** *(from the missions and the fact that people speak Spanish)*

● **What languages do you hear in your community?** *(Answers will vary.)*

★**THINKING FURTHER:** *Compare and Contrast* **Compare some historical buildings in your community to those in San Antonio. How are they alike? How are they different? What do they tell about your community's past?** *(Students should support their answers with examples.)*

Technology CONNECTION

ADVENTURES CD-ROM
Enrich the lesson with the *Key Places* segment on the CD-ROM.

Second-Language Support

DIALOGS Second-language learners may gain confidence from understanding that all communities have celebrations that reflect the heritage of the people who live there. Have students think of special parties and holidays in which they have participated. Help them brainstorm a list of special foods, clothes, music, and activities that are related to those celebrations. Encourage students to share that information with a partner and then with the rest of the class if they are comfortable doing so.

DID YOU KNOW?

How much candy did you get?

Many Mexican games are popular in San Antonio. A favorite one involves a piñata. A piñata is a hanging paper animal filled with candy. It is used to celebrate special events. Children are blindfolded and take turns hitting the piñata with a stick. When it breaks open, the candy falls to the ground. Children then pick up the candy.

Fiesta in San Antonio

You can learn a lot about a community by watching its celebrations. San Antonio has many celebrations, festivals, and events all year long. The celebrations show the many different cultures that make up this city. "That's one thing I like about San Antonio," says Susann. "There's always something special going on."

For Susann and her grandmother, there is one festival they like most of all. It is a weeklong event called Fiesta. *Fiesta* means "festival" in Spanish. Fiesta includes San Jacinto Day. It celebrates the day Texas won freedom from Mexico on April 21, 1836.

Fiesta is the biggest celebration of the year. Many volunteers help to make it a success. A volunteer is someone who does something by choice, without pay. Volunteers help organize parades and many other activities. For ten days the city becomes a big party. There are over 150 different events to see.

San Antonio's Fiesta Parade includes floats covered with flowers. In the past people threw flowers in a playful battle.

130

Memories of San Antonio

A few years ago there was a writing contest during Fiesta. People were asked to write about their memories of San Antonio's past. Mrs. Shupp was so excited about this, she entered the contest. Here is what she said about her memories of the Fiesta Parade. What do you remember most about celebrations in your community?

MANY VOICES PRIMARY SOURCE

Story by Barbara Shupp written in 1985.

To our family the Fiesta Parade was the **consolidation** of all the events of the year. Neither rain nor shine could keep us away. My love for the parade was probably why I went to work that morning even though I didn't feel well. It was the big day of the parade and I wouldn't let a sore throat stop me from going! As I stood waiting for the parade, I began to shake. The weather was warm, but I was freezing. What should I do? I didn't want to miss the parade, but I felt too sick to stay outside. Then it came to me—I would go sit inside the nearby movie house. As I sat watching a movie, I could hear the marching band come down the street. Even though I couldn't see the flag, I had a lump in my throat when it went by. Who would have thought that the parade's number one fan would be watching a movie as it went by!

---

consolidation: coming together

131

Thinking About Memories of San Antonio Point out the photo of Mrs. Shupp. Then ask students why the memories of older people are important to all of us.

Learning from the Primary Source Have students discuss Mrs. Shupp's account of the Fiesta Day Parade.

Suggested Questions

- *Why did Mrs. Shupp go to work even though she was sick?* (She didn't want to miss the parade.)

- *Why did she sit in the movie theater instead of watching the parade?* (She was too sick to stay outside but didn't want to miss the parade altogether. From the theater, she could hear the band.)

- *What part of the parade was the most meaningful to Mrs. Shupp? How do you know?* (The fact that Mrs. Shupp got a lump in her throat when the flag went by indicates that it was the most meaningful part of the parade for her.)

Curriculum CONNECTION

LINKS TO LANGUAGE ARTS Invite students to interview family members and neighbors about the history of their community. File the written interviews in a "community history" binder for everyone to share.

- Have students plan the questions they will ask at their interviews. Suggest that in addition to specific questions, students ask open-ended ones such as "Is there any special memory you would like to share?"

- Have students plan how they will record their interviews. Students who will write their interviews in a notebook may want to work with a partner. Others may want to use a tape recorder to help them remember what was said.

Field Trip

Arrange a visit to a senior-citizens center and invite residents to share memories of their community with your students. Before the visit, help students write down their questions and practice asking them. If permissible, suggest that students take photos of their new friends and add them—along with the written interviews—to the community history binder.

Discussing Living Together As students look at the picture, point out that the first Texas cowboys were Spanish. Help students focus on the many aspects of Spanish culture evident in San Antonio and other parts of our country today.

Suggested Questions
- **Why is Mrs. Shupp glad Susan is growing up in San Antonio?** *(She loves the city and its interesting people.)*

Discussing WHY IT MATTERS Help students sum up what they have learned about San Antonio's rich past.

Suggested Questions
- **What are two examples of San Antonio's Spanish and Mexican heritage?** *(Many people speak Spanish as well as English. The city's architecture and festivals also reflect its multicultural heritage.)*

⭐ 3 CLOSE

SUM IT UP
Have students answer these questions.

Suggested Questions
- **What culture does Fiesta celebrate?** *(Spanish, Mexican, Mexican American)*

- **How has San Antonio changed since Mrs. Shupp was young? How has it stayed the same?** *(It has grown from a small town to the tenth-largest city in the U.S. It is still a place where different people live together.)*

EVALUATE
✓ **Answers to Think About It**
1. There are many Mexican Americans and Spanish-speaking people. The missions and other historic buildings are still standing.
2. its beauty, Fiesta, different people living together
3. with Fiesta, parades, and Mexican games
4. Students can compare and contrast the size, buildings, people, history, and celebrations of San Antonio and the local community.
5. Students should focus on shared community experiences.

Write About It Have students suppose they are visiting San Antonio during Fiesta week and write a journal entry that describes their experiences.

The Livestock and Rodeo show is one way people celebrate in San Antonio.

Living Together

Mrs. Shupp likes to talk about things she remembers from growing up in San Antonio. "One thing hasn't changed," Mrs. Shupp notes. "You still meet interesting people. San Antonio has always been a place where different people live together. I am glad that Susann is growing up in San Antonio today."

WHY IT MATTERS

You have learned about San Antonio's rich past. You have also seen how people in San Antonio celebrate their culture.

Every community has its own special past. People enjoy remembering their past and joining in celebrations. These are some of the reasons that people like living in communities.

✓ Reviewing Facts and Ideas

SUM IT UP
- San Antonio has grown into a large, busy city.
- San Antonio celebrates its cultures with many festivals and events like Fiesta.
- One way to learn about the past is to listen to people who remember it.
- San Jacinto Day celebrates Texas's independence from Mexico on April 21, 1836.

THINK ABOUT IT
1. What signs of San Antonio's past can still be seen today?
2. What is one thing Mrs. Shupp likes about living in San Antonio?
3. **FOCUS** How do people celebrate San Antonio's culture?
4. **THINKING SKILL** How is San Antonio *like* your community today? How is it *different*?
5. **WRITE** Think about something you want to remember about your community. Write about that memory.

132

MEETING *Individual* **NEEDS**

RETEACHING (Easy) Invite students to draw or paint illustrations of Fiesta in San Antonio or of similar celebrations in your community.

EXTENSION (Average) Have students create a radio commercial advertising a local festival. Encourage students to act out the commercial for the class.

ENRICHMENT (Challenging) Ask students to find out about other cultural groups that live in and around San Antonio today. Encourage them to write brief reports discussing the history of those groups.

132

CITIZENSHIP
MAKING A DIFFERENCE

From the Community Garden

SAN ANTONIO, TEXAS— Tiffany Rogers started volunteering at the Children's East Community Garden in San Antonio just a few years ago. Back then she could not tell a cucumber plant from a tomato plant. Now she raises her own vegetables such as carrots and spinach. She even brings them home for dinner!

For Tiffany the garden is very special. It is a place where she helps the community by growing plants and vegetables for herself and others.

Volunteers are given a small piece of land by community leaders. Local businesses help with seeds and tools. About 20 children and 40 adults work in the garden.

People like Vernon Mullins teach Tiffany and others about planting, weeding, and watering. Mr. Mullins likes his job because he, too, is making a difference in his community.

"Working in the community garden, we all become friends," he said. "If one person sees another person needs help, they pitch in. We also give the food we grow to needy people in the community."

Working in the community garden has taught Tiffany how to make a difference in her community. It has also taught her a lot about plants. And it sure keeps Tiffany busy. "You get lots of exercise and you don't waste time sitting home," she said.

"You get lots of exercise . . . "

Tiffany Rochelle Rogers

133

CITIZENSHIP

WORKING TOGETHER Give students an opportunity to become involved in a cooperative gardening project.

- If there is a community garden in your area, students can volunteer to work in it. Appoint a committee to report on where the garden is, when it is open, and how children can become involved.

- Students can plant a garden in the schoolyard or a nearby park. Enlist the aid of parent volunteers to help contact local officials for permission to use the land and local businesses for contributions.

- If an outdoor garden is not feasible, consider a classroom garden grown under lights. Children can make planters by decorating coffee cans, milk cartons, and other containers. They can plant seeds from a variety of fruits and vegetables. And they can invite other classes to visit their garden when it begins to grow, so they can enjoy it too.

Lesson Objective

★ Understand that in a community project, each person makes a difference.

Identifying the Focus Be sure students understand why the community garden is special to the people who work there and the rest of the community.

Suggested Questions

● *Why is the garden very special to Tiffany?* (It gives her a chance to help herself and her community by growing plants and vegetables.)

Why It Matters Help students understand that as people share skills and energy, they make new friends and strengthen the community.

Suggested Questions

● *Who works in the garden?* (about 20 children and 40 adults, all volunteers)

● *How do community leaders help the garden? How do local businesses help?* (Community leaders allocate land for the garden; local businesses donate seeds and tools.)

● *How do new gardeners learn what to do?* (People like Vernon Mullins teach them.)

● *Why does Vernon Mullins like working in the garden?* (He can make friends, enjoy a spirit of teamwork, help his community and needy people.)

● *What does Tiffany Rogers learn from working in the garden?* (She learns how to help her community, work with other people, and use her time productively. She also learns about plants.)

★**THINKING FURTHER:** *Making Conclusions* **How do we help ourselves when we help our community?** (Students should realize that helping the community makes people feel good about themselves.)

Lesson Overview
We can use graphs to present information visually.

Lesson Objective
★ Interpret bar graphs and line graphs.

1 PREPARE

MOTIVATE Ask students to think about the sizes of familiar groups of people, such as a family or a class. Use the capacity of a local stadium or theater to help students comprehend a larger group of people. Then compare the numbers of those groups with the number of people in your town.

SET PURPOSE Explain that graphs are pictures that show amounts—population or rainfall, for example. Explain that in this lesson students will learn how to read two kinds of graphs—*bar graphs* and *line graphs*.

DISCUSSING HELPING YOURSELF
Point out the *Helping Yourself* box on p. 135. Suggesst that students refer to it as they work on this lesson.

2 TEACH

Why the Skill Matters Remind students that *population* is the number of people in a group. The graphs they will be using in this lesson show two ways to learn about population.

Reading a Bar Graph Have students read the headings on the graph and look at the bars. Explain that the longer the bar is, the larger the number it represents. Be sure students understand that bar graphs are used to illustrate and compare amounts. Show students that a bar graph can be horizontal as well as vertical by drawing a horizontal version of the graph on the chalk board.

Resource **REMINDER**

Practice Book: *p. 31*

STUDYSKILLS

Reading Bar and Line Graphs

VOCABULARY
bar graph   line graph

WHY THE SKILL MATTERS
In the last lesson you learned about San Antonio today. In studying San Antonio it is helpful to compare its population with those of other large cities in Texas. It is also useful to see how San Antonio's population has changed over time. One way to view this information is to use graphs.

READING A BAR GRAPH
Suppose you want to compare the populations of San Antonio and other Texas cities. Look at the bar graph at right. A bar graph uses bars of different heights to show amounts. This bar graph shows the populations of three of the largest cities in Texas.

Look at the bottom of this bar graph. Which cities does it name? Look at the numbers on the left side of the graph. The numbers stand for populations.*

Now "read" the graph. First find the bar for San Antonio. Slide your finger to the top of the bar. Now slide your finger across to the number at the left. The number is just below one million. The population of San Antonio is about one million people.

Now find the bar for Houston. About how many people live in Houston?**

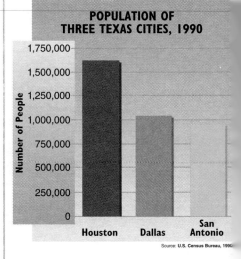

POPULATION OF THREE TEXAS CITIES, 1990

Number of People

1,750,000
1,500,000
1,250,000
1,000,000
750,000
500,000
250,000
0

Houston   Dallas   San Antonio

Source: U.S. Census Bureau, 1990

READING A LINE GRAPH
Another kind of graph is a line graph. A line graph shows how something changes over time. Look at the line graph on the next page. It shows how the population of San Antonio has changed over time.

The dots for each year are connected by a line. The line shows you a picture of what happened to San Antonio's population.

134   *Houston, Dallas, San Antonio   **Houston has about 1,700,000 people.

Curriculum CONNECTION

LINKS TO MATH: MORE GRAPH WORK
● Have students write their birthdays under the headings winter, spring, summer, and autumn. Then ask them to work together to make a vertical bar graph using the birthday data. Ask students to read the completed graph, answering questions such as: Which season has the most birthdays? How do you know?

● Use a line graph to show how money in a piggy bank changes over time. Along the left side of the graph, mark spaces to show one dollar increments; along the bottom, mark spaces for six weeks. Let students suggest how much money is added to or subtracted from the bank each week. Have them place a dot on the graph to reflect the data. Students can draw a line to connect the dots and then pose questions and answer them.

*It has increased (from about 3,500 people in 1850 to about 936,000 people in 1990).
**Bar graph; line graph; the population increased (from about 53,000 to 936,000 people).

Run your finger along the line. Note the dates at the bottom and the numbers at the left. How has the city's population changed between 1850 and 1990?*

TRYING THE SKILL

You may find it useful to refer to the Helping Yourself box as you continue to study the graphs. Which graph would you use to find the population of Dallas in 1990? Which would you use to compare San Antonio's population in 1900 with its population in 1990?

HELPING Yourself

- **Bar graphs** compare amounts. **Line graphs** show how amounts change over time.

- To read a graph, use the words and numbers on the left and bottom.

What happened during this time?**

REVIEWING THE SKILL

1. Which city on the bar graph has the largest population? Tell how you know.

2. What is the earliest year shown on the line graph? How can you tell?

3. About how many people lived in San Antonio in 1950?

4. What would you tell someone to do to make it easier to read a graph?

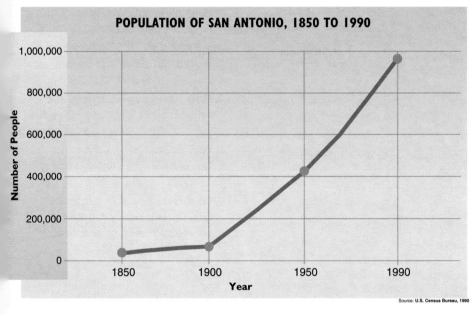

POPULATION OF SAN ANTONIO, 1850 TO 1990

Number of People / Year

Source: U.S. Census Bureau, 1990

135

Reading a Line Graph Have students read the headings on the graph and look at the line. Explain that the higher the line goes on the graph, the larger the number it stands for. Explain that line graphs show how amounts change over time. Tell students that it is easier to read numbers from the graph if they use a finger to go from the dot across to the number on the left.

Trying The Skill Remind students to read the statements in the *Helping Yourself* box as they work independently.

Suggested Questions

- *How many cities are shown on the bar graph?* (3)

- *How many cities are shown on the line graph?* (1)

- *Which kind of graph is better to use for comparing different amounts?* (bar)

- *Which kind of graph is better for seeing how amounts have changed over time?* (line)

- *What does the line graph tell you about San Antonio between the year 1950 and the year 1990?* (The population of the city increased by 600,000 people.)

- *Does San Antonio have more people or fewer people than Houston? Which graph did you use to find out?* (fewer; the bar graph)

3 CLOSE

SUM IT UP

Ask students to explain in their own words the differences between bar graphs and line graphs. Have students share their answers to the questions.

EVALUATE

✓ **Answers to Reviewing the Skill**

1. Houston, because its bar is higher

2. 1850, because that is the year in the lower left.

3. 400,000

4. Slide your finger from the top of the bar to the number on the left or from the dot on the line to the number across from it.

MEETING *Individual* NEEDS

RETEACHING (Easy) Have students redraw the lesson bar graph to make it horizontal. Show them how to label the left side with city names and the top with population numbers. Or provide them with a page on which these lines have already been drawn and labeled.

EXTENSION (Average) Invite students to use a bar graph to compare the number of pets owned by classmates. Demonstrate how to list each type of pet along the bottom of the graph, and place numbers along the left side.

ENRICHMENT (Challenging) Challenge students to graph two sets of data: one for comparison and one to show change over time. Students can graph, for example, the size of your class over a three-year period (line graph); or the number of toy stores, clothing stores, and restaurants in a nearby mall (bar graph).

Discussing Major Events Use the following questions to help students practice reading a time line.

Suggested Questions

- **When did the Spanish start their first missions in Texas?** *(1720)*
- **When did Texas gain its independence from Mexico?** *(1836)*
- **When did Texas join the United States?** *(1845)*
- **How long was Texas an independent country?** *(9 years)*

Answers to
THINKING ABOUT VOCABULARY

1. independence
2. missions
3. volunteers
4. cactus
5. Fiesta

Answers to
THINKING ABOUT FACTS

1. The missionaries taught the Coahuiltecan the Catholic religion and the Spanish language. Gradually, the Coahuiltecan culture disappeared.

2. 1845; the battle of The Alamo was fought and Texas won its independence from Mexico.

3. People built the River Walk to keep the river from flooding. There are shops and parks along the River Walk; the area is good for farming because the climate is warm and water from the San Antonio River is available for irrigation.

Resource REMINDER

Assessment Book: *Chapter 5 Test*

CHAPTER 5 REVIEW

Major Events

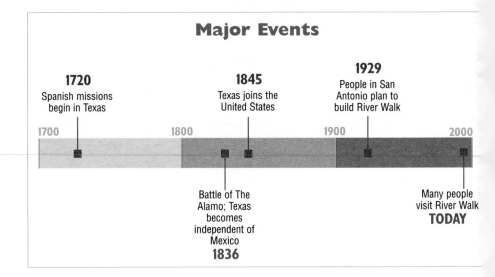

1720
Spanish missions begin in Texas

1845
Texas joins the United States

1929
People in San Antonio plan to build River Walk

1700   1800   1900   2000

Battle of The Alamo; Texas becomes independent of Mexico
1836

Many people visit River Walk
TODAY

THINKING ABOUT VOCABULARY

Number a piece of paper from 1 to 5. Beside each number write the word that best completes each sentence.

cactus   missions
Fiesta   volunteers
independence

1. Texas won its _____ from Mexico in 1836.

2. To teach Native Americans about Spanish culture and religion, the missionaries set up _____ .

3. Thanks to the unpaid work done by _____, the party went well.

4. The dry desert is home to many types of _____ plants.

5. _____ is a celebration of Texas's independence from Mexico.

136

THINKING ABOUT FACTS

1. How did the missionaries change the lives of the Coahuiltecan people? What happened to the Coahuiltecan culture?

2. In what year did Texas join the United States? What events took place before this happened?

3. How has the area around the San Antonio River changed since the 1950s? Why is it good for farming?

4. Why is Spanish a common language in San Antonio today?

5. How do people in San Antonio celebrate their culture? What cultural celebrations take place in your community or one nearby?

Suggestions for Think and Write

SIGNS OF SUCCESS

WRITING A STORY A story about a mission child would describe a highly scheduled day of prayer, meals, religious instruction, and work.

WRITING A THEME SONG Students' songs should mention the Spanish missions, the Coahuiltecans, the San Antonio River, the state of Texas, and the importance of Spanish culture and language. If possible, students should include several Spanish words in their songs.

WRITING AN ADVERTISEMENT Be sure students' advertisements focus on the River Walk, the Spanish heritage, and the surrounding farmlands.

For performance assessment, see Assessment Book, Chapter 5.

THINK AND WRITE ◀▦▶

WRITING A STORY
Write a brief story about a typical day of a child living at a mission long ago.

WRITING A THEME SONG
Write a theme song to be performed at Fiesta. In it describe San Antonio's past and present.

WRITING AN ADVERTISEMENT
Suppose you work for an advertising company and have been asked to create a magazine advertisement about San Antonio. Write an advertisement to tell people what is special about San Antonio.

APPLYING STUDY SKILLS

READING BAR AND LINE GRAPHS
Answer the following questions to practice the skill of reading bar and line graphs. Use the graphs on pages 134–135.

1. What is the difference between a bar graph and a line graph?
2. Which city has the larger population, Houston or Dallas? Which graph tells you this?
3. Did more people live in San Antonio in 1850 or in 1950?
4. Which graph tells you about changes over time?
5. What information about yourself could you show on a line graph?

4. San Antonio was settled by Spanish-speaking people and many Mexican immigrants make San Antonio their home.
5. They hold a week-long Fiesta, eat traditional Mexican foods, play Mexican music and games. Students can describe a cultural celebration in your community.

Answers to APPLYING STUDY SKILLS

1. A bar graph uses bars of different sizes to show the differences in amounts of things. A line graph uses a line to show how something has changed over time.
2. Houston; the bar graph
3. in 1950
4. the line graph
5. Students may suggest any topic that shows change over time. For example, they may suggest their height or how much money they have saved.

Summing Up the Chapter

Fill in a copy of the Venn Diagram below. In the circle on the left, write the words that describe San Antonio in the 1700s. In the circle on the right, write the words that describe San Antonio today. Where the circles meet, write the words that describe both time periods. How has San Antonio changed since the 1700s? How is it still the same?

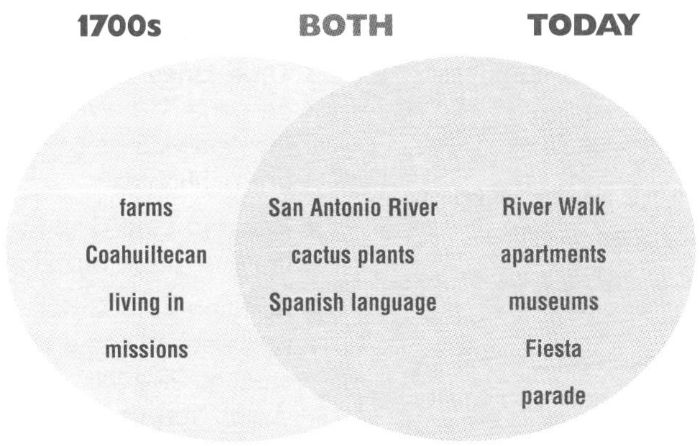

1700s	BOTH	TODAY
farms	San Antonio River	River Walk
Coahuiltecan	cactus plants	apartments
living in	Spanish language	museums
missions		Fiesta
		parade

137

Suggestions for Summing Up the Chapter

- Prepare copies of the diagram for the class. Or ask students to draw two large circles on the page to create a diagram like the one above. Explain that the diagram is a compare/contrast chart. Each circle represents a different time period and the place where the circles overlap represents both periods.
- After students have completed their diagrams, draw a diagram on the chalkboard and invite the class to complete it. Correct answers are written in red.
- Have students use the information in the diagram to write summary statements that tell how San Antonio has changed and remained the same over time.

Answers to
THINKING ABOUT VOCABULARY

1. technology
2. Bay
3. mission
4. artifacts
5. decision
6. kiva
7. desert
8. volunteers
9. mesa
10. museum

Suggestions for
THINK AND WRITE

- **Writing a Review** Students should explain that places like Mesa Verde National Park and Jamestown Settlement are important because they help us learn about our country's history and the people who lived here long ago.

- **Writing an Essay** Students should identify the special event, explain the reasons that it is important to them and to the community, and provide specifics such as when and how the event is celebrated.

- **Writing a Newspaper Article** Students should use the 5 Ws to tell *when* the missionaries went to Texas, *why* they went, *whom* they met there, *what* problems they faced, and *where* they settled.

UNIT 2 REVIEW

THINKING ABOUT VOCABULARY

Number a sheet of paper from 1 to 10. Beside each number write the word from the list that best completes each sentence.

artifacts   kiva   technology
Bay   mesa   volunteers
decision   mission
desert   museum

1. _____ is the use of tools and materials to serve people's needs.
2. Ships heading into Jamestown sailed on the Chesapeake _____ .
3. A _____ was a community where Native Americans lived and practiced the Catholic religion.
4. Scientists often use _____ to learn about how a group of people lived long ago.
5. The tour book listed many places to visit. We had to make a _____ about where to go first.
6. A _____ was a room used by the Anasazi for religious purposes.
7. The climate is usually hot and dry in a _____ .
8. _____ work for free in different places within communities.
9. A _____ is a landform that looks like a high, flat table.
10. At a _____ people can look at objects of art, science, or history.

138

THINK AND WRITE

WRITING A REVIEW
Suppose you have just visited Mesa Verde National Park and Jamestown Settlement. Write a paragraph reviewing why such places are important.

WRITING AN ESSAY
Write one paragraph explaining a special event in your community that is important to you. It could be a parade or a holiday celebration.

WRITING A NEWSPAPER ARTICLE
Suppose you went with the Spanish missionaries to Texas. Write an article that reports on the land, the people, and the problems you faced.

BUILDING SKILLS

1. **Making Decisions** What is the first step to take in making a decision?
2. **Making Decisions** Identify a decision you made today and how you made it.
3. **Time Lines** Look at the time line on page 113. Which happened first, the "starving time" or the marriage of Pocahontas?
4. **Bar and Line Graphs** What does the line graph on page 135 show?
5. **Bar and Line Graphs** Suppose you want to show how many students like various kinds of fruit. Would you use a line graph or a bar graph? Why?

Ongoing Unit Project

OPTIONS FOR ASSESSMENT

This ongoing project, begun on page 64D, can be part of your assessment program, along with other forms of evaluation.

PLANNING Students should choose artifacts they learned about in the unit. Descriptions of each artifact's importance and its relationship to present-day objects should be included.

SIGNS OF SUCCESS

- Time lines will reflect an understanding of the communities studied, their place in history, and any relationships to communities today.

- Groups should reach consensus on the artifacts to include; a variety of artifacts should be displayed.

- Artifacts should be correctly placed on the time line.

 FOR THE PORTFOLIO Individual artifact pages can be included in each student's portfolio.

YESTERDAY, TODAY &

TOMORROW

At Mesa Verde you can see how the Anasazi lived long ago. At Jamestown Settlement you can see how the colonists and the Powhatan lived. What would you save for people of the future to show how you live today? Why?

READING ON YOUR OWN

Here are some books you might find at the library to help you learn more.

THE MUD FAMILY
by Betsy James
Read of a time when an Anasazi girl made mud dolls that gave rain to her community.

SAN ANTONIO
by Sally Lee
Explore the history, festivals, and neighborhoods of San Antonio.

SARAH MORTON'S DAY: A DAY IN THE LIFE OF A PILGRIM GIRL
by Kate Waters
Join a girl named Sarah as she works and plays in a colonial village in 1627.

UNIT PROJECT

Creating an Infographic

1. Create an Infographic showing how people lived in Jamestown long ago.
2. In a group, discuss facts to include in your Infographic.
3. Decide how you will present these facts. Use the Infographic on pages 84-85 as a guide.
4. Have each group member choose one part of the Infographic to complete.
5. Include colorful drawings to show what life in Jamestown was really like.

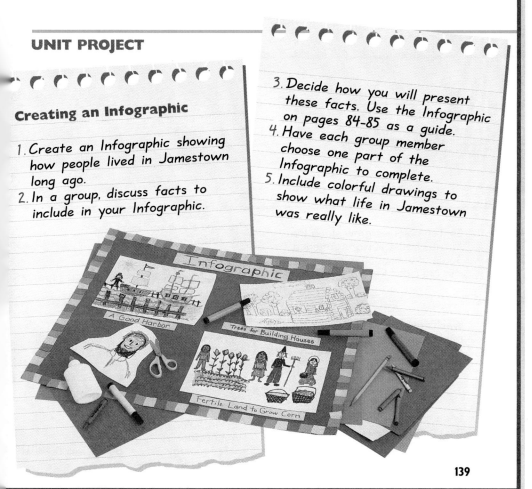

Answers to BUILDING SKILLS

1. thinking about your goal

2. Students should describe how they defined their goal, listed two or three choices, and then made a choice that helped them fulfill their goal.

3. the "starving time"

4. It shows that the population of San Antonio, Texas, has grown from a few thousand in 1850 to almost one million in 1990.

5. a bar graph; because bar graphs are best for comparing amounts

Suggestions for YESTERDAY, TODAY, AND TOMORROW

Invite students to list several of the artifacts they learned about in this unit. Ask them to brainstorm three or four categories in which to classify the artifacts. Students will understand that certain types of artifacts, such as tools, crafts, clothing, and shelter, help us understand how people used to live. As they consider what items to leave for the future, encourage them to choose items from these categories.

Suggestions for READING ON YOUR OWN

The library books suggested under Reading On Your Own will help students explore the unit topics in more depth. Invite students to choose one of these books to read and report on to the class. Additional recommendations are listed in the Annotated Bibliography in the Unit Organizer on page 64B. You may also want to assign specific books for partners or small reading groups to read aloud and discuss.

139

Unit Project: *Create an Infographic*

OBJECTIVE: The Infographic can help students develop a more concrete idea of what life was like in Jamestown.

MATERIALS: drawing paper, crayons, markers

• Direct groups to brainstorm facts to use in their infographics about Jamestown.

• Then invite students to present these facts. Remind students to use the *Infographic* about Mesa Verde on page 84 as a guide. Which details in the Mesa Verde *Infographic* would they like to incorporate in their Infographics about Jamestown?

• Each group member should complete one part of the Infographic. Encourage students to add colorful drawings to help illustrate what life was like in Jamestown.

OPTIONS FOR ASSESSMENT

This project can be part of your assessment program.

PLANNING Let students know they should choose the information they consider most important to present in their Infographics. Tell them their Infographics should reflect the way people lived in Jamestown.

SIGNS OF SUCCESS

• Infographics should reflect students' understanding of how resources, geography, problems, and people contributed to the way people lived in Jamestown.

• Group members should be able to explain how they chose their information and graphics.

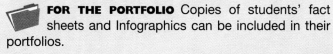 **FOR THE PORTFOLIO** Copies of students' fact sheets and Infographics can be included in their portfolios.

Building a Government

PAGES 140–203

UNIT OVERVIEW

People and the government work together to make lives better for people in communities. Our country's first government was started in the colonial city of Philadelphia. In 1790, the United States capital became Washington, D.C. People who know about government can be responsible citizens of their community and country.

Adventures with National Geographic pp. 142–143

UNIT PLANNING GUIDE

CHAPTER	SUGGESTED PACING	CHAPTER OVERVIEW	CHAPTER RESOURCES
6 A New Country Is Born pp. 144–163	8–10 days	English colonies grew along the Atlantic coast of North America. Some of these communities grew into big cities like Philadelphia.	*Practice Book* pp. 33–35 *Anthology* pp. 54–65 *Project Book* p. 14 *Transparency:* Graphic Organizer *Technology:* Videodisc/Video Tape, CD-ROM
7 Countries Have Capitals pp. 164–183	9–11 days	Washington, D.C., is the capital of the United States of America and it is the center of the national government.	*Practice Book* pp. 37–40 *Anthology* pp. 66–77 ● *Project Book* p. 15 *Technology:* Videodisc/Video Tape, CD-ROM *Transparency:* 9 ● *Outline Map* p. 14 *Desk Map* United States *Geo Big Book* pp. R6–R7
8 Citizens Make Communities Work pp. 184–201	8–10 days	Each community and state across the country has a government too. Governments make laws that help people live safely and fairly.	*Practice Book* pp. 42–44 *Anthology* pp. 71–82 *Project Book* pp. 16–17 *Technology:* Videodisc/Video Tape, CD-ROM *Desk Map* United States

ASSESSMENT OPPORTUNITIES

UNIT ASSESSMENT

Unit Review pp. 202–203
   Unit Projects pp. 202–203

Assessment Book
   Unit Test Unit 3 Test
   Performance Assessment Unit 3

DAILY ASSESSMENT

Geo Adventures Daily Geography Activities

CHAPTER ASSESSMENT

Meeting Individual Needs pp. 145, 151, 153, 159, 165, 169, 175, 177, 181, 185, 189, 191, 197
Write About It pp. 151, 153, 159, 169, 175, 181, 189, 197
Chapter Reviews pp. 162–163, 182–183, 200–201

Assessment Book
   Chapter Tests Ch. 6 Test, Ch. 7 Test, Ch. 8 Test
   Performance Assessment Ch. 6, Ch. 7, Ch. 8

ANNOTATED BIBLIOGRAPHY

Classroom Library

■ Waters, Kate. *The Story of the White House*. New York: Scholastic Inc., 1991. Brief text and colorful photos describe the history and special qualities of the White House.

Student Books

Colman, Warren. *The Bill of Rights*. Chicago, IL: Children's Press, 1987. This is a brief and simplified explanation of the meaning of the Bill of Rights. **(Average)**

Bunting, Eve. *The Wall*. New York: Clarion Books, 1990. A boy and his father visit the Vietnam Veterans Memorial in Washington, D.C. **(Average)**

■ Giblin, James Cross. *George Washington: A Picture Book Biography*. New York: Scholastic, Inc., 1992. Read the story of George Washington's life—from boyhood to Presidency. **(Challenging)**

Krementz, Jill. *A Visit to Washington, D.C.* New York: Scholastic Inc., 1987. A young boy and his family tour some of the main attractions of Washington, D.C. **(Easy)**

Levy, Elizabeth. *. . . If You Were There When They Signed the Constitution.* New York: Scholastic, Inc., 1987. An interesting question-and-answer format provides information on the Constitution. **(Challenging)**

Logan, Suzanne. *The Kids Can Help Book*. New York: The Putnam Publishing Group, 1992. This book suggests ways children can make a difference in their community. **(Challenging)**

■ Pinkney, Andrea Davis. *Dear Benjamin Banneker*. San Diego, CA: Harcourt Brace, 1994. This is a biography of the accomplished African American astronomer and mathematician who helped plan the city of Washington, D.C. **(Average)**

Quackenbush, Robert. *James Madison & Dolly Madison and Their Times*. New York: Pippin Press, 1992. This brief biography of our country's fourth President and his wife makes clear why he is known as one of the "founding fathers" of the United States. **(Challenging)**

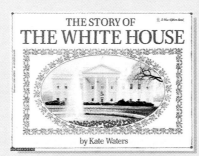

THE STORY OF
THE WHITE HOUSE
by Kate Waters

ANDREA DAVIS PINKNEY
Dear Benjamin Banneker
Illustrated by BRIAN PINKNEY

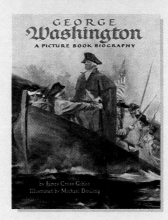

GEORGE Washington
A PICTURE BOOK BIOGRAPHY

by James Cross Giblin
Illustrated by Michael Dooling

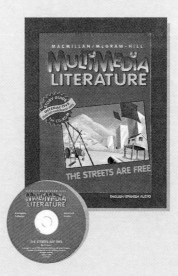

MACMILLAN/McGRAW-HILL
MULTIMEDIA LITERATURE
THE STREETS ARE FREE

Teacher Books

Brenner, Barbara. *If You Were There in 1776*. New York: Bradbury Press, 1994. This book offers background information on what life was like in the late eighteenth century.

Jorgensen, Karen L. *History Workshop: Reconstructing the Past with Elementary Students* Portsmouth, NH: Heinemann, 1993. This book explains how to teach history so that it builds on children's curiosity about the past.

Read Aloud Books

■ DiSalvo-Ryan, DyAnne. *City Green*. New York: Morrow Junior Books, 1994. A young girl starts a clean-up project to turn an empty lot into a community garden.

Maestro, Betsy and Giulio Maestro. *A More Perfect Union: The Story of Our Constitution*. New York: Lothrop, Lee & Shepard, 1987. Colorful illustrations and simple text tell the story of how the Constitution was drafted.

Technology Multimedia

Our Nation's Capital City. 1 filmstrip, cassette. No.5320. This is a fun-and-fact-filled tour of Washington, D.C. Knowledge Unlimited. (800) 356-2303.

The Streets Are Free. CD-ROM, Story 4. The children of San José, Venezuela join together to solve their problem—a place to play. Macmillan/McGraw-Hill Multimedia Literature. Toll Free: 1-800-442-9685.

Free or Inexpensive Materials

For a "Bill of Responsibilities" modeled after the Bill of Rights, send to: Mack Trucks, Inc., Attn: Linda K. Peters; Box M; 2100 Mack Blvd.; Allentown, PA 18105-5000.

■ *Book excerpted in the Anthology*

■ *Book featured in the student bibliography of the Unit Review*

☐ *National Geographic technology*

Ideas for Active Learning

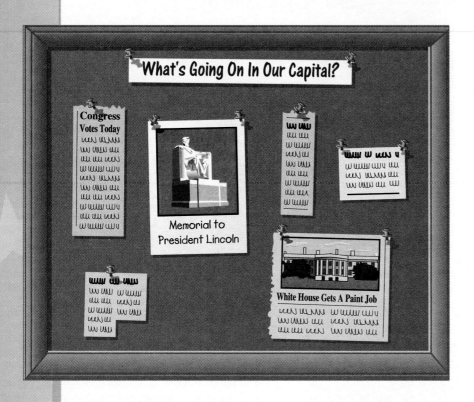

What's Going On In Our Capital?

Congress Votes Today

Memorial to President Lincoln

White House Gets A Paint Job

Building a Government

Help students to create a bulletin board titled "What's Going On In Our Capital?"

- Ask students to scan current newspapers and magazines for articles and pictures that relate to the federal government and to events and issues in Washington, D.C. They can cut out the articles and pictures and place them on the bulletin board.

- Have students use a highlighter or marker to underline key words in the title and article, such as Washington, the Supreme Court, voters, the White House, and the names of elected officials. Encourage discussion about the bulletin board entries, and invite students to make changes to the display as current events change.

Thanks to: Frances Shoup, Bunker Hill Elementary School, Houston, Texas

Wax Museum

ON YOUR OWN 30 MINUTES OR LONGER

Materials: paper; pencil; tape recorders and tapes; costume props such as hats, dress-up clothing and shoes

1. Brainstorm a list of people who have been important in the formation of the United States. Have each student choose a person to portray.
2. Have students research their person. Tell them to write their information as though they were really that person.
3. Tell students to read their reports aloud and tape-record them. They should begin with "My name is . . . My job is . . ." Then, in 3 minutes or less, they should tell how their person contributed to the formation of the United States.
4. Invite students to dress like their person on presentation day. They can use costume props or create costumes.
5. Invite visitors to hear students' taped reports on presentation day. Have students stand very still as their report plays and invite the guests to walk around and listen as a group.

Enriching with Multimedia

 RESOURCE: *Internet Project Handbook*

- Look at the **Internet Project Handbook** for student projects related to this unit or have students go on-line at http://www.mmhschool.com, Macmillan/McGraw-Hill School's home page on the World Wide Web.

RESOURCE: *Videodisc/Video Tape 2*

- Enrich Unit 3 with the Videodisc *glossary* and *map* segments.

Search Frame 53585

Building a Government

- Discuss with students how members of your local and state government are chosen and talk about some of their responsibilities. Then list the names of your state's governor, your local mayor, and members of your city council for students.

- Encourage students to share their list with their families, and to extend the list of local government leaders as they watch the news or read newspapers together. Students should then select a local community issue that is in the news, and list the names and titles of the government leaders who are involved in the issue. Students may also want to write a few sentences telling how they feel about the issue.

Community Constitution

CURRICULUM CONNECTION **Art/Language Arts**

RESOURCE: Project Book p. 13.

Throughout this unit, students will work in groups to create a set of laws tailored to their community.

1. After each chapter, students can work in assigned groups to create laws that will make their community a better place to live. Laws can relate to information from the chapters and issues of concern to students. Groups can store this work in a folder.
2. When all ideas are developed, conduct a class debate on the pros and cons of each law. Students can then vote on the laws that they want to include in their constitution.
3. Once the laws are adopted, record the constitution on a large sheet of construction paper.
4. As an alternative or extension activity, students can create a constitution for their school community.

 Assessment suggestions for this activity appear on p. 202.

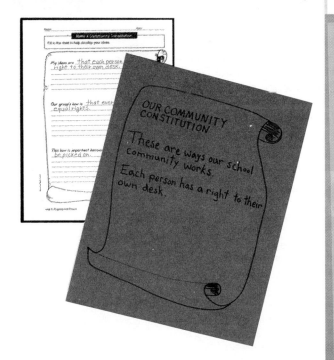

UNIT THREE

PAGES 140-203

Introducing the Unit

Invite students to read *Why Does It Matter?* and to look at the photographs on this spread. Then use the questions below to lead class discussion.

Exploring Prior Knowledge Help students review what they learned in Chapter 4 about Jamestown and the other English colonies.

Suggested Questions

- *What is the name of the first English colony in America?* (Jamestown)

- *What group of people lived in the Jamestown area when the English arrived?* (the Powhatan)

- *In what part of North America were the English colonies that became our first states?* (along the Atlantic coast)

- *How do you suppose those colonies became the United States of America?* (Students can share what they know about the Revolutionary War and other aspects of our early history.)

Looking Ahead Students will learn how the colonists fought for independence from England. They will read about the men who drafted the Declaration of Independence and about the Constitution. They will explore the capital city of Washington, D.C., and the importance of responsible citizenship.

Background INFORMATION

ABOUT THE PHOTOGRAPHS

- **THE HULBERT FLAG** This flag, once flown in Long Island, New York, is an example of early flag design. Other early flags show the stars in a circle. Each star and each stripe represents one of the original thirteen states. Today there are fifty stars in the blue field, representing the fifty states.

- **THE CAPITOL BUILDING** Located on a hill in Washington, D.C., the Capitol Building houses the United States Senate and House of Representatives, which make the laws for the country. Tourists can visit the congressional offices for their own state.

  Refer to *Background Information, About the Capitol,* on p. 171 for more information about the Capitol building.

UNIT THREE

Building a Government

WHY DOES IT MATTER?

People in our country work together to make laws that help us live safely and fairly. Some were made a long time ago. Some of the laws were made much more recently. In this unit you will learn about how people and government work to make lives better for people in communities.

As a citizen of the United States of America, you have important rights and responsibilities. By learning about government and citizenship, you will be better able to make a difference to your country and your community.

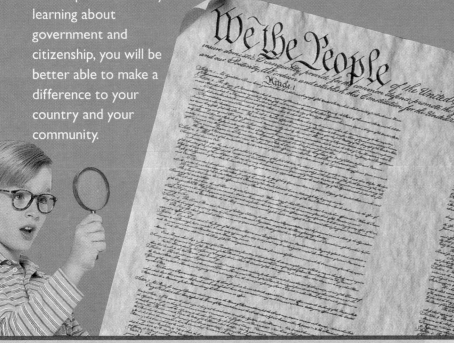

Discussing the Photographs Encourage students to study the photographs for clues about the beginnings of our country. Explain that the American flag, the Capitol, and the Constitution are legacies from our country's early history.

Suggested Questions

● **What is the girl in the picture doing?** *(She is pledging allegiance to the flag; she is promising to be loyal to her country.)*

● **Look at the flag in the picture. How is it different from American flags you have seen? How is it the same?** *(The flag is different because it has only thirteen stars; it is the same because it has both stars and stripes and is red, white, and blue.)*

● **Look at the picture of the Constitution. Which words tell us that this document applies to all citizens of the United States?** *("We the people. . .")*

Discussing WHY DOES IT MATTER Have volunteers read aloud the *Why Does It Matter?* passage.

Suggested Questions

● **What is the name of our country? What does the name mean?** *(Our country is the United States of America. This name means that many separate states are united in North America to form one country.)*

● **Why do people make laws?** *(to help us live safely and fairly)*

Background INFORMATION

ABOUT THE PHOTOGRAPHS

● **THE CONSTITUTION** The handwritten Constitution of the United States was drafted in 1787 at the Constitutional Convention in Philadelphia. Among the most famous delegates to the Convention were Benjamin Franklin, George Washington, James Madison, and John Hancock. This important document outlines the laws and structure of the United States government. Today the original document is preserved in the National Archives in Washington, D.C.

● Refer to *Background Information* on p. 156 and *Citizenship* on p. 157 for more information about the Constitution.

Introducing
When the White House Is Home

Exploring Prior Knowledge Have students who have visited the White House or seen pictures of it describe what it looks like.

Links to the Unit In Unit 3, students will learn about people who helped build our nation and its capital. Explain that students will examine the history of the White House and our Presidents.

When the White House Is Home Be sure students understand that the White House is where the President of the United States lives. Many members of Presidents' families have enjoyed their stay here. First Families have enjoyed working in the gardens, swimming and playing tennis on the grounds, eating dinner, doing homework, reading books, and watching television like any other American family.

Resource **REMINDER**

National Geographic Poster

Geo Adventures *Daily Geography Activities*

Technology: *Adventures CD-ROM*

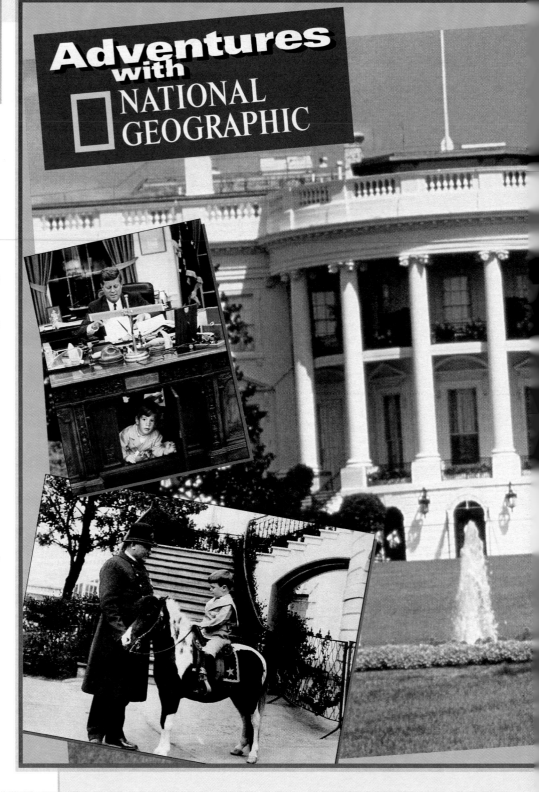

Adventures with NATIONAL GEOGRAPHIC

Background INFORMATION

MORE ABOUT LIVING IN THE WHITE HOUSE The White House has been the home of consecutive Presidents of the United States and their families since John Adams, our second President. The children who have lived here played games, brushed their teeth, and went to school like children everywhere.

• Tad Lincoln was 7 when he moved into the White House, and his brother William was 10. One story tells how Tad bombarded the door of the Cabinet Room with a toy cannon during an important meeting. President Lincoln allowed time for his family. He loved to wrestle with his boys and helped them raise dogs, ponies, and goats.

• Franklin Roosevelt's children kept a badger, a bear, a raccoon, cats, dogs, rats, guinea pigs, snakes, and a pony as pets. They slid down the stairways on trays from the White House kitchen. They also bicycled, skated, and walked on stilts through the halls of the immense mansion. Mrs. Roosevelt once said she didn't think any family had ever enjoyed the White House as much as her family.

• John and Jacqueline Kennedy moved into the White House when Caroline was 3 and John, Jr., was 2 months old. They had a tree house, a swing, a pet canary, a pony, and a dog who was the gift of Soviet premier Nikita Krushchev. Mrs. Kennedy made a special effort to protect the privacy of her children.

• Amy Carter also had a pet pony, and she enjoyed a treehouse in a twisted old cedar tree on the south lawn of the White House.

WHEN THE WHITE HOUSE IS HOME

The White House belongs to all Americans. But some kids have a special connection to the President's house. It's their home! Young Tad Lincoln liked to read there with his father, Abraham Lincoln. Quentin Roosevelt, Teddy Roosevelt's son, rode his pony in the driveway. "John John" Kennedy enjoyed hiding under the desk of his dad, John Kennedy. And Amy Carter, Jimmy Carter's daughter, played with her nephew in a tree house on the lawn. Kids who live in the White House give up a lot of privacy for the privilege of living there. But White House kids get to make history.

GEO JOURNAL

It's your first night in the White House. Describe your thoughts about being there.

143

Have students link the information in the text with each of the photographs. Explain that the White House policeman holds the reins for Quentin Roosevelt. Be sure students notice the secret door under John F. Kennedy's desk. This door could be shut to create what John, Jr., called "My house."

Explain that the small map shows the location of Washington, D.C. You may want to have students locate your community in relation to the White House.

Ask students to consider the differences between living in the White House and living in a regular neighborhood. Explain that one of the biggest problems the First Family has is protecting their privacy.

Everyone wants to know how the President and his family lives. Photographers and reporters are frequently hoping for access to family events. Today, reporters, or anyone, may not enter the White House grounds without a pass. Secret Service guards are posted at the entrances in gatehouses linked by an iron fence. Some members of presidential families want to share their experiences with the public. One White House teenager, Susan Ford, took a series of photographs of life inside the White House.

Using the Geo Journal Invite students to draw a picture of their new room or their first night at dinner.

Technology CONNECTION

ADVENTURES CD-ROM
Enrich this lesson with the CD-ROM activity, *When the White House Is Home.*

Curriculum CONNECTION

LINKS TO LANGUAGE ARTS Ask students to write essays that compare the lives of children in the White House with their own lives.

- Ask students to begin by making a compare/contrast chart listing similarities and differences in the two homes. Students can use information from their texts and the background material on the facing page. They can also draw conclusions and find information in library books about the White House and the children who have lived there.
- Have students refer to their compare/contrast charts when writing their essays. Remind them to tell about several ways children's lives in the White House are probably the same as theirs, and several ways they are probably different.

6 CHAPTER ORGANIZER

A New Country Is Born
PAGES 144–163

CHAPTER OVERVIEW

Long ago English colonies grew along the Atlantic coast of North America. Some of the communities grew into big cities like Philadelphia. It was there that Thomas Jefferson wrote the Declaration of Independence and George Washington became the first President of the United States.

CHAPTER PLANNING GUIDE
Suggested pacing: 8–10 days

LESSON	LESSON FOCUS	LESSON RESOURCES
1 BEN FRANKLIN AND PHILADELPHIA pages 146–151	Ben Franklin Makes a Difference	*Practice Book* p. 33 *Anthology* pp. 54–59 *Technology:* Videodisc/Video Tape, CD-ROM
LEGACY pages 152–153	Our Country's Flag: Linking Past and Present	*Technology: Adventures* CD-ROM
2 OUR FIRST PRESIDENT pages 154–159	The Birth of a Nation	*Practice Book* p. 34 *Anthology* pp. 60–65 *Technology:* Videodisc/Video Tape
THINKING SKILLS pages 160–161	Comparing and Contrasting	*Practice Book* p. 35 *Transparency:* Graphic Organizer
CHAPTER REVIEW pages 162–163	Students' understanding of vocabulary, content, and skills is assessed.	*Assessment:* Ch. 6 Test, Performance Assessment Ch. 6 *Transparency:* Graphic Organizer

OPTIONS FOR STUDENT ACTIVITIES

Citizenship pp. 150, 153, 157

Curriculum Connection pp. 148, 149, 153, 158

Using the Anthology pp. 148, 157

ASSESSMENT OPPORTUNITIES

Meeting Individual Needs pp. 145, 151, 153, 159

Write About It pp. 151, 153, 159

Chapter Review pp. 162–163

Assessment Book

Chapter Test Ch. 6 Test

Performance Assessment Ch. 6

Using Geo Adventures Use **Geo Adventures** Daily Geography Activities to assess students' understanding of geography skills.

Using the Vocabulary Cards The vocabulary words for each lesson are available on *Vocabulary Cards* for review and practice.

GETTING READY FOR THE CHAPTER

Research the Founding of Your Town or City GROUP 30 MINUTES OR LONGER

Objective: To arouse interest in the birth of our nation and its leaders.

Materials: *Project Book* p. 14

1. Ask students if they know how old their town or city is. Invite them to share their ideas about how their hometown or home city looked when it was first founded.
2. Divide the class into groups and have them use classroom resources to research the founding of your town or city. Suggest each group assign a specific job to each member. One member could be responsible for finding the name of the first mayor, another for finding the year the town or city was founded, another for finding pictures of how it looked long ago, and so on.
3. Have each student fill out Project Book p. 14.
4. Encourage groups to compare and pool their information.
5. As an extension, you might involve students in a Founding Day celebration on the anniversary of the founding of your city or town.

SECOND-LANGUAGE SUPPORT

As second-language learners work through this activity, encourage them to take notes that they can refer to throughout the process.

Additional Second-Language Support Tips: pp. 146, 159

Introducing the Chapter

Use the map on p. 145 to point out the location of Philadelphia and New York. Explain that in this chapter, students will learn about the role both cities played in the birth of our nation.

THINKING ABOUT GEOGRAPHY AND HISTORY

Help students match the colors on the map to the colors on the time line to see where each event happened. Be sure students understand that all three events mark the beginning of the United States.

1776

Suggested Questions

- *Why is 1776 an important date to all Americans? (The Declaration of Independence was signed on this date.)*

- *Where was the Declaration of Independence signed? (in Philadelphia)*

- *What is independence? What country do you think the colonies wanted independence from? (freedom; from England)*

- *The Declaration was a written statement from the colonies to the English government. What do you think it said? (that the colonies wanted to make their own laws, that they were unhappy with English rule, that they would fight for freedom)*

Resource REMINDER

 Technology: *Videodisc/Video Tape 2*

CHAPTER 6

A New Country Is Born

THINKING ABOUT GEOGRAPHY AND HISTORY

As you have read, English colonies grew along the Atlantic coast of North America long ago. Some colonial communities, among them Philadelphia and New York, grew into busy cities.

From the time line and map, you can see that some major events happened in Philadelphia and New York. Match the triangles on the map to the picture that has the same color. In Chapter 6 you will meet some of the people who made Philadelphia and New York important and see how their ideas helped form our country, the United States of America.

1776

The Declaration of Independence is signed

144

1787

The Constitution is written

Background INFORMATION

LINKING THE TIME LINE TO HISTORY

- The picture shows Benjamin Franklin and Thomas Jefferson signing the Declaration of Independence. It was Jefferson who wrote the Declaration, which states the American ideal of government—a government that protects the natural rights of all its citizens.

- George Washington was made general of the Continental Army in 1775. He accepted no pay for the position until after the American Revolution was over. After several defeats, Washington and his troops camped and regrouped at Valley Forge in 1777 and then went on to win the war.

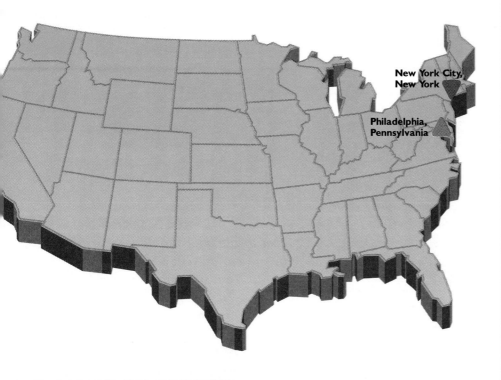

New York City, New York

Philadelphia, Pennsylvania

1787

Suggested Questions

- **What important event happened in 1787?** *(The Constitution was written.)*

- **Where did it happen?** *(in Philadelphia)*

- **What do you know about the Constitution?** *(Invite students to share their prior knowledge about the Constitution.)*

- **The Constitution was written how many years after the Declaration of Independence was signed?** *(11 years)*

1789

Suggested Questions

- **Who was George Washington?** *(our first President)*

- **When and where did he take office?** *(in 1789, in New York City)*

- **George Washington became President how many years after the Declaration of Independence was signed? How many years after the Constitution was written?** *(13 years; two years)*

Technology CONNECTION

VIDEODISC/VIDEO TAPE 2
Enrich Chapter 6 with the Videodisc *map* and *glossary* segments.

Search Frame 53777

1789

George Washington becomes our first President

145

Meeting *Individual* Needs

RETEACHING (Easy) Have students locate the areas on the map that were colonized by English settlers. For reference, students can turn to the *Infographic* on p. 106

EXTENSION (Average) Bring in books showing the Philadelphia of yesterday and today. Have students illustrate two new boxes for the time line: one showing Philadelphia in 1775 and the other showing the city as it looks today.

ENRICHMENT (Challenging) Invite students to write Declarations of Independence based on their own ideas of human rights. Have them explain what a good government should do for its people. As they read the chapter, they can add to or change their declarations.

LESSON 1

PAGES 146–151

Lesson Overview
Philadelphia played an important role in U.S. history.

Lesson Objectives
★ Evaluate Philadelphia's place in U.S. history.

★ Describe Benjamin Franklin's contributions to his community and country.

★ Discuss the *American Revolution* and the *Declaration of Independence.*

1 PREPARE

MOTIVATE Read the *Read Aloud* and have students look at the picture. Invite observations about details that reveal characteristics of colonial times.

SET PURPOSE Remind students that the U.S. was not a country in the early 1700s. Then point out the *Read to Learn* question and *Vocabulary* list. Explain that in this lesson, students will discover how both relate to the birth of our country.

2 TEACH

Discussing Welcome to Philadelphia! Have students turn to the *Infographic* on p. 106 to review what they learned about the 13 colonies. Point out that Pennsylvania is in the middle of the colonies. This location was one reason why its capital, Philadelphia, was so important in colonial times.

Suggested Questions

● **What country ruled the colonies in the early 1700s? In which colony was Philadelphia?** *(England; Pennsylvania)*

★**THINKING FURTHER:** *Using Prior Knowledge* **Philadelphia is on the Delaware River, which flows into the Atlantic Ocean. Why did that location help Philadelphia grow?** *(It provided opportunities for trade.)*

Resource REMINDER

Practice Book: *p. 33*

Anthology: *Ben and Books, pp. 54–59*

Technology: Adventures *CD-ROM; Videodisc/Video Tape 2*

The Bettmann Archive

Ben Franklin and Philadelphia

Focus Activity

READ TO LEARN
How did Ben Franklin make a difference in Philadelphia?

VOCABULARY
almanac
tax
American Revolution
Declaration of Independence

PLACE
Philadelphia, Pennsylvania

PEOPLE
Benjamin Franklin
Thomas Jefferson

146

READ ALOUD
"Most of the shop fronts were painted red, blue, green, or yellow, and the big swinging signs in front of them were brilliant with paint. . . . The people of Philadelphia wore bright colors and had a taste for fine clothes."

Welcome to Philadelphia!
These are the words of a writer named Margaret Cousins. She describes what life was like in the city of Philadelphia, Pennsylvania in the early 1700s. At that time there were 13 English colonies in America. The colonies had many cities. The biggest, busiest city of all was Philadelphia. About 38,000 people lived there, more people than in Boston and New York City put together.

Philadelphia became one of the most important communities in our country's history. Many things happened there that led the colonies to become the United States of America. Let's take a look at what Philadelphia was like back in colonial days.

Reading STRATEGIES *and* Language DEVELOPMENT

REREADING After students read pp. 150 and 151, which provide an overview of the American Revolution, have them jot down any questions they have and then reread each section to find the answers. Explain that rereading helps us understand and remember information.

CAPITALIZATION Remind the class that a proper noun names a specific person, place, or thing. Examples: Benjamin Franklin, Philadelphia, American Revolution. Then have students turn to p. 148 and look at lines 3 and 4. Point out that the word *almanac* is used twice—once with a capital letter and once without. Challenge students to explain why.

Second-Language Support

TAKING NOTES Ben Franklin's sayings (p. 148) may be challenging for second-language learners. Have them work in heterogeneous groups to retell the sayings in their own words and then write them down.

Meet Ben Franklin

Everyone in Philadelphia was talking about one person—Benjamin Franklin. He seemed to be everywhere, doing just about everything.

Ben Franklin grew up in Boston, Massachusetts, in a family of 17 children. When he was 12, his father sent him to live and work with his older brother James, a printer. Ben quickly learned a lot about printing. But he did not get along with his brother. When he was 17, he left for Philadelphia.

When he arrived in Philadelphia in 1723, Ben found an exciting city. He talked to everyone and soon made many friends. He loved his new city, and he set out to make it even better.

As a young man, Ben Franklin learned to use the printing press.

Cigna Museum & Art Collection

147

Discussing Meet Ben Franklin Tell students that the printing press in the picture was used by Ben Franklin. The painting is a portrait of Franklin.

Suggested Questions

- *In which colony did Ben Franklin grow up?* (Massachusetts)

- *How did Ben learn about printing?* (by working for his brother James, a printer)

- *How old was Ben when he left Boston? Why did he leave?* (He was 17; he didn't get along with his brother.)

★**THINKING FURTHER:** *Making Conclusions* **Why do you think Ben decided to move to Philadelphia?** (It was the biggest, busiest city in the colonies.)

Technology CONNECTION

VIDEODISC/VIDEO TAPE 2
Enrich the lesson with the *Pennsylvania map* segments.

Search Frame 53670

Background INFORMATION

MORE ABOUT PHILADELPHIA

- The name *Philadelphia* comes from two Greek words meaning "brotherly love." The city was founded by William Penn, an English Quaker who came to America seeking religious freedom.

- Penn intended Philadelphia to be a place where people of all religions, races, and beliefs could live together in harmony. His belief in brotherly love was evident in his transactions with the people of the Delaware nation. He paid them for their land and established a relationship of friendship and respect.

- Philadelphia became a haven for escaped slaves when the first Abolitionist Society was established there in 1775.

- Philadelphia played such a key role in U.S. history that it is called the "Birthplace of American Independence."

- In 1774 the First Continental Congress met in Philadelphia's Carpenters' Hall to unite the colonies in their dealings with England. In 1776 the Second Continental Congress adopted the Declaration of Independence in Philadelpia's Independence Hall. And in 1787 the U.S. Constitution was ratified there.

MORE ABOUT BEN FRANKLIN

Although Franklin went to school only until age 10, his education never stopped. As an apprentice, he worked up to 14 hours a day, then stayed up to read. He taught himself grammar, arithmetic, navigation, philosophy, and several foreign languages during the course of his life. Franklin not only said "the doors of wisdom never shut," he also proved it.

Discussing Poor Richard's Almanac Tell students that in addition to his almanac, Ben Franklin published a newspaper. The picture shows the papers being delivered in a wheelbarrow.

Suggested Questions

- **What kind of information would you find in an almanac?** *(calendar, weather predictions, information about the sun and moon)*

- **What did people like most about Franklin's almanac?** *(the advice)*

Learning from the Primary Source Help students understand what the sayings mean and why they are helpful.

Suggested Questions

- **Which saying warns against wasting time? Money?** *(Lost time is never found again; a penny saved is a penny earned.)*

- **What did Franklin mean when he said "When the well's dry, we know the worth of water"?** *(We don't appreciate what we have until we lose it.)*

- **Think about these sayings: "Little strokes fell great oaks," and "Well done is twice done." How do they apply to schoolwork?** *(No assignment is too big if you just keep at it; check your work before you hand it in.)*

- ★**THINKING FURTHER:** *Making Conclusions* **What can we learn from this saying: "The honey is sweet, but the bee has a sting"?** *(Some things we like may be harmful.)*

Poor Richard's Almanac

Ben quickly found work in Philadelphia as a printer. A few years later, in 1732, he wrote and printed *Poor Richard's Almanac*. An almanac is a book that comes out every year with lots of information in it. His almanac had a calendar, weather predictions, and information about the moon and sun. It was most popular for the helpful advice it gave readers. Read the following sayings from his almanac. Which sayings have you heard of?

From *Poor Richard's Almanac*, written by Benjamin Franklin, 1732-1757.

- Early to bed and early to rise, makes a man healthy, wealthy and wise.
- Lost time is never found again.
- Don't throw stones at your neighbors', if your own windows are glass.
- A penny saved is a penny earned.
- Little strokes fell great oaks.
- Well done is twice done.
- When the well's dry, we know the worth of water.
- The honey is sweet, but the bee has a sting.

148

Curriculum CONNECTION

LINKS TO WRITING Franklin wrote the first American autobiography. "The next thing most like living one's life over again seems to be . . . putting it down in writing," he said. Invite students to write about a past event in their lives that they would like to "live over again."

LINKS TO DRAMA In colonial times, people played games like charades, often acting out sayings from Franklin's almanacs. Invite students to do the same, using the sayings on this page plus others they find in the library.

Using the ANTHOLOGY

BEN AND BOOKS, pages 54–59 Students will enjoy acting out this play about how Benjamin Franklin educated himself.

Background INFORMATION

ABOUT THOMAS JEFFERSON Provide the following information when students read about the Declaration of Independence (p. 150) and the Bill of Rights (p. 159).

- Jefferson was an outspoken advocate of popular rule and the rights of the individual. He was one of the leaders in the fight to add the Bill of Rights to the U.S. Constitution.
- While serving as our third President, Jefferson helped define the responsibilities of the Federal government as separate from those of the state and local governments.
- Jefferson died on July 4, 1826, the 50th anniversary of the Declaration of Independence.

Helping His Community

The almanac sold so many copies that soon Ben Franklin was a rich man. He didn't have to work as much as he used to. Franklin decided to spend his time doing things he loved, including helping Philadelphia and the colonies. Look at the chart on this page to learn about some of his many great ideas.

The Inventions of BEN FRANKLIN

The first lending library in the colonies was started by Franklin.

Franklin did many experiments with electricity. To save buildings from fires, he invented lightning rods, which conduct lightning straight into the ground.

The Franklin stove used much less wood and gave off more heat than fireplaces.

Franklin helped organize Philadelphia's first volunteer fire department. Volunteers carried leather pails to help fight fires.

Franklin created bifocal glasses to help people see close-up, for reading, as well as at a distance.

Thinking About Helping His Community Have students look at the pictures and read the captions aloud. Point out that the lightning rod was the result of Franklin's famous kite experiment, which is discussed in *Curriculum Connections, Links to Science,* on p. 45.

Suggested Questions

- *Which of Franklin's inventions demonstrates his saying that "An ounce of prevention is worth a pound of cure"?* (the lightning rod)

- *Which invention was used to keep houses warm?* (the Franklin stove)

- *Why are bifocal glasses useful?* (They help people see close up and at a distance.)

- *How did Franklin help people share his love of books?* (He started the first lending library.)

- *How did he use the power of teamwork to help Philadelphia?* (He organized the city's first volunteer fire department.)

- *Which of his inventions are still used by people in your community today?* (bifocal glasses, lightning rods)

★**THINKING FURTHER:** *Making Conclusions* **Ben Franklin never took money for his inventions. He wanted people to use them for free. What does that tell you about the kind of person he probably was?** (He was probably a generous man, more interested in helping people than in acquiring wealth.)

Curriculum CONNECTION

LINKS TO SCIENCE Tell students that Ben Franklin began inventing things as a child. One early invention was a swimming aid: paddles attached to the arms and legs.

Invite students to work in groups to make inventions of their own. They can follow these steps:

- Look around your community. What invention could help people at work or play? Make a list of ideas.
- Choose one idea and talk about how to make it. Draw up a plan and a list of materials.
- Make a model of your invention. Test it to make sure it works. Then share your invention with your class.

Background INFORMATION

FRANKLIN THE STATESMAN Benjamin Franklin was a major political figure in Revolutionary times. Provide the following information as students read p. 150.

- In 1766 Franklin appeared before the British Parliament to protest the Stamp Act, which imposed *taxes* the colonists considered unjust. The act was repealed, but "taxation without representation" continued to be a major reason for colonial dissent.
- Franklin offered to pay for the tea destroyed in the Boston Tea Party if the British would repeal the tax on tea, but his offer was ignored.
- During the Revolution Franklin convinced France to aid the colonies. Many historians believe that without that help, America would have lost the war.

Discussing Fighting for Freedom

Have students look at the pictures. The painting shows Thomas Jefferson (in the red waistcoat) presenting the Declaration of Independence to John Hancock, president of the Continental Congress. Tell students that the original Declaration is on display, along with the Constitution, in the National Archives in Washington, D.C.

Suggested Questions

- **What kinds of problems did the colonies have with England?** *(They wanted to make their own laws. They didn't want to pay taxes to England. They wanted their own government.)*

- **When did the American Revolution begin? What did the colonies want?** *(1775; independence)*

- **Why did the leaders of the colonies meet in 1776?** *(to work together to win the war)*

- **What is the Declaration of Independence? Who wrote it?** *(a statement about why the colonies should be free; Thomas Jefferson)*

- **What happened on July 4, 1776?** *(The Declaration of Independence was adopted.)*

- ★**THINKING FURTHER:** *Making Decisions* **Suppose you were deciding where the colonial leaders should meet in 1776. What city would you choose? Why?** *(Students might decide Philadelphia was a good choice; it was the largest colonial city and centrally located within the 13 colonies.)*

Fighting for Freedom

In Franklin's time the colonies grew and began to have problems with their English rulers. The colonists felt that they should make their own laws. They did not want to pay taxes to the English government. A tax is money that people pay to support the government. By the 1770s many colonists wanted to have their own government.

In 1775 the American Revolution broke out. Fighting began between the colonists and the English. The colonies wanted independence, or to be a free country.

It was the summer of 1776. The leaders of the colonies met in Philadelphia to work together to win the war. Ben Franklin was there. His wise advice and experience were highly valued. Thomas Jefferson from Virginia was also there. Jefferson wrote a statement about why the colonies should be free. It was called the Declaration of Independence. On July 4, 1776, the leaders all agreed to adopt it.

The artist John Trumbull painted *The Declaration of Independence, 4 July 1776* (bottom).

150

The United States of America

Most Americans were happy about the Declaration of Independence. But the real celebration could not take place yet. Freedom had not yet been won. People from every colony marched off to war against the English. Many battles were fought. Many lives were lost. Finally, in 1781, America won its independence. The 13 colonies were now the states of a new country, the United States of America.

WHY IT MATTERS

Philadelphia was an important city during the American Revolution. Ben Franklin worked to help his city and all the colonies. On July 4, 1776, Ben Franklin was one of 56 leaders to adopt the Declaration of Independence. This date is still important to us today. It is the birthday of our country.

In 1776, the Liberty Bell rang to celebrate the adoption of the Declaration of Independence.

✓✓ Reviewing Facts and Ideas

SUM IT UP

- Ben Franklin arrived in Philadelphia in 1723. He did many things to help the city.
- Starting in 1775 the American Revolution was fought to free the colonies from England. The colonies wanted to make their own laws and to stop paying taxes to England.
- On July 4, 1776, the Declaration of Independence was adopted.
- In 1781 the American Revolution ended.

THINK ABOUT IT

1. Why did the colonies fight against England?
2. **FOCUS** How did Ben Franklin make a difference in Philadelphia?
3. **THINKING SKILL** _Predict_ what might have happened if the American colonies had lost the American Revolution.
4. **WRITE** Suppose that you are writing your own almanac. Write two sayings that would be helpful to people today.

151

Thinking About The United States of America Reinforce the main points of this section.

Suggested Questions

- **Who fought in the Revolutionary War?** (People from every colony fought the English.)

- **When did the war end?** (1781)

- ★**THINKING FURTHER:** _Cause and Effect_ **What was the cause of the American Revolution? What was the effect?** (The colonies were unhappy with English rule and wanted independence; they attained independence and formed the United States of America.)

Discussing WHY IT MATTERS Be sure students understand Philadelphia's role in the birth of our country.

Suggested Questions

- **Why was Philadelphia an important city during the Revolution?** (Colonial leaders met there to work together to win the war. The Declaration of Independence was signed there.)

⭐ 3 CLOSE

SUM IT UP

Have students answer these questions.

Suggested Questions

- **What was the American Revolution?** (a war for independence between the colonies and England, which resulted in the birth of the United States)

- **Why was the Declaration of Independence important to the colonies?** (It unified them and explained why they should be free.)

EVALUATE
✓ **Answers to Think About It**

1. They wanted independence.
2. Possible answers: He organized a fire department and lending library; he invented the Franklin stove, the lightning rod, and bifocal glasses.
3. We might be British citizens today.
4. Have students use Franklin's sayings as models for their own.

Write About It Ask students to write a paragraph explaining why we celebrate the Fourth of July each year.

Meeting _Individual_ Needs

RETEACHING (Easy) Have students draw pictures illustrating Ben Franklin's contributions to his community and country.

EXTENSION (Average) Have students do research to make a landmark map of Philadelphia, using the CD-ROM if possible. Ask them to include a key that explains the significance of each historic site.

ENRICHMENT (Challenging) Divide the class into research and writing groups to make a newspaper for July 4, 1776. Tell students to include feature articles about the main event of the day, summaries of what led up to that historic event, and editorials predicting the consequences.

LEGACY

Lesson Overview

Our flag is a symbol of our country.

Lesson Objective

★ Understand that the flag is a legacy from our country's past that will live on in the future.

1 PREPARE

MOTIVATE Remind students that they learned about map symbols on pp. G6–G7. Then explain that in this lesson they will learn about another kind of symbol—one that represents our country.

SET PURPOSE Write these headings on the chalkboard: *What I Know; What I Want to Know; What I Learned.* Then ask children what they know about the American flag and what they want to know about it. Write their responses on the board in the appropriate columns. Tell students that they will fill in the last column at the end of this lesson.

2 TEACH

Understanding the Concept of a Legacy Explain that the "Stars and Stripes" has been a symbol of freedom to Americans since Revolutionary times.

Examining the Pictures Have students look at the pictures.

Suggested Questions

● **What does the American flag symbolize?** *(our country's land, people, history, and hopes)*

● **The flag on the moon is metal. Why do you think metal was used instead of cloth?** *(Metal is more durable than cloth.)*

Legacy

LINKING PAST AND PRESENT

Our Country's Flag

What is red, white, and blue and has been waving in our country since the American Revolution? It is "Old Glory," our country's flag.

Before 1777 each colony had its own flag. But the colonies came under one flag when they became the United States of America.

The legacy of our "Stars and Stripes" celebrates the land, people, and history of the United States. It is a symbol of the past and future hopes of our country.

As you look at the legacy of our flag, see how it has stayed the same and changed.

In 1969 our "Stars and Stripes" waved far away on the moon.

152

Background INFORMATION

MORE ABOUT OUR COUNTRY'S FLAG

● The design for the original "Stars and Stripes" was adopted by the First Continental Congress on June 14, 1777. Today we celebrate June 14 as Flag Day.

● The 13 stars and stripes on our first flag stood for the 13 colonies. In 1794 two more stars and stripes were added when Kentucky and Vermont joined the Union.

● By 1818 it was clear that the flag could not keep expanding with the growth of the nation. Congress decided to limit the number of stripes to 13 and to add a star for each new state that joined the Union.

● New stars are added to the flag on the Fourth of July that follows a state's admission to the Union. Today our flag has 50 stars. The 50th star was added in 1960 to mark Hawaii's entry into the Union.

The rattlesnake was a colonial symbol used in 1775.

Betsy Ross is said to have made our first flag. Today a copy of that flag, with 13 stars and 13 stripes, is flown outside the Betsy Ross House in Philadelphia.

153

- **Look at the picture of the colonial flag in 1775. Below the snake is a motto: "Don't tread [step] on me." What do you think the snake represents? What do you suppose the motto means?** (The snake represents danger; the motto is a warning. Together they convey the idea that if provoked, the colony will strike back.)

- **A sign on Betsy Ross's house says "Birthplace of Old Glory." To what does "Old Glory" refer?** (It refers to the American flag. At this point, you may wish to note that we do not know if Betsy Ross really made our first official flag. But we do know that she was making flags for the government as early as May 1777.)

⭐ 3 CLOSE

SUM IT UP

Have students sum up the lesson by filling in the *What I Learned* column on the chalkboard.

EVALUATE

Write About It Have students write a paragraph explaining why our flag is a legacy that we should respect.

Technology CONNECTION

ADVENTURES CD-ROM
Enrich the lesson with the CD-ROM activity *It's a Grand Old Flag.*

⭐CITIZENSHIP

HONORING THE FLAG Tell students that the United States has a flag code, which gives the basic rules for honoring our flag. Then divide the class into groups to research and report on the proper procedures for displaying, folding, saluting, and caring for the flag.

Curriculum CONNECTION

LINKS TO READING It is said that Betsy Ross not only made our first flag, but also convinced George Washington that the stars should have five points rather than six because she could make them with one snip of the scissors. Students can read the whole story in *A Flag for Our Country* by Eve Spencer (Steck-Vaughn, 1993).

MEETING *Individual* NEEDS

RETEACHING (Easy) Have students draw a picture of their state flag and write a caption explaining what it symbolizes.

EXTENSION (Average) Have students research and report on the symbol of our country's independence: the Great Seal of the United States.

ENRICHMENT (Challenging) Have students make a flag for their community that includes symbols of its past, present, and future.

LESSON 2
PAGES 154-159

Lesson Overview
George Washington led our country during its formative years.

Lesson Objectives
★ Understand the role of George Washington in U.S. history.

★ Appreciate the significance of the *Constitution.*

★ Describe the three branches of the national government.

★ 1 PREPARE

MOTIVATE Ask students if they recognize the man in the picture and invite them to share what they know about George Washington. Then have one volunteer read the *Read Aloud* and another the *Read to Learn* question. Encourage speculation about why people looked to Washington to help bring the country together.

SET PURPOSE Tell students that in this lesson they will discover why George Washington is known as the "Father of Our Country." Then direct attention to the *Vocabulary* words and remind students to watch for them as they read.

★ 2 TEACH

Discussing Meet George Washington Tell students that the army leader quoted in this section is General "Lighthorse" Harry Lee, who served with Washington during the Revolution.

Suggested Questions

● **Why was George Washington a hero to the American people?** *(He led the Revolutionary army to victory.)*

● **Why did Washington refuse to be king?** *(He thought the new country should have a leader chosen by the people. Also, he wanted to rest.)*

Resource REMINDER

Practice Book: *p. 34*

Anthology: *Washington the Great, p. 60; If You Were There When They Signed the Constitution, pp. 61–65*

Technology: *Videodisc/Video Tape 2*

Our First President

READ ALOUD
The American Revolution was over. A new country called the United States was born. But who would lead this country? What kind of government would it have? There was one person many hoped could help the states reach an agreement. That man was George Washington.

Meet George Washington

People had good reason to pin their hopes on George Washington. During the American Revolution, he led the whole army. The army did not have a lot of money or supplies. But Washington's courage and leadership helped win the war. Afterward, he was praised by many people. One army leader described him as ". . . first in war, first in peace, and first in the hearts of his countrymen."

Some people even thought Washington should be crowned the king of the new country. Washington said the new country should not have a king. It should have a leader chosen by the people. Besides, he did not want to be king. He just wanted to go to his home in Virginia when the war ended. "I will rest under my own vine and my own fig tree," he said.

Focus Activity

READ TO LEARN
How did George Washington help our country start a new government?

VOCABULARY
Constitution
elect
compromise
Congress
President
Supreme Court
Bill of Rights

PEOPLE
George Washington
James Madison

154

Reading STRATEGIES *and* Language DEVELOPMENT

SEQUENCING Explain that dates help us keep track of when important events took place in history. When students read *Sum It Up* on p. 159, have them note the dates that are mentioned. Then have them use those dates, plus what they learned in the lesson, to put the events in time-order sequence. *(Washington led the Army in the Revolution; the Constitution was written in 1787; Washington became President in 1789; the Bill of Rights was added to the Constitution in 1791; today our government is still based on the Constitution.)*

CAPITALIZATION Point out the capitalized words in the *Vocabulary* list. Explain that we use a capital letter when we refer to the President of the United States, a branch of government such as Congress, and historic documents such as the Constitution. When students read the lesson, have them find the following terms and explain why they are capitalized: Senate, House of Representatives, Supreme Court (p. 157); Bill of Rights (p. 159).

A Leader Is Needed

In 1787 the new country was facing new troubles. Many of the problems were about money. All the states were printing money to help pay the costs of the war. Each state had its own kind of money. The states started arguing with each other over these matters. They realized they needed a new government to make laws for printing money.

Leaders from the states decided to hold a meeting in Philadelphia. Their goal was to solve these problems. One of the leaders was George Washington. He was ill, but he knew he was needed once again to help his country.

George Washington and other leaders traveled to Philadelphia in 1787. At their meeting they discussed laws to help the country, including laws for making money.

Discussing A Leader Is Needed

Point out the pictures of the Massachusetts Pine Tree shilling, the first American coin, and the Rhode Island three-dollar banknote, issued by the state. Then explain that the painting shows George Washington with two colonial leaders from Virginia: Patrick Henry and Edmund Pendleton.

Suggested Questions

● **Why did all the states print money after the American Revolution?** *(to help pay the costs of the war)*

● **What did the leaders hope to accomplish in Philadelphia?** *(They hoped to solve the country's problems by forming a new government.)*

★**THINKING FURTHER:** *Making Conclusions* **Why was it a problem for different states to have different kinds of money?** *(Help students understand how difficult it would be to trade between states without a standard currency.)*

Technology CONNECTION

VIDEODISC/VIDEO TAPE 2
Enrich the lesson with the *Presidents' Day* segment.

Search Frame 53585

Background INFORMATION

NEW TROUBLES FOR A NEW NATION After their experience with British rule, Americans distrusted the idea of a strong central government. The new nation was governed under the Articles of Confederation, which set up a weak central government and let the states act independently.

● Congress had the authority to make laws and declare war but not to levy taxes. Without money to operate, Congress was virtually powerless.

● The states printed their own money, raised their own armies, and made their own laws. People could not get used to thinking of themselves as Americans. They put the interests of their states above the interests of the country. The result was chaos, with states arguing over trade, boundaries, and taxes.

Background INFORMATION

THE FATHER OF OUR COUNTRY With almost 20 years of public service, George Washington helped shape the nation we live in today.

● As commander of the Continental armies, Washington was a symbol of the fight for independence. He served without pay and emerged from the war a national hero.

● As president of the Constitutional Convention, he used his prestige to keep the meetings from breaking up during the four long months of debate.

● As the first President of the United States, he set precedents that became national policy in the years to come. His refusal to run for a third term established the "no third term" tradition that was broken only once, by Franklin Roosevelt in 1940.

U.S. Capitol Historical Society

Leaders came from each state to write the Constitution. James Madison (above) suggested a type of government with three different branches.

Writing the Constitution

The summer of 1787 was the hottest summer anyone in Philadelphia could remember. In spite of the heat, an important meeting was taking place to create a new government.

Imagine what it was like when the leaders met. The men wore wigs, long coats, ruffled shirts, and vests. Their pants came to their knees. Flies buzzed around and could bite right through their knee-high stockings.

Somehow none of that was important. The leaders were forming a new government. Their job was to write a Constitution. The Constitution states the laws and the plan for how the government of our country works.

One of the first things they did was to elect someone to lead the meeting. To elect is to choose by voting. George Washington was elected to be in charge.

156

A New Plan

Many leaders were at the meeting. Ben Franklin was there. So was James Madison. He spent the whole time taking careful notes. That's how we know what went on at the meeting.

Madison suggested a plan for three branches, or parts, of government. The leaders argued about the plan but worked out some compromises. A compromise is an agreement reached when each side gives up some demands.

When the Constitution was finally signed, Washington called it a miracle. Look at the chart below to see the three branches of our country's government.

Ben Franklin, over 80 years old, was carried to the meeting.

Our Country's National Government

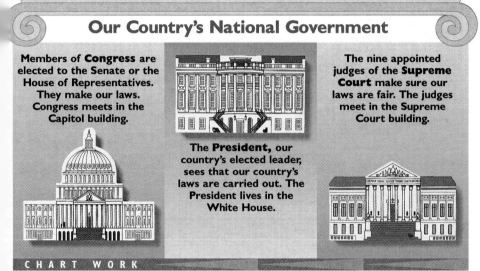

Members of **Congress** are elected to the Senate or the House of Representatives. They make our laws. Congress meets in the Capitol building.

The **President,** our country's elected leader, sees that our country's laws are carried out. The President lives in the White House.

The nine appointed judges of the **Supreme Court** make sure our laws are fair. The judges meet in the Supreme Court building.

CHART WORK

The Constitution describes the job of each branch of government.

1. What are the two parts of Congress?
2. Who is the leader of our country?
3. In what building does Congress meet? In what building does the President work?
4. How do you think the three branches work together?

CHART WORK: 1. House of Representatives, the Senate. 2. the President. 3. Capitol; White House 4. All three branches work together: Congress makes the laws, the Supreme Court makes sure the laws are fair, and the President makes sure the laws are enforced

157

Understanding A New Plan Help students understand that a government that represents people with different viewpoints must be able to compromise.

Suggested Questions

- ***What is a compromise?*** *(an agreement reached when each side gives up some demands)*
- ***What did the leaders argue about before they signed the Constitution? How did they settle their argument?*** *(Madison's plan for a three-part government; by compromising)*
- ***James Madison is called the "father of the Constitution." What are two things he did to earn that title?*** *(took notes at the meeting and proposed a government with three branches)*

★**THINKING FURTHER:** *Making Conclusions* ***Why did Washington call the signing of the Constitution a "miracle"?*** *(because many arguments had to be resolved before it was signed; because the nation finally had a plan for a working government)*

More CHART WORK

Be sure students understand that the plan of government set forth in the Constitution is the same plan we follow today.

Suggested Questions

★**THINKING FURTHER:** *Classifying* ***Which members of our government are elected? Which are appointed?*** *(Elected:* President, *members of Congress; appointed:* Supreme Court *justices. At this point, you may wish to explain that Supreme Court justices are appointed by the President but must be approved by the Senate.)*

CITIZENSHIP

LINKING PAST AND PRESENT As the supreme law of the land, the Constitution not only shapes U.S. history, it also reflects it.

- **AHEAD OF ITS TIME** The Constitution put into practice the ideals expressed in the Declaration of Independence. It was the first written constitution in history.
- **A PRODUCT OF ITS TIME** The Constitution created a government run by the people and for the people. But that government represented only one group of people—white male property owners. For many years, they were the only Americans who had the right to vote.

- **A LIVING DOCUMENT** The Constitution has survived for over 200 years because it is flexible enough to change with the times. Today, all citizens over the age of 18 have the right to vote. Constitutional amendments have changed our government from one that represented some of the people to one that represents all the people.

MAKING CONNECTIONS Work with students to write a constitution that reflects the rights and responsibilities of students and teachers in your school

Using the ANTHOLOGY

...IF YOU WERE THERE WHEN THEY SIGNED THE CONSTITUTION, pages 61–65 Students will explore issues considered during the Constitutional Convention.

Discussing Our First President
Point out Washington's signature at the bottom of the page. Then have students discuss the picture and the text.

Suggested Questions
- **What is the difference between a president and a king?** (A president is elected; a king usually inherits the title.)

- **Who was the first President of the United States?** (George Washington)

- **What evidence shows that people approved of their first President?** (They reelected him.)

★THINKING FURTHER: *Using Prior Knowledge* **Why do you think Washington chose Thomas Jefferson to help run the government?** (Students should remember that Jefferson wrote the Declaration of Independence.)

Extending Did You Know? Tell the class that all U.S. coins bear the Latin motto: *e pluribus unum,* meaning "out of many, one." Invite speculation about what the motto means. Then explain that it refers to the creation of our nation from the 13 colonies. Invite students to research other images and words that appear on our currency.

Have you seen these faces before?

Many of the leaders from our country's past are still honored. Just take a look at the money we use today. Do you recognize any of the faces on these bills and coins?*

Wherever George Washington traveled in the colonies, he was often greeted by large crowds of people.

Our First President

As you can see on the chart on page 157, the Constitution made the President the leader of our country. The President would be different than a king. The President would be elected.

In February 1789, George Washington was elected the first President of the United States. A few months later, he rode to New York City for a special ceremony to become the President. In every town and city he passed through, people surrounded his carriage and cheered. There were parades and celebrations at just about every stop. When he reached New York City, the crowds were so thick that it was hard for carriages to move.

One of Washington's most important jobs was to choose good leaders to help him. Thomas Jefferson was one of the leaders chosen to help run the government. After four years Washington was elected President again.

158

Background INFORMATION

MORE ABOUT OUR FIRST PRESIDENT
- The leaders Washington chose to help him came to be known as the President's Cabinet. The first Cabinet members were Secretary of State Thomas Jefferson, Secretary of the Treasury Alexander Hamilton, Secretary of War Henry Knox, and Attorney General Edmund Randolph.

- Washington wanted to retire after his first term, but his Cabinet members persuaded him to accept reelection. The country was not on its feet yet, they argued, and only Washington could keep it from collapsing.

- Washington stepped down from public life in 1797. He died two years later, at his home in Mount Vernon.

Curriculum CONNECTION

LINKS TO LANGUAGE ARTS After students read p. 159, explain that the Bill of Rights consists of the first ten amendments to the Constitution, which protect our basic rights and freedoms. They cannot be violated by the government, but they can be restricted under certain circumstances.

In 1919, the Supreme Court ruled that freedom of speech may be limited when exercising it creates a "clear and present danger to society." Ask students if they can think of such an instance. (Example: Yelling "Fire" in a crowded theater when there is no fire.) Then divide the class into teams to debate the issue.

Appoint nine students to act as Supreme Court justices. They will evaluate the arguments and render a verdict.

WHY IT MATTERS

George Washington was an important leader in our country's history. He led the American Army during the American Revolution. He also helped write the Constitution. The Constitution is very important to all Americans. It has the most important laws of our country. But people found that it was not enough. It did not protect all people's freedom and rights.

In 1791 the Bill of Rights was added to the Constitution. It lists our most important rights. These include the right to free speech and the right to practice religion freely.

Throughout the history of our country, other changes have been made to the Constitution. But the ideas written in the summer of 1787 still guide us today.

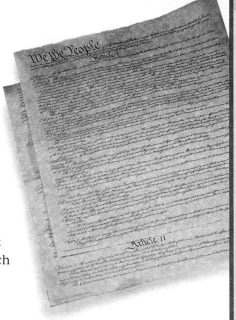

The Constitution and the Bill of Rights still guide our country.

✓// Reviewing Facts and Ideas

SUM IT UP

- George Washington led the American Army in the American Revolution. He became our country's first President in 1789.

- Leaders gathered in 1787 in Philadelphia to write the Constitution. James Madison took notes at the meeting.

- Today, the Constitution is still the plan for how our government works.

- The Bill of Rights was added to the Constitution in 1791.

THINK ABOUT IT

1. What problems did the new country have?

2. **FOCUS** How did George Washington help our country start a new government?

3. **THINKING SKILL** Suppose you had to form a government. How would you _decide_ how to make laws? What would your new government be like?

4. **WRITE** Many people consider George Washington a hero. Write a paragraph about how he might be a hero to you.

159

Second-Language **Support**

DRAMATIZATION Dramatizing scenes from history can benefit second-language students. Create short skits of lesson events and have students present them to small groups and then the entire class.

Meeting _Individual_ Needs

RETEACHING (Easy) Tell students that Washington's birthday has been celebrated in the U.S. since Revolutionary times. Ask them to write a speech that would be suitable for one of those celebrations.

EXTENSION (Average) Have students make a chart with the names of the President, the Senators and Representatives from their state, and the nine Supreme Court justices.

ENRICHMENT (Challenging) Have students research, write, and act out a skit in which the following people explain their decision to sign the Constitution: George Washington, Benjamin Franklin, James Madison.

Understanding WHY IT MATTERS
Review the contributions George Washington made to the United States. Point out that the _Bill of Rights_ was passed during his first administration.

Suggested Questions

- _**What are three ways in which George Washington helped his country?**_ _(He led the army to victory in the Revolution, helped write the Constitution, and served two terms as President.)_

- ★**THINKING FURTHER:** _Making Conclusions_ _**Why is the Bill of Rights an important part of our Constitution?**_ _(It protects our basic rights and freedoms.)_

⭐ 3 CLOSE

SUM IT UP
Have students answer these questions.

Suggested Questions

- _**Why do we celebrate George Washington's birthday today?**_ _(He was our first President.)_

- _**What did our nation's leaders accomplish in Philadelphia during the summer of 1787?**_ _(They agreed on a plan for a new government and stated that plan in the Constitution.)_

- _**Which part of the Constitution protects our freedom of speech and religion?**_ _(Bill of Rights)_

EVALUATE
✓ **Answers to Think About It**

1. The states were printing their own money. They were arguing about finances and other matters.

2. He led the meeting at which the Constitution was written. He was the first President of the United States.

3. Students should identify alternatives and predict consequences before making their decisions.

4. Students should cite Washington's contributions to his country.

Write About It Have students read "Washington the Great" on p. 60 of the _Anthology,_ and listen to it on the _Anthology Cassette._ Then have them work in groups to make up new verses to the song.

Lesson Overview
When we *compare* and *contrast,* we see how things are alike and different.

Lesson Objective
★ Compare and contrast items.

1 PREPARE

MOTIVATE Display a dictionary and an atlas. Ask students how they are alike and different. Write their responses on the chalkboard under the headings *Alike* and *Different.* Then tell students that they have just compared and contrasted two items. Write *Compare* and *Contrast* beside the appropriate headings on the board.

SET PURPOSE Tell students that in this lesson they will practice comparing and contrasting items. In the process, they will discover why this skill is useful.

DISCUSSING HELPING YOURSELF Direct students to the *Helping Yourself* box on page 161. Have volunteers read it aloud.

2 TEACH

Why the Skill Matters Explain that comparing and contrasting can help us understand information and make decisions. Then have students read the text.

Using the Skill As students read the text, help them recall what they learned about the Declaration of Independence and the Constitution.

Suggested Questions

● **What is one thing the Declaration of Independence and the Constitution have in common?** *(Both were written in Philadelphia.)*

● **Contrast the purpose of the Declaration of Indendence with the purpose of the Constitution.** *(Declaration: to state independence; Constitution: to set up the new government's laws and plans)*

Resource REMINDER

Practice Book: *p. 35*
Transparency: *Graphic Organizer*

THINKINGSKILLS

Comparing and Contrasting

VOCABULARY
compare
contrast

WHY THE SKILL MATTERS

You have just learned about two very important documents in the history of our country, the Declaration of Independence and the Constitution. A document is a written statement that gives information about something. Suppose you wanted to better understand both documents. To do this you might want to compare and contrast them.

To compare things is to see how they are alike. To contrast things is to see how they are different. Comparing and contrasting can help you decide how the Declaration of Independence and the Constitution are important to the history of the United States.

USING THE SKILL

In comparing and contrasting these two documents, your first step might be to think about the Declaration of Independence. You know it was written in 1776. Then think about the Constitution. It was written in 1787, 11 years later. That's one difference. People gathered to write the Declaration of Independence in Philadelphia. They also gathered to write the Constitution in Philadelphia. That's one thing the documents have in common.

The Declaration was written during the American Revolution to simply state the goal of independence. The

The Granger Collection

Field Trip

Take students on a field trip to a local historical society or government building and encourage them to compare and contrast some of the historical paintings. Have students describe what these paintings tell about the history and culture of the area.

As an alternative, display a painting of our first President and a photograph of our current President. Have students work in groups to compare and contrast the two illustrations.

Constitution was written after the Revolution was over, to set up the laws and plan for the new government. That's another way they are different. Each document was written for a different purpose.

TRYING THE SKILL

When our country was being formed, people did not have cameras. But we can get an idea of the way people looked from paintings and notes. Look at the two paintings

The Granger Collection

HELPING Yourself

- To **compare** is to see how things are alike. To **contrast** is to see how they are different.
- Choose one piece of information about the first thing. Then check the second thing for the same information. Is it alike or different?

of Thomas Jefferson. Use your new skill to compare and contrast the paintings. You can use the Helping Yourself box for some tips as you try this skill.

What should you do first? You could look at the clothes Jefferson is wearing in each painting. How are his clothes alike? How are they different? How else can you compare and contrast the two paintings?*

REVIEWING THE SKILL

1. What did you do to compare and contrast the two pictures?

2. What is the difference between comparing and contrasting?

3. Look at the chart of the three branches of government on page 157. How are the President and the Supreme Court alike? How are they different? How do you know?

4. When is it helpful to compare and contrast? Why?

*Both outfits are black with a white shirt; his shoes and neckpiece are different; compare his position, hair color, age, and the activity he is doing.

Trying the Skill Have students refer to the *Helping Yourself* box as they work. Tell them to look carefully at both pictures when choosing points to compare and contrast.

Suggested Questions

- ***Look carefully at both pictures. What can you find to compare and contrast aside from Thomas Jefferson?** (Students could compare and contrast details about the rooms, furnishings, and so on.)*

⭐ 3 CLOSE

SUM IT UP

Have students explain how to compare and contrast items.

EVALUATE
✓ **Answers to Reviewing the Skill**

1. First, looked at the first picture, chose one feature, looked at the other picture to see if the same feature was present; continued to repeat this procedure, each time noting similarities and differences.

2. Comparing means to show how things are alike; contrasting means to show how they are different.

3. *Alike:* Both are parts of our national government. *Different:* The President is elected; Supreme Court judges are appointed. There is one President; there are nine judges. The President sees that our country's laws are carried out; the Supreme Court makes sure they are fair. We know how the President and Supreme Court are alike and different by comparing and contrasting.

4. when we need to evaluate information; when we need to understand the significance of information

---

Background INFORMATION

USING THE GRAPHIC ORGANIZER You may want to have students work with this Graphic Organizer transparency to help them organize their information.

Discussing Major Events Ask questions about the time line to help students understand the cause and effect relationship between events

Suggested Questions

- *What happened in 1723?* (Ben Franklin moved to Philadelphia.)

- *What happened in 1775? How did events in 1781 change America?* (In 1775, the American Revolution began, and in 1781, Americans won their independence from England.)

- *Why did people want to write a constitution for the new United States? What events had happened that led to writing this document?* (They had become unhappy with the English government, they fought a war for independence and won it, and they needed to decide on their own form of government.)

Answers to
THINKING ABOUT VOCABULARY

1. In the American Revolution, colonists fought for their independence from England.

2. People vote to elect government representatives.

3. The Bill of Rights was added to the Constitution to protect important rights of all American citizens.

4. The first President of our country was George Washington.

5. The best way to settle an argument is to make a compromise.

6. The Declaration of Independence told England that colonists had decided to form a new country.

Resource **REMINDER**

Assessment Book: *Chapter 6 Test*

CHAPTER 6 REVIEW

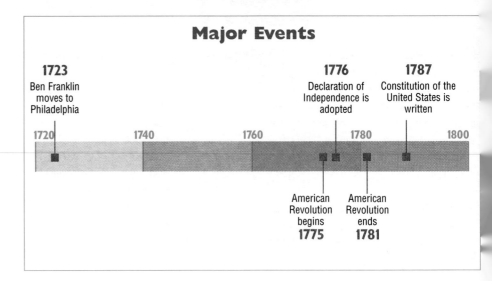

Major Events

1723	1776	1787
Ben Franklin moves to Philadelphia	Declaration of Independence is adopted	Constitution of the United States is written

1720   1740   1760   1780   1800

American Revolution begins **1775** American Revolution ends **1781**

THINKING ABOUT VOCABULARY

Number a sheet of paper from 1 to 10. For each word listed below, write a sentence using the word correctly. The sentence should show that you know what the word means.

American Revolution   elect
Bill of Rights   President
compromise   Supreme Court
Congress   tax
Constitution
Declaration of Independence

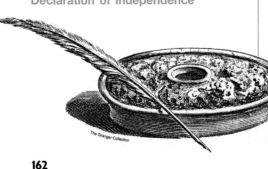

The Granger Collection

162

THINKING ABOUT FACTS

1. What are some of the things for which Benjamin Franklin is remembered?

2. What is the Declaration of Independence? Who wrote it? When was it adopted?

3. In what year did the American Revolution begin? How long did it last?

4. What important things did George Washington do for our country? Which do you think was his greatest achievement?

5. Into what three different parts does the Constitution divide our government? Name another document important to our freedom. Tell what it does.

Suggestions for **Think and Write**
SIGNS OF SUCCESS

WRITING A NEWSPAPER STORY Newspaper articles should convey the excitement over the beginning of our country. Students should know that the Constitution was written at the Constitutional Convention during a hot summer in 1787. Leaders from every state were present, including Ben Franklin, James Madison, and George Washington. The new government had three branches, the Congress, the President, and the Supreme Court.

WRITING AN INTERVIEW Students should ask and answer questions about relations with England, the Declaration of Independence, the Revolutionary War, and the Constitution.

WRITING ABOUT A LEGACY Legacies students might choose include: The Constitution and our government; the original thirteen states; the flag; the national anthem; an important historical building or site.

For performance assessment, see Assessment Book, Chapter 6.

THINK AND WRITE

WRITING A NEWSPAPER STORY

Write a newspaper article about the creation of the Constitution. Discuss the meetings, the leaders involved, the disagreements that took place, and how Americans reacted to it.

WRITING AN INTERVIEW

Choose a person from this chapter to interview about the beginning of our country. Write the interview. Include your questions and the answers you think your subject may have given.

WRITING ABOUT A LEGACY

A legacy is something that we value in our lives today that is also a valued part of our past. Our flag is one example of a legacy. Write two paragraphs describing something that you consider to be a legacy.

APPLYING THINKING SKILLS

COMPARING AND CONTRASTING

Answer the following questions to practice the skill of comparing and contrasting.

1. What does it mean to compare and contrast two things?

2. How were Thomas Jefferson and George Washington alike? How were they different?

3. Compare and contrast the pictures of Benjamin Franklin on pages 147 and 157.

4. Compare and contrast the flags on pages 152 and 153. How has our flag changed?

5. What kinds of things might you want to compare and contrast?

Summing Up the Chapter

Review the chapter and then fill in a copy of the word map below. For each document, list the year it was written, its purpose, and any other important information. Then compare and contrast these documents.

Documents of the United States

Declaration of Independence	Constitution	Bill of Rights
written by Thomas Jefferson in 1776 in Philadelphia; adopted on July 4,1776; declared why the colonies should be free	laws and plan for how the government of our country works; written in 1787; George Washington led the meeting	added to the Constitution in 1791; list of our rights and freedoms

163

Suggestions for **Summing Up the Chapter**

- Prepare copies of the diagram for the class or help students draw their own diagrams.
- Ask students to complete the diagram by finding information about each topic. Tell them to list the author, purpose, and date of each document. Suggested answers are annotated in red.
- Invite the entire class to compare and contrast the documents. Have volunteers explain why our country's leaders felt each document was needed at the specific time it was written. Ask them also to tell why each document is important for all Americans today.

---

7. The English collected a tax on goods shipped from America.

8. The Constitution describes how our government works.

9. The Congress is a group of people who help make our laws.

10. The Supreme Court decides whether new laws follow the rules of the Constitution.

Answers to THINKING ABOUT FACTS

1. He helped write the Constitution; he invented the Franklin stove; he discovered that lightning was electricity; he wrote and published an almanac that gave helpful advice.

2. It is a paper that states that the colonists no longer want to be ruled by England; Thomas Jefferson wrote it; July 4, 1776.

3. 1775; six years

4. He led the colonial army to victory against England; he helped write the Constitution; he was our first President.

5. the President, the Supreme Court, and Congress; the Bill of Rights; it guarantees rights such as freedom of speech and religion.

Answers to APPLYING THINKING SKILLS

1. to tell how they are different and alike

2. They were both early leaders of our country. They both helped write the Constitution. Thomas Jefferson was a gentleman, an architect and inventor. He wrote the Declaration of Independence. George Washington was a farmer and a military man. He was our first president.

3. Both pictures show Franklin. The first shows him as a young man, standing; the second shows him at age 80, seated.

4. The original flag had thirteen stars and thirteen stripes to represent the thirteen states. The number of stars on the flag has changed to 50. Each star represents a present-day state in the union.

5. When students compare and contrast, be sure they describe at least one similarity and one difference.

Countries Have Capitals
PAGES 164–183

CHAPTER OVERVIEW

Washington, D.C., is the capital of the United States of America and the center of the national government. Planning and building the capital was one of the government's first jobs. The buildings in the capital belong to everyone in the United States.

CHAPTER PLANNING GUIDE
Suggested pacing: 9–11 days

LESSON	LESSON FOCUS	LESSON RESOURCES
1 A CAPITAL FOR THE U.S.A. pages 166–169	The Creation of Washington, D.C.	*Practice Book* p. 37 *Anthology* pp. 66–70 *Technology:* Videodisc/Video Tape, CD-ROM *Desk Maps* United States
2 OUR NATION'S CAPITAL TODAY pages 170–175	A City of Museums and Monuments	*Practice Book* p. 38 *Anthology* pp. 76–77
Infographic pages 172–173	A Capital to Remember	*Technology: Adventures* CD-ROM
GEOGRAPHY SKILLS pages 176–177	Reading Grid Maps	*Practice Book* p. 39 *Transparency:* 9 *Technology:* Videodisc/Video Tape *Outline Map* p. 14
GLOBAL CONNECTIONS pages 178–181	A Capital in Senegal	*Practice Book* p. 40 *Technology: Adventures* CD-ROM *Geo Big Book* pp. R6–R7
CHAPTER REVIEW pages 182–183	Students' understanding of vocabulary, content, and skills is assessed.	*Assessment:* Ch. 7 Test, Performance Assessment Ch. 7 *Transparency:* Graphic Organizer

OPTIONS FOR STUDENT ACTIVITIES

Citizenship pp. 168, 174, 179

Curriculum Connection pp. 174, 180

Expanding the *Infographic* p. 173

Using the Anthology pp. 168, 174

ASSESSMENT OPPORTUNITIES

Meeting Individual Needs pp. 165, 169, 175, 177, 181

Write About It pp. 169, 175, 181

Chapter Review pp. 182–183

Assessment Book

Chapter Test Ch. 7 Test

Performance Assessment Ch. 7

Using the Floor Map Use the Floor Map and the Project Book with Lesson 1 by inviting students to imagine that the floor map is a "country" and that they must decide where the country's capital should be built.

Using Geo Adventures Use **Geo Adventures** Daily Geography Activities to assess students' understanding of geography skills.

Using the Vocabulary Cards The vocabulary words for each lesson are available on *Vocabulary Cards* for review and practice.

GETTING READY FOR THE CHAPTER

Lead a Tour GROUP 30 MINUTES OR LONGER

Objective: To introduce students to the purpose and history of our country's capital.

Materials: *Project Book* p. 15, crayons, markers

1. Have students work in small groups. Choose one student in each group to be the recorder.
2. Tell students that each group will plan a tour of important public places in their community. Discuss that public places are places that all the people who live in the community can use and enjoy. Some examples are schools, libraries, post offices, and parks.
3. As groups discuss places they might include on their tours, have the recorder list the ideas.
4. Have group members review the list. Then let each choose one place to describe, using Project Book p. 15.
5. Encourage each group to decide in which order to present the places they described. They can then "lead" their tours by presenting the information to the class.

> ### SECOND-LANGUAGE SUPPORT
> Second-language learners may benefit from working with an English-proficient peer during part or all of this activity.
>
> Additional Second-Language Support Tips: pp. 168, 170

Introducing the Chapter

Invite students to share what they know about Washington, D.C. Remind them that rural areas often grow into urban centers and explain that Washington, D.C. was once a rural area near the Potomac River.

THINKING ABOUT GEOGRAPHY AND HISTORY

Help students understand the relationship between this time line and the one for Chapter 6. Then have them locate Washington, D.C., on the map. Explain that in this chapter they will discover how it became our nation's capital.

1791

Suggested Questions

● **When and how did Benjamin Banneker help his country?** *(In 1791, he helped complete plans for the new capital.)*

★**THINKING FURTHER:** *Making Conclusions* **Why do you think our country's leaders decided to build a new capital city?** *(Accept any reasonable answers.)*

Resource REMINDER

 Technology: *Videodisc/Video Tape 2*

Countries Have Capitals

THINKING ABOUT GEOGRAPHY AND HISTORY

Washington, D.C., is our country's capital. It is the center of our national government. In Chapter 7 you will learn about the beginnings of our capital city. Choosing its location and building it were among the first jobs of the United States government.

Today our capital has memorials and buildings that belong to everybody in the United States. As you will see, these structures honor important people and events in our country's history.

1791

Benjamin Banneker helps complete plans for the new capital city

1800

John and Abigail Adams move into the White House

164

Background INFORMATION

ABOUT THE TIME LINE

● The picture shows Benjamin Banneker using a surveying device. He was an assistant to Andrew Ellicott, the surveyor who laid out the boundaries of Washington, D.C. Banneker was recommended for the job by Secretary of State Thomas Jefferson. In addition to being a surveyor, Banneker was a mathematician, astronomer, and farmer.

● John Adams was our second president. His wife, Abigail Adams, urged her husband to support the rights of women, who could not vote, hold public office, or attend college in those times.

● The Lincoln Memorial is a white marble structure that was built in the 1920s. The great hall inside is surrounded by 36 Doric columns, representing the 36 states in the Union when Lincoln died.

The Smithsonian Institution in Washington, D.C., is the largest, most famous museum in the U.S.

Washington, D.C.

TODAY

Many people visit the monuments and museums of Washington, D.C.

165

Suggested Questions

● **Who was President in 1800? How do you know?** *(John Adams was President. Students should know that the President lives in the White House.)*

★**THINKING FURTHER:** *Sequence* **What happened between the years of 1791 and 1800?** *(The White House was built.)*

Suggested Questions

● **What can people do in Washington, D.C., today that they could not do in 1791?** *(They can visit monuments and museums.)*

● **What do you think you might find in a museum in Washington, D.C.?** *(Possible answers include historical records and documents, items from Presidents' lives, and early American flags. Invite students who have been to Washington, D.C., to share their experiences.)*

 Technology CONNECTION

VIDEODISC/VIDEO TAPE 2
Enrich Chapter 7 with the Videodisc *map* and *glossary* segments.

Search Frame 53777

Meeting *Individual* Needs

RETEACHING (Easy) Have students explain how Washington, D.C., was named. Ask students to list reasons for honoring George Washington.

EXTENSION (Average) Ask students to write a dialog between two early U.S. leaders. In the dialog, leaders can discuss why a new capital city is needed, where it might be, and what kinds of buildings it might need. Tell students to base their dialog on what they have already learned.

ENRICHMENT (Challenging) Have students research the memorials and monuments shown in the *Infographic* on pages 172 to 173. Ask them to make a time line illustrating the structures and telling when they were built.

LESSON 1

Lesson Overview

Many people helped make Washington, D.C., our nation's permanent *capital*.

Lesson Objectives

★ Understand how Washington, D.C., became our nation's capital.

★ Identify the people who built our capital.

★ Describe life in Washington, D.C., in 1800.

1 PREPARE

MOTIVATE Read the *Read Aloud*. Have students name its source by reading the first paragraph under "A Capital Is Needed." Next direct attention to the *Vocabulary* word and have students read the second paragraph to find its meaning.

SET PURPOSE Have students turn to the *Infographic* on p. 106. Remind them that the 13 colonies became our country's first states. Then direct students to the *Read to Learn* question. Explain that they will discover the answer when they read the lesson.

2 TEACH

Discussing A Capital Is Needed

Call attention to the picture of the White House under construction. If necessary, explain that the White House is the place where the President lives and works.

Suggested Questions

● **Who was John Adams?** *(the second President of the United States and the first to live in the White House)*

● **What is a capital?** *(the place where the government of a country or state is located)*

● **Why did our nation's leaders have trouble deciding where to build the capital?** *(They argued about whether it should be in the North or the South.)*

Resource REMINDER

Practice Book: *p. 37*

Anthology: *What Are You Figuring Now?, pp. 66–70*

Technology: *Videodisc/Video Tape 2; Adventures CD-ROM*

Desk Maps: *United States*

BUILDING THE FIRST WHITE HOUSE

White House Historical Association

WASHINGTON D.C. 1798

A Capital for the U.S.A.

Focus Activity

READ TO LEARN

Who helped to build our country's capital?

VOCABULARY

capital

PEOPLE

John Adams
Abigail Adams
Pierre L'Enfant
Benjamin Banneker

PLACES

White House
Washington, D.C.

READ ALOUD

"I pray heaven to bestow [give] the best of blessings on this house and on all that shall hereafter inhabit [live in] it. May none but honest and wise men ever rule under this roof."

A Capital Is Needed

The words above were written by President John Adams in 1800. They were written in a letter to his wife, Abigail, the day after he moved into the White House. John Adams was the second President of the United States and the first President to live in the White House.

Just a few years earlier, the leaders of the United States had trouble deciding where to build a capital city for the new country. A capital is the place where the government of a country or state is located.

Thomas Jefferson, who was from the South, thought the capital should be in one of the southern states. Leaders from the North thought Boston or New York would be a good choice. Others thought Philadelphia should be the capital.

166

Reading STRATEGIES *and* Language DEVELOPMENT

MAIN IDEA Remind students that identifying the main idea of a paragraph can help us understand what it is about. Explain that the main idea may be stated directly, or it may be implied. In the first paragraph of p. 167, for example, the main idea is stated; in the *Primary Source* on p. 168, it is implied. After students read each passage, help them find its main idea. (P. 167: . . . its [the capital's] *location was a compromise*. P. 168: *Washington, D.C., was not what Abigail Adams had expected*.)

POSSESSIVES Write the following on the chalkboard: *Who helped to build the capital of our country?* Point out that the word *of* signifies possession: the capital belongs to our country. Explain that another way to show possession is by adding an apostrophe and an *s* to a singular noun. Then direct attention to the *Read to Learn* question. Have students note that it means the same as the quesion on the board but uses the possessive noun *country's* to show to whom the capital belongs.

Planning a City

In 1790 members of Congress agreed that the capital should not be in any one state. Instead, it should be separate and belong to all the people of the country. Look at this map to see where the new capital was to be. As you can see, its location was a compromise. The new capital was really in the middle of the northern and southern states of our country.

Thirteen
Original
States

Washington, D.C.

President Washington hired a French builder named Pierre L'Enfant (pee AIR lah FAHN) to draw up plans for the new capital.

L'Enfant came to America in 1777. He was in the army and fought for the colonists during the American Revolution. L'Enfant designed a grand city, with wide streets and magnificent buildings. But he didn't get along with other planners. He left in the middle of the planning. And he took his plans with him!

Here is our capital city long ago. The new streets and buildings were built on land that once was a forest.

Thinking About Planning a City

Review the definition of *compromise*, which students learned in *Chapter 6* (p. 157).

Suggested Questions

- ***Why did Congress decide that the capital should not be part of any state?*** *(to solve the arguments over which state it should be in; so it would belong to all the people)*

- ***Where did Congress decide the new capital should be? Why was that a compromise?*** *(in the middle of the northern and southern states; because neither the North nor the South could claim the capital)*

- ***How did Pierre L'Enfant help the American colonies?*** *(He fought in the Revolution.)*

- ***How did he help the United States?*** *(He planned the new capital.)*

- ***What problem did he cause the United States?*** *(He left in the middle of his work on the capital and took his plans with him.)*

Technology CONNECTION

VIDEODISC/VIDEO TAPE
Enrich the lesson with the *Washington, D.C.*, maps.

Search Frame 53696

167

Background INFORMATION

ABOUT JOHN ADAMS
- John Adams was one of the first colonial leaders to advocate independence from England. He was a signer of the Declaration of Independence and played a leading role in its adoption.
- Adams served as Vice President during both of Washington's terms. He became our second President in 1797.
- The White House was under construction during most of his Administration. He occupied it for only a few months at the end of his term.
- John Adams died in 1826, on the Fourth of July. He had lived to see his eldest son, John Quincy Adams, become the sixth President of the United States.

Background INFORMATION

ABOUT THE CAPITAL
- Congress made the decision to locate the new capital on the banks of the Potomac River. President Washington chose the exact site, and Maryland and Virginia donated the land.
- The White House was the first building to be occupied in Washington, D.C., but it was not finished when John and Abigail Adams moved in.
- The Presidential home was damp and drafty. Setting up house required ingenuity, and the First Lady rose to the challenge. When she needed a place for laundry, she solved the problem by using the East Room. It was better, she said, than having people see the President's wash hanging outside.

Life in the New Capital

Luckily, a man named Benjamin Banneker (BAN ih kur) had a good memory. Banneker had been one of L'Enfant's assistants. He had also worked hard on the plans for the new city. He sat down with other planners. Together they redrew L'Enfant's plans.

The new capital was named after George Washington. It was called Washington, D.C. The *D.C.* stands for District of Columbia.

The first building to be built in the new capital was the White House. In 1800 Abigail Adams was eager to start life in the new house. In her letters to her sister Mary, Abigail described life in the new capital. Read the letter below. What does it tell you about living in Washington, D.C., in 1800?

Benjamin Banneker was honored on a United States stamp.

MANY VOICES
PRIMARY SOURCE

Letter written by Abigail Adams in 1800.

My DEAR SISTER:

I expected to find it a new country, with scattered houses over a space of ten miles, and trees and stumps in plenty with a castle of a house. I found the President's House is in a beautiful situation in front of which is the Potomac [River]. . . . The country around is romantic but wild, a wilderness at present.

168

WHY IT MATTERS

Abigail Adams's letters give us a look into the past. If she could have looked into the future, she might have been very surprised. There have been many changes to the White House since she lived there. Every year has also brought other changes to our country's capital. In the next lesson you will look at Washington, D.C., today.

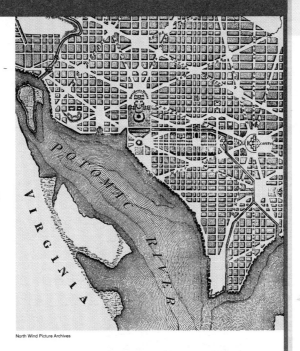

Early plans for Washington, D.C., included wide streets and open areas.

North Wind Picture Archives

Reviewing Facts and Ideas

SUM IT UP

- John Adams was the second President of the United States. In 1800 he and his wife Abigail became the first people to live in the newly built White House.

- The leaders of the country compromised and chose Washington, D.C., as the location for the capital. The new capital city would be in the middle of the country and would not be part of any one state.

- Pierre L'Enfant drew up the first plans for the capital. When he left in the middle of planning, Benjamin Banneker helped to redraw the plans.

THINK ABOUT IT

1. Why did people disagree about where the new capital should be? How did they compromise?

2. **FOCUS** Who helped to build our country's capital?

3. **THINKING SKILL** Suppose you had to choose a location for the United States capital today. Where should it be? How would you _decide_?

4. **GEOGRAPHY** Leaders chose to build the new city along the Potomac River. Most cities at that time were located on or near rivers. Why do you think that was so?

169

Meeting _Individual_ Needs

RETEACHING (Easy) Have students design a stamp to commemorate a person, place, or event that played a role in the birth of our nation. Students can draw their stamp and write a caption explaining their choice.

EXTENSION (Average) Have students expand what they have learned about the Key People in this lesson by doing library research and/or using the CD-ROM. Students can use their findings to make time lines of important events in the lives of the people they researched.

ENRICHMENT (Challenging) Have students use their _Desk Maps_ to identify and label the states that made up our country when Washington, D.C., became the capital. Direct them to label the capital city in red and write a short paragraph explaining why it was chosen.

Understanding WHY IT MATTERS

Tell students that the picture shows L'Enfant's original plans for the capital.

Suggested Questions

★**THINKING FURTHER: _Making Pre-dictions_ _What would Abigail Adams have seen if she could have looked into the future at Washington, D.C., today?_** (Answers should reflect the idea that she would have seen a busy modern city that is very different from the place where she lived.)

⭐ 3 CLOSE

SUM IT UP

Have students work with partners to answer the following questions.

Suggested Questions

- _**Who were the first people to live in the White House?**_ (John Adams, the second President of the United States, and his wife, Abigail)

- _**Why did the leaders of our country choose Washington, D.C., as the capital?**_ (It was a compromise that settled arguments about which state and region the capital should be in.)

- _**What did Pierre L'Enfant and Benjamin Banneker contribute to the United States?**_ (L'Enfant drew up the plans for the capital; Banneker helped put them into effect.)

EVALUATE
✓ **Answers to Think About It**

1. They wanted the capital to be in their state or region. They compromised on a location that was not in any state and was midway between the North and the South.

2. Pierre L'Enfant, Benjamin Banneker

3. Be sure students give reasons for their decisions.

4. Rivers facilitated transportation to, from, and within cities and afforded opportunities for trade. _Human/Environment Interaction_

Write About It Ask students to add a paragraph to Abigail Adams's letter, comparing life in the new capital with life in Philadelphia.

LESSON 2

Lesson Overview

In Washington, D.C., today, we can learn about our country's past and present.

Lesson Objectives

★ Compare and contrast Washington, D.C., in the past and present.

★ Describe places of interest in our nation's capital.

★ Appreciate what our capital city represents to people.

⭐ 1 PREPARE

MOTIVATE Tell the class that the picture shows the place where Congress meets. Then have students read the *Read Aloud*. Afterward, provide the *Background Information* on p. 171 about the National Zoo.

SET PURPOSE Initiate responses to the *Read to Learn* question by engaging students in the *Using Visuals* activity at the bottom of this page. As students look at the pictures, help them generate a definition of the *Vocabulary* word.

⭐ 2 TEACH

Discussing Come See the Capital
Help students recall what they learned about the capital in the last lesson.

Suggested Questions

● **Why does Washington, D.C., belong to all Americans?** *(It is the capital of the United States.)*

★**THINKING FURTHER:** *Compare and Contrast* **How has Washington, D.C., changed since 1790? How has it stayed the same?** *(More people live and work there; buildings, streets, and modern transportation have replaced forests, dirt paths, and horses and carriages. The city is still our capital where government officials work; some early buildings still remain.)*

Resource REMINDER

Practice Book: *p 38*

Anthology: *Dear Mr. President, pp. 76–77*

🔘 **Technology:** *Adventures CD-ROM*

Our Nation's Capital Today

READ ALOUD

"It's great to live in Washington. There are a lot of things to see and do. My favorite place to go to is the National Zoo."

Focus Activity

READ TO LEARN

What interesting things can you see and do in our capital today?

VOCABULARY

memorial

PLACES

Capitol
Washington
  Monument
Jefferson Memorial
Lincoln Memorial
Vietnam Veterans
  Memorial
Lafayette Park

170

Come See the Capital

Gary Senn is a third grader who lives in Washington, D.C. Not far from his home, the President and other leaders of the United States are busy every day. They are making decisions that are important to the future of our country and the world. Washington, D.C., is home to many people. But it is the capital for all Americans.

Washington, D.C., has changed a lot since it was first built. Many more people live and work here. There are many shops and office buildings where forests once grew. Wide streets have replaced dirt paths and roads. Today cars and buses carry people through the city. There are no more horses and carriages. But you can still see some of the buildings that were built long ago.

Reading STRATEGIES *and* Language DEVELOPMENT

USING VISUALS Tell students that the pictures in the lesson can help them answer the *Read to Learn* question. Allow time for the class to examine the visuals. Then have students use what they learned from the pictures to suggest answers to the question.

HOMOPHONES After students read p. 171, explain that *capitol* and *capital* are *homophones*—words that sound the same but have different meanings and spellings. Then divide the class into teams for a homophone hunt. Challenge each team to find other words on p. 171 that have homophones.

Second-Language Support

USING PROPS Mnemonic devices can help students with spelling. Point out the dome in the picture of the Capitol and tell them to think of it when trying to remember if the word is spelled with an *o* or an *a*.

Getting Around Town

Look at the map below. Find Anacostia. Here is where Gary Senn and his family live. Gary can walk to his school. To travel to other places in the city, Gary can take the Metro. The Metro is a train system that runs underground. People in Washington are proud of how fast and clean the Metro is.

Not very far from Gary's home is the Capitol. The Capitol is the building where Congress meets. *Capitol,* the word for the building, sounds like *capital,* the word for the city. But, as you can see, these words are spelled differently. Since 1800 Congress has met to make laws inside the Capitol.

Gary Senn is a third grader living in Washington, D.C.

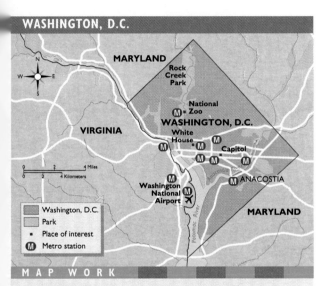

WASHINGTON, D.C.

MARYLAND
Rock Creek Park
National Zoo
WASHINGTON, D.C.
White House
Capitol
VIRGINIA
ANACOSTIA
Washington National Airport
MARYLAND
Potomac River

- Washington, D.C.
- Park
- • Place of interest
- Ⓜ Metro station

MAP WORK

Washington, D.C., is bordered by the states of Maryland and Virginia.

1. Which different rivers run through Washington, D.C.?

2. In which direction is the National Zoo from Rock Creek Park?

3. Why do you think many people travel by Metro?

MAP WORK: 1. Potomac, Anacostia **2.** south **3.** It is quicker and less expensive than traveling by car in traffic.

171

Thinking About Getting Around Town Have students look at the map to see Gary Senn's community in relation to the rest of Washington, D.C.

Suggested Questions

- *What is the Metro?* (an underground train system)

- *How do people in Washington, D.C., get around?* (walk, drive, take a bus or the Metro)

- *What is the difference between a capital and the Capitol?* (A capital is where a state or national government is located. The Capitol is the building where the U.S. Congress meets.)

★ THINKING FURTHER: *Sequencing* **Put these events in order: Congress starts meeting in the Capitol; Congress agrees on a place for a capital city; the White House is built.** (Congress agrees on a capital city; the White House is built; Congress starts meeting in the Capitol.)

More **MAP WORK**

Point out the place where the Anacostia and Potomac rivers meet and explain that George Washington chose that exact site for the capital city. Then ask these questions.

Suggested Questions

- *In which direction does Gary travel to get from his home to the National Zoo?* (northwest)

★ THINKING FURTHER: *Using Prior Knowledge* **What buildings would you visit if you wanted to see where Congress works and the President lives?** (Capitol, White House)

Background INFORMATION

ABOUT THE NATIONAL ZOO Owned by the federal government and operated by the Smithsonian Institution, the National Zoo has more than 2,000 animals. Two of the most famous are Ling-Ling and Hsing-Hsing, the giant pandas China gave the U.S. in 1972. Another famous resident is our country's national bird—the bald eagle.

Global CONNECTION

AN INTERNATIONAL CITY Washington's Massachusetts Avenue is known as Embassy Row because many ambassadors live there. The international nature of the neighborhood is reflected in the diverse architectural styles of the embassies and the national flags on display. The embassies themselves are considered foreign territories, belonging to the countries they represent.

Background INFORMATION

ABOUT THE CAPITOL

- George Washington and Pierre L'Enfant chose the site of the Capitol, a hill that L'Enfant called "a pedestal waiting for a monument."

- Today the Capitol is not only the place where Congress meets, it is also a museum of U.S. history, with artifacts, statues, and paintings from our nation's past. One painting, *The Declaration of Independence* by John Trumbull, is shown on p. 150 of this book.

- About 10 million people visit the Capitol each year. Many come to see Congress in action. A flag flies above the north wing when the Senate is in session and above the south wing when the House of Representatives meets.

Tell students that all four memorials are located in the National Mall—a two-mile area of Washington with many places of interest.

Discussing A Capital to Remember Have a volunteer read aloud the first column of text. If necessary, explain that a monument is one type of memorial. As students examine the *Infographic,* help them understand why it is important to remember our country's past.

Suggested Questions

- **What is a memorial? Why do we call the Washington Monument a memorial?** *(A reminder of a person or event; it reminds us of George Washington.)*

- **Why is it important to remember George Washington?** *(He helped the colonies win the Revolution and served as our first President.)*

Technology CONNECTION

ADVENTURES CD-ROM

Enrich the *Infographic* with the *Take Me to the Mall* activity.

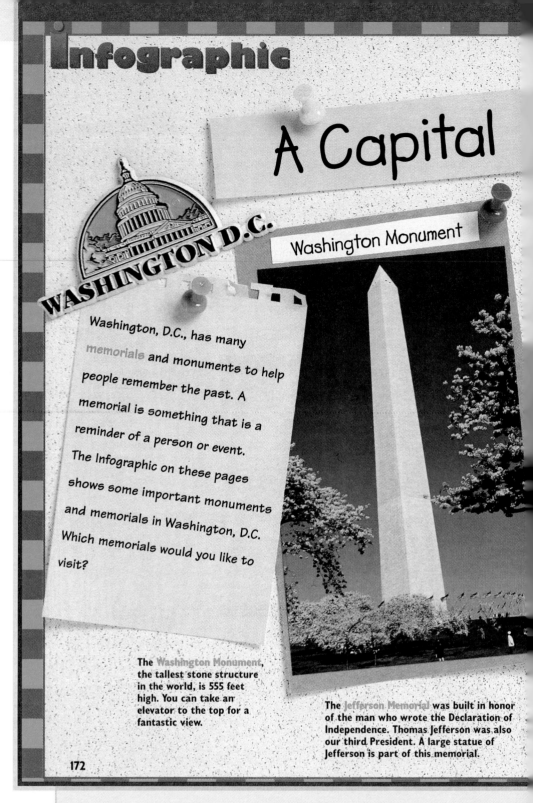

Infographic

A Capital

WASHINGTON D.C.

Washington Monument

Washington, D.C., has many memorials and monuments to help people remember the past. A memorial is something that is a reminder of a person or event. The Infographic on these pages shows some important monuments and memorials in Washington, D.C. Which memorials would you like to visit?

The Washington Monument, the tallest stone structure in the world, is 555 feet high. You can take an elevator to the top for a fantastic view.

The Jefferson Memorial was built in honor of the man who wrote the Declaration of Independence. Thomas Jefferson was also our third President. A large statue of Jefferson is part of this memorial.

172

Background INFORMATION

MORE ABOUT THE MEMORIALS

- Proposals for a monument to honor Washington date back to the end of the Revolution, but construction did not begin until the middle 1800s. Among other obstacles to the project had been Washington himself—he objected to the expense!

- Inside the Jefferson Memorial are quotations from his writings, including the passage from the Declaration of Independence proclaiming that all men are created equal.

- Dominating the Lincoln Memorial is the statue by Daniel Chester French. Flanking the statue are Lincoln's Gettysburg Address and Second Inaugural Address.

Almost 100 years after the Civil War ended, the Lincoln Memorial was the site of another famous speech by another great American. It was there that Dr. Martin Luther King, Jr., delivered his "I Have a Dream" speech before a crowd of 200,000 people.

- The Vietnam Veterans Memorial was dedicated on Veterans' Day, 1982—nine years after the longest war in U.S. history ended. It was designed by Maya Ying Lin, a 21-year-old architecture student. The Wall was built with money contributed by the American people and raised by Vietnam veterans. Etched in the black granite are the names of 58,132 Americans—all lost in Vietnam.

to Remember

Lincoln Memorial

The Lincoln Memorial was built in honor of President Abraham Lincoln. He was President during the Civil War. He helped free African Americans from slavery. A large statue of Lincoln looks over the Reflecting Pool.

Vietnam Veterans Memorial

Jefferson Memorial

The names of all American soldiers who died in the Vietnam War are on the walls of the Vietnam Veterans Memorial. People leave flowers and notes to help remember those killed in the war.

173

- *Which memorial honors the man who wrote the Declaration of Independence? In what other way did he serve his country* (Jefferson Memorial; served as third President)

- *Who was Abraham Lincoln? Why do we honor him?* (He was President during the Civil War; he helped free African Americans from slavery.)

- *How does the Vietnam Veterans Memorial help us remember every American who was lost in the Vietnam War?* (All the names appear on the walls.)

- *Why do people leave notes and flowers at the Vietnam Veterans Memorial?* (as reminders and signs of appreciation for those who were lost in the war)

- *If you looked down at the Reflecting Pool, which memorial would you see?* (You would see the Lincoln Memorial. Tell students that at the other end of the Reflecting Pool is the Washington Monument, which is also reflected in the water.)

- ★**THINKING FURTHER:** *Making Conclusions Why is it important for a capital to have memorials?* (so people will remember their country's history, take pride in it, and learn from it)

Expanding the Infographic

LINKS TO READING Students can read these books to learn about the people the memorials help us remember:

- *George Washington: A Picture Book Biography* by James Cross Giblin (Scholastic, 1992). This biography of Washington also serves as an overview of the events surrounding the birth of our nation.

- *Thomas Jefferson: A Picture Book Biography* by James Cross Giblin (Scholastic, 1994). This book traces the course of Jefferson's life from childhood to his final years. Included are excerpts from his writings and a "tour" of his beloved home, Monticello.

- *The Picture Book of Abraham Lincoln* by David Adler (Holiday House, 1989). This biography will help students understand Lincoln's place in United States history.

- *The Wall* by Eve Bunting (Clarion, 1990). This sensitive story, told from the viewpoint of a child, can help students understand what the Vietnam Veterans Memorial means to Americans.

Field Trip

Take students on a trip to a memorial or monument in the community. As preparation, provide background information about the person or event the structure commemorates. As a follow-up, use the *Curriculum Connection* activity on p. 174.

If a field trip is not possible, display a picture of a local memorial and discuss it with the class.

Discussing The Government at Work As students look at the pictures, explain that Lafayette Park was named for a French hero of the American Revolution, the Marquis de Lafayette.

Suggested Questions

● *How do many people in Washington, D.C., make a living?* (They work for the government.)

● *Why do you think people go to Lafayette Park to express their opinions?* (It is near important government buildings such as the White House.)

● *Why do people in our country have the right to express their opinions?* (That right is guaranteed by the Constitution.)

● *Why is it important for people to make their opinions known to government leaders?* (Guide students to understand that government officials need to be aware of public opinion in order to serve the people they represent.)

● *What is one important problem our country still has to solve?* (homelessness)

★**THINKING FURTHER:** *Making Decisions* *What would you suggest to help people get homes?* (Answers will vary.)

Links to ART

In Memory Of...

The design for the Vietnam Veterans Memorial was the idea of a young woman named Maya Ying Lin. Her design reminds us of all the Americans who died in the Vietnam War.

As a class make a drawing for a memorial to honor someone who made a difference in your community in the past.

The Government at Work

Early in the morning Washington, D.C., is already bustling. Thousands of people are going to work. Many of them work for the government.

Right across from the White House lawn is another interesting place in Washington, D.C.— Lafayette Park. This park is public. *Public* means anyone can go there. On many days you can see people holding large signs. They are expressing their opinions. They want the President and other leaders to know how they feel about certain issues. Thanks to our Constitution, people in our country are free to share their opinions.

You might see some people who live in Lafayette Park. They live there because they have no homes. They are a reminder that our country still has problems to solve.

In Lafayette Park people often make signs that express their opinions (left). Many people work for our government in buildings in Washington, D.C. (above).

Curriculum CONNECTION

LINKS TO ART: IN MEMORY OF . . . Have students think of people who have made a difference in their community. Write the names on the board and have children discuss each one. Help them establish criteria for deciding which person to honor with a memorial. Then have students vote for the person of their choice.

Using the ANTHOLOGY

DEAR MR. PRESIDENT, pages 76–77 When the *Washington Post* invited America's children to write letters to the President, almost 11,000 children responded. This selection presents seven of those letters.

Tell students that they will have an opportunity to write letters of their own in the *Citizenship* activity that follows.

CITIZENSHIP

USING CURRENT EVENTS Initiate a class discussion about problems our country has today. Help children narrow the list to five problems they think are most important. List them on chart paper.

Explain that the first step in solving any problem is to learn about it. Informed citizens can make a difference by expressing their concerns, ideas, and opinions to their elected leaders.

Divide the class into five groups. Have each group learn about one problem on the list. Then suggest that group members use their findings to write letters to the President expressing their thoughts about the problems facing our country.

WHY IT MATTERS

The President of the United States and Gary Senn have at least two things in common. They both live in Washington, D.C. They are both Americans.

Many different people live and work in our country's capital. There are also interesting things to see and do there. Some places will show you how our government works today. There are also memorials and monuments to remind us of important people and events in our country's past.

In different countries around the world, capital cities are important to people. Capitals are not only centers of government. They are also places where people are proud to learn about their country. In the next lesson you will learn about a capital city in Africa.

The President is one of the elected people who work in Washington, D.C.

Reviewing Facts and Ideas

SUM IT UP

- Washington, D.C., is a busy city today. Many people live and work there.

- Memorials and monuments, such as the Washington Monument, remind us of our country's past.

- In Washington, D.C., people work hard trying to make our country a better place for all Americans.

THINK ABOUT IT

1. What is a memorial?

2. **FOCUS** What interesting things can you see and do in our capital today?

3. **THINKING SKILL** _Sort_ different places to visit in Washington, D.C., into two groups: memorials and buildings.

4. **GEOGRAPHY** Look at the map of Washington, D.C., on page 171. In what direction would you travel to go from Washington National Airport to the White House?

175

Meeting *Individual* Needs

RETEACHING (Easy) Have students illustrate places of interest in Washington, D.C., for a travel guide. For reference, students can use the Key Places segment on the *CD-ROM* and the *Classroom Library* selection for this unit: *The Story of the White House* by Kate Waters (Scholastic, 1991).

EXTENSION (Average) Have students write captions for the pictures their classmates have drawn. They can obtain information from the sources listed above.

ENRICHMENT (Challenging) Have students write an introduction to the travel guide, telling how Washington, D.C., has changed over time. For reference, students can look back at this lesson and the last and consult the sources listed above.

Understanding WHY IT MATTERS
Be sure students understand why Washington, D.C., is a special place for all Americans.

Suggested Questions

- **Who is the man in the picture?** (President Clinton)

- **What makes Washington, D.C., a special kind of community?** (It is our nation's capital, where we can see how our government works as well as reminders of our country's past.)

- **Why are capital cities important to people around the world?** (They are centers of government; they are places where people can learn about and take pride in their countries.)

3 CLOSE

SUM IT UP
Use the questions below to help students review the lesson.

Suggested Questions

- **What kind of community was Washington, D.C., in its early years? What kind of community is it today?** (rural; urban)

- **What is the purpose of a memorial?** (to remind people of the past; to honor people who have served the public)

- **How do many people who work in Washington, D.C., help all Americans?** (by working for the government)

EVALUATE
✓ **Answers to Think About It**

1. something that reminds us of a person or event in the past

2. see memorials that honor Washington, Jefferson, Lincoln, and the veterans of the Vietnam War; visit the Capitol and White House; take the Metro; go to Lafayette Park

3. Memorials: Washington Monument; Jefferson, Lincoln, and Vietnam Veterans memorials. Buildings: White House, Capitol.

4. northwest *Location*

Write About It Have students plan a tour of Washington, D.C. Tell them to make a list of the places they would include on the tour and write a sentence explaining the significance of each one.

Lesson Overview
Grid maps help people locate places.

Lesson Objectives
★ Explain what a grid map is.
★ Practice using a grid map.

1 PREPARE

MOTIVATE Have students examine the map of the National Mall. Ask them how it is different from other maps they have seen. Call attention to the numbers and letters surrounding the map and the boxes that divide it. Explain that this kind of map is called a *grid map.* If possible, project *Transparency 9* on the wall to provide an enlarged view.

SET PURPOSE Have students suppose they were visiting a community they had never been to before. How would they locate the places they wanted to see? Explain that in such circumstances, a grid map is useful. Tell students that they will learn to use one in this lesson.

DISCUSSING HELPING YOURSELF Tell the class that the *Helping Yourself* box (p. 177) explains how to read a grid map.

2 TEACH

Why the Skill Matters Have a volunteer read the text aloud. Then review the definition of *grid map.*

Using the Skill Explain that like a book, a map can have an index. A book index helps us locate information in a book. A map index helps us locate places on a map. Have students read the text to find out how to use the grid map index.

Suggested Questions
● *In what box is the White House located?* (A6)

● *Along what avenue would you walk to get from the White House to the National Gallery of Art?* (Pennsylvania Ave.)

Resource REMINDER
Practice Book: *p. 39*
Technology: *Videodisc/Video Tape 2*
Transparency: *#9*
Outline Maps: *p. 14*

GEOGRAPHYSKILLS

Reading Grid Maps

VOCABULARY
grid map
index

WHY THE SKILL MATTERS

You have read about some places to visit in Washington, D.C. You have already seen a map of our capital city. But sometimes it is hard to find different places on a map. A grid map can help. A grid map has a grid, or a set of crisscrossing lines, to help you locate places on the map.

USING THE SKILL

Look at the grid map below. You can see two sets of lines. One set runs across, the other set runs up and down the map. The two sets crisscross to form boxes, or a grid. This grid map shows you the area in our capital called the National Mall. It is an area where many memorials, monuments, museums, and also government buildings are located.

Suppose you want to find the Library of Congress. It has many books. It is the biggest library in the world. First look at the index. An index is a list that tells you where to find information. Indexes are usually in alphabetical order.

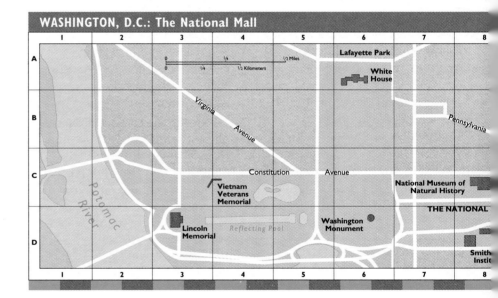

WASHINGTON, D.C.: The National Mall

176

Background INFORMATION

ABOUT THE SMITHSONIAN The Smithsonian Institution operates over a dozen museums. Some of the most popular are discussed below.

● The National Air and Space Museum has more visitors annually than any museum in the U.S. Displays include the Wright brothers' first plane, a Skylab space station, and a moon rock visitors can touch.

● The National Museum of Natural History is especially popular with children for such attractions as the Discovery Room (with exhibits children can handle), the Insect Zoo (with thousands of live insects), and Dinosaur Hall (with dinosaur skeletons). Outside the museum is "Uncle Beazley," a life-size fiberglass triceratops children can climb.

● The National Museum of African Art has the largest collection of African Art in the U.S. Of interest to many people is an exhibit that shows how African cultures have influenced modern European and American art.

Look in the index for the Library of Congress. Find D13 next to its name. D13 is the letter and number of a box on the grid. Find the letter D along the side of the map. Then move your finger across until it is over number 13. Your finger is now in box D13. Can you find the library in this grid box?

TRYING THE SKILL

Use the Helping Yourself box as you find more places on the grid

HELPING Yourself

- **Grid maps** have crisscrossing lines that help you find places.
- The **index** lists the grid box in which places appear.
- To find a grid box, point to the grid letter on the side of the map. Slide your finger over to reach the right grid number.

map. To find the Capitol, look in the index. What grid boxes is it in? Find the Capitol on the map. Next look at box D6. What place of interest is located here?*

REVIEWING THE SKILL

1. In what box is the Supreme Court located? How did you know?

2. Which buildings can be found in two boxes?

3. Why is it helpful to use a grid map?

Trying the Skill Remind students to use the *Helping Yourself* box as they work on their own.

Suggested Questions

- **Where is Union Station?** *(A12–A13)*

- **What place of interest is in box D6? What memorial is northwest of that place?** *(Washington Monument; Vietnam Veterans Memorial)*

- **What building do you face if you sit in Lafayette Park?** *(the White House)*

3 CLOSE

SUM IT UP
Have students explain how to use a grid map in their own words.

EVALUATE
√ **Answers to Reviewing the Skill**
1. C13; by looking at the index

2. Capitol, National Air and Space Museum, National Gallery of Art, Smithsonian Institution, Union Station.

3. to find places on a map

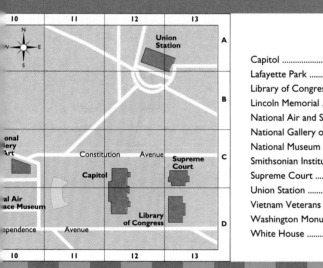

INDEX	
Capitol	C12–D12
Lafayette Park	A6
Library of Congress	D13
Lincoln Memorial	D3
National Air and Space Museum	D9–D10
National Gallery of Art	C9–C10
National Museum of Natural History	C8
Smithsonian Institution	D8–D9
Supreme Court	C13
Union Station	A12–A13
Vietnam Veterans Memorial	C3–C4
Washington Monument	D6
White House	A6

Technology CONNECTION

VIDEODISC/VIDEO TAPE 2
Enrich the lesson with the *Washington, D.C.*, segment.

Search Frame 23537

177

Background INFORMATION

ABOUT THE LIBRARY OF CONGRESS

- Established in 1800 as a research library for Congress, the Library of Congress has grown from one room to three buildings, housing close to 100 million items, including books, maps, movies, and music.

- American publishers send two copies of every book they publish to the Library of Congress, so the collection grows bigger every day.

- Among the many historical items of interest on display at the Library of Congress are George Washington's papers and Thomas Jefferson's first draft of the Declaration of Independence.

Meeting *Individual* Needs

RETEACHING (Easy) Have students label the places of interest on the grid map of Washington, D.C., which appears on p. 14 of the *Outline Maps*.

EXTENSION (Average) Have students plan a boat trip down the Potomac River. Tell them to chart their course by writing down the boxes through which the boat will pass.

ENRICHMENT (Challenging) Have students tell which boxes they would pass through to get from Union Station to the buildings that house the three branches of the national government.

GLOBAL CONNECTIONS

PAGES 178–181

Lesson Overview

Dakar is the capital of Senegal and the sister city of Washington, D.C.

Lesson Objectives

★ Describe the capital city of Senegal.

★ Compare and contrast Dakar with Washington, D.C.

★ Explain the relationship of sister cities.

1 PREPARE

MOTIVATE Use the world map in the *Atlas* or *Geo Big Book* to show students Senegal in relation to the United States. Explain that in addition to being the capital of Senegal, Dakar is its commercial center and one of Africa's busiest ports. Many different items are bought and sold in Dakar's markets, including baskets like those in the picture.

SET PURPOSE Read the *Read Aloud* and point out that it helps us answer the *Read to Learn* question. Then have students read the lesson to find out how the capital of Senegal is similar to and different from the capital of our country. Finally, call on a volunteer to define the *Vocabulary* word.

2 TEACH

Discussing A Capital Connection
Have students answer the questions.

Suggested Questions

● **What is an ambassador?** *(someone who is sent to another country to represent his or her own country)*

● **Where is Senegal?** *(west coast of Africa)*

★**THINKING FURTHER:** *Making Conclusions* **How does the Sister Cities program help cities around the world?** *(It gives them a way to share ideas and solutions to problems.)*

Resource REMINDER

Practice Book: *p. 40*
Technology: Adventures *CD-ROM*
Geo Big Book: *pp. R6–R7*

A Capital in Senegal

READ ALOUD

"Dakar is a great place. Everyone smiles and helps each other."

A Capital Connection

These words come from Damian Padilla (puh DEE yuh). He is a 19-year-old ambassador for his school in Washington, D.C. An ambassador is someone who is sent to another country to represent his or her country. Damian went to learn about life in Dakar, Senegal. The country of Senegal is located on the west coast of the continent of Africa along the Atlantic Ocean. Damian also hoped to tell the Senegalese people all about life in Washington, D.C.

Dakar and Washington, D.C., have some things in common. They are both the capitals of their countries. Dakar and Washington, D.C., are also part of a program called Sister Cities. This program links cities in the United States with cities in other countries. People from these cities share ideas. They help each other solve problems.

Focus Activity

READ TO LEARN
What is life like in Dakar, Senegal?

VOCABULARY
mayor

PLACE
Dakar, Senegal

178

Reading STRATEGIES *and* Language DEVELOPMENT

COMPARE AND CONTRAST At the end of this lesson, students will be asked to compare and contrast Dakar and Washington, D.C. To help them prepare for that question, distribute copies of a Venn diagram with the following labels: *Washington, D.C., Dakar, Both.* If necessary, show students how to use the diagram. Then suggest that they fill it out as they read the lesson.

IRREGULAR PLURALS Remind students that we usually add *s* or *es* to a singular noun to make it plural. Then write the following words from the lesson on the chalkboard: *city, cities; country, countries.* Explain that when a noun ends in a consonant and *y*, we change the *y* to *i* and add *es* to make it plural. For reinforcement, write the word *similarity* on the board and have a volunteer demonstrate how to make it plural.

Governing Senegal

"I had a great time in Senegal," said Damian. "I even met the mayor of Dakar." A mayor is the head of a city government.

Damian learned that the governments of the United States and Senegal have things in common. Senegal's government has a parliament (PAHR luh munt), which is similar to our Congress. It has a supreme court, just as we do. Both countries are also led by a president elected by the people.

Look at the grid map below. In Dakar parliament meets in a building called the Palais (pa LAY) de l'Assemblée (de lah sum BLAY) Nationale (NAH see ah nahl). In which box is it located?*

Damian Padilla (left) met the mayor of Dakar (right).

DAKAR, SENEGAL

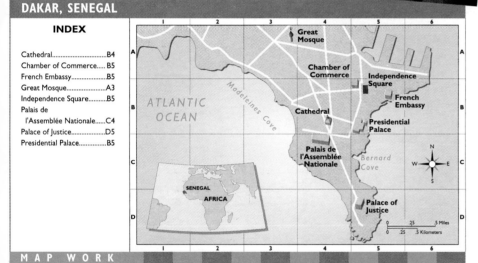

INDEX

Cathedral.................................B4
Chamber of Commerce.......B5
French Embassy....................B5
Great Mosque.......................A3
Independence Square..........B5
Palais de
  l'Assemblée Nationale......C4
Palace of Justice..................D5
Presidential Palace..............B5

MAP WORK

Dakar is the capital of Senegal, a country in western Africa.

1. In which grid box is the Palace of Justice, or Supreme Court building?

2. How would you find Independence Square on the map?

3. How is Dakar similar to Washington, D.C.?

MAP WORK: **1.** D5 **2.** Look for the place on the index to find the grid box; find the grid box letter at the side of the map; follow it over to the correct grid box number; look for the place in the grid box. **3.** Government buildings are located near each other.

179

Discussing Governing Senegal

Help students understand that both Senegal and the United States have representative forms of government.

Suggested Questions

● **What does the picture show?** (It shows Damian and the mayor of Dakar. You might take this opportunity to explain that like Dakar, Washington, D.C., and most other U.S. cities are governed by mayors.)

● **What are three similarities between our government and the government of Senegal?** (Both have an elected president, both have a supreme court, our Congress is similar to Senegal's parliament.)

★THINKING FURTHER: *Compare and Contrast* **How are a mayor and a president alike and different?** (Alike: Both are heads of government. Different: A mayor heads a city government; a president heads a national government.)

More MAP WORK

Have students answer these questions.

● **In which grid box is the Presidential Palace?** (B5)

● **In what direction is the Chamber of Commerce from the Presidential Palace?** (north)

Background INFORMATION

THE PEOPLE OF DAKAR

● Dakar's population changes with the seasons. Many farmers move to the city to work during the dry season (November to June), when they cannot cultivate their fields. They return to their farms when the rainy season approaches.

● Residents of Dakar include immigrants from other African countries as well as from Lebanon and France. The city also attracts many foreign students, who come to study at the University of Dakar.

● A more traditional method of education in Dakar and other communities is provided by *griots*—storytellers versed in the art of oral history. Griots pass down Senegalese traditions from one generation to the next.

CITIZENSHIP

MORE ABOUT SISTER CITIES

● Sister Cities International is a nonprofit agency, whose Honorary Chairman is the President of the United States. It was founded in 1956 to foster friendship among children of the world. Today, over 900 U.S. communities have sister cities around the world.

● Many sister cities have penpal programs for children and exchange-student programs for older students, who live with host families in foreign countries. When they return home, students often visit schools to share their experiences.

● Your class can invite an exchange student for a visit or find out about the penpal program by writing to Sister Cities International, 120 South Payne St., Alexandria, VA 22314.

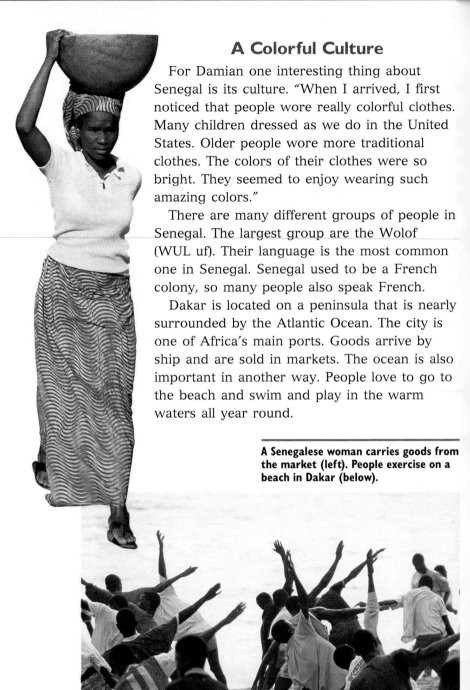

A Colorful Culture

For Damian one interesting thing about Senegal is its culture. "When I arrived, I first noticed that people wore really colorful clothes. Many children dressed as we do in the United States. Older people wore more traditional clothes. The colors of their clothes were so bright. They seemed to enjoy wearing such amazing colors."

There are many different groups of people in Senegal. The largest group are the Wolof (WUL uf). Their language is the most common one in Senegal. Senegal used to be a French colony, so many people also speak French.

Dakar is located on a peninsula that is nearly surrounded by the Atlantic Ocean. The city is one of Africa's main ports. Goods arrive by ship and are sold in markets. The ocean is also important in another way. People love to go to the beach and swim and play in the warm waters all year round.

A Senegalese woman carries goods from the market (left). People exercise on a beach in Dakar (below).

180

Living in Two Worlds

You have read about life in Dakar. What do you think someone from Senegal might say about living in the United States? Abdoulaye Diouf (ahb DOO lay DOOF) is a student from Senegal. He lives in Washington, D.C. "I was nervous when I first got here. It was my first time in the United States. But now I'm having fun," he said.

Abdoulaye sees some similarities and differences between the two cities. "In Dakar they are building houses more like American houses," he said. "And in Washington, D.C., the buses are faster."

WHY IT MATTERS

Like Washington, D.C., other cities in our country have sister cities around the world. People from these cities learn about and help each other. Both Damian and Abdoulaye learned that, like two sisters, Dakar and Washington, D.C., have a lot in common.

The Senegalese flag flies over the home of the president of Senegal. It is called the Presidential Palace.

Reviewing Facts and Ideas

SUM IT UP

- Dakar is the capital of Senegal.
- The Sister Cities program helps people in different cities around the world meet and work together to solve problems.
- The governments of Senegal and the United States have things in common.
- People speak Wolof and French in Senegal. Wolof is the main language.

THINK ABOUT IT

1. How are the governments of Senegal and the United States similar?

2. **FOCUS** What is life like in Dakar, Senegal?

3. **THINKING SKILL** *Compare* and *contrast* Dakar and Washington, D.C.

4. **GEOGRAPHY** Is Senegal in the Northern or Southern Hemisphere?

181

Thinking About Living in Two Worlds Have students look at the picture and then read the text.

Suggested Questions

★**THINKING FURTHER:** *Compare and Contrast* **According to Abdoulaye Diouf, how are Dakar and Washington, D.C., similar and different?** *(New houses in Dakar are like American houses. Buses in Washington are faster than buses in Dakar.)*

Understanding WHY IT MATTERS Direct attention to the last sentence, which contains the main idea of the lesson.

Suggested Questions

- **What did Damian and Abdoulaye learn about Dakar and Washington, D.C.?** *(The cities have a lot in common.)*

⭐ 3 CLOSE

SUM IT UP
Have students answer these questions.

Suggested Questions

- **What is Senegal's capital?** *(Dakar)*

- **If you went to Dakar, what language would you hear most often?** *(Wolof)*

EVALUATE
✓ **Answers to Think About It**

1. Both have a president, national legislature, and supreme court.

2. Students should mention characteristics unique to Dakar plus those that reflect its status as a capital city and major port.

3. Both are sister cities and capitals, where government buildings are close together and populations are diverse. Dakar is surrounded by the ocean on three sides and its main language is Wolof. Washington, D.C., is surrounded by land and its main language is English.

4. Northern *Location*

Write About It Have students write a paragraph explaining why it is important to get to know people in communities around the world.

Meeting *Individual* Needs

RETEACHING (Easy) Have students work in groups to brainstorm a list of things people in Dakar and Washington, D.C., could learn from each other.

EXTENSION (Average) Have students work with partners to write a letter from Damian to Abdoulaye and vice versa. Each letter should describe a typical day in the country the student is visiting.

ENRICHMENT (Challenging) Tell students that Senegal attained its independence from France in 1960. Have them use the library and/or the CD-ROM to learn about the challenges that faced the new country. Ask students to share their findings with the class in a written report.

Answers to
THINKING ABOUT VOCABULARY

1. capital
2. Capitol
3. memorials
4. grid map
5. index

Answers to
THINKING ABOUT FACTS

1. That location was midway between the northern and southern states.

2. He remembered the architectural plans made for the new capital by Pierre L' Enfant. Banneker redrew them.

3. 1800

4. The Capitol is the name of the building that houses the government in Washington, D.C. A capital is the city that is the center of government for a state or country.

5. We build memorials to honor people who have helped others and made our country great. In Washington, there are memorials to Lincoln, Jefferson, Washington, and to the soldiers who fought in the Vietnam War. Students can list one or two memorials in your town or state.

Resource **REMINDER**

Project Book: *p. 14*
Assessment Book: *Chapter 7 Test*

CHAPTER 7 REVIEW

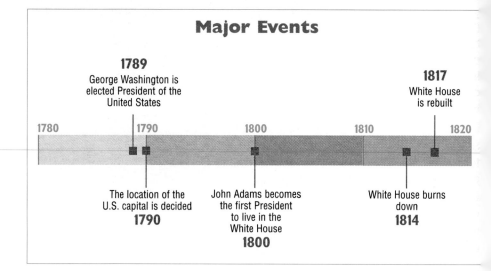

Major Events

1789 George Washington is elected President of the United States

1817 White House is rebuilt

1780 — 1790 — 1800 — 1810 — 1820

The location of the U.S. capital is decided **1790**

John Adams becomes the first President to live in the White House **1800**

White House burns down **1814**

THINKING ABOUT VOCABULARY

Number a sheet of paper from 1 to 5. Write the word or words that best complete the sentences in the paragraphs below.

capital   index
Capitol   memorials
grid map

Washington, D.C., is the __1__ of the United States. There you can visit the __2__ building where Congress works. You can also see many different __3__ that honor important people and events.

When visiting Washington, D.C., it would be helpful to use a __4__. It is made up of a set of crisscrossing lines to help you locate different places to visit. To learn where you can find the information on the map, you would look in the __5__.

THINKING ABOUT FACTS

1. Why is our capital located where it is?

2. How was Benjamin Banneker important to the building of Washington, D.C.?

3. In what year did President Adams move into the White House?

4. What is the difference between the Capitol and the capital?

5. Why do we build memorials? What are some memorials in Washington, D.C.? What are some memorials in your community?

182

Suggestions for **Think and Write**
SIGNS OF SUCCESS

WRITING TO PERSUADE Students should name the person they wish to honor with a memorial, itemize what that person has done to benefit the school or community, include details about the type of memorial that would be built, and tell where it would be located.

WRITING A JOURNAL ENTRY Journal entries should list the buildings and memorials necessary in a new capital city and their purpose. A design for a capital city would include memorials to famous people and events, and government buildings such as a Capitol and a presidential home.

WRITING A TRAVEL BROCHURE Students' travel brochures should include the White House, the Capitol Building, the Lincoln, Jefferson, and Vietnam memorials, the Washington Monument, and other sites on the Mall.

For performance assessment, see Assessment Book, Chapter 7.

THINK AND WRITE

WRITING TO PERSUADE

Write a letter about a person from your school or community who you think should be honored. The letter is to persuade local leaders that this person should have a memorial. Include the things this person has done, and the type and location of the memorial you have in mind.

WRITING A JOURNAL ENTRY

Suppose the President has asked you to plan a new capital. Write a journal entry about a day at this new job.

WRITING A TRAVEL BROCHURE

Write a travel brochure about Washington, D.C. List places to visit and describe one.

APPLYING GEOGRAPHY SKILLS

READING GRID MAPS

Answer the following questions using the map on pages 176–177 to practice your skill of reading grid maps.

1. What is a grid map?

2. How is an index helpful in reading a grid map?

3. In which box is the White House located? What building is located in box C8? How did you find the answer to each question?

4. Through which boxes does Virginia Avenue run?

5. When might you use a grid map?

Answers to APPLYING GEOGRAPHY SKILLS

1. a map that helps you locate sites in grids marked with letters and numbers

2. The index tells you which numbered or lettered columns to look in to find the location you are looking for.

3. A6; National Museum of Natural History; students should understand that they connected the horizontal and vertical columns to find each box location.

4. A2, A3, B3, B4, C4, C5

5. when you want to specify smaller areas of a larger map; when you are looking for someone's street on a road map

Summing Up the Chapter

Review the chapter before completing a copy of the main idea map below. Fill in at least one fact under every heading. Then write a paragraph explaining the development of Washington, D.C.

Location
built between the northern and southern states; not part of any one state

Washington, D.C., Today
many more buildings and people; Metro

Washington, D.C.

Planners
Pierre L'Enfant; Benjamin Banneker

Sister City
Dakar, Senegal; similarities in government; both capital cities

183

Suggestions for Summing Up the Chapter

- Create copies of the main-idea map and pass them out to the class. Students can also make their own copies of the map.

- Review main ideas and supporting details. Explain that main ideas express the most important idea about a topic.

- After students have written main ideas, you may want to have them list several details before beginning to write. Explain that details will help explain and expand each topic. Detail notes will give students a good basis for writing about the development of Washington, D.C.

- Students' paragraphs should describe how the site of the new capital was chosen between the north and the southern states; how Benjamin Banneker redrew the plans originally conceived by Pierre L'Enfant; how the plan included the wide avenue with the Capitol Building on the hill; and how Washington grew into a big city with modern transportation and office buildings.

Citizens Make Communities Work

PAGES 184–201

CHAPTER OVERVIEW

Each community and state across the country has a government. Governments make laws that help people live safely and fairly. People also help each other by doing volunteer service. Learning about government and citizenship makes people responsible for their communities.

CHAPTER PLANNING GUIDE
Suggested pacing: 8–10 days

LESSON	LESSON FOCUS	LESSON RESOURCES
1 COMMUNITY GOVERNMENT pages 186–189	A Look at Local Government	*Practice Book* p. 42 *Anthology* pp. 71–75 *Technology:* Videodisc/Video Tape *Desk Maps* United States
STUDY SKILLS pages 190–191	Using the Library	*Practice Book* p. 43 *Technology: Adventures* CD-ROM
2 CITIZENS IN ACTION pages 192–197	Working Together for Change	*Practice Book* p. 44 *Anthology* pp. 78–82 *Anthology Cassette:* America, The Pledge of Allegiance
CITIZENSHIP Viewpoints pages 198–199	Should Voting Be Required?	
CHAPTER REVIEW pages 200–201	Students' understanding of vocabulary, content, and skills is assessed.	*Assessment:* Ch. 8 Test, Performance Assessment Ch. 8 *Transparency:* Graphic Organizer

OPTIONS FOR STUDENT ACTIVITIES

Citizenship pp. 188, 193, 195, 199

Curriculum Connection pp. 187, 194, 195, 196

Using the Anthology p. 195

ASSESSMENT OPPORTUNITIES

Meeting Individual Needs pp. 185, 189, 191, 197

Write About It pp. 189, 197

Chapter Review pp. 200–201

Assessment Book

   Chapter Test Ch. 8 Test

   Performance Assessment Ch. 8

Using Geo Adventures Use **Geo Adventures** Daily Geography Activities to assess students' understanding of geography skills.

Using the Vocabulary Cards The vocabulary words for each lesson are available on *Vocabulary Cards* for review and practice.

GETTING READY FOR THE CHAPTER

Make a Do and Don't Poster

Objective: To understand the importance of laws.

Materials: *Project Book* pp. 16–17, glue

1. Name a familiar situation in which students need to follow rules, for example, a fire drill or a field trip. Encourage students to discuss the rules that apply to the situation. Discuss who made the rules and what might happen if they are not followed.

2. Give each student a copy of Project Book pp. 16 and 17. Explain that students should first choose and cut out one of the scenes, or use the blank area to draw a scene of their own. They can then make a poster by gluing the scene onto the next page and writing two "Do's" and two "Don'ts" for that situation.

3. Have students share the rules they wrote. Why should people follow their rules? How did they think of their rules? What would happen if people didn't follow their rules?

> ### SECOND-LANGUAGE SUPPORT
> As second-language learners work through this activity, they may feel more comfortable sharing thoughts and information with small groups or with a partner before they speak to the whole class.
>
> Additional Second-Language Support Tip: p. 196

Introducing the Chapter

Ask students what your school would be like without people who worked together and followed rules. Explain that every community needs organization in the form of rules and government.

THINKING ABOUT GEOGRAPHY AND CITIZENSHIP

Help students locate their community in relation to those identified on the map. Then discuss the pictures on the following page.

LOCAL GOVERNMENT

Suggested Questions

- **Look at the picture of the children in Larchmont, New York. What are two ways in which the local government affects their lives?** *(The local government makes decisions about school and about transportation for schoolchildren.)*

- **What safety features in your community help you travel to and from school?** *(Possible answers: crosswalk helpers, stop signs, crosswalks, bicycle paths.)*

- **What would you like to know about local government?** *(Students may want to know who helps to run the local government, what kinds of laws they make, where it is located, and how people voice their ideas.)*

Resource REMINDER

Technology: *Videodisc/Video Tape 2*

CHAPTER 8

Citizens Make Communities Work

THINKING ABOUT GEOGRAPHY AND CITIZENSHIP

Citizens work together to make their communities better places. One way they do this is through government. Large or small, each community and state across our country has a government. In Chapter 8 you will learn what governments do. You will also see other ways people help each other and their communities.

Larchmont, New York

Frankfort, Kentucky

Los Angeles, California

184

Background INFORMATION

LINKING THE MAP TO THE PHOTOGRAPHS

- Local governments head a variety of different-sized communities such as cities, counties, towns, and rural districts. The governments of most cities have an elected mayor and a city council that makes the laws for the community.

- State governments are headed by an elected governor and a state congress, which passes state law.

- The Federal government is made up of the executive, legislative, and judicial branches, which students learned about in Chapter 6.

State government in Kentucky meets in the State Capitol.

Local government makes decisions about schools in communities like Larchmont, New York.

Government taxes pay for highways like this one in Los Angeles, California.

185

Suggested Questions

- *In what Kentucky community does the state government meet?* (Frankfort, the capital)

- *Where is the capital of your state? How far is it from your community?* (Help students locate your state capital on a map and approximate its distance from the local community.)

- *What do you think are the responsibilities of the state government?* (Students may say the state government pays for the state colleges, state roads, and state parks.)

Suggested Questions

- *Where is Los Angeles?* (in southern California)

- *Do you think highways are a good way to spend tax money? Why or why not?* (Most students will say "yes" because the roads connect one community to another.)

Technology CONNECTION

VIDEODISC/VIDEO TAPE 2
Enrich Chapter 8 with the Videodisc *map* and *glossary* segments.

Search Frame 53777

Meeting *Individual* Needs

RETEACHING (Easy) Have students make name tags for the mayor of your city, governor of your state, and President of the United States.

EXTENSION (Average) Help students understand why every community needs a government. Ask them to write essays about experiences with school or community clubs. Have them write what the rules of the club are, how the rules were made, and why they are important.

ENRICHMENT (Challenging) Invite students to write what they know about local government in your community. Students can write about their own experiences with local officials or laws. They can also write about the structure of the government.

LESSON 1

PAGES 186–189

Lesson Overview
Communities have governments to handle matters that concern the public.

Lesson Objectives
★ Identify the basic functions of state and local governments.

★ Understand why all communities have governments and laws.

★ Discuss the need for law enforcement.

★ 1 PREPARE

MOTIVATE Direct attention to the signs in the picture. Point out that signs remind us to observe laws, which help keep people and property safe. In this instance, the signs help protect school-children crossing the street. Have students read the *Read Aloud* and consider the questions it raises.

SET PURPOSE Have students read the *Read to Learn* question. Point out that they have just discussed one reason that communities have governments: to make laws. Tell students they will learn other reasons as they read the lesson. Then preview the *Vocabulary* words.

★ 2 TEACH

Discussing State and Local Governments Help students compare state and local governments.

Suggested Questions
● **Who is the head of the state government?** *(governor)*

● **What is a local government?** *(one that governs a city or community)*

● **What does a city council do? How do people become members of a city council?** *(makes city laws; elected)*

Resource REMINDER

Practice Book: *p. 42*
Anthology: *City Green, pp. 71–75*
Technology: *Videodisc/Video Tape 2*
Desk Maps: *U.S.*

Community Government

READ ALOUD

These are some signs you might see in your community. Have you ever thought about where they come from? Who decides where to put the signs? Who decides on the laws?

Focus Activity

READ TO LEARN
Why do communities have governments?

VOCABULARY
governor
local government
city council
town meeting

PLACES
Shapleigh, Maine
New England

State and Local Governments

In the last chapter you read about our country's government. But the country's government does not make all of the laws.

Every state in our country has its own government. At the head of each state's government is the governor. A governor is elected by the people of the state. The governor and other state leaders make laws for the state. The state government is responsible for such things as fixing state highways and cleaning state parks.

A community can make its own laws too. Local government is the government in each city or community. Many local governments are led by a mayor. The mayor chooses people to help run the community. Many cities also have a city council. A city council is a group of elected people who make the laws for the city.

186

Reading STRATEGIES *and* Language DEVELOPMENT

MAKING GENERALIZATIONS Explain that we can make a generalization to sum up a group of related facts. Then suggest that as students read the lesson, they make a list of facts that relate to the *Read to Learn* question. By the end of the lesson, students should be able to sum up their facts with a generalization that answers the question.

BASE WORDS Direct attention to the words *governor* and *government* in the *Vocabulary* list and have students note that they both contain the base word *govern*. Explain that you can make a base word into a new word by adding a prefix or suffix to it. Then have students identify the suffix in each word, look up the meaning of each suffix in the dictionary, and use that information to write a definition for each word.

Welcome to Shapleigh

Potholes, parking, and parks. What do these three things have in common? They are all things a local government takes care of. Does the community want potholes in the local roads to be paved over? If so, how will they be paid for? Are streets too crowded? How can more parking spaces be built? Local governments are responsible for these things. And, as a group of students in Shapleigh (SHAP lee), Maine, found out, local government can also help to build a park.

Look at the map on this page. Shapleigh is a community in the northeast part of our country known as New England. Since colonial times, many communities in this area have held town meetings. Town meetings are a type of local government. They are usually held once a year. People come to a town meeting to decide on the laws and rules that are important to their community. Everyone in the community can come and have a say in what happens. At the end of the town meeting, people vote.

Shapleigh, Maine
NEW ENGLAND

Every year there is a town meeting in Shapleigh, Maine. Community members meet in Town Hall to discuss important issues.

Discussing Welcome to Shapleigh
Remind students that the term *New England* was first used in colonial times by John Smith, whom they learned about in *Chapter 4*. Today, the six New England states are Maine, New Hampshire, Vermont, Massachusetts, Rhode Island, and Connecticut. Have students label those states on their *Desk Maps*. Then have them find their own community in relation to Shapleigh.

Suggested Questions

● **What are some of the responsibilities of a local government?** *(to make local laws; to take care of local roads, parks, and other public places; to handle local problems)*

● **Where is Shapleigh, Maine?** *(in New England, in the Northeast)*

● **What type of local government does Shapleigh have?** *(town meetings)*

● **What do people discuss at town meetings? How do they make decisions?** *(laws and other community issues; by voting)*

● **Why is it important for people to take part in their local government?** *(to express their views and participate in making decisions)*

★**THINKING FURTHER:** *Using Prior Knowledge* **How do local governments get money to take care of community needs?** *(They levy taxes.)*

Background INFORMATION

MORE ABOUT STATE GOVERNMENTS

● Each state has a constitution that divides power into three branches: executive, legislative, and judicial.

● State governments make laws, levy taxes, and establish standards for public health, safety, and education.

● Most of the money in a state's budget goes toward education, highways, public welfare, health care, and unemployment insurance. All states get aid from the federal government and give aid to local governments.

MORE ABOUT LOCAL GOVERNMENTS

● The most common form of city government is the mayor-town council form.

● Local governments handle a variety of matters, including law enforcement, fire protection, sanitation and schools.

Curriculum CONNECTION

LINKS TO RESEARCH Have students do research to learn the names and titles of their state and local officials. They can use their findings to make government family trees for the state and local governments.

LINKS TO SPEAKING AND LISTENING To help students appreciate the importance of law enforcement, invite a police officer to talk to the class. Allow time for questions and answers after the talk.

Field Trip

Take students for a walk around the neighborhood. Have them discuss the signs they see and categorize them according to function: those that help protect people; those that help protect property.

Thinking About At the Town Meeting Help students understand that a town meeting is the truest form of democratic government because decisions are made directly by the people rather than by their representatives.

Suggested Questions

● ***What kinds of compromises might people at a town meeting make?*** *(Help students think of issues that usually require compromise, such as raising and spending taxes, making laws, deciding on public officials.)*

● ***Why did Mr. Brown's class go to the town meeting? How did they prepare for it?*** *(to convince people to let them build a park on unused land; by studying and planning)*

★ **THINKING FURTHER:** *Sequencing* ***How did Shapleigh get the new park? Use the pictures, plus what you have read, to tell the sequence of events in order.*** *(First, the students discovered the land was going to waste. Then they studied and planned. Next they convinced people at the town meeting to let them build the park. After that, the land was cleared. Then the students and other people did gardening work such as raking. Finally, the park was built.)*

Technology CONNECTION

VIDEODISC/VIDEO TAPE 2
Enrich the lesson with the glossary segment on government.

Search Frame 32772

At the Town Meeting

All around New England, early March is an exciting time. The town meetings are about to be held. There will be many discussions and many compromises.

Mr. Jim Brown teaches sixth graders in Shapleigh. A few years ago his students decided that some land in Shapleigh was going to waste. When the yearly town meeting was about to happen, Mr. Brown's students decided to take action. They studied and planned. Then they convinced people at the town meeting that they could build a park on the land. And the result, a beautiful park, has improved their community!

With the help of students and others, a new park was built in Shapleigh.

188

188

Students Speak Up

Taking part in the town meeting was important for Mr. Brown's students. "I was surprised," said Adam Pierce. "We made a difference in how people thought about the park in Shapleigh. We changed their opinions."

"It felt good that Shapleigh was getting something out of our hard work," said Wendy Wehmeyer. "I knew it would be nice to have a park for people to enjoy the trees and flowers." A vote by citizens at the town meeting showed that they agreed with Mr. Brown's students.

WHY IT MATTERS

Your community and state have their own governments. They decide on many things that matter to you, like your schools, libraries, parks, streets, and your safety.

You are not old enough to vote yet. Still, you can take part in your government. The next lesson shows you how. You will also see how citizens can improve their communities.

Wendy Wehmeyer and Adam Pierce helped build the new park.

Reviewing Facts and Ideas

SUM IT UP

- The state government makes state laws. A governor is the head of each state government.
- Many local governments have a city council to make laws. Mayors are the heads of many local governments.
- Some communities have town meetings where people vote on important issues.
- Everyone can get involved in community decisions.

THINK ABOUT IT

1. What is a town meeting?
2. **FOCUS** Why do communities have governments?
3. **THINKING SKILL** *Compare* and *contrast* local government with state government.
4. **WRITE** Suppose you are going to a town meeting. Write a speech with your classmates about something you would like to tell your community's leaders.

189

SKILLS LESSON

Lesson Overview
The library contains books and other useful sources of information.

Lesson Objective
★ Explain how to use the library.

1 PREPARE

MOTIVATE Make a three-column chart on the chalkboard with these headings: *What I Know About the Library, What I Want to Know About the Library, What I Learned About the Library.* Have students discuss their experiences at the library and use the information they generate to fill out the first column of the chart. Then ask students what they want to learn about the library and write their questions in the second column. Finally, explain that the third column will be filled out at the end of the lesson.

SET PURPOSE Have students read the lesson to find the answers to their questions about the library. Remind them to watch for the *Vocabulary* words.

DISCUSSING HELPING YOURSELF Have students read the *Helping Yourself* box on p. 191.

2 TEACH

Why the Skill Matters Help students appreciate the resources libraries offer.

Using the Skill Suggest that students jot down definitions of the *Vocabulary* words as they read the text.

Suggested Questions

- **What are reference books? In which part of the library are they found?** (*books containing many facts; reference section*)

- **What kind of information can you find in an encyclopedia?** (*facts about people, places, things, and events*)

Resource REMINDER

Practice Book: *p. 43*

 Technology: *Adventures CD-ROM*

STUDYSKILLS

Using the Library

VOCABULARY

research	nonfiction
reference	fiction
encyclopedia	author
guide word	

WHY THE SKILL MATTERS

The students of Shapleigh wanted to learn about gardening before they planted grass and trees in their park. To find the information they wanted, they did research. To research is to look for information. The library is often a good place to do research.

USING THE SKILL

At the library there are books of all kinds. Many libraries also have computer and CD-ROM technology. If you need help, a librarian can show you the library's resources.

The Shapleigh students wanted to find information about gardening. If you were going to help them, where would you look?

The first place you might go is the reference section. Reference books have many facts in them. You can look things up, but you usually cannot take reference books home.

One useful reference is the encyclopedia. Encyclopedias are books or sets of books with facts about people, places, things, and events. If you find encyclopedias on CD-ROM, you can view information on a computer screen.

The topics in an encyclopedia are listed in alphabetical order. If you wanted information on gardening, where would you look? You might use the encyclopedia with the letter G on the cover. Encyclopedias also have guide words on the top of each page. Guide words tell the first subject and the last subject that appear on a page.

After reading about gardening in an encyclopedia, you might decide to learn more about planting trees and flowers. Where could you go in the library to do more research?

Next you could go to the nonfiction section. Nonfiction books are about real people, places, and events. They are grouped by topics such as environment, history, and science. Suppose the librarian suggests a book called *My Garden Companion* by Jamie Jobb. It is a nonfiction book on growing different kinds of plants. To find it you would look at the environmental books in the nonfiction section of the library.

While you're at the library, you might go to the fiction section. Books of fiction are made-up stories

---

Field Trip

Take students on a trip to a public library. If possible, arrange for a librarian to conduct a tour of the fiction, nonfiction, and reference sections.

- In the fiction section, have students locate favorite storybooks. In nonfiction, point out the call numbers and explain how they are used. In reference, show students different kinds of source books such as biographical dictionaries and specialized encyclopedias.

- Familiarize students with the library's filing system. Show them how to locate books using the card catalog, computer, or both.

If a trip to a public library is not possible, visit the school library instead.

*Encyclopedia volume will vary, depending on the name of your state. For books about your community, students could look in the nonfiction and reference sections.

of people, places, and events.

Fiction books are grouped on the shelves in alphabetical order by the last name of the author. The author is the person who wrote the book.

TRYING THE SKILL

Suppose you want to research your own community and its government. Where would you begin your research? Use the Helping Yourself box to guide you in using the library.

Which encyclopedia should you use to research your state? Where

HELPING Yourself

- The library is helpful for **researching** information and finding books.
- **Encyclopedias are in the reference** section.
- Other books can be divided into **fiction** and **nonfiction**.

would you look in the library for a book about your community?*

REVIEWING THE SKILL

1. Where would you go in your community if you needed to do research? Why?

2. What are some of the resources that are in the library? Which ones have you used before?

3. How are guide words helpful in finding information on a page?

4. What is a fiction book? How are fiction books organized on shelves in the library?

- *How are topics listed in an encyclopedia?* (alphabetical order)

- *What do guide words tell you?* (the first and last subject on a page)

- *How are books of nonfiction and fiction alike and different?* (Alike: both are about people, places, and events. Different: fiction is made up; nonfiction is real.)

- *How are nonfiction books grouped? How are books of fiction grouped?* (by topic; by last name of author)

Trying the Skill Remind students to refer to the *Helping Yourself* box as they work independently. To extend this activity, have volunteers use the school library to find a map of their state and current population statistics for their community. Afterward, have them tell the class what section of the library contained the books they needed (reference) and what books contained the map (atlas) and statistics (almanac).

⭐ 3 CLOSE

SUM IT UP

Have students sum up what they learned about using the library. Use the information they generate to fill out the third column of the *KWL* chart.

EVALUATE
✓ **Answers to Reviewing the Skill**

1. library; because it has books and other resources useful for research

2. All libraries have books. Many also have computer and CD-ROM technology.

3. They tell the first and last subjects on a page.

4. a made-up story about people, places, and events; by author's last name

Technology CONNECTION

ADVENTURES CD-ROM
Enrich the skills lesson by having students use the CD-ROM to become familiar with multimedia reference tools.

MEETING *Individual* NEEDS

RETEACHING (Easy) Have students write down one question about the state or local government, exchange questions with a partner, and then do library research to find the answers. When they give their partners the answers, students should explain how they found them.

EXTENSION (Average) Divide the class into groups for a reference scavenger hunt. Make a list of 10 topics, and give a copy of the list to each group. Send groups to the school library at separate intervals to find sources of information about each topic. Have them write down each source they find. The group that finds the greatest number of sources in 30 minutes wins.

ENRICHMENT (Challenging) Have students work in groups to create a pamphlet called *Using Your Library*. They can model it on the lesson and include the *Vocabulary* words plus the tips in the *Helping Yourself* box. Display the completed pamphlet in the school library.

LESSON 2

PAGES 192-197

Lesson Overview
People can be good citizens in many ways.

Lesson Objectives
★ Recognize citizens' responsibilities to the community.
★ Identify community leaders who make a difference.
★ Understand the significance of voting and elections.

1 PREPARE

MOTIVATE Have students use the *Vocabulary* term to explain what the child in the picture (top, left) is doing. Then discuss the *Read Aloud*. Ask students what they think the *Pledge of Allegiance* means. If you wish, use the *Language Development* activity at the bottom of this page to facilitate the discussion.

SET PURPOSE Remind students that they have learned about some of the rights we have in our country. Then point out that we also have responsibilities. One important responsibility is to be a good citizen. Direct attention to the *Read to Learn* question and ask students to suggest answers. Tell them that they will explore the subject further as they read the lesson.

2 TEACH

Discussing Being a Good Citizen
Use the *Anthology Cassette* to help students understand the significance of the Pledge of Allegiance.

Suggested Questions
● **What are we promising when we "pledge allegiance"?** *(to be loyal)*

● **Why do we pledge allegiance to our country's flag?** *(It is one of our country's most important symbols.)*

Resource REMINDER

Practice Book: *p. 44*
Anthology: *Julio in the Lion's Den, pp. 78–82*
📼 **Anthology Cassette:** *America; Pledge of Allegiance*

Citizens in Action

READ ALOUD
"I pledge allegiance to the flag of the United States of America and to the Republic for which it stands, one Nation under God, indivisible, with liberty and justice for all."

Being a Good Citizen

What do these words mean? You have probably heard and said the Pledge of Allegiance many times. When you "pledge allegiance," you are promising to be loyal. The flag is one of the most important symbols of our country. When you promise to be loyal to the flag, you are really promising to be loyal to your country.

One of the most important things you can do for your country is to be a good citizen. Being a good citizen may mean taking part in your government. What else does being a good citizen mean to you? In this lesson we will see some of the many ways you can be a good citizen in your community and your country.

Focus Activity

READ TO LEARN
What can people do to be good citizens?

VOCABULARY
Pledge of Allegiance

PLACES
Tampa, Florida
Portland, Oregon
Oakland, California

192

Reading STRATEGIES *and* Language DEVELOPMENT

CAUSE AND EFFECT After the class has read p. 193, write the following sentences on the board: *Some people cannot leave their homes. Alberta Reed delivers their meals to them.* Then check students' understanding of cause and effect by asking them to combine the sentences, using one of these words: *because, since, so, therefore.* Continue to have students combine the sentences until all the words have been used. For reinforcement, have students identify the word in each new sentence that signals cause or effect.

SYNONYMS Remind the class that a *synonym* is a word that has the same or almost the same meaning as another word. Then work with students to think of synonyms for the following words in the *Read Aloud*: *pledge* (promise), *allegiance* (loyalty), *liberty* (freedom).

Citizens Get Involved

In this book you have read about many communities. All communities have one thing in common. They work best when people work together and help each other.

When you pick up litter, you are helping your community. When you help someone cross the street, you are helping your community. There are many ways to help people.

Alberta Reed lives in Tampa, Florida. She helps people by being a volunteer for a group called Meals on Wheels. Volunteers for Meals on Wheels deliver meals to people who cannot leave their homes.

Once a week Alberta Reed drives to the Meals on Wheels center. She picks up meals and delivers them to people in their homes. "These people cannot go out and shop or cook," she says. "Sometimes the meal I bring them is the only meal they get that day. They really just like seeing someone. I always smile and talk with them."

One way you can help your community is by picking up litter (below). Alberta Reed (top) and other volunteers deliver meals to people in their communities.

193

Thinking About Free Bicycles

Have students look at the pictures and then read the text to find out how free bikes got on the streets of Portland.

Suggested Questions

- **In what community does Joe Keating live? What group does he lead?** *(Portland, Oregon; United Community Action Network)*

- **What does the group do?** *(It puts free bikes on the streets for people to use.)*

- **Why does it help the environment when people use bikes instead of cars?** *(It reduces air pollution from car exhaust.)*

- **How do you think the bikes help make Portland more livable?** *(They provide an alternate means of transportation and reduce traffic.)*

★**THINKING FURTHER:** *Making Conclusions* **How do the citizens of Portland cooperate to make the free-bike project work?** *(They return the bikes to major streets so other people can use them. At this point, you may wish to provide the* Background Information *below so students can see other ways in which the citizens cooperate to make the project work.)*

Free Bicycles

Good citizens work together to improve their community. In Portland, Oregon, Joe Keating had a great idea on how to be a good citizen and improve community life.

Mr. Keating leads a group called the United Community Action Network. He decided to put free bicycles on the streets of Portland. A person could use a bicycle and then leave it at the end of the trip. Someone else who came along could use it next!

"We wanted to make Portland more livable and to protect the environment," he said. "The bikes worked perfectly for both goals."

Look at the special license plates Mr. Keating and others put on the backs of the bicycles. What do these license plates tell us about being a responsible citizen in the community of Portland?*

Free community bicycles are available for use by people on main streets in Portland, Oregon.

Background INFORMATION

ABOUT THE UNITED COMMUNITY ACTION NETWORK

- Joe Keating launched the free-bike project with 10 broken-down bicycles donated by neighbors. He and his friends worked with local children at a community center to repair the bikes. They used supplies donated by a local car shop to paint the bikes yellow, which made the bikes stand out.

- As word of the project spread, more people donated bikes. Soon there were over 200 on the streets, and people in all walks of life were riding them—even the mayor!

- Today many people in Portland are involved with the project. The county provides a warehouse to store the bikes, a trucking company supplies trucks to transport them, and local citizens do all the repairs.

Curriculum CONNECTION

LINKS TO LANGUAGE ARTS Have students work with partners to interview neighbors and family members who do volunteer work in the community. (Examples: scout leaders, crossing guards, Little League coaches.) Help students generate a list of questions such as the following:

- Why did you decide to do volunteer work?

- How much time do you spend on it each week?

- How does your work help our community?

- How does our community help you do your work?

Tell students to make appointments for their interviews. Remind them to take their questions plus paper and pencils. After their interviews, invite students to share what they learned with the class.

Becoming a Leader

Some good citizens also get involved in government. John Russo lives in Oakland, California. A few years ago he decided he wanted to be elected as a member of the City Council. He worked to tell people his ideas about improving community life in Oakland. He knocked on people's doors. He talked to anyone who would listen to his ideas about making Oakland a better place to live.

Since he was elected, Councilman Russo has been making laws to help find housing for people who don't have homes. He's also trying to get other citizens to do volunteer work.

Students can be active in government too. They can discuss issues with government leaders. "I talk to children all the time," said Councilman Russo. "Even though they can't vote, children are important citizens. They will be the leaders in the future!"

Links to MATHEMATICS

And the Winner Is . . .

Many people do not vote. They do not think their vote makes a difference. But many elections have been decided by just a few votes.

Suppose you wanted to run for president of your class. One other person is running against you. How many votes would you need to win the election?

Councilman John Russo talks with children in Oakland, California.

195

195

Discussing Becoming a Leader

Guide students to see how elected officials can make a difference in their communities.

Suggested Questions

- **Where does John Russo live? What job does he do for his community?** *(Oakland, California; he is a member of the City Council.)*

- **How did he get elected to the City Council?** *(He let people know his ideas for improving life in Oakland.)*

- **How has Councilman Russo been helping his community?** *(He's been making laws to get housing for homeless people and encouraging people to do volunteer work.)*

- **Why does he think it is important to talk to children? Why do you think it is important for children to talk to elected officials?** *(Children are the future leaders of our country. Students' answers should reflect the idea that it is important for all citizens, including children, to express their views to their representatives.)*

- **What would you like to say to your local representative?** *(Answers will vary. At this point, you may wish to refer to the Field Trip activity below.)*

★ **THINKING FURTHER:** *Making Conclusions* **Why is it important for all citizens in our country to vote?** *(Use the Links to Mathematics activity to help students understand that even one vote can determine the outcome of an election.)*

Curriculum CONNECTION

LINKS TO MATHEMATICS: AND THE WINNER IS . . . To find out how many votes they would need to win the election, students should count the number of children in the class (including themselves), divide that number by 2, and add 1 to the quotient.

Using the Anthology

JULIO IN THE LION'S DEN, pages 78–82 This excerpt can lead to a discussion about the qualifications an elected leader needs. Ask students which of the three characters they think should be class president and have them explain their reasons. Then have students vote for the person they would elect.

CITIZENSHIP

UNDERSTANDING GOVERNMENT

- Obtain a sample ballot and voter registration card from your County Registrar of Voters. Make copies for students.
- Show students how to fill out a voter registration card. Explain that all citizens follow this procedure to become registered voters.
- Use the ballot to show students the types of issues on which people vote. Point out the sections that call for votes on federal, state, and local issues.

Field Trip

Take students to City Hall to speak with a local official. Before the trip, have them decide on issues they want to discuss. As an alternative, invite an official to visit the class.

Learning from Music Use the *Anthology Cassette* to help students understand how the song "America" affirms the idea that the United States belongs to all of its people.

Suggested Questions

● **Why do we sing the song "America"?** *(to show pride in our country)*

● **What do the words "My country" tell us about the United States?** *(It belongs to all of its citizens. Point out that this means we all share certain rights and responsibilities.)*

● **Why does the song mention the Pilgrims?** *(They are an important part of our country's history.)*

● **Which words refer to principles on which our country was founded?** *(liberty, freedom)*

★**THINKING FURTHER:** *Making Decisions* **Suppose you were writing another verse to this song. How would you express your pride in your country?** *(Answers will vary.)*

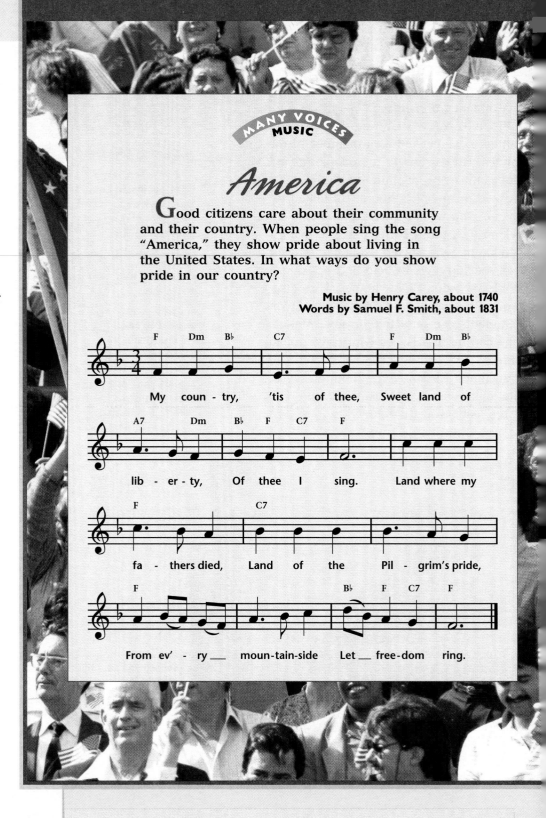

MANY VOICES
MUSIC

America

Good citizens care about their community and their country. When people sing the song "America," they show pride about living in the United States. In what ways do you show pride in our country?

Music by Henry Carey, about 1740
Words by Samuel F. Smith, about 1831

My coun-try, 'tis of thee, Sweet land of lib-er-ty, Of thee I sing. Land where my fa-thers died, Land of the Pil-grim's pride, From ev'-ry ___ moun-tain-side Let ___ free-dom ring.

Background INFORMATION

MORE ABOUT "AMERICA"

● Samuel Francis Smith was studying to become a minister when he decided to write a patriotic song about the United States. He wrote the words to "America" in less than half an hour, to a melody he found in a book of German hymns. He did not know at the time that it was the same melody used in the British national anthem, "God Save the Queen."

● "America" was first sung in 1831, the year it was written, at a Fourth of July celebration in Boston. Surprised but pleased when the song soon became popular, Smith said, "I am glad to have done something for the cause of American freedom."

Curriculum CONNECTION

LINKS TO MUSIC Invite students to perform a medley of patriotic songs at a school assembly. Teach them the remaining verses of "America" plus other patriotic songs such as "America the Beautiful" and "Yankee Doodle." Students can dress up on performance day in sashes made from red, white, and blue crepe paper.

Second-Language Support

TAKING NOTES Use this opportunity to work with second-language learners on the Pledge of Allegiance. Distribute copies of the Pledge and have students circle any unfamiliar words. Then work with them to write synonyms above the circled words. Afterward, have students read both versions of the Pledge aloud.

WHY IT MATTERS

The next time you pledge allegiance or sing a song like "America," think about what it means to be a good citizen. One important thing makes our country and our communities strong: people working together to help each other.

Firefighters and volunteers who visit nursing homes are examples of people who help others.

Reviewing Facts and Ideas

SUM IT UP

- There are many ways to be a good citizen.
- Volunteering to help others is one important part of citizenship.
- Students can be good citizens by talking and writing to their leaders about things that are important to their community.
- Voting is an important part of citizenship.

THINK ABOUT IT

1. Why do communities need good citizens?
2. **FOCUS** What can people do to be good citizens?
3. **THINKING SKILL** Suppose there are two people running for mayor of your town. How would you *decide* for whom to vote?
4. **WRITE** Think of a project you would like to start in your community. Make a sign asking others to help you with your project.

197

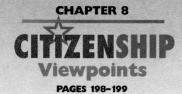
Lesson Objective
★ Compare and analyze viewpoints about whether citizens should be required to vote.

Identifying the Issue Have the class read the text on this page. Then take a preliminary poll to see how many students do or do not think voting should be required. Tell them they will vote again at the end of the lesson.

Discussing Three Different Viewpoints Have volunteers read aloud the viewpoints on p. 199.

SUZANNE HEE

Suggested Questions

- **What is Suzanne Hee's viewpoint about voting?** (She thinks it should be required.)

- **Why does she think it is important for people to vote?** (When people vote, they have a say in issues that affect them and their society.)

DEBBIE MACON

Suggested Questions

- **Why does Debbie Macon think that people should not be required to vote?** (She thinks freedom of choice is as important as the right to vote. Requiring people to vote would violate that freedom.)

- **What does Debbie think we should do to increase voting?** (She thinks we should provide people with more information so they will vote voluntarily.)

JOEL ROSCH

Suggested Questions

- **What is Joel Rosch's viewpoint about voting?** (He thinks people should be required to vote but that voting should take place when people have time off from their jobs.)

- **What does he mean when he says that voting is a small price to pay for living in a democracy?** (A democracy can't function if people don't vote.)

CITIZENSHIP
VIEWPOINTS

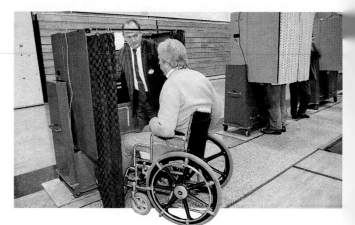

Citizens of the United States vote in booths like this one.

SHOULD VOTING BE REQUIRED?

United States citizens 18 years or older have the right to vote. In most states voters must also register before their first election and any time they move. To register means giving proof of your citizenship and address.

Although United States citizens have the right to vote, many don't use this right. In our country only five out of ten people vote.

Some people suggest that citizens should be made to vote. Suzanne Hee's viewpoint on the next page expresses this idea. Others like Debbie Macon believe that it is best not to vote if you are not informed. Still others, like Joel Rosch, say that voting should be made easier. If Election Day was a national holiday, for example, people would find it easier to vote.

Consider the viewpoints at right, then answer the questions that follow.

198

Background INFORMATION

MORE ABOUT VOTING

- The Fifteenth Amendment was adopted in 1870 to protect the voting rights of African Americans. But those rights were violated in many southern states through physical force and other means. The civil rights movement of the 1960s focused national attention on those violations, and the Civil Rights Act of 1965 finally brought an end to them. The Act made it a federal offense to prevent any U.S. citizen from voting and gave federal agents the power to enforce the law.

- The Nineteenth Amendment was ratified in 1920, giving women the right to vote. The fight for women's suffrage had been going on since 1848, when the first women's rights convention in the world was held in Seneca Falls, New York. At that time, women were not only denied the right to vote, they were also denied the right to own property, to attend most colleges, and to work at many kinds of jobs.

Three DIFFERENT Viewpoints

1 **SUZANNE HEE**
Researcher, Los Angeles, California
Excerpt from Interview, 1994

I think voting should be required. Voting should be what each citizen gives back to society for all that he or she receives from society. I think it is very important for people to know about the issues that affect them and have a say on those issues. I don't think people realize that their votes count.

"... voting should be required."

2 **DEBBIE MACON**
Community Leader, West Bloomfield, Michigan
Excerpt from Interview, 1994

I believe that every citizen should be encouraged to vote, but not required. In our country freedom of choice is as important as the right to vote. Many times people don't vote because they feel they don't have enough information. If people have enough information, they will vote on their own without forcing them.

"... freedom of choice ..."

3 **JOEL ROSCH**
Teacher, Raleigh, North Carolina
Excerpt from Interview, 1994

Forcing people to vote is a good idea, but there have to be certain conditions. People should not have to take time off from their jobs. Instead, voting should take place when people have time off. Democracy involves not only rights but responsibilities. If we are going to live in a democracy, going out to vote is a small price to pay.

"... not only rights but responsibilities."

BUILDING CITIZENSHIP

1. What is the viewpoint of each person?
2. How are they alike? In what ways are they different?
3. What other opinions might people have on this issue?

SHARING VIEWPOINTS
Discuss what you agree or disagree with in these and other viewpoints. Be sure to give reasons to support your opinions. Then as a class try to write one statement about which you can all agree.

199

✓ Answers to Building Citizenship

1. **Suzanne Hee** — People owe it to themselves and society to vote, so voting should be required;
Debbie Macon — We should encourage people to vote by giving them adequate information, but we shouldn't require people to vote because that would interfere with their freedom of choice;
Joel Rosch — We should require people to vote but we should make sure that voting takes place when people have time off from work.

2. All three people think it's important to vote. Suzanne and Joel think people should be required to vote. Debbie thinks people should be encouraged, but not required, to vote.

3. Answers will vary.

Sharing Viewpoints Have students assess the merits and drawbacks of the viewpoints they heard. Encourage them to express their own ideas as well. Then poll students to see how many now think voting should or should not be required. Ask them to explain how sharing viewpoints affected their original ideas on the subject. Finally, help students formulate a statement about voting that they can all support.

Debating Viewpoints The *Citizenship* activity below will give students an opportunity to debate the issue they have been discussing. Remind students that community members and government officials often have debates in order to reach compromises that satisfy the parties concerned.

CITIZENSHIP

RECOGNIZING PERSPECTIVES Have students suppose they are attending a community town meeting. The issue is how to increase voting. Some people think voting should be required by law. Others think voting should be encouraged but not required. Still others think voting should be required under certain conditions.

Poll students to see which viewpoint they support. Then divide the class into three groups accordingly. Have each group draw up a list of reasons to support its viewpoint. Then have each group appoint two representatives to debate the issue. Explain that the goal of the debate is to find a way to increase voting. To accomplish that goal, the debaters need to reach a compromise they can all support.

EXERCISING THE RIGHT TO VOTE Students can hold an election of their own by taking part in the Election Day activity on p. T4.

Answers to
THINKING ABOUT VOCABULARY

1. Pledge of Allegiance
2. town meeting
3. local government
4. city council
5. governor

Answers to
THINKING ABOUT FACTS

1. to help build state schools and roads with state taxes, to enforce state laws about the environment, safety, and state courts

2. Students should be aware of your local government and the name of your mayor or town manager.

3. city council members, mayors and selectmen

4. When saying the pledge, people promise to obey the laws of our country and to help to make it a better place to live.

5. People want to help make their communities better. When people become involved in local government, they know what is happening in their own community and they have some power to improve things.

Resource REMINDER

Project Book: *pp. 16–17*

Assessment Book: *Chapter 8 Test*

CHAPTER 8 REVIEW

THINKING ABOUT VOCABULARY

On a sheet of paper write the word or term from the list below that matches the statement.

city council   Pledge of Allegiance
governor   town meeting
local government

1. We say this when we salute the flag.
2. This type of local government is common in New England.
3. Town meetings are an example of this type of government.
4. This group works with the mayor to make community laws.
5. This person is the elected head of our state government.

THINKING ABOUT FACTS

1. What is the role of the state government?
2. What type of local government does your community have? Who heads your local government?
3. Who are some of the leaders in a local government?
4. Why is the Pledge of Allegiance important?
5. Why do you think people get involved in their local government?

THINK AND WRITE

WRITING A VOLUNTEER LISTING
Think of ways you and your classmates could help others. Write a list on posterboard to display in your classroom. Your list could include ways to help people in class, in school, or in the community. For example, you and your classmates could help improve the school grounds by picking up litter.

WRITING ABOUT A MEETING
When town meetings are held, someone writes a record of what happened. Suppose you are writing a record of a class meeting about classroom rules. Your record must note who was at the meeting, what was discussed, and any decisions that were made.

WRITING A JINGLE
Suppose you work for your state or local government. Your job is to create a jingle, or a saying set to music, that will get people to vote. Write a jingle about the importance of voting, or about voting and citizenship.

Suggestions for Think and Write
SIGNS OF SUCCESS

WRITING A VOLUNTEER LISTING Students should understand that volunteer work is any work that is unpaid. Posters should show an understanding of the kinds of work needed to be done in your community or school and the kinds of work suitable for third graders.

WRITING ABOUT A MEETING Minutes should include names of teachers and students in the class, logical topics that might be discussed, arguments for and against any decision described, and a description of the rules or decisions made.

WRITING A JINGLE Remind students that jingles usually rhyme and have catchy tunes to help people remember them. Students' jingles should describe the responsibility of each citizen to know about political issues and to vote on them.

For performance assessment, see Assessment Book, Chapter 8.

APPLYING STUDY SKILLS

USING THE LIBRARY

Answer the following questions to review your skill of using the library.

1. What type of research materials can you find in the library?

2. What is the difference between nonfiction and fiction books? Give an example of each.

3. Where would you look to find out about the history of voting in the United States?

4. How would you go about finding a fiction book by Mark Twain?

5. Why do you think it is important to divide the library into fiction, nonfiction, and reference sections?

Answers to APPLYING STUDY SKILLS

1. encyclopedias, almanacs, atlases, dictionaries, and nonfiction books

2. A nonfiction book is a book that tells about facts. Encyclopedias and books about science or history are nonfiction books. A fiction book tells a story that is imagined. *The Wizard of Oz* is fiction.

3. In a history book, an encyclopedia (under the United States), or a book about voting; you can find books about voting by using the card catalog or computer index.

4. You would look in the fiction section under *T* for Twain.

5. so that it is easier to find the kind of book you are looking for; so people won't mix up fact with fiction

---

Summing Up the Chapter

Review the chapter before completing a copy of the main idea pyramid below. Read the chapter theme at the top and the main ideas in the middle of the pyramid. Fill in the bottom with details that support each main idea. Then answer the following question: Why are good citizens important to a community?

Good citizens take part in their government.

Communities and states have their own government.	Being a good citizen is important to your community and country.
governor is head of state and enforces state laws; mayor is head of local government; may include city council, community laws, and town meetings	To be a good citizen, people can volunteer, talk and write to leaders, vote and help each other and their community.

201

Suggestions for Summing Up the Chapter

- Prepare copies of the main-idea pyramid and distribute them to the class. Or invite students to draw diagrams like the one shown.

- Suggest that students restate each main idea as a question. For example, students can ask themselves, *What are some parts of community and state governments? How is being a good citizen important to your community and country?* They can find answers to the questions when reviewing Chapter 8.

- Discuss students' answers to the questions in class. Students should understand that a community is only as good as its citizens, because people make the government work.

Answers to
THINKING ABOUT VOCABULARY

1. T		**6.** T	
2. F		**7.** T	
3. T		**8.** F	
4. F		**9.** F	
5. T		**10.** T	

Suggestions for
THINK AND WRITE

Writing About Art Descriptions should include details about the structures, as well as vivid language.

Writing a Profile Students should describe what one person did to help his or her country. They should also tell what characteristics the person had that made them a good leader.

Writing a Poem Students' poems do not have to rhyme but they should have a distinct rhythm and contain words that provide strong visual images.

Answers to
BUILDING SKILLS

1. List what you know about one of the topics.

2. Students should cite at least one similarity and one difference.

3. A grid map is divided into vertical and horizontal columns that are labeled with letters or numbers.

UNIT 3 REVIEW

THINKING ABOUT VOCABULARY

Number a sheet of paper from 1 to 10. Read the definition of each underlined word or words. Write **T** if the definition is true and **F** if it is false. If the definition is false, write a sentence that correctly defines the underlined word or words.

1. <u>Town meetings</u> are a type of local government.

2. A <u>city council</u> is a group of people who are hired to give advice to local governments.

3. The <u>Constitution</u> is a statement about the laws and plans for how our government works.

4. The <u>capital</u> is a building in Washington, D.C.

5. The <u>Declaration of Independence</u> is a statement about why the colonies should be free.

6. A <u>memorial</u> honors an important person or event.

7. To <u>elect</u> is to choose by voting.

8. A <u>tax</u> is money you are paid by the government.

9. A <u>compromise</u> is the constitutional way we run the Supreme Court.

10. The <u>Bill of Rights</u> is a list of our country's most important rights.

THINK AND WRITE

WRITING ABOUT ART
Describe the memorials and monuments in the Infographic on pages 172–173.

WRITING A PROFILE
Choose one important person from this unit. Write a paragraph describing this person.

WRITING A POEM
Write a short poem or song about our country and the importance of being loyal.

BUILDING SKILLS

1. **Compare and Contrast** What is the first step in comparing and contrasting two things?

2. **Compare and Contrast** Look at the pictures of George Washington on page 155 and Thomas Jefferson on page 160. How are they alike? How are they different?

3. **Grid Map** How does a grid map work?

4. **Grid Map** Look at the grid map on pages 176–177. Where is the Reflecting Pool?

5. **Using the Library** How could you research more information about the memorials in Washington, D.C.?

Ongoing Unit Project

OPTIONS FOR ASSESSMENT

This ongoing project, begun on page 140D, can be part of your assessment program, along with other forms of evaluation.

PLANNING Let groups know that their laws should relate to issues studied in the unit, as well as those of concern in your community. Groups should be able to provide clear reasons why their laws should be passed.

SIGNS OF SUCCESS

• Groups reach consensus on the laws they want to include in the constitution and all group members add to the class debate.

• Students communicate their understanding of the role of laws through clear discussions of their ideas.

• Laws chosen for the constitution reflect students' understanding of their rights and responsibilities as citizens.

 FOR THE PORTFOLIO A record of group work can be included in each child's portfolio.

YESTERDAY, TODAY & *TOMORROW*

George Washington is honored by the Washington Monument and on quarters and dollar bills. In what other ways do we honor him? Do you think we will honor presidents in the future? In what ways might we honor them?

READING ON YOUR OWN

Here are some books you might find at the library to help you learn more.

GEORGE WASHINGTON: A PICTURE BOOK BIOGRAPHY
by James Cross Giblin
An exciting book that tells the story of the father of our country.

DEAR BENJAMIN BANNEKER
by Andrea Davis Pinkney
A biography of the man who helped plan the city of Washington, D.C.

THE STORY OF THE WHITE HOUSE
by Kate Waters
Tour the White House and learn what it was like over two hundred years ago.

When looking for a location on a grid map, you will be given the letters or numbers for two columns. With your fingers, you can follow the columns across or up and down. The location you are looking for will be in this square where the two columns meet.

4. D3–D5

5. You would look up Washington, D.C., in the encyclopedia. You could also look for book titles in the card or computer catalog.

Suggestions for YESTERDAY, TODAY, AND TOMORROW

As students consider methods of honoring presidents in the future, help them understand that cities, buildings, streets, and parks are often named after famous people. Invite them also to discuss the various monuments and memorials built for different presidents.

Suggestions for READING ON YOUR OWN

There are many biographies of the founding fathers and stories about the early United States suitable for third grade readers. Help students list the important people and events from this unit before they visit the library to find books for independent reading. The suggestions listed under *Reading On Your Own* will guide students' search. There are additional titles listed in the Unit Bibliography on the Unit Organizer on page 140B. Encourage students to write reports and to share what they have learned in class discussion. Invite students who have read biographies of the same people to present their reports at the same time.

UNIT PROJECT

Make a Citizenship Mobile

1. In a group, make a list of what it means to be a good citizen.
2. Have each group member draw and cut out a shape on a piece of colored paper.
3. On each shape, write one thing that a good citizen does.
4. Decorate your shapes with different colors and glitter.
5. Punch a hole in the top of each shape. Attach each shape to a piece of string.
6. Wrap colorful pipe cleaners around a wire hanger. Attach the strings to the hanger.

203

Unit Project: *Make a Citizenship Mobile*

OBJECTIVE: This project will increase students' awareness of the actions and qualities that make a good citizen.

MATERIALS: oaktag or cardboard, string, wire hangers, glitter, glue, hole puncher, colored pipe cleaners

• Divide the class into groups of five and have each group member list their ideas about what it means to be a good citizen. Have members of each group share their ideas and choose one from each member's list.

• Give each group a sheet of oaktag, five lengths of string, and a wire hanger. Have each member cut out a different shape and write his or her idea on it.

• Then have them punch a hole in each one, tie a string through the hole and attach the shapes to the hanger to create a mobile.

OPTIONS FOR ASSESSMENT

This project can be part of your assessment program.

PLANNING Make sure students understand that each one should contribute his or her own ideas about being a good citizen. The mobiles should reflect the ideas of the entire group.

SIGNS OF SUCCESS

• Students' individual lists should reflect ideas from the unit as well as their own ideas about good citizenship.

• Group members should be able to explain why the actions and qualities described on their mobiles are important for good citizenship.

 FOR THE PORTFOLIO Students' individual lists may be included in their portfolios.

Communities on the Move
PAGES 204–267

UNIT OVERVIEW

The United States has always been a country of movement and change. Americans move from one place in the country to start new communities in other places. People also move from other countries to live in the United States. Technology has changed transportation and communication. Today people travel in jets and get news over the telephone.

☐ *Adventures with National Geographic* pp. 206–207

UNIT PLANNING GUIDE

CHAPTER	SUGGESTED PACING	CHAPTER OVERVIEW	CHAPTER RESOURCES
9 **Building New Lives** pp. 208–239	16–18 days	The United States has always been a country of movement and change. Immigration has helped the country to change.	**Practice Book** pp. 46–50 ▢ **Anthology** pp. 84–90, 95–101 **Project Book** pp. 19–20 **Transparency:** Graphic Organizer ◉ **Technology:** Videodisc/Video Tape, CD-ROM **Desk Maps** United States, World **Geo Big Book,** pp. 8–9 ● **Inflatable Globe**
10 **Changing the Way People Live** pp. 240–265	11–13 days	Technology has changed the way people travel and get news. Today transportation and communication are faster than ever.	**Practice Book** pp. 52–55 **Anthology** pp. 91–94, 102–112 **Project Book** pp. 21–23 ● **Transparency:** 9 ◉ **Technology:** Adventures CD-ROM **Desk Maps** United States, World

ASSESSMENT OPPORTUNITIES

Internet CONNECTION

The **Internet Project Handbook** and the Home Page at **http://www.mmh-school.com** contain on-line student activities related to this unit.

UNIT ASSESSMENT
Unit Review pp. 266–267
Unit Projects pp. 266–267

Assessment Book
Unit Test Unit 4 Test
Performance Assessment Unit 4

DAILY ASSESSMENT
Geo Adventures Daily Geography Activities

CHAPTER ASSESSMENT

Meeting Individual Needs pp. 209, 215, 223, 229, 231, 236, 241, 247, 249, 255, 261, 263
Write About It pp. 215, 223, 229, 236, 247, 255, 261, 263
Chapter Reviews pp. 238–239, 264–265

Assessment Book
Chapter Tests Ch. 9 Test, Ch. 10 Test
Performance Assessments Ch. 9, Ch. 10

ANNOTATED BIBLIOGRAPHY

Classroom Library

■ Say, Allen. *Grandfather's Journey*. Boston, MA: Houghton Mifflin Co., 1993. A Japanese immigrant struggles with his love for America and Japan; a Caldecott-Winner selection.

Student Books

■ Choi, Sook Nyul. *Halmoni and the Picnic*. Boston, MA: Houghton Mifflin Co., 1993. A Korean American girl gets help from her third-grade class in making her grandmother feel welcome to the United States. **(Average)**

Freedman, Russell. *Immigrant Kids*. New York: E. P. Dutton, 1980. Text and period photos chronicle the life of immigrant children in the late 1800s and early 1900s. **(Challenging)**

■ Geis, Jacqueline. *The First Ride: Blazing the Trail for the Pony Express*. Nashville, TN: Ideals Children's Books, 1994. Read about how the pony express evolved. **(Average)**

■ Harvey, Brett. *Immigrant Girl*. New York: Holiday House, 1987. A young girl and her family emigrate from Russia to start a new life in New York City in 1910. **(Challenging)**

■ Knight, Amelia Stewart. *The Way West: Journal of a Pioneer Woman*. Morristown, NJ: Simon & Schuster, 1993. Excerpts from the journal kept by the author present the difficulties of traveling west to Oregon in the 1800s. **(Challenging)**

Lawrence, Jacob. *The Great Migration: An American Story*. New York: HarperCollins Publishers, 1993. A series of dramatic paintings combine with text to portray the northern migration of African Americans. **(Average)**

Marzollo, Jean. *Happy Birthday, Martin Luther King*. New York: Scholastic Inc., 1993. This biography of Martin Luther King, Jr., is simply told, with award-winning illustrations. **(Easy)**

■ Provensen, Alice, and Martin Provensen. *The Glorious Flight: Across the Channel with Louis Blériot*. New York: Viking Penguin Inc., 1983. This is the story of the man who produced the *Blériot XI*, which flew the English Channel in 1909. **(Easy)**

Teacher Books

Jorgensen, Karen L. *History Workshop: Reconstructing the Past with Elementary Students*. Portsmouth, NH: Heinemann, 1993. This book explains how to teach history to build on children's curiosity about the past.

Levinson, Nancy. *Turn of the Century: Our Nation One Hundred Years Ago*. New York: Lodestar Books, 1994. This is a detailed portrayal of what life in America was like one hundred years ago.

Read Aloud Books

Herold, Maggie. *A Very Important Day*. New York: Morrow Junior Books, 1995. People from all over the city go downtown to be sworn in as citizens of the United States.

Singer, Marilyn. *Family Reunion*. New York: Macmillan Publishing Co., 1994. An extended family gathers for their annual family picnic; presented in lively rhyme.

Technology Multimedia

Away We Go: All About Transportation. Video. RB854. Compare transportation in the past to present modes of transportation. Rainbow Educational Media. (800) 331-4047.

Follow the Drinking Gourd. Video. An enslaved family follows the Big Dipper to freedom in the North. *Anansi*. Video. Anansi, the spider, held all of the stories in Africa's jungle long ago. Story Lane Theater, Macmillan/McGraw-Hill. (800) 442-9685.

Kentucky Pioneers. Video. No. 2788-106. Explore one family's travels to Kentucky in 1790. Britannica Videos. (800) 554-9862.

Free or Inexpensive Materials

For a scrapbook of cartoon panels and facts about transportation that begins with the days of chariots, send to: United Transportation Union; Public Relations Dept., 14600 Detroit Avenue; Cleveland, Ohio 44107-4250.

■ Book excerpted in the Anthology

■ Book featured in the student bibliography of the Unit Review

☐ *National Geographic technology*

Ideas for Active Learning

Keep On Movin'

Immigrants came to New York City by Ship in the 1900's

Many people travled by train to find jobs in the North.

Communities on the Move

Help students to create a bulletin board titled "Keep On Movin'." Ask them to make collages on horizontal strips of paper that illustrate how people have moved both to and across the United States. Each collage should include two illustrations. One illustration will show the kind of transportation used; the other will show the person or people who used the transportation.

- Ask students to include written information on the collage that tells the person's destination, and a date telling when the person used the transportation. The collages may include drawings or photographs cut from magazines, cut out arrows or yarn, and photocopies of portions of maps.

- Have students sequence their work in time order and then post the collages on the bulletin board.

Thanks to: Nancy Burkhardt, Cathedral Center, Erie, Pennsylvania

Designing a T-shirt

ON YOUR OWN   30 MINUTES OR LONGER

Materials: white paper, wax crayons, water color paint

1. After studying the unit, have students design paper T-shirts that highlight some aspect of movement in or to the United States.
2. First have students sketch their ideas on scrap paper.
3. Then cut out paper T-shirts from white paper and distribute them to students.
4. Next have students transfer their sketches onto T-shirts and then color them using crayons.
5. Using one color of watercolor paint, brush the paint on in one direction. Cover the entire T-shirt and let dry. The crayon design will show through the paint.
6. The finished T-shirts can be taped to yarn and hung up to look like a laundry line.

Enriching with Multimedia

RESOURCE: *Internet Project Handbook*

- Look at the **Internet Project Handbook** for student projects related to this unit or have students go online at http://www.mmhschool.com, Macmillan/McGraw-Hill School's home page on the World Wide Web.

RESOURCE: *Adventures* CD-ROM

- Enrich Unit 4 with the *time line* and *map-building* resources and the Unit Activities on the *Adventures* CD-ROM.

New Ideas In Communication

- Throughout the unit, students will learn about changes in transportation and communication over time. Work with the class to chart technological advances in communication from 1860 to 1960. Then add headings for the decades 1960 to 2000+.

- Students and their families can study the chart, and family members can circle any technology that came into use during their lifetime. Families can then work together to complete the chart with technological innovations since 1960 and predictions of advances that might occur by the year 2010. Families can discuss how the advances in communication changed their lives and how the predicted inventions might affect them.

NEW IDEAS

1960	1970	1980	1990	2000+
push-button phones	video games			
area codes				

Technology-Migration Time Lines

CURRICULUM CONNECTION Art/Language Arts

RESOURCE: Project Book p. 18.

For this unit, students can work individually and in groups to create time lines connecting changing technology with movements of people.

1. After each lesson, students can describe and depict the period of immigration or the types of transportation or communication studied. This work can be stored in a folder.
2. Once the unit is complete, students can gather in small groups to create their time lines. One time line will show the evolution of transportation and communication and the other will represent periods of migration.
3. To create the time lines, groups can tape sheets in chronological order. They can then connect the time lines by using string to link technology with periods of migration.
4. Each group member can then discuss an aspect of the time line.

 Assessment suggestions for this activity appear on p. 266.

UNIT FOUR

Introducing the Unit

Invite students to look at the pictures and talk about what they see. Then have them read the *Why Does It Matter?* passage silently.

Exploring Prior Knowledge Remind students that they already know about the English colonists who moved to Jamestown and about the Spanish missionaries who settled in Texas.

Suggested Questions

- **Tell about one kind of transportation that has changed from yesterday to today.** *(Students will know that people used to travel on boats, on horseback, and by foot. They will know that today we use engines to power trains, cars, boats, and planes.)*

- **Tell one thing you know about the Statue of Liberty.** *(Students may have visited the Statue of Liberty or know that it is a large statue that represents freedom.)*

Looking Ahead Students will investigate how the United States has grown as a nation of immigrants. They will read about families past and present who have moved here from all over the world to build better lives. They will also learn how the United States has expanded over two centuries, and how developments in communication and transportation have helped the United States grow.

UNIT CONTENTS

204

Background INFORMATION

ABOUT THE PHOTOGRAPHS

- **THE STATUE OF LIBERTY** The Statue of Liberty stands on Liberty Island in New York Harbor. This 152-foot-tall statue was designed by F. A. Bartholdi and presented to the United States by France in 1884 as a symbol of liberty, an ideal shared by the people of both nations. Millions of immigrants entering the United States were welcomed by the Statue, and it has become a symbol of freedom for people around the world.

- **CONESTOGA WAGON** The covered wagon was named after the Conestoga Valley in Pennsylvania, where it was first built. These wooden wagons covered with canvas carried the entire household of pioneer families migrating west. The wheels could be removed so that the wagons could float across rivers like a boat. They were usually drawn by six horses and were also called "camels of the prairie."

UNIT FOUR

Communities on the Move

WHY DOES IT MATTER?

Our country has a history of movement and change. From colonists long ago to people today, the United States has always been a country on the move. Whether they have come from communities within our country or from far away, people on the move have helped make our country a special place.

Another important part of our country's history is change. As you will see, the changing technology of transportation and communication has helped our country become what it is today: a land of many people and many exciting ideas.

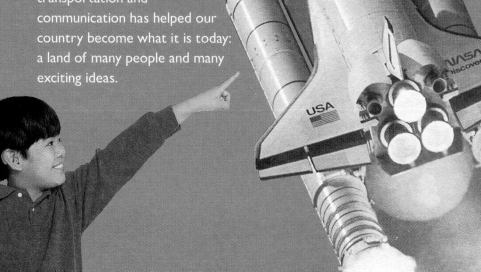

Discussing the Photographs Help students connect each photograph to a time and place.

Suggested Questions

- ● ***In what ways has our country changed over time? What things haven't changed?*** *(Students will recognize the covered wagon as an old way of traveling and the space shuttle as modern. They will recognize that the Statue of Liberty hasn't changed—except that it has aged.)*

- ★**THINKING FURTHER:** *Compare and Contrast* **Look at the two forms of transportation. What might it be like to travel in each one? How are they different?** *(Students will note that the wagon has to be pulled by an animal and moves very slowly along the ground. The space shuttle travels through space at enormous speeds, burns fuel, and only carries specially trained people.)*

Discussing WHY DOES IT MATTER? Have students read the *Why Does It Matter?* passage aloud. Then ask them to make generalizations about how our country has changed.

Suggested Questions

- ● ***What does it mean to be on the move?*** *(to move from one place to another)*

- ● ***Remember what you learned about the rights protected by the Constitution. Why might these laws make people want to move to the United States?*** *(Students may know that people move here to find freedom of religion and speech, and to have the right to vote.)*

- ★**THINKING FURTHER:** *Cause and Effect* **How could better transportation help a country grow?** *(Better transportation could help people move more easily from place to place. People could also ship equipment and natural resources farther and more quickly.)*

Background INFORMATION

ABOUT THE PHOTOGRAPHS

- ● **SPACE SHUTTLE** This reusable space craft was first launched in 1982, barely 80 years after the Wright brothers' first flight at Kitty Hawk, N.C. The space shuttle has the two rocket boosters and a giant fuel tank. After the first two minutes of flight, the boosters use up their fuel. They disengage from the shuttle and parachute safely to Earth. After eight minutes, fuel in the giant tank is depleted and the tank falls away to burn up in Earth's atmosphere.

The space shuttle is used for communications, defense, weather, and scientific explorations. Most of the launches are from the John F. Kennedy Space Center at Cape Canaveral, FL.

Introducing
On the Oregon Trail

Exploring Prior Knowledge Ask students to share what they know about pioneers. Some students may have watched films or read books about pioneer life. Sharing stories of pioneer adventures will spark students' interest in this unit.

Links to the Unit As students continue with Unit 4, they will study pioneer life along the Oregon Trail. They will learn how and why families traveled under difficult circumstances to resettle in the West.

On the Oregon Trail Have students look at the pictures and read the text on the facing page. Discuss each picture with students, asking volunteers to explain what is happening in each scene. Be sure students understand that the photographs show people today, dressed in pioneer garb, recreating life on the Oregon Trail.

Explain that the small map at the bottom of the spread shows the route of the Oregon Trail. Be sure that students understand that people traveled across the United States on this dirt trail, carrying all of their household goods in wagons.

Point out the large rock in the center picture. It is called Chimney Rock, and is one of the most famous landmarks along the Oregon Trail. Because there were no road signs or highways, pioneers had to rely on natural landmarks to guide them. When they reached Chimney Rock, they knew they were about to cross the vast open plains. They also knew that their old homes and farms now lay behind them forever.

Resource **REMINDER**

National Geographic Poster
Geo Adventures *Daily Geography Activities*
Technology: *Adventures CD-ROM*

Adventures with NATIONAL GEOGRAPHIC

206

Background INFORMATION

THE OREGON TRAIL TODAY Modern-day "pioneers" can take short trips on the Oregon Trail in a wagon train led by the Howard family of Bayard, Nebraska.

- Travel time is about 11 miles a day, the same rate at which the pioneers traveled.
- Children take turns driving the wagon, walking behind it, and riding packhorses, just as pioneer children did.
- Meals are prepared on the trail, with authentic pioneer recipes and cookware.
- Nights are spent sleeping in covered wagons, tents, or sleeping bags out on the prairie under the stars. Campsites include historic spots such as Chimney Rock.

ON THE OREGON TRAIL

Your wagon bumps along. So many other wagons have come this way, there are ruts carved into the ground! Sometimes you ride; sometimes you walk. When it gets dark, you help light a fire to cook supper. Is it 1841, or today? It's hard to tell. Modern kids who take part in re-creating the 2,000-mile wagon trip on the Oregon Trail share an experience that thousands of settlers had as they headed west over 100 years ago. They find out what it's like to travel through prairie and desert without a motel in sight.

GEO JOURNAL

Would you like to travel on the Oregon Trail today? Why or why not?

207

Direct attention to the inset on p. 206. Explain to students that each night, the pioneers stopped to cook their evening meal. Be sure students notice Chimney Rock in the background between the two wagons.

The two children in the inset at the top of this page are dressed for Oregon Trail Days, an annual celebration that has been held in Gering, Nebraska, for 75 years. Six-year-old Shannon Simpson and her five-year-old brother Wade won first prize for their costumes.

The inset at the bottom of this page shows a section of the Oregon Trail in Wyoming. On this hill, as in many places along the trail, families struggled to pull their wagons along the route. In the picture, students can see the deep ruts left by wagon wheels in the sandstone road.

Using the Geo Journal Before students answer the question, you may wish to share with them the *Background Information* about the Oregon Trail on page 206.

Technology CONNECTION

ADVENTURES CD-ROM
Enrich the discussion with *On the Oregon Trail.*

Curriculum CONNECTION

LINKS TO ART Looking at additional pictures will familiarize students with the dress and homes of people who traveled the Oregon Trail. It will also help them understand the geography of the land the pioneers crossed.

- Have students visit the library to find more pictures of the Oregon Trail. Suggest students look in the encyclopedia and in illustrated nonfiction books.
- Ask students to draw copies of the pictures or help them photocopy pictures that are hard to draw.
- Invite students to write captions desciribing the illustrations and post them on an Oregon Trail bulletin board. Explain to students that they can add reports, maps, and artwork to the bulletin board as they progress though the Unit.

Building New Lives

PAGES 208–239

CHAPTER OVERVIEW

From the colonists long ago to people today, the United States has always been a country of movement and change. Whether they came from communites within the country or from far away, people have moved to start new communities. Immigration has helped the country to change.

CHAPTER PLANNING GUIDE
Suggested pacing: 16–18 days

LESSON	LESSON FOCUS	LESSON RESOURCES
1 THE OREGON TRAIL pages 210–215	Traveling West to a New Frontier	*Practice Book* p. 46 *Anthology* pp. 84–86 ◉ *Technology:* Videodisc/Video Tape *Desk Map* United States
THINKING SKILLS pages 216–217	Classifying	*Practice Book* p. 47 *Transparency:* Graphic Organizer
2 COMING TO AMERICA pages 218–223	Immigrants from Around the World	*Practice Book* p. 48 ▭ *Anthology* pp. 87–90 ◉ *Technology:* Adventures CD-ROM *Inflatable Globe*
3 MOVING TO NORTHERN CITIES pages 224–229	The Great Migration	*Practice Book* p. 49 ▭ *Anthology* p. 95 ◉ *Technology:* Videodisc/Video Tape, CD-ROM
LEGACY pages 230–231	A Family Reunion: Linking Past and Present	◉ *Technology:* Adventures CD-ROM
4 IMMIGRATION TODAY pages 232–236	Building a New Life in the U.S.A.	*Practice Book* p. 50 ▭ *Anthology* pp. 96–101 *Desk Maps* United States, World *Geo Big Book* pp. 8–9
Infographic page 234	United States Immigration Today	◉ *Technology:* Videodisc/Video Tape
CITIZENSHIP **Making a Difference** page 237	Helping New Immigrants	◉ *Technology:* Adventures CD-ROM
CHAPTER REVIEW page 238–239	Students' understanding of vocabulary, content, and skills is assessed.	*Assessment:* Ch. 9 Test, Performance Assessment Ch. 9 *Transparency:* Graphic Organizer

OPTIONS FOR STUDENT ACTIVITIES

Citizenship pp. 214, 221, 228, 230, 233, 235, 237

Curriculum Connection pp. 212, 216, 219, 222, 225, 228, 235

Expanding the *Infographic* p. 234

Using the Anthology pp. 220, 233

ASSESSMENT OPPORTUNITIES

Meeting Individual Needs pp. 209, 215, 223, 229, 231, 236

Write About It pp. 215, 223, 229, 236

Chapter Review pp. 238–239

Assessment Book

  Chapter Test Ch. 9 Test

  Performance Assessment Ch. 9

Using the Floor Map You can use the Floor Map and the Project Book with Lesson 1 by inviting students to create a travel route between two places on the map. Have them discuss modes of transportation and potential obstacles.

Using Geo Adventures Use **Geo Adventures** Daily Geography Activities to assess students' understanding of geography skills.

Using the Vocabulary Cards The vocabulary words for each lesson are available on *Vocabulary Cards* for review and practice.

GETTING READY FOR THE CHAPTER

Design a Welcome Symbol

Objective: To think about the people who have helped build our country.

Materials: *Project Book* pp. 19–20

1. Discuss what it is like to move to a new place. Have any students had the experience of moving to a new home? Did they have to move far away? What are some of the challenges of moving? What are some of the new and exciting experiences?
2. Talk with the class about how to make newcomers feel more comfortable, and how to help make them feel like an important part of the community.
3. Invite each student to design a welcome symbol for newcomers by filling in Project Book p. 19. They can then draw their symbol on Project Book p. 20. Point out that the design they choose can be a welcoming message or a symbol of your community.

SECOND-LANGUAGE SUPPORT

As second-language learners work through this activity, they may feel more comfortable sharing thoughts and information with small groups or with a partner before they speak to the whole class.

Additional Second-Language Support Tips: pp. 220, 236

Introducing the Chapter

Ask volunteers to share information about different cultural backgrounds in the community. Explain that students will be learning how people from all over the world have come to settle in the United States.

THINKING ABOUT GEOGRAPHY AND HISTORY

Help students link the events on the time line with cities and regions on the map. Help them understand how immigrating and migrating people gradually settled the entire country.

1840s – 1850s

Suggested Questions

- **Where in the United States is Oregon City?** (on the northern west coast)

- **Tell one thing you know about covered wagons.** (Many students will be familiar with covered wagons from movies or stories.)

- **The people who traveled on the Oregon Trail were moving into territory unknown to them. What do you think their journey was like? Why?** (Be sure students support their answers.)

1880–1920

Suggested Questions

- **What happened in the years 1880 to 1920?** (Many people moved to the United States from around the world.)

- **Over what body of water did the people in the picture travel?** (the Atlantic Ocean)

Resource REMINDER

Technology: *Videodisc/Video Tape 3*

CHAPTER 9

Building New Lives

THINKING ABOUT GEOGRAPHY AND HISTORY

Long ago, people traveled over the oceans to start new communities in the United States. They also moved within our country to start new communities. This is still true today. This time line and map show how our history is filled with people on the move throughout our country.

In Chapter 9 you will learn how our country has grown and changed. You will also meet some of the many people who helped make the United States a special country.

1840s–1850s

OREGON CITY

Many people move west along the Oregon Trail and settle in cities

1880–1920

NEW YORK CITY

People from around the world move to cities in the United States

208

Background INFORMATION

LINKING THE MAP TO THE PHOTOGRAPHS

- By the middle 1800s, the eastern states were becoming crowded. The United States government, hoping to secure the western territories for the Union, encouraged families to establish new farms and businesses there. Pioneers packed wagons with household items and slowly made the journey across the Great Plains.

- Immigration was at its peak at the turn of the century. Many Europeans fled desperate political or economic situations, leaving everything behind to resettle in the United States. In 1892 an official inspection station was set up on Ellis Island, where doctors checked immigrants for illnesses and officials approved their immigration papers.

egon City, Oregon

New York City, New York

Chicago, Illinois

San Diego, California

1890s–1940s

CHICAGO

African Americans from the South move to Chicago and other cities in the North

TODAY

SAN DIEGO

People still move to San Diego and other cities in the United States, looking for a better life

209

★**THINKING FURTHER:** *Making Conclusions* **Why do you think families would leave their homes and move to a new land?** *(Students may conclude that families had difficult lives where they lived and hoped to find better ones.)*

1890s–1940s

Suggested Questions

● **What happened during this time?** *(Many African Americans moved from the South to cities in the North.)*

● **What kind of transportation do you think was important?** *(a train)*

TODAY

Suggested Questions

● **What are the people in the picture doing? Why?** *(Students may guess that they are promising to be loyal to the United States.)*

● **What difficulties might people have when they first move to the United States?** *(They might not be able to speak English or they might not know anyone in the country.)*

★**THINKING FURTHER:** *Recognizing Point of View* **Why do you think people move to the United States today?** *(Students can explain why they think the United States is a good place to live.)*

Technology CONNECTION

VIDEODISC/VIDEO TAPE 3
Enrich Chapter 9 with the Videodisc *glossary* segments.

Search Frame 53777

Meeting *Individual* Needs

RETEACHING (Easy) Have students combine this time line with the time lines in *Chapters 5* and *6* to illustrate the growth of the United States over time.

EXTENSION (Average) Invite students to write stories from the point of view of one of the people on the move. Have them tell what it is like to leave a home and travel to someplace completely unfamiliar.

ENRICHMENT (Challenging) Ask students to write brief essays summarizing the time line. Challenge them to explain why early immigrants arrived on the East Coast and why many recent immigrants arrive on the West Coast.

LESSON 1

PAGES 210–215

Lesson Overview
The Oregon Trail opened the West to pioneers in the mid-1800s.

Lesson Objectives
★ Explain why people moved west on the Oregon Trail.
★ Describe life in a wagon train.
★ Compare aspects of pioneer life with aspects of life today.

1 PREPARE

MOTIVATE Tell students that the *Read Aloud* was written in 1853, when the pioneers were settling the West. Then explain that the states west of the Mississippi River were not part of our country at that time.

SET PURPOSE Have students discuss the *Read to Learn* question and tell how the picture relates to it. During the discussion, challenge students to use the *Vocabulary* words in context.

2 TEACH

Discussing Leaving Home Have students answer these questions.

Suggested Questions

● **What is a prairie?** *(flat or rolling land covered with tall grasses)*

● **What is a pioneer?** *(someone who leads the way to a new area)*

● **Who lived on the prairies when the pioneers arrived?** *(Native Americans)*

★**THINKING FURTHER:** *Making Conclusions* **Why do you think Rebecca Ketchum compared the prairies to the ocean?** *(Like the ocean, the prairies seem to go on forever. Also, the prairie grass rolls and ripples like waves in the ocean.)*

Resource REMINDER

Practice Book: *p. 46*
Anthology: *Diary of Mrs. Amelia Stewart Knight, pp. 84–86*
Technology: *Videodisc/Video Tape 3*
Desk Maps: *United States*

Focus Activity

READ TO LEARN
What was it like to travel west on the Oregon Trail?

VOCABULARY
prairie
pioneer
diary

PLACES
Oregon Trail
Independence, Missouri
Oregon City, Oregon

210

The Oregon Trail

READ ALOUD
"The prairie, oh, the broad, the beautiful, the bounding [hilly], rolling prairie! Imagine the ocean, when the waves are rolling mountains high, becoming solid and covered with beautiful green grass and you have some faint idea of it."

Leaving Home

These words were written in 1853 by a young woman named Rebecca Ketchum. She was describing the prairie in the middle of the United States. A prairie is flat or rolling land covered with tall grasses. Many Native American groups lived west of the Mississippi River on these prairie lands.

People in the East heard that these areas had rich land for farming. In the 1840s and 1850s, many people left their homes to move west. They became pioneers. Pioneers are people who are among the first to explore and settle an area not known to them. Their adventures are part of our country's history.

Reading STRATEGIES *and* Language DEVELOPMENT

USING VISUALS Write the following old saying on the chalkboard: *A picture is worth a thousand words.* Then challenge students to prove the truth of that statement by examining the pictures in this lesson and explaining what they reveal about life on the Oregon Trail.

QUOTATION MARKS Remind students that the quotation marks surrounding the *Read Aloud* tell us that we are reading Rebecca Ketchum's exact words. Then call attention to the word that appears in brackets on the second line. Explain that the brackets tell us the word is not part of the original quotation. It was added by someone else for a certain reason. Invite students to speculate about who might have added the word and why.

*They traveled in groups to help each other and protect themselves from attacks.

CHAPTER 9 • LESSON 1

Moving West

The map on this page shows some of the routes that thousands of pioneers used to move west. As you can see, the Oregon Trail was one of these routes. Pioneers traveled together in groups of wagons called wagon trains. Why do you think they traveled in groups?*

Many wagon trains left from Independence, Missouri. This community had shops that sold supplies and animals for the long journey west.

Many pioneers began their trip west from Independence, Missouri.

TRAILS TO THE WEST, 1840-1860

CANADA

0   250   500 Miles
0   250   500 Kilometers

Oregon City

CASCADE RANGE

Oregon Trail

ROCKY MOUNTAINS

Fort Hall

SIERRA NEVADA

California Trail

Sacramento

Old Spanish Trail

Oregon Trail

Santa Fe Trail

Independence

APPALACHIAN MOUNTAINS

Los Angeles

Santa Fe

PACIFIC OCEAN

ATLANTIC OCEAN

Gulf of Mexico

MEXICO

- California Trail
- Old Spanish Trail
- Oregon Trail
- Santa Fe Trail

ent-day boundaries are shown.

MAP WORK

Pioneers could take several different trails to travel west.

1. How many trails are shown on this map? Which is the longest trail?

2. At what place do the Santa Fe Trail and Old Spanish Trail meet?

3. Where might a trip on the Oregon Trail be difficult? Why?

MAP WORK: 1. four; the Oregon Trail **2.** Santa Fe **3.** It would be difficult in areas that are mountainous because it would be hard to pass over the rough terrain.

211

Talking About Moving West Have students look at the picture and read the caption. Then discuss the text.

Suggested Questions

● *How did the pioneers travel?* (in wagon trains)

★ **THINKING FURTHER:** *Making Conclusions* **Why is it reasonable to conclude that Independence, Missouri, was one of the westernmost settlements in the days of the pioneers?** *(If there had been settlements farther west, the pioneers would have departed from them.)*

More MAP WORK

Have students use the map to answer these questions.

Suggested Questions

● *How many miles long was the Oregon Trail?* (2,000)

● *Where did the Oregon Trail meet the California Trail?* (at Fort Hall)

● *How would a traveler from Santa Fe get to Los Angeles?* (by taking the Old Spanish Trail)

Technology CONNECTION

VIDEODISC/VIDEO TAPE 3
Enrich the lesson with the *Oregon Trail* map.

Search Frame 42488

Background INFORMATION

OREGON FEVER The first white settlers to reach the Pacific Northwest were fur traders and missionaries. Their glowing reports of the fertile Willamette Valley spread through the East. By the early 1840s, pioneers in the grip of "Oregon fever" were traveling westward.

● The first wagon train to travel on the Oregon Trail left Missouri in May 1842 and arrived in Oregon six months later. About 100 people made the journey. By 1852 there were 10,000 pioneers on the Oregon Trail.

● The pioneers moved west for many reasons, but most came for the opportunity to own land. Farmland in the East was crowded and expensive. In the West, it could be had for little or nothing. Oregon became a U.S. territory in 1848, and by 1850 the government was issuing land grants to encourage settlement.

THE OREGON TRAIL Some of the landmarks that guided the pioneers on the Oregon Trail can still be seen today.

● At Fort Laramie, Wyoming, travelers bought supplies, repaired equipment, and prepared to enter the Rocky Mountains. Today the fort is a living history museum.

● The names of more than 5,000 pioneers are carved on Independence Rock, a granite boulder in Wyoming that is also known as "the Great Registry of the Desert."

● The Oregon and California trails met at Fort Hall, Idaho. A replica of the fort near the original site is open to tourists.

● Travelers to the Willamette Valley prepared for the final part of their journey at the Whitman Mission in Washington. Today it is a National Historic Site.

Understanding A World of Wagons Have students look at the picture and tell what the people are doing.

Suggested Questions

- **How far did the pioneers travel? How long did the trip take?** *(2,000 miles; over five months)*

- **What kinds of animals traveled with the pioneers? What did the animals do?** *(oxen, mules, horses; pulled the wagons)*

- **What kinds of problems made life hard for the pioneers?** *(They had to cross rivers and mountains and cope with bad weather and sickness.)*

- **Why do you think the pioneers formed a circle at night?** *(for protection)*

- **How did they help each other?** *(They discussed problems, shared food, worked together to repair equipment and care for animals.)*

- **What responsibilities did the children have?** *(They helped cook, wash dishes, milk cows, tie up the animals.)*

★**THINKING FURTHER:** *Compare and Contrast* **How was life in a wagon train like life in your community today? How was it different?** *(Like: People shared problems and worked for the common good; children had responsibilities and sometimes school lessons. Different: The wagon train was a traveling community, with no modern conveniences.)*

Extending Did You Know? Have students measure a five-mile distance on a community map. Then help them visualize that area of the community as it would look if it were occupied by a five-mile-long wagon train.

How long is that train?

A wagon train sometimes had as many as 1,000 travelers. There were 3,000 or 4,000 cows and other animals. Wagon trains sometimes stretched for five miles, with over 100 wagons!

A World of Wagons

The wagon trains were a useful way to make the long, difficult journey. The 2,000-mile trip took over five months. The wagons were pulled by oxen, mules, and horses. They crossed rivers and mountains. They ran into snow, rain, and mud. Many pioneers got sick and died along the way.

At night the wagons were set up front-to-end in a big circle. Children would play together in the middle of the circle. People would meet to discuss their problems. Perhaps someone had a broken wagon wheel, another's mule was sick, another was out of flour. Everyone helped each other. Even children had responsibilities. They helped cook and wash dishes. They milked the cows and helped tie up the animals at night. Sometimes children had school lessons from parents or older brothers and sisters.

Settling in for the night often meant a hot meal and rest before the next day's difficult journey.

212

212

Background INFORMATION

KEEP MOVING The pioneers who set out on the Oregon Trail had to leave in spring to avoid being trapped in the mountains by winter storms. For the same reason, they had to keep on the move. The wagon train stopped only twice a day: at noon and at night.

The travelers covered 15 to 20 miles a day. Many walked the entire journey. Those in the lead left notes for the others if there was danger ahead. They also sent back water when they reached a spring after a dry spell.

The pioneers who made it across the Oregon Trail used to say they had "seen the elephant." The "elephant" was the mighty American continent; the pioneers felt like tiny fleas upon its back.

Curriculum CONNECTION

LINKS TO SCIENCE To save time and work, pioneer women strung up milk bottles inside their wagons. The constant bumping churned the cream at the top of the bottle, turning it into butter.

Students can work together to churn cream into butter. Pour a pint of cream into a glass jar and seal tightly. Have students take turns shaking the jar vigorously, about 10 times each. Within 15 minutes, they will have butter.

Life on the Trail

Life on the trail was oftentimes uncertain. Native Americans lived in many of the areas along the way. In fact, the Oregon Trail was not made by the pioneers. It went along a path that had been used years before by Native Americans. Sometimes Native Americans gave settlers advice about traveling along the trail. But sometimes the two groups fought with each other over the land.

One way we know about the pioneers is from the diaries they kept. A diary is a written record of what someone has done or thought each day. Read the following words from a diary written by a 14-year-old girl named Sallie Hester. How was a day on the Oregon Trail different from one of your days?

Pioneers carved their names and dates of passage on big rocks to record their journey for others.

MANY VOICES PRIMARY SOURCE

Diary written by Sallie Hester, May 21, 1849.

Camped on the beautiful Blue River with plenty of wood and water and good grazing for our cattle. Our family all in good health. We had two deaths in our train within the past week of **cholera** (KAHL ur uh). When we camp at night, we form a **corral** with our wagons. We sleep in our wagons on feather beds. We live on bacon, ham, rice, dried fruits, molasses, packed butter, bread, coffee. Occasionally some of the men kill an antelope and then we have a feast; and sometimes we have fish on Sunday.

cholera: disease of the intestines
corral: fenced-in area for animals

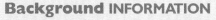

Thinking About Life on the Trail

Have students use the map of Native American cultural groups on p. 73 to identify the Native Americans that inhabited the areas through which the pioneers traveled.

Suggested Questions

- **Who made the Oregon Trail?** (Native Americans)

- **How did Native Americans help the pioneers?** (by giving them advice about traveling on the trail)

- **Why do you think the two groups sometimes fought over the land?** (The pioneers were moving onto lands that Native Americans had occupied for centuries. The Background Information below will help students understand the conflict.)

- **Why do diaries help us learn about the pioneers?** (They are written records of the pioneers' actions and thoughts.)

Learning from the Primary Source For another first-person account of pioneer life, students can read "Diary of Mrs. Amelia Stewart Knight" on pp. 84–86 in the *Anthology*.

Suggested Questions

- **Where and when did Sallie Hester write this diary entry?** (banks of the Blue River, May 21, 1849)

- ★**THINKING FURTHER:** *Compare and Contrast* **How was bedtime on the Oregon Trail different from bedtime in your house?** (Answers should include the fact that the pioneers camped out and slept in wagons.)

Background INFORMATION

CHANGES In the early days of the Oregon Trail, some Native Americans helped the pioneers, guiding them through difficult routes and river crossings. But the westward expansion put an end to peaceful relations.

The settlers farmed on Native American hunting grounds and staked claims on their sacred burial grounds. They depleted the natural resources on which the Indians relied. Conflicts were inevitable. By 1850 fighting between Native Americans and settlers had begun. The U.S. Army was called in to put the Indians down.

The fighting lasted more than 30 years. One by one, different groups of Indians were forced onto reservations. Some refused to go. The *Background Information* at the right discusses one of those groups

Background INFORMATION

"I WILL FIGHT NO MORE FOREVER" The Nez Percé of Oregon's Wallowa Valley lived in harmony with the settlers until the government tried to move them to a reservation in 1877. Then fighting broke out.

Under the leadership of Chief Joseph, the Nez Percé tried to retreat to Canada. They traveled for over a thousand miles, battling the army along the way. When they were almost at the Canadian border, the army surrounded them in a surprise attack. After a five-day battle, Chief Joseph surrendered. "My heart is sick and sad," he said. "From where the sun now stands, I will fight no more forever."

Discussing New Communities
Gold was discovered in California in 1848 and in southwestern Oregon in 1850. The discoveries brought thousands of people to the West, many via the Oregon Trail. Mining towns sprang up overnight, bringing cash into the territory.

Suggested Questions

● *Why might some pioneers have been both happy and sad when they reached the end of the trail?* (They might have been happy that the journey was over but sad if they lost any friends or family along the way.)

● *Why did many of the pioneers settle around Oregon City?* (It was the largest city in Oregon.)

● *What are three ways people planned to make a living in the West?* (farming, opening shops, looking for gold)

● *Why was life difficult for many pioneers when they arrived in the West?* (Many of them had no money and few belongings.)

★THINKING FURTHER: *Compare and Contrast* **Look at the picture of Oregon City in the 1850s. How would a picture of Oregon City be different today?** (It would show modern buildings and transportation.)

Newly arrived pioneers built farms and houses (top). Communities like Oregon City grew quickly (bottom).

New Communities

After many months and thousands of miles, most of the pioneers reached Oregon. Some of them had lost family and friends along the way. One traveler wrote, "Our journey across the Plains was a long and hard one. We lost everything but our lives."

Most pioneers were planning to settle around Oregon City, Oregon. Many new cities were starting up. Oregon City was the largest. Some people were planning to farm the rich land. Others were planning to open up shops. Some were looking for gold in Oregon and California. Once there, though, life was not easy. Many people arrived with no money and few belongings. They were starting new lives.

214

CITIZENSHIP

RECOGNIZING PERSPECTIVES Invite students to read the following books and then discuss the points of view they present about westward expansion.

● *Little House on the Prairie,* Laura Ingalls Wilder (Harper Collins, 1935). In this book, students will encounter some of the pioneers' negative opinions about Native Americans. Explain that one cause of prejudice is a lack of understanding of different ways of life.

● *Brother Eagle, Sister Sky* by Susan Jeffers (Dial Books, 1991). This is an illustrated adaptation of a speech delivered by Chief Seattle, one of the leaders of the Northwest Nations, during treaty negotiations with the U.S. government in the mid 1850s.

Background INFORMATION

MORE ABOUT NEW COMMUNITIES George Washington Bush was one of the leaders of a wagon train that made the long journey across the Oregon Trail. But when Bush and his family finally reached Oregon, they were turned away. The reason: Bush was an African American. The Oregon settlers had just passed a law prohibiting African Americans from settling in the area.

Bush and his family headed north toward Puget Sound. Other members of the wagon train chose to join them. Together, they founded the state of Washington.

To learn more about Bush and the experiences of other African American settlers, students can read *Black Heroes of the Wild West* by Ruth Pelz (Open Hand Publishing, 1990).

Our Country Grows

In 1869 a railroad was built across the country. Soon railroads replaced the Oregon Trail. Today people still move to different parts of the country looking to start new lives. But the ways people travel have certainly changed! How do people travel between communities in our country today?*

WHY IT MATTERS

Earlier in this book you read that English settlers came to Jamestown hoping to build new communities in our country. In the same way, the pioneers who traveled west along the Oregon Trail dreamed of building better lives.

The history of our country is filled with stories of people moving to new communities. As you read the next lesson, think about what it would be like to come to a new community, in a new land, to build a better life.

Trails were filled with ruts and holes, which often damaged wagon wheels.

✔// Reviewing Facts and Ideas

SUM IT UP

- In the 1840s and 1850s many pioneers traveled west on the Oregon Trail.
- The route over the prairie and mountains was difficult.
- Stories of people moving to new communities are part of our country's history.

THINK ABOUT IT

1. What was the Oregon Trail?
2. **FOCUS** What was it like to travel west on the Oregon Trail?
3. **THINKING SKILL** Can you _predict_ what responsibilities you might have had on a wagon train? In what ways are they like yours today?
4. **WRITE** Write a diary entry describing a day you spent traveling with your family.

215

Discussing Our Country Grows

Turn to p. 244 for *Background Information* about the first transcontinental railroad, which is referred to on the first line of this section.

Suggested Questions

- **Why did people stop using the Oregon Trail in the late 1800s?** *(Railroads replaced the trail.)*

Understanding WHY IT MATTERS

Help students understand what the pioneers had in common with other settlers of the United States.

Suggested Questions

★**THINKING FURTHER:** *Compare and Contrast* **What do the following groups of people have in common: the Jamestown settlers, the pioneers, the people from other countries who came to the United States?** *(They all moved to new places, hoping to build better lives.)*

⭐ 3 CLOSE

SUM IT UP

Have students write their answers to the questions below.

Suggested Questions

- **Why did the pioneers leave their homes to move west?** *(to farm on the rich land; to build better lives)*

- **Why was life hard on the Oregon Trail?** *(The terrain was rugged; there was no time for rest; bad weather and sickness were constant threats.)*

EVALUATE
✓ **Answers to Think About It**

1. one of the routes the pioneers used to move west

2. Students should mention how the pioneers traveled, the difficulties they encountered on the trail, and the interaction between the travelers.

3. Accept any reasonable answers.

4. Encourage students to include information about where they went, how long the trip took, and how they traveled.

Write About It Have students write a letter from a pioneer child to a friend back home comparing and contrasting life in the wagon train with life at home.

Meeting *Individual* NEEDS

RETEACHING (Easy) Have students work with partners to draw two pictures of life on the Oregon Trail. One picture should be titled "On the Move" and show the pioneers traveling on the trail. The other picture should be titled "At Rest" and show the pioneers camped out at night.

EXTENSION (Average) Have students use their *Desk Maps* to trace the Oregon Trail and then label the states that are there today.

ENRICHMENT (Challenging) Have students use library resources to do research on Oregon City, Oregon, or Independence, Missouri. Ask students to make a chart comparing and contrasting life in those cities today and in the days of the pioneers.

SKILLS LESSON

PAGES 216–217

Lesson Overview
Classifying is the process of sorting items into categories.

Lesson Objective
★ Recognize similarities and differences among a collection of items.

1 PREPARE

MOTIVATE On a chart, write the words *Writing* and *Reading*. Have students sort items in the classroom by placing them in the proper category: writing (pencil, paper, chalk) or reading (books, posters). Explain that this process is called *classifying*.

SET PURPOSE Explain that classifying involves grouping similar items together. Have students suggest new categories under which to sort the classroom objects.

DISCUSSING HELPING YOURSELF Have volunteers read aloud the tips in the *Helping Yourself* box on p. 217.

Resource REMINDER

Practice Book: *p. 47*
Transparency: *Graphic Organizer*

THINKING SKILLS

Classifying

VOCABULARY
classifying

WHY THE SKILL MATTERS

Heading west on the Oregon Trail required careful planning. Travel conditions were very difficult. Pioneers had to plan what to carry with them in their wagons. If a wagon was too heavy to pull, the oxen would get tired and sick. On the other hand, the pioneers were going on a long journey across the country. There were no repair shops or stores with supplies along the way. Pioneers had to bring the things they needed for the trip and for the new homes and farms they were going to build.

One skill that can help in making choices like these is classifying. Classifying is grouping similar things together. Classifying helps to sort many items.

USING THE SKILL

Look at the pictures on the next page. They show some of the different things people wanted to bring with them on the Oregon Trail.

Suppose you were traveling west in the 1840s. Not everything shown in the picture can fit in your wagon. To plan what to take, you could classify the items into things that you will surely need and things that could be given up.

First select an item that you think is necessary. Supplies of food, such as flour and sugar, are necessary. Find other items that are also needed, such as the hammer and nails for repairs. What items are not needed? A favorite old piece of furniture is not absolutely necessary. Could the doll stay behind if there were no room? Continue to sort the items into two groups, those that are needed and those that are not.

216

Background INFORMATION

ALONG THE WAY For life on the trail and in their new homes, pioneers carried supplies such as the following:

- rifles and ammunition for hunting and protection;
- hundreds of pounds of flour, sugar, bacon, coffee, salt, dried fruit and rice, plus barrels to store water during desert crossings;
- pots and pans; knives, forks, and spoons; bowls, dishes, and cups;
- tents, blankets, and extra clothing; needles and thread for sewing;
- axes, saws, grease for wagon wheels;
- plows, hoes, shovels, seed for planting a first crop.

Many families started their journey with items that were hard to leave behind such as china, portraits, books, or toys. But overloaded wagons soon broke down, and unnecessary items had to be discarded. The Oregon Trail was littered with piles of precious possessions, abandoned along the way.

Curriculum CONNECTION

LINK TO MATHEMATICS Food supplies for each child on the trail included 100 pounds of flour, 50 pounds of bacon, 15 pounds of sugar, 15 pounds of coffee, 10 pounds of rice, and 10 pounds of dried fruit. Have students figure out how many pounds of food had to be packed for each child. How many pounds for a family of three children? (100 + 50 + 15 + 15 + 10 + 10 = 200; 200 x 3 = 600).

*Needle and thread are for mending clothes; coffee pot and knife are used for cooking; a doll and a guitar would be fun for a child to have.

TRYING THE SKILL

There is more than one way to classify the items shown in the picture. Suppose your goal is to find items for mending and making clothes. Which items are those? Which items are useful for cooking? Which items would help a child enjoy a long trip?*

Use the Helping Yourself box to guide you in classifying.

HELPING Yourself

- Classifying is grouping similar things together.
- Look for items with similar features. Classify them in a group.
- There may be more than one way to classify a group of items.

REVIEWING THE SKILL

1. What is classifying?
2. Which items would you classify as being useful for wagon repairs? Which ones are not useful?
3. Look through the items in your desk or school bag. How could you classify them?
4. Why do you think it is helpful to classify things?

217

2 TEACH

Why the Skill Matters Have students discuss ways they use classifying to create order, such as arranging laundry in drawers or food in cupboards. Classifying helps us organize items so they are easier to find and use.

Using the Skill Create two columns on the chalkboard, one titled *Need* and the other titled *Want*. Ask students to classify the items pictured in the text and to explain the reasoning behind their decisions.

Suggested Questions

- *Which items should be classified as needs?* (sugar, flour, pot, pan, needle, thread, scissors, fabric, hammer, knife, nails, saw)

- *Which items should be classified as wants?* (furniture, vase, toy, doll, book, guitar)

Trying the Skill Have students work with partners to reclassify the items in the picture into the following categories: Food, Toys, Tools. Remind students to use the *Helping Yourself* box if necessary.

3 CLOSE

SUM IT UP

Have students share their new classifications with the class and explain the reasoning behind their classification decisions.

EVALUATE
✓ **Answers to Reviewing the Skill**

1. placing similar items together in the same group and naming the group

2. useful: hammer, knife, nails, saw. Not useful: sugar, flour, pots, pans, furniture, vase, needle, thread, scissors, fabric, toy, doll, book, guitar

3. writing materials, reading materials, food, clothing

4. Possible answers: to keep items organized so they can be easily found when needed; to select the best items to take along on a trip; to make it easier to be sure you have packed everything you need.

Background INFORMATION

USING THE GRAPHIC ORGANIZER You may want to have students work with this Graphic Organizer transparency to help them organize their information.

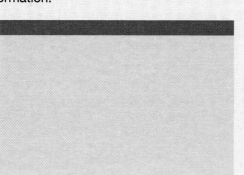

LESSON 2

PAGES 218-223

Lesson Overview
Millions of Europeans emigrated to the U.S. in the early 1900s.

Lesson Objectives
★ Understand why immigrants came to the U.S. in the early 1900's.

★ Appreciate the contributions of different cultural groups to the U.S.

1 PREPARE

MOTIVATE Direct students to the *Read Aloud* and then the picture. Explain that the Statue of Liberty wears the crown of justice and carries the torch of liberty. Invite students to tell what they know about "Miss Liberty" and what she symbolizes to people all over the world. Then take this opportunity to revisit the *Background Information* about the Statue of Liberty on p. 204.

SET PURPOSE Have students read the *Read to Learn* question and speculate about the answer. Then preview the *Vocabulary* words and remind students to watch for them as they read.

2 TEACH

Discussing Journey by Sea Have students answer the questions.

Suggested Questions

● **What is the name of the "lady" Joseph saw?** *(the Statue of Liberty)*

★THINKING FURTHER: *Compare and Contrast* **What did the immigrants in the 1900s have in common with the pioneers in the 1800s?** *(Both groups were seeking to build better lives.)*

Resource REMINDER

Practice Book: *p. 48*

 Anthology: *When I First Came to This Land, p. 87; Immigrant Girl, pp. 88–89*

Technology: *Adventures CD-ROM*

Inflatable Globe

Coming to America

READ ALOUD

"That was the first time I saw the Statue of Liberty, when I was standing on deck. And I had a hat on, and the wind came along and took my hat off. I said to my mother in Italian, 'Mama, there goes my hat!' And I said to her, 'Look at the lady, the lady over there!'"

Focus Activity

READ TO LEARN
Why did Immigrants come to America?

VOCABULARY
immigrant
oral history

PLACES
New York City
Ellis Island

Journey by Sea

These are the words of Joseph Allatin (a lah TEEN). The "lady" he saw was the Statue of Liberty. Joseph was six years old. His family had left Italy in 1894. The family sailed across the Atlantic Ocean to make new lives in the United States. The Statue of Liberty is in the harbor of New York City. It brought great joy to people like Joseph. It meant that they had arrived in the United States.

The Statue of Liberty is still a symbol that our country welcomes many immigrants. An immigrant is someone who comes to live in a new country. Like the pioneers who moved west in the 1840s and 1850s, immigrants were seeking a new life. During the early 1900s, they came to the United States looking for freedom. They also came because they could not find good jobs in their own country.

218

Reading STRATEGIES *and* Language DEVELOPMENT

SEQUENCE There are many opportunities for students to recognize sequence of events in this lesson. Explain that *sequence* means the logical order in which things happen. As students read have them tell a partner the sequence of events in some immigrants' lives. Ask them to look for signal words like *first, during, once, then, never,* and *often* to help organize events in the order in which they occurred.

ABBREVIATIONS Remind students that abbreviations are shortened forms of words. Explain that words that are abbreviated—shortened—are almost always abbreviated the same way. For example, *Mr.* (page 220) is always the spelling used for the abbreviation of *Mister.* Have students review the abbreviations of other similar words, such as *street, avenue, doctor.*

Arriving in New York

Once the ships carrying immigrants arrived in New York, they sailed past the Statue of Liberty to Ellis Island. Ellis Island was an immigration center. Officers there decided if people could stay in the United States. Immigrants who were sick might be forced to return to their country.

Many Americans today had a relative who came through Ellis Island. Lauren Buchter (BUHK ter) is 11 years old. Her great-grandfather came from Austria in 1902. He went through Ellis Island and then lived in New York City. Lauren's great-grandmother followed in 1916.

Lauren lives in New York City today. She never knew her great-grandparents. But she likes to learn about her past by talking to her grandfather, Jerry Selinfreund (SE lihn froynd). He was born a few years after his parents came to New York City.

When she asks her grandfather questions, Lauren is listening to oral history. Oral history is telling people what life was like in the past.

Children of all ages arrived with their families at Ellis Island (top). Lauren Buchter learns about the past from her grandfather (below). Here he is as a young boy long ago (left).

219

Suggested Questions

● **Where did Lauren's great-grandparents and many other immigrants live when they came to America?** (on the Lower East Side in New York City)

● **Where did the immigrants on the Lower East Side come from?** (many different places)

● **What language did the immigrants speak?** (many different languages)

● **How was life hard for the immigrants?** (Their apartments were crowded and people were poor.)

● **What is a tenement?** (a run-down apartment building)

★**THINKING FURTHER:** *Compare and Contrast* **How might life be more difficult for someone who didn't speak English when they arrived?** (It might be hard to get a job. It would be hard to read street signs and talk to people in some of the stores. It would be hard to understand the customs of your new country.)

The Lower East Side

Like many other immigrants, Lauren's great-grandparents went to live on New York City's Lower East Side. It was very crowded. Most people lived in small, run-down apartment buildings called tenements.

"Even though living conditions were tough, my mother did not mind," said Mr. Selinfreund. "She lived in a tenement. She had to walk up to the fifth floor."

Immigrants came from many countries. They came for different reasons. Lauren's great-grandparents came for religious freedom.

Immigrants on the Lower East Side had different cultures. They also spoke many different languages. Having their children learn English was important. "My mother spoke many languages," Mr. Selinfreund said. "But none of them was English. That was one of the hardest parts. But she was so happy to be in the United States."

The Lower East Side was a community alive with very crowded apartments and busy streets.

Background INFORMATION

WHY IMMIGRANTS LEFT Use the *Inflatable Globe* or *Atlas* pp. R10–R11 to point out the countries named below.

● In Ireland, disease destroyed the potato crop. As this was the main source of income, millions of people died of starvation or fled to America in desperation.

● The largest wave of immigrants to New York City were from southern and eastern Europe. (Poland, Italy, Russia, Romania, Hungary, Turkey, and Greece) In many of these countries, ruling nobles controlled the wealth. Most people lived in poverty, and many were persecuted for their religious beliefs and cultural backgrounds.

● Many immigrants came from Germany, Sweden, and Denmark looking for farmlands. They continued on from New York to emigrate west.

Using the Anthology 📖

IMMIGRANT GIRL, pages 88–90 This selection is excerpted from a fact-based story of a young girl who emigrates to New York City in the early 1900s to escape religious persecution in Russia.

WHEN I FIRST CAME TO THIS LAND, page 87 If available, use the *Anthology Cassette* to play this song. Students can sing along while reading the lyrics in the *Anthology*.

Second-Language Support

DIALOGS Second-language learners can benefit from participating in oral-history research. Work with students to list questions they can ask their relatives about coming to America. Then suggest that children ask the questions in their native tongue, translate the answers into English, and share them orally in small groups.

Work and Play

Most immigrants worked very hard. Often they did several jobs to make a living. "My father was a glazier *(window-maker)* and a religious leader," said Mr. Selinfreund. "He also taught dancing. He even drove a taxi and became a button-maker."

Many women and children worked, too. Some worked in factories. Children sold pencils, candy, or newspapers on the streets. But life was not all work for children. The streets were also their playgrounds. They played tag and stickball. Instead of a baseball bat, they used a broomstick. Many neighbors came out to play or watch. But everything stopped when the soda man came by selling cold sodas!

Life was both difficult and fun. Children often worked to earn money to help their families (top). But there was also time to play street games like stickball (bottom).

Discussing Work and Play Explain that people had to work very hard for several reasons. Like the pioneers and the colonists, they were starting new lives with very few possessions.

Suggested Questions

● ***What did Mr. Selinfreund's father do for work?*** *(He was a glazier, religious leader, dance teacher, taxi-driver, and button-maker.)*

● ***What did children do to help make money?*** *(Children worked in factories or sold pencils, candy, or newspapers on the streets.)*

● ***What did children do for fun on the Lower East Side?*** *(They played tag and stickball.)*

★**THINKING FURTHER:** *Compare and Contrast* **How was community life on the Lower East Side different from and the same as yours?** *(Students can compare and contrast elements such as how children help out, games they play, living conditions, languages spoken, the size of the community.)*

CITIZENSHIP

LINKING PAST AND PRESENT Today on the Lower East Side, people speak many different languages. One can see signs in Hebrew next to signs in Spanish, Italian, English, Chinese, and Ukrainian. The businesses also reflect the varied flow of immigrants into the community. Two of the oldest neighborhoods in the Lower East Side are Little Italy and Chinatown.

● **LITTLE ITALY** Many Italian families settled in Little Italy. There are still outdoor cafes as well as stores that sell traditional products. The Italians celebrate their culture each year with the San Gennaro and Saint Anthony festivals.

● **CHINATOWN** A few blocks south of Little Italy is Chinatown. Signs in Chinese advertise fresh ginger and other spices and vegetables. Chinese New Year is celebrated each year in Chinatown with a colorful parade and loud firecrackers.

Have students prepare reports that compare distinctive areas of their communities where people share and celebrate a common culture and heritage. Encourage students to illustrate their reports with pictures of representative music, art, and food.

Immigrants arrived with suitcases filled with personal items. Their few belongings were all they had to start new lives.

A Country of Immigrants

The early 1900s was a time when many immigrants came to our country. They came from many different places around the world. The graph on this page shows you how many people came during this time period. Most came through New York. Others arrived in such cities as Boston and San Francisco.

Immigrants came from many different cultures. The one thing they had in common was hope—hope that life in the United States would be better.

Each group of immigrants has brought many important things to our country. They brought different languages, religions, and other parts of culture. They have made our country rich and strong.

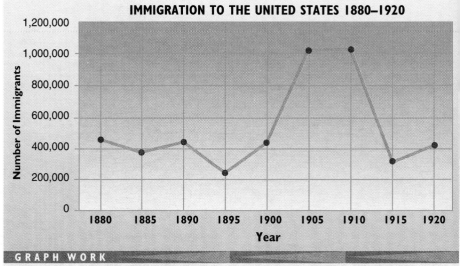

IMMIGRATION TO THE UNITED STATES 1880–1920

GRAPH WORK

The United States grew as more and more immigrants came each year.

1. About how many immigrants came to the United States in 1905? About how many came in 1920?

2. What happened to the number of immigrants who came between 1900 and 1905?

3. What can you say about the pattern of immigration between 1880 to 1920?

Source: U.S. Census Bureau

GRAPH WORK: 1. just over 1 million immigrants; about 430,000 **2.** They increased from about 450,000 to just over 1 million. **3.** At times it increased and at other times it decreased.

222

Oral History

When Lauren is older, she may tell her children about how she lived in New York too. Then she will continue her family's oral history. "It's fun to hear my family stories," said Lauren. "It helps explain who I am today."

Do you have older people in your family or community? Ask them about their lives. Then you, too, will be learning from oral history.

WHY IT MATTERS

In the early 1900s, millions of new people came to the United States. They formed new communities. But immigration was not new for our country. Immigrants have been coming to our country for hundreds of years.

Today people still move here from other countries. People here also move from place to place. There is one thing you can say about our country—it is always changing!

Visitors to Ellis Island can learn about immigration and our country's history.

✔// Reviewing Facts and Ideas

SUM IT UP

- In the early 1900s, millions of immigrants came to the United States. Life was often difficult for the new immigrants.

- Immigrants came from many different countries.

- Many immigrants settled in New York's Lower East Side. Others settled in communities throughout the country.

- One way we learn about the past is through oral history.

THINK ABOUT IT

1. Why was the Statue of Liberty important for immigrants?

2. **FOCUS** Why did immigrants come to America?

3. **THINKING SKILL** *Classify* the years shown on the graph on page 222 into two groups. Group 1 is when over one million people immigrated. Group 2 is when under one million people immigrated. What have you learned?

4. **WRITE** Write a short poem about the Statue of Liberty.

223

Discussing Oral History Help students understand that everyone has stories about history to tell.

Suggested Questions

- *How can Lauren keep the story of her family's history alive?* (by telling it to her children)

Discussing WHY IT MATTERS Remind students that the colonists were immigrants, and point out that each year many new immigrants come to settle in our country.

Suggested Questions

- *When did millions of immigrants begin coming to the United States?* (in the early 1900s)

- *What is one thing that immigrants today have in common with immigrants of the past?* (the hope of building better lives)

⭐ 3 CLOSE

SUM IT UP
Suggested Questions

- *How was life difficult for immigrants in the early 1900s?* (They lived in crowded apartments and worked long hours.)

- *What were the immigrants hoping for?* (better lives and freedom)

- *Why is oral history important?* (because it tells us about people's personal experiences and about history)

EVALUATE
✔ **Answers to Think About It**

1. The Statue of Liberty represents the freedom found in America. It is one of the first things that immigrants see when they land in New York.

2. to be free, to build better lives

3. that there were only 2 points when over 1 million people emigrated to the United States

4. Students' poems should reflect what the Statue of Liberty represents to people around the world.

Write About It Encourage students to write poems that compare their lives with those of children who lived on the Lower East Side in the early 1900s.

Meeting *Individual* NEEDS

RETEACHING (Easy) Ask students to draw pictures of life on the Lower East Side in the early 1900s. Ask them to write captions about their illustrations.

EXTENSION (Average) Have groups of students do library research and/or use *Adventures* CD-ROM to expand what they learned about the Key Places in this lesson. Students can share their findings in a simulated documentary that follows an immigrant family from its arrival at Ellis Island to its first week on the Lower East Side.

ENRICHMENT (Challenging) Invite students to make a class scrapbook of stories about people who have emigrated to the United States. In the scrapbook, students can paste drawings of people they have read about in history books; photographs of friends and relatives; and written stories about the people, telling where they came from, when they came and why, and how they built their new lives.

LESSON 3

PAGES 224–229

Lesson Overview
During WWI thousands of African Americans moved from the South to the North.

Lesson Objectives
★ Describe the African American migration from the South to the North.

★ Appreciate African American contributions to the United States.

★ Understand the role of Martin Luther King, Jr., in U.S. history.

1 PREPARE

MOTIVATE Remind students that in *Chapter 4* they learned that many African people were sold into slavery in the colonies. Explain that in this lesson students will learn about some of their descendants.

SET PURPOSE Provide students with the *Background Information* about Jacob Lawrence on p. 227. Then direct attention to the *Read Aloud* and explain that it is a quote from Lawrence. Next have students read the *Read to Learn* question. Tell them that they will learn about the *Great Migration* in this lesson. Finally, preview the *Vocabulary* words.

2 TEACH

Thinking About People on the Move Have students explain how the picture relates to the section title.

Suggested Questions

● **What is the Great Migration?** *(the movement north of many African Americans)*

● **What is the difference between migration and immigration?** *(Migration is the movement of people within a country. Immigration is the movement of people to a country.)*

Resource REMINDER

Practice Book: *p. 49*

Anthology: *Ancestry, p. 95*

Technology: *Videodisc/Video Tape 3; Adventures CD-ROM*

Moving to Northern Cities

READ ALOUD

"The Great Migration is part of my life. I grew up knowing about people on the move. . . . There was always talk in my house of other families arriving from the South."

Focus Activity

READ TO LEARN
What was the Great Migration?

VOCABULARY
migration
Great Migration
Civil War

PLACES
Chicago, Illinois

PEOPLE
Jacob Lawrence
Abraham Lincoln
Martin Luther King, Jr.

People on the Move

These are the words of an artist named Jacob Lawrence. He is describing a great journey. It was made by many African Americans in the early 1900s. During this time many African Americans left their homes in the southern part of the United States. They hoped to build new lives in northern cities.

In the last lesson you read about people moving from other countries to the United States. That type of movement, as you know, is called immigration. Another type of movement is called migration. Migration is the movement of people from one part of a country or area to another.

In this lesson you will learn more about Jacob Lawrence. You will also learn about the Great Migration, the movement north of many African Americans.

224

Reading STRATEGIES *and* Language DEVELOPMENT

USING VISUALS Have students compare the pictures on p. 226 with the pictures on p. 227. Ask them what the pictures tell us about lifestyles in the South and North. Then have students look at the picture on p. 228. What does it tell us about the Great Migration?

WORDS OFTEN CONFUSED The words *migration* and *immigration* are often confused because they look alike. One way to distinguish between them is to remember that the prefix *im-* means "in" or "into." *Immigration* is the act of moving into a country. *Migration* is the act of moving within a country. Encourage students to name other pairs of often-confused words and think of mnemonic devices to distinguish between them. For example, we can distinguish between *principle* and *principal* by remembering that the school principal is our pal.

The Civil War

Since colonial times most African Americans had been living as slaves. They were forced to work for the people who owned them. They were not allowed to read and write. They were not free people.

Look at the map below. From 1861 to 1865 the Northern and Southern parts of the United States went to war against each other.

This war was called the Civil War. People in the South wanted to be separate from the North. People in the North wanted both sides to stay together as one country. During the war President Abraham Lincoln wanted to end slavery. Finally, in 1865, the war ended. Slavery was over. African Americans were free.

Abraham Lincoln said, "slavery must die that the nation might live."

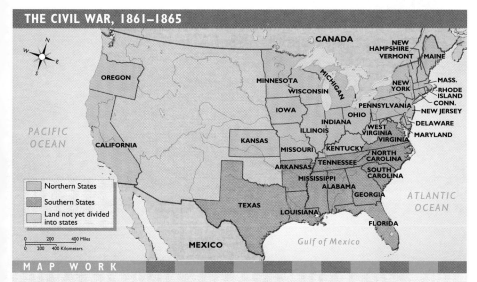

THE CIVIL WAR, 1861–1865

Northern States
Southern States
Land not yet divided into states

MAP WORK

During the Civil War the Northern states fought against the Southern states.

1. Locate Texas on the map. Was it part of the Northern or Southern states?

2. Which Northern states shared a border with Southern states?

3. Can you name any states today that did not exist during the Civil War?

MAP WORK: **1.** Texas was a Southern state. **2.** Missouri, Kentucky, West Virginia, Maryland
3. Alaska, Montana, Washington, amongst others

225

Discussing the Civil War Help students understand some of the economic reasons that led to the Civil War: As an agricultural society, the South had an economic investment in slavery. The North did not have the same investment because it was largely industrial.

Suggested Questions

● *How had most African Americans in the United States been living since colonial times?* (as slaves)

● *Why do you think enslaved people were not allowed to read or write?* (Answers should reflect the idea that knowledge is power.)

● *What happened in 1865?* (The Civil War ended, and African Americans gained their freedom.)

★THINKING FURTHER: *Making Conclusions* **What do you think President Lincoln meant when he said, "Slavery must die that the nation might live"?** (The nation was so divided over the issue of slavery it was in danger of breaking apart.)

More **MAP WORK**

Tell students that the Civil War caused families, friends, and neighbors to turn upon each other. It even divided a state.

Have students use the map to find the Northern state (West Virginia) and the Southern state (Virginia) that had been one state before the Civil War.

Curriculum CONNECTION

LINKS TO READING The following books will help students understand the horrors of slavery and the heroic efforts people made to escape it.

● *Follow the Drinkin' Gourd* by Jeannette Winter (Knopf, 1988). This account of a family fleeing to the North reveals the courage of fugitive slaves and those who helped them.

● *Go Free or Die* by Jeri Ferris (Macmillan/McGraw-Hill, 1988). This biography of Harriet Tubman focuses on her early years and ends with her flight to freedom. An epilogue recounts her work on the Underground Railroad.

● *Nettie's Trip South* by Ann Turner (Macmillan, 1987). Written in the form of a letter, this book chronicles the reactions of a northern white girl who encounters slavery for the first time on a trip to the South.

Background INFORMATION

ABRAHAM LINCOLN AND THE CIVIL WAR

● When Abraham Lincoln won the election of 1860, the Southern states refused to recognize an antislavery President. They began to secede from the Union even before he was inaugurated.

● In his campaign for President, Lincoln had said, "A house divided against itself cannot stand." Less than five weeks after taking office, he was called upon to act on those words.

● The Civil War lasted from 1861 to 1865. Lincoln spent those years directing military affairs and bolstering morale in the North. He devoted what little free time he had to visiting wounded soldiers and consoling grieving families.

Explain that many African Americans put themselves in great jeopardy to fight the injustices they faced.

Suggested Questions

● *In what ways was life difficult for African Americans after the Civil War?* *(They had few chances for good jobs or education, and they were treated unfairly.)*

● *What do the pictures tell us about the kinds of jobs many African Americans had at that time?* *(The pictures show that many African Americans worked on farms or did domestic work such as sewing.)*

● *When did the Great Migration begin?* *(in the early 1900s)*

● *Why did many African Americans move to northern cities?* *(They hoped they would be able to build better lives.)*

★ THINKING FURTHER: *Using Prior Knowledge* *Why might African Americans have expected to be treated more fairly in the North than in the South?* *(The South fought to preserve slavery; the North fought to abolish it.)*

Difficult Lives

Although they were free, African Americans living in the South still had a difficult time after the Civil War. There were very few chances for good jobs or education. They still were not treated fairly.

In the early 1900s, African Americans heard there were good jobs and better opportunities in northern cities like Chicago, Detroit, New York, and Philadelphia. Thousands of people moved north hoping for a better life. The Great Migration began.

Many African Americans in the South lived in rural communities where they were not treated fairly.

226

Background INFORMATION

LIFE IN THE SOUTH For years after the Civil War, African Americans were banned from most spheres of public life in the South. Segregation was legalized through Jim Crow laws and a series of Supreme Court decisions, including the "separate but equal" ruling in 1896.

● African Americans could not eat in the same restaurants as whites, go to the same schools, or attend the same events. In many places they were prevented from voting.

● Many African Americans were sharecroppers, renting land from white landowners and paying in crops. Often, they paid so much that they had barely enough left to feed their families. Other ways of making a living were limited. Most jobs that involved working with white people were prohibited to African Americans.

MORE ABOUT THE GREAT MIGRATION Several factors contributed to the Great Migration.

● The early 1900s was a time of increased hostility toward African Americans in the South. Lynchings were an ever-present danger.

● A series of floods and insect infestations caused serious crop damage, making life difficult for farmers throughout the South.

● The outbreak of WWI in 1914 created a shortage of labor in northern industries. Factory owners sent agents to southern towns to recruit workers. The promise of new opportunities convinced many African Americans to leave their homes and move north.

Starting Over

Starting a new life in the North was exciting for many African Americans. One woman wrote of her life in Chicago, Illinois: "I am well and thankful to be in a city. . . . The people are rushing here by the thousands. The houses are so pretty, we [have] a nice place. Hurry up and come to Chicago. It is wonderful. . . ."

As communities grew in the North, there were more opportunities to find jobs. People worked in iron and steel mills. Some made buildings. Many worked in factories where they made products like bricks and glass. Others worked on railroads. Their lives were improving. As their community grew, some people started their own businesses. Many people were happy with their decision to migrate to the North.

These photos of life in the North were taken in the 1920s by the photographer James Van Der Zee.

227

Thinking About Painting the Great Migration If possible, bring in *The Great Migration* (HarperCollins, 1992), which illustrates Lawrence's Migration series.

Suggested Questions

● ***When did Jacob Lawrence's parents migrate to the North? To what city did they move?*** *(1917; Philadelphia)*

● ***Why do you think Lawrence decided to do a series of paintings about the Great Migration?*** *(Accept any reasonable answers. For example: He might have been interested in the subject because of his parents' experience.)*

★ **THINKING FURTHER:** *Making Conclusions* ***What can we learn from Lawrence's paintings?*** *(We can learn about an important time in our nation's history and what it was like to live during that time.)*

Learning from the Primary Source Have students examine the painting.

Suggested Questions

● ***To what cities are the people in the picture going?*** *(Chicago, New York, St. Louis)*

● ***How are they getting there?*** *(by train)*

● ***Why do you think Lawrence made the train station look so crowded?*** *(to show that many people took part in the Great Migration)*

Painting the Great Migration

You have read about the artist Jacob Lawrence. About 1917 his parents migrated north to Philadelphia. As a young boy Jacob Lawrence became interested in painting. He knew he wanted to be an artist. Later, in 1941, he made a series of paintings about the Great Migration. Look at the painting on this page. Describe what it tells about the Great Migration.

Painting by Jacob Lawrence, completed in 1941.

228

Curriculum CONNECTION

LINKS TO ART Share with students the following quote from Jacob Lawrence: "People all over the world are still on the move, trying to build better lives for themselves and their families." Then invite students to create a three-panel mural called "People on the Move."

● Divide the class into three groups. Assign each group one of the following subjects for their panel: pioneers moving west, immigrants moving to the United States, African Americans moving north. Then work with students to make a storyboard of their ideas.

● Invite students to illustrate their panels on butcher paper taped to the walls. When the mural is finished, let each group present its panel and explain what it shows.

CITIZENSHIP

CIVIL RIGHTS During the 1950s and 1960s Americans from all walks of life came together to put an end to segregation. The following books can help students learn about two heroes of the civil rights movement.

● *A Picture Book of Rosa Parks,* David Adler (Holiday House, 1993). Rosa Parks was arrested when she refused to give up her seat to a white passenger on a bus in Montgomery, Alabama. The events that followed marked the beginning of the civil rights movement.

● *I Have a Dream,* Margaret Davidson (Scholastic, 1986). Dr. Martin Luther King, Jr., led the year-long bus boycott to protest the arrest of Rosa Parks. His leadership then and in the years that followed was an inspiration to America.

Martin Luther King, Jr.

As African Americans soon found out, life was still difficult in the North. Although they did have a better chance for work and education, they still faced unfair treatment. They often received less pay than a white worker for the same job.

Unfair treatment continued in both the North and South. In the 1950s and 1960s thousands of people joined together to work for change. One African American leader was Martin Luther King, Jr. He spent his life working to make sure all people were treated fairly.

WHY IT MATTERS

You have read about immigration and migration. Our country's history includes many stories of people moving to new communities to build new lives. In the next lesson you will learn how people today still move to the United States with hopes of starting new lives.

Martin Luther King, Jr., wanted to make laws fair for all Americans.

✔ Reviewing Facts and Ideas

SUM IT UP

- The Civil War was fought between the North and South from 1861 to 1865.
- President Abraham Lincoln helped to end slavery.
- The Great Migration took place during the early 1900s.
- Martin Luther King, Jr., worked to end the unfair treatment of people.

THINK ABOUT IT

1. Why did African Americans migrate to the North?
2. **FOCUS** What was the Great Migration?
3. **THINKING SKILL** How is migration *like* immigration? How is it *different*?
4. **GEOGRAPHY** Look at the map on page 225. In what direction is Maine from Florida?

229

Discussing Martin Luther King, Jr. For *Background Information* about Martin Luther King, Jr., refer to p. T8.

Suggested Questions

- ***What is an example of the unfair way African Americans were treated in the North?*** *(They were often paid less than white workers for the same job.)*

- ***When did thousands of people begin to work together for change?*** *(1950s and 1960s)*

- ***How did Martin Luther King, Jr., help all Americans?*** *(He worked to make sure everyone was treated fairly.)*

Thinking About WHY IT MATTERS
Be sure students understand why the Great Migration is an important part of U.S. history.

Suggested Questions

- ***What did the people who took part in the Great Migration contribute to the cities they moved to?*** *(their labor, skills, and culture)*

⭐ 3 CLOSE

SUM IT UP
Have students answer the questions.

Suggested Questions

- ***Who was President during the Civil War?*** *(Lincoln)*

- ***Which parts of the country were most affected by the Great Migration?*** *(the North and the South)*

- ***Why do we celebrate Martin Luther King Day as a national holiday?*** *(He helped make life better for all Americans.)*

EVALUATE
✔ **Answers to Think About It**
1. They wanted to build better lives.
2. the movement north of many African Americans in the early 1900s
3. Like: It involves moving from one place to another. Different: Migration is movement within a country. Immigration is movement to a country.
4. northeast *Location*

Write About It Have students write a caption explaining the painting on p. 228.

Meeting *Individual* NEEDS

RETEACHING (Easy) Have students ask their grandparents or other senior citizens about their memories of the civil rights movement. Students can share what they learn with their classmates.

EXTENSION (Average) Have students work with partners to write a series of letters between a friend who took part in the Great Migration and a friend who stayed at home.

ENRICHMENT (Challenging) Have students work in groups of three to expand what they have learned about the Key People in this lesson. Groups can obtain information from library books and *Adventures* CD-ROM. Have them use their findings to write a three-part report telling what each Key Person contributed to the United States.

LEGACY

Lesson Overview
Family reunions help keep the Pressley family strong.

Lesson Objective
★ Link family values yesterday and today.

1 PREPARE

MOTIVATE Review the meaning of the word *legacy.* Then have students think about family activities they do year after year.

SET PURPOSE Have several volunteers explain what they usually do to celebrate their birthdays. Point out that this ritual is part of their own history, or legacy.

2 TEACH

Understanding the Concept of a Legacy Help students understand that family traditions are legacies passed between generations. Explain how traditions are built when people create a ritual and other family members continue it. Even a simple family tradition, like reading a bedtime story, tells us about families.

Discussing A Family Reunion Help students link the legacy of the Pressley family with the legacy of our country.

Suggested Questions

● **When did some members of the Pressley family move north?** *(during the Great Migration)*

● **When they moved, who did they leave behind?** *(other members of the family)*

● **How do they keep in touch with family members?** *(They have a reunion every year.)*

★**THINKING FURTHER:** *Predicting*
How might the Pressley family continue their family legacy? *(Possible answers: by having more reunions; by listening to oral histories; by sharing experiences.)*

Legacy
LINKING PAST AND PRESENT

A Family Reunion

During the Great Migration, some members of the Pressley family in South Carolina moved north to Philadelphia.

Today people in this family live in many different communities. Every year they return to South Carolina to have a family reunion. At the reunion they see people they care about. They also learn about their family history. It is a special time.

Today, as in the past, families sometimes move. They may move to new communities in the United States or even to another country.

At the airport Felicia Green welcomes cousins traveling to the reunion from faraway places.

230

CITIZENSHIP

LINKING PAST AND PRESENT Invite students to paint portraits of one of their older family members or close friends.

● Students can bring in photocopies of photographs or ask another person to describe the family member.

● Have students illustrate the person involved in a family tradition or activity.

● Exhibit the paintings in a portrait gallery for other students to enjoy. You also may want to encourage each student to share his or her portrait with the class while telling a story about it.

Felicia's scrapbook includes a page on fun at the family reunion. Whether it's storytelling (top left), singing or playing baseball, there's lots to do!

It doesn't matter who wins in the tug of war, as long as it's fun for everyone.

231

Examining the Pictures As students study the pictures, help them understand how the activities can become legacies.

Suggested Questions

● **What can you see people doing in the pictures?** *(telling stories, playing games, singing)*

● **How does the family reunion make the Pressley family stronger?** *(Possible answers: They get to know each other better, learn family history, and help each other.)*

★**THINKING FURTHER:** *Making Decisions* **Suppose you were at a family reunion of your own. What kinds of things would you like to do?** *(Encourage students to give reasons for their choices.)*

Global CONNECTION

FAMILY CELEBRATIONS Have students find out about family celebrations around the world, such as Boxing Day in the United Kingdom and El Día de los Muertos in Mexico.

● Have students create illustrated reports explaining the traditions associated with the event.

● Encourage students to use *Adventures* CD-ROM to create maps that show the countries the holiday is celebrated in.

MEETING *Individual* NEEDS

RETEACHING (Easy) Ask students to explain how a family reunion becomes a legacy. Have them also explain why people like to celebrate family reunions.

EXTENSION (Average) Have students think about the kinds of things family members share at a reunion. Then ask them to look at each picture on pp. 230–231 and write a conversation between the people in the pictures.

ENRICHMENT (Challenging) Have students suppose that they were planning a family reunion. Ask them to write a plan that describes how long the reunion will be, what games they will play, and other events such as singing and storytelling.

LESSON 4

PAGES 232-236

Lesson Overview
The U.S. still attracts immigrants today.

Lesson Objectives
★ Discuss immigration to the United States today.

★ Appreciate the contributions of various cultural groups to the United States.

★ Understand the process of becoming a U.S. citizen.

1 PREPARE

MOTIVATE Ask students to read the *Read Aloud.* Then have volunteers talk about times they have moved to new places.

SET PURPOSE Direct students to the *Read to Learn* question and invite speculation about the answer. Then point out the *Vocabulary* word.

2 TEACH

Discussing Moving to a New Country Tell students that the girl in the picture is Delores Stivalet.

Suggested Questions

● **Where did Delores Stivalet's family move to? Where did they move from?** *(to San Diego, California; from Veracruz, Mexico)*

★**THINKING FURTHER:** *Making Conclusions* **What do you think might be exciting for Delores? What might be difficult? Explain your answers.** *(Possible answers: making new friends, exploring a new neighborhood; going to a new school, learning a new language.)*

Resource REMINDER

Practice Book: *p. 50*

Anthology: *Halmoni and the Picnic, pp. 96–99; In a Neighborhood in Los Angeles, pp. 100–101*

Technology: *Videodisc/Video Tape 3*

Desk Maps: *United States, World*

Geo Big Book: *pp. 8–9*

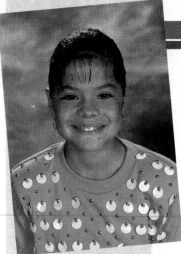

Focus Activity

READ TO LEARN
What is it like to immigrate to the United States today?

VOCABULARY
oath

PLACES
San Diego, California
Veracruz, Mexico

Immigration Today

READ ALOUD

"I like it in the United States. School is a little bit hard for me now. But it's getting better. I have new friends. But sometimes I miss my old friends."

Moving to a New Country

These are the words of a student named Delores Stivalet (STEE va lay). She and her family moved to San Diego, California, from Veracruz, Mexico, just a few years ago. Delores was 11 years old. It was an exciting time for her and her family.

Maybe you and your family at one time moved to a new community. If so, you know how the move made you feel. Perhaps you were excited, nervous, or a little sad. On the first day of school, you may have been shy.

Perhaps you or someone you know has moved to the United States from another country. Moving to a new country can be very hard. There are many things to learn and many changes to make. In this lesson you will see how immigrants like Delores and her family build new lives in the United States.

232

Reading STRATEGIES *and* Language DEVELOPMENT

REREADING Remind students that when we encounter information about sequence, or steps in a process, it is always a good idea to reread the passage. Encourage students to reread the chart on p. 235 to be sure they understand the information and the sequence.

QUOTATION MARKS Remind the class that we use quotation marks to show that a person is speaking. Then have students read the quotations in the *Infographic* on p. 234. Help them understand the function of the single quotation marks in Oyeyinka Oyelaran's statement.

Settling in San Diego

For Delores and her family, moving to a new country like the United States was challenging. Her family felt that there were better schools and more jobs for people in the United States. "If you really want to do something in the United States," her father said, "you can do it. That's why we moved here."

Delores's new community in San Diego has a lot in common with Veracruz. They both have busy ports with beautiful beaches. The climate is warm in both cities.

There are also many differences between the two cities. In San Diego, Delores and her family have to learn English. "I am learning to speak English," said Delores. "But we still speak Spanish at home."

Veracruz and San Diego are port cities. In Veracruz a woman sells goods (top). San Diego has many tall office buildings (bottom).

Thinking About Settling in San Diego Ask students to discuss what they remember about Mexico City. Have them compare Mexican and United States communities.

Suggested Questions

● **Why did Delores's father want to move to the United States?** (He felt there were better jobs and schools here and more opportunity.)

● **What is Delores learning to help her in her new city?** (She is learning to speak English.)

● **How is San Diego like Veracruz?** (They both have warm climates, busy ports, and beautiful beaches.)

● **How are San Diego and Veracruz different?** (In Veracruz, people speak Spanish.)

★THINKING FURTHER: *Making Conclusions* **Why do you think Delores's family speaks Spanish at home?** (It is their native language and an important part of their culture.)

233

CITIZENSHIP

LAND OF OPPORTUNITY The statement below, made by Henry Cisneros, can help the class understand why the U.S. is known as the "land of opportunity." Before reading the quotation aloud, remind students that they met Cisneros in Chapter 5, Lesson 3: *San Antonio Today.* Explain that he made this statement in 1984 when he was a potential candidate for Vice President.

"When my grandfather crossed into Texas from Mexico, he could never have imagined that someday one of his own would be interviewed for the Vice Presidency of the United States. The fact that this is happening is a testimony to the openness of American society and is proof that if we have faith in people and give them the tools to work with, they will achieve."

Using the Anthology 🖿

HALMONI AND THE PICNIC, PAGES 96–97 Invite students to read this selection about some of the challenges that face newcomers to the United States.

IN A NEIGHBORHOOD IN LOS ANGELES, PAGES, 100–101 Have students read the poem in English and then listen to it in Spanish on the *Anthology Cassette.* Spanish-speaking students can read aloud with the recording. Students who do not speak Spanish can follow along in their texts.

Infographic

Discussing United States Immigration Today Have one group of students use their *Desk Maps* of the world to color the country from which each student came. Have another group use their *Desk Maps* of the U.S. to color the state in which each student lives.

Suggested Questions

- **From which countries did the students emigrate?** *(India, Poland, Nigeria)*

- **How is life in the U.S. different from life in Poland for Joanna Jawdosiuk?** *(Everything seems big here.)*

- **How is life in the U.S. different from life in India for Aditya Nochur?** *(It's colder here and there is snow.)*

- **How is life in the U.S. different from life in Nigeria for Oyeyinka Oyelaran?** *(He misses some favorite foods but has learned to like some new foods.)*

★**THINKING FURTHER:** *Compare and Contrast* **What is similar about the lives of the immigrants? What is different?** *(Similar: They are all immigrants, they all find life here different from their old lives. Different: They come from very different cultures, different climates, they speak different languages, and now live in different parts of America.)*

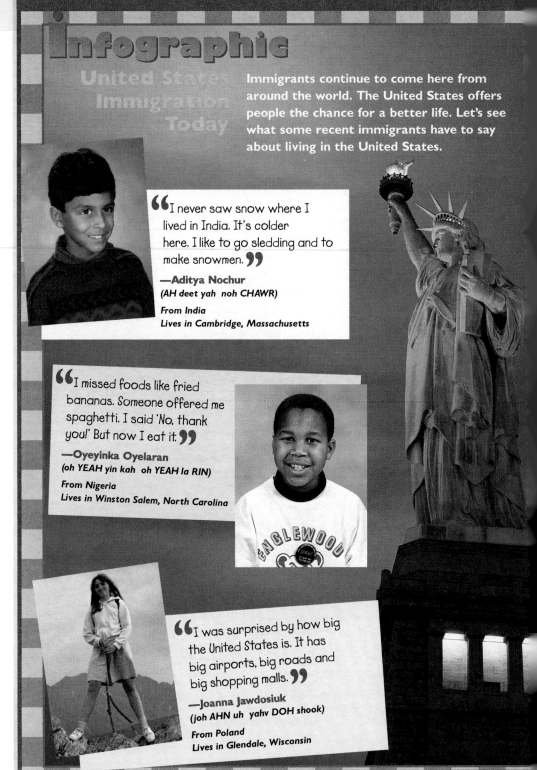

Infographic
United States Immigration Today

Immigrants continue to come here from around the world. The United States offers people the chance for a better life. Let's see what some recent immigrants have to say about living in the United States.

> "I never saw snow where I lived in India. It's colder here. I like to go sledding and to make snowmen."
>
> —**Aditya Nochur**
> *(AH deet yah noh CHAWR)*
> **From India**
> **Lives in Cambridge, Massachusetts**

> "I missed foods like fried bananas. Someone offered me spaghetti. I said 'No, thank you!' But now I eat it."
>
> —**Oyeyinka Oyelaran**
> *(oh YEAH yin kah oh YEAH la RIN)*
> **From Nigeria**
> **Lives in Winston Salem, North Carolina**

> "I was surprised by how big the United States is. It has big airports, big roads and big shopping malls."
>
> —**Joanna Jawdosiuk**
> *(joh AHN uh yahv DOH shook)*
> **From Poland**
> **Lives in Glendale, Wisconsin**

Expanding the Infographic

COMPARING CULTURES

- Have students work in small groups to research one of the immigrants' homelands. Ask each group to make a chart comparing and contrasting the foreign country with the United States.

- Invite group members to share their findings with the class, using their charts and other visual aids such as the world map in the *Atlas* or *Geo Big Book*.

- Help students make a master chart comparing and contrasting all four countries: the United States, India, Nigeria, and Poland. Students can use what they have learned to create chart headings such as the following: Geography, Language, Food, Transportation, Housing, Work, Entertainment.

Becoming a Citizen

From the Infographic you can see that people immigrate to the United States from different countries around the world. Many of these immigrants, like Delores and her family, hope to become citizens of the United States.

Study the chart below. It shows how some adult immigrants can become citizens of the United States today.

BECOMING A CITIZEN OF THE UNITED STATES OF AMERICA

EP 5: Receive a rtificate of citizenship.

STEP 1: Fill out form about you and your life.

TEP 4: Take an oath of yalty to the United tates. An oath is a tatement or promise in hich a person swears hat what he or she said true.

STEP 3: Meet with Judge, who can grant citizenship.

STEP 2: Answer questions in English about United States of America history and government.

235

Learning About Becoming a Citizen Explain that only citizens can vote. Point out that there are other rights and responsibilities that only citizens can enjoy.

Suggested Questions

- *What do many immigrants hope for when they move here?* (to become citizens of the United States)

- *Why do you think many immigrants want to become citizens?* (Possible answer: only citizens can vote.)

- *Why do most people who wish to become citizens have to be able to speak English?* (in order to answer questions about the U.S.)

- *What is an oath?* (a promise that something is true)

- *What is an oath of loyalty?* (a promise to be faithful to the United States and to be a good citizen)

★**THINKING FURTHER:** *Sequence Look at the chart. If you were an immigrant wanting to become a citizen, what would you do first?* (Learn English or fill out the form.)

CITIZENSHIP

OATH OF LOYALTY Explain that the oath new citizens take includes these promises:

- I declare that I give up my loyalty to any other country.
- I will support, defend, and be faithful to the Constitution of the United States.
- I will join the armed forces or fight in the army when the law requires it.
- I will also do other work for my country when it is required by law.
- I swear that I am freely choosing to promise these things.

Curriculum CONNECTION

HERITAGE DAY Help students organize a Cultural Heritage Day.

- Plan a feast of ethnic foods, and have students bring in favorite dishes.
- Make a chart with "hello" printed in different languages. Have students label the countries in which each language is spoken and paint national flags beside each label.
- Help partners and groups learn folk stories and songs from their own or other cultures. Encourage them to share them with the class.

Discussing WHY IT MATTERS Remind students that America is a nation of immigrants.

Suggested Questions

● **What do immigrants today have in common with our country's earliest immigrants?** *(They come to the U.S. to find freedom and build better lives.)*

3 CLOSE

SUM IT UP

Have students work with partners to prepare their responses.

Suggested Questions

● **Why might life be difficult in a new community?** *(It might be difficult to find work, adjust to a new school, and so on.)*

● **What is one way immigrants help the United States grow?** *(Possible answers: by becoming citizens; by bringing their skills and traditions.)*

EVALUATE

✓ Answers to Think About It

1. Answers will vary.

2. It is exciting because there are many opportunities here. It is hard because you have to learn English and get used to a new culture.

3. First you fill out a form about yourself and your life, then you answer questions in English about U.S. history and government, then you meet with a judge, then you take an oath of loyalty, then you receive a certificate of citizenship.

4. Students can give helpful suggestions about where to shop, how to find playgrounds, and how to take the bus.

Write About It Ask students to write a journal entry describing the first day of school for a student who has just come to this country.

WHY IT MATTERS

Immigration is even older than our country. From the early English settlers to the Ellis Island immigrants, people kept coming to this land to build new lives. The United States is still growing because of new immigrants and new citizens. The Statue of Liberty stands in New York harbor as a symbol of hope and friendship to all.

Taking the **oath** is an exciting event for immigrants who hope to build new lives in the United States.

✓ Reviewing Facts and Ideas

SUM IT UP

● Many people immigrate to the United States from different countries around the world.

● Immigrants face a new language and a new way of life in their new country.

● Immigrants continue to help the United States grow.

THINK ABOUT IT

1. Name some countries where immigrants to the United States come from.

2. **FOCUS** What is it like to immigrate to the United States today?

3. **THINKING SKILL** What is the *sequence* of steps needed to become a citizen?

4. **WRITE** Write a paragraph describing your community to someone who just moved there.

236

MEETING *Individual* NEEDS

RETEACHING (Easy) Ask students to tell what it means when we say that the United States is a country of immigrants.

EXTENSION (Average) Have students write letters to new immigrants to welcome them. Have them suggest ways to make new friends and tell about exciting things to do in your community.

ENRICHMENT (Challenging) Have students research the process of becoming a citizen and explain to the class the steps in the process.

Second-Language Support

MAKING CONNECTIONS Second-language learners may identify with the experiences Delores had in moving to the United States. Encourage them to discuss ways of making new students feel welcome at school.

CITIZENSHIP
MAKING A DIFFERENCE

Helping New Immigrants

LOS ANGELES, CALIFORNIA—Hee Jin Kang [HEE JIN KAYNG] is 11 years old. She immigrated to the United States from Korea. Hee Jin likes her new home and school. But she misses her family in Korea, especially her grandparents. "My biggest problem," says Hee Jin, "is learning English. It's not easy for me to talk with other students. So it's hard for me to make friends."

Keith Soon Kim is much older than Hee Jin. But he knows how she feels. He, too, was once an immigrant from Korea. He then became a citizen. But he did not forget how hard his early days here had been. He wanted to help new immigrant children. He wanted them to have an easier time learning about the United States.

Mr. Kim decided to work with Korean children in schools in Los Angeles. He started after-school clubs for these students. Club members practice speaking English. They also learn about American culture. Mr. Kim works with the parents of these students, too. Many Korean immigrant parents do not speak English. He helps parents and teachers communicate more easily with each other.

Today Mr. Kim continues to help Korean American immigrants. He started a camp and a leadership program for college students. Mr. Kim works hard to help young people, "because I want them to be good American citizens," he says.

". . . I want them to be good American citizens."

Keith Soon Kim

237

Lesson Objective
★ Recognize that community members help one another.

Identifying the Focus Help students understand how responsible citizens help immigrants feel at home and become good citizens.

Suggested Questions
● **How old is Hee Jin Kang? Where is she from?** (11 years old; Korea)

● **Why is it hard for Hee Jin to make friends?** (because she doesn't speak English very well yet)

● **How are Keith Soon Kim and Hee Jin Kang alike and different?** (They are both immigrants from Korea; Mr Kim is older and is a citizen.)

● **How has Mr. Kim helped Korean immigrants?** (He started after-school clubs where children practice English and learn about American culture; he made it easier for parents to talk to teachers; he started a camp and leadership program for college students.)

● **Why does Mr. Kim help Korean American immigrants?** (He wants them to become good American citizens.)

★**THINKING FURTHER:** **How do you predict Hee Jin Kang's life will change in a few years?** (She will probably speak English well, make new friends, feel more at home here.)

CITIZENSHIP

HELPING NEW RESIDENTS Explain to students that there are many local and national organizations to help new immigrants to the United States.

● Have students research such organizations, and choose one to focus on. Encourage them to use the library and other resources to get information.

● Ask them to prepare a report, including any brochures or literature from the organizations as visuals. Tell students to be sure to include information about how the organization helps people in your community or state.

Technology CONNECTION

ADVENTURES CD-ROM
Enrich the lesson with the CD-ROM activity, *All in the American Family.*

Answers to
THINKING ABOUT VOCABULARY

1. oral history
2. oath
3. prairie
4. classify
5. migration
6. immigrant
7. pioneer
8. Great Migration
9. Civil War
10. diary

Answers to
THINKING ABOUT FACTS

1. The pioneers moved west to build new lives. Some planned to farm the rich land, others to open shops, and still others to look for gold.

2. Diaries are written by real people who tell what happened to them every day. Reading a diary is like visiting with someone who lived long ago.

3. Immigrants came to the U.S. in the early 1900s to find freedom and opportunities to improve their lives.

4. African Americans wanted to leave the south after the Civil War because they were still not treated fairly. Many went north because they heard there were jobs in the factories. Most found a better life and free education for their children, but life was still hard for many.

5. Immigrants fill out a form, pass a test about the United States, meet with a judge, and take an oath of loyalty to the United States.

Resource REMINDER

Assessment Book: *Chapter 9 Test*

CHAPTER 9 REVIEW

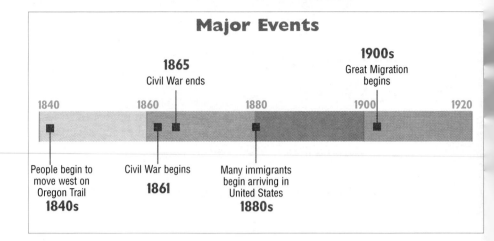

Major Events

1865
Civil War ends

1900s
Great Migration begins

1840   1860   1880   1900   1920

People begin to move west on Oregon Trail
1840s

Civil War begins
1861

Many immigrants begin arriving in United States
1880s

THINKING ABOUT VOCABULARY

Number a sheet of paper from 1 to 10. Beside each number write the word or words from the list that best fit each definition.

Civil War   immigrant   oral history
classify   migration   pioneer
diary   oath   prairie
Great Migration

1. People telling what life was like in the past
2. A statement in which a person swears to tell the truth
3. Flat or rolling land covered with tall grasses
4. To group similar things together
5. The movement of people from one part of a country to another
6. Someone who comes to live in a new country
7. A person who leads the way into a land not known to them
8. The movement north of African Americans in the early 1900s
9. The war between the northern and southern states from 1861–1865
10. A written record of what someone has done or thought each day

THINKING ABOUT FACTS

1. Why did pioneers travel west in groups known as wagon trains?
2. How do diaries help us learn about the past?
3. Why did immigrants come to the United States in the early 1900s?
4. What led to the Great Migration? Did the people who migrated north find what they hoped for?
5. What are some of the steps adult immigrants take to become citizens of the United States?

238

Suggestions for Think and Write
SIGNS OF SUCCESS

WRITING INTERVIEW QUESTIONS Students should write direct, specific questions that lead to informative reponses showing how children's lives have changed from past to present.

WRITING A WELCOME GUIDE Welcome guides should include illustrations or other visuals as well as written information that would be useful to an immigrant. The presentation of material should reflect awareness of the fact that new immigrants may not speak English.

WRITING A COMPARISON Students' work should show a clear understanding of the similarities and differences between the reasons for the two migrations. Students should understand that both groups of people were seeking to build better lives, but that many of their reasons for needing to do so were different.

For performance assessment, see Assessment Book, Chapter 9.

THINK AND WRITE

WRITING INTERVIEW QUESTIONS
Choose an older person to interview. To prepare, write some questions to ask about the person's childhood.

WRITING A WELCOME GUIDE
Create a guide to your community for new immigrants. Include helpful information such as where to buy groceries, how to get a library card, and how to get emergency help.

WRITING A COMPARISON
Write a paragraph comparing the reasons for two migrations: the move west and the Great Migration.

APPLYING THINKING SKILLS

CLASSIFYING
Review the classifying skill on pages 216–217 before answering the following questions.

1. How do you classify things?
2. How could you classify the things in your school?
3. List items you would take on an overnight camping trip. Classify the items into those needed for survival and those not needed.
4. Look at your list again. How else could you classify the items on it?
5. What are things you classify during a normal day?

Answers to
APPLYING THINKING SKILLS

1. You sort them into categories of like things.
2. For example, according to size, how they are made, who owns them, or how they are used.
3. Things needed for survival might be a blanket or sleeping bag, matches, knife, flashlight, and food. Things not needed for survival might include a book, hairbrush, teddy bear, and guitar.
4. Students might classify items into the following categories: soft things and hard things; things that produce light and things that don't; heavy things and light things.
5. For example, foods eaten for breakfast, lunch, dinner, or deserts; school clothes and play clothes, friends and strangers.

Summing Up the Chapter

The movement of people into and within the United States is classified into four groups on the main idea map below. Review the chapter. Then complete a copy of the map by listing several reasons why each group migrated or immigrated. What goal did these groups have in common?

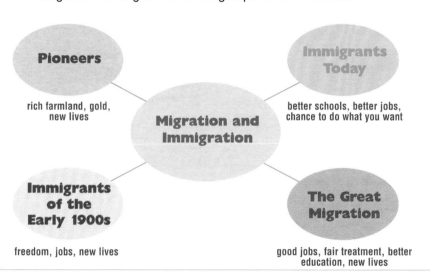

Pioneers
rich farmland, gold, new lives

Immigrants Today
better schools, better jobs, chance to do what you want

Migration and Immigration

Immigrants of the Early 1900s
freedom, jobs, new lives

The Great Migration
good jobs, fair treatment, better education, new lives

239

Suggestions for Summing Up the Chapter

- Have students copy the map on their papers or prepare copies to distribute to the class.
- Help students frame main-idea sentences such as the following:
  Why did the pioneers move west on the Oregon Trail?
  Why did immigrants come to the U.S. in the early 1900s?
  Why did African Americans move north during the Great Migration?
  Why do immigrants come to the United States today?
- Have students look through the chapter to answer the questions. Tell them to write their answers on their diagrams. Then discuss the common goal of all four groups of people: to improve their lives.

Changing the Way People Live

PAGES 240–265

CHAPTER OVERVIEW

Technology has changed the way people travel and get news. At one time people moved around the country by coach or canal. They sent messages by mail and then later by telegraph. Today transportation and communication are faster and now people fly in jets and talk on the telephone.

CHAPTER PLANNING GUIDE
Suggested pacing: 11–13 days

LESSON	LESSON FOCUS	LESSON RESOURCES
1 ON THE GO pages 242–247	Transportation Then and Now	*Practice Book* p. 52 *Anthology* pp. 91–94, 102–107
GEOGRAPHY SKILLS pages 248–249	Reading Transportation Maps	*Practice Book* p. 53 *Transparency:* 9 *Technology:* Adventures CD-ROM
2 KEEPING IN TOUCH pages 250–255	The World of Communication	*Practice Book* p. 54 *Anthology* pp. 102, 108–112 *Desk Map* United States
GLOBAL CONNECTIONS pages 256–261	A Tunnel in Europe	*Practice Book* p. 55 *Technology:* Adventures CD-ROM *Desk Map* World
LEGACY pages 262–263	Here We Go: Linking Past and Present	
CHAPTER REVIEW pages 264–265	Students' understanding of vocabulary, content, and skills is assessed.	*Assessment:* Ch. 10 Test, Performance Assessment Ch. 10 *Transparency:* Graphic Organizer

OPTIONS FOR STUDENT ACTIVITIES

Citizenship pp. 247, 251, 262

Curriculum Connection pp. 244, 252, 254, 258, 260, 262

Using the Anthology p. 250

ASSESSMENT OPPORTUNITIES

Meeting Individual Needs pp. 241, 247, 249, 255, 261, 263

Write About It pp. 247, 255, 261, 263

Chapter Review pp. 264–265

Assessment Book

Chapter Test Ch. 10 Test

Performance Assessment Ch. 10

Using Geo Adventures Use **Geo Adventures** Daily Geography Activities to assess students' understanding of geography skills.

Using the Vocabulary Cards The vocabulary words for each lesson are available on *Vocabulary Cards* for review and practice.

GETTING READY FOR THE CHAPTER

Make a "Ways To Go" Mural GROUP 30 MINUTES OR LONGER

Objective: To arouse interest in transportation and communication.

Materials: *Project Book* pp. 21–23, mural paper, scissors, glue, crayons

1. Have students work in groups. Explain that each group will make its own mural showing different ways people can travel.
2. Give each student one copy of Project Book pp. 21, 22, and 23. Use the pages to start a discussion. How do people travel on land, by air, and by water? You might suggest some unconventional means of travel such as hot-air balloons, skate boards, and rafts. What are some of the reasons that people need to travel?
3. Have students draw on Project Book pp. 21, 22, and 23 as many ways to travel as they can think of.
4. Invite group members to work together to make the group mural. Suggest they start by designing three sections, representing land, sea, and air. Encourage each group to share its mural with the class.

> **SECOND-LANGUAGE SUPPORT**
> Second-language learners may benefit from working with an English-proficient peer during part or all of this activity.
>
> Additional Second-Language Support Tips: pp. 242, 254

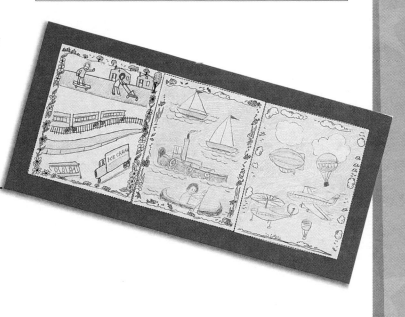

Introducing the Chapter

Ask students to consider for a moment what life would be like without cars, airplanes, telephones, and televisions. Help students understand that their great-great grandparents would have been astounded by our fast-moving technological world.

THINKING ABOUT GEOGRAPHY AND TECHNOLOGY

Invite students to link locations on the map with the inventions or accomplishments represented by the time line.

1807

Suggested Questions

- **What happened in 1807?** *(The first steamboat traveled upriver from New York City.)*

- **What was the name of the first steam-powered boat?** *(the* Clermont*)*

1839

Suggested Questions

- **What kinds of transportation were used on the National Road?** *(horses and wagons)*

- **Why do you think the road was called the National Road?** *(Students may guess that it was built by the government or that it went across part of the nation.)*

 Resource **REMINDER**

Technology: *Videodisc/Video Tape 3*

CHAPTER
10

Changing the Way People Live

THINKING ABOUT GEOGRAPHY AND TECHNOLOGY
Two hundred years ago, moving to a new community may have meant a difficult trip and no news from old friends and neighbors. Since then, new methods of transportation and communication have made traveling and staying in touch much easier.

In Chapter 10, you will learn how technology has changed the ways we travel and get news. Technology is not only part of our history, it is part of our lives today and tomorrow.

1807

HUDSON RIVER, NEW YORK
The first steam-powered boat, the *Clermont*, travels upriver from New York City

1839

VANDALIA, ILLINOIS
The National Road, started in the East, reaches Vandalia, Illinois

240

Background INFORMATION

DISCUSSING THE TIME LINE

- Robert Fulton's *Clermont* burned coal to create steam power and used sails to help power the boat. Combining these two technologies enabled the *Clermont* to navigate against the current.

- The National Road from Baltimore to Illinois may seem primitive today but it made overland travel easier for many people who wanted to settle west of the original thirteen states.

- Samuel Morse's telegraph sent messages using Morse Code. Messages were tapped on the device shown in the picture. These signals were received and decoded on the other end of the wire.

- The Wright brothers' flight lasted less than a minute but it proved their theories of flight and led to the further development of the airplane.

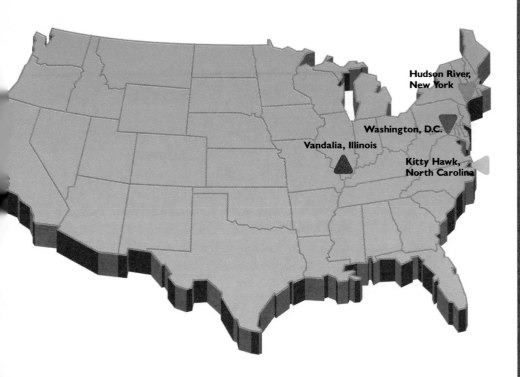

Hudson River, New York

Washington, D.C.

Vandalia, Illinois

Kitty Hawk, North Carolina

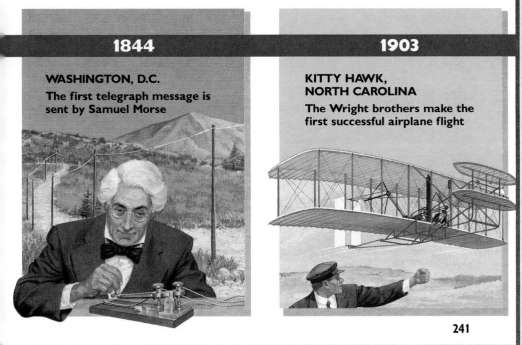

1844

WASHINGTON, D.C.

The first telegraph message is sent by Samuel Morse

1903

KITTY HAWK, NORTH CAROLINA

The Wright brothers make the first successful airplane flight

241

★**THINKING FURTHER:** *Compare and Contrast* **The National Road was the first big road built in the United States. How does it compare to roads we use today?** *(It looks like it is a narrow dirt road used by horses. Today we travel with automobiles on paved highways.)*

1844

Suggested Questions

● **What did Samuel Morse do in 1844?** *(He sent the first telegraph message.)*

● **From where was the message sent?** *(from Washington, D.C.)*

● **What is a telegraph?** *(Students may say that the telegraph is used for sending messages over wires.)*

1903

Suggested Questions

● **What happened in 1903?** *(The Wright brothers made the first successful airplane flight.)*

● **What did the Wright brothers' plane look like?** *(It was a small plane made of wood with two levels of wings.)*

● **Where did the Wright brothers test their plane?** *(in Kitty Hawk)*

Technology CONNECTION

VIDEODISC/VIDEO TAPE 3
Enrich Chapter 10 with the Videodisc *glossary* segments.

Search Frame 53777

Meeting *Individual* Needs

RETEACHING (Easy) Have students review the pictures. Ask them to tell how each event relates to a type of transportation or communication we use today.

EXTENSION (Average) Ask students to draw a picture for the year 1923 with the caption: "Vladimir Zworykin invents the television." Then have them illustrate a panel for 1982 with the caption: "The first successful flight of the reusable space shuttle." Have students discuss how technology has changed our lives over time.

ENRICHMENT (Challenging) Invite students to choose one picture from the time line. Ask them to write detailed explanations of how the event or invention changed people's lives. Encourage students to read the chapter and do additional research.

LESSON 1

Lesson Overview

New types of transportation changed the way people live in communities.

Lesson Objectives

★ Analyze changes in transportation.

★ Describe the influence of technology on transportation.

★ Evaluate the effects of transportation on communities in the past and present.

1 PREPARE

MOTIVATE Use the *Read Aloud* and the picture to initiate a discussion about transportation in the past and present. During the discussion, call attention to the *Vocabulary* word and work with students to define it.

SET PURPOSE Direct attention to the *Read to Learn* question. Elicit responses by using the *Making Predictions* exercise at the bottom of this page.

2 TEACH

Discussing Transportation Before 1800 Help students see how limited transportation was before 1800.

Suggested Questions

● *How did people travel long distances before 1800? How did they travel over water?* (They rode horses or mules or used wagons pulled by animals; they used canoes and other boats.)

★THINKING FURTHER: *Compare and Contrast* **What is one way your life would be different without buses, cars, and trains?** (Answers should reflect the idea that most activities would take place near home.)

Resource REMINDER

Practice Book: *p. 52*

Anthology: *Childtimes, pp. 91–94; Amelia Takes to the Skies, pp. 103–107*

On the Go

READ ALOUD

In the last chapter you read about people moving to new communities. What were some of the ways they traveled? They bumped along in wagons over the Oregon Trail. They sailed long distances on ships across the Atlantic Ocean. They also chugged along in trains to cities in the North.

Focus Activity

READ TO LEARN
In what ways has transportation changed over time?

VOCABULARY
fuel

PEOPLE
Robert Fulton
Peter Cooper
Henry Ford
Wilbur Wright
Orville Wright
Elisha Otis
Amelia Earhart
Eduardo San Juan
Mae Jemison

PLACES
National Road

Transportation Before 1800

You probably travel somewhere almost every day. You may walk, ride a bike, or take a bus to get to school or to visit friends. Maybe you ride in a car or on a train. Can you imagine what your life would be like without these forms of transportation?

Before 1800, people walked to get most places. There were no cars or trains. If people had to go far, they rode on horses or mules, or used wagons pulled by animals. People also used canoes and boats if they had to travel over water.

Often travel over land was difficult because there were few roads in the United States. There were only paths and trails. They were nothing like the wide, smooth roads you often see in our country today.

242

Reading STRATEGIES *and* Language DEVELOPMENT

MAKING PREDICTIONS Have students respond to the *Read to Learn* question by predicting what they will learn about how transportation has changed over time. To make their predictions, students can use the picture on this page, the information in the *Read Aloud*, and their own knowledge about transportation today.

LANGUAGE HISTORY Tell students that the word *automobile* was first used sometime around 1890. It comes from the Greek word *auto*, meaning "self," and the French word *mobile*, meaning "moving." Challenge students to think of other words that use those word parts.

Second-Language Support

GRAPHIC ORGANIZERS Second-language learners can benefit from connecting pictures with new vocabulary. Have students pair up to make an illustrated glossary of transportation terms that are new to them.

Steam-Powered Engines

People had always traveled along waterways. But it was hard for boats to travel against the currents of the water. Robert Fulton thought there must be a way that technology could improve travel by water. He worked for years on the idea of using steam engines to power boats. Finally, in 1807, he got to test his idea. People lined the Hudson River in New York to watch Fulton's boat, the *Clermont*. Everyone was excited to see the boat move up the river.

The National Road

In the early 1800s people began to build new roads. Some of these new roads were covered with stone. Other roads were made from logs and planks of wood. Each new road made it easier to travel between places. One road became the busiest of all. It was called the National Road. It was built over many years, by many people. From the map below you can see that it helped people to move west.

This drawing shows Robert Fulton's steamboat, the *Clermont*, chugging up the Hudson River.

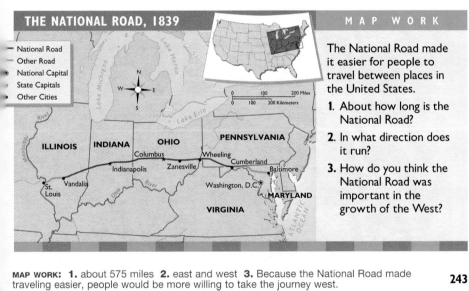

THE NATIONAL ROAD, 1839

- — National Road
- — Other Road
- ⊛ National Capital
- • State Capitals
- • Other Cities

MAP WORK

The National Road made it easier for people to travel between places in the United States.

1. About how long is the National Road?

2. In what direction does it run?

3. How do you think the National Road was important in the growth of the West?

MAP WORK: 1. about 575 miles **2.** east and west **3.** Because the National Road made traveling easier, people would be more willing to take the journey west.

243

Discussing Steam-Powered Engines Be sure students understand what a current is.

Suggested Questions

● *How did Robert Fulton improve water travel? (by using steam engines in boats)*

● *What could steamboats do that was hard for other boats to do? (travel against currents)*

Discussing the National Road Explain that the American frontier shifted westward in stages. By the time the National Road was completed, most of the land east of the Mississippi had been settled. During the mid-1800s, westward expansion continued along the Oregon Trail, which students learned about in *Chapter 9*. For *Background Information* about the National Road, see p. 244.

Suggested Questions

★THINKING FURTHER: *Making Conclusions* **Why do you think people began building roads in the 1800s?** *(The country was expanding, and roads were needed for travel.)*

More MAP WORK

Point out the map key.

Suggested Questions

★THINKING FURTHER: *Making Decisions* **In 1840, how would you get from the capital of Ohio to Mississippi?** *(Take the National Road from Columbus, Ohio, to Vandalia, Illinois; use the connecting road from Vandalia to St. Louis; take a steamship down the Mississippi River to Mississippi.)*

Curriculum CONNECTION

LINKS TO SCIENCE The steam engine revolutionized water transportation. It provided a source of energy other than wind or muscle power and could easily travel against the current.

Students can do a simple experiment at home to experience the force of a current:

● Put a toy boat or any object that floats in a bathtub of water. Lift the drain to let the water out.

● Watch the object float toward the drain. Try to push it in the opposite direction. Notice that the current pulls it toward the drain as you try to push it away.

Background INFORMATION

MORE ABOUT STEAMBOATS

● In 1769 Scottish engineer James Watt patented a steam engine that could be used to power boats. Fulton used an engine made by Watt in the *Clermont*.

● In 1787 American inventor John Fitch demonstrated the first workable steamboat in the U.S. He also started the first commercial steamboat service but lacked the funds to keep operating.

● The *Clermont* was the first commercially successful steamboat. With it came a new era in transportation, which lasted half a century. The Mississippi, Missouri, and Ohio rivers became major trade and transportation routes, bringing growth and prosperity to port cities like Cincinnati, Pittsburgh, St. Louis, Memphis, and New Orleans.

Thinking About Railroads from Coast to Coast Have students look at the picture. Then point out the Cascade Mountains on a physical map of the United States so students can see how far west railroads extended by 1885.

Suggested Questions

- **When were steam engines first used in railroad trains? How did trains move before?** *(around 1825; pulled by horses)*

- **What was the Tom Thumb? What made it special?** *(It was one of the first railroad engines; it could travel over hills and around curves, and it went fast.)*

- **Why did Peter Cooper set up a race between the Tom Thumb and a horse-drawn train?** *(He wanted people to know how fast his engine was.)*

- **What happened at the race?** *(The Tom Thumb broke down, and the horse-drawn train won.)*

★**THINKING FURTHER:** *Making Conclusions* **When railroads were being built, decisions had to be made about what towns they would go through. Why do you think most towns wanted to be chosen as railroad stops?** *(It was good for business, and it gave people access to other communities.)*

Links to
MATHEMATICS

How Fast Is that Train?

Peter Cooper's *Tom Thumb* was a powerful little steam engine. It could travel at speeds of 18 miles an hour. A train pulled by horse traveled at only 6 miles an hour.

How much faster was the steam engine than the horse? How far could the engine go in 2 hours?*

Railroads from Coast to Coast

It was not long before steam engines were also used in other forms of transportation. Around 1825 steam engines in the United States were used for the first time to power railroad trains. Before then trains were pulled by horses.

One of the first railroad engines was called the *Tom Thumb*. Peter Cooper built the engine so it would be able to travel over hills and around curves. Cooper was proud of the *Tom Thumb*. He wanted people to know how fast his engine was. He set up a race. His engine would race against a "gallant gray" horse pulling a train car. When the day came for the big event, Cooper was disappointed! The mighty *Tom Thumb* broke down. The horse went on to cross the finish line.

But the age of the railroad was coming. Soon steam-powered railroads ran between most big cities. They made it easier for people to travel. Railroads also made it easier to move goods across the country.

The year is 1885. These construction workers are in front of railroad tracks built along the Cascade Mountains.

Background INFORMATION

MORE ABOUT THE NATIONAL ROAD
- The National Road was the first road built with federal funds. Construction took 28 years, from 1811 to 1839.
- The National Road brought pioneers from East to West and points in between for many years. It fell into a period of disuse in the middle 1800s with the arrival of railroads but came back to life at the turn of the century with the advent of autos. Today it is part of U.S. Route 40, which runs across the country.

MORE ABOUT RAILROADS Congress began granting federal lands for railroad development in 1850 to attract settlers to undeveloped parts of the country. In 1862 Congress authorized the building of the first transcontinental railroad. It would span the country, linking East to West.

Over 20,000 people toiled on the railroad. Most were immigrants from China, Ireland, and Mexico. Using hand tools, explosives, and muscle power, they cut down forests and blasted through mountains. In all, they laid 1,775 miles of rail.

The railroad was finished in 1869, at Promontory Point, Utah. A gold spike was driven into the last railroad tie to mark the occasion.

Curriculum CONNECTION

LINKS TO MATHEMATICS: HOW FAST IS THAT TRAIN?
Have students do the subtraction (18 - 6 = 12) and multiplication (18 x 2 = 36) to find the answers.

The Auto and the Airplane

With roads and steamboats and railroads, traveling long distances kept getting easier. Soon another invention changed the way people traveled between communities.

In 1908 a man named Henry Ford made a car he called the Model T. For the next several years Ford worked on making cars cheap enough so that many people could afford to buy them. People could now travel on their own to different places in less time than ever before. How do you think automobiles changed the way people live in your community?

Another invention that changed the way we live was the airplane. Wilbur and Orville Wright were brothers who owned a bicycle shop. Together they completed the world's first airplane flight in Kitty Hawk, North Carolina. Airplanes made people think that anything was possible.

Henry Ford's Model T (top) and the Wright Brothers airplane (bottom) changed forever the way people travel.

245

Discussing the Auto and the Airplane Explain that people had been trying to build a "horseless carriage" since the late 1700s. The auto industry was officially born in 1886, when the first successful gasoline engine was invented by Gottlieb Daimler and Karl Benz.

Suggested Questions

● *What was the Model T?* (a car invented by Henry Ford)

● *How did Henry Ford make it possible for many people to own cars?* (by making them more affordable)

● *Look at the picture at the top of the page. What does it tell us about one of the ways people used the Model T?* (People used the Model T for recreational activities like picnics.)

● *How did Orville and Wilbur Wright change the way we live?* (They proved that humans could fly in airplanes.)

● *Look at the picture of the Wright brothers' airplane. How was it different from airplanes today?* (It was open, not closed; only one person could fly in it; it was light enough for humans to lift.)

★ THINKING FURTHER: *Cause and Effect What are two ways our lives would be different without cars? Without airplanes?* (Accept any answers that show how cars and airplanes affect our lives.)

Background INFORMATION

MORE ABOUT THE AUTO Mass production and the moving assembly line allowed Ford to make automobiles that the general public could afford. By 1928 he had sold more than 15 million cars and changed the American way of life. (Students will read more about Ford and the assembly line in *Chapter 12.*)

Farmers were the first large-scale group of auto buyers. With cars, they were no longer isolated in rural areas. They could visit and shop in once-inaccessible places.

In urban areas, cars meant that workers no longer had to live near their jobs. As roads improved they began leaving the crowded cities and commuting to work by car. By the 1920s the move to the suburbs was on.

MORE ABOUT THE AIRPLANE The Wright brothers' first flight lasted only 12 seconds, but it proved their theories about flight, which are the basis for aviation today.

● When Orville and Wilbur Wright first became interested in flight, they studied all the information they could find on the subject. They concluded that most of it was wrong and began developing their own theories.

● The Wrights experimented with gliders on the windswept dunes of North Carolina's Kitty Hawk for three years, testing and revising their ideas.

● Their first flight in 1903 generated little interest from the public or government. But in 1908 the War Department took the "flying machine" seriously enough to commission military planes from the Wrights.

Understanding Faster and Further
Invite students to share what they know about space travel.

Suggested Questions

- **To what places in space have people sent machines?** (the moon and Mars)

- ★**THINKING FURTHER: Making Predictions How can we be sure that transportation will continue to change?** (Technology keeps changing.)

More CHART WORK

Suggested Questions

- **Who made elevators safe enough for people to ride in?** (Elisha Otis)

- **What do you think elevators were used for before they carried people?** (to carry freight)

- **What did Amelia Earhart try to do in 1937?** (fly around the world)

- **What invention did the astronauts use on the moon? Who designed that invention?** (lunar rover vehicle, or moon buggy; Eduardo San Juan)

- ★**THINKING FURTHER: Sequencing What does Mae Jemison do before she launches a space shuttle? What can she do after launching the shuttle?** (She prepares the space shuttle; she can travel in it.)

Faster and Further

Transportation and technology are always changing. Today people travel in space. There are even machines that have landed on the moon and the planet Mars. Look at the chart below. It shows that the history of transportation has many exciting people and events. What did Eduardo San Juan (ed WAHR doh san WAHN) do?*

PEOPLE IN TRANSPORTATION

Elisha Otis invented an elevator with a safety clamp in 1852. This led to the first passenger elevator and encouraged the building of skyscrapers.

In 1932 Amelia Earhart was the first woman to make a cross-Atlantic flight alone. In 1937, she disappeared on a flight around the world.

Eduardo San Juan, a scientist and engineer, designed the lunar rover vehicle. Called the "moon buggy," it carried astronauts across the moon's surface in 1971 and 1972.

Mae Jemison became an astronaut in 1988. She was the first African American woman to prepare, launch, and travel in space shuttles.

CHART WORK

Many people have helped to shape the way we travel today.

1. Who was the first woman to fly alone in a plane across the Atlantic Ocean?

2. How do you think elevators changed the way people live in communities?

3. In what ways is the work of Eduardo San Juan and Mae Jemison similar?

CHART WORK: **1.** Amelia Earhart **2.** People can work and live in tall buildings. Without elevators it would be difficult to get up and down. **3.** Both worked in helping to develop transportation in outer space.

246

Background INFORMATION

MORE ABOUT PEOPLE IN TRANSPORTATION

- Elisha Otis was born in 1811 in Vermont. To demonstrate his safety elevator, Otis ascended with it, then ordered the hoisting cable cut. The safety clamp kept the platform in place, and Otis emerged unharmed, astonishing the assembled crowd.

- Amelia Earhart was born in 1897 in Kansas. She began flying when she was about 22. In 1937 she set out to fly around the world with navigator Fred Noonan. Their plane disappeared near Howland Island in the central Pacific Ocean. No trace of it, or its occupants, was ever found.

  Students can learn more about Amelia Earhart by reading "Amelia Takes to the Skies" on pp. 103–107 of their *Anthology*.

- Eduardo San Juan was born in 1925 in the Philippines. His LRV (lunar rover vehicle) was first used in the Apollo 15 mission (1971) and then in the Apollo 16 and 17 missions (1972). The LRV was nicknamed "moon buggy" because its large balloon-like tires made it resemble dune buggies used on sand.

- Mae Jemison was born in 1956 in Alabama. She is a medical doctor with degrees in chemical engineering and African and Afro-American studies. Jemison was aboard the space shuttle *Endeavor* in 1992 during its one-week mission to study the effects of zero gravity. She took with her an Alvin Ailey dance poster to honor the work of other African Americans.

*Fewer cars are used for transportation so air pollution is decreased.

Public Transportation

Sometimes new types of transportation bring new problems. Most forms of transportation today use fuel. Fuel is something that is burned to provide power. Gas and oil are examples of fuel. But burning fuel can cause pollution and use up our natural resources.

Today people are working to solve these problems. Public transportation is one solution that saves fuel. When people share buses and trains instead of taking their own cars, there are fewer vehicles on roads. How do you think public transportation helps the environment?*

WHY IT MATTERS

The United States has always been a country of people on the move. Today people move faster and further than ever before. Transportation is one way to bring people closer together. In the next lesson you will see other ways that bring people in communities closer together.

Public transportation is helpful in fighting pollution by saving fuel.

✔// Reviewing Facts and Ideas

SUM IT UP

- In the 1800s Americans began to build many roads.
- Robert Fulton developed steam engines to power boats.
- Steam engines were also used for railroad trains.
- Henry Ford made cars that many people could afford.
- The Wright Brothers made the first successful airplane flight.
- New types of transportation change the way people live.

THINK ABOUT IT

1. How did the steam engine change transportation?
2. **FOCUS** In what ways has transportation changed over time?
3. **THINKING SKILL** *Classify* into groups different ways people travel. Make a chart. What headings could you use?
4. **GEOGRAPHY** Look at the map on page 243. What direction is Vandalia from Cumberland?

247

☆ CITIZENSHIP

APPRECIATING PUBLIC TRANSPORTATION Have students brainstorm reasons for using public transportation. List each reason on the board. Then have students use the list to make posters encouraging people to use public transportation. If possible, display the posters in local meeting places such as community centers and libraries.

MEETING *Individual* NEEDS

RETEACHING (Easy) Have students make a collage showing different forms of transportation. They can include drawings of their own plus pictures cut out of old magazines.

EXTENSION (Average) Have students interview a senior citizen about how transportation has changed in his or her lifetime.

ENRICHMENT (Challenging) Have students make an illustrated time line showing major events in transportation from 1800 to the present.

Discussing Public Transportation
Be sure students understand that fuels are natural resources that can run out.

Suggested Questions

- **What problems do we have today because of changes in transportation? What causes those problems?** *(pollution and loss of natural resources; burning fuel)*
- **How can we save fuel and reduce pollution?** *(Take public transportation.)*

Understanding WHY IT MATTERS
Have students discuss how changes in transportation have affected the way people live, work, and play.

Suggested Questions

★**THINKING FURTHER:** *Cause and Effect* **Think about the changes in transportation discussed in this lesson. Choose one of those changes and suppose it never took place. How would your life be different?** *(Answers will vary.)*

3 CLOSE

SUM IT UP
Have students answer these questions.

Suggested Questions

- **What road linked the East with the West in the 1800s?** *(National Road)*
- **What did steamboats and railroads have in common?** *(steam engines)*
- **How did Henry Ford help bring communities closer together?** *(He made cars that people could afford.)*
- **What legacy did the Wright brothers leave us?** *(the airplane)*

EVALUATE
✔ **Answers to Think About It**

1. It made it possible for boats and railroads to travel farther and faster.
2. Students should itemize the changes in transportation they read about in the lesson.
3. Possible headings include *Land, Water, Air; Public, Private.*
4. West *Location*

Write About It Have students write two stories about taking a trip to see a friend in another community. One story should take place in 1850; the other should take place today.

SKILLS LESSON
PAGES 248–249

Lesson Overview
Transportation maps show routes
and methods of travel.

Lesson Objective
★ Use a transportation map.

1 PREPARE

MOTIVATE Have students talk about
the routes they take to school and the
types of transportation they use. Then
ask them how that information could be
illustrated. Guide students to see that
routes and methods of travel can be
shown on transportation maps.

SET PURPOSE Tell students that in
this lesson they will learn how to read a
transportation map that shows routes
and methods of travel in 1860.

DISCUSSING HELPING YOURSELF
Have a volunteer read aloud the *Helping Yourself* box on the next page.

2 TEACH

Why the Skill Matters Call on a volunteer to read the text aloud. Then have
students look at the map on the next
page. Direct attention to the title and the
map key. Ask students to explain why a
map like this would have been helpful to
pioneers planning to travel from the East
to the West.

Using the Skill Have students look
at the map key. Ask them to rank the
three forms of transportation from
fastest to slowest (railroads, canals,
roads). Then have students read the
text to find out how to use the map.

Resource REMINDER
Practice Book: *p. 53*
Technology: Adventures *CD-ROM*
Transparency: *#9*

GEOGRAPHYSKILLS

Reading Transportation Maps

VOCABULARY
transportation map

WHY THE SKILL MATTERS

By the middle of the 1800s there
were several different ways for people
to travel. You can see these different
ways by reading a transportation
map. A transportation map shows the
routes people can use to travel from
place to place. Transportation maps
often show roads, railroads, and other
kinds of transportation all on the
same map.

Use the Helping Yourself box on
the following page to guide you in
reading transportation maps.

USING THE SKILL

Look at the map on the next page.
It shows some other ways people
traveled in the United States in 1860.
Look at the map key. Find the
symbols for roads, railroads, and
canals. Canals are
waterways dug across
the land and used for
boat travel.

Look at the painting of the Erie
Canal below. Canals helped people
move goods between bodies of
water. A trip that had taken up to six
weeks on rough trails and rivers took
about a week on the Erie Canal. Find
the Erie Canal on the map on the
next page. It connects the Hudson
River and Lake Erie.

Suppose that you wanted to travel
from Cumberland, Maryland, to
Vandalia, Illinois. The red line shows
you that the National Road connected
these two cities. With your finger
follow the route from Cumberland to
Vandalia on the map. You will pass
through Maryland, Virginia,
Pennsylvania, Ohio, Indiana, and
Illinois. The brown line shows you
that a railroad connected Cumberland
and Vandalia.

The Granger Collection

248

Background INFORMATION

MORE ABOUT THE ERIE CANAL The Erie Canal was the first major waterway built in the U.S. It was the brainchild of New York State Governor DeWitt Clinton. Opponents of the project called it "Clinton's Ditch."

• The Erie Canal was built entirely with hand tools. Construction began
  in 1817 and ended in 1825. Barges carrying freight were towed
  through the 363-mile canal by horses and mules on shore.

• By providing a link between the Great Lakes and the eastern
  seaboard, the canal played a vital role in the growth of the Midwest
  and the economic development of the East. Towns like Buffalo,
  Rochester, Syracuse, and Albany became major cities, and New York
  City became the nation's leading port.

• The success of the Erie Canal led to the construction of many other
  canals in the United States. By the mid-1800s, however, railroads
  were beginning to replace them as major transportation routes.

*road or railroad; Pittsburgh, Pennsylvania, and Wilmington, North Carolina, among others

TRYING THE SKILL

The map shows more than one way to get from one place to another. Suppose you wanted to travel north from Augusta, Georgia, to Boston, Massachusetts. What were two ways you could get there? If you wanted to take a train trip from the city of Philadelphia, where were two places you could go?*

REVIEWING THE SKILL

1. What types of transportation are shown on the map below?

HELPING Yourself

- A **transportation map** shows various ways to travel.
- The map key shows the symbols for different kinds of transportation on the map.
- Sometimes there is more than one way to travel between two places.

2. In what ways can people travel now that were not possible in 1860?

3. What kinds of transportation could people use to travel from Augusta to Montgomery in 1860? How do you know?

4. Look at the cities on the map. In 1860 most cities were near railroads or along the water. Why do you think that was so?

5. When is it helpful to use a transportation map?

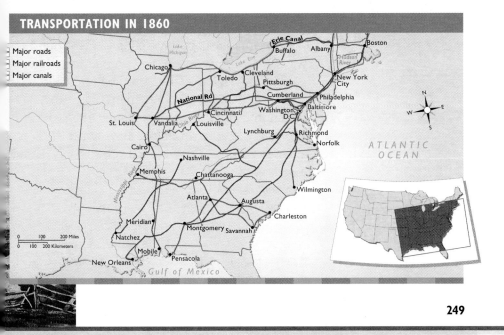

TRANSPORTATION IN 1860

Key: Major roads, Major railroads, Major canals

(Map labels: Lake Michigan, Lake Erie, Erie Canal, Buffalo, Albany, Boston, Chicago, Cleveland, Toledo, Pittsburgh, Hudson River, New York City, National Rd, Cumberland, Philadelphia, Baltimore, Cincinnati, Washington D.C., St. Louis, Vandalia, Ohio River, Louisville, Lynchburg, Richmond, Norfolk, ATLANTIC OCEAN, Cairo, Nashville, Chattanooga, Wilmington, Memphis, Mississippi River, Atlanta, Augusta, Charleston, Meridian, Montgomery, Savannah, Natchez, Mobile, Pensacola, New Orleans, Gulf of Mexico)

0 100 200 Miles
0 100 200 Kilometers

249

Suggested Questions

- **What was the fastest way to get from Chicago to St. Louis in 1860?** (railroad)

- **What were two ways to get from Buffalo to Albany?** (railroad, canal)

Trying the Skill Have the class review the information in the *Helping Yourself* box before students begin working individually.

Suggested Questions

- **How could a shopkeeper in Cincinnati get goods to Toledo?** (canal)

- **What were two ways to get from Vandalia to Washington, D.C.?** (road, railroad)

3 CLOSE

SUM IT UP

Ask students why it is useful to know how to read a transportation map. Then have them discuss transportation maps that would be useful to people today; for example, road maps and subway maps.

EVALUATE

✓ **Answers to Reviewing the Skill**

1. road, railroads, canals

2. by car, plane, subway

3. railroad and road; by reading the map

4. Both locations facilitate trade.

5. when planning a trip

Technology CONNECTION

ADVENTURES CD-ROM
Enrich the lesson with the map segment of the CD-ROM.

MEETING *Individual* NEEDS

RETEACHING (Easy) Have students show younger children how to use the transportation map.

EXTENSION (Average) Have students bring in different kinds of transportation maps, which they can get from the library and bus and train stations. Students can display their maps and explain how to use them.

ENRICHMENT (Challenging) Have students create a transportation map of your community, using the CD-ROM if possible. They can start with a simple outline map, next draw the map key, and then the transportation routes.

LESSON 2
PAGES 250–255

Lesson Overview
Advances in communication helped bring communities closer together.

Lesson Objectives
★ Explain how advances in communication have brought communities together.

★ Sequence events in the history of communication.

1 PREPARE

MOTIVATE Use the *Read Aloud* and the *Read to Learn* question to generate a discussion about communication in the past and present. Ask students how they think television might have changed their grandparents' lives. Then expand the discussion to include speculation about the effects of other changes in communication over time.

SET PURPOSE Make a word web on the board with *communicate* in the center and the other *Vocabulary* words branching out from it. Tell students they will be able to add more words to the web as they read the lesson.

2 TEACH

Thinking About Communicating Long Ago Have students look at the picture, speculate about what is happening, and then read the text to find out.

Suggested Questions

● **What form of communication did people use in the past that we still use today?** (newspapers)

★**THINKING FURTHER:** *Making Conclusions* **What is the man in the picture doing?** (The man is a town crier. He is reading the news aloud.)

Resource REMINDER

Practice Book: *p. 54*

Anthology: *Success!, p. 102; The First Ride, pp. 108–112*

Desk Maps: *United States*

Keeping in Touch

READ ALOUD
The whole family gathered in the living room. Everyone was so excited as the switch was turned on. Slowly, like a miracle, a picture appeared on the screen and voices came out of the box.

Your grandparents probably remember a scene like this from the first time they watched television. In this lesson you will read about how television and other inventions have changed our lives.

Focus Activity

READ TO LEARN
In what ways has communication changed over time?

VOCABULARY
communicate
pony express
telegraph
satellite

PEOPLE
Samuel Morse
Alexander Graham Bell
Guglielmo Marconi

Communicating Long Ago

From the earliest days people have found ways to communicate. To communicate is to pass along feelings, thoughts, or information to someone. Today there are many ways to communicate with people around the world. What did people do before telephones, radios, and televisions? People used other ways to get information and share ideas.

Newspapers long ago were an important source of news. But they were expensive and hard to get. Town criers stood on street corners and yelled out the main news stories. News stories were also posted in public places where people could read them.

250

Reading STRATEGIES *and* Language DEVELOPMENT

CAUSE AND EFFECT Remind students that the cause of something is the reason it happened; the *effect* is the result of what happened. As students read the lesson, help them make cause-and-effect statements.

CONTRACTIONS After students learn about the *telegraph* (p. 252) and the Morse Code (p. 252, *Background Information*), distribute copies of the Morse Code, which can be found in any encyclopedia. Point out that one punctuation mark is missing from the code: the apostrophe. Explain how we use apostrophes to make contractions. Then write a coded message containing several contractions on the board. Invite students to decode the message and add apostrophes where needed.

Using the ANTHOLOGY

THE FIRST RIDE, pages 108–112 Students can read this fact-based story about the *pony express* and then discuss it in class.

Riding the Pony Express

Pioneers often left friends and family behind as they moved to new communities and built new lives. These people wanted news from their families and old communities.

In the 1800s mail service was not reliable. But in 1860 a group of men developed a mail service called the pony express. The pony express was a team of daring horseback riders. They rode across the western United States to deliver mail from one place to another. They would hand off the mail to another rider, who would continue the route. Look at the map below. Find the route of the pony express. People in Sacramento, California, could get mail from people in St. Joseph, Missouri, in just 10 days.

Pony express riders traveled by horse both day and night, no matter what the weather.

THE PONY EXPRESS, 1860–1861

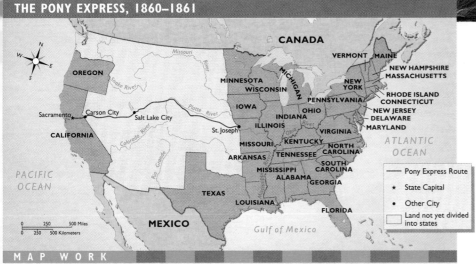

	Pony Express Route
★	State Capital
•	Other City
	Land not yet divided into states

MAP WORK

At each city riders used fresh horses to carry the mail to the next city.

1. About how many miles is the trip from St. Joseph to Carson City?

2. Along what river does the pony express route travel?

3. Where might the trip be most difficult for riders?

MAP WORK: **1.** about 1900 miles **2.** along the Platte River **3.** in mountainous areas or in desert areas

251

Discussing Riding the Pony Express Have students discuss the picture and the text.

Suggested Questions

● **How did the pioneers communicate with the friends and family they left behind?** (by mail)

● **What was mail service like in the 1800s?** (slow and unreliable)

● **What was the pony express?** (a team of horseback riders who rode across the western United States to deliver mail)

● **How long did the pony express take to get a letter from Sacramento, California, to St. Joseph, Missouri?** (10 days)

● **About how long would it take for a letter to travel the same distance today?** (two days)

★**THINKING FURTHER: Using Prior Knowledge** **How do we get mail today? Who is in charge of the mail: the national, state, or local government? What makes you say so?** (Most people get mail through the post office, which is run by the national government since it involves interstate commerce.)

More MAP WORK

Have students use their desk maps to trace the route of the pony express. Then have them label the states through which they would pass if they traveled that route today.

Background INFORMATION

MORE ABOUT THE PONY EXPRESS The pony express was like a relay race on horseback. A rider set off from one station, rode 10 to 15 miles to another station, changed horses in 2 minutes, and rode on to the next station, where the same procedure was repeated. A new rider took over every 75 miles. In this way, the pony express moved mail at a rate of 200 miles a day.

Field Trip

Help students learn about present-day mail service by taking them on a trip to the local post office. Make arrangements for a postal worker to explain how the mail is delivered, sorted, and processed. As an alternative, invite a postal worker to class to talk about the post office.

CITIZENSHIP

APPRECIATING THE POST OFFICE Have students make a flowchart showing what happens to a letter from the time it is mailed to the time it is received. They can use what they learned on their field trip plus information from the library. Display their chart at the post office.

Global CONNECTION

Postal networks have existed around the world since ancient times. In the 400s B.C. the Greek historian Herodotus wrote this description of Persia's messengers: "Neither snow, nor rain, nor heat, nor gloom of night stays these couriers from the swift completion of their appointed rounds." Today that quotation is inscribed on New York City's main post office building. It is not, as many people think, the official slogan of the U.S. postal service.

This **telegraph** register (left) was used by Samuel Morse (right) in 1844. It received and printed codes sent by wire.

Communication by Wire

The pony express was a new step for communication. But soon an invention was to change everything. Samuel Morse was one of the early inventors of the machine called the telegraph. The telegraph used special codes to send words long distances over wires. In 1844 Morse had workers run a wire from Washington, D.C., to Baltimore, Maryland. He then sat in the Capitol building and tapped out the first telegraph message: *"What hath* [has] *God wrought* [made]*!"* The telegraph worked! By 1861 telegraph wires ran across the country. People could now get news from far away places in minutes. The pony express was no longer needed.

It was not too much longer before another invention changed how people communicated. In 1876 Alexander Graham Bell built a working telephone. People could now speak to each other directly from far away places.

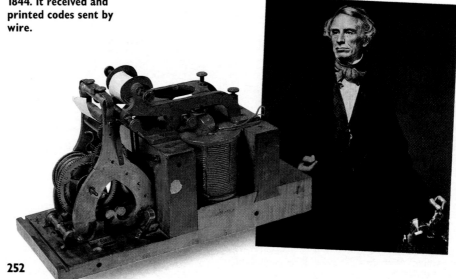

252

On the Air

The telegraph and the telephone were exciting inventions. Messages could travel in seconds! But there was one problem. The messages had to run through wires. It was impossible to connect all places around the world with wires.

Guglielmo Marconi (goo LYEHL moh mahr KOH nee) was an Italian inventor. He wanted to find a way to send signals without using wires. He studied the ideas and inventions of other people who had been working on the same idea. Finally, in 1895 Marconi invented the wireless telegraph. Now, even ships at sea could send signals back and forth to each other. The wireless telegraph then led to the invention of the radio.

Later, scientists invented a way to send pictures through space. That led to the invention of the television. Today, televisions and radios are in many homes. We can instantly see clear pictures and hear voices from all over the world.

The radio (above) was a popular form of communication before television. Alexander Graham Bell (bottom) built this telephone in 1875.

Understanding On the Air Like most inventors, Marconi picked up on the ideas of his predecessors. He once said, "I doubt very much whether there has ever been a case of a useful invention [which was] the work of one man."

Many people contributed to the development of television, but no single person can be called its inventor.

Suggested Questions

- *How did the telegraph and telephone send messages? Why was that sometimes a problem?* (They sent messages through wires; wires couldn't always be used to connect places.)

- *What did Guglielmo Marconi invent?* (the wireless telegraph)

- *Why was his invention so important?* (It eliminated the need for wires, so people could send messages anywhere.)

- ★**THINKING FURTHER:** *Cause and Effect* *What invention made it possible for Marconi to invent the wireless telegraph? What two inventions did the wireless lead to?* (telegraph; radio, television)

Background INFORMATION

THE WIRELESS On Dec. 12, 1901, Marconi transmitted the Morse Code letter *S* from England to Canada. It was history's first transatlantic wireless communication.

- The first practical use of the wireless was for communicating with ships. In 1909 the S.S. *Republic* radioed for help after colliding with another ship. It was the first time the radio was used in a sea rescue, and almost all the passengers were saved.

- Today radio signals reach around the world and beyond. "The era of satellite communication could not have occurred without wireless radio," said former astronaut John Glenn. "Because of Marconi's development of wireless radio, we can . . . learn about our solar system and perhaps someday the universe."

ABOUT TELEVISION Experimental television began in the 1920s, but TV did not develop on a wide scale until after WWII. In the early days of television, few people had sets. In many communities, neighbors gathered at the home of the nearest TV owner to see their favorite programs. People also watched sets in store windows.

A turning point in the television industry occurred in 1947, with the first telecast of the World Series. About 4 million people watched—a huge audience at the time. The telecast convinced many viewers who did not have their own sets to buy them.

By the early 1950s TV had replaced radio as the main source of news and entertainment for the American public. Today 98 percent of homes in the U.S. have a TV set.

Discussing Latest Connections

Encourage students to share what they know about computers, videotape machines, and CD-ROMs.

Suggested Questions

● **What is a satellite?** *(a spacecraft used to connect radio, telephone, and television communications)*

● **When were communications satellites first used?** *(in the 1960s)*

● **How do satellites help us learn about people in other countries?** *(They make it possible for us to talk to people in other countries, to listen to them on radios, and to see them on TV.)*

● **Look at the picture. What do satellites help scientists learn about?** *(faraway places like the sun, Venus, and Mars)*

More CHART WORK

Have students examine the time line.

● **When was the first television broadcast? How many years later could a TV show be carried by satellite?** *(1936; 26 years)*

● **Which was widely used first: fax machines or videotape machines?** *(videotape machines)*

● ★**THINKING FURTHER:** *Making Conclusions* **When was the first telegraph invented? Why do you think the pony express was still needed 16 years later?** *(The first telegraph was invented in 1844, but telegraph wires didn't run across the country until 1861.)*

Satellites are used by scientists to help them learn about faraway places like the sun, Venus, and Mars.

Latest Connections

Look at the time line. You can see that people have continued to look for new ways to improve communication. In the 1960s the first communications satellites were used. A satellite is a spacecraft that is used to connect radio, telephone, and television communications. Satellites make it possible for people to communicate in seconds across oceans to other countries.

Can you think of other machines that people use to communicate with each other? Computers and faxes are used every day to send and receive information.

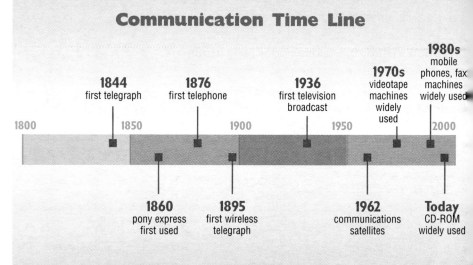

Communication Time Line

1844 first telegraph	
1876 first telephone	
1936 first television broadcast	
1970s videotape machines widely used	
1980s mobile phones, fax machines widely used	

1800   1850   1900   1950   2000

Below timeline	
1860 pony express first used	
1895 first wireless telegraph	
1962 communications satellites	
Today CD-ROM widely used	

CHART WORK

Every year people are finding newer and faster ways to communicate with each other around the world.

1. What happened in 1860?

2. How many years after the invention of the telephone was the mobile phone being used by people?

3. Can you think of an invention in communication that might be in people's homes in the future?

254   **GRAPH WORK:** **1.** Pony express is first used. **2.** more than 100 years later
3. video telephones, multi-media centers, virtual reality machines

---

Background INFORMATION

ABOUT SATELLITES Explain that a satellite is something that orbits a planet. The moon is a satellite that orbits earth. Most artificial satellites also orbit earth or some other body in space.

Communications satellites pick up radio signal messages from one place and transmit them to another. They make it possible for TV audiences around the world to see the same program at the same time and for telephone users to have international conference calls.

Second-Language Support

MAKING CONNECTIONS Activate prior knowledge to facilitate comprehension of content material. Have students list different modes of communication, guess when each developed, and then read the lesson to check their ideas.

Curriculum CONNECTION

LINKS TO LANGUAGE ARTS Thomas Edison is considered the greatest inventor in history. He patented 1,093 inventions, among them the lightbulb and phonograph, and he improved many existing inventions, including the telephone and typewriter.

Students can use the encyclopedia and these books to learn about Edison: *Thomas Edison and Electricity* by Steve Parker (HarperCollins, 1992); *The Story of Thomas Alva Edison, Inventor* by Margaret Davidson (Scholastic Inc., 1990).

When they finish their reading, students can work in groups to make an Age of Edison time line illustrating his major inventions. Suggest that they put a star beside the inventions that relate to communication.

WHY IT MATTERS

t has always been important for people to communicate. It used to take days to get a message across the country by pony express. Now it can happen in less than a second.

Over the years people have found new and better ways to share ideas and information. As people communicate more quickly with each other, they learn more about communities and the world around them. By communicating more easily around the world every day, people learn about many cultures and new ideas. By working together to understand each other and to use new ways of communication, people can solve many problems in our world today.

Just fifteen years ago, few people used personal computers. Today they are used by many people at work and home.

Reviewing Facts and Ideas

SUM IT UP

- People have always found ways to communicate.
- The pony express used horses and daring riders to speed mail across the western part of the country.
- Samuel Morse invented a way to send messages across wires.
- Guglielmo Marconi invented a way to send messages without wires.
- Radios and televisions soon followed. Communication continues to improve today with satellites and computers.

THINK ABOUT IT

1. How did people receive news long ago?

2. **FOCUS** In what ways has communication changed over time?

3. **THINKING SKILL** Make your own time line about some of the changes in communication. Put the events in the correct _sequence_.

4. **WRITE** Write a newspaper headline about the invention of the personal computer.

255

Understanding WHY IT MATTERS
Have students discuss the picture and then the text.

Suggested Questions

- *Do you know someone who uses a personal computer? How does it help them do their work? (Encourage students to share what they know about computers.)*

★THINKING FURTHER: *Cause and Effect* *What are the names of three people who made it possible for us to communicate with people around the world today? Why is it important for us to do so? (Morse, Bell, Marconi; we learn about different communities and cultures, share ideas, and work together to solve problems.)*

3 CLOSE

SUM IT UP
Have students answer these questions.

Suggested Questions

- *What forms of communication used before 1800 are still used today? (letters, newspapers, books)*

- *What invention put the pony express out of business? (telegraph)*

- *In what kinds of places was Marconi's invention most useful? (places where wires were hard or impossible to connect; for example, the ocean or mountainous areas)*

EVALUATE
✓ **Answers to Think About It**

1. from town criers, news stories posted in public places, and newspapers

2. Students should itemize the changes in communication that they read about in the lesson.

3. Students can use the answers to the second question as the basis for their time lines.

4. Students can use their own knowledge plus the picture and caption on this page to write their headlines.

Write About It Have students choose one of the ways communication has changed since 1800 and explain how it brought communities closer together.

Meeting *Individual* Needs

RETEACHING (Easy) Have students make a poster illustrating different forms of communication from 1800 to the present.

EXTENSION (Average) Have students use the library to do research on Morse, Bell, or Marconi and then write a report about that inventor.

ENRICHMENT (Challenging) Have students write a newspaper article about an invention that changed communication. The article should sound as if it were written when the invention was introduced, and it should answer these questions: What is the invention? Who invented it? When and where was it demonstrated? Why is it important? How will it affect people's lives? Students can use an encyclopedia to get the information they need.

GLOBAL CONNECTIONS

Lesson Overview
The English Channel Tunnel is bringing communities in England and France closer together.

Lesson Objectives
★ Describe the impact of the English Channel Tunnel on England and France.

★ Use a transportation map and a bar graph.

1 PREPARE

MOTIVATE Have students use their *Desk Maps* to identify England as an island separated from France and the rest of the continent by the English Channel. Then direct attention to the *Read Aloud*. Ask students why it would be dangerous to be in a ship or plane on a foggy day. Challenge them to think of another way to cross the Channel.

SET PURPOSE Have students read the *Read to Learn* question and invite speculation about the answer. Then point out the *Vocabulary* term and explain that the picture shows the English Channel Tunnel, which students will learn about in the lesson.

2 TEACH

Discussing Two Countries and a Channel Have students answer the questions.

Suggested Questions
● **What is a channel?** *(a narrow waterway between two larger bodies of water)*

● **What bodies of water does the English Channel connect?** *(Atlantic Ocean and North Sea)*

Resource REMINDER
Practice Book: *p. 55*

Technology: *Adventures CD-ROM*

Desk Maps: *World*

A Tunnel in Europe

Focus Activity

READ TO LEARN
What is the English Channel Tunnel?

VOCABULARY
channel

PLACES
France
England
English Channel

256

READ ALOUD
"Fog in Channel. Continent Cut Off."

These words appeared in a newspaper headline in England long ago. It describes what happened when fog prevented ships from sailing across the English Channel.

But thanks to technology, things have changed. Today people do not have to rely on ships and planes to cross the English Channel.

Two Countries and a Channel

In 1994 the first passengers boarded the *Eurostar* train. They were about to take a special trip. It was the first time France and England were connected by railroad. Look at the map on the next page. England is an island off the continent of Europe. It is separated from the rest of Europe by the English Channel. A channel is a narrow waterway between two larger bodies of water. The English Channel connects the Atlantic Ocean and the North Sea.

England and France are only about 21 miles apart at their closest points. But to travel between these two countries, people had to take a ship or fly. Now the English Channel Tunnel has connected them in a new way.

Reading STRATEGIES *and* Language DEVELOPMENT

CONTEXT CLUES Remind the class that one way to find the meaning of a new word is to look at the other words in a sentence for clues. Then have students identify the words in the *Read Aloud* that provide clues to the meaning of the word *channel*. They should cite the words *ships* and *sailing*, which let us know that a channel is a body of water.

LANGUAGE HISTORY Tell students that another name for the English Channel Tunnel is *Chunnel.* Write the name on the board with a slash between the syllables: *Chun/nel.* Ask students which part of the name comes from the word *channel* and which part comes from the word *tunnel.* Then write the words *brunch* and *smog* on the chalkboard. Challenge students to figure out the two words each blended word comes from. *(breakfast, lunch; smoke, fog)*

A Dream of Many Years

For over 200 years people have dreamed of linking England with France. In 1802 a French scientist came up with a plan for two long tunnels with a little island in between. The horse-drawn carriages could stop at the island to get fresh horses! The plan never came to life. Over the years many other plans were made. However, some people in England were afraid to connect their country with the rest of Europe. They thought they were safer as an island. But in 1986 the decision was made to build the tunnel. It took eight years to complete.

A ferry trip across the English Channel includes a view of these chalk cliffs at Dover, England.

THE ENGLISH CHANNEL TUNNEL

Legend:
— English Channel Tunnel
— Railroad
··· Ferry Route
▒ Highway
✈ Airport
⊛ National Capital
○ Other City

MAP WORK

Before the English Channel Tunnel was built, people travelled between England and France by ferry or plane.

1. About how far is it from Folkestone to Calais?

2. What are two ways to get from Calais to Paris?

3. What might be some differences in traveling by ferry instead of by tunnel?

MAP WORK: **1.** about 26 miles **2.** car and railroad **3.** Ferry takes longer. By ferry you can see water and landforms.

257

Understanding A Dream of Many Years The tunnel project provided about 15,000 jobs for people in England and France. The potential for employment was one reason that the two countries finally decided to build the tunnel.

Suggested Questions

● **Why do you think people dreamed of connecting England and France for so many years?** *(so they could trade and visit more easily)*

● **Why weren't plans to link the countries carried out in the past?** *(Some English people thought it would be safer to remain an island, separate from the rest of Europe.)*

● **When was the decision made to build the tunnel? When was the tunnel completed?** *(1986; 1994)*

★**THINKING FURTHER:** *Making Conclusions* **Why do you think some people thought England was safer as an island than as part of Europe?** *(Help students understand that being an island made it harder for enemies to invade England.)*

More MAP WORK

Have students use the map to answer the question.

Suggested Questions

● **If you didn't want to fly, how would you get from London, England, to Paris, France?** *(railroad to Folkestone, English Channel Tunnel to Calais, railroad to Paris)*

Background INFORMATION

ABOUT THE ENGLISH CHANNEL The Channel Tunnel crosses the narrowest part of the English Channel: the Strait of Dover.

● The English Channel is the busiest sea passage in the world, but crossing it can be a challenge. About 25 heavy fogs occur each year, and the seas are often rough. The roughness is caused by strong winds and by currents from the Atlantic Ocean and North Sea that meet in the Channel.

● The Channel has protected England from invasions for centuries. In the 16th century it helped to keep the Spanish Armada from conquering England. In the 19th century it stopped Napolean from invading. And in the 20th century it protected England from Hitler's navy.

ABOUT ENGLAND AND FRANCE

● England and France had a long history of political enmity that began with the Norman Conquest in 1066. In 1337 the two countries embarked on the Hundred Years' War, a series of battles that lasted until 1453. And in 1793 they began fighting the Napoleonic Wars, which finally ended in 1815.

● By the turn of the century, England and France had become allies. They signed a treaty of friendship in 1904 and fought together during both World Wars.

● Today the English Channel Tunnel can be seen as a symbol of trust between two countries. Both England and France expect to derive economic boosts from the increased tourism and trade the tunnel will bring.

Thinking About Building the Tunnel Have students discuss the pictures and then read the text. When they finish this section, you may wish to tell them that 90 acres worth of soil—the equivalent of 68 football fields—was piled along the French and English coasts.

Suggested Questions

● **What kind of machine was used to dig the tunnel?** *(tunnel-boring machine)*

● **Why were the French and English workers excited when they reached the breakthrough site?** *(The digging of the tunnel was completed.)*

● **Why was the breakthrough site in the middle of the tunnel?** *(The tunnel-boring machines had started from opposite ends and worked toward the middle.)*

● **What happened to the earth that was dug to make the tunnel?** *(It was piled along the French and English coasts.)*

● **What will be built in those areas?** *(parks)*

★**THINKING FURTHER:** *Making Conclusions* **Look at the words in the picture of the party. Which words mean the same thing? How do you know?** *(*Welcome *and* bienvenue *mean the same thing. Students should realize that* welcome *would be written in both languages since both English and French workers had the party.)*

Special machines dug a tunnel below the channel (left). When the digging was done, English and French workers had a big party (right).

Building the Tunnel

Finally we reach the breakthrough site. The two machines that dug this tunnel started from opposite sides of the Channel and worked toward the middle. [The] cutterhead—a huge wheel with . . . teeth—chews into the last trace of rock separating England from France.

These are the words of a writer named Cathy Newman. She was describing the moment when workers broke through the rock that separated the two halves of the tunnel. It was an important moment. The digging of the tunnel was completed. French and English workers hugged each other.

A special machine called the "tunnel-boring machine" was used to dig the tunnel. Many pounds of earth were dug up from the bottom of the English Channel to make the tunnel. That earth was then piled along the English and French coasts. These areas will be used to build parks.

258

Background INFORMATION

MORE ABOUT BUILDING THE TUNNEL

● To save time and money, the tunnel-boring machines (TBMs) worked from both sides of the Channel toward the middle.

● When the work was finished, the huge machines were buried because it would have been too difficult to remove them. Each TBM was the length of two football fields!

● The tunnel was bored in the seabed, 140 feet below the water. To help students understand how tunnel walls can withstand the weight of the water and/or earth above them, use the *Curriculum Connection* activity at right.

Curriculum CONNECTION

LINKS TO SCIENCE Work with students to perform an experiment that illustrates why tunnel walls are curved rather than straight. You will need four blocks and two pieces of thin cardboard. Tell students that the two pieces of cardboard represent tunnel walls.

● Anchor a curved piece of cardboard between two blocks to form an arch. Then put two blocks on top of the arch. Explain that the curved "walls" support the load because the weight is evenly distributed and shared between the two curved sides.

● Replace the arch with a flat piece of cardboard placed across the blocks. Put two blocks in the middle of the cardboard. Explain that the straight "walls" do not support the load because the weight is concentrated in the middle.

All Aboard!

The English Channel Tunnel is more than one tunnel. It is really three tunnels. Trains from England to France run through one tunnel. Trains from France to England run through the second tunnel. The third tunnel is just for workers and service crews. The service crews help keep the tunnel safe.

Two different trains run through the tunnel. *Eurostar* is the train for passengers without cars. The other train is called *Le Shuttle* (le shuh TELL). It carries people with their cars. It also carries trucks filled with goods that will be sold in other countries.

The tunnels are actually dug in the ground below the bottom of the English Channel (right). Trains (below) travel through the tunnel faster than cars on the highway.

259

Discussing All Aboard Tell students that *Le Shuttle* means "the shuttle." Then discuss the meaning of the word *shuttle* in English and French.

Suggested Questions

● **Why is there one tunnel for trains from England to France and another tunnel for trains from France to England?** *(so the trains won't crash)*

● **Who uses the third tunnel?** *(workers and service crews)*

● **Look at the pictures and read the captions. Where were the tunnels dug?** *(in the ground below the bottom of the English Channel)*

● **If you were in a rush to get from England to France, would you travel by car or by train? Why?** *(You would travel by train because it's faster than by car.)*

★ **THINKING FURTHER:** *Classifying*
What are the names and uses of the two trains that run through the tunnel? *(Eurostar: for passengers without cars; Le Shuttle: for people with cars and trucks with goods.)* **On which train would a bus full of tourists ride?** *(Le Shuttle)*

Technology CONNECTION

***ADVENTURES* CD-ROM**
Enrich the lesson with the maps of Great Britain and France on the CD-ROM.

Global CONNECTION

THE RAILROAD CONNECTION With the English Channel Tunnel, England is now connected by rail to the high-speed trains that form a transportation network through much of Europe.

● European express trains are among the best in the world, and they carry much of the continent's passenger traffic. Inter-City express trains link major cities in nine Western European countries.

● Travel between countries in Europe is as common as travel between states in the U.S. By the time they graduate from high school, most students have made at least one trip to a neighboring country. They are also fluent in at least one other language besides their own.

Background INFORMATION

TRAVEL TIME The figures below will give students a sense of the travel time between France and England by train, plane, and ferry. Have them use their desk maps to locate the places below, then trace and measure the distances between them.

● Paris to London: about 3 hours by train; about 1 hour by plane.

● Calais, France, to Dover, England: 75 minutes by ferry.

● Calais, France, to Folkstone, England: 35 minutes by train (of that time, 19 minutes is spent in the tunnel).

Understanding A Big Change

Help students understand the impact of the tunnel on people in France and England.

Suggested Questions

- **What are two ways the tunnel helps people in France and England?** *(It helps people visit and do business more easily.)*

- **What are three differences between the French and English?** *(They have different cultures, histories, and languages.)*

★**THINKING FURTHER:** *Making Decisions* **If you could build a tunnel between two places that you have learned about in this book, which places would you choose? Why?** *(Encourage students to give reasons for their answers.)*

Learning from Literature Explain that the boy in the picture is Adam Westgarth. His poem is from a book of poems written by students in France and England to celebrate the opening of the tunnel.

Suggested Questions

- **How has Adam been feeling about the tunnel?** *(anxious and curious)*

- **Why is he excited about the tunnel?** *(He can travel "as quick as a flash" from London to Paris.)*

- **To what animal does he compare tunnel users? Why?** *(a mole because it lives underground)*

★**THINKING FURTHER:** *Compare and Contrast* **To what would you compare tunnel users?** *(Encourage students to make up similes and metaphors of their own.)*

A Big Change

Because of the tunnel, people in England and France can do business with each other more easily. Goods can be trucked from one country to the other without having to be loaded and unloaded onto a boat or plane.

The French and English have different cultures, different histories, and different languages. But now they can visit each other more easily. The poem below was written by a ten-year-old English boy named Adam Westgarth. In what ways do you think he is excited about the tunnel?

The Channel Tunnel
Poem written by Adam Westgarth in 1994.

At last, the Channel Tunnel has arrived
We have been waiting,
Anxiously, curiously for a long while.
Deep, deep down we will **burrow**
Into the sea,
Like a mole underground.
From London to Paris we can travel
With no delay;
Just straight down the tracks,
Going at tremendous speed
As quick as a flash,
We will be there.

burrow: dig

260

Curriculum CONNECTION

LINKS TO ART Since the first plan in 1802, there have been 25 more proposals to link England and France by building a tunnel under the English Channel. Each proposal was defeated for the same reason—England's desire to protect itself by remaining an island.

Have students work in pairs to consider the benefits and drawbacks of living on an island. Tell them to draw a picture of an island; add pictures of places where people live, work, and play; and give their island a name. When they finish, help students arrange their "islands" on the floor. Then have them debate the pros and cons of establishing a link to any of the other islands.

After the class discussion, have students decide whether they want to link their islands to any others. Then have them share their decisions with the class and explain the reasons for them. Students who wish to establish connections can make paper tunnels or bridges to the islands of their choice.

GRAPH WORK: **1.** about 33 miles long **2.** Traffic in a tunnel would not be delayed by bad weather conditions.

WHY IT MATTERS

In this chapter you have read about changes in transportation and communication. Each of these changes has brought people closer together in different ways.

Trains, planes and automobiles have allowed people to travel between places faster than ever. The telegraph allowed people to send messages quickly to each other over wires. Today the computer lets people around the world communicate quickly without wires. And in Europe the English Channel Tunnel makes it easier for people in England and France to share ideas and lives every day.

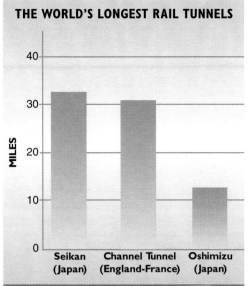

THE WORLD'S LONGEST RAIL TUNNELS

MILES

- Seikan (Japan)
- Channel Tunnel (England-France)
- Oshimizu (Japan)

GRAPH WORK

Japan has two of the three longest tunnels in the world.

1. About how long is the Seikan Tunnel?
2. Can you think of one way a tunnel might be better for travel than a bridge?

✓ Reviewing Facts and Ideas

SUM IT UP

- England is separated from the rest of Europe by the English Channel.
- For hundreds of years people dreamed of ways to connect England and France.
- The English Channel Tunnel has made it easier to travel between England and France.

THINK ABOUT IT

1. What are two ways to cross the English Channel today?
2. **FOCUS** What is the English Channel Tunnel?
3. **THINKING SKILL** List in *sequence* some of the new kinds of transportation that have been invented since 1800.
4. **GEOGRAPHY** Look at the world map in the Atlas on pages R10 and R11. What are some other places a tunnel might be built?

261

Understanding WHY IT MATTERS

Help students appreciate the advances made in transportation and communication during the last 200 years.

Suggested Questions

★**THINKING FURTHER: Compare and Contrast How could a message get from England to France in 1800? How could it get from England to France today?** *(In 1800 a verbal or written message could be carried from England to France by boat; today the same message could be carried by boat, plane, or train, telephone, fax, or computer.)*

More GRAPH WORK

The Channel Tunnel is the world's longest *undersea* tunnel.

Suggested Questions

- **What is the second-longest tunnel in the world?** *(the Channel Tunnel)*
- **About how long is the Oshimizu Tunnel?** *(about 13 miles long)*

3 CLOSE

SUM IT UP

Have students write their answers to the questions below.

Suggested Questions

- **What separates England from the rest of Europe?** *(the English Channel)*
- **If you were traveling from England to France, would you take a ferry, plane, or train? Why?** *(Have students give reasons for their answers.)*

EVALUATE
✓ **Answers to Think About It**

1. boat, plane, train
2. a tunnel under the English Channel connecting England and France
3. steamships, railroads, cars, airplanes, spacecraft
4. Accept any reasonable answers. *Location*

Write About It Have students work with partners to write down what a French and English worker might have said to each other when they met at the tunnel breakthrough site.

MEETING *Individual* NEEDS

RETEACHING (Easy) Have students write a newspaper headline about the opening of the English Channel Tunnel.

EXTENSION (Average) Have students write and illustrate an advertisement for *Le Shuttle* or *Eurostar*.

ENRICHMENT (Challenging) Have students compare trains of today with trains of the late 19th century. They can start by comparing the train shown on page 244 with the one on page 259. Then they can do research to learn more about trains in the past and present. Students can present their findings in a then-and-now report about trains.

Lesson Overview
People can have fun with transportation.

Lesson Objective
★Evaluate transportation as a legacy that can be fun.

1 PREPARE

MOTIVATE Have students talk about activities they do for fun. Focus the discussion on those that involve transportation, such as bike riding and boating. Have students note that transportation is not only a way to meet our needs. It is also a way to have fun.

SET PURPOSE Label a two-column chart on the chalkboard: *Land* and *Water*. Under each heading, students should group the activities they discussed. Tell them to add more activities as they read the lesson.

2 TEACH

Understanding the Concept of a Legacy Ask students who taught them how to skate, swim, or ride a bike. Point out that that person learned the skill from someone in the past. In the future, students may teach the skill to someone else. In this way, the legacy of having fun with transportation is carried on through the years.

Examining the Pictures Call on a volunteer to read the text. Then have students look at the pictures and read the captions aloud.

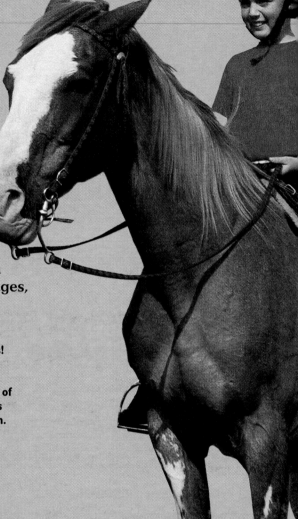

Legacy
LINKING PAST AND PRESENT

HERE WE GO

Modern ways of transportation help people travel between communities quickly. But for many people transportation is more than just traveling from one place to another. Transportation is also a legacy of fun and excitement. Look at the pictures here. See why being on the move has been fun for people of all ages, yesterday and today.

Look out pony express! In some communities today, people still use horses as a main form of transportation. Others ride horses just for fun.

262

Curriculum CONNECTION

LINKS TO LANGUAGE ARTS One way to have fun with transportation is to invent "crazy contraptions" for people to enjoy on land or water. To get the ball rolling, write the following examples on the chalkboard:

- rubber water wings for floating in water
- motorized jumropes for mile-high leaps
- bikes with umbrellas for riding in rain

Have students work in pairs to come up with crazy contraptions of their own. Then invite them to write and illustrate advertisements for their creations.

CITIZENSHIP

SAFETY FIRST Have students work in groups to make illustrated posters of safety tips for skaters, swimmers, and bike riders. Remind students to consider the following questions as they work on their posters:

- What protective gear is needed?
- When and where can the activity be done safely?
- Should adults be present?

Moving on! In the 1920s children rode carts they made from wooden boxes and baby carriage wheels (left). Today children keep rolling with in-line skates.

Whether paddling a canoe on a warm river or ice skating on a frozen lake, people enjoy having fun on the go in all kinds of weather.

Suggested Questions

- **Why do you think the child on the horse is wearing a helmet?** *(in case of a fall)*

- **Where are people more likely to go horseback riding for fun: in urban, suburban, or rural communities? Why?** *(rural because there is more open space than in the other types of communities)*

- **How has the child on skates protected himself from falls?** *(by wearing a helmet and knee pads)*

- **Which is done more often as an outdoor sport: in-line skating or iceskating? Why?** *(in-line skating because it can be done year-round, not just in winter)*

- **Why are the children in the canoe wearing life vests?** *(in case the canoe tips over)*

- **What are some other ways to have fun getting around in the water?** *(Possible answers: swimming; floating on rafts; using sailboats, rowboats, and other kinds of boats.)*

⭐ 3 CLOSE

SUM IT UP

Have students work with partners to write summary statements about the lesson.

EVALUATE

Write About It Have students write a story called "On the Move." The main character of the story is a child who spends an entire weekend having fun with transportation. Students can work in groups to fill in the details.

Meeting *Individual* Needs

RETEACHING (Easy) Have students draw pictures of people having fun with transportation. Use their pictures to make a "Here We Go" bulletin board display.

EXTENSION (Average) Have students make a *Fun on Wheels* poster with pictures of such items as bicycles, roller skates, scooters, GoKarts, skateboards, and in-line skates. Have students write a caption for each picture they include.

ENRICHMENT (Challenging) Have students research and report on the history of ice skates, roller skates, or bicycles.

Answers to THINKING ABOUT VOCABULARY

1. communication
2. telegraph
3. pony express
4. satellites
5. Channel

Answers to THINKING ABOUT FACTS

1. Before 1800: walking, riding horse-back or in horse-drawn carriages, sailing in boats; Since 1800: steam-powered boats and trains, automo-biles, airplanes; answers will vary.

2. air pollution; using public trans-portation or riding bicycles instead of driving cars

3. a team of horseback riders who delivered mail across the West; the telegraph

4. telephones, faxes, computers, let-ters; all but letters

5. by making it easier for people in both countries to visit each other and do business together

Resource REMINDER

Project Book: *pp. 21–23*
Assessment Book: *Chapter 10 Test*

CHAPTER 10 REVIEW

Major Events

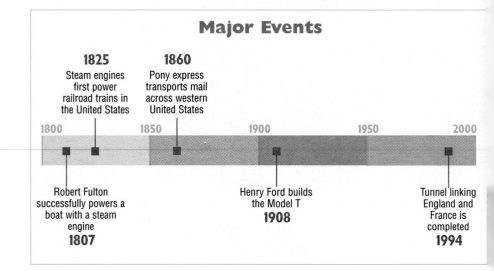

1825 Steam engines first power railroad trains in the United States

1860 Pony express transports mail across western United States

1800 — 1850 — 1900 — 1950 — 2000

Robert Fulton successfully powers a boat with a steam engine **1807**

Henry Ford builds the Model T **1908**

Tunnel linking England and France is completed **1994**

THINKING ABOUT VOCABULARY

Number a sheet of paper from 1 to 5. Write the word or words that best complete each sentence in the paragraph below.

Channel satellites
communication telegraph
pony express

Various means of transportation and __1__ have developed over time. In 1844, the __2__ first sent messages over wires. Later, in 1860 the __3__ delivered mail across the western U.S. In the 1960s __4__ enabled people to communicate around the world in seconds. And in the 1990s some high-speed trains travel below the English __5__.

THINKING ABOUT FACTS

1. What types of transportation were available before 1800? Name several types of transportation developed since then. Which do you think influenced people's lives the most? Why?

2. What environmental problem is partly caused by modern transportation? What is one way to help prevent this problem?

3. What was the pony express? What invention replaced it?

4. What are four ways people communicate today? Which of these ways were not available to people before 1800?

5. How has the English Channel Tunnel changed the lives of people in England and France?

264

Suggestions for Think and Write

SIGNS OF SUCCESS

WRITING A JOURNAL ENTRY Journal entries should in-clude a date and specific details about the event such as where and when it happened. Entries should also include personal observations about the event, speculations about its consequences, and/or reflections about what led up to it.

WRITING TO CONVINCE Students should cite the limita-tions of telegraphs that use wires and the advantages of the wireless telegraph. Students should also anticipate and refute arguments that might be used by people who do not agree with them.

WRITING A RADIO REPORT Reports should explain that the tunnel was built under the English Channel to con-nect England and France by railroad. Before the English Channel Tunnel was built, travel between England and France was limited to ship or plane. Many people like the tunnel because it opens up new opportunities for trade. Others dislike it because they feel that being connected to mainland Europe jeopardizes England's safety.

For performance assessment, see Assessment Book, Chapter 10.

THINK AND WRITE

WRITING A JOURNAL ENTRY

Suppose you are Robert Fulton or one of the Wright brothers. Write a journal entry about the first time your invention worked.

WRITING TO CONVINCE

Write a letter to convince people that they need the wireless telegraph. Explain why this invention is needed when people can already send messages over telegraph wires.

WRITING A RADIO REPORT

Write a radio report about the English Channel Tunnel. Explain what it is, why it is important, and why people like or dislike it.

APPLYING GEOGRAPHY SKILLS

READING TRANSPORTATION MAPS

Answer the following questions about the map on page 249 to practice your skill of reading transportation maps.

1. What do transportation maps show?

2. What types of transportation are shown on the map key?

3. What kind of transportation can you use to get from Chicago to St. Louis?

4. Which cities are not on a railroad line? How could you travel there?

5. How are transportation maps different from grid maps? How are they alike?

Answers to APPLYING GEOGRAPHY SKILLS

1. the routes of different kinds of transportation; how to travel using transportation

2. major roads, railroads, and canals

3. railroad

4. The following cities are not on a railroad line and would have to be reached by road: New Orleans, Natchez, Nashville, Louisville.

5. Transportation maps show how to travel by many different kinds of transportation. They have a map key which shows transportation symbols. A transportation map may be a grid map also. Both maps may have grids, show cities, distances, and roads.

Summing Up the Chapter

The chart below shows major changes in transportation and communication since 1800. Complete a copy of the chart by listing the missing development or person most responsible for it. How have we benefited by these changes in transportation and communication?

Person	Development
Robert Fulton	steamboat
Samuel Morse	telegraph
Alexander Graham Bell	telephone
Guglielmo Marconi	wireless telegraph
Henry Ford	Model T automobile
Wright Brothers	airplane
Eduardo San Juan	"moon buggy"
French and English (1994)	English Channel Tunnel

265

Suggestions for Summing Up the Chapter

- Prepare copies of the chart and pass them out to the class.

- Explain that each person in the left-hand column is responsible for a major development in transportation or communication. Students should write that development in the right-hand column. Each development in the right-hand column can be credited to the person most responsible for it. Students should write the name of that person in the left-hand column.

- Discuss the question with the entire class. Have volunteers describe how we have benefited from each development on the list. Also ask them to tell how the person contributed to the development.

Answers to
THINKING ABOUT VOCABULARY

1. fuel	6. migration
2. pioneers	7. channel
3. diary	8. oral history
4. oath	9. pony express
5. immigrants	10. prairie

Suggestions for
THINK AND WRITE

Writing a Journal Entry Have students work in pairs to list questions about life on a wagon train. (Example: What was it like to be constantly on the move?) Students can use those questions as a guide when writing their journal entries.

Writing an Advertisement Students can use one of the following formats to write convincing advertisements. *Contrast:* show life before and after the development in transportation or communication. *Explanation:* specify how the development will improve people's lives. *List:* itemize examples of improvements the development will bring.

Writing About Perspective Paragraphs should have a main idea and supporting details that show how life would be different today without buses, cars, airplanes, computers, or telephones.

Answers to
BUILDING SKILLS

1. Think about what items have in common.

2. Categories might include: items belonging to the school, students,

UNIT 4 REVIEW

THINKING ABOUT VOCABULARY

Number a sheet of paper from 1 to 10. Beside each number write the word or words from the list below that best completes each sentence.

channel	oath
diary	oral history
fuel	pioneers
immigrants	pony express
migration	prairie

1. Much of our pollution is caused by burning _____ .

2. Many _____ traveled west in wagon trains on the Oregon Trail.

3. By reading a _____, we can learn about someone's personal life.

4. When people become citizens of the United States they must take an _____ of allegiance.

5. Many _____ came to the United States hoping to begin new lives.

6. The _____ north of African Americans began around 1900.

7. Some bodies of water are connected by a _____ .

8. By listening to _____, we can learn what life was like in the past.

9. It was difficult for the _____ riders to cross the western United States to deliver mail.

10. Flat or rolling land covered with tall grasses is known as _____ .

266

THINK AND WRITE

WRITING A JOURNAL ENTRY
Suppose that you are crossing the United States by wagon train with your family in the 1850s. Write a journal entry describing what life is like during your trip West.

WRITING AN ADVERTISEMENT
Choose one of the developments in communication or transportation discussed in Chapter 10. Then create an advertisement to convince people that this development will make their lives better.

WRITING ABOUT PERSPECTIVE
Write a paragraph about how your life might be different today if there were no buses, cars, airplanes, computers, or even telephones.

BUILDING SKILLS

1. **Classifying** What is the first step to take when classifying items?

2. **Classifying** Classify items in your classroom into three groups.

3. **Transportation Maps** Look at the map on page 257. What are two ways to get from London to Dover?

4. **Transportation Maps** Look at the map again. How can you travel from Calais to Lille?

5. **Transportation Maps** When might you or your family need to use a transportation map?

Ongoing Unit Project

OPTIONS FOR ASSESSMENT

This ongoing project, begun on page 204D, can be part of your assessment program, along with other forms of evaluation.

PLANNING Let students know that they will use information from the unit for their time lines. They will need to describe how different modes of transportation and communication were important and affected migration.

SIGNS OF SUCCESS

• Work will reveal an understanding of why advances in transportation and communication enables our country to grow today as in the past.

• Groups will reach consensus on work to include on the time line and information will be placed in chronological order.

• Students will understand the links between changes in transportation and communication and movements of people.

 FOR THE PORTFOLIO Individual research sheets can be placed in each child's portfolio.

YESTERDAY, TODAY &
TOMORROW

In this unit, you have read about changes in where and how people lived in the past. Why do people move to new places today? What further changes in communication and transportation could we make in the future?

READING ON YOUR OWN

Here are some books you might find at the library to help you learn more.

THE FIRST RIDE: BLAZING THE TRAIL FOR THE PONY EXPRESS
by Jacqueline Geis
The story of the Pony Express and how it blazed a trail through dangerous territory.

THE GLORIOUS FLIGHT
by Alice and Martin Provenson
Louis Bleriot has a wish: He wants to fly. Read how he makes his dream come true.

GRANDFATHER'S JOURNEY
by Allen Say
A Japanese immigrant struggles with his love for both the United States and Japan.

and the teacher; items that can be moved and those that can't; items invented recently and items people might have had one hundred years ago.

3. railroad, highway
4. railroad
5. Accept any reasonable answer.

Suggestions for
YESTERDAY, TODAY, AND TOMORROW

Initiate a class discussion by asking students to share stories of family or friends who have moved. Thinking about true moving stories will help students make generalizations about why people move today. As students consider what changes may occur in the future, remind them that much of the new technology of the last 100 years amazed and surprised people when it was first invented. Encourage students to suggest amazing and incredible inventions that would be useful to people of the future. Students' ideas may predict future trends.

Suggestions for
READING ON YOUR OWN

Help students locate the library books suggested under *Reading On Your Own.* You will find additional titles listed in the Unit Bibliography on the Unit Organizer on page 204B. Invite students to choose books for independent reading. Ask students to think carefully about the people and events in the books they read. Have them share information about their topics by role-playing a character from the story and retelling the story or historical event in the words of that character.

UNIT PROJECT

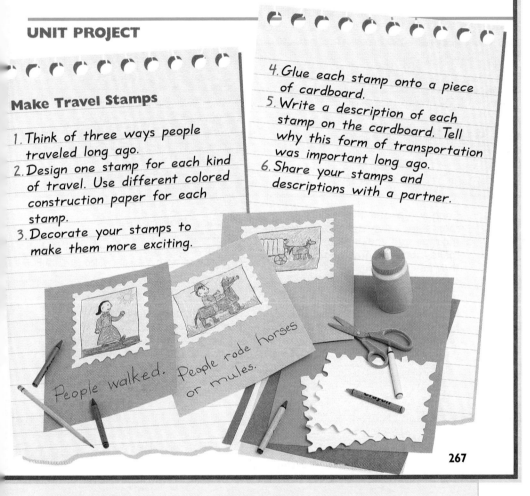

Make Travel Stamps

1. Think of three ways people traveled long ago.
2. Design one stamp for each kind of travel. Use different colored construction paper for each stamp.
3. Decorate your stamps to make them more exciting.
4. Glue each stamp onto a piece of cardboard.
5. Write a description of each stamp on the cardboard. Tell why this form of transportation was important long ago.
6. Share your stamps and descriptions with a partner.

People walked. People rode horses or mules.

267

Unit Project: *Make Travel Stamps*

OBJECTIVE: Making these stamps will help students review what they learned in the unit about the ways in which transportation has changed over time.

MATERIALS: construction paper, scissors, crayons or markers, glue, cardboard

- Invite students to brainstorm about the ways people traveled in the past. Each student should come up with at least three ways. Encourage students to revisit the unit to get ideas.

- Have each student draw pictures on colored paper for three stamps, cut out their stamps, and mount them on cardboard. Instruct students to write descriptions for their stamps explaining how the chosen form of transportation was important to people of the past.

- After partners have shared their stamps and descriptions, display the stamps around the room or bind them together along with the descriptions to make a class album.

OPTIONS FOR ASSESSMENT

The stamps can be part of your assessment program.

PLANNING Let students know that their stamps should illustrate and describe ways of travel they learned about in the unit.

SIGNS OF SUCCESS

- Students' descriptions should accurately explain their pictures.
- Students should proofread their descriptions to make sure grammar, spelling, and punctuation are correct.

 FOR THE PORTFOLIO Students' stamps and descriptions may be included in their portfolios.

5

Working Together

PAGES 268–327

UNIT OVERVIEW

People are an important resource of our country because the work they do contributes to the country's growth. People produce a good or provide a service when they work at their job. Jobs pay the workers money with which to buy other goods and services. There are many different types of jobs but most jobs require that people work together.

Adventures with National Geographic pp. 270–271

UNIT PLANNING GUIDE

CHAPTER	SUGGESTED PACING	CHAPTER OVERVIEW	CHAPTER RESOURCES
11 Work and Money pp. 272–297	15–17 days	Long ago people made or grew most things they needed. Today most people work at jobs to make money to buy the things they need or want.	**Practice Book** pp. 57–60 **Anthology** pp. 114–125 ● **Project Book** p. 25 **Transparency:** Graphic Organizer **Technology:** Videodisc/Video Tape, CD-ROM
12 Producing Goods pp. 298–325	14–16 days	Many of the goods that people produce are made from natural resources. It is important to use natural resources carefully.	**Practice Book** pp. 62–66 **Anthology** pp. 126–135 **Project Book** pp. 26–27 **Technology:** Adventures CD-ROM **Desk Maps** United States, World **Geo Big Book** pp. 8–9

Internet CONNECTION

The **Internet Project Handbook** and the Home Page at **http://www.mmh-school.com** contain on-line student activities related to this unit.

ASSESSMENT OPPORTUNITIES

UNIT ASSESSMENT

Unit Review pp. 326–327
  Unit Projects pp. 326–327

Assessment Book
  Unit Test Unit 5 Test
  Performance Assessment Unit 5

DAILY ASSESSMENT

Geo Adventures Daily Geography Activities

CHAPTER ASSESSMENT

Meeting Individual Needs pp. 273, 278, 287, 289, 295, 299, 305, 307, 311, 318, 323
Write About It pp. 278, 287, 289, 295, 305, 311, 318, 323
Chapter Reviews pp. 296–297, 324–325

Assessment Book
  Chapter Tests Ch. 11 Test, Ch. 12 Test
  Performance Assessments Ch. 11, Ch. 12

ANNOTATED BIBLIOGRAPHY

Classroom Library

■ Schwartz, David. *If You Made a Million*. New York: Lothrop, Lee & Shepard Books, 1989. This book is a description of the various forms which money can take, and how it can be used to buy, save, and earn.

Student Books

Aliki. *How a Book Is Made*. New York: Thomas Y. Crowell, 1986. Learn about the stages in making a book, from manuscript to bound copies. **(Average)**

■ Greenberg, Melanie Hope. *Aunt Lilly's Laundromat*. New York: Dutton Children's Books, 1994. While Aunt Lilly works in her laundromat in Brooklyn, she thinks about her island home, Haiti. **(Easy)**

■ McFarland, Cynthia. *Cows in the Parlor: A Visit to a Dairy Farm*. New York: Atheneum, 1990. This colorful photo-essay describes a typical day at a dairy farm. **(Average)**

Machotka, Hana. *Pasta Factory*. Boston, MA: Houghton Mifflin Co., 1992. This photo-essay describes a pasta factory and the pasta-making process. **(Average)**

Mitgutsch, Ali. *From Grain to Bread*. Minneapolis, MN: Carolrhoda Books, Inc., 1981. Explore the step-by-step process of planting wheat seeds, harvesting the crop, grinding wheat, and baking bread. **(Easy)**

■ Mitchell, Margaree King. *Uncle Jed's Barbershop*. New York: Simon & Schuster, 1993. A young girl's uncle fulfills his dream of opening his own barbershop, despite the obstacles that faced African Americans in the early twentieth century. **(Average)**

■ Smucker, Anna Egan. *No Star Nights*. New York: Alfred A. Knopf, 1989. The author recalls her own childhood growing up in a West Virginia steel mill town. **(Average)**

■ Williams, Vera. *Music, Music, for Everyone*. New York: William Morrow and Co. Inc., 1984. Rosa and her friends form a band and play at a neighborhood party. **(Average)**

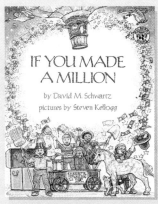

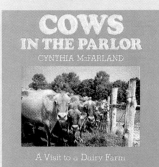

Teacher Books

Johnson, Neil. *All in a Day's Work: Twelve Americans Talk About Their Jobs*. Boston, MA: Little, Brown and Co., 1989. Adults discuss their work and the value of it.

Wilkinson, Elizabeth. *Making Cents: Every Kid's Guide to Making Money*. Boston, MA: Little, Brown & Co., 1989. This useful resource contains ideas and projects about ways students can earn money.

Read Aloud Books

Schotter, Roni. *A Fruit and Vegetable Man*. Boston, MA: Little, Brown and Co., 1993. An unexpected surprise comes to Sun Ho, a young boy who enjoys helping at the fruit and vegetable store in his neighborhood.

Torres, Leyla. *Saturday Sancocho*. New York: Farrar, Straus & Giroux, 1995. A young girl takes her grandmother to the outdoor market for the right ingredients for sancocho stew.

Technology Multimedia

Down on the Farm: Yesterday and Today. Video. RB8110. How a farm was in the 18th century is compared with a modern farm. Rainbow Educational Media. (800) 331-4047.

John Henry. Video. The greatest steel-driver competes against the steam drill. *Mose the Fireman.* Video. Mose saves New York and digs the first subway tunnel. Story Lane Theater, Macmillan/McGraw-Hill. (800) 442-9685.

Making the Things We Need. Video. No. 4489-106. This is a presentation of the processes of goods and services. Britannica Videos. (800) 554-9862.

Free Or Inexpensive Materials

For a comic book-style pamphlet that illustrates the importance of saving, send to: Federal Reserve Bank of New York; Public Information Dept., 33 Liberty Street; New York, NY 10045.

■ *Book excerpted in the Anthology*

■ *Book featured in the student bibliography of the Unit Review*

☐ *National Geographic technology*

Ideas for Active Learning

BULLETIN BOARD

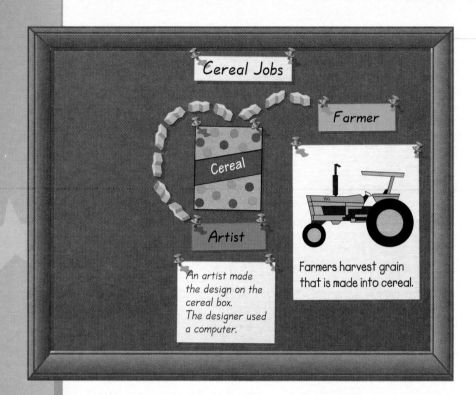

Cereal Jobs

Farmer

Cereal

Artist

An artist made the design on the cereal box. The designer used a computer.

Farmers harvest grain that is made into cereal.

Working Together

Help students create a bulletin board titled "Cereal Jobs" that will illustrate the many jobs and tools that go into the creation of a product.

- Attach an empty cereal box to the center of the bulletin board. Have students prepare index cards with labels identifying the jobs that were performed in order to get the box of cereal to the table.

- Encourage students to illustrate their cards and include captions that explain the role of the job in the production of the cereal box.

TEACHER EXCHANGE

Thanks to: Sandra W. Austin, Bates Elementary School, Louisville, Kentucky

Making Business Brochures 👥 GROUP 🕐 30 MINUTES OR LONGER

Materials: construction paper, crayons, glue, scissors, magazines, posterboard

1. Have students design a brochure about their community.
2. Tell students that brochures are used by communities to promote themselves. Brochures help businesspeople to decide whether they want to move their business to a community.
3. Ask each student to select something about the local community that he or she would like to promote. Tell students to concentrate on those aspects that would be important to businesses, such as good transportation.
4. Using arts and crafts supplies, have groups of students create brochures.
5. Suggest to students that they may want to write something on their brochures that explains why their community is special.
6. Send the finished brochures to the local chamber of commerce.

Enriching with Multimedia

RESOURCE: *Internet Project Handbook*

- Look at the **Internet Project Handbook** for student projects related to this unit or have students go online at http://www.mmhschool.com, Macmillan/McGraw-Hill School's home page on the World Wide Web.

RESOURCE: *Videodisc/Video Tape 3*

- Enrich Unit 5 with the Videodisc *glossary* segments.

Search Frame 53777

SCHOOL-TO-HOME

Working Together

- Throughout the unit, students will learn about how work supports the community, and the different kinds of work people do to produce goods and services. Ask students what work they might like to do as adults, and list their responses on paper for students to take home.
- Students and their families can use the Help-Wanted section of the local newspaper to see what jobs are available for each profession students listed. They may also look at advertisements for schools or other instruction opportunities to see where people could learn about the professions on the list. Suggest that students and their families work together to write a summary of what they have learned about different types of jobs and the required training. Encourage them to decorate their summaries with ads clipped from the newspapers.

ONGOING UNIT PROJECT

Consumer Catalog

CURRICULUM CONNECTION Art/Economics

RESOURCE: Project Book p. 24.

For this unit, students will work individually and in groups to create a catalog of consumer goods.

1. After Chapter 11, students can create a list of products they would like to sell. They can store this work in a folder.
2. After Chapter 12, students can research the jobs and materials needed to make those products.
3. When their research is complete, students can work in groups to determine which products will be included in a group catalog. They can then describe the products and create visuals for them.
4. This work can be compiled into a catalog and each group member can discuss catalog products.

Assessment suggestions for this activity appear on p. 326.

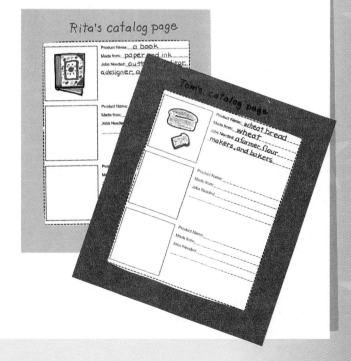

Introducing the Unit

Allow time for students to study the pictures and read the *Why Does It Matter?* passage to themselves.

Exploring Prior Knowledge Remind students that they have already learned about using natural resources and the development of technology.

Suggested Questions

- ***What have you learned about how people use natural resources?*** *(Students will recall that people use natural resources to grow food and to make clothing, shelter, and other useful items—such as the Anasazi making pots from clay, and the Jamestown settlers using shells to build their homes.)*

- ***You have learned how technology improved transportation in our country. How does technology help people do their jobs today?*** *(Students can discuss how modern transportation helps people to get to work and to transport goods. They may also mention items such as computers, X-rays, televisions, and telephones.)*

- ***What experiences have you had with earning or saving money?*** *(Invite students to share their experiences of working for pay or saving allowances.)*

Looking Ahead Students will learn how the economy functions. They will read how people obtain natural resources, turn them into useful products, and then sell them to others who need them. They will understand how people save money and reinvest it in a community economy, and how countries use money to trade natural resources and products.

National Museum of American Art, Smithsonian Institution

Background INFORMATION

ABOUT THE PICTURES

- **WHEAT** This painting by Thomas Hart Benton, entitled "Wheat" (1967), shows wheat ready for harvest. The artist has shown that the first two rows of wheat have been harvested.

- **HEAVY MACHINERY** Technology has revolutionized the workplace. Heavy machines such as the bulldozer illustrated are used in mining operations, construction, and farming. The bulldozer is an earth-moving machine that has a large, steel blade attached to the front of a powerful tractor.

The gear wheels pictured above are used to multiply either force or speed in a machine.

UNIT FIVE

Working Together

WHY DOES IT MATTER?

As you know, people are an important resource in our country. The work that people do contributes to our country's growth. In this unit you will learn about the different types of jobs people have to make a living. You will also learn how people use money.

Some people help other people for a living. Still others turn natural resources into products that people can use. As you will see, most jobs require people to work together.

269

Discussing the Photographs Invite students to make predictions about the unit based on the pictures on this spread.

Suggested Questions
- **Think about the changes that have happened in transportation. How do you think these changes have helped people grow wheat?** *(Students may understand that people can use machines to do tasks more easily and rapidly.)*

Discussing WHY DOES IT MATTER? Ask a volunteer to read aloud the *Why Does It Matter?* passage. Ask students to discuss how working with others makes work easier.

Suggested Questions
- **Why are people an important resource?** *(They can help each other get work done. They can work together to build houses, grow food, share ideas, and create laws.)*

- **What are some jobs that help other people?** *(health-care-related jobs, firefighting, teaching)*

- **What are some jobs that use natural resources to make products?** *(furniture and house building, cooking, automobile manufacturing)*

- ★**THINKING FURTHER:** *Making Conclusions* **Why is it often easier to work with other people?** *(Many people can give their time and energy, and it is nice to share ideas and successes.)*

Background INFORMATION

ABOUT THE PHOTOGRAPHS
- **SAVINGS BANK** People have always saved money at home and sometimes in little savings banks like the antique one shown. The first commercial savings bank in the United States was the Bank of North America, established in 1781 in Philadelphia. Banks are businesses that safeguard people's money and use it to make loans to and investments with others. Banks generally pay interest to their depositors for the use of their money.

Adventures
with
NATIONAL
GEOGRAPHIC

Introducing
Kidz Biz

Exploring Prior Knowledge Ask students to state definitions of the word *businessperson*. Then ask them to tell what they think a *businesskid* might be.

Links to the Unit In Unit 5, students will explore how people work together in businesses. They will investigate how people work to help others and make a profit. They will also plan their own inventions and businesses.

Kidz Biz Ask students to read Kidz Biz on page 271. Help them link information in the paragraph with each picture in this spread. Point out the small map and ask students to note the location of each businesskid's home. Help them discover which businesskid lives closest to your community.

After students have read the text, discuss the name Chris Webb chose for his business. Ask students to brainstorm names for the other kids' businesses. Be sure they consider what kind of product is being made, how people might use it, and who is making it.

Resource REMINDER

National Geographic Poster
Geo Adventures *Daily Geography Activities*
Technology: *Adventures CD-ROM*

Background INFORMATION

MORE ABOUT BUSINESSKIDS

- Teenager Chris Webb was excited by the special effects he saw in the movie *Star Wars*. He hopes someday to design special effects for films. Besides making movable Teddy Bears, Chris builds his own hairy monsters and goblins out of painted foam rubber. He placed one set of goblins in a haunted Halloween forest at the Green Mountain Audubon Nature Center in Vermont. These scary monsters moved when Chris controlled them by radio!

- Casey Golden has been playing golf since he was five. He found out that golf tees are made of wood, and golfers often lose them or leave them behind. He wanted to help save trees, so he worked on a biodegradable golf tee— one that would melt into the golf course without hurt-

ing nature. His idea has caught on, and his whole family is part of the business now.

- Brandi Champion is a sixth grader who plans to go to college. She plans to pay for her education by herself. She sells her dolls at crafts fairs, and puts all of the money she earns in the bank.

- Celesly Shabi learned to weave when she was 11. She enjoys planning the design and seeing how it comes out. Celesly sells her rugs and exhibits them. One of them won first place and best-of-show in the young artists' division of the 1991 Navajo Nation Window Rock Fair in Arizona.

Kidz Biz

Being young didn't stand in Chris Webb's way when he created "Imagination Industries." This teenager from Vermont makes teddy bears that move—and he sells them. Other "businesskids" have also come up with great ideas. Casey Golden, of Colorado, makes biodegradable golf tees from grass seeds, apple sauce, and other materials. Brandi Champion, of Maryland, creates dolls out of mops. Celesly Shabi, of Arizona, weaves traditional Navajo rugs, a skill she learned from her mom. What business would you like to go into?

GEO JOURNAL

Write and draw an advertisement to sell a product you invent yourself.

271

Explain that the large picture in this spread shows Chris Webb at work. He is taking apart teddy bears from the Vermont Teddy Bear Company. To make the bear move, he inserts a small motor like those used in a model airplane. Soon the movement of the head, arms, and legs can be controlled by remote control.

The picture on the lower left shows Brandi Champion with one of her mop dolls. Brandi ties the mop strings together to create the dolls arms. Then she makes a head by inserting a piece of cloth and painting on a face.

Casey Golden is shown holding one of his biodegradable golf tees. It was made from a hardened mixture of peat moss, grass seed, applesauce, and paste.

Celesly Shabi is shown holding a skein of the heavy yarn used in weaving Navajo rugs.

Using the Geo Journal You may want to provide students with colored construction paper and markers so they can make their advertisements enticing.

Technology CONNECTION

ADVENTURES CD-ROM
Have students use the *Travel* function to find the places mentioned in Kidz Biz.

Curriculum CONNECTION

LINKS TO LANGUAGE ARTS Have students read about student businesskids and report on what they discover.

- Have them visit the library to find articles about student inventors and businesses. Suggest students look in children's magazines like *National Geographic World* and *Cobblestone.* They can also look in the nonfiction section of the library under *inventors* and *business.* Remind students to ask the reference librarian for help if they have difficulty finding information.

- Ask each student to write a profile of a businesskid. The profile should include a picture of the businesskid and of his or her product or service. The profile should also describe how they got started and how other people helped in the work.

- Display the profiles in a classroom reading corner so students can read them in spare class-time.

11 CHAPTER ORGANIZER

Work and Money
PAGES 272-297

CHAPTER OVERVIEW

Long ago people made or grew most things they needed. Today most people work at jobs to make money to buy the things they need or want. There are many ways to work and make money. Some workers provide services to the community and others produce goods.

CHAPTER PLANNING GUIDE
Suggested pacing: 15–17 days

LESSON	LESSON FOCUS	LESSON RESOURCES
1 JOBS AND MONEY pages 274–278	Earning, Saving, and Spending Money	*Practice Book* p. 57 *Anthology* pp. 114–119
CITIZENSHIP **Making a Difference** page 279	The Pencilmania Business	
2 PEOPLE AT WORK pages 280–287	The Many Ways to Make a Living	*Practice Book* p. 58 *Anthology* pp. 120–125 *Technology:* Videodisc/Video Tape
Infographic pages 284–285	At the Workplace	*Technology:* Adventures CD-ROM
LEGACY pages 288–289	Working at Home: Linking Past and Present	*Technology:* Adventures CD-ROM
THINKING SKILLS pages 290–291	Identifying Cause and Effect	*Practice Book* p. 59 *Transparency:* Graphic Organizer *Technology:* Videodisc/Video Tape
GLOBAL CONNECTIONS pages 292–295	Life in Japan	*Practice Book* p. 60 *Technology:* Videodisc/Video Tape, CD-ROM
CHAPTER REVIEW pages 296–297	Students' understanding of vocabulary, content, and skills is assessed.	*Assessment:* Ch. 11 Test, Performance Assessment Ch. 11 *Transparency:* Graphic Organizer

OPTIONS FOR STUDENT ACTIVITIES

Citizenship pp. 275, 279

Curriculum Connection pp. 277, 283, 288, 290

Expanding the *Infographic* p. 284

Using the Anthology p. 286

ASSESSMENT OPPORTUNITIES

Meeting Individual Needs pp. 273, 278, 287, 289, 295

Write About It pp. 278, 287, 289, 295

Chapter Review pp. 296–297

Assessment Book

Chapter Test Ch. 11 Test

Performance Assessment Ch. 12

Using the Floor Map Use the Floor Map and the Project Book with Lessons 1, 2, or 3 by inviting students to build a farm, a factory, and other businesses. Students should discuss how they chose locations for these places.

Using Geo Adventures Use **Geo Adventures** Daily Geography Activities to assess students' understanding of geography skills.

Using the Vocabulary Cards The vocabulary words for each lesson are available on *Vocabulary Cards* for review and practice.

GETTING READY FOR THE CHAPTER

Make a Jobs Collage GROUP 30 MINUTES OR LONGER

Objective: To think about how people earn and spend money.

Materials: *Project Book* p. 25, magazines, scissors, glue, oaktag

1. Have students work in small groups. Give each group a few magazines and explain that they will use them to make collages that show a variety of jobs.
2. Suggest that students find and cut out pictures of people at work, as well as pictures that show the results of a particular job. For example, a photo of a delicious pie might suggest a baker, a recipe writer, or the photographer who took the picture. Encourage each group to keep a list of their ideas.
3. To make the collages, have the groups select, arrange, and glue onto oaktag the pictures they have cut out. Have them label each picture with the name of a job it matches.
4. Finally, have each group member choose one of the jobs from the group collage to write about on Project Book p. 25.

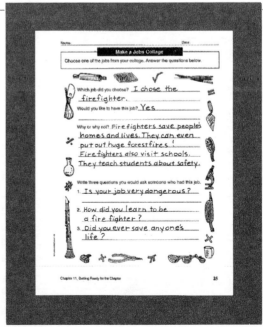

Introducing the Chapter

Initiate a discussion about why people work and what kinds of work they do. Students can share their own experiences with paid and unpaid work.

THINKING ABOUT GEOGRAPHY AND ECONOMICS

Explain that when we talk about economics we mean how people make money and spend it. Ask students to link locations on the map with the places they read about on the opposite page.

WORKING IN SPOKANE, WASHINGTON

Suggested Questions

- *What is the boy in the picture doing?* (He is raking leaves.)

- *Do you think he is getting paid for his work? Why or why not?* (He may be raking leaves to help his family or he may be raking a neighbor's lawn to earn money.)

- ★THINKING FURTHER: *Classifying* *What kinds of jobs can young people do to help their families and to earn money?* (Students may suggest yardwork, taking care of pets, housecleaning, or baby-sitting.)

WORKING IN JAPAN

Suggested Questions

- *What is the woman in the picture doing?* (selling magazines and newspapers)

- *What country does she work in?* (Japan)

 **REMINDER**

Technology: *Videodisc/Video Tape 3*

CHAPTER 11

Work and Money

THINKING ABOUT GEOGRAPHY AND ECONOMICS

Long ago people made or grew most things they needed. Today things have changed. Most people work at jobs to make money to buy things they need and want. In Chapter 11 you will see the many different jobs people have in communities around our country and in other countries too.

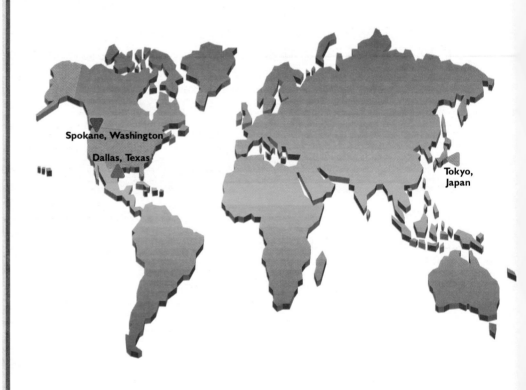

Spokane, Washington

Dallas, Texas

Tokyo, Japan

272

Background *Information*

LINKING THE MAP TO THE PHOTOGRAPHS

- In suburban Spokane, many jobs center around the upkeep of single-family homes. Whether the job is paid or unpaid, work around the home contributes to the economy by keeping the community safe and clean. Yardwork is only one way that students can participate in the economy.

- Selling magazines and newspapers is only one task in the complicated industry of publishing. Using modern technology—such as a word processor and a facsimile machine—helps writers, editors, and publishers to receive work from distant places and produce printed material all around the world.

- The sports industry provides jobs for workers in large communities and small. It is a part of the entertainment industry and attracts large audiences in arenas and stadiums, as well as by radio and television.

Spokane,
Washington,
work around the
house may include
raking leaves.

**Basketball players in
Dallas, Texas, have a
difficult job, but one
that is fun and exciting.**

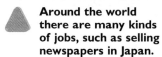

**Around the world
there are many kinds
of jobs, such as selling
newspapers in Japan.**

273

★**THINKING FURTHER:** *Compare and
Contrast* **How is this job like a job
someone might have in your community? How is it different?** *(Possible answer: Someone in my community sells newspapers and magazines.
The lady shown here is selling mainly
newspapers printed in Japanese, but
here the newspapers are in English.)*

WORKING IN DALLAS, TEXAS

Suggested Questions

● **What do the men in this photograph do for a living?** *(They play
basketball.)*

● **In what kinds of communities do
they work?** *(urban)*

● **What do you know about profes-
sional basketball? What more
would you like to learn?** *(Invite students to share their knowledge and
their questions.)*

★**THINKING FURTHER:** *Making Decisions* **Which kind of work pictured
here interests you most? Why?**
*(Students can give personal reasons
for interest in a specific job.)*

Technology CONNECTION

VIDEODISC/VIDEO TAPE 3
Enrich Chapter 11 with the Videodisc *map*
and *glossary* segments.

Search Frame 53777

Meeting *Individual* **Needs**

RETEACHING (Easy) Invite students to draw pictures of someone
working in your community.

EXTENSION (Average) Have students write "interviews" with one of the
people in the pictures. Ask them to describe what the person does and
why the person likes the job. Ask them also to describe how the job
helps other people and how other people help this person work.

ENRICHMENT (Challenging) Ask students to write essays about making money. Have them answer the question: "Why do we need money?"
Explain that students will learn more about money as they read the
chapter.

LESSON 1

Lesson Overview
Many people work to make a business flourish.

Lesson Objectives
★ Investigate the human resources of a community.

★ Explain why people earn, save, and spend money.

★ Explain the interdependence of people and products in a community.

1 PREPARE

MOTIVATE Have a volunteer read the *Read Aloud.* Tell students that the man in the picture is Mr. Flythe. Ask them what kinds of questions they would like to ask him.

SET PURPOSE Review the *Vocabulary* words with students. Then direct their attention to the *Read to Learn* question and invite speculation about the answers.

2 TEACH

Thinking About Making a Living
Help students understand that Mr. Flythe makes a living by providing goods and services for his community.

Suggested Questions

● **What are goods?** *(They are things that people make or grow.)*

● **What goods does Mr. Flythe sell?** *(bicycles and bicycle parts)*

● **What is a service?** *(a job that helps others)*

● **What services does Mr. Flythe offer?** *(He sells and repairs bicycles.)*

Resource **REMINDER**

Practice Book: *p. 57*

Anthology: *Music, Music for Everyone, pp. 114–119*

Jobs and Money

READ ALOUD
Mr. Skip Flythe (Flīth) works in a bicycle shop. He has sold hundreds and hundreds of bicycles to children. "I'll tell you something," he says. "There's nothing more exciting than selling a bike to a child."

Focus Activity

READ TO LEARN
Why do people earn, save, and spend money?

VOCABULARY
goods
services
employer
interest
consumer
economy

PLACE
Raleigh, North Carolina

Making a Living

Mr. Flythe has worked at the Flythe Cyclery shop in Raleigh (RAW lee), North Carolina for many years. His grandfather first opened the store back in the 1920s. What if his grandfather walked into the store today? He might be surprised at how it has changed. The style of bicycles has changed. And so have the prices. Bicycles are much more expensive today. But some things have remained the same. The sign on the front hasn't changed. There are still plenty of bicycles in the store. And, like his grandfather, Mr. Flythe provides goods for the people of Raleigh to buy. Goods are things that people make or grow. Mr. Flythe also offers a service by selling and repairing goods such as bicycles. A service is a job that helps others by providing something they need or want.

274

Reading STRATEGIES *and* Language DEVELOPMENT

CLASSIFYING Remind students that classifying means to sort items or ideas into categories. In this lesson, the categories of goods and services are discussed. Help students classify *goods* and *services* into the proper categories as they read about them in the text. Goods include bicycles, bicycle parts, helmets, food, clothes, books. Services include tire repair, bicycle maintenance, lawn-mowing, baby-sitting, car-washing, housekeeping, doctor's services, free bicycle workshop.

PREFIXES AND SUFFIXES Explain that a suffix is an ending (a letter or letters) added to a word that changes the meaning of the word. Write the *Vocabulary* words *employer* and *consumer* on the chalkboard and ask a volunteer to underline the suffix in each word. Explain that the suffix *-er* means "a person or thing that." You may want to have students find the dictionary definitions for the words *employ* ("to hire") and *consume* ("to use"). Then have students explain how the added suffix changes each word.

Why People Work

"I've been in this business ever since I was a little boy," says Mr. Flythe. "Whenever I was free, I was in the store with my grandfather. Then the business was my father's. Now it's mine. And one of my sons seems interested in joining the business. I've been warning him—it's a lot of hard work. But he still seems interested!"

Raleigh, North Carolina

Maybe Mr. Flythe's children will work in the bicycle shop. Or maybe they'll do some other work to earn money. Most people work to earn money. Then they use that money to pay for a place to live. They also use it to buy food, pay for visits to the doctor, and buy clothes and books. What are other reasons people need money?

Mr. Flythe does not work all by himself. He needs other people to help him sell and repair bicycles. So he hires other people to work for him. This means he is an employer. An employer is someone who hires and pays other people to work. There are six other people who work at Flythe Cyclery.

Like his grandfather long ago, Mr. Flythe provides a service by selling bicycles to people in Raleigh.

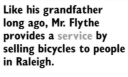

275

Thinking About Why People Work

Explain that people work to make money so that they can buy goods and services and because work is satisfying and interesting. Invite students to talk about jobs that interest them.

Suggested Questions

- ***How did Mr. Flythe start working in the bicycle store?*** *(He visited his grandfather in the shop, worked with his father, and then inherited the business.)*

- ***Who helps Mr. Flythe in his business?*** *(He has six helpers.)*

- ***How does an employer get people to work for him or her?*** *(The employer hires and pays the workers.)*

★**THINKING FURTHER** *Sequence* **Mr. Flythe spends some of the money he makes in his community grocery store. Where might the grocery store owners spend their money?** *(in a community clothing, book, or even bicycle store)*

Background INFORMATION

ABOUT EMPLOYERS AND EMPLOYEES

- Employers carefully choose workers and teach them any skills required by the business. Often employers help pay for employees' health insurance. They also pay money into an account for employees who are laid off or get hurt on the job. Employers usually make important business decisions and plan the direction of the company. A good employer makes sure that employees are happy in their jobs so that they will be motivated to do their best for the company.

- Employees are expected to perform their jobs according to the rules of the company. Employees are often encouraged to make suggestions about how to improve goods or services. As employees' skills increase, they are often given more responsibility and better pay.

★CITIZENSHIP

BUSINESS AND THE COMMUNITY Invite a local shop owner to talk with the class about the responsibilities of owning a business. Ask the speaker to explain how the business is run and how it serves the community.

Second-Language Support

GRAPHIC ORGANIZERS Second-language learners can increase their vocabularies by creating "word banks" of goods and services. Have students make charts of goods that their families might buy and services that their families might need. Then have students use telephone directories to find other goods and services that they can add to their word banks.

DID YOU KNOW?

How did the piggy bank get its name?

The answer has nothing to do with pigs! The name comes from *pygg,* (pronounced like the word *pig*), an old Scottish word for a kind of clay used to make jars. People stored money at home in these jars. The jars made from this clay became known as pyggy banks. Later the name changed to piggy banks and the jars were even shaped like pigs.

Elissa Zellinger worked at different jobs to earn money to buy a bicycle.

Saving Money

Elissa Zellinger is a 14-year-old girl who lives in Raleigh. She has visited Flythe Cyclery many times to look at the bicycles. "Looking at those bikes kept me going," says Elissa. Slowly, she has saved her allowance and money from jobs outside her home.

Elissa was saving her money in a piggy bank. Her parents had a better idea. They took her to a bank and helped her open an account. If you save money in a bank, the bank gives you extra money called interest. The interest is payment for lending money to the bank. "I need every extra penny of interest," says Elissa.

Mr. Flythe has used banks for his business too. He keeps the money the store earns in the bank. He has also borrowed money from the bank to help the business grow. He pays interest to the bank for his loan.

Being a Consumer

Finally Elissa saved enough money. She did some research to find out which bikes were the best buys. Elissa wanted to be a smart consumer. Consumers are people who buy goods and services. "I've worked hard to save money," says Elissa. "I want to make sure I don't throw it away!"

Mr. Flythe knows what Elissa means. "Children who have earned and saved their own money are my best consumers. I give a free workshop for children on bicycle safety and repair. Children who have saved their money are always the ones who take my class!"

Elissa loves her new bike. She even knows how to fix a tire or a slipped chain. She also knows she has to wear her helmet and be alert when she rides her bicycle. And she has also learned a lot about how our economy works. Economy is the making and consuming of goods and services.

Elissa is a smart consumer. She asked many questions before deciding which bicycle to buy.

Thinking About Being a Consumer Ask students to discuss how earning and saving can teach people the value of money.

Suggested Questions

- **What is a consumer?** *(someone who buys goods or services)*

- **What is a smart consumer?** *(someone who finds out which products are the best to buy)*

- **Why did Elissa want to be a smart consumer?** *(She had worked hard to save money and wanted to be sure she spent it in the best possible way.)*

- **What is the economy?** *(It is the providing and consuming of goods and services.)*

- **What did Elissa learn about the economy?** *(She learned that people work to earn money, and save to buy the things they need and want.)*

★**THINKING FURTHER:** *Cause and Effect* **What is the effect of working hard to save money for something you want?** *(You try to be a smart consumer and take very good care of your purchase.)*

277

Field Trip

Plan a trip to a bank and ask a teller or manager to explain how accounts are opened, how interest is added to the account, how to deposit and withdraw money, how records are kept, and how patrons can check their balances. Be sure students understand that money in the bank is constantly in circulation.

Curriculum CONNECTION

LINKS TO READING As preparation for the *Field Trip*, invite students to read the *Classroom Library* selection for this unit: *If You Made a Million* by David M. Schwartz (Mulberry Books, 1989). Told with humor and imagination, this introduction to banking is enjoyable and informative.

Background INFORMATION

ABOUT THE FREE-ENTERPRISE SYSTEM Our country's economy is a free-enterprise system, also called "private enterprise."

- According to the free-enterprise system, people can own or operate businesses for profit, with little governmental control.

- In a free-enterprise system, businesses compete with one another. Through competition, each business tries to satisfy the consumer more effectively than the competition.

- High quality and reasonable prices are major benefits of the free-enterprise system. Businesses must dedicate themselves to keeping the quality of their products high and their prices reasonable or they will not be competitive.

WHY IT MATTERS

Flythe Cyclery is part of Raleigh's economy. Mr. Flythe and his employees provide a service and sell goods. They also earn money. They spend that money in their community. That money helps other businesses grow.

Some people do jobs that don't earn money. For example, some people work in their homes raising their families. That's an important job too. Everyone who works contributes something to a community and to its economy.

Elissa plays a role in her community's economy by earning money and buying goods.

✓✓ Reviewing Facts and Ideas

SUM IT UP

● Goods are things people make or grow.

● A service is a job that helps other people by providing something they need or want.

● People who buy goods are called consumers.

● Interest is money paid for a loan.

● Economy is the making and consuming of goods and services.

THINK ABOUT IT

1. What is the difference between an employer and a consumer?

2. **FOCUS** Why do people earn, save, and spend money?

3. **THINKING SKILL** <u>Compare</u> and <u>contrast</u> Mr. Flythe's job with the job of a teacher or principal.

4. **WRITE** Suppose you want to earn money over the summer. Write a brochure advertising what services you can offer your neighbors. Make sure your brochure tells why people should hire you and what you will charge.

278

CITIZENSHIP
MAKING A DIFFERENCE

The Pencilmania Business

NEW YORK CITY, NEW YORK— Would you like a monster pencil holder, an eraser shaped like a clown, or a holiday bunch of lollipops and pencils? Jason Walder and José Rodriguez can help you. They are 12-year-old students at Public School 169 in New York City. They're in classes for students who have special learning needs. And they are "super salesmen" of a program called Pencilmania.

Pencilmania is a made-up word that means "crazy about pencils." Students in Pencilmania need not be crazy about pencils, but they are serious about learning to run a business. Every day at lunch, they sell pencils and gift items.

The students give some of the money they earn to the Make a Wish Foundation to help children who are very sick. The money also pays for class trips to museums and concerts.

"Selling the pencils is just one part of the business," Jason learned.

The students use catalogs and decide what and how many of each kind of pencil to order. When the pencils arrive, they make sure they have received everything they ordered. They advertise their goods with posters, fliers, and announcements over the school loudspeaker.

José enters the daily earnings on a computer. "I also help decide how much each item should sell for so we can make money. But what I like most is helping the customers decide what they want. And I like to count money. It helps me in math."

The hard work is rewarding. Jason explained, "I am proud I learned how to make good decisions." And José added, "We learned how to work together to get our job done."

Pencilmania

279

CITIZENSHIP

USING CURRENT EVENTS Point out that Pencilmania is a small, student-run business that benefits the community. Many small businesses in communities all over the United States also donate a percentage of their profits to worthy causes, such as public radio or television, scholarships, or environmental funds. Encourage students to conduct community research to find companies that donate some of their profits to specific causes. To obtain information, students can use local media resources and write letters of inquiry to local businesses.

Lesson Objective
★ Analyze how a business can benefit the community.

Identifying the Focus Running a business can help students earn money, learn business skills, practice math, help others, and feel proud of making decisions together.

Discussing Pencilmania Have students talk about money-raising ventures they have helped with in school, scout groups, or other community groups. Ask them to share what they liked about the work and how the money they earned was used.

Suggested Questions

● **Who are Jason Walder and José Rodriquez?** *(They are 12-year-old students who live in New York City, New York.)*

● **What do they do to make money?** *(They sell pencils and make gift items.)*

● **What do they do with the money they make?** *(Part of it goes to the Make a Wish Foundation, part of it helps to pay for class trips to concerts and museums.)*

● **What does José use a computer for?** *(He uses it to record the daily earnings.)*

● **Why do José and Jason like the work?** *(They help others; José likes to count money and help customers; Jason is proud of making good decisions; Both Jason and José like to work together.)*

★**THINKING FURTHER:** *Sequencing*
What are the steps in the process of ordering and selling pencils? *(Look in catalogs to decide which pencils to order; check the order when it comes in; advertise with posters, fliers, and announcements; help the customers decide; count the money.)*

LESSON 2

PAGES 280–287

Lesson Overview
People work together in many businesses to produce goods and perform services.

Lesson Objectives
★ Describe different ways people make a living.

★ Explain how technology influences the way people make a living.

★ Understand that people need to work together to do their jobs.

1 PREPARE

MOTIVATE Have a volunteer read the *Read Aloud*. Ask students what skills people might need to work on a textbook.

SET PURPOSE Review the *Vocabulary* words with students. Then direct them to the *Read to Learn* question and invite speculation about the answer.

2 TEACH

Discussing Where Did This Book Come From? Point out the picture of Iris Kim and help students understand that every product is the result of people's work.

Suggested Questions
● **Where does Iris Kim work?** *(She works at a publishing company.)*

● **What does she do for a living?** *(She is an editor. She helps with all the steps in making textbooks.)*

★ **THINKING FURTHER:** *Compare and Contrast* **How is Iris Kim's job different from Mr. Flythe's? How is it the same?** *(Iris Kim works with many other people to make a product. Mr. Flythe sells and repairs products. They both provide goods and services to other people.)*

Resource REMINDER
Practice Book: *p. 58*

Anthology: *On the Job, pp. 120–121; Uncle Jed's Barbershop, pp. 122–125*

Technology: *Videodisc/Video Tape 3; Adventures CD-ROM*

People at Work

Focus Activity

READ TO LEARN
What are some different ways a person can make a living?

VOCABULARY
publishing
editor
designer
producer

READ ALOUD
"When I was a child, I didn't think much about where textbooks came from. I didn't think about who wrote them or how they were printed. Now I think about textbooks a lot! Working on textbooks is how I make my living."

Where Did This Book Come From?

These are the words of Iris Kim. She works at the publishing company in New York City that made this book. Publishing companies make books, magazines, CD-ROMs, and other things people can read. Ms. Kim is an editor. An editor helps with all the steps involved in making a book.

Like Ms. Kim at your age, you may not have given thought to your textbooks. But many people work hard to make the books that appear on your desk at the start of each school year. For Ms. Kim and the people she works with, making textbooks is more than just a way to make a living. They hope that readers, like you, will learn from the books. In this lesson you will learn some of the steps involved in making a book like this one.

280

Reading STRATEGIES *and* Language DEVELOPMENT

MAKING CONCLUSIONS Point out to students that we are making conclusions by getting information from what we read and by using what we know from life. As students read the lesson, help them make conclusions that answer the *Read to Learn* question.

ABBREVIATIONS Remind students that an abbreviation is a shortened form of a word. Some technological terms are too long or complicated to use in everyday speech. People abbreviate these words to make them easier to use. Point out *CD-ROM* on p. 280 and explain that this abbreviation stands for Compact Disk–Read Only Memory. This means that the disk is meant to be read only—you cannot add information to it. Invite students to brainstorm other technology abbreviations (VCR, FAX, TV) and find out their meanings.

Planning a Book

One of the first steps in making a textbook is to decide what the book should be about. The authors and editors make this decision together. Ms. Kim does research to find interesting and important topics for the textbooks she helps plan. Textbook authors and editors also pay attention to what teachers want their students to learn. The authors and editors learn what people have liked about their books in the past. It is also important to find out what changes to the book people would like to see in the future.

As an *editor* Iris Kim must research information. She also discusses writing ideas with writers and other editors.

Thinking About Planning a Book
On chart paper, begin an outline of the people who help publish textbooks and the skills and ideas they contribute.

Suggested Questions

- **What is one of the first steps in making a textbook?** *(deciding what to include)*

- **Who makes the decisions about what to include?** *(The authors and editors work together to decide.)*

- **How do they make these decisions?** *(They do research, they talk to teachers, and they think about what should be kept or changed from their other books.)*

★**THINKING FURTHER:** *Making Conclusions* **Why do you think there are so many people helping to plan a textbook?** *(Some people help to add ideas to make the book interesting and other people help to check that the book is accurate.)*

Technology CONNECTION

VIDEODISC/VIDEO TAPE 3
Enrich the lesson with the glossary entries on *Occupations.*

Search Frame 53777

Background INFORMATION

MORE ABOUT WRITING A BOOK Explain to students that technology allows many people across the country to work on texbooks. To find information, a writer might:

- interview an expert by visiting him or her or calling him or her on the phone. Some social-studies experts work at museums. Others are people who are skilled workers, have lived in an area for a long time, or were eyewitnesses to an event. Most people who know about a subject or skill are eager to share their knowledge with a writer.

- read many library books on a subject. Other authors and editors who write encyclopedias, magazine articles, and other nonfiction books help writers double-check their facts and think about ideas from different perspectives. Reference librarians help writers find the exact information they need; they may fax the writer information too.

- watch a television program or a video on a subject. Photographers, writers, actors, and musicians have all worked together to film information about many different topics and supply that information to the people who make the textbook.

- gather information from many sources around the world, including on-line services and Internet sites.

Discussing How Does it Read?
Help students understand that parts of
a book often have to be revised many
times before they are ready to be
printed. Explain that the editorial
process is similar to a student's
process when producing a first draft.

Suggested Questions

● **What does an editor do?** *(An editor
reads the author's work and makes
suggestions about how to improve it.)*

● **What tools does Iris Kim use to
edit a textbook?** *(a pen and a computer)*

● **How do computers help editors?**
*(They help them make changes
quickly and help keep track of what is
on every page.)*

How Does It Read?

After the first version of the book is written,
many changes are made. The editor reads each
lesson and makes suggestions about how to
improve them. "Then I try to make all the
changes work," says Ms. Kim. "I used to do my
work on a typewriter. Now I use computers
and other new technologies. I can make many
more changes in much less time. I try to make
each lesson interesting for students to read!"

Sometimes more information is needed, so
Ms. Kim does more research. Sometimes all the
information will not fit in the lesson. Then Ms.
Kim must decide what information to leave out.
There are also pictures and maps. Deciding
what is most important is the editor's job.
Computers help editors keep track of what
is on each page.

**After Ms. Kim receives a
page from a writer, she
makes many corrections
and changes.**

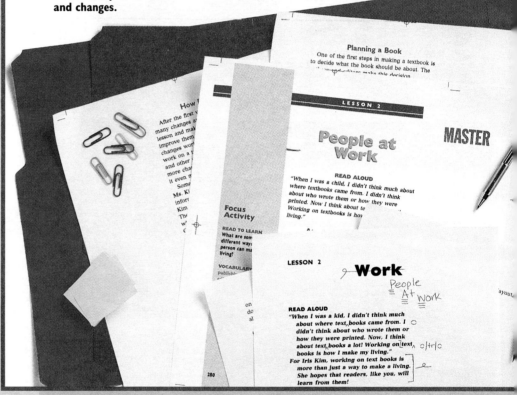

Background INFORMATION

MORE ABOUT TECHNOLOGY The people who publish
textbooks are a community of workers. The tools they use
to create books have changed from those of just a few
years ago.

● Writers write on a word processor. They send their writing on a computer disk to editors. In the past, writers
used typewriters and made carbon copies or photocopies of their work.

● Writers can use reference materials in the library. Now
they can locate information on databases through the
Internet.

● Writers and editors can exchange long-distance messages between computers over the telephone and now
via E-mail and modems.

● Designers design pages on the computer and send the
finished computer disk to the printer. Designers used
to plan the pages with pencil and paper. They would
cut and paste the copy and the pictures by hand.

● Authors and editors can send paper copies of their research or writing over a fax machine.

● Modern transportation systems using trucks and airplanes can guarantee and trace delivery of an entire
manuscript from across the country in one day.

The designer decides where the photos and drawings will go on each page (top). The pages are then sent to the printer and made into a book (bottom).

How Does It Look?

Next, designers look at the pages. Designers make sure that each page looks right. They use a computer to help them decide where pictures will fit. "I try to make these pages exciting to look at," says a designer of this book. "Learning should be fun, so I choose pictures and designs that I think children will enjoy and learn from."

Then there are people who make sure the book will be printed correctly. All in all, about 75 people have worked on the book you are holding in your hands right now! By making a textbook that will be used by consumers, Ms. Kim and others are producers. A producer is a maker of goods or services.

283

Discussing How Does it Look?
Use the *Curriculum Connection* activity below to help students understand and experience book design and layout.

Suggested Questions
● **What do book designers do?** *(They make sure that the pages of a book look attractive.)*

● **How do designers decide where pictures and writing will fit?** *(They move them around by hand and on a computer screen.)*

● **Why should the pages in a book look appealing?** *(so people are interested in reading them and so they are clear and easy to read)*

● **How many people worked on your textbook?** *(about 75)*

● **Why are these people called producers?** *(They have worked together to make something for consumers.)*

★**THINKING FURTHER:** *Sequence*
Who are the last people to work on a textbook? *(the designers and the printers)*

Curriculum CONNECTION

LINKS TO SCIENCE Designers and editors plan how to illustrate the pages. They order photographs or sketches from an artist who may create them on computer or with traditional materials.

● The designer puts the author's manuscript disk in the computer. Using a design program, the size and style of the letters are chosen, and sentences and paragraphs moved. The designer can see every change on the screen and know exactly what the page will look like.

● Pictures are entered into the computer with an electronic eye called a *scanner*. Or computer art may be created on the screen. Once the pictures are on the screen, the designer can enlarge or reduce them.

Have students research the way a scanner electronically changes images into digits that the computer can read. You may suggest that they use computer magazines as well as encyclopedias for information. Then have students work in small groups to create an oral report, using visuals if appropriate.

Infographic

Help students understand that there are many different kinds of jobs in your community and in the world.

Discussing At the Workplace Use the *Infographic* to help students recognize the enthusiasm that people share for meaningful work. Ask volunteers to read aloud each quote. Then discuss how each person's work gives him or her a personal sense of satisfaction, while earning money and providing a service or goods for other people.

Suggested Questions

- **Who made your textbook?** *(editors and authors, designers and printers)*

- **Do you know who made your clothing or shoes?** *(Some students may know which country their clothing came from.)*

★**THINKING FURTHER:** *Making Conclusions* **Do you think it is important to know about the work other people do? Why or why not?** *(Be sure students support their answers.)*

Reading the Quotes Help students recognize the talents and interests that led each person to their unique job.

Suggested Questions

- **Why does Dena Abergel like her job?** *(She gets to express herself and it makes her happy.)*

- **Why does Kim Guyette like her job?** *(It involves every step in the process of making something.)*

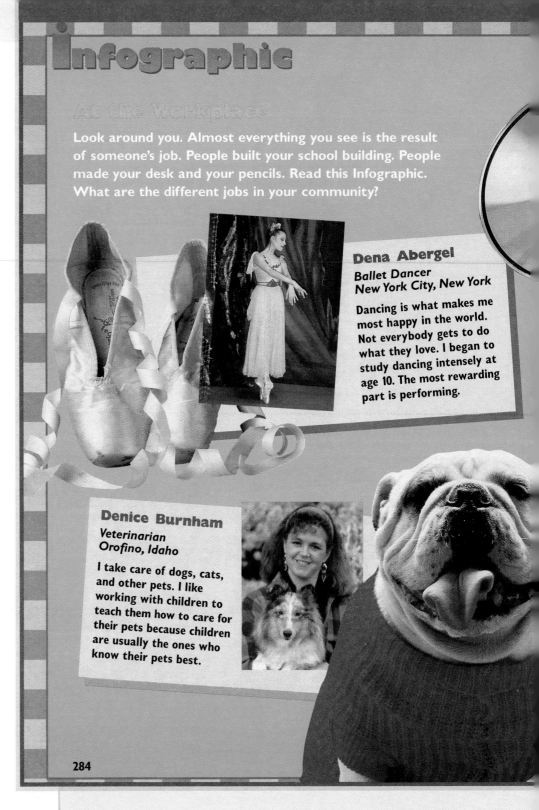

Infographic

At the Workplace

Look around you. Almost everything you see is the result of someone's job. People built your school building. People made your desk and your pencils. Read this Infographic. What are the different jobs in your community?

Dena Abergel

Ballet Dancer
New York City, New York

Dancing is what makes me most happy in the world. Not everybody gets to do what they love. I began to study dancing intensely at age 10. The most rewarding part is performing.

Denice Burnham

Veterinarian
Orofino, Idaho

I take care of dogs, cats, and other pets. I like working with children to teach them how to care for their pets because children are usually the ones who know their pets best.

284

Expanding the Infographic

LINKS TO LANGUAGE ARTS Have students create a display that includes pictures of people in your community and quotes about their jobs.

- Have students work in pairs to interview neighbors and relatives about the skills and technological tools they need for their jobs and how their work helps the community. Then they can copy brief quotes and display them next to drawings or photographs of the workers.

- Invite students to bring in photographs of themselves to display along with written statements about what kind of work they would like to do and how the job would provide goods or services to the community. Students can also research and report about specific job training, responsibilities, and skills.

- Encourage students to conduct research to compare and contrast the jobs in the *Infographic* that existed in the past to the same jobs in the present. How are they alike? How are they different?

- If possible, make arrangements for other classes to visit yours so students can share what they have learned about people and jobs.

Alfredo Estrada
**Third-Grade Teacher
El Paso, Texas**

There's a lot of work involved in teaching. I like the challenge of trying to make learning exciting. I use computer games to teach writing, spelling, and math. I also use laser discs to teach science.

Leon Harris
**Television Anchorperson
Stone Mountain, Georgia**

I make news stories understandable. A story can happen and within minutes I'm talking about it. When I get nervous I just imagine I'm talking to my son.

Kim Guyette
**Furniture Maker and Woodworker
Waterbury Center, Vermont**

I build tables from start to finish. Working with wood is challenging because you don't know exactly how each piece will come out.

285

- **Which workers provide a service?** (everyone except Kim Guyette)

- **Which workers make goods?** (Kim Guyette)

- **Whose job was invented in the last 100 years?** (Leon Harris)

★**THINKING FURTHER:** *Making Decisions* **Which of these jobs interests you the most? Why?** (Help students express how their talents and interests might be best used in the work force.)

Technology CONNECTION
ADVENTURES CD-ROM
Enrich the lesson with the CD-ROM activity, *Hi Ho! Hi Ho! It's Off to Work We Go.*

Background INFORMATION

Share these additional quotes from some of the workers in the *Infographic* about using technology on the job.

- **Denice Burnham** "My job has changed somewhat because of new diagnostic tools from treating animals and deciding what kinds of problems they have. For instance, now I can refer an animal with a possible brain tumor to the university veterinary school for a CAT scan—a series of computerized X rays over the entire body."

- **Kim Guyette** "I use a radial arm saw to do the cutting. We use different saws on different parts of the tables. The table is then sanded with a hand-held sanding machine. The sanding evens out the wood and makes it feel smooth. If the table is supposed to have a certain

shape, like a rounded or beveled edge, we do that with an electric tool called a *router,* or shaper."

- **Dena Abergel** "Videos have changed the way we train and practice. Now every ballet performance is taped. We watch them to check on how we are performing. We also look at videos of ballets being performed when we are first learning a part. We learn much faster this way."

Discussing I Like My Job Invite students to discuss stories about jobs and work that they have enjoyed reading. Then have them read *Many Voices*.

Learning from Literature Have volunteers take turns reading the selection aloud.

Suggested Questions

● **Who wrote the story Uncle Jed's Barber Shop?** *(Margaree King Mitchell)*

● **What job did Uncle Jed have?** *(He was a barber.)*

● **Did Uncle Jed provide a good or a service?** *(a service)*

● **Who provides other services in your community?** *(teachers, doctors, lawyers, dentists, accountants)*

I Like My Job!

For people to do a good job, it's important that they enjoy their work. Read the story below about a man who loves his job.

UNCLE JED'S BARBERSHOP

Story by Margaree King Mitchell, 1993.

Jedediah Johnson was my granddaddy's brother. Everybody has their favorite relative. Well, Uncle Jedediah was mine.

He used to come by our house every Wednesday night with his clippers. He was the only black barber in the county. Daddy said that before Uncle Jed started cutting hair, he and Granddaddy used to have to go thirty miles to get a haircut.

After Uncle Jed cut my daddy's hair, he **lathered** a short brush with soap and spread it over my daddy's face and shaved him. Then he started over on my granddaddy.

I always asked Uncle Jed to cut my hair, but Mama wouldn't let him. So he would run the clippers on the back of my neck and just pretend to cut my hair. He even spread lotion on my neck. I would smell wonderful all day.

lathered: filled with soap

286

Using the ANTHOLOGY

ON THE JOB, pages 120–121 This selection offers three interviews with people who do very different kinds of work. After students read the interviews, have them discuss any questions they have about the people and their jobs.

UNCLE JED'S BARBERSHOP, pages 122–125 Students will enjoy the book from which the *Many Voices* selection was taken. It is the story of Jedediah Johnson, an African American who spent much of his life saving for his own barbershop. If you wish, read the book aloud with children. At that time, you can answer any questions about discrimination that they might have.

Second-Language Support

MAKING CONNECTIONS Second-language learners can develop vocabulary as they think about the kinds of work that went into making their textbook. After reading the lesson together, have students look through their book and list the different jobs that were done in order to produce it. Next to each job, have students write down the skills that are needed to do it. Afterward, encourage students to produce a small book of their own about the history of the local community.

WHY IT MATTERS

In this lesson you have met people doing different things to earn a living. All of these people depend on other people to do their jobs. "I wouldn't be able to do my job by myself," says Ms. Kim. "Authors, designers, artists, and other editors all work on books with me. And the most important people of all are the students who read them. Without them, I wouldn't be able to work on books like this one at all!"

Ms. Kim and many other people have worked together to make this textbook.

✔ Reviewing Facts and Ideas

SUM IT UP

- Publishing companies make books. Authors, editors, and designers are some of the people who work on books.
- Technology has changed the way editors and designers do their jobs.
- A producer is a maker of goods and services.
- There are many different ways to make a living. People need to work together to do their jobs.

THINK ABOUT IT

1. What is a producer?
2. **FOCUS** What are some different ways a person can make a living?
3. **THINKING SKILL** Look around your classroom. List some jobs needed to produce the things you observe. _Classify_ the jobs into at least three groups. What do these groups tell you about making a living?
4. **WRITE** Write a letter to the editor of this book telling what you like and don't like about the book.

287

MEETING _Individual_ NEEDS

RETEACHING (Easy) Ask students to create a simple outline of the people who collaborate to publish a textbook.

EXTENSION (Average) Invite students to make a map of one business street in your community. Have them draw outlines of the buildings and fill in information describing the goods and services each business provides.

ENRICHMENT (Challenging) Invite students to talk with an older family member or neighbor about how technology has changed their profession over the past twenty years. Encourage them to find out how these changes have improved people's lives and how change may have been difficult.

Discussing WHY IT MATTERS Be sure students understand how important it is for people to work together.

★**THINKING FURTHER:** _Cause and Effect_ **Why can't Ms. Kim do her job by herself?** (She needs the ideas and skills of other people who can write, edit, design, and draw.)

⭐ 3 CLOSE

SUM IT UP
Have students write their answers to the questions below.

Suggested Questions

- **What is one way writing a book is different today than 100 years ago?** (People can now write, edit, and design on computers; they can send information long distances immediately, so they can work together while living in different places.)

- **Who are some producers in your community?** (Students may list factory workers, small manufacturers, farmers, or individual artists and writers in your community.)

- **How do consumers help people make their livings?** (When consumers buy products or services, they pay money to other people, who can then spend it someplace else.)

EVALUATE
✔ **Answers to Think About It**

1. a person who makes goods or services
2. Students may answer with examples from this lesson or with professions in your community.
3. for example, paper: lumberjacks to cut the trees, workers in the pulp mill or recycling factory, packagers, designers, truck drivers and distributors, school-supply sales people
4. Encourage students to list their favorite chapters and to list suggestions for improvements.

Write About It Have students write a letter to one of the people in the _Infographic_ telling why they are interested in their job.

LEGACY
PAGES 288–289

Lesson Overview
Throughout history people have worked at home.

Lesson Objective
★ Learn about working at home in the past and in the present.

1 PREPARE

MOTIVATE Ask students to talk about the kinds of work people do in their homes. Have them tell about household chores and responsibilities. Ask volunteers to describe businesses that friends or relatives run from their homes.

SET PURPOSE Ask students to review some of the ways in which technology has changed people's lives. Ask how technology has changed life in the home.

2 TEACH

Understanding the Concept of a Legacy Remind students that legacies are traditions from the past. Help them understand that the legacy of working in the home probably began when humans first lived in caves. This lesson will help students understand how traditions can continue even as they change with the times.

Examining the Pictures Have students examine the pictures and read the captions.

Suggested Questions

● *How did people work at home long ago?* (They lived above their business or had a backyard workshop.)

● *What jobs do people do at home to care for their homes and families?* (They clean the house, do the laundry, shop and prepare food, take care of small children.)

● *What high-tech jobs do people do at home today?* (They use computers to run businesses.)

Legacy
LINKING PAST AND PRESENT

Working AT Home

Working at home is a legacy that goes back long ago. People often lived above their shop or business or had a workshop in their backyard.

Today many people still work at home. As in the past some people work at home to care for their family and home. Still others work at home using computers and other high-tech machines to help run a business.

Cooking, cleaning and managing expenses are some of the many tasks homemakers do.

288

Curriculum CONNECTION

LINKS TO LANGUAGE ARTS
Ask partners to interview four or five neighbors to find out what kinds of work they do in the home. Students can ask what kinds of jobs they do, how long they have been working at home, and how technology helps them in their work. Remind students to include people who have home offices, those who work both in and outside the home, and homemakers. Suggest that students ask questions such as the following:

● What do you do at home? What jobs do children do?

● When did you start working at home?

● In general, how many hours do you work at home? Do you work during the day or the evening?

● How do computers help you work at home?

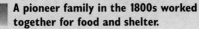
A pioneer family in the 1800s worked together for food and shelter.

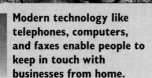

Modern technology like telephones, computers, and faxes enable people to keep in touch with businesses from home.

Craftmakers often work at home. Dressed as a colonist, a woman shows how candles were made (left). Today, an Arapaho woman sews quilts (below).

- **What jobs did the pioneers have to do to care for their families and homes?** *(They had to make everything themselves including homes and clothes, and they had to grow their own food.)*

- **How has homemaking become easier over the years?** *(People can now buy food, cook on convenient stoves, and use electric appliances, like vacuum cleaners and dishwashers.)*

- **What kind of work in the home interests you the most?** *(Students can mention any of the occupations on these pages or other home businesses they are familiar with.)*

★THINKING FURTHER: *Compare and Contrast* **How is working at home today the same as it was 100 years ago? How is it different?** *(People still care for their homes and families and still run businesses in their homes. Today people have technology to help them clean, cook, and run businesses.)*

⭐ 3 CLOSE

SUM IT UP

Be sure students understand that no matter how much technology changes working at home, past and present are linked through the legacy of working at home.

EVALUATE

Write About It Ask students to write a newspaper article describing the history of working in the home.

MEETING *Individual* NEEDS

RETEACHING (Easy) Have students make illustrated lists of the tasks family members do to care for their homes and family and the tools they use.

EXTENSION (Average) Ask students to interview someone in their neighborhood who works in the home. Explain that the person may be a homemaker or someone with a home business. Have students find information about the kind of work they do, why the person values working at home, and how technology has made the person's work easier.

ENRICHMENT (Challenging) Tell students that technology is helping more and more people to set up offices in the home. Challenge them to write essays predicting how their community might be different if many more people had home businesses.

Technology CONNECTION

ADVENTURES CD-ROM
Enrich the lesson with the *Time Line* segment on the CD-ROM.

SKILLS LESSON

PAGES 290–291

Lesson Overview

When we identify cause and effect, we identify what makes something happen and what results.

Lesson Objective

★ Recognize cause and effect.

1 PREPARE

MOTIVATE To demonstrate cause and effect, clap two chalkboard erasers together. Ask students to comment on what happened. Point out that clapping the erasers together is a cause; the chalk dust is the effect.

SET PURPOSE The *Vocabulary* words *cause* and *effect* are defined in the lesson. Tell students that in this lesson they will practice identifying cause-and-effect relationships.

DISCUSSING HELPING YOURSELF Direct student's attention to the *Helping Yourself* box on p. 291. Ask a volunteer to read aloud the steps.

2 TEACH

Why the Skill Matters Help students review the definitions of *cause* and *effect*.

Suggested Questions

- *What is a cause?* (something that makes something else happen)

- *What is an effect?* (something that happens as the result of something else)

Using the Skill Encourage students to make statements about the events in the paragraph, explaining *cause* and *effect*.

- *What words can you look for that might show a cause?* (because of, as a result of, *and* since)

- *What words can you look for that might show an effect?* (as a result, so, therefore)

Resource REMINDER

Practice Book: *p. 59*

Transparency: *Graphic Organizer*

 Technology: *Videodisc/Video Tape 3*

THINKINGSKILLS

Identifying Cause and Effect

VOCABULARY

cause   effect

WHY THE SKILL MATTERS

In the last lesson you read about how technology has changed publishing. It is now easier for authors, editors, and designers to do their jobs. People can work all over the country, using fax machines and computers to send their work in.

New technology is one cause of these changes. A cause is something that makes something else happen. Some of the changes are effects of the new technology. An effect is what happens as a result of something else.

Understanding cause and effect connections helps you to make good decisions. For example, you know that opening your window on a cold day will cause cold air to come into the room. That will have the effect of making the room colder. You can then decide if you want to open the window or not. Look at the Helping Yourself box for some tips on how to find causes and effects as you read.

290

USING THE SKILL

One way to understand the connection between events is to look for clues as you read. Some words and phrases that may show you a cause are *because of*, *as a result of*, and *since*. Some that indicate effects are *as a result*, *so*, and *therefore*. As you read the story that follows, look for words to help you identify causes and effects.

> *Lisa Groome just took a new job. Since she is still learning how to do her new job, Lisa has to work late.*
> *Lisa is more excited about her work than she was at her old job. It is more rewarding. As a result, Lisa is happier.*

In the first paragraph, the word *since* connects two ideas. One idea is that Lisa is learning her new job. The other idea is that she is working late. *Since* shows you that Lisa's learning the job is the cause of her working late. Working late is an effect of learning the job.

Read the second paragraph again. Notice the phrase *as a result*, which indicates an effect. *As a result* shows that Lisa's happiness is an effect of her new job being more rewarding. The rewarding job is the cause of her happiness.

Curriculum CONNECTION

LINKS TO LANGUAGE ARTS In a story circle, help students make up a continuous story about money changing hands in a community to illustrate cause-and-effect connections.

- Begin by writing the cause-and-effect clue words on the chalkboard to help students remember them.

- Cut a green piece of construction paper and write $5 on it.

- Tell students that they will be making up a story about five dollars that travels through a community. Spending the five dollars is the cause. When the five dollars is spent, certain effects occur.

- Give one student the five-dollar bill. Ask the student to explain how he or she will spend it and the effects that will occur. In turn, students should pass the five dollars around the circle, explaining how they will spend it (the cause) and what effects the spending will have.

*Having a new job that makes more money; family will have to move; look for words that show causes like *because of, as a result of,* and look for words that show effects like *as a result* and *therefore.*

TRYING THE SKILL

Suppose that your mother or father is going to take a new job. Since the new job pays more money, your family will be able to save money for an exciting vacation. But the new job is located in another town, so you and your family will have to move.

What is the cause of your family being able to take a vacation? What is the effect of the job being in another town? How can you tell?*

HELPING Yourself

- **A cause** is an event that makes something happen. An **effect** is what happens because of something else.
- Look for words that show causes—*because of, as a result of, since.*
- Look for words that show effects—*as a result, therefore, so.*

REVIEWING THE SKILL

1. What is a cause? What is an effect?

2. Suppose your community builds a new library. What might be some effects of the library on your community?

3. As a result of technology, editors can change what is written more easily. Is the technology a cause or an effect? How do you know?

4. Why is it helpful to think about cause and effect when making a decision or solving a problem?

Trying the Skill Remind students to use the *Helping Yourself* box as they answer the questions independently. Then ask a volunteer to tell which clue words helped them recognize cause and effect. (*since* and *so*)

3 CLOSE

SUM IT UP
Ask students to practice making additional statements about cause and effect.

EVALUATE
✓ **Answers to Reviewing the Skill**

1. A cause is why something happens. An effect is something that happens as a result of something else.

2. For example: People might read more books. There might be a story time for children. People might have to pay more taxes to pay for it.

3. The technology is a cause. The phrase *as a result of technology* tells us this.

4. Knowing the cause of a problem can help you solve it. Knowing the effect of something can help you know what might work and what might not work.

Technology CONNECTION

VIDEODISC/VIDEO TAPE 3
Enrich the lesson with the glossary segment.

Search Frame 53777

Background INFORMATION

USING THE GRAPHIC ORGANIZER You may want to have students work with this Graphic Organizer transparency to help them organize their information.

GLOBAL CONNECTIONS

PAGES 292–295

Lesson Overview
Modern technology and ancient traditions affect the way people live and work In Japan.

Lesson Objectives
★ Describe how people live and work in Japan.

★ Understand how technology has influenced the way people in Japan make a living.

1 PREPARE

MOTIVATE Point out the picture of a subway in Japan. Then direct attention to the *Read Aloud*. Invite students to compare and contrast the Tokyo transportation system with one in their city, or in a city they know.

SET PURPOSE Review the *Vocabulary* words with students. Direct attention to the *Read to Learn* question and invite speculation about the answers.

2 TEACH

Discussing A Growing Country
Point out Montana on a U.S. map. Explain that Japan is about the size of Montana and that 125 million people live there. Then direct attention to the entire map of the U.S. Tell students that 250 million people live in our country. Have students compare the sizes of the two areas.

Suggested Questions

● *What city is the capital of Japan?* (Tokyo)

● *How big is Japan? How many people live there?* (about the size of the state of Montana; about 125 million)

★THINKING FURTHER: *Predicting*
Think of what you know about capital cities. What do you predict a visitor to Tokyo could see? (government buildings, historical monuments and statues, transportation systems)

Resource REMINDER

Practice Book: *p. 60*

Technology: *Videodisc/Video Tape 3; Adventures CD-ROM*

Focus Activity

READ TO LEARN
How do people live and work in Japan?

VOCABULARY
journalist
high-tech

PLACE
Tokyo
Japan

292

Life in Japan

READ ALOUD
It is early Monday morning in Tokyo, Japan. Tokyo is one of the largest cities in the world. The subway platform is crowded. A train pulls into the station, silent and fast. The doors open and people start moving into the cars. Then the "pusher" comes along. He gently pushes people into the train to pack it more tightly. In Tokyo, the work day has begun.

A Growing Country
Tokyo (TOH kee yoh) is the capital of Japan. Japan is a small country in terms of land. Japan is a large country in terms of population. About 125 million people live in Japan. That number is about half the number of people living in the United States of America. To understand how crowded Japan is, picture half the people in our country moving to Montana!

Japan has been called "the land of the rising sun" because it is in the most eastern part of the continent of Asia. People there are among the first in the world to see the sun rise each day. Today "the land of the rising sun" has another meaning. The Japanese have worked hard to build up their country. So, they might see their country as a rising sun growing every day.

Reading STRATEGIES *and* Language DEVELOPMENT

CAUSE AND EFFECT Ask a volunteer to review the definitions of *cause* and *effect*. Help students identify causes and effects by pointing out the *effect* of technology on Japanese culture and the *cause* of Japanese culture becoming more like other countries in the world.

COMPARATIVES/SUPERLATIVES Remind students that comparative adjectives compare two nouns. Superlative adjectives compare more than two nouns. Point out the superlatives in this lesson: *largest* (p. 292), *latest* (p. 294), and *most important* (p. 295). Help students discover how these adjectives would be written as comparatives: *larger, later, more important*. Then ask them to find descriptive words in the lesson and use them in sentences in the superlative form.

On the Job in Japan

Tsutomu Yamaguchi (tsew TOH mew yah mah GEW chee) is a journalist. A journalist writes for a newspaper, a magazine, or for a television news program. Mr. Yamaguchi lives in Japan and writes for a newspaper called the *Yomiuri Shimbun* (yoh mee ur ree SHIM bewn). "Working as a journalist is very challenging and exciting," says Mr. Yamaguchi. "I like finding stories and responding quickly to the news."

Mr. Yamaguchi also finds his job to be very hard at times. "The news is endless," he says. "And it is difficult to work on sad stories."

Just as Ms. Kim's job as an editor in the United States has changed because of technology, so has Mr. Yamaguchi's job. "We are very proud of our technology. We can get news stories and information faster than ever before. There is more information to understand," says Mr. Yamaguchi. "But it is still people who write the stories and make the decisions."

Mr. Yamaguchi is a journalist who has worked in Japan and around the world.

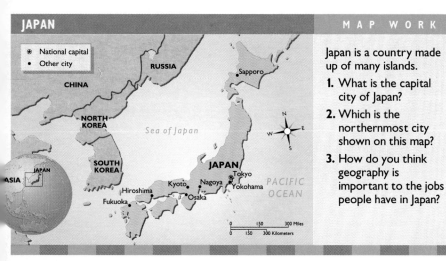

JAPAN

- ⊛ National capital
- • Other city

RUSSIA
CHINA
Sapporo
NORTH KOREA
Sea of Japan
SOUTH KOREA
ASIA
JAPAN
JAPAN
Tokyo
Kyoto Nagoya Yokohama
Hiroshima
Osaka
Fukuoka
PACIFIC OCEAN

0 150 300 Miles
0 150 300 Kilometers

MAP WORK

Japan is a country made up of many islands.

1. What is the capital city of Japan?
2. Which is the northernmost city shown on this map?
3. How do you think geography is important to the jobs people have in Japan?

MAP WORK: 1. Tokyo **2.** Sapporo **3.** Because Japan is surrounded by water on many sides, fishing and shipping are two very important businesses.

293

Discussing On the Job in Japan

Ask students to discuss what they know about the field of journalism in the United States.

Suggested Questions

- **Where does Tsutomu Yamaguchi live?** *(in Japan)*

- **What business does he work for?** *(He works for the* Yomiuri Shimbun, *a Japanese newspaper.)*

- **What is a journalist?** *(someone who finds out the news and writes about it)*

- **What does Mr. Yamaguchi like about his work? What does he dislike?** *(He likes to find news stories and to respond quickly; the news is endless and is often filled with sad stories)*

★**THINKING FURTHER:** *Using Prior Knowledge* **How is news reporting different today than it was 100 years ago?** *(Today we can get news stories and pictures from around the world immediately by satellite. One hundred years ago people had to send information by telegraph.)*

More MAP WORK

On a globe, point out the International Dateline. Explain that if you travel east from Japan, you eventually run into yesterday!

Suggested Questions

- **What body of water is Tokyo near?** *(the Pacific Ocean)*

- **What continent is Japan part of?** *(Asia)*

Background INFORMATION

JOURNALISM TODAY In the early days of reporting, a journalist might have written about an event weeks or months after it happened. Today Mr. Yamaguchi uses modern technology to report news events quickly.

- Mr. Yamaguchi may travel to a news event by car, train, or airplane. Once there, he can pick up a radio receiver and send a news story immediately to one of many newspaper wireless or aviation stations. From these stations, the news can be relayed to the main office.

- If Mr. Yamaguchi travels near one of the paper's offices, he can use computers and photo transmitters to send his article to the main office. His story arrives ready for printing within hours or minutes of when it happened.

Global CONNECTION

- *Yomiuri Shimbun* has offices in 36 cities around the world, including five in the United States. Reporters in these countries research and write about international news. *Yomiuri Shimbun* also receives news stories from other papers and magazines from around the world and from international news bureaus.

- Many Japanese living abroad want to read the news in Japanese. Using high-tech equipment, *Yomiuri Shimbun* now prints its daily newspapers overseas. They send page copies and printing information instantly across the Pacific Ocean on an undersea fiber-optics cable. Pages are received in the United States as facsimiles. They are turned into film for printing within hours. *Yomiuri Shimbun* also prints the daily paper in Bangkok and London, sending information via satellite.

Thinking About Old and New Invite students to talk about familiar Japanese products and traditions. Then help them compare life in Japan with life in your community.

Suggested Questions

- **What does high-tech mean?** *(use of the latest technology to make electronics and other goods)*

- **What high-tech businesses does Japan have?** *(Japanese businesses make cars, televisions, computers, and video and recording machines.)*

- **Is Noh theater an ancient or modern form?** *(It is very old.)*

- **What U.S. tradition is popular in Japan?** *(baseball)*

★**THINKING FURTHER: Classifying** **Which businesses and professions are special Japanese traditions? Which are traditions or businesses that are also seen in the U.S.?** *(Noh theater and Japanese pottery are Japanese traditions; cars, televisions, computers, video and recording machines, baseball, and newspapers can be found in America.)*

Technology CONNECTION

VIDEODISC/VIDEO TAPE 3
Enrich the lesson with the map of Japan.

Search Frame 53730

Old and New

If you look around your home, the chances are you'll find something made in Japan. Like American companies, Japanese companies are also known for making high-tech products. High-tech is the use of the latest technology to make electronic and other goods. Japan makes cars, televisions, computers, video and recording machines, and other high-tech goods.

Japan has changed as quickly as technology has changed. It has kept much of its old culture as well. Look at the pictures on this page. They show some parts of Japanese culture. In his free time Mr. Yamaguchi likes to take part in a kind of theater called *Noh*. Actors in Noh theater wear masks that have been part of Japanese culture for hundreds of years. Mr. Yamaguchi also likes to make pottery. "In recent years, though, I haven't had time. I work long hours," says Mr. Yamaguchi. "When I have free time, I like to spend it with my family."

Noh theater is a very old tradition that is still popular in Japan.

Many people read the *Yomiuri Shimbun* (left). Baseball is popular in Japan.

294

Background INFORMATION

MORE ABOUT TRADITIONS

- Noh Theater has been an unchanged tradition since the 1300s. The language is old, the wooden masks are passed down from generation to generation, and many stories are about older beliefs. Because the players wear masks, their bodies must dance to convey action and emotion.

- Japanese potters have a long tradition of creating beautiful pots and ceremonial tea cups by hand. Some Japanese potters create pots as tall as 3 feet high. The Japanese craftsman Soetsu Yanagi thought society needed many different artisans to provide handmade crafts. He said, "To me the greatest thing is to live beauty in our daily life and to crowd every moment with things of beauty."

- Baseball has been a favorite sport in Japan since the 1930s. The *Yomiuri Shimbun* sponsored an American baseball game in Japan, and Babe Ruth captured the admiration of the Japanese people.

- Japanese gardens are traditional places of rest in crowded cities like Tokyo. Parks are usually carefully planned, with walkways, fish ponds, rock gardens, and statues.

Curriculum CONNECTION

LINKS TO ART Use the books below to introduce students to origami, the classic Japanese art of paper-folding.
- *Classic Origami* by P. D. Tuyen (Sterling, 1995)
- *Origami Playtime* by Nobuyashi Enomoto (Charles Tuttle Co., 1992)

A Changing Country

"In some ways, Japan is becoming more and more like other countries," says Mr. Yamaguchi. "My son is fifteen years old and his favorite music is American. But in other ways, Japan will always be different. For one thing, no other country speaks Japanese. It is a difficult language."

WHY IT MATTERS

You have read about some people who work for an American publishing company. You have also read about someone working for a Japanese newspaper company. What are some of the differences? Some things are very similar. Both work places have been changed by technology. And in both countries, as everywhere, people are the most important resource.

Japanese traditions like this style of house remain strong today, but Japan is changing as contact with other countries continues.

✓// Reviewing Facts and Ideas

SUM IT UP

- Japan is a small country with a large population.
- Journalists write for newspapers, magazines, or television news programs.
- Japan is known for making high-tech products.
- Japan has kept much of its traditional culture.

THINK ABOUT IT

1. What does a journalist do for a living?

2. **FOCUS** How do people live and work in Japan?

3. **THINKING SKILL** What is the *cause* of Mr. Yamaguchi's being able to receive information more quickly? What are the *effects* of technology on his job?

4. **WRITE** Write a two-paragraph newspaper article about something that happened at your school this week.

295

Discussing A Changing Country
Point out that a country can change while keeping its traditions.

Suggested Questions

- **How will Japan always be different from other countries?** *(No other country speaks Japanese.)*

Discussing WHY IT MATTERS Have students answer this question.

Suggested Questions

★**THINKING FURTHER:** *Predicting* **How do you predict technology might change news reporting in the future?** *(Possible answers: Paper may become scarce and newspapers may be read on home computers, or interactive television may let us choose the news stories we want to hear more about.)*

⭐ 3 CLOSE

SUM IT UP
Invite students to answer this question in class discussion.

Suggested Questions

- **About how big is Japan? About how many people live there?** *(Possible answer: Japan is as big as Montana; half as many people live there as in the United States.)*

EVALUATE
✓ **Answers to Think About It**

1. researches the news and writes about it

2. They speak Japanese; they maintain many traditions from the past, while living and working with the most up-to-date technology.

3. Cause: Modern satellites and computers can relay information quickly. Effect: He can report stories from all over the world.

4. Help students focus their articles on a news event. Encourage them to write details about the people, place, and event, and to tell why it is important news.

Write About It Invite students to write some questions they would like to ask Mr. Yamaguchi.

Answers to
THINKING ABOUT VOCABULARY

1. journalist
2. high-tech
3. economy
4. employer
5. interest

6. consumer
7. designer
8. producers
9. goods
10. service

Answers to
THINKING ABOUT FACTS

1. to make money to buy food, shelter, and clothing

2. Goods are manufactured items. Services are ways that people help other people.

3. Smart consumers find out how a product is made, how it works and lasts, how much it should cost, and how it compares with other products on the market before they buy.

4. because people keep the economy going by earning and spending money.

5. the Noh theater and traditional Japanese pottery

Resource REMINDER

Project Book: *p. 25*
Assessment Book: *Chapter 11 Test*

CHAPTER 11 REVIEW

THINKING ABOUT VOCABULARY

Number a sheet of paper from 1 to 10. Beside each number write the word or term from the list below that best completes each sentence.

consumer	high-tech
designer	interest
economy	journalist
employer	producers
goods	service

1. A good _____ makes sure that all the information in a news story is correct.

2. Some _____ products include fax machines and CD-ROMs.

3. People who produce and consume goods and services help our _____ to grow.

4. An _____ is someone who hires and pays other people to work.

5. A savings account in a bank earns extra money called _____.

6. When you buy something you are acting as a _____.

7. A _____ makes sure pages in a book look good.

8. _____ make things that consumers buy.

9. Books, cars, and sneakers are all examples of _____ people buy.

10. A doctor provides a _____ by helping people stay healthy.

THINKING ABOUT FACTS

1. Why do most people work?

2. What is the difference between goods and services?

3. What does it mean to be a smart consumer?

4. Why are people the most important resource in any economy?

5. Describe two ways in which Japan has kept its traditional culture.

THINK AND WRITE

WRITING A HOW-TO PARAGRAPH
Write a paragraph describing the steps involved in making a textbook such as this one.

WRITING A RESUME
A resume is a list of the jobs people had, with a description of each job. Write a short resume about yourself. Describe the different jobs or responsibilities you have.

WRITING ABOUT HOME
Look at the Legacy lesson on pages 288-289. Write a paragraph describing how working at home is different today than long ago.

296

Suggestions for Think and Write
SIGNS OF SUCCESS

WRITING A HOW-TO PARAGRAPH Steps should include the following: Editors and authors plan the book; authors write it; editors check the work, make changes, and send it to designers; designers plan how the pages will look and send the designed pages to the printers; the printers print the book. Students should describe how much of the work is done on computer.

WRITING A RESUME Finished resumes should have specific information about students' accomplishments, "work" experience, and interests. Information should be categorized or arranged in a recognizable manner.

WRITING ABOUT HOME Students' paragraphs should cite a main idea and include supporting details showing the change from past to present.

For performance assessment, see Assessment Book, Chapter 11.

APPLYING THINKING SKILLS

IDENTIFYING CAUSE AND EFFECT
Read the paragraph below and answer the questions that follow.

Twinkles Sports Shop was losing business because a huge new discount store was selling products at a lower price. It seemed that everyone was buying balls, bats, and skateboards there. Fortunately, the owner of Twinkles had an idea. She invited Muscles Malone, a famous football hero, to sign autographs and give tips on kicking and catching. As a result, Twinkles is full of customers now and sales are better than ever.

1. Define cause and effect.
2. What caused Twinkles Sports Shop to lose business?
3. What was the effect of Muscles Malone coming to Twinkles?
4. What do you think might be the effect of two stores selling the same products?
5. Why is it important to be able to tell the difference between causes and effects?

Answers to APPLYING THINKING SKILLS

1. Cause is why something happens. Effect is what happens as a result of something else.
2. A huge new discount store was selling products at a lower price.
3. More customers came into the store and bought products. Sales are now better than ever.
4. They might compete with one another to make their stores cheaper or more interesting.
5. You may need to know why something happened if you want either to allow or to prevent its reoccurrence. You may want to know the effects of your actions or someone else's so that you can plan your actions carefully.

Summing Up the Chapter

Read the headings on the diagram below. Then review the chapter to find at least two pieces of information to include under each heading. When you have filled in a copy of the diagram, use it to write a sentence or two about how our economy works.

People
1. Needed to produce goods and services
2. Needed to be consumers

Money
1. Needed in order to buy goods
2. Needed to pay for services

Jobs
1. Exist so that many needs and many wants are met.
2. Make our economy grow.

OUR ECONOMY AT WORK

A strong economy is the result of people making and consuming all kinds of goods and services.

297

Suggestions for Summing Up the Chapter

- Prepare copies of the diagram for the class or ask students to copy the numbers and headings onto their papers. Tell students to ask themselves why people, money, and jobs are needed to make the economy work. Have them write reasons under each heading to complete the chart.
- Ask a volunteer to define the word *economy*. When students have written their sentences about the economy, discuss the word again and invite students to read their descriptions. Help the class create one statement that summarizes how our economy works. Suggested answers are annotated in red.

12 CHAPTER ORGANIZER

Producing Goods
PAGES 298–325

CHAPTER OVERVIEW

Many of the goods that people produce are made from natural resources. Bread is produced from wheat and lumber comes from trees grown in forests. It is important for everyone to use natural resources carefully so that our resources do not run out.

CHAPTER PLANNING GUIDE
Suggested pacing: 14–16 days

LESSON	LESSON FOCUS	LESSON RESOURCES
1 ON THE FARM pages 300–305	How Wheat Is Produced on Farms	*Practice Book* p. 62 *Anthology* pp. 126–127 *Anthology Cassette:* Harvest *Desk Map* United States
STUDY SKILLS pages 306–307	Reading Flow Charts	*Practice Book* p. 63
2 MINING THE LAND pages 308–311	Getting and Using Mineral Resources	*Practice Book* p. 64 *Anthology* p. 128
3 ON THE ASSEMBLY LINE pages 312–318	The Business of Making Things	*Practice Book* p. 65 *Anthology* pp. 129–134 *Technology:* Adventures CD-ROM
CITIZENSHIP Making a Difference Page 319	Inventor and Friend	
GLOBAL CONNECTIONS pages 320–323	Partners in Trade	*Practice Book* p. 66 *Anthology* p. 135 *Desk Map* World *Geo Big Book* pp. 8–9
Infographic page 322	U.S. Trade Around the World	*Technology:* Adventures CD-ROM
CHAPTER REVIEW pages 324–325	Students' understanding of vocabulary, content, and skills is assessed.	*Assessment:* Ch. 12 Test, Performance Assessment Ch. 12 *Transparency:* Graphic Organizer

OPTIONS FOR STUDENT ACTIVITIES

Citizenship pp. 303, 304, 309, 310, 315, 316, 319

Curriculum Connection pp. 302, 306, 313

Expanding the *Infographic* p. 322

Using the Anthology p. 316

ASSESSMENT OPPORTUNITIES

Meeting Individual Needs pp. 299, 305, 307, 311, 318, 323

Write About It pp. 305, 311, 318, 323

Chapter Review pp. 324–325

Assessment Book

Chapter Test Ch. 12 Test

Performance Assessment Ch. 12

Using Geo Adventures Use **Geo Adventures** Daily Geography Activities to assess students' understanding of geography skills.

Using the Vocabulary Cards The vocabulary words for each lesson are available on *Vocabulary Cards* for review and practice.

GETTING READY FOR THE CHAPTER

Write a "Mystery Goods" Riddle
ON YOUR OWN   15 TO 30 MINUTES

Objective: To help students understand that goods are produced by farming, mining, and manufacturing.

Materials: *Project Book* pp. 26–27

1. Recall with students some of the goods they read about in the previous chapter.
2. Now ask students to raise their hands when they think they know the answer to this riddle.
   Clue #1: This food is good for you. It tastes good, and it's fun to make too.
   Clue #2: It grows on a plant that is tall, but the pieces you eat are quite small.
   Clue #3: This movie-time munch has lots of crunch!
3. After students have guessed the answer—popcorn—invite them to make up their own "mystery goods" riddles using Project Book p. 26. Then have them draw a picture that shows the answer underneath the clues.
4. Let students share their riddles with the class. Let them know that in the next chapter they will learn more about how goods are produced.

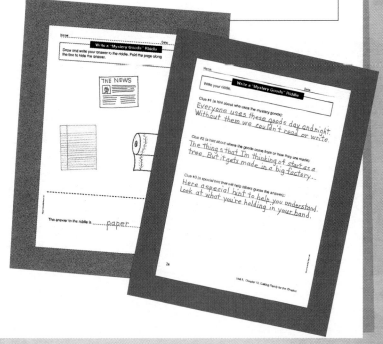

298B

Introducing the Chapter

Remind students that Native American communities were dependent upon the natural resources from the land around them. Ask students to consider how modern production affects the resources a community can obtain.

THINKING ABOUT GEOGRAPHY AND ECONOMICS

As students locate regions on the map, explain that countries have different natural resources and therefore make different products.

AUTOMOBILES

Suggested Questions

● **Where are the automobiles in the picture being sent?** *(to Holland)*

● **What do you know about the making of automobiles? What more would you like know?** *(Students may know where certain models of cars are made; they may want to know how they are shipped and sold.)*

★**THINKING FURTHER:** *Making Conclusions* **Why do you think Holland buys automobiles from another country?** *(Cars are not made in Holland.)*

OIL

Suggested Questions

● **What is the structure in the picture?** *(It is an oil-drilling rig on a floating offshore platform.)*

Resource **REMINDER**

 Technology: *Videodisc/Video Tape 3*

CHAPTER 12

Producing Goods

THINKING ABOUT GEOGRAPHY AND ECONOMICS

Many things that people need are made from natural resources. The availability of these resources influences what can be produced. So, caring for our resources is important not only to people who work with them but to all of us. In Chapter 12 you will see how people work to turn resources into many different products.

Amsterdam, Netherlands

Port Arthur, Texas

Saõ Paulo, Brazil

The United States exports computers to countries around the world.

298

Background INFORMATION

● Automobiles are the most important means of personal transportation for millions of people, and the auto industry provides many jobs for the powerful industrial countries. Japan is the world's leading exporter of automobiles, while Holland and Norway are leading importers.

● Crude oil, or petroleum, is a flammable liquid found in deposits underground and is used for fuel and as a raw material for chemical products. It is taken from underground by the use of a drilling rig either on land or at sea. The Gulf of Mexico is one of the major petroleum producing areas in the world.

● Shoes used to be made by hand by shoemakers in small shops. The earliest known shoemaker in the U.S. was Thomas Beard, who worked in Salem, Massachusetts, in 1629. Today over 180 different kinds of machines are used to produce shoes in large factories. Technology has made more shoe styles and sizes available to a greater section of the population.

Oil is produced in the United States.

Automobiles are imported to the Netherlands.

Shoes made in Brazil are traded throughout the world.

★**THINKING FURTHER:** *Classifying*
Oil is a valuable natural resource. What are some of the uses for oil? *(heat for our homes, fuel for cars and planes, asphalt for our streets)*

Suggested Questions

● ***What is the man in the photograph doing?*** *(packing shoes)*

• ***In what country does he work?*** *(Brazil)*

● ***Where will the shoes be sent?*** *(to countries around the world)*

★**THINKING FURTHER:** *Cause and Effect* ***Why do you think other people want to buy Brazilian shoes?*** *(These shoes are of high quality or low cost and other countries don't have a large shoe industry.)*

Suggested Questions

● ***Where was the computer in the picture made?*** *(in the United States)*

● ***What skills are needed to build computers?*** *(training in computer technology which requires many years of school)*

● ***What more would you like to know about how computers are made?*** *(Invite students to share their questions.)*

★**THINKING FURTHER:** *Making Conclusions* ***Why do you think people and countries trade with each other?*** *(Each one has something the other wants or needs.)*

Technology CONNECTION

VIDEODISC/VIDEO TAPE 3
Enrich Chapter 12 with the Videodisc *map* and *glossary* segments.

Search Frame 53777

Meeting *Individual* Needs

RETEACHING (Easy) Have students look at the map. Ask them to point out routes that each item may take as it is imported or exported.

EXTENSION (Average) Invite students to discuss how the items in the pictures might be traded between countries. Ask students how many pairs of shoes might be traded for a computer or a car. Have them explain how money might be used to trade.

ENRICHMENT (Challenging) Have students write paragraphs briefly describing the limited natural resources of a Native American community. Have them tell how production has improved and how this has effected the availability of natural resources and goods.

LESSON 1

PAGES 300–305

Lesson Overview
Farmers use hard work, traditional skills, and modern technology to grow our food.

Lesson Objectives
★ Identify natural, human, and technological resources in farming.

★ Discuss specialized farming.

★ Describe how technology has influenced farming in the U.S.

★ Interpret a product map.

1 PREPARE

MOTIVATE Ask a volunteer to read the *Read Aloud*. Then point out that the man in the picture is Jon Lofgreen. Invite students to share what they know about farmers and farming.

SET PURPOSE Review the *Vocabulary* words with students. Then direct them to the *Read to Learn* question and inview speculation about the answer. Explain that in this lesson students will learn about farming in our country.

2 TEACH

Discussing A Farm in Kansas Help students locate Kansas on a map. Remind them that Kansas has good soil and a good climate for farming.

Suggested Questions
● **Who is Jon Lofgreen?** *(He is a farmer in Kansas)*

● **What does Mr. Lofgreen grow?** *(crops like wheat and alfalfa, and animals like cows)*

★**THINKING FURTHER:** *Cause and Effect* **What effect does the soil and climate of Kansas have on the way of life there?** *(The rich soil and good climate created a way of life that depended on farming.)*

Resource REMINDER

Practice Book: *p. 62*

Anthology: *The Cow, p. 126; Picking Berries, p. 127*

Anthology Cassette: *Harvest*

Desk Map: *United States*

On the Farm

READ ALOUD
"Sometimes my job is hard on my children. I come home tired and dirty. But the children bring me lunch and help in the fields. They see me working with the land, growing things. They learn a lot about nature, the economy, and hard work. I think they're proud of me."

Jon Lofgreen is a farmer. Across our country, there are many different kinds of farming. In this lesson you will see what life on one farm in Kansas is like.

A Farm in Kansas
Sometimes Jon Lofgreen just likes to stand in the middle of his wheat farm near Norton, Kansas. Kansas has good soil and a good climate for growing crops. Mr. Lofgreen looks around and sees his land surrounding him in all directions. Crops such as wheat and alfalfa grow on that land. Four hundred cows also graze on that land. This land has supported the Lofgreen family for over 100 years. But sometimes when Mr. Lofgreen stands and looks across his farm, he's not thinking about that. He's just looking at the beauty of the wheat blowing in the wind, covering the rolling hills.

Focus Activity

READ TO LEARN
How is wheat produced on farms?

VOCABULARY
agriculture
harvest
fertilizer
product map
process

PLACE
Norton, Kansas

300

Reading STRATEGIES *and* Language DEVELOPMENT

MAKING CONCLUSIONS In this lesson, students will learn about conclusions that Mr. Lofgreen might draw from seeing wheat prices on his computer. Have students note that Mr. Lofgreen uses what he knows about wheat prices in the past plus the information about prices that he sees on his computer to decide when and where to sell his crop. Have students explain what other conclusions Mr. Lofgreen could draw from information on his computer.

CONTRACTIONS Remind students that contractions are formed when a letter or letters are left out of a word. An apostrophe is used in place of the missing letters. Write *can't* and *she's* on the chalkboard and show students the words from which the contractions are formed. Then ask them to find the contractions in the lesson. They will find *he's* on p. 300, *doesn't* on p. 301, and *here's* on p. 303. Ask volunteers to tell what letters are replaced by the apostrophe in each contraction.

Busy All Year

Of course, agriculture doesn't leave much time for gazing or standing around. Agriculture is the business of growing crops and raising animals. "We do several different kinds of farming here," says Mr. Lofgreen. "But most of the land is used for growing wheat. The harvest is gathered in about ten days at the end of June. But the rest of the year is spent getting ready for those ten days!"

The harvest is the ripe crops that are gathered. It takes planning, hard work, and help from nature to produce a good harvest. "Toward the end of September, we plant the crop in the brown soil. We use machines to plant the wheat and spread fertilizer," says Mr. Lofgreen. Fertilizers are chemicals that are used to help plants grow.

In the winter the wheat freezes. The fields turn brown again, but the plants are still working. They are producing seeds. In the spring the plants begin to turn dark green.

There are many jobs to do on a farm. Seth Lofgreen feeds a calf (below). Mr. Lofgreen loads wheat stored in a silo (bottom).

301

Discussing Busy All Year Help students draw a yearly calendar and chart the sequence of farming tasks and events.

Suggested Questions

- **What is agriculture?** *(It is the business of growing crops and raising animals.)*

- **What is the harvest?** *(It is the ripe crops that are gathered.)*

- **How long does it take to plant and grow the wheat?** *(Wheat is planted in September and harvested the following June.)*

- **How long does it take to gather the harvest?** *(about ten days)*

- **How does Seth Lofgreen help out on the farm?** *(He helps feed the animals.)*

★**THINKING FURTHER:** *Compare and contrast* **How do the chores of children who live on farms compare and contrast to chores you do?** *(The chores may be different depending on where students live, but they are the same in that they help out the family and they need to be done.)*

Background INFORMATION

MORE ABOUT WHEAT Explain that wheat is a cereal grain, like rice, corn, barley, oats, sorghum, millet, triticale, and rye. It is the most important food crop in the world, and wheat fields cover more of Earth's surface than any other crop.

When growing, wheat looks like a tall grass. During harvesting, the wheat kernel is removed. Then it is ground into flour and used for baking breads, cereals, pasta, pizza dough, crackers, and cakes. Some wheat is also used for animal food, and the straw is used for livestock bedding.

Global CONNECTION

WHEAT AROUND THE WORLD

- Scientists believe that wheat was first discovered in the Middle East. Ancient people gathered wild stalks and ate the kernels before they learned to make porridge.

- As trade routes expanded, farming techniques and wheat seeds were shared by many communities throughout Europe and Asia. By about 4000 B.C. many people in Asia, Europe, and northern Africa were planting and harvesting wheat crops.

- Christopher Columbus introduced wheat to the Americas when he traveled to the West Indies in the 1400s.

- Today wheat is grown in Canada, France, China, India, the former Soviet Union, the Ukraine, and the United States.

Help students understand the sequence in which wheat is grown, processed, and distributed.

Suggested Questions

● **What color is the wheat when it is ready to be gathered?** (golden)

● **What machine helps the farmers cut and clean the wheat?** (a combine)

● **What processes happen to the wheat after it is cut and cleaned?** (It is put in storage tanks, then it is ground, made into products, and sold around the world.)

★**THINKING FURTHER:** *Making Conclusions* **Why do you think Mr. Lofgreen sells the wheat instead of grinding it and making bread?** (His job is to grow and harvest the wheat; he gets paid for his work by selling it.)

More **MAP WORK**

Tell students that the map shows some, but not all, of the products grown in each state.

Suggested Questions

● **What products come from Texas?** (Wheat, cotton, dairy, fruits, and vegetables)

● **What states are the greatest cotton producers?** (the southern states)

● **What farm products are grown in Hawaii?** (fruits and vegetables)

Wheat is used to make many products you might eat, such as breads and cereals.

Farm Products

By mid–June, the wheat has turned from dark green to light green, and then to a golden color. The wheat is ready to be gathered. Farmers use a machine called a combine to cut the wheat, clean it, and put it in a holding tank. From there, trucks haul the wheat to storage tanks. Finally it is sold to companies that grind the wheat into flour. The flour is then made into bread, cakes, pasta, and other foods.

These foods are then sold all over the world. Wheat is just one of many crops grown in our country. Look at the product map below. A product map shows the places where goods are made or grown. This map shows crops that are grown in the United States.

UNITED STATES FARM PRODUCTS

Corn • Dairy
Cotton • Wheat
Fruits and Vegetables

MAP WORK

Farmers throughout the United States supply many different types of products.

1. What are some of the different crops grown in the United States?

2. What products are grown in Florida?

3. In what ways do you think states in our country rely on each other for food products?

302 MAP WORK: **1.** corn, cotton, wheat, fruits, vegetables **2.** fruits and vegetables **3.** People need products that are not produced in their own state.

Curriculum CONNECTION

LINKS TO RESEARCH Explain that farmers today grow specialized crops. This means that they research crops that will grow best in the soil and climate of their region. Corn, for example, needs warm moist conditions, and wheat grows best in the cooler and drier climates of the northern plains.

Have research groups choose regions from the product map. Ask them to look in library books or an encyclopedia to find out the climate and geography of each region. Students can also discover other crops farmed in each state. Have them share what they learn with the class and discuss how climate and soil affect what farmers grow in your state or region.

Curriculum CONNECTION

LINKS TO HEALTH: WHY EAT WHEAT? Invite students to experience one stage in the wheat-growing process. At a health food store, obtain some whole wheat kernels.

● Plant the wheat grass kernels in a small amount of soil or between two paper towels. Keep the seeds wet and watch them grow into soft grass.

Second-Language **Support**

USING VISUALS Using pictures to summarize reading will help second-language learners build comprehension. Have students draw the different stages of the wheat harvest and write a caption for each picture. Then invite students to summarize the wheat-farming process, using their pictures as props.

From milking cows to growing cranberries, farmers rely on technology to help make their work easier and faster.

New Ways of Farming

Sometimes Mr. Lofgreen is out in the fields, riding the combine or giving directions to workers. Other times he sits at a computer to do his farming. Here's what he says about how farmers today depend on technology to make a living. "I look at my computer and I can know in a second that wheat is selling for $3.69 a bushel. My computer helps me make decisions about when and where to sell my crop. I can see what's happening with other crops, in other parts of the world."

Look at the pictures on this page. Some farmers raise cattle. Others grow cranberries. Many farmers are now using new technology like computers and high-tech combines to help raise their crops and animals.

Links to HEALTH

Why Eat Wheat?

Many breakfast cereals contain grains such as wheat. Grains are the seeds of cereal plants. Wheat and other grains give you important vitamins and minerals. They help your muscles, blood, nerves, bones, and teeth stay healthy.

Look at the nutrition labels on the containers and packaging of foods you eat. Which foods list wheat as one of the first three ingredients?

303

Discussing New Ways of Farming
Be sure students understand that Mr. Lofgreen sells huge volumes of wheat. A variation of even a few cents per bushel can make a great difference in his profits.

Suggested Questions

- *What tasks does Mr. Lofgreen do on the farm?* (He rides the combine, directs workers, and works on the computer.)

- *What can Mr. Lofgreen read on his computer?* (the prices of wheat around the world)

- *How does it help Mr. Lofgreen to know the price of wheat immediately?* (He can choose to sell his wheat when he can get the best price.)

★ THINKING FURTHER: *Predicting*
Mr. Lofgreen reads on his computer that many American farmers lost their wheat crop in floods. Do you think his wheat will become more or less valuable? Explain your answer. (It will sell for more money because it is more valuable.)

Background INFORMATION

FARMING TODAY Explain how technology has changed farming into big business. Young people who plan to be farmers attend special agricultural colleges. They learn how to operate and maintain machines, and use computers to manage finances associated with huge volumes of crops.

CITIZENSHIP

LINKING PAST AND PRESENT Farmers often share expensive equipment and labor. Communities of farmers in the late 1800s usually bought a steam engine tractor to share. Today, independent teams of combines travel through the wheat region, helping farmers harvest and thresh their crops.

Have partners research farmers' cooperatives in the past and today. Invite them to present their reports, using visuals such as time lines or Venn diagrams.

Learning from Music To help students understand what the words in the song are describing, you may want to bring in rutabagas, sweet potatoes, and parsnips or pictures of them.

Suggested Questions

● *How have people celebrated the harvest throughout history?* (with singing and dancing)

● *How can you guess that this song was written long ago?* (because it's about digging vegetables by hand)

● *What other songs about farming or the harvest do you know?* (Students may know "Old MacDonald," for example.)

★ **THINKING FURTHER:** *Classifying* *Harvest is usually in the fall. What fall celebrations can you think of? How are they related to the harvest?* (Students should indicate that at Thanksgiving, people give thanks for the harvest; they may also mention local harvest festivals.)

MANY VOICES — MUSIC

Throughout the history of our country, the harvest has been important to people. Some people celebrate the harvest with dancing and singing. Read the following song. Have you ever planted any of these crops?

Harvest

Georgia Folk Song

1. Time to gath-er har-vest. __ Oh, Em-ma, oh! ____
2. Dig-ging sweet _ po-ta-toes. __ Oh, Em-ma, oh! ____
3. Dig-ging ru-ta-ba-gas. __ Oh, Em-ma, oh! ____
4. Dig-ging big _ fat par-snips. __ Oh, Em-ma, oh! ____

You turn a-round, dig a hole in the ground,__

Oh, Em - ma, oh!

304

Background INFORMATION

CULTURAL PERSPECTIVES Point out that many different cultures have celebrated the harvest and spring planting.

● Some Native American tribes celebrated the first corn crop of the summer with the Green Corn Dance. In 1621, colonists celebrated their first harvest in the Americas with the first thanksgiving feast.

● Ancient Persians, Egyptians, Greeks, and Romans all colored eggs in the springtime to symbolize the earth's new beginnings. Today people in the Ukraine, Europe, and the United States include colored eggs in their springtime holidays and traditional observances.

● Invite students to make up their own songs celebrating springtime in your community, or dances about planting local crops.

CITIZENSHIP

HOW GOVERNMENT HELPS BUSINESS Explain that the United States government recognizes the importance of farming and helps farmers by:

● publishing bulletins with crop marketing news.

● helping farmers to get loans to buy expensive machines.

● sharing the cost of soil conservation with farmers. The government will sometimes pay farmers to rest their fields.

● buying surplus crops. When there is too much wheat, the price may drop and farmers may go out of business. The government buys the surplus and stores it until it is needed.

To Your Table

Farmers rely on each other. "The alfalfa I grow helps feed cattle on someone else's farm," points out Mr. Lofgreen. "The food on my table comes from another farm."

Many people other than farmers help make the food you see at your table. Some people process the food. To process is to change something into a different form. People process wheat to make bread and oranges to make orange juice. People at factories put the food into packages. Truckers drive the packages to stores. Stores sell the products to consumers.

WHY IT MATTERS

Native Americans farmed corn and other crops hundreds of years ago. Today Mr. Lofgreen makes a living from farming, as his great-great grandparents did. Farming is one of the important ways people make a living in our country.

Milk from cows is processed to make cheese and other dairy products.

Reviewing Facts and Ideas

SUM IT UP

- Agriculture is the business of growing and raising crops. One example of agriculture is wheat farming.
- There are many different kinds of farming in our country.
- There are many different jobs involved in getting food from the farm to your table.

THINK ABOUT IT

1. What are two ways people earn their living in agriculture?
2. **FOCUS** How is wheat produced on farms?
3. **THINKING SKILL** What do you think might _cause_ a bad harvest? What _effect_ would this have on farming?
4. **GEOGRAPHY** Look at the product map on page 302. What kinds of farming are done in California?

305

Discussing To Your Table Explain that in all businesses people work together to create and sell products.

Suggested Questions

- **What does Mr. Lofgreen grow that helps feed cattle?** _(alfalfa)_
- **What does it mean to process food?** _(to change it into another form)_

Discussing WHY IT MATTERS Remind students that America has always been a nation of farmers. Native Americans farmed the lands. Early Europeans came to find good farming land. Explain that farmers will always be important because they grow our food.

Suggested Questions

- **Why is farming an important job?** _(Farmers grow our food.)_
- **What kinds of workers help farmers bring us food?** _(people who process food and other products made from crops)_

3 CLOSE

SUM IT UP

Have students answer these questions.

Suggested Questions

- **What three examples of agriculture can you name?** _(raising cattle, growing corn, growing vegetables or fruit)_
- **Choose one item in your lunch. How do you think the food came from the farm to you?** _(Answers should reflect the process involved in producing the item.)_

EVALUATE

✓ **Answers to Think About It**

1. For example, people could work in the fields, or grow or process crops.
2. Farmers plant wheat in the fall. It turns brown and freezes but grows green again in the spring. Then it turns golden before being harvested at the end of June.
3. Possible causes: drought, too much rain, too many insects. Possible effects: plants dry up, are washed away, are damaged.
4. fruits, vegetables, cotton _Human-Environment Interaction_

Write About It Have students write an article about a day in the life of a farmer.

SKILLS LESSON

PAGES 306–307

Lesson Overview

A flow chart shows the sequence of events followed to complete a process successfully.

Lesson Objective

★ Examine flow charts and learn techniques for reading them.

1 PREPARE

MOTIVATE Invite students to make a list of the steps in the process of farming wheat. There may be some steps that students are unsure of. Explain that reading the flow chart in this lesson will help them understand the order of events.

SET PURPOSE Have students discuss what steps in a process are, for example, steps that you might follow to make or build something. Tell them that in this lesson, they will learn how to read a flow chart.

DISCUSSING HELPING YOURSELF Explain that the steps in the *Helping Yourself* box are a guide to reading a flow chart.

2 TEACH

Why the Skill Matters Initiate a discussion about the importance of following steps in a process. Remind students that to complete many jobs, or to build or grow something, it is important to know the order of steps to follow.

Suggested Questions

● **Why are Jon Lofgreen and his workers busy all year?** *(They follow the various steps required to grow wheat.)*

● **What is a flow chart used for?** *(It shows the sequence of steps in a process.)*

● **Why is a flow chart a good way to illustrate growing wheat?** *(Growing wheat is a process that follows a certain order and requires that tasks be done in a certain sequence.)*

Resource **REMINDER**

Practice Book: *p. 63*

STUDYSKILLS

Reading Flow Charts

VOCABULARY
flow chart

WHY THE SKILL MATTERS

For ten busy days in June, wheat is harvested on Jon Lofgreen's farm. But he and the other workers are busy the rest of the year too. As you have read, more than one step is involved in growing wheat. The order in which these steps are taken is important. A flow chart can be used to show the sequence of steps that are followed to produce a final product. Flow charts show the steps of an activity in order. Look at the Helping Yourself box for some tips on how to read flow charts.

USING THE SKILL

Suppose you want to see the sequence of steps in growing wheat. Look at how the flow chart below shows these steps and their order.

To read the flow chart, first look at its title. What is this flow chart about? Next notice that each step has a picture and a label. How many steps are shown in this flow chart?*

The steps of an activity are shown in order in a flow chart. As you can see here, the first step in growing wheat is plowing the field. An arrow leads you to the next step—which is planting the wheat. The steps that follow are harvesting the wheat and finally selling it.

It is very important to follow the steps in order. If you plow the field after planting the wheat, you will not end up with much wheat to harvest!

GROWING WHEAT

1 Plow field. 2 Plant wheat. 3 Harvest wheat. 4 Sell wheat.

*The flow chart has four steps.

Curriculum CONNECTIONS

LINKS TO READING Students will enjoy reading the following books, which explain wheat farming and pasta making from start to finish: *Siggy's Spaghetti Works* by Peggy Thompson (Morrow, 1993) and *Pasta Factory* by Huna Machotka (Houghton Mifflin, 1992).

LINKS TO SPEAKING AND LISTENING Tell students the classic story of the Little Red Hen or bring in the book and have volunteers read it aloud. Then have students work in groups to make a flow chart illustrating the events in the story.

*Flour is emptied into a bin; eggs, milk and flour are mixed together to make dough; dough is dried and cut into shapes.

TRYING THE SKILL

You have learned about some of the steps followed by wheat farmers. Farmers grow wheat in order to sell it. One wheat product is pasta. The flow chart on this page shows some of the steps in making pasta.

What is the first step in making pasta? What happens after flour is emptied into a bin? What happens after dough is formed into big sheets?*

HELPING Yourself

● **A flow chart shows all of the steps of an activity in order.**

● **Study the title, pictures, and labels.**

● **Follow the arrows to read flow charts in order.**

REVIEWING THE SKILL

1. What is a flow chart?

2. Look at the flow chart for making pasta. What is the last step shown?

3. Suppose you are making a flow chart of the steps you follow in making a sandwich. What would you show as the first step?

4. When is it helpful to read a flow chart?

Using the Skill Invite students to study the flow chart and to quietly tell themselves the steps in the process. You might explain that the people in step 4 represent brokers, who sell large quantities of wheat.

Suggested Questions

● **What is the flow chart about?** (growing wheat)

● **What is the first step in the flow chart?** (plowing the field)

● **What is the next step?** (planting the wheat)

● **How do you know this is the next step?** (An arrow leads you to it.)

Trying the Skill Because this flow chart is more complex than the one that precedes it, you may want to encourage students to follow the arrows with their fingers while reading. Remind students that the *Helping Yourself* box will help them also.

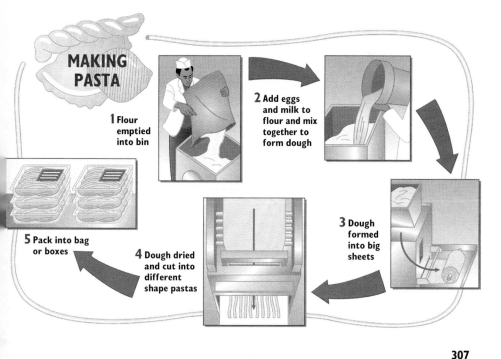

MAKING PASTA

1 Flour emptied into bin

2 Add eggs and milk to flour and mix together to form dough

3 Dough formed into big sheets

4 Dough dried and cut into different shape pastas

5 Pack into bag or boxes

307

★ 3 CLOSE

SUM IT UP

Encourage students to brainstorm other processes that might be illustrated in a flow chart. Have them discuss how a flow chart might be helpful to workers building the English Channel Tunnel or to someone who is just learning how to sell bicycles.

EVALUATE
✓ **Answers to Reviewing the Skill**

1. a chart that shows the sequence of steps in a process

2. packing the pasta

3. possible answer: laying out two slices of bread

4. It's helpful to read a flow chart when you want to know the order of steps in a complicated process.

MEETING *Individual* NEEDS

RETEACHING (Easy) Remind students that farmers work most of the year. Then have them draw a flow chart for growing wheat, beginning with the step of harvesting the wheat. The flow chart should show continuous activity on a farm through the winter.

EXTENSION (Average) Bring in soil and beans and demonstrate how to plant and care for a seedling. Then ask students to begin flow charts to illustrate the steps in order. As the class cares for the plant over a period of weeks, have them add steps to their flow charts.

ENRICHMENT (Challenging) Have students make flow charts of processes from previous chapters. For example, they can chart the process of publishing a textbook or selling pencils in a school.

LESSON 2
PAGES 308-311

Lesson Overview
Minerals like copper are nonrenewable resources that must be used carefully.

Lesson Objectives
★ Distinguish between renewable and nonrenewable natural resources.
★ Understand how mining provides access to mineral resources.
★ Distinguish between public and private property.

1 PREPARE

MOTIVATE Have students share what they remember from *Chapter 2* about natural resources. Ask a volunteer to read the *Read Aloud*. Then invite students to name minerals that are important to everyday life in our country. Note that the picture shows a truck hauling minerals from a mine.

SET PURPOSE Review the *Vocabulary* words with students. Then direct them to the *Read to Learn* question and invite speculation about the answer.

2 TEACH

Thinking About An Important Resource Be sure students understand the definition of *mineral*.

Suggested Questions
● **How do miners make their living from the land?** *(They remove minerals from below Earth's surface.)*

● **What is a renewable resource?** *(a resource that can be replaced by nature)*

● **What does nonrenewable resource mean?** *(That is a resource that can be used up completely.)*

★ **THINKING FURTHER: Classifying**
What kinds of resources do farmers use? What kinds of resources do miners use? *(renewable resources like soil and water; nonrenewable resources like copper and gold)*

Resource REMINDER
Practice Book: *p. 64*
Anthology: *Down in a Coal Mine, p. 128*

Mining the Land

READ ALOUD
Every state has certain symbols. For example, you may know the name of your state bird or state tree. Did you know that some states also have a state mineral? In this lesson you will read about why minerals are so important to people in our country.

An Important Resource
Look at the pictures at the bottom of page 309. They show some everyday objects. Can you guess what these objects have in common? They all are made from the same mineral, copper.

Like farmers, miners also make their living from the land. They remove minerals from the land. There is one important difference, though. Many of the resources that farmers use are renewable resources. A renewable resource is one that can be replaced by nature, if used carefully. The soil and water used to grow wheat are renewable resources. Minerals are nonrenewable resources. That means they cannot be replaced. Once nonrenewable resources are used up they are gone forever.

Focus Activity

READ TO LEARN
What are some ways we get and use mineral resources?

VOCABULARY
renewable resource
nonrenewable resource
public property
private property

308

Reading STRATEGIES *and* Language DEVELOPMENT

CAUSE AND EFFECT Invite students to practice recognizing cause and effect in this lesson. They can write sentences explaining the effects of open-pit mining, the effects of using nonrenewable resources, and the effects of conserving and recycling resources.

QUOTATION MARKS Students are familiar with quotation marks used to show the words that someone speaks. Have them look at the quotation on p. 309 and tell which words Mr. Romero said and how the words of a real person can give important information. Then explain that quotation marks are also used to enclose phrases or sayings. Have them find an example in the lesson ("boom towns," p. 311). Be sure students understand that these quotation marks indicate a common phrase.

Working in a Mine

Andy Romero knows a lot about the importance of natural resources. He is a copper miner in a community in Arizona. From the picture here you can see that Mr. Romero drives a truck in an open-pit mine. Copper that lies close to Earth's surface is removed by open-pit mining. "Natural resources like copper help keep our company in business and are important in making products people need," Mr. Romero says.

There are also other ways to mine copper. Some companies send miners deep down below the surface to dig for copper. Look at the chart on the next page to see what happens after copper is mined.

Andy Romero (top) drives a big truck at a mine. He is one of the many people who make copper available for all types of products (bottom). Copper is one of several minerals used to make a penny.

Thinking About Working in a Mine Remind students of Mr. Flythe's bicycle shop. Help them appreciate miners as workers who provide raw materials for products like bicycles, cars, and electrical parts.

Suggested Questions

● *Who is Andy Romero?* (He is a copper miner in Arizona.)

● *In what kind of copper mine does he work?* (an open-pit mine)

● *How does he help in the process of mining?* (He drives a truck.)

● *What are two ways to mine copper?* (If it is close to the surface, you can dig it from an open-pit mine. If it is down deep, miners go far below the surface to dig.)

● *What do you think will happen to the copper after it is mined?* (It will be shipped to a manufacturing company to make some kind of product such as wire or jewelry.)

★THINKING FURTHER: *Predicting*
Will Mr. Romero's company be able to dig copper from the mine forever? Why or why not? (No, because copper is a nonrenewable resource.)

309

Background INFORMATION

MORE ABOUT COPPER

● Copper is an excellent electrical conductor. More than half of the copper produced is used to make electrical wire for televisions, telephones, electric motors, and generators.

● Copper doesn't rust or corrode. When exposed to the elements, copper forms a thin green film which protects it from further corrosion. The Statue of Liberty is green because it is made of hammered copper that is covered with a naturally oxidized film.

● The United States mines about one-seventh of the copper in the world, most of it in Arizona. We import copper from Canada, Chile, and Peru.

CITIZENSHIP

UNDERSTANDING ENVIRONMENTAL CONCERNS Encourage students to design a bulletin board about natural resources and how to conserve them.

● Make a chart of good advice for energy conservation. Ideas might include turning off the lights when you are not in a room; walking and bicycling instead of driving; riding in a carpool or taking public transportation; sealing windows in winter; recycling of aluminum and glass.

● Students can research alternative sources of energy. Ask them to make illustrations with captions describing how solar power, nuclear power, hydroelectric power, and wind generators create energy.

Help students compare the size of our country again with the size of a smaller country like Japan or Italy.

Suggested Questions

• *What resources are obtained by mining?* (*iron, gold, silver, limestone, coal, and oil, for example)*

• *Are these renewable resources? Why or why not?* (They are nonrenewable resources because they can be used up and won't be replaced by nature.)

★THINKING FURTHER: *Classifying*
What is one example of public property in your community? What is one example of private property? (Accept appropriate responses.)

More CHART WORK

Ask students to discuss the sequence of events.

Suggested Questions

• *What is the first important step in making copper wire?* (mining rocks that contain copper)

• *What is the next important step?* (removing copper from rocks)

• *What happens after the copper is cast into bars?* (It is rolled into rods.)

★THINKING FURTHER: *Compare and Contrast How is making copper wire like making a textbook?* (Many people share their skills and hard work to produce something that many others will use.)

World of Resources

Copper is just one resource that people remove from Earth. Iron, gold, silver, limestone, coal, and oil are also mined. Our country is very rich in natural resources.

Some resources are on public property. Public property is land that has been set aside for all people to use. National parks and forests are public property.

Other resources are on private property. Private property is land that is owned by people or companies. Some people own land to build homes on it. Mining companies have bought a lot of land in order to mine it.

Minerals include (clockwise from top) gold, iron pyrite, and forms of copper.

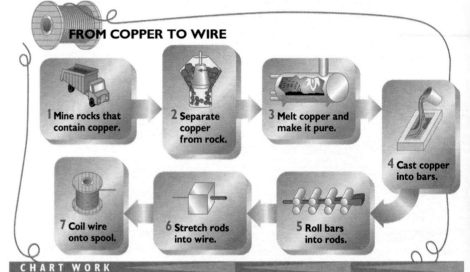

FROM COPPER TO WIRE

1 Mine rocks that contain copper.
2 Separate copper from rock.
3 Melt copper and make it pure.
4 Cast copper into bars.
5 Roll bars into rods.
6 Stretch rods into wire.
7 Coil wire onto spool.

CHART WORK

There are several steps involved before copper is made into wire.

1. What is the first step in the process of making copper wire?

2. What happens after the copper is made pure?

3. What are two questions you could ask to learn more about making copper products?

CHART WORK: **1.** Mine rocks that contain copper. **2.** It is cast into copper bars. **3.** Does the copper come from an open-pit mine? How long does it take to melt copper to make it pure?

310

Background INFORMATION

ABOUT JOBS IN THE MINING INDUSTRY

• Geologists study rock formations.

• Mining engineers design mines.

• Chemists and physicists find new techniques for mining or refining.

• Mechanics fix machines.

• Electricians help design and maintain machinery and electrical systems.

• Miners and truck drivers dig and load the mineral onto trucks and carry it to the refinery.

★CITIZENSHIP

PUBLIC AND PRIVATE PROPERTY Guide students in a discussion of public and private property that they know about. Are there any city parks, public pools, or city parking lots in the community? What private property can students identify? How do those places differ from public property?

Have students make a community map and identify public and private property in their community.

Boom Town to Ghost Town

Earth's resources provide jobs for many people. Sometimes "boom towns" grow when a resource is discovered. Many people move quickly to these towns to try to make money mining gold, oil, or other resources. Once the resource runs out, the jobs disappear.

People cannot make natural resources. But some companies make products that are like those found in nature. For example, plastic is sometimes used instead of metal.

WHY IT MATTERS

There are many mining jobs. People have to find where the minerals are. Some people are in charge of safety in the mines. Other people change minerals into forms people can use.

We use natural resources in many different ways. But we must use them carefully to be sure they will be here for a long, long time.

This ghost town in California was once a busy community. People hoped to get rich by finding valuable minerals.

✓// Reviewing Facts and Ideas

SUM IT UP

- Mining is the removing of minerals from the earth.
- Renewable resources can be replaced by nature. Once nonrenewable resources are used, they are gone forever.
- Public property is land that has been set aside for all people to use. Private property is land that is owned by people or companies.

THINK ABOUT IT

1. Give an example of public property in your community. Give an example of private property.
2. **FOCUS** What are some ways we get and use mineral resources?
3. **THINKING SKILL** Suppose oil was discovered near your town. What might be some of the *effects* of this discovery?
4. **WRITE** Write a paragraph describing the process of making wire.

311

Discussing Boom Town to Ghost Town Have students discuss the picture and then the text.

Suggested Questions

- **What is a boom town?** *(a town that grows quickly because a natural resource is discovered there)*

- **How do many people make money from a natural resource?** *(They mine resources and sell what they find.)*

Discussing WHY IT MATTERS Be sure students understand we need to use natural resources wisely.

Suggested Questions

- **Why is it important to be careful about how we use natural resources?** *(They won't last forever.)*

3 CLOSE

SUM IT UP
Have students answer these questions.

Suggested Questions

- **What are two kinds of mines?** *(open-pit mines and deep mines)*

- **Are minerals renewable or nonrenewable resources? Explain your answer.** *(Nonrenewable; they can't be replaced.)*

EVALUATE
✓ **Answers to Think About It**
1. for example, public: the library, the streets, and parks; private: houses and businesses
2. We mine them and melt them and make them into products.
3. Companies might try to buy the property. Some people would get rich. Others would move to your town and buy property in the hopes of finding oil.
4. Answers should include the steps in sequence from the flow chart on p. 310.

Write About It Ask students to write a report about someone who works in a mineral mine. Have them explain the job that person does and how he or she cooperates with other workers.

MEETING *Individual* NEEDS

RETEACHING (Easy) Have students make a chart of renewable and nonrenewable resources and some of the products made from each.

EXTENSION (Average) Tell students that many minerals are mined and refined in the same manner as copper. Then have them make illustrated flow charts showing how gold is mined and made into a piece of jewelry.

ENRICHMENT (Challenging) Challenge students to find out from a nearby state, regional, or national park or forest its regulations concerning natural resources. Have students ask if visitors can collect stones or firewood and if companies can cut trees or mine for minerals. Remind them also to ask the park officials to explain why specific resources are protected.

LESSON 3

Lesson Overview
Manufacturing is important to the economy of our country.

Lesson Objectives

★ Understand that an assembly line is an example of division of labor.

★ Examine how technology has changed manufacturing.

★ Compare and contrast different kinds of manufacturing.

1 PREPARE

MOTIVATE Have a volunteer read the *Read Aloud*. Ask students why dividing jobs and sharing tasks makes work easier and faster.

SET PURPOSE Point out the *Vocabulary* words that relate to work in a factory. Then direct students to the *Read to Learn* question and invite speculation about the answer and about the connection between the cars in the picture and factories.

2 TEACH

Thinking About A Factory in Detroit Help students visualize workers on an automobile assembly line. Explain that each worker repeats the same task as an item such as a car part moves in front of them on a conveyor belt.

Suggested Questions

● ***What is manufacturing?*** *(the business of making things)*

● ***In what place are things manufactured?*** *(in a factory)*

● ***Where does Marge Gendron work?*** *(an automobile factory in Detroit)*

● ***What is an assembly line?*** *(It is a line of workers and machines all working together to make a product.)*

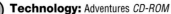

Resource REMINDER

Practice Book: *p. 65*

Anthology: *Working on an Assembly Line, pp. 129–130; No Star Nights, pp. 131–134*

Technology: Adventures *CD-ROM*

On the Assembly Line

READ ALOUD

Suppose your class is making teddy bears to sell at a fair. Instead of each person making a complete bear, everyone has a special job. For example, one person will cut the fabric. Another will sew on the faces. Your class has just discovered a smart way to make a product. In this lesson you will read more about smart ways companies make things.

Focus Activity

READ TO LEARN
How do factories work?

VOCABULARY
manufacturing
factory
assembly line
robot
mill

PLACE
Detroit, Michigan

A Factory in Detroit

Whether you're making teddy bears or cars, you are manufacturing. Manufacturing is the business of making things. Manufacturing used to be done mostly by hand in factories. A factory is a place where things are manufactured. Today manufacturing is often done by people as well as by high-tech machines in factories.

Marge Gendron works in manufacturing at an automobile company in Detroit, Michigan. Most cars are built on assembly lines in factories like hers. An assembly line is a line of workers and machines all working together to make a final product. Different tasks are done at each stop along the way.

312

Reading STRATEGIES *and* Language DEVELOPMENT

REREADING Remind students that rereading is a good strategy to use when a text presents many facts. Have students practice the strategy with the text on p. 316. Explain that before rereading it is a good idea to make a list of questions. Have students list two or three questions they had while reading *Manufacturing Today*. Then invite them to reread to discover the answers. Encourage students to practice this strategy on other pages of the lesson.

ROOT WORDS Students will remember that many words in our language were created using Latin root words. Understanding Latin root words can help readers figure out unfamiliar words. Encourage students to consider how the words *factory*, on p. 312, and *manufacturing*, on p. 312, are related. Explain that they both contain the Latin root *factor*, meaning "make." Explain also that *manus* is a Latin root meaning "hand."

Assembly Lines Long Ago

The cars that roll off the assembly line today look very different from the first cars in our country. The assembly line is not a new idea for the automobile industry. In fact, assembly lines got their start in the early 1900s as a way to make cars.

At first only a few people could afford to buy cars. Cars took so much time to build that they were very expensive. But Henry Ford knew that many people would want to buy cars if they were less expensive. He started one of the first assembly lines. Soon it took less time to make cars. Then the price of cars went down and people rushed to buy them. In 1924 a Model T cost $290.

From filling bottles (top) to making automobiles (bottom), people had different jobs on assembly lines **long ago.**

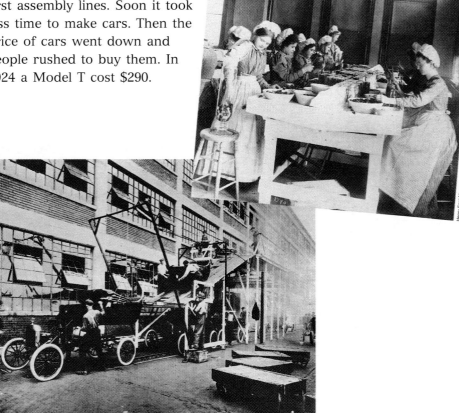

Henry Ford Museum

313

Thinking About Assembly Lines Long Ago Be sure students understand that Henry Ford's use of the assembly line revolutionized manufacturing in America.

Suggested Questions

- ***When did assembly lines begin?*** *(in the 1900s)*

- ***Why were the first cars so expensive?*** *(They took a long time to build.)*

- ***What did Henry Ford know?*** *(that people would buy cars if they were cheap enough)*

- ***How did he make cars less expensive?*** *(He started making them on an assembly line.)*

- ★**THINKING FURTHER:** *Cause and Effect* **In what ways did Henry Ford help America grow?** *(He helped people afford cars. He also invented the assembly line, which helped people make many products more easily.)*

Background INFORMATION

HENRY FORD AND THE ASSEMBLY LINE Henry Ford wanted to create a car that was affordable to everyone. He perfected the moving assembly line. Before the assembly line, workers had to move around to collect tools and do different tasks. Now they stood in one place and repeated the same task on each car that moved along a conveyor belt in front of them. Because the labor was divided in this way, it took less time to assemble a car.

This division of labor meant that many people could now afford the cheaper cars. The assembly line was also used in many other factories, and the United States became a leader in manufacturing.

Curriculum CONNECTION

LINKS TO ART Help students understand how assembly lines speed up production.

- Bring in colored beads, separated by color, and a ball of string. Tell students that they will cut one-foot lengths of string and thread beads onto each string in the following order: 3 red, 5 green, 2 blue, 4 white, and 3 yellow.

- Have two or three groups form assembly lines. In each assembly line, the first worker can cut string and tie a knot in the bottom of it. The next workers in line can each add one color of bead to the string.

- Ask the remaining students to work at another table to manufacture necklaces individually.

- After 10 minutes, have students compare their work. Ask which group made more necklaces per worker.

Marge Gendron works in a factory where she checks automobile bumpers.

Making a Car Today

The assembly line Marge Gendron works on today is different from the one Henry Ford first used. Today's assembly lines use robots. Robots are machines made to do tasks. Marge feels lucky that her job is still done by people. "Otherwise," she says, "I'd be out of work!"

From the chart below you can see that a car has many parts. Ms. Gendron works at the "bumper station." There she checks that the bumpers are safely made. She also makes sure the bumpers have no scratches or paint marks. If she finds a problem, it is also her job to fix the bumper. One hour after she checks the bumper, it is attached to a finished car.

PARTS OF A CAR

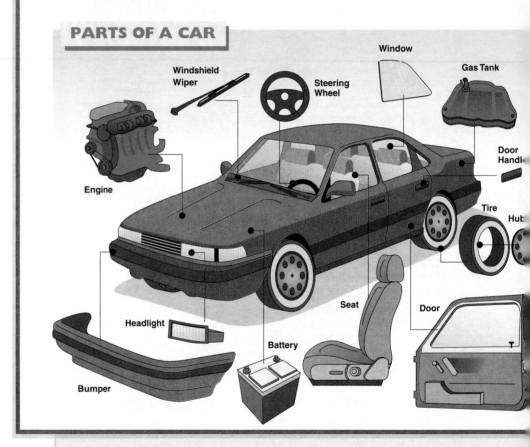

Window

Windshield Wiper

Steering Wheel

Gas Tank

Engine

Door Handle

Tire

Hub

Headlight

Seat

Door

Bumper

Battery

Proud of a Product

Marge Gendron has been working at the same company for almost 30 years. "Sometimes it's been rough to do the same job day after day," she says. "Each bumper weighs about 30 pounds. That's a lot of bending and lifting. I feel proud when I see people driving our cars. I like to think that we do a good job. My best friend works next to me. I also like to hear people say we make beautiful cars."

Look at the pictures on this page. What do they tell you about how manufacturing is changing the jobs people like Marge Gendron do?

Robots do many jobs on assembly lines, including welding (top) and safety testing (bottom).

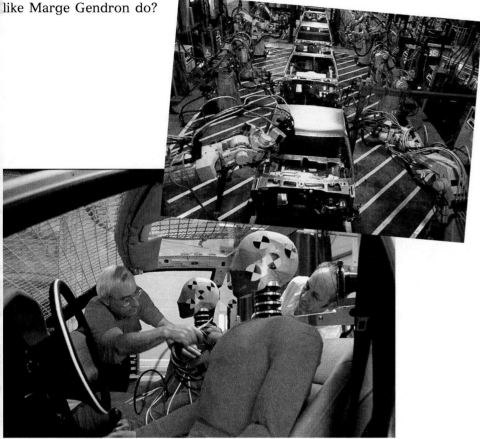

Discussing Proud of a Product
Invite students to think about lifting an object weighing 30 pounds.

Suggested Questions

● *How long has Marge Gendron been working at the same company?* (almost 30 years)

● *Why is it difficult to do her job?* (She lifts 30 pounds many times a day.)

● *Why does Marge like her job?* (She likes to do good work, and she is proud when people drive or admire her company's cars.)

● *When have you felt proud of finishing a difficult job?* (Help students understand why people enjoy the results of hard work.)

Technology CONNECTION

ADVENTURES CD-ROM
Enrich the lesson by inviting students to investigate industries in their state.

315

CITIZENSHIP

CHANGES IN THE WORKPLACE Explain that technology has also caused some problems for workers.

● Machines have replaced workers in many fields. For example, automated bank machines are replacing tellers, and robots and electronic devices have replaced many assembly line workers. Some businesses provide retraining for employees who lose their jobs.

Have students find out about local and state job training programs. Then have them prepare a report to present to the class.

Field Trip

FACTORIES AT WORK Arrange a field trip to a factory in your community. If possible, arrange for students to see assembly-line workers as well as the automated assembly of a product. Encourage them to take notes on what they see, and if permitted, to photograph steps in the assembly process. In the classroom, have students create a display of the tasks on the assembly line.

Manufacturing Today

Cars are just one of the many products manufactured in our country. Many companies are in the manufacturing business. Manufacturing is one of the biggest kinds of business in our country. Millions of people work in manufacturing. They make thousands of different products. Some of the most important products are transportation equipment, such as trains, cars, and buses. Chemicals, machines, medicines, food, toys, computers, and books are some other examples.

Not all things are manufactured on assembly lines. Can you think of something in your school that was not manufactured on an assembly line? How about your school building? It was most likely built by workers using tools, not on an assembly line. Or perhaps the blanket in your bedroom was made by hand by someone in your family.

Not all products are made in a factory. The house you live in and baked goods you eat were most likely made by hand.

A Manufacturing Town

The jobs people have are not only important to them, but they are also important to their family and community. The story below is about a steel mill in West Virginia. A mill is a place where people use machines to make natural resources into finished products. How do you think the jobs that people do at this steel mill influence the community?

LITERATURE

No Star Nights

**Excerpt from the story
by Anna Egan Smucker, 1989.**

We went to school across from the mill. The smokestacks towered above us and the smoke billowed out in great puffy clouds of red, orange, and yellow, but mostly the color of rust. Everything—houses, hedges, old cars— was a rusty red color. Everything but the little bits of **graphite**, and they glinted like silver in the dust. At recess when the wind whirled these sharp, shiny metal pieces around, we girls would crouch so that our skirts touched the ground and kept our bare legs from being stung.

We would squint our eyes when the wind blew to keep the graphite out. Once a piece got caught in my eye, and no matter how much I blinked or how much my eye watered it wouldn't come out. When the eye doctor finally took it out and showed it to me, I was amazed that a speck that small could feel so big.

—————————————
graphite: soft, black mineral

Discussing a Manufacturing Town Explain that in a small manufacturing town, most of the people work at the factory. Often towns are built around a factory as people move there to find work.

Suggested Questions

● **What is a steel mill?** *(a place where people use machines to make steel)*

● **Where is the mill in this story?** *(West Virginia)*

★**THINKING FURTHER:** *Sequencing*
What must happen before the steel is made? Who may use the steel after the factory produces it? *(Miners bring the minerals from which steel is made; an automobile company may use the steel.)*

Learning from Literature Have students read the selection and then discuss these questions.

Suggested Questions

● **What did the smokestacks of the mill look like?** *(Smoke billowed out rust-colored smoke.)*

● **How did the smoke from the mill affect the town?** *(Everything in the town was a rusty color.)*

● **What is graphite?** *(Shiny bits of metal that were part of the smoke spewed out by the smokestacks.)*

● **What effect did the graphite have on the narrator?** *(Bits and pieces could sting her leg; she once had a particle in her eye.)*

317

Background INFORMATION

ALTERNATIVE ENERGY

● **SOLAR ENERGY** Scientists estimate this will be a renewable resource for about 5 billion years. The sun's energy can be collected by flat panels called solar panels. However, solar panels large enough to provide electricity for a city would have to be spread over large areas of land. The sun doesn't shine constantly so no energy can be produced at night.

● **NUCLEAR ENERGY** is created by a chain reaction of splitting atoms. Nuclear reactors today furnish energy for our major cities. Unfortunately, radioactive waste is harmful to living things and remains so for thousands of years. Some scientists are working on developing safer nuclear energy.

● **HYDROELECTRIC POWER** One-third of the world's electricity is hydroelectric. Tremendous pressure from water at the bottom of dams spins turbines and produces energy. This alternative source is the cheapest and the cleanest. Hydroelectic power can't provide more energy without damming the world's wild rivers.

● **WIND ENERGY** Before electricity, windmills were used to power mills and water pumps on farms. Some scientists are hoping to harness wind power on the Great Lakes, the east coast of the United States, and the Aleutian Islands. However, wind power is not reliable.

Nuts and bolts are manufactured from natural resources like iron.

Using Resources

In manufacturing products, people need to use natural resources. Trees are used to make paper. Sand is used to make glass. Iron is used to make steel. Coal and oil are used to make the energy that runs the factories. So in manufacturing, people must also be sure to use resources carefully.

WHY IT MATTERS

A factory hires people like Marge Gendron to make products. It also creates jobs for even more people outside of the company. Suppose a company makes computers. Other people are hired to ship the computers. Still other people are needed to sell the computers. And someone else may design programs to be used on the computer. As you can see, most of the jobs in your community and around our country are connected to each other in many ways.

✓ Reviewing Facts and Ideas

SUM IT UP

- Manufacturing is the business of making things.

- Many factories use assembly lines to make things faster and less expensively. On an assembly line different steps are done in order to make a finished product.

- Manufacturing is one of the most important types of businesses in our country today.

THINK ABOUT IT

1. List ten different things manufactured in our country today.

2. **FOCUS** How do factories work?

3. **THINKING SKILL** *Classify* these items—books, water, coal, cars, trees, computers, copper. Are they manufactured, or are they natural resources?

4. **GEOGRAPHY** Many types of manufacturing companies are located near big cities. Why do you think this is so?

318

CITIZENSHIP
MAKING A DIFFERENCE

Inventor and Friend

HOUSTON, TEXAS—One day Josh Parsons, age 10, made a close friend. It started with baseball. Josh's father coached Josh's Little League team, the Mustangs.

One day just before the season started, Mr. Parsons told Josh about a boy named David Potter. David wanted to try out for the Mustangs. He was a very good hitter and catcher. "This was unusual," Josh says, "because he has arms only to the elbows." When David was 4 years old, he lost his hands and lower arms in an accident.

Like Josh, David loved baseball. On his own he learned to swing a bat. He also taught himself to catch a ball. He used a glove attached to his elbow. But David could not find a way to throw a ball.

"I had an idea," says Josh. "I thought of making something to help him throw. It could be shaped like a scoop. I told my idea to my Dad. We made a model of it."

Josh and his father went to David's house. They wanted to show him the invention. "I didn't know

him. He didn't know me. At first he was shocked. Then he tried the throwing arm on. It fit perfectly over his elbow. We went into his yard and my dad threw the ball to him. He threw it back. The arm worked!"

With his new throwing arm, David tried out for and won a place on the Mustang team. Today both boys are still playing baseball. And Josh is still inventing. He made another throwing arm for a boy in Montana. "This one," says Josh "is good for throwing snowballs in the winter and baseballs in the summer."

Josh Parsons

"I thought of making something to help him . . ."

319

CITIZENSHIP

HELPING OTHERS Have students consider how they can share their own skills to make a difference in your community.

- Students can begin by listing people they know who need extra help with physical tasks. They may know elderly people, for example, who walk slowly or can't read or hear as well as they used to.

- Some may want to invent products that help others. Invite these students to look at library books showing inventions that help people who are physically challenged. Then ask them to design inventions that could help someone they know.

- Other students may want to write about skills they might use to help others, such as reading to someone who is visually impaired, or working with dogs as canine companions.

- If possible, help students find ways to create and deliver their inventions or share their skills.

Lesson Objective
★ Illustrate how one boy used his special skills to make a difference in someone else's life.

Identifying the Focus Students will read how Josh invented a product that improved David's life. Explain that good citizens use their skills to help other people.

Why It Matters Point out that often when we are helping others we develop our own skills and talents.

Suggested Questions
- ● *How old is Josh Parsons?* (10 years old)

- ● *What happened to David Potter when he was 4 years old?* (He lost his arms in an accident.)

- ● *What did David want to do?* (He wanted to play baseball and try out for the Mustangs.)

- ● *How did Josh want to help him?* (He thought of inventing a scoop to help David throw.)

- ● *How is Josh a good citizen?* (He went out of his way to help someone else.)

★**THINKING FURTHER:** *Cause and Effect* **How did Josh's help affect David's life? What do you think was the effect of David's success on Josh?** (David was able to try out and win a place on the Mustangs; Josh probably felt happy for David, proud of his invention, and satisfied because he used his skill to help someone else.)

GLOBAL CONNECTIONS

PAGES 320–323

Lesson Overview
Communities around the world share resources, skills, and products through trade.

Lesson Objectives
★ Investigate domestic and international trade.

★ Distinguish between imports and exports.

★ Understand the interdependence of people and products in the world.

1 PREPARE

MOTIVATE Tell students that the quotation in the *Read Aloud* is from a song called "It's a Small World." Invite students to read the entire song, which is on p. 135 of the *Anthology,* and then sing along with it on the *Anthology Cassette.*

SET PURPOSE Write the *Read to Learn* question on the chalkboard. Then ask students what they would like to learn about trade. Finally, review the *Vocabulary* words and remind students to watch for them in the lesson.

2 TEACH

Discussing Not Only Baseball Cards Explain that buying something is a form of trade. Money is used to represent the value of something, and it can be used when trading for products or resources. Point out the picture and tell students that Canada is one of our country's biggest trading partners.

Suggested Questions
● **What is trade?** *(the buying and selling of goods and services)*

● **Why do countries trade?** *(People in each country want something the other country has.)*

Resource REMINDER

Practice Book: *p. 66*

Anthology: *It's a Small World, p. 135*

Technology: Adventures *CD-ROM*

Desk Maps: *World*

Geo Big Book *pp. 8–9*

Focus Activity

READ TO LEARN
Why is trade important?

VOCABULARY
trade
domestic trade
export
import
international trade

PLACE
Canada

320

Partners in Trade

READ ALOUD
"There's so much that we share that it's time we're aware, It's a small world after all."

You've read a lot in this book about how important our natural resources are. People in communities work together to share them and to make the most of them. People are also working to protect natural resources. In this lesson you will see how the words to the above song are true.

Not Only Baseball Cards
What do you think of when you hear the word trade? Perhaps you think about swapping sandwiches with a friend. Or you may think about trading baseball cards. For businesses and governments, *trade* means something a little different. Trade is the buying and selling of goods and services. In some ways, though, trade is not that different from trade in the lunchroom or in the schoolyard. People and countries trade for the same reasons. They trade because each side has something the other wants.

Reading STRATEGIES *and* Language DEVELOPMENT

MAKING CONCLUSIONS Remind students that readers make conclusions by combining new information with information they already know. As students read the lesson, invite them to draw conclusions about why different countries are interested in obtaining different products and about the ways in which countries around the world are dependent upon each other. Encourage students to share the prior knowledge and new information that helped them make the conclusion.

PREFIXES Write the words *export* and *import* on the chalkboard. Explain that these words are opposites. Thinking about prefixes will help students differentiate between them. The prefix *ex-* means "out" or "from." Therefore *export* refers to goods sent out of the country. The prefix *im-* means "in" or "into." Therefore *import* refers to goods brought into the country.

Trade Across Borders

Earlier in this chapter you read that Kansas has good soil and a good climate for agriculture. But it does not have many big cities with manufacturing. Detroit, Michigan has a lot of automobile factories. But it does not grow much wheat. So people in Kansas buy cars made in Detroit. People in Detroit eat bread made from wheat grown in Kansas. This exchange is called domestic trade, or trade within one country.

Most countries can't produce everything they need. Instead they import goods that are made or grown in another country. To import is to buy goods from another country. Then often they export what they've made or grown to other countries. To export is to sell and ship goods to another country.

One of our country's biggest trading partners is Canada, our neighbor to the north. We import fish, wood, and other products from Canada. We export computers, fruits, and other products to Canada.

The United States imports products like fish and wood from Canada and exports products including computers and automobiles.

Thinking About Trade Across Borders Explain that domestic trade occurs when U.S. companies buy goods from one another or when people buy and sell from stores. When companies engage in international trade, governments help them write trade agreements guaranteeing each country a fair deal.

Suggested Questions

- **What do people produce in Kansas?** *(wheat and other crops)*

- **What do people produce in Detroit, Michigan?** *(cars)*

- **What is it called when people in Kansas and people in Detroit buy each other's products?** *(domestic trade)*

- **What does it mean to import goods?** *(to buy them from another country)*

- **What does it mean to export goods?** *(to sell them to another country)*

★**THINKING FURTHER:** *Classifying* **What products and resources do we import from Canada? What do we export to Canada?** *(We import fish, wood, and aluminum; we export computers and crops.)*

Background INFORMATION

MONEY AND TRADE Be sure students understand that buying and selling goods is a form of trade. Explain that money is a contract. It promises that whoever receives it can get something later of equal value.

- Early communities traded extra foods and tools. They may have traded firewood for cloth or animal skins and milk for arrowheads. This system of trading goods for goods was called barter.

- The earliest forms of money were made of varied resources. Ancient Chinese people used shells of a certain shape. Some Native Americans wove money beads into belts; others used feathers, or shells. Africans traded with lumps of salt and Mexicans used cacao beans.

- People realized that metal money was best because it didn't wear out. About 2000 years ago the ancient Lydians began to make coins from gold and silver. They marked them with a lion's head. The Chinese made early coins of iron.

- U.S. money was once made from gold and silver. The amount of metal in the coin determined how much it was worth. Later, notes representing a certain value in gold were issued by banks.

- Invite students to look up *currency* in the encyclopedia and study the different kinds of money used around the world.

Infographic

Help students understand that countries around the world are linked through trade. Explain that governments often regulate the amount and types of trade between countries to make sure that their country is not spending too much money outside of the country or exporting too many valuable natural resources.

Discussing U.S. Trade Around the World Have students look at the *Infographic* and explain which items are natural resources and which are manufactured products. Help students understand that specialized manufactured products, such as airplanes and leather products, are valuable because they are made from specific natural resources and require skills or technology that are not available in the other country.

Suggested Questions

● **What is international trade?** *(trade between countries)*

● **Why do countries trade?** *(to buy resources and products they need or to sell surplus resources and products)*

● **What does Argentina export to the United States?** *(fish and shoes)*

● **What does the Nigeria export to the United States?** *(oil and fabric)*

● **What does the United States export to Nigeria?** *(medicine and computers)*

★**THINKING FURTHER:** *Making Conclusions* **Why do you think Australia and the United States both sell computers to each other?** *(Each country has special kinds of computers that the other country wants.)*

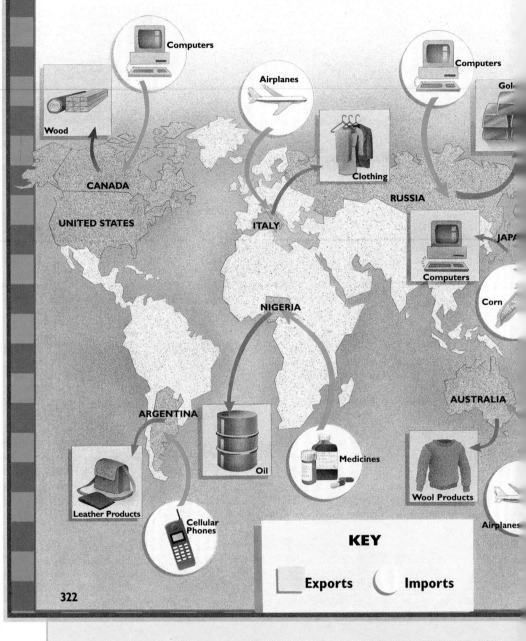

Infographic

U.S. Trade Around the World

International trade is the importing and exporting of goods between countries. Look at this Infographic to see some of the products the United States trades with other countries of the world.

Computers

Airplanes

Computers

Gol

Wood

Clothing

CANADA

RUSSIA

UNITED STATES

ITALY

JAP

Computers

Corn

NIGERIA

AUSTRALIA

ARGENTINA

Oil

Medicines

Wool Products

Leather Products

Cellular Phones

Airplanes

KEY

Exports ▢   Imports ◯

322

Expanding the Infographic

WATCH IT WORK Assist the class in a world-trade activity.

● Divide the class in half and ask one half to form small groups to represent the seven countries represented on the *Infographic*. The other half of the class will represent citizens of the United States.

● You may want to ask students to research more information about the products their country exports. Ask groups to illustrate five to ten cards with pictures of exported products. Tell students to duplicate pictures of each product.

● Invite citizens of different countries to meet with citizens of the United States to discuss trade deals. Explain that each side must tell the other why their product is valuable. They must also explain why people in their country want the products from the other country.

The World at Home

Look at the picture on this page. If you visited a port, you might see many different products being imported and exported from around the world. Sugar might come from sugarcane grown in the Philippines or India. Coffee probably comes from beans grown in Colombia in South America. The wheat being loaded might be headed for Japan or Russia.

WHY IT MATTERS

People in communities in the United States and around the world depend on each other in many ways. One of these ways is trade. By working with each other in the years ahead, people in all communities can continue to make our planet a better place to live and work.

The port of Los Angeles handles trade between the United States and other countries.

✔ Reviewing Facts and Ideas

SUM IT UP

- Trade is the business of buying and selling goods and services.
- To export is to sell goods to another country. To import is to buy goods from another country.
- The United States trades with Canada and other countries all over the world.
- Domestic trade is trade within one country.
- International trade is importing and exporting of goods between countries.

THINK ABOUT IT

1. What is the difference between imports and exports?

2. **FOCUS** Why is trade important?

3. **THINKING SKILL** Suppose the United States could not trade with other countries. What are some *effects* this might have on life in our country?

4. **GEOGRAPHY** Look at the map on page R10. What ocean would a ship carrying coffee have to cross to get from Colombia to the western United States?

323

Discussing the World at Home

Have students recall port cities they learned about this year. Then have them read about the imports and exports that go through the port of Los Angeles.

Suggested Questions

- **What is one way that products are imported and exported around the world?** (shipped from ports.)

Discussing WHY IT MATTERS Remind students that trade brings nations together.

Suggested Questions

- **Why do people depend on each other around the world?** (They need to trade goods and natural resources with each other.)

3 CLOSE

SUM IT UP

Use the world map in the *Atlas* or *Geo Big Book* to point out the countries named in the lesson. Have students name the product(s) the U.S. trades with each country.

Suggested Questions

- **What do we import from Canada? What do we export to Canada?** (fish, aluminum; computers, crops)

- **What is an example of domestic trade?** (People in Detroit buy bread made with Kansas wheat and people in Kansas buy Detroit's cars.)

EVALUATE
✓ Answers to Think About It

1. Imports are bought from other places; exports are sold to other places.

2. People need goods and resources from around the world to improve their lives and work.

3. We might not use as much aluminum or steel. We might not drink as much coffee, eat as much sugar, olive oil, or fish. We would not have as much oil to use for energy.

4. the Pacific Ocean *Movement*

Write About It Ask students to choose one businessperson from this unit and write a paragraph describing how importing or exporting goods might help the person's business.

MEETING *Individual* NEEDS

RETEACHING (Easy) Have students use their *Desk Maps* to label the countries discussed in this lesson and the imports we get from them.

EXTENSION (Average) Invite students to explore the idea of specialization. Ask them to write paragraphs describing their own special skills or talents. Have them read their paragraphs and invite the class to discuss how students can trade their specialized skills. For example, a student with cooking skills might offer cooking classes or sell burritos or cookies, and may be able to trade these skills with someone who can teach in-line skating.

ENRICHMENT (Challenging) Ask students to bring from home lists of processed food products that are imported from other countries or packaged in other states. (Students may need adult help reading labels.) Then make a class chart of foods your community imports or trades domestically.

Answers to
THINKING ABOUT VOCABULARY

1. trade
2. factory
3. manufacturing
4. harvest
5. agriculture
6. fertilizer
7. process
8. robot
9. import
10. assembly line

Answers to Thinking About Facts

1. F; In Kansas, the harvest is ready in the fall.
2. T
3. F; Minerals like copper are examples of nonrenewable resources.
4. T
5. F; International trade is trade between countries; domestic trade is trade within a country.

Resource REMINDER

Project Book: *p. 26–27*
Assessment Book: *Chapter 12 Test*

CHAPTER 12 REVIEW

THINKING ABOUT VOCABULARY

Number a sheet of paper from 1 to 10. Beside each number write the word or term from the list below that matches the statement.

agriculture	import
assembly line	manufacturing
factory	process
fertilizer	robot
harvest	trade

1. The buying and selling of goods and services
2. A place where things are manufactured
3. The business of making things
4. The ripe crops that are gathered
5. The business of growing crops and raising animals
6. Chemicals used to help plants grow
7. To change into a different form
8. Machine made to do tasks instead of people
9. To buy goods from another country
10. A line of workers and machines all working together to make a final product

THINKING ABOUT FACTS

Number a sheet of paper from 1 to 5. Write **T** if a statement is true. If it is false, rewrite it to make it true.

1. In Kansas the wheat harvest is usually ready during the summer.
2. Today many farmers in the United States make use of computers and high-tech combines to help grow their crops.
3. Minerals like copper are examples of renewable resources.
4. The use of assembly lines lowers the cost of making products such as cars and trucks.
5. Domestic trade is trade between countries.

THINK AND WRITE

WRITING ABOUT A FARM
Write a story in which you describe what it might be like to live and work on a Kansas wheat farm.

WRITING ABOUT BUSINESS
Write a paragraph explaining why the assembly line helped reduce the cost of making automobiles.

WRITING A SHORT STORY
Write a story about a young boy or girl who lives near a copper mine. Describe how the mine and the people who work there are important to their community. You can refer to "Many Voices" on page 317 for help.

324

Suggestions for Think and Write
SIGNS OF SUCCESS

WRITING ABOUT A FARM Stories should be set in large open tracts of land. They should describe the seasonal process of planting wheat in the spring, fertilizing it, watering it, and harvesting it in the fall. Stories should tell how big machines help with the work and how farmers keep accounts on computers.

WRITING ABOUT BUSINESS Students should understand that on an assembly line, workers do one job repeatedly as the automobiles pass them on a conveyor belt. Workers do not waste time changing tools or tasks. More cars can be made in less time, so they are less expensive.

WRITING A SHORT STORY The short stories should have a clear story sequence. The events should include accurate information from within the chapter.

For performance assessment, see Assessment Book, Chapter 12.

APPLYING STUDY SKILLS

READING FLOW CHARTS

Answer the following questions about the chart on page 310 to practice your skill of reading flow charts.

1. Explain how to read a flow chart.
2. What is the first step shown on the flow chart? What is the last step?
3. What happens right after the copper is separated from rock?
4. What happens just before the melted copper is rolled into rods?
5. Why is a flow chart a good way to explain how wire is made?

Answers to
APPLYING STUDY SKILLS

1. You follow the arrows from one step to the next. This will help you understand the order of steps in a process.
2. Mine rocks that contain copper. Coil wire onto spools.
3. It is melted to make it pure.
4. It is cast into bars.
5. A flow chart can show pictures of each process. It helps organize the information and makes it easier to visualize and understand.

Summing Up the Chapter

Review the chapter to find information about each type of work shown in the theme diagram below. Next fill in a copy of the diagram with a main idea about each type of work. Then write a short paragraph describing one way in which goods are produced from natural resources.

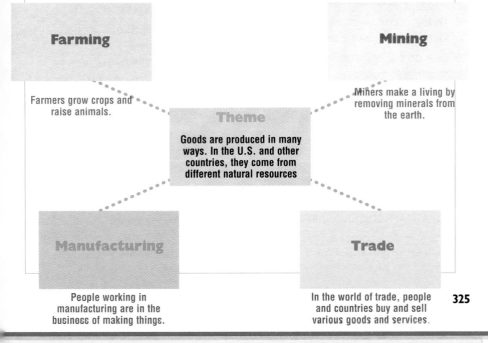

Farming

Farmers grow crops and raise animals.

Mining

Miners make a living by removing minerals from the earth.

Theme

Goods are produced in many ways. In the U.S. and other countries, they come from different natural resources

Manufacturing

People working in manufacturing are in the business of making things.

Trade

In the world of trade, people and countries buy and sell various goods and services.

325

Suggestions for Summing Up the Chapter

- Have students write headings on their papers in a diagram like the one above. Or prepare copies of the diagram and distribute them to the class. Tell students to write one main-idea sentence under each heading.
- In their paragraphs, students should write about every worker who helps in the process of obtaining the natural resources or turning them into the products we use.
- Invite students to share their paragraphs with the class. Ask other students to tell how people sell the products and use them.

Answers to
THINKING ABOUT VOCABULARY

1. consumers   6. C
2. C   7. designer
3. public property   8. product map
4. robots   9. C
5. C   10. C

Suggestions for
THINK AND WRITE

Writing About Jobs Students' writing should show consideration of their own talents and interests. They should describe how their abilities might be used to help other people or to make a profit. Paragraphs should also describe the responsibilities and rewards of a specific job. Students may enjoy illustrating their paragraphs with a future self-portrait.

Writing a Paragraph Be sure students understand that farmers have always needed to exchange services. For example, farmers probably needed to help each other plow and harvest, build shelters, shear sheep, herd cattle, or take care of children. They may have needed to share tools, seeds, and food or clothing. Students' writing should describe the process of trade, and show a basic awareness of the relative value of goods and services.

Writing About Working Together Encourage students to review many of the graphics in the chapter. Their paragraphs should include at least three examples of how people work together here and with other countries to create an international network of goods and services.

UNIT 5 REVIEW

THINKING ABOUT VOCABULARY

consumers   imports
designer   product map
employer   public property
export   robots
fertilizer   services

Number a sheet of paper from 1 to 10. Beside each number write **C** if the underlined word is used correctly. If it is not, choose the word or term from the list above that correctly completes the sentence.

1. During a sale, Andy's Bike Shop is always filled with <u>employers</u>.

2. The more money you save in a bank, the more <u>interest</u> you earn.

3. We enjoy camping on <u>private property</u> such as national parks.

4. Today <u>consumers</u> are used in factories to make cars and trucks.

5. One of the first <u>assembly lines</u> made automobiles.

6. The United States <u>imports</u> computers and cars from Japan.

7. A <u>journalist</u> makes sure that every page in a book looks good.

8. A <u>flow chart</u> shows the places where goods are made or grown.

9. The <u>economy</u> is the making and consuming of goods and services.

10. The farmer brings his <u>harvest</u> to be sold at the market.

THINK AND WRITE

WRITING ABOUT JOBS
In this unit you read about a variety of jobs. Write a paragraph explaining why you might choose to have any one of these jobs.

WRITING A PARAGRAPH
Suppose that you lived long ago, before the use of money. Write a paragraph describing how farmers might have obtained goods and services.

WRITING ABOUT WORKING TOGETHER
You have seen how people work together in many ways. Write a paragraph describing how the United States trades with other countries.

BUILDING SKILLS

1. **Cause and Effect** List three words that show causes. List three words that show effects.

2. **Cause and Effect** What is one effect of saving your money in a bank?

3. **Cause and Effect** What is one effect of using an assembly line?

4. **Flow Charts** Why is a flow chart a good way to learn about how things are made?

5. **Flow Charts** Look at the flow chart on page 307. What happens after the dough is dried and cut?

Ongoing Unit Project

OPTIONS FOR ASSESSMENT
This ongoing project, begun on page 268D, can be part of your assessment program, along with other forms of evaluation.

PLANNING Let students know that they will keep a record of information about the products and should have clear reasons they want to include products in the catalog.

SIGNS OF SUCCESS
- Students will use information and terminology from the chapter.
- Groups will reach consensus about the products to include in the catalog.
- Catalog descriptions will be clear, reflecting students' knowledge about the products and who will buy them.
- Students will understand who benefits from the sale of these products.

 FOR THE PORTFOLIO Each child's research can be added to a portfolio.

YESTERDAY, TODAY & *TOMORROW*

Assembly lines, computers, robots, and high-tech machines have changed farming and manufacturing. Name two ways a farmer might use a robot in the future. How might a farmer use computers?

READING ON YOUR OWN

Here are some books you might find at the library to help you learn more.

COWS IN THE PARLOR
by Cynthia McFarland
Where does milk come from? Visit Clear Creek Farm and learn about dairy farming.

AUNT LILLY'S LAUNDROMAT
by Melanie Hope Greenberg
Step into Aunt Lilly's laundromat and learn about working hard and keeping dreams alive.

IF YOU MADE A MILLION
by David Schwartz
Here's your chance to learn about making and spending a lot of money.

Answers to BUILDING SKILLS

1. cause: because, as a result of, since; effect: as a result, so, therefore

2. For example: You collect interest; you have a large sum of money when you need it.

3. For example: Products are made more quickly; products are made less expensively.

4. A flow chart presents the steps of a process in order. A flow chart is easy to read.

5. The pasta is packed into bags or boxes.

Suggestions for YESTERDAY, TODAY, AND TOMORROW

Be sure students understand that robots are machines that do human work by working automatically. Explain that robots may be automated trucks or big machines, or they may be sensitive instruments that can do delicate and precise work.

Suggestions for READING ON YOUR OWN

Bring in library book from the list under Reading On Your Own. You will find additional suggestions listed in the Annotated Bibliography on the Unit Organizer on page 268B. Encourage students to choose books about interesting topics and to read them independently. Invite students to report on their reading by presenting oral or written reports. Encourage them to include flow charts to describe step by step processes and invite other students to ask questions about a topic after listening.

UNIT PROJECT

Have a Career Fair

1. Have each group member choose one career they would like to research.
2. Write several facts and draw pictures for each career on a piece of cardboard.
3. Make a display showing the different careers in your group.

4. Share displays in a Class Career Fair. Have group members describe why they chose each career.

Unit Project: *Have A Career Fair*

ORGANIZING THE CAREER FAIR

OBJECTIVE: This project will help students review the unit and start them thinking about careers that might interest them in the future.

MATERIALS: cardboard, crayons or markers

- Divide the class into groups of three. Invite each group to brainstorm careers individual members will research. Each group member should choose one career.

- Give each student a sheet of cardboard and show them how to fold it into three sections to make a stand. Then students write facts and draw pictures about the careers and attach them to the cardboard stand.

- Display the stands around the classroom. Have each student tell the class about his or her career and reasons for choosing it.

OPTIONS FOR ASSESSMENT

The project can be part of your assessment program.

PLANNING Tell students that their information should be accurate and specific.

SIGNS OF SUCCESS

- Students should be able to explain why they chose their careers.

- Students should be able to name the research sources they used.

- Each student in each group should research a different career.

 FOR THE PORTFOLIO The completed career reports may be included in students' portfolios.

Using Prior Knowledge Help students complete a word web on the chalkboard. In the center of the web, write the name of your community. Draw radiating lines from this circle and connect them to periphery circles labeled: *history*, *geography*, *government*, *transportation*, *work*, and *play*.

Ask students to think of what they have learned about their community this year. Students can then make suggestions while you fill in the circles with the information they volunteer.

Looking at the Picture Ask students to look at the picture on page 328. Ask if students can draw conclusions about the children in the picture: How do the children feel about their community?

Explain to students that they will be reading about activities completed by Mrs. Green's class in Toms River. Reading about the students in Toms River will help them focus on special issues in their own community.

Curriculum CONNECTION

LINKS TO ART Invite students to create letter cards like those shown in the photograph.

- Provide students with colored construction paper (8 1/2 x 11 inches), rulers, pencils, and scissors.
- Have students sketch the outlines of capital letters in the name of your community onto construction paper.
- Students can cut out the letters and paste them onto construction paper of a contrasting color.
- Have the class practice holding the letters in sequence so that your community name is easy to read. Ask students to display the name of your community proudly at a sports events or school assembly.

Background INFORMATION

MORE ABOUT TOMS RIVER

- Toms River is the county seat of Ocean County, New Jersey, a county that boasts 45 miles of oceanfront and 150 miles of waterfront. The area has many fine swimming beaches and wildlife preserves
- The Garden State Parkway, which students can note on the map on p. 330, allows residents to travel easily to neighboring cities. Toms River is 70 miles south of New York City and 60 miles east of Philadelphia. It is near two airports and is connected to bus and train lines.
- Toms River has a Seaport Maritime Museum (that displays the history of boat building in the region), the Ocean County Historical Museum, and the Ocean County Courthouse (which looks as it did in 1850 when it was built).

SPECIAL SECTION
EXPLORING YOUR COMMUNITY

Welcome to Toms River, New Jersey! It's the end of the school year for Mrs. Green's third-grade class at Walnut Street Elementary School. In social studies, the students have studied communities. Now the class wants to do something very special.

More and more people move to Toms River every year. So Mrs. Green's class decided to make a Community Welcome Center. It will be on display at their school. Making the Welcome Center will be a great way for Mrs. Green's class to learn about their community. It will also help people who are new to the community to learn about Toms River.

You can learn how to make your own Community Welcome Center. Read this section to learn how to do it.

Exploring Your Community Have students read the text on page 329. Then invite them to describe how it might feel to move to your community. Have students consider all of the new information that new neighbors have to learn. They have to learn street signs and business locations, meet new friends, begin a new job, and learn how they can participate in community government. They are also probably eager to learn about interesting places to visit and things to do.

Point out that in any community, long-time residents can help newcomers feel more at home. In some communities, the Chamber of Commerce will give new families books of coupons to introduce them to local businesses. Many good neighbors welcome newcomers by inviting them to community gatherings and by offering to give directions or advice.

Ask students to tell in their own words why a community might need a Welcome Center. Then explain to the class that this Special Section includes ideas for making a Welcome Center. Encourage students to begin thinking about helpful information and publications they might like to include. Suggest that they begin by creating a list of questions that they might have if they had just arrived in a new community.

Curriculum CONNECTION

LINKS TO DRAMATIC ARTS To help spark students' interest in a Community Welcome Center, have them role play the arrival of a new community member.

- Have small groups work together to create original role plays.

- Suggest that students choose a community setting for each role play. Explain that one or two students can play newcomers to the community. Other students can play community members who introduce the newcomers to landmarks, businesses, people, or events. Tell students to keep their role plays simple. They can do this by focusing on one or two scenes that show people helping each other.

- Invite students to find basic props and give them time to practice their role plays.

- Students will enjoy performing the role plays for the class. You may want to discuss the story line of each role play. This will help students empathize with newcomers. It will also help them brainstorm ideas to include in a Community Welcome Center.

Making a Map Invite students to read the text on page 330. Then have them look at Rashad's and Jaime's map. Have students tell what kinds of landmarks and symbols are included in the map and help them review map-reading skills. Ask them which direction Walnut Elementary school lies from Toms River and which Parkway runs north and south (Garden State).

Ask a volunteer to tell the class why using a map might be more helpful to a newcomer than asking for directions from someone. Explain that your class will be making a map of your community. Ask students to talk about the layout of your town and to list the important landmarks, streets, or buildings a newcomer might want to locate.

You may want to have students flip though their books to review the different kinds of maps they have studied. Invite volunteers to describe physical maps, grid maps, political maps, and transportation maps. Encourage students to consider what kind of map would best show the layout of your community. Remind students that a rural community may best be shown by a physical map that shows some streets. An urban community may best be mapped with a grid map.

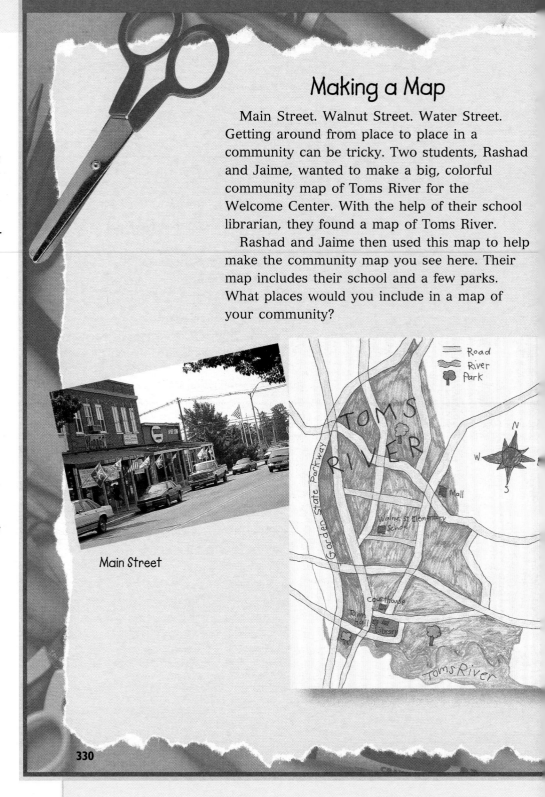

Making a Map

Main Street. Walnut Street. Water Street. Getting around from place to place in a community can be tricky. Two students, Rashad and Jaime, wanted to make a big, colorful community map of Toms River for the Welcome Center. With the help of their school librarian, they found a map of Toms River.

Rashad and Jaime then used this map to help make the community map you see here. Their map includes their school and a few parks. What places would you include in a map of your community?

Main Street

330

CITIZENSHIP

Invite students to make a Community Resource Book to include in the Welcome Center.

- Ask students to suggest categories for important parts of any community. Categories might include, for example, *government, recreation, education, arts, history, community service* and *businesses*. Write their suggestions on the chalkboard. Then brainstorm people and places in your community that fall into each category.

- Assign pairs of students items from the list. Explain that for each item, they should write a short description of why the person or place is important, an address, and a telephone number.

- Have students carefully write their entries on separate sheets of paper. Ask volunteers to design an introductory page for each category, an index page, and a cover page. Students may also want to use colored tabs to make the book easy to use.

- Help students separate the entries into the appropriate sections. Staple the book together along one edge or fix the pages in a plastic report cover.

Helping Our Environment

Joseph, Cyndi, and Jaclyn wanted the Welcome Center to include a poster about protecting their environment. So first they researched information about the environment. They spoke with people in the state government who could tell them about environmental problems. They learned about water pollution problems in Toms River. They also learned how they could help fight water pollution. Look at their poster below. What does it say about fighting pollution in Toms River?* What would you want to say in a pollution poster for your community?

KEEP TOMS RIVER CLEAN

*Help keep rivers and parks clean by putting trash in waste baskets.

331

Using Prior Knowledge Help students review what they have learned about protecting the environment. On chart paper, have students create a list of natural resources they have studied. Then, as you point to each item on the list, have a volunteer tell how we use the resource and how we can protect it from overuse or pollution.

Helping our Environment Give students a few minutes to read *Helping Our Environment* and to look at the pictures. Ask students to look at the poster that Joseph, Cyndi, and Jaclyn drew. Discuss how the poster illustrates how or why people keep Toms River clean.

Ask students to explain how a poster can be effective. Encourage them to consider the kinds of information you need before you can teach others about environmental issues. Tell students they will be creating posters about the environment later on (see *Curriculum Connection*).

Be sure students understand that protecting the environment is important in every community and that newcomers will want to know how they can help.

Background INFORMATION

CLASS VISITOR/FIELD TRIP

- Contact a local environmental group about environmental problems in your community. Invite an informed speaker in to talk about environmental problems close to your school.
- Ahead of time, help students research information about the geography, animals, and plants of the area so they are prepared to ask questions. Students can discuss with the speaker how people can help solve any environmental problems.
- If possible, take students to visit any local site that they have studied. You may also want to take students to a bird or animal rescue center to show them how environmental problems affect wildlife.

Curriculum CONNECTION

LINKS TO ART/LANGUAGE ARTS Invite students to make posters about what they have learned about environmental problems. They need heavy paper, markers, and magazines to cut up. Posters should include:

- a description of problems and the land, animals, and plants affected by them
- persuasive language telling people why they should care. Posters may have rhyming slogans or huge letters.
- information about how people can become part of the solution; phone numbers to call; organizations to join; things to do every day to help protect the environment

Encourage students to use a pencil to sketch in words. Then they can proofread for spelling and grammar.

Using Prior Knowledge Ask students to look at the time line and to discuss the events. Be sure students understand how the history of communities which they learned about in previous chapters will help them understand Ryan's time line. Have students tell how the Revolutionary War, the railroad, and freeways and parkways affected other U.S. communities. Then you can predict how these changes may have affected Toms River.

The History of Toms River You may want to share additional information about the history of Toms River. Explain that the town was first known as Tom's River in 1712, and there are few written records from that time. One record is an epic poem written by Tom Luker. One of the verses says:

> Luker means river
> In Indian tongue
> And along this river,
> My new life begun.
> This little shire
> May never know fame,
> But at this time
> It bears my name.

When Tom married a Native American woman, the Native Americans gave them a triangular piece of land near the river. Tom built a house near the bend of the river and built a business ferrying people, horses, and wagons across. In his poem, Tom tells us that *Luker* means "river" in the local Native American tongue. So *Tom Luker* means "Tom River."

Tell students that in Toms River, the county Museum and Research Center is in a Victorian house. The rooms are decorated with furniture and tools from the past. The museum also has nearly 3,000 books and many exhibits showing how people long ago made glass, charcoal, and boats and how they processed lumber and cranberries. Many people in the community volunteer their time to help others learn about local history. These volunteers are interested in local history and were pleased to help Ryan research his question.

The History of Toms River

Why is Toms River called Toms River? Ryan was curious. So he did some research at the local historical museum to answer this question. He found out that no one knows for sure. Some people think Toms River was named by an English settler called Captain William Toms in the 1660s. Others think that Toms River is named for a man named Tom Luker. This man married the daughter of a local Native American chief. Still others think it is named for a Native American known as "Old Indian Tom." He lived in the area in the late 1700s.

One thing was certain, though. Ryan was excited about all the information he gathered at the museum. What questions about your community would you like to research?

From the Collection of Richard Steele/Ocean County Library

Ocean County Cultural & Heritage Com

Photos Taken Around 1900

332

Background INFORMATION

REPORTS ON THE COMMUNITY Ask the class to research information about the history and geography of their community.

- Throughout the year, students have discussed and researched the history of their community. Invite students to share their past work in a class discussion about your town or city. Encourage students to talk about questions that are still unanswered. Then help them gather into focus groups centered around their interests. Some students may be interested in geography, others in natural resources and others in the history of a building or a street name.

- Have groups or partners research a topic. They may use the library or historical museum, and can talk with community members.

- Suggest that students present a report to the class as an oral report, a written report, a play, an illustrated story, a flow chart, or a poster.

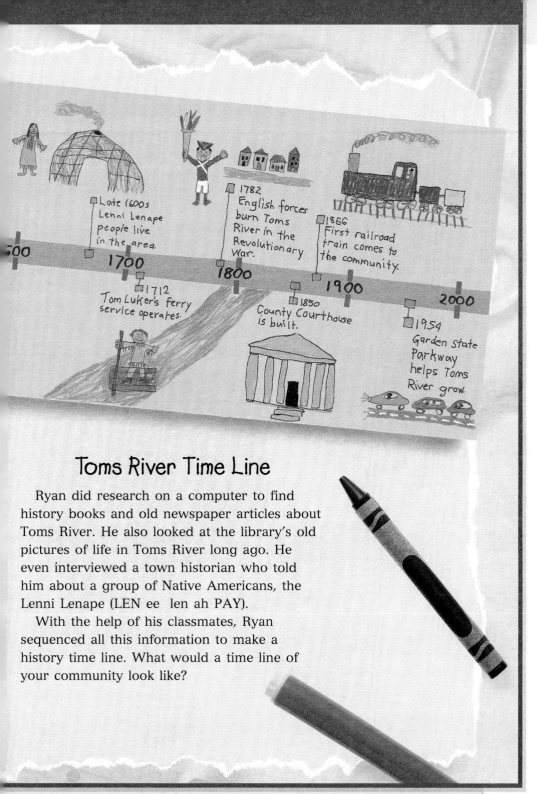

Late 1600s
Lenni Lenape
people live
in the area.

1782
English forces
burn Toms
River in the
Revolutionary
War.

1866
First railroad
train comes to
the community.

1700

1800

1900

2000

1712
Tom Luker's ferry
service operates.

1850
County Courthouse
is built.

1954
Garden state
Parkway
helps Toms
River grow.

Toms River Time Line

Ryan did research on a computer to find history books and old newspaper articles about Toms River. He also looked at the library's old pictures of life in Toms River long ago. He even interviewed a town historian who told him about a group of Native Americans, the Lenni Lenape (LEN ee len ah PAY).

With the help of his classmates, Ryan sequenced all this information to make a history time line. What would a time line of your community look like?

Using Prior Knowledge Remind students that many Unit Openers in their books introduced historical events by showing them on a time line. Turn to one of these time lines and ask students to explain how the pictures and dates helped them understand the sequence of events. Have them tell why it is important to understand the order in which historical events occurred.

Toms River Time Line Invite students to read the text and to look at Ryan's time line of Toms River. Be sure students understand that Ryan researched his information through several different sources.

Explain to students that they will make a time line of local history to include in the Welcome Center. Ask students to discuss why a newcomer to your community might want to understand local history. Be sure students understand that people who are just settling in a new community may not have time to read a long history of the area. Point out that reading a simple time line will help new community members understand some of the important events that made your community what it is today.

Curriculum CONNECTION

LINKS TO MATHEMATICS: MAKE A TIME LINE You may want to work with the entire class to develop a time line of local historical events.

- Have students look through their reports on the community for important dates. Write students' suggestions on the chalkboard. If students remember important dates mentioned by older community members, include these in the list.
- Ask students to research additional dates in the school library or by talking with a local historian.
- Invite volunteers to rewrite the dates in chronological order. Then ask the class to agree on five to seven of the most important events. Explain that these events will be included on a time line.

Provide students with paper, pencils, rulers, and crayons so that each student can illustrate the time line.

LINKS TO MATHEMATICS: MAKE A FAMILY TIME LINE Help the class understand how events in your local history correspond to events in the lives of people they know.

- Invite students to create time lines for the history of their families. Ask them to find out when and where their older family members and their siblings were born. They can also include other important dates, such as moving to a new community or house, or graduating from school.
- Have students compare their family time line with the time line of the community.

Using Prior Knowledge In earlier chapters, students investigated many different kinds of work performed by people in different communities. Ask students to create a list on the chalkboard of jobs they remember. Invite students to circle the jobs that people do in your community.

A Video Look at Work Give students several minutes to read *A Video Look at Work* and to look at the pictures. Have volunteers describe what they see in each picture and tell what they know about the person's line of work.

Point out that many people may move to your community because they like the climate, schools, or people. Many people, especially people with families, will move to a community only after they have found a job. Others may find work soon after they arrive. Invite students to discuss how interviews with community members might help a newcomer find work.

Be sure students understand that knowing about individuals and their work will help a newcomer understand the community better. Have students list three jobs that many people in your community have. Invite them to explain how knowing what people do in these jobs helps you understand them better.

A Video Look at Work

Sarah knew that many people move to communities like Toms River to find jobs and make a living. She decided that she would make a video of the different people and their jobs in Toms River.

With the help of people at the Chamber of Commerce, Sarah contacted different workers. She then interviewed them on videotape to learn about their jobs. By including her video in the Welcome Center, Sarah wants to help people learn about the different jobs in Toms River. What would you include in a video about jobs in your community?

Dr. Zimmerman
Astronomer

Mr. Rush
Teacher

Ms. Wauters
Environmental Lawyer

334

Background INFORMATION

Students learned in Unit 5 that many different kinds of workers are needed to make businesses function smoothly. As a class project, you may want to have students research the many workers who help manufacture, test, ship, and sell a product.

For example, students can visit a bicycle store and talk to the owner. Students can find out where specific parts come from. They can write letters (or make toll-free calls) asking questions about how and where the parts are manufactured. They can also find out information about the people who ship or sell the parts to the store, people who assemble the bikes, and people who print catalogs and advertisements. Then students can make a detailed chart showing all of the people who help in just one business.

Curriculum CONNECTION

LINKS TO ART Students can include words and pictures of many different workers in the Welcome Center. Invite students to contact the Chamber of Commerce for the names of businesses who would welcome students.

- If you have video equipment available, help students videotape interviews with workers. Remind students to carefully plan their questions. Suggest they give workers a copy of the questions in advance so that everyone is prepared before filming begins.

- As an alternative, students can make audiotapes or written transcripts of interviews. They can place these in an exhibit area along with photographs or drawings of the people they talked to.

Fun All Year!

Winter, spring, summer, or fall—there are many ways people have fun in Toms River. Nathan decided to make a calendar of these events. He read local newspapers and magazines. He spoke with his schoolmates. Soon he had plenty of information to include in his calendar.

Look at Nathan's Community Calendar of Events. How are these events like those in your community? How are they different?

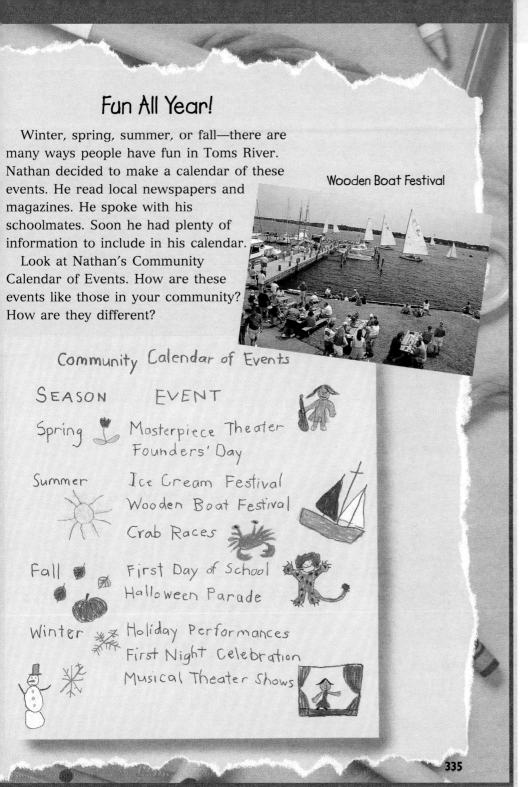

Wooden Boat Festival

Community Calendar of Events

SEASON	EVENT
Spring	Masterpiece Theater Founders' Day
Summer	Ice Cream Festival Wooden Boat Festival Crab Races
Fall	First Day of School Halloween Parade
Winter	Holiday Performances First Night Celebration Musical Theater Shows

335

Fun All Year Ask students to tell how they find out about special events in the community. You may want to ask students to bring in events calendars from local newspapers or community centers. Discuss how events are listed and what kinds of pictures are shown.

Ask students to consider how knowing about community events will help new-comers feel at home. Point out that sports events and performances are fun to attend with new friends. Newcomers may also find an excellent way to make new friends by participating in a parade or festival.

Remind students that people who have lived in a community for a long time also enjoy learning about new ways to have fun. Explain that students will have a chance to create their own events calendars to share fun activities with everyone in the community. (See *Curriculum Connections, Links to Art* below.)

Curriculum CONNECTION

LINKS TO LANGUAGE ARTS: SEASONAL CELEBRATIONS
In large communities, there are usually too many seasonal celebrations to count. Invite students to share general ideas about what they like about the different seasons.

Then have each student write a detailed description of a favorite celebration or seasonal event. Ask them to explain why we celebrate the event in a particular season. Then, invite students to illustrate their descriptions and share them with the class.

LINKS TO ART: A COMMUNITY CALENDAR OF EVENTS
An events calendar will help residents remember where and when to have fun. On a large piece of chart paper, students can write the four seasons and list several of the most enjoyable community celebrations. Post this calendar in the Welcome Center. Students can also create a detailed monthly calendar.

- Invite students to work in small groups to illustrate the months of the year. On one page, groups can draw pictures of festivals or seasonal celebrations that happen during their assigned month. Encourage students to share their reports with each other so that everyone gets to make recommendations.
- Photocopy the illustrations and make copies of a calendar grid. Have students work in an assembly line to collate the pages.
- Punch three holes in the top of each page and tie the pages together with yarn.

Using Prior Knowledge Ask volunteers to give clear definitions of the words *government* and *citizenship*. Write their suggestions on the chalkboard. Ask new volunteers to give several examples to further explain each word.

Being a Good Citizen After students have read *Being a Good Citizen* and looked at the pictures, focus the discussion on class projects. Have students explain in their own words how Yifan and Anna chose topics and researched them. Ask students to tell how these topics could help others learn about Toms River.

Help students brainstorm topics for reports. Invite students to create a list of good citizens and community leaders. Encourage them also to list questions about community government that have remained unanswered. Encourage students to choose ideas from these lists for research projects.

Explain to students that they will be creating their own class projects that teach about local government. The suggestions below will help students organize and present their research.

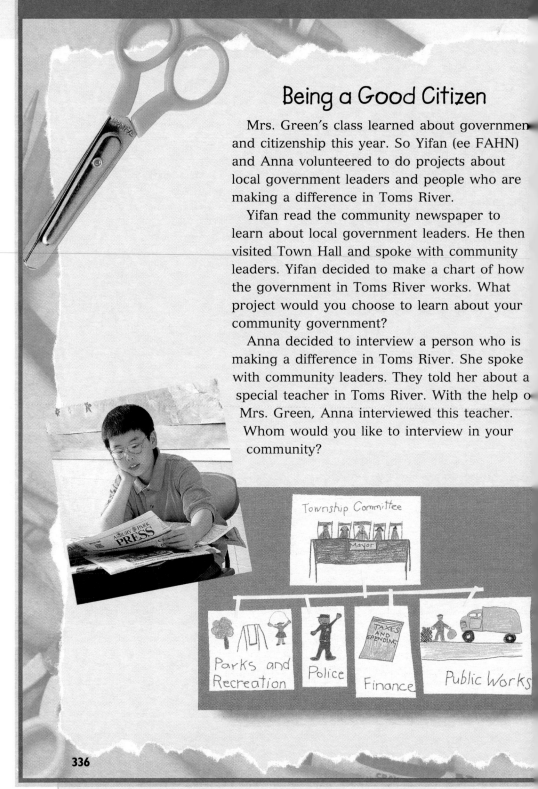

Being a Good Citizen

Mrs. Green's class learned about government and citizenship this year. So Yifan (ee FAHN) and Anna volunteered to do projects about local government leaders and people who are making a difference in Toms River.

Yifan read the community newspaper to learn about local government leaders. He then visited Town Hall and spoke with community leaders. Yifan decided to make a chart of how the government in Toms River works. What project would you choose to learn about your community government?

Anna decided to interview a person who is making a difference in Toms River. She spoke with community leaders. They told her about a special teacher in Toms River. With the help of Mrs. Green, Anna interviewed this teacher. Whom would you like to interview in your community?

Township Committee · Mayor

Parks and Recreation · Police · Finance · Public Works

336

Curriculum CONNECTION

Have students interview community members who make a difference.

- Remind students that in public school, teachers' salaries are paid by the state government. Create a list of people whose jobs are funded by federal, local, or state government. These jobs include postal workers, road repair crews, sanitation workers, county health employees, public school teachers, librarians, law enforcement officials, firefighters, and members of the military.

- When the list is complete, ask students to work in groups to list questions they would like to ask government workers. Students may want to find out who pays workers' salaries, how they are hired, what the job entails, and how workers make a difference in your community.

- Invite visitors to the classroom or help students set up appointments to visit a local library, clinic, police station, or fire station. Have students include their interviews in the Welcome Center.

Computers for All

In this interview Anna spoke with a teacher named Mrs. Clare Devine. Anna met with Mrs. Devine at the computer lab at North Dover Elementary School in Toms River. The lab is a big room with many computers. Mrs. Devine teaches students how to use the computers. She and her students started a program to teach older Americans how to use computers.

Q: Why did you start this program?

Mrs. Devine: I know that many people, especially older people, are nervous or afraid of working with computers. They did not grow up using them in school, as children do today. My students know a lot about computers. I thought they would enjoy teaching others.

Q: What do older Americans learn in the classes?

Mrs. Devine: Each class shows the older people a different way to use the computer. Also, the students show them their favorite computer games. We also taught them how to "talk" to someone on the Internet.

Q: Do older Americans like the classes?

Mrs. Devine: Yes, I think so. This year at the last class, they bought ice cream for everyone.

Q: What do you like best about this project?

Mrs. Devine: Everyone wins. Older people see that working with computers is not as hard as they thought. Many children don't spend much time with older people. Working together, students and older people get to know each other.

North Dover Elementary School

337

Using Prior Knowledge Remind students that they read about volunteers in Chapter 8. Ask someone to define the word *volunteer.* Then ask students to give examples of volunteer work that was discussed in class. Have them explain why someone who volunteers their time to help others is a good citizen.

Computers for All Invite students to read the interview with Mrs. Devine and to look at the pictures of her class. Help students understand that when people teach each other new skills, they are also building a stronger community. Point out that many young people spend hours learning from older people. Teaching older people can help students feel good about the skills they know. Teaching anyone a skill is one way people share with others in our communities.

You may also want to explain that in many cultures, older people live with their children and grandchildren. In the United States, we have to set aside special time to share with older people. Have students tell about enjoyable times they spend with older people.

CITIZENSHIP

TEACHING OTHERS Invite students to share their skills with younger students.

- Help students brainstorm a list of skills that they could teach. For example students could teach a song, a string game, knitting, how to draw a cat, or how to use a measuring tape.

- Invite students to give practice demonstrations in class to prepare for teaching a younger class.

- Help students organize the classroom into skill areas. For example, musicians and singers can gather in one corner of the classroom, artists in another, math experts in a third, jugglers and joke-tellers in a fourth. Students can paint signs to describe their area of expertise.

- Invite the second grade for a visit. Younger students can choose a skill they would like to learn and have fun learning from third-grade experts.

Using Prior Knowledge Invite students to assemble all of their writing and artwork generated during this Special Section lesson. Have students show their work to the class and explain how it will help a newcomer learn about your community.

Hello Around the World After students have read the text on page 338 and looked at the pictures, ask them to share their experiences with pen pals. If students are currently writing to pen pals, ask if they would like to share part of a letter with the class. Encourage students to explain what they have learned about another community through corresponding with someone far away.

Tell students that they will be making a Welcome Kit to share with people far away. Explain that the Welcome Kit will tell other people why we like living in our community. Invite students to discuss plans for a Welcome Kit. Ask students to think about the student projects they have seen. Have them consider which might be included in a Welcome Kit and how large projects might be reduced in size or length for easier mailing.

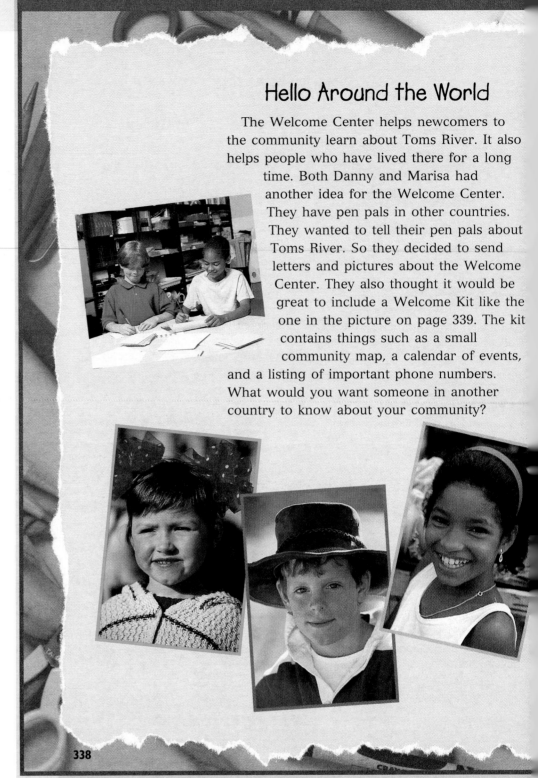

Hello Around the World

The Welcome Center helps newcomers to the community learn about Toms River. It also helps people who have lived there for a long time. Both Danny and Marisa had another idea for the Welcome Center. They have pen pals in other countries. They wanted to tell their pen pals about Toms River. So they decided to send letters and pictures about the Welcome Center. They also thought it would be great to include a Welcome Kit like the one in the picture on page 339. The kit contains things such as a small community map, a calendar of events, and a listing of important phone numbers. What would you want someone in another country to know about your community?

338

Curriculum CONNECTIONS

LINKS TO LANGUAGE ARTS Ask students to work in small groups to write letters to students in a distant community. Encourage students to write personal accounts of fun and interesting experiences they have had. Have them also tell about sights or events they would like to show a newcomer and people they would like to introduce them to. Remind students to also include questions they want answered about life in another community.

LINKS TO ART: MAKE A WELCOME KIT Invite students to work as a class to develop a Welcome Kit. Encourage students to brainstorm original ideas about what to include. You may also want to use some of the following suggestions. Students can:

- design an interesting and beautiful cover.
- create small community maps showing important landmarks and routes.
- design a fold-out brochure that includes a calendar of events and important phone numbers.
- design a community newsletter that includes excerpts from citizenship interviews and student illustrations.
- collate and copy students' letters; copy maps and brochures.
- collect the parts of the Welcome Kit and package them for mailing.
- mail copies of the Welcome Kit to friends and relatives in distant communities.

Communities Are Special

This year in social studies, Mrs. Green's class learned a lot about communities in the United States and around the world. They read about the geography of different places. They learned about the history of different communities. They also learned about people who make a difference to their community.

By making the Welcome Center below, Mrs. Green's class learned that their community is a special place. When you explore your own community, you will see that it, too, is special.

Communities Are Special Ask students to read the text on page 339. As they look at the completed Welcome Center, ask them to make comparisons between it and the one in your classroom.

Help students summarize what they have learned in this Special Section. (While creating the Welcome Center and Welcome Kit, students learned about new community events. They listened to interviews and stories and learned of the experiences of classmates and community members.)

Ask students to tell what new and surprising things they have learned about the area in which you live. Point out that sharing our community with others often helps us learn more about it.

Be sure that students understand that every community is special for a different reason. Help them understand that it is through living in a place and getting to know its land and people that we truly come to appreciate it.

★ CITIZENSHIP

There are many ways students can share their welcome kit with people in the community.

- Invite parents in for a special hour in the afternoon or evening. Invite them to view the Welcome Center and listen to the reports on our community.
- Make copies of the Welcome Kit and bring them to the Chamber of Commerce. Ask the Chamber of Commerce to share them with visitors and people who are beginning new lives in your town. Also, ask the Chamber of Commerce to let students know how their kits have helped others.
- Arrange for a bulletin board display at your local library or community center. Bring in copies of the Welcome Kit and display it.

Curriculum CONNECTION

LINKS TO LANGUAGE ARTS: LETTER TO THE EDITOR Invite groups of students to develop a letter to the editor of your local paper explaining why your community is special. Students can choose roles such as to:

- review Unit 1 for ideas about geography and community; review Unit 2 for ideas about living in communities; review Unit 3 for ideas about American history and your community; review Unit 4 for ideas about welcoming newcomers; review Unit 5 for ideas about the economy and your community.
- record and organize ideas into a first draft; act as editor to proofread the first draft; locate addresses for local newspapers; write the final draft, address, and send the letter; check the newspaper to see if the letter was printed.

REFERENCE SECTION

The Reference Section has many parts, each with a different type of information. Use this section to look up people, places, and events as you study.

R4 Atlas

An atlas is a collection of maps. An atlas can be a book or a separate section within a book. This Atlas is a separate section with maps to help you study the geography in this book.

R2

The *Adventures* CD-ROM can be used to enrich the Reference Section.

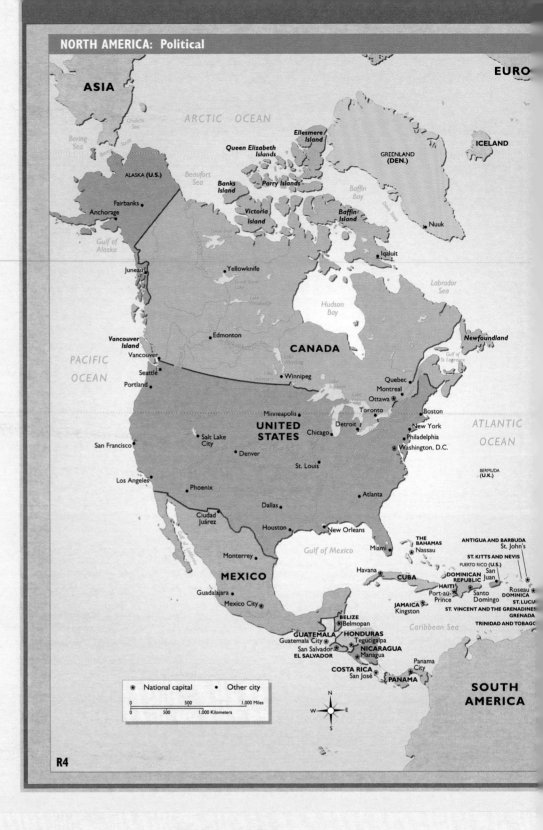

EURO

ASIA

ARCTIC OCEAN

Chukchi Sea

Bering Sea

Ellesmere Island

Queen Elizabeth Islands

GREENLAND (DEN.)

ICELAND

ALASKA (U.S.)

Beaufort Sea

Banks Island

Parry Islands

Baffin Bay

Fairbanks

Anchorage

Victoria Island

Baffin Island

Davis Strait

Nuuk

Gulf of Alaska

Iqaluit

Juneau

Yellowknife

Labrador Sea

Great Bear Lake

Hudson Bay

Vancouver Island

Edmonton

CANADA

Newfoundland

Vancouver

Gulf of St. Lawrence

PACIFIC OCEAN

Seattle

Winnipeg

Quebec

Montreal

Portland

Ottawa ✸

Lake Superior

Toronto

Boston

ATLANTIC OCEAN

Minneapolis

Detroit

New York

UNITED STATES

Chicago

Philadelphia

San Francisco

Salt Lake City

Washington, D.C. ✸

Denver

St. Louis

BERMUDA (U.K.)

Los Angeles

Phoenix

Atlanta

Dallas

Ciudad Juárez

Houston

New Orleans

THE BAHAMAS

ANTIGUA AND BARBUDA
St. John's

Miami

Nassau

ST. KITTS AND NEVIS

Monterrey

Gulf of Mexico

Havana

PUERTO RICO (U.S.)

CUBA

DOMINICAN REPUBLIC

San Juan

MEXICO

HAITI

Roseau

Guadalajara

Port-au-Prince

Santo Domingo

DOMINICA

ST. LUCIA

Mexico City ✸

JAMAICA

Kingston

ST. VINCENT AND THE GRENADINES

GRENADA

BELIZE

✸ Belmopan

TRINIDAD AND TOBAGO

GUATEMALA

HONDURAS

Caribbean Sea

Guatemala City ✸

Tegucigalpa

San Salvador ✸

NICARAGUA

EL SALVADOR

Managua

Panama City

COSTA RICA

San José ✸

PANAMA

SOUTH AMERICA

✸ National capital   • Other city

0   500   1,000 Miles
0 500 1,000 Kilometers

N
W   E
S

R4

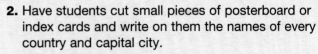

North America: Political Map

ASK ABOUT DISTANCES
GROUP

Objective: To use a map scale to measure distances.

Materials: paper, scissors, pencils, *Geo Big Book*

30 MINUTES OR LONGER

1. Have students cut paper measuring scales based on the map mileage scale in the *Atlas* or *Geo Big Book*.

2. Invite volunteers to pose questions to the class about distances. Students might ask, for example, "How far is it from Washington, D.C., to Managua?" or "How long is the island of Cuba?"

3. Let students who find the answer ask the next question. Be sure to give every student a chance to ask questions.

PLAY A NAME GAME
PARTNER

Objective: To recognize countries and capitals in North America and Central America.

Materials: posterboard, scissors, pens, *Outline Map*

30 MINUTES OR LONGER

1. Enlarge a copy of the North America *Outline Map* or draw your own map, omitting the city and country names. Paste it onto a piece of posterboard.

2. Have students cut small pieces of posterboard or index cards and write on them the names of every country and capital city.

3. To play, partners can shuffle the cards and place them face down. They can take turns choosing cards and placing them on the appropriate country.

The **Geo Big Book**, with dry markers, may be used with all Atlas Activities.

Caribbean Sea

Barranquilla
Maracaibo
Valencia
Caracas

CENTRAL
AMERICA

VENEZUELA

Georgetown
Paramaribo
Cayenne

Medellín

GUYANA

Bogotá

SURINAME
FRENCH
GUIANA
(FR.)

Cali

COLOMBIA

Quito

ECUADOR

Guayaquil

Manaus

Belém

Iquitos

PERU

Recife

Trujillo

Callao
Lima

BRAZIL

Cuzco

Salvador
(Bahía)

Arequipa

BOLIVIA

La Paz

Brasília

Sucre

Belo
Horizonte

PACIFIC
OCEAN

PARAGUAY

Antofagasta

Rio de Janeiro

Tucumán

São Paulo

Asunción

CHILE

ATLANTIC
OCEAN

Pôrto Alegre

Córdoba

Rosario

Valparaíso

URUGUAY

Santiago

Buenos Aires

Montevideo

ARGENTINA

Rio de la Plata

Concepción

| ⊛ | National capital | • | Other city |

N
W—E
S

0   250   500 Miles
0 250 500 Kilometers

FALKLAND
ISLANDS
(U.K.)

Strait of Magellan

Punta Arenas

SOUTH GEORGIA
(U.K.)

R5

South America: Political Map

FIND CITIES IN SOUTH AMERICA

Objective: To practice reading map keys.

Materials: chalkboard or chart paper, *Geo Big Book*

1. As students look at the map in the *Atlas* or *Geo Big Book,* have them name countries in South America. Write their suggestions in a horizontal line on the chalkboard or on chart paper.

2. Ask students to tell you the names of capital cities in each country as you write them under the country names. Have students explain how they used the map key to find the capital.

3. Have students locate other cities in each country. Write their suggestions on the chart.

MAKE A PUZZLE

Objective: To practice map-making skills.

Materials: paper, crayons, scissors, boxes

1. Have groups make jigsaw puzzles of South America. Have students draw the outline of South America, draw country boundaries (and color each country differently), and label countries and capitals.

2. Have students cut apart the paper to make puzzle pieces. Ask some groups to cut the puzzle along the lines of country boundaries. Have others cut the puzzle randomly.

3. Invite students to assemble their puzzles. Have them exchange puzzles with another group.

The **Geo Big Book**, with dry markers, may be used with all Atlas Activities.

R5

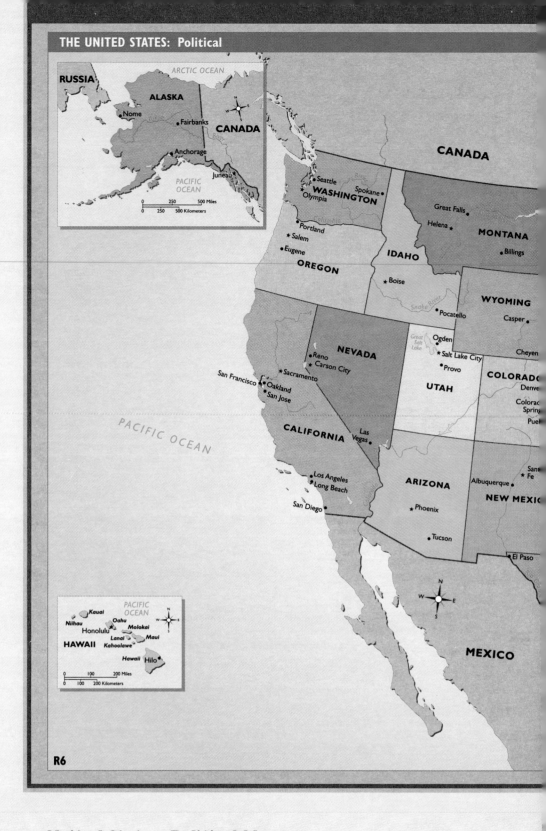

THE UNITED STATES: Political

RUSSIA

ALASKA

ARCTIC OCEAN

• Nome
• Fairbanks

CANADA

• Anchorage

Juneau

PACIFIC
OCEAN

0   250   500 Miles
0 250 500 Kilometers

CANADA

• Seattle   Spokane •
★ Olympia
WASHINGTON

Great Falls •

Helena ★

MONTANA

• Billings

• Portland
★ Salem
• Eugene

OREGON

IDAHO

• Boise

Snake River

WYOMING

• Pocatello

Casper •

Great
Salt
Lake

Ogden •
★ Salt Lake City
• Provo

Cheyen

COLORADO

• Reno
★ Carson City

NEVADA

UTAH

Denve

San Francisco
★ Sacramento
• Oakland
• San Jose

Colorac
Sprin

Pue

PACIFIC OCEAN

CALIFORNIA

Las
Vegas •

• Los Angeles
• Long Beach

San Diego •

ARIZONA

• Phoenix

Albuquerque •

San
★ Fe

NEW MEXIC

PACIFIC
OCEAN

• Kauai
Niihau   Oahu   Molokai
Honolulu   Lanai   Maui
Kahoolawe
HAWAII   Hawaii   Hilo

0   100   200 Miles
0   100   200 Kilometers

• Tucson

El Paso •

MEXICO

R6

United States: Political Map

PARTNER

READ THE MAP
Objective: To read map symbols and recognize state capitals.
Materials: pencil, prepared lists of states

30 MINUTES
OR LONGER

1. Prepare worksheets with the names of the fifty states.

2. Discuss the meaning of the map symbols.

3. Ask students to write the name of the capital city next to the name of each state on their worksheet.

4. Invite partners to choose two states. Have them write short rhymes to help remember the name of the capital. Ask students to teach their rhymes to the class to help all students remember state capital names.

GROUP

HOW FAR IS IT?
Objective: To use a map scale to measure distances.
Materials: paper, scissors, *Geo Big Book*

1. Have students make measuring strips based on the map scale in the *Atlas* or *Geo Big Book*.

30 MINUTES
OR LONGER

2. Ask them to write a list of 10 distances they would like to find out. Students may want to know, for example, the length of a state, the distance between their community and Washington, D.C., or the length of the entire United States.

3. Have students work in groups to measure the distances and write them in chart form to share with the class.

The **Geo Big Book**, with dry markers, may be used with all Atlas Activities.

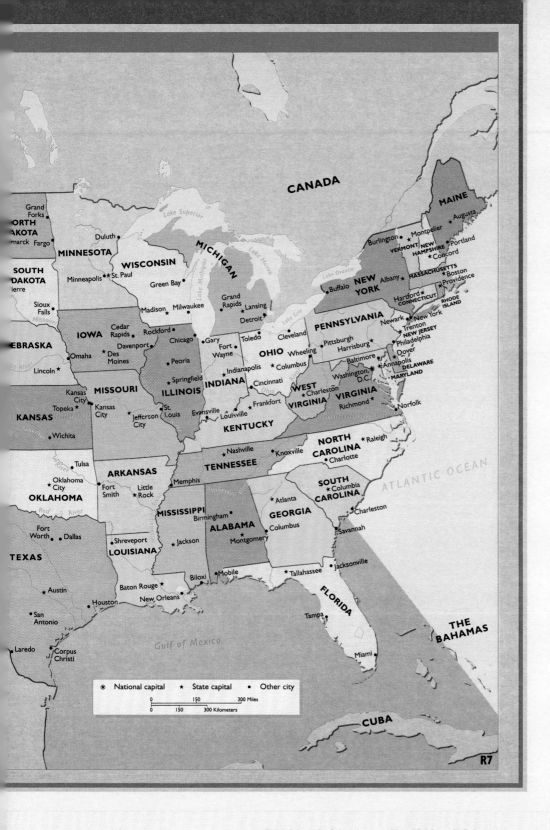

United States: Political Map

MARK THE PORTS

Objective: To develop map symbols.

Materials: tracing paper, pencils, desk map

30 MINUTES OR LONGER

1. Trace the outline of the United States and its major rivers and bays or use the *Desk Maps.* Hand out copies to the class.

2. Ask partners or groups to invent a symbol to signify a port city. Have them draw symbols on their maps to show New York City, New Orleans, Los Angeles, San Francisco, Washington, D.C., Boston, Seattle, Miami, and Galveston.

3. Ask volunteers to explain why cities probably were built in these locations.

MAKE A STATE MAP

Objective: To practice making political maps.

Materials: chart paper, marker

GROUP

30 MINUTES OR LONGER

1. Review the concept of state and local government. Remind students that each state is divided into political regions called counties.

2. Using a library map as your guide, make a large outline map of your state and work with groups of students to draw the political boundaries. Be sure students understand which states border yours, which county they live in, the names of bordering counties, and which county houses the state government.

The **Geo Big Book**, with dry markers, may be used with all Atlas Activities.

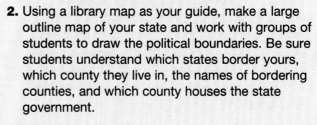

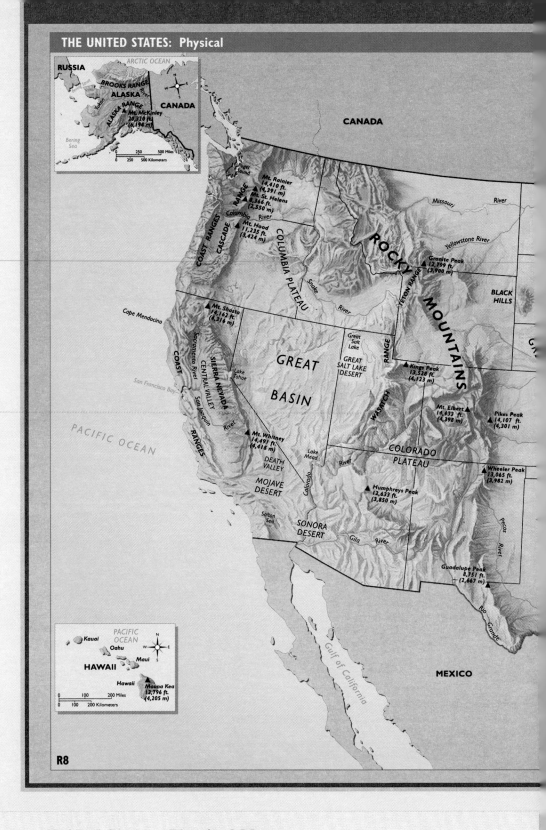

THE UNITED STATES: Physical

ARCTIC OCEAN

RUSSIA

BROOKS RANGE

ALASKA

CANADA

ALASKA RANGE

Mt. McKinley
20,320 ft.
(6,194 m)

Bering
Sea

CANADA

Mt. Rainier
14,410 ft.
(4,391 m)

Mt. St. Helens
8,366 ft.
(2,550 m)

COAST RANGES

CASCADE RANGE

Columbia River

Mt. Hood
11,235 ft.
(3,424 m)

COLUMBIA PLATEAU

Snake River

Missouri   River

ROCKY MOUNTAINS

Yellowstone River

Granite Peak
12,799 ft.
(3,900 m)

TETON RANGE

BLACK
HILLS

Cape Mendocino

Mt. Shasta
14,162 ft.
(4,316 m)

Great
Salt
Lake

GREAT
SALT LAKE
DESERT

RANGE

Kings Peak
13,528 ft.
(4,123 m)

WASATCH

Sacramento River

COAST

SIERRA NEVADA

CENTRAL VALLEY

Lake
Tahoe

GREAT

BASIN

San Joaquin   River

Mt. Elbert
14,433 ft.
(4,398 m)

Pikes Peak
14,107 ft.
(4,301 m)

San Francisco Bay

PACIFIC OCEAN

Mt. Whitney
14,491 ft.
(4,418 m)

DEATH
VALLEY

Lake
Mead

Colorado   River

COLORADO
PLATEAU

RANGES

MOJAVE
DESERT

Colorado

Humphreys Peak
12,633 ft.
(3,850 m)

Wheeler Peak
13,065 ft.
(3,982 m)

Pecos   River

Salton
Sea

SONORA
DESERT

Gila   River

Guadalupe Peak
8,751 ft.
(2,667 m)

Rio Grande

Gulf of California

MEXICO

PACIFIC
OCEAN

Kauai

Oahu

Maui

HAWAII

Hawaii

Maona Kea
13,796 ft.
(4,205 m)

0   100   200 Miles
0   100   200 Kilometers

R8

United States: Physical Map

ON
YOUR
OWN

15 TO 30
MINUTES

EXPLORING NATURAL BORDERS

Objective: To compare physical and political maps.

1. Have students study the map to find and describe state boundaries created by rivers and lakes. They can glance at the United States political map on pages R6–R7 to find state names. (Examples include borders created by the Mississippi, Missouri, Chatta-hoochee, Savannah, Delaware, Potomac, Ohio, Columbia, and Colorado rivers, and Lake Michigan.)

2. You may also want to have students list the states that contain major landforms such as the Rocky Mountains, the Great Plains, and the Appalachian Mountains.

PARTNER

30 MINUTES
OR LONGER

VISUALIZE GEOGRAPHY

Objective: To visualize geographical terms.

Materials: paper, crayons or paints, *Geo Big Book*

1. Assign pairs of students a geographical term from the physical map in the *Atlas* or *Geo Big Book*. Terms may be unfamiliar (*cape, range, strait, gulf*) or familiar (*mountain, plain, river, plateau*).

2. Ask students to look up unfamiliar terms in an encyclopedia. Have all students draw pictures of the landforms or bodies of water described.

3. As you study the map with students, read the names of geographic areas and ask students to hold up the appropriate illustrations.

The **Geo Big Book**, with dry markers, may be used with all Atlas Activities.

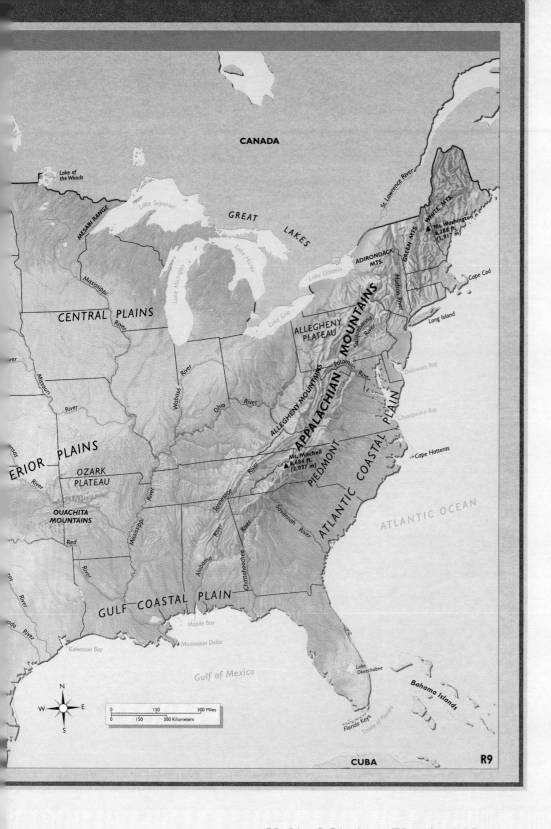

Map labels:
CANADA
Lake of the Woods
Lake Superior
GREAT LAKES
MESABI RANGE
Mississippi River
Lake Michigan
Lake Huron
Lake Erie
Lake Ontario
St. Lawrence River
GREEN MTS.
WHITE MTS.
▲ Mt. Washington 6,288 ft. (1,917 m)
Cape Cod
ADIRONDACK MTS.
Hudson River
Long Island
CENTRAL PLAINS
Missouri River
Wabash River
Ohio River
ALLEGHENY PLATEAU
ALLEGHENY MOUNTAINS
APPALACHIAN MOUNTAINS
Susquehanna River
Potomac River
Delaware Bay
ERIOR PLAINS
OZARK PLATEAU
OUACHITA MOUNTAINS
Red River
Arkansas River
Mississippi River
Tennessee River
▲ Mt. Mitchell 6,684 ft. (2,037 m)
PIEDMONT
Chesapeake Bay
Cape Hatteras
ATLANTIC COASTAL PLAIN
ATLANTIC OCEAN
Savannah River
Alabama River
Chattahoochee River
GULF COASTAL PLAIN
Mobile Bay
Mississippi Delta
Galveston Bay
Colorado River
Gulf of Mexico
Lake Okeechobee
Bahama Islands
Florida Keys
Straits of Florida
N W E S
0 150 300 Miles
0 150 300 Kilometers
CUBA
R9

United States: Physical Map

TRAVEL OVER LAND AND SEA

Objective: To link geography with history.

ON YOUR OWN

Materials: tracing paper, crayons or colored pencils

30 MINUTES OR LONGER

1. Have groups of students trace the physical map, using crayons or colored pencils to indicate different landforms and bodies of water.

2. Have groups draw one of the following routes on their map: the Oregon Trail, the Pony Express, the Transcontinental Railroad.

3. Invite group members to share their maps with the class and point out the route they drew. Ask them to explain how the different geographic features along the route might have helped or hindered travelers.

HAVE FUN WITH GEOGRAPHY

Objective: To relate geography to everyday life.

ON YOUR OWN

Materials: mural paper, paints, crayons

30 MINUTES OR LONGER

1. On mural paper draw the outline of the United States. Draw simple outlines of mountain ranges, deserts, lakes, and rivers. Invite students to color in these areas and the oceans, adding drawings of trees and other symbols of terrain and vegetation.

2. Have students brainstorm ways to have fun in different geographical regions. Have them draw small pictures of people having fun. Cut out the pictures and paste them onto the mural map in the appropriate areas.

The **Geo Big Book**, with dry markers, may be used with all Atlas Activities.

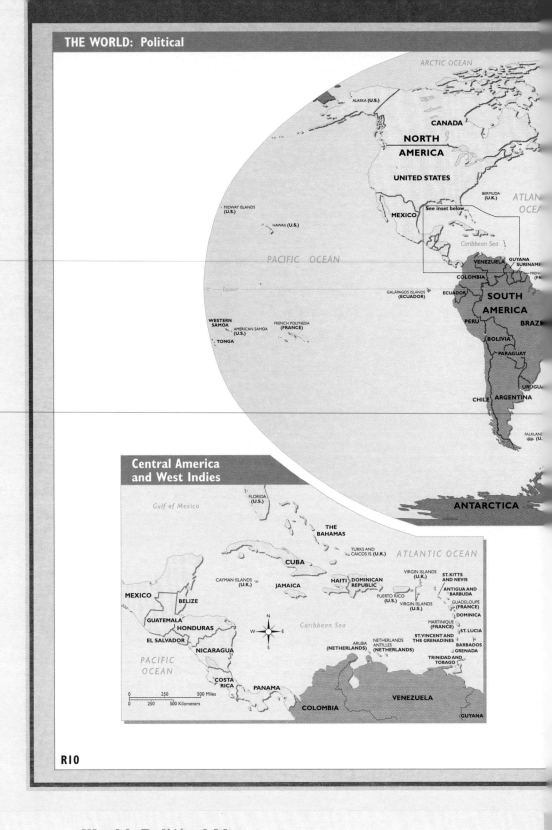

THE WORLD: Political

ARCTIC OCEAN

ALASKA (U.S.)

CANADA

NORTH AMERICA

UNITED STATES

BERMUDA (U.K.)

ATLANTIC OCEAN

MIDWAY ISLANDS (U.S.)

MEXICO

See inset below

HAWAII (U.S.)

Caribbean Sea

VENEZUELA   GUYANA   SURINAME

FRENCH (FR.)

COLOMBIA

PACIFIC OCEAN

Equator

GALÁPAGOS ISLANDS (ECUADOR)

ECUADOR

SOUTH AMERICA

WESTERN SAMOA

AMERICAN SAMOA (U.S.)

FRENCH POLYNESIA (FRANCE)

PERU

BRAZIL

BOLIVIA

TONGA

PARAGUAY

URUGUAY

CHILE   ARGENTINA

FALKLAND (U.

ANTARCTICA

Central America and West Indies

FLORIDA (U.S.)

Gulf of Mexico

THE BAHAMAS

TURKS AND CAICOS IS. (U.K.)

ATLANTIC OCEAN

CUBA

VIRGIN ISLANDS (U.K.)   ST. KITTS AND NEVIS

CAYMAN ISLANDS (U.K.)

JAMAICA

HAITI   DOMINICAN REPUBLIC

PUERTO RICO (U.S.)   VIRGIN ISLANDS (U.S.)

ANTIGUA AND BARBUDA

GUADELOUPE (FRANCE)

DOMINICA

MEXICO

BELIZE

MARTINIQUE (FRANCE)   ST. LUCIA

GUATEMALA

HONDURAS

Caribbean Sea

EL SALVADOR

ST. VINCENT AND THE GRENADINES

NICARAGUA

ARUBA (NETHERLANDS)

NETHERLANDS ANTILLES (NETHERLANDS)

BARBADOS

GRENADA

PACIFIC OCEAN

TRINIDAD AND TOBAGO

0   250   500 Miles

0   250   500 Kilometers

COSTA RICA

PANAMA

VENEZUELA

COLOMBIA

GUYANA

R10

World: Political Map

GROUP

15 TO 30 MINUTES

WHERE IN THE WORLD?

Objective: To practice using directions.

Materials: Geo Big Book

1. Invite students to play "Where in the World?" using the World Map in the *Atlas* or *Geo Big Book*. The game begins with one student making a statement such as, "I am thinking of a country located in a big continent northeast of Africa."

2. To narrow their choices, guessing students can ask *yes* or *no* questions concerning directions. For example: "Is the country south of China?"

3. Invite the student who guesses correctly to choose another mystery country.

PARTNER

15 TO 30 MINUTES

BEYOND THE BORDERS

Objective: To understand political boundaries.

Materials: pencil, paper, Geo Big Book

1. If available, display the *Geo Big Book* for this activity. Direct students' attention to the Abbreviation Key. Explain that some countries' political borders include islands or territories which lie far away from the mainland.

2. Have pairs of students study the map and list islands and/or territories that belong to the U.S., the U.K., France, Italy, Spain, and the Netherlands.

3. Have students use the map scale to measure the distance between the territories and mother countries.

The **Geo Big Book**, with dry markers, may be used with all Atlas Activities.

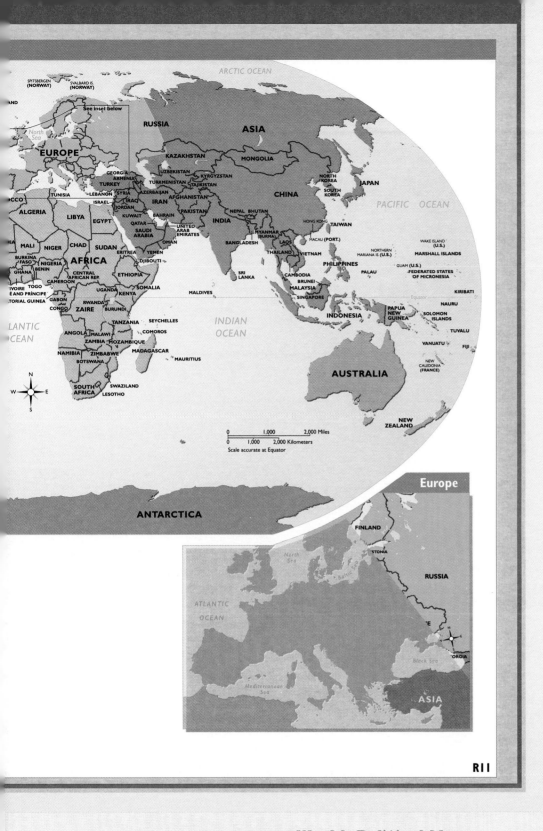

ARCTIC OCEAN

SPITSBERGEN
(NORWAY)

SVALBARD IS.
(NORWAY)

RUSSIA

ASIA

See inset below

North
Sea

EUROPE

KAZAKHSTAN

MONGOLIA

GEORGIA
ARMENIA
TURKEY

UZBEKISTAN
KYRGYZSTAN

NORTH
KOREA

JAPAN

TUNISIA

LEBANON
ISRAEL
JORDAN

SYRIA
AZERBAIJAN
IRAQ
IRAN

TURKMENISTAN
TAJIKISTAN

AFGHANISTAN

KUWAIT
BAHRAIN
QATAR

PAKISTAN

CHINA

SOUTH
KOREA

TAIWAN

PACIFIC   OCEAN

ALGERIA

LIBYA

EGYPT

SAUDI
ARABIA

UNITED
ARAB
EMIRATES

OMAN

NEPAL

INDIA

BHUTAN

HONG KONG

MACAU (PORT.)

WAKE ISLAND
(U.S.)

MALI

NIGER

CHAD

SUDAN

ERITREA

YEMEN

BANGLADESH

MYANMAR
(BURMA)

LAOS

NORTHERN
MARIANA IS. (U.S.)

MARSHALL ISLANDS

BURKINA
FASO

NIGERIA

AFRICA

DJIBOUTI

THAILAND

VIETNAM

GUAM (U.S.)

GHANA

BENIN

CENTRAL
AFRICAN REP.

ETHIOPIA

SRI
LANKA

CAMBODIA

PHILIPPINES

PALAU

FEDERATED STATES
OF MICRONESIA

IVOIRE
É AND PRINCIPE

CAMEROON

UGANDA

SOMALIA

BRUNEI

TORIAL GUINEA

GABON

RWANDA

KENYA

MALDIVES

MALAYSIA

SINGAPORE

KIRIBATI

CONGO

ZAIRE

BURUNDI

NAURU

LANTIC
OCEAN

TANZANIA

SEYCHELLES

INDIAN
OCEAN

INDONESIA

PAPUA
NEW
GUINEA

SOLOMON
ISLANDS

ANGOLA

MALAWI

COMOROS

Equator

TUVALU

ZAMBIA

MOZAMBIQUE

VANUATU

FIJI

NAMIBIA

ZIMBABWE

MADAGASCAR

MAURITIUS

NEW
CALEDONIA
(FRANCE)

BOTSWANA

N

SOUTH
AFRICA

SWAZILAND

LESOTHO

AUSTRALIA

W   E

S

0   1,000   2,000 Miles

0   1,000   2,000 Kilometers

NEW
ZEALAND

Scale accurate at Equator

ANTARCTICA

Europe

FINLAND

North
Sea

STONIA

RUSSIA

ATLANTIC
OCEAN

Baltic Sea

E

ORGIA

Black Sea

Mediterranean
Sea

ASIA

R11

World: Political Map

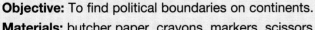
COUNTRIES AND CONTINENTS

Objective: To find political boundaries on continents.

Materials: butcher paper, crayons, markers, scissors

30 MINUTES
OR LONGER

1. On butcher paper, draw large proportional outlines of the continents and cut them out. Divide the class into small groups and give one paper continent to each group.

2. Have each group outline the political borders on one continent and color in each country with its own identifying color.

3. Exhibit the world map by reassembling it on a blue background.

MAP A TRIP

Objective: To measure and comprehend distances.

Materials: paper, pencils, ruler, *Desk Map*, markers

1. Have students draw a simple map of the world or use the *Desk Map.* Then have them mark at least seven capital cities to visit on a "world tour."

2. Have students number the cities in the order they will be visited and draw lines connecting them. Then have students use the map scale to mark the approximate mileage between locations. Explain that traveling about 1000 miles by jet takes about 2 hours, and have students write down the approximate travel time. Tell them to write a daily itinerary.

30 MINUTES
OR LONGER

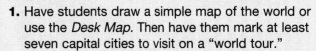

The **Geo Big Book**, with dry markers, may be used with all Atlas Activities.

Dictionary of GEOGRAPHIC TERMS

HILL (hil) Rounded, raised landform; not as high as a mountain.

GULF (gulf) Body of water partly surrounded by land; larger than a bay.

PENINSULA (pə nin'sə lə) Land that has water on all sides but one.

MESA (mā'sə) Landform that looks like a high, flat table.

LAKE (lāk) Body of water completely surrounded by land.

PLAIN (plān) Large area of flat land.

PORT (pôrt) Place where ships load and unload goods.

CANAL (kə nal') Waterway dug across the land to connect two bodies of water.

BAY (bā) Body of water partly surrounded by land.

HARBOR (här'bər) Protected place by an ocean or river where ships can safely stay.

BEACH (bēch) Land covered with sand or pebbles next to an ocean or lake.

ISLAND (i'lənd) Land that is surrounded on all sides by water.

MOUNTAIN (moun′tən) High landform with steep sides; higher than a hill.

CANYON (kan′yən) Deep river valley with steep sides.

VALLEY (val′ē) Area of low land between hills or mountains.

RIVER (ri′vər) Long stream of water that empties into another body of water.

PLATEAU (pla tō′) High flat area that rises steeply above the surrounding land.

COAST (kōst) Land next to an ocean.

CLIFF (klif) High steep face of rock.

OCEAN (ō′shən) A large body of salt water.

Gazetteer

This Gazetteer is a geographical dictionary that will help you to pronounce and locate the places discussed in this book. The page numbers tell you where each place appears on a map or in the text.

A

Africa (af′ri kə) A continent located in the Eastern and Southern hemispheres. (m. G5, t. 59)

Antarctica (ant ärk′ti kə) A continent in the Southern Hemisphere. (m. G5)

Arctic Ocean (ärk′tik ō′shən) A large body of water located in the Northern Hemisphere. (m. G5)

Argentina (är jən tē′nə) A country in southern South America. (m. 322, t. 322)

Asia (ā′zhə) A continent in the Eastern and Northern hemispheres. (m. G5, t. 292)

Atlantic Ocean (at lan′tik ō′shən) A large body of water located to the east of North and South America. (m. G5, t. 37)

Australia (ôs trāl′yə) An island continent in the Southern Hemisphere between the Pacific and Indian oceans. (m. G5, t. 322)

B

Baltimore (bôl′tə môr) Port city on the Chesapeake Bay in the state of Maryland. (m. 243, t. 252)

Belgium (bel′jəm) A country in Western Europe on the North Sea. (m. 257)

Bothell (bäth′əl) A suburban community near Seattle, Washington. (t. 18)

Brazil (brə zil′) The largest country in South America. (m. R5, t. 299)

C

Calais (ka lā) City that is connecting point for English Channel Tunnel in France. (m. 257)

Canada (kan′ə də) A very large country located in the northern part of North America, bordering the United States. (m. 211, t. 321)

Capitol (kap′i təl) The building in Washington, D.C., where Congress meets. (m. 171, t. 171)

Chesapeake Bay (ches′ə pēk bā) A bay, partly enclosed by Maryland and Virginia. (m. 99, t. 99)

Chicago (shi kä′gō) A port city in northeastern Illinois. It is the largest city in the state. (m. 23, t. 227)

Colombia (kə ləm′bē ə) A country in the northwestern part of South America. (m. R5, t. 323)

Cuajimalpa (kwä hē mäl′pə) A suburban community near Mexico City, Mexico. (t. 25)

Cumberland (kəm′bər lənd) The most eastern city on the National Road. It is located in Maryland. (m. 243, t. 248)

pronunciation key

a	at	ī	ice	u	up	th	thin
ā	ape	îr	pierce	ū	use	th	this
ä	far	o	hot	ü	rule	zh	measure
âr	care	ō	old	ù	pull	ə	about, taken,
e	end	ô	fork	ûr	turn		pencil, lemon,
ē	me	oi	oil	hw	white		circus
i	it	ou	out	ng	song		

D

Dakar (dä kär') The capital and largest city in the country of Senegal. (m. 179, t. 178)

Detroit (di troit') The largest city in Michigan. It is an important automobile manufacturing center. (m. 23, t. 312)

E

Eastern Hemisphere (ēs'tərn hem'is fîr) The half of Earth east of the Atlantic Ocean that includes Europe, Africa, Asia and Australia. (m. 58, t. 58)

Ellis Island (el'is ī'lənd) A small island located near New York City. It was the first stop for millions of immigrants who came to the United States from 1892 to 1954. (t. 219)

England (ing'glənd) Part of the United Kingdom, an island country off the continent of Europe. (m. 257, t. 256)

English Channel (ing'glish chan'əl) A narrow waterway between England and France. It connects the Atlantic Ocean and the North Sea. (m. 257, t. 256)

Equator (i kwā'tər) An imaginary line around the middle of Earth between the Northern Hemisphere and the Southern Hemisphere. (m. G4, t. G4)

Erie Canal (îr'ē kə nal') A narrow waterway located in New York State connecting the Hudson River with Lake Erie. (m. 249, t. 248)

Europe (yùr əp) The smallest of Earth's seven continents. (m. G5, t. 256)

F

Folkestone (fōk'stən) City that is the connecting point for the English Channel Tunnel in England. (m. 257)

Four Corners (fôr kôr'nərz) The only place in the United States where four states meet. The states are Arizona, New Mexico, Utah, and Colorado. (m. 79, t. 78)

France (frans) A country in western Europe on the Atlantic Ocean and the Mediterranean Sea. (m. 257, t. 256)

G

Galveston (gal'və stən) A port city located on the Gulf of Mexico in the southeast part of Texas. (m. 10, t. 9)

H

Hudson River (hud' sən riv'ər) A river that flows in the eastern part of New York State. (m. 249, t. 243)

I

Independence (in di pen'dəns) A community in Missouri that marked the beginning of the Oregon Trail in the 1840s. (m. 211, t. 211)

India (in'dē ə) A country located in South Asia. (R11, t. 234)

Indian Ocean (in'dē ən ō'shən) A large body of water located east of Africa. (m. G5)

Italy (it'ə lē) A country in southern Europe. (m. 322, t. 322)

J

Jamestown (jāmz'toun) A community in southeastern Virginia along the James River. Settled in 1607, it was the first permanent English colony established in North America. (m. 99, t. 98)

Jamestown Settlement (jāmz'toun set'əl mənt) A living history museum showing how the English colonists and the Powhatan lived in the 1600s. (t. 108)

R15

Japan (jə pan') A country of islands in the Pacific Ocean off the eastern coast of Asia. (m. 293, t. 292)

Jefferson Memorial (jef'ər sən mə môr'ē əl) A building in Washington, D.C. dedicated to the memory of President Thomas Jefferson. It was completed in 1943. (t. 172)

L

Lafayette Park (läf ē et' pärk) A public park located near the White House in Washington, D.C. (m. 176, t. 174)

Lake Erie (lāk îr'ē) The most southern of the five Great Lakes. It is located on the border between Canada and the United States. (m. 41, t. 248)

Lake Huron (lāk hyür'ən) The second largest of the five Great Lakes. It is located on the border between Canada and the United States. (m. 41)

Lake Michigan (lāk mish'ə gən) The third largest of the five Great Lakes. It is located between the states of Michigan and Wisconsin. (m. 41)

Lake Ontario (lāk on târ'ē ō) The smallest of the five Great Lakes. It is located on the border between Canada and the United States. (m. 41)

Lake Superior (lāk sə pîr'ē ər) The largest of the five Great Lakes. It is located on the border between Canada and the United States. (m. 41)

Lincoln Memorial (ling'kən mə môr'ē əl) A building in Washington, D.C., that honors President Abraham Lincoln. (m. 176, t. 173)

M

Mesa Verde (mā'sə vûr'dē) The ruins of an Anasazi community built into the side of a cliff and located in the southwestern part of the state of Colorado (m. 79, t. 80)

Mesa Verde National Park (mā'sə vûr'dē nash'ə nəl pärk) A national park in the state of Colorado that was an Anasazi community long ago. (m. 89, t. 88)

Mexico (mek'si kō) A country in North America that borders the southern United States. (m. 25, t. 24)

Mexico City (mek'si kō sit'ē) The capital of Mexico. (m. 25, t. 25)

Mississippi River (mis ə sip'ē riv'ər) One of the longest rivers in North America. It flows south from northern Minnesota into the Gulf of Mexico. (m. 40-41, t. 37)

N

National Mall (nash'ə nəl môl) An area in Washington, D.C. where many monuments, memorial, museums, and government buildings are located. (m. 176-177, t. 176)

National Road (nash'ə nəl rōd) A highway built in the 1800s that ran from Cumberland, Maryland to Vandalia, Illinois. It opened the way for people to move west. (m. 243, t. 243)

New England (nü ing'glənd) The northeastern part of the United States. It includes Maine, Vermont, New Hampshire, Massachusetts, Connecticut, and Rhode Island. (m. 187, t. 187)

New Orleans (nü ôr'lē ənz) The largest city in the state of Louisiana. It is an important Mississippi River port. (m. R7, t. 17)

New York City (nü yôrk sit'ē) The largest city in the United States, located in southeastern New York. (m. 249, t. 218)

Nigeria (nī jîr'ē ə) A country in West Africa. (m. 322, t. 234)

North America (nôrth ə mer'i kə) A continent in the Northern and Western hemispheres. (m. G5, t. 59)

R16

Northern Hemisphere (nôr′thərn hem′i sfîr) The half of Earth north of the equator. (m. 59, t. 58)

North Pole (nôrth pōl) The place farthest north on Earth. (m. G5)

Norton (nôr′tən) A farming community in northern Kansas. (m. 302, t. 300)

O

Oakland (ōk′lənd) A port city in western California. It is on San Francisco Bay directly opposite the city of San Francisco. (m. R6, t. 195)

Oregon City (ôr′i gən sit′ē) A city located in the northwestern part of Oregon. In the 1840s it marked the end of the Oregon Trail. (m. 211, t. 214)

Oregon Trail (ôr′i gən trāl) A route that pioneers used in their move west in the 1840s. It ran from Independence, Missouri to Oregon City, Oregon. (m. 211, t. 211)

P

Pacific Ocean (pə sif′ik ō′shən) A large body of salt water bordering the west side of the United States. (m. G5, t. 37)

Paracas (pə räk′əs) A fishing community located in the country of Peru in South America. (m. 53, t. 52)

Peru (pə rü′) A country on the western coast of South America. (m. 53, t. 52)

Philadelphia (fil ə del′fē ə) A port city in southeastern Pennsylvania. It is the largest city in the state. (m. 147, t. 146)

Phillipines (fil′ə pēnz) An island country located in Southeast Asia, separated from the mainland by the South China Sea. (m. R11, t. 323)

Poland (pō′lənd) A country in Eastern Europe on the Baltic Sea. (m. R11, t. 234)

Portland (pôrt′lənd) A port city in northwestern Oregon on the Columbia River. (m. R6, t. 194)

R

Raleigh (rô′lē) The capital city of the state of North Carolina. (m. 275, t. 274)

River Walk (riv′ər wôk) A riverside park along the San Antonio River in Texas. It has sidewalks, trees, restaurants, and shops. (m. 120, t. 118)

Rochester (räch′ə stər) A rural farming community located in northern Indiana. (m. 23, t. 19)

Rocky Mountains (rok′ē moun′tənz) The longest mountain range in North America. It stretches from Alaska into Mexico. (m. 40, t. 38)

Russia (rush′ə) A country in Eastern Europe and Northern Asia. (m. 322, t. 322)

S

Sacramento (sak rə men′tō) The capital of the state of California. It also served as the western-most stop on the route of the pony express. (m. 251, t. 251)

St. Joseph (sānt jō′zef) A city in Missouri that was the eastern-most stop on the route of the pony express. (m. 251, t. 251)

R17

San Antonio (san an tō′nē ō) A port city located in south Texas, connected to the Gulf of Mexico by the San Antonio River. (m. 120, t. 118)

San Antonio River (san an tō′nē ō riv′ər) A river that flows southeast from the city of San Antonio, Texas, into the Gulf of Mexico. (m. 120, t. 118)

San Diego (san dē ā′gō) A port city in southern California. (m. 126, t. 232)

Senegal (sen′i gôl) A country in western Africa. (m. 179, t. 178)

Shapleigh (shap′lē) A rural community in the state of Maine. (m. 187, t. 187)

South America (south ə mer′i kə) A continent in the Southern and Western hemispheres. (m. G5, t. 52)

Southern Hemisphere (suth′ərn hem′i sfîr) The half of Earth south of the equator. (m. 59, t. 58)

South Pole (south pōl) The place farthest south on Earth. (m. G5)

T

Tampa (tam′pə) A port city in west-central Florida on the Gulf of Mexico. (m. R7, t. 193)

Tokyo (tō′kyō) The capital of Japan and its largest city. (m. 293, t. 292)

Toms River (tomz riv′ər) A suburban community in the state of New Jersey. (m. 329, t. 329)

V

Vandalia (vân dal′ē ə) The western-most city on the National Road. It is located in the state of Illinois. (m. 243, t. 248)

Veracruz (ver ə krüz′) A port city on the eastern coast of Mexico. (t. 232)

Vietnam Veterans Memorial (vē et näm′ vet′ər ənz mə môr′ē əl) A place in Washington, D.C., that has the names of more than 58,000 Americans who died in the Vietnam War. (m. 176, t. 173)

Virginia (vər jin′yə) A southern state on the Atlantic Ocean. It was one of the original 13 colonies. (m. 99, t. 98)

W

Washington, D.C. (wô′shing tən) Capital city of the United States. (m. 171, t. 168)

Washington Monument (wô′shing tən mon′yə mənt) A tall tower in Washington, D.C., that honors President George Washington. (m. 176, t. 172)

Western Hemisphere (wes′tərn hem′i sfîr) The half of Earth that includes North and South America. (m. 58, t. 58)

White House (hwīt hous) The home of the President of the United States, located in Washington, D.C. (m. 171, t. 166)

Biographical Dictionary

Biographical Dictionary

The Biographical Dictionary tells you about the people you have learned about in this book. The Pronunciation Key tells you how to say their names. The page numbers let you see where each person first appears in the text.

Adams, Abigail (ad′əmz), 1744–1818 Wife of President John Adams and mother of another president, John Quincy Adams. (p. 166)

Adams, John (ad′əmz), 1735–1826 The second President of the United States, 1797-1801. He was the first President to live in the White House. (p. 166)

Banneker, Benjamin (ban′i kər), 1731–1806 Surveyor who helped to draw plans for designing the city of Washington, D.C. in 1791. (p. 168)

Bell, Alexander Graham (bel, al ig zân′dər grā′əm), 1847–1922 Inventor who built the first working telephone in 1876. (p. 252)

Cisneros, Henry (sēs nâr′rōs), 1947– Mayor of San Antonio, Texas, 1981-1989. First person of Mexican heritage to be mayor of a large U.S. city. (p. 128)

Cooper, Peter (kü′pər), 1791-1883 Inventor who built the *Tom Thumb* in 1830, one of the first railroad steam engines. (p. 244)

pronunciation key

a	at	ī	ice		up	th	**th**in
ā	ape	îr	pierce	ū	use	th	**th**is
ä	far	o	hot	ü	rule	zh	measure
âr	care	ō	old	ù	pull	ə	about, taken,
e	end	ô	fork	ûr	turn		pencil, lemon,
ē	me	oi	oil	hw	white		circus
i	it	ou	out	ng	song		

Biographical Dictionary

Earhart, Amelia
(âr′härt, â mēl yuh), 1898–1937 First woman to fly alone across the Atlantic and Pacific oceans. (p. 246)

Ford, Henry (fôrd), 1863–1947 Maker of the Model T car in 1908. He made his cars so that many people could afford them. (p. 245)

Franklin, Benjamin (frang′klin), 1706–1790 American colonial leader, writer, and scientist. (p. 147)

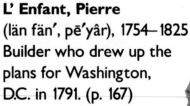

Fulton, Robert (ful′tən), 1765–1815 Inventor who built the *Clermont,* one of the first steamboats, in 1807. (p. 243)

Jefferson, Thomas (jef′ər sən), 1743–1826 Colonial leader who wrote the Declaration of Independence and was third President of the United States. (p. 150)

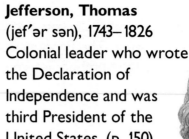
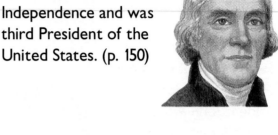

Jemison, Mae (jem′ə sən, mā), 1956– In 1992 she became the first African American woman to travel in space. (p. 246)

King, Martin Luther, Jr. (king), 1929–1968 Leader who worked to make laws fair for all people. (p. 229)

L' Enfant, Pierre (län fän′, pē′yâr), 1754–1825 Builder who drew up the plans for Washington, D.C. in 1791. (p. 167)

Lawrence, Jacob
(lôr'əns), 1917– Artist who made a series of paintings about the Great Migration in 1941. (p. 224)

Lin, Maya Ying (lin, mī'ə ying), 1959– Artist who designed the Vietnam Veterans memorial in Washington, D.C. (p. 174)

Lincoln, Abraham
(ling'kən), 1809–1865 The sixteenth President of the United States, 1861–1865. He led the North during the Civil War and wanted to end slavery. (p. 225)

Lyons, Oren (lī'ənz, ôr'ən), 1931– A teacher and leader of the Iroquois people. (p. 74)

Madison, James
(mad'ə sən), 1751–1836 The fourth President of the United States, 1809–1817. In 1787, he made a plan for three different parts of government. (p. 157)

Marconi, Guglielmo
(mär kō'nē, gül yêl'mō), 1874–1937 Inventor of the wireless telegraph in 1895. (p. 253)

Morse, Samuel (môrs), 1791–1872 Inventor who built one of the earliest telegraphs in 1844. (p. 252)

Otis, Elisha
(ōt'əs, e lī'shə), 1811–1861 He invented an automatic safety clamp in 1852 that led to the first elevators. (p. 246)

pronunciation key

a at; ā ape; ä far; âr care; e end; ē me; i it; ī ice; îr pierce; o hot; ō old; ô fork; oi oil; ou out; u up; ū use; ü rule; ù pull; ûr turn; hw white; ng song; th thin; <u>th</u> this; zh measure; ə about, taken, pencil, lemon, circus

Pocahontas (pō kə hon′təs), 1595?–1617 Daughter of Chief Powhatan who helped the English colony of Jamestown to survive. (p. 105)

Smith, John (smith), 1580?–1631 English colonial leader in Virginia who helped the Jamestown settlement to survive during hard times. (p. 102)

Powhatan (pou ə tan′), 1550?–1618 Chief of the Powhatan who lived on Chesapeake Bay near the English settlement at Jamestown. (p. 102)

Washington, George (wô′shing tən) 1732–1799 The first President of the United States, 1789–1797. During the American Revolution he led the colonial army. (p. 154)

Rolfe, John (rälf), 1585–1622 Leader of Jamestown colony who grew a new kind of tobacco that could be sold for a lot of money. (p. 105)

Wright, Orville (rīt), 1871–1948 With his brother Wilbur, he built the world's first successful airplane. (p. 245)

San Juan, Eduardo (san hwän′, əd währ′dō), 1925–1988 Designer of the vehicle that astronauts drove on the moon in 1971 and 1972. (p. 246)

Wright, Wilbur (rīt), 1867–1912 With his brother Orville, he built the world's first successful airplane. (p. 245)

Glossary

Glossary

This Glossary will help you to pronounce and understand the meanings of the vocabulary in this book. The page number at the end of the definition tells where the word first appears.

A

agriculture (ag'ri kul chər) The business of growing crops and raising animals for food. Farmers are an important part of the **agriculture** business. (p. 301)

almanac (ôl'mə nak) A book that comes out every year with information on many different subjects. *Poor Richard's Almanac* was popular long ago. (p. 148)

ambassador (am bas'ə dər) A person who is sent to represent his or her country in another country. The **ambassador** studies the different cultures of the countries she visits. (p. 178)

American Revolution (ə mer'i kən rev ə lü'shən) The war fought by the American colonies to end English rule, 1775-1783. The American colonies defeated the English in the **American Revolution**. (p. 150)

artifact (är'tə fakt) A human-made object left behind by a group of people who lived long ago. The Anasazi left behind many **artifacts** at Mesa Verde. (p. 87)

assembly line (ə sem'blē līn) A line of workers and machines all working together to make a final product. Airplanes and televisions are two products made on an **assembly line**. (p. 312)

author (ô'thər) The writer of a book or other printed work. An **author** does research before writing a book. (p. 191)

B

bar graph (bär graf) A graph that uses bars of different heights to show amounts of things. The **bar graph** showed the population of three cities in Florida. (p. 134)

bay (bā) A part of a sea or lake that is partly surrounded by land. The English sailed in ships over the Chesapeake **Bay** to get to Jamestown. (p. 99)

Bill of Rights (bil uv rīts) A list of our country's most important rights and freedoms that was added to the Constitution in 1791. The **Bill of Rights** includes the right to free speech and the right to practice religion freely. (p. 159)

C

cactus (kak'təs) A plant that grows in hot, dry, sunny places. There are many **cactus** plants in the desert. (p. 122)

canyon (can'yən) A deep valley with steep sides. The river ran a few miles through the **canyon**. (p. 80)

pronunciation key

a	at	ī	ice	u	up	th	thin
ā	ape	îr	pierce	ū	use	th	this
ä	far	o	hot	ü	rule	zh	measure
âr	care	ō	old	ù	pull	ə	about, taken,
e	end	ô	fork	ûr	turn		pencil, lemon,
ē	me	oi	oil	hw	white		circus
i	it	ou	out	ng	song		

capital (kap′i təl) A place where the government of a state or country is located. People decided that the **capital** of our country should be located between the northern and southern States. (p. 166)

Capitol (kap′i təl) The building in Washington, D.C., where Congress meets to make laws. Both the House of Representatives and the Senate meet in the **Capitol**. (p. 171)

cardinal directions (kârd′ ən əl di rek′ shenz) Cardinal directions are north, south, east, and west. The airplane pilot used the compass rose to find the **cardinal directions** on the map. (p. G8)

cause (kôz) Something that makes something else happen. The **cause** of the sunburn was too much sun. (p. 290)

channel (chan′əl) A narrow waterway between two larger bodies of water. The ships sailed through the **channel** before reaching the ocean. (p. 256)

citizen (sit′ə zən) A member of a community or country. Communities need **citizens** to work together to solve problems. (p. 11)

city council (sit′ē koun′səl). Group of elected people who make the laws for a city. The **city council** meets in the town hall on Main Street. (p. 186)

Civil War (siv′əl wôr) The war between the North and the South, 1861-1865. After the **Civil War**, African Americans were free from slavery. (p. 225)

classifying (klas′ə fī ing) The grouping together of similar things. The movers **classified** the furniture into two groups: heavy pieces and light pieces. (p. 216)

cliff (klif) The high, steep face of a mountain or rock. The Anasazi lived in homes built into the **cliffs**. (p. 80)

climate (klī′mit) The weather a place has over a long period of time. Alaska has a cold **climate**. (p. 39)

coast (kōst) The land next to an ocean. There are many beaches and ports along the California **coast**. (p. 52)

coastal plain (kōs′təl plān) The flat land along a coast. The settlers built farms along the **coastal plain**. (p. 100)

colonist (kol′ə nist) Someone who lives in a colony. The **colonists** built a community at Jamestown. (p. 103)

colony (kol′ə nē) A place that is ruled by another, distant country. The King of England hoped that the **colony** at Jamestown would provide great riches. (p. 103)

communicate (kə mū′ni kāt) To share ideas, thoughts, or information with someone. Telephones help people **communicate** quickly. (p. 250)

community (kə mū′ni tē) A place where people live, work, and have fun together. It is usually made up of several different neighborhoods. Many people in Michael's **community** have fun by going to the beach during the summer. (p. 8)

compare (kəm pâr′) To see how things are alike. The students will **compare** the different jobs people have in the community to understand how they are alike. (p. 160)

compass rose (kum′ pəs rōz) A guide to the cardinal directions on a map. Mary used the **compass rose** to find that the river was south of her community. (p. G8)

compromise (kom′prə mīz) To settle an argument by agreeing that each side will give up some of its demands. In making fair laws people often work together and **compromise**. (p. 157)

Congress (kong′ris) The part of the United States government that makes laws for our country. Members of **Congress** are elected by citizens. (p. 157)

Constitution (kon sti tü′shən) The plan of government for the United States that explains what the different parts of government are and outlines the most important laws. Today the **Constitution** is still important in helping people make laws in our country. (p. 156)

consumer (kən sü′mər) People who buy goods and services. **Consumers** buy the products that are made or grown by producers. (p. 277)

continent (kon′tə nent) A very large body of land. Canada and the United States are both located on the **continent** of North America. (p. G5)

contrast (kən trast′) To see how things are different. At the museum, the visitors saw the differences in Jacob Lawrence's paintings by **contrasting** them. (p. 160)

culture (kul′chər) The way of life of a group of people including that group's language, music, foods, holidays, and beliefs. The language the Iroquois speak and the dances they participate in are all part of their **culture**. (p. 25)

D

decision (di sizh′ən) The act of choosing one thing rather than another. When you choose what food to eat, you are making a **decision**. (p. 92)

Declaration of Independence (dek lə rā′shən uv in di pen′dəns) A document written by Thomas Jefferson in 1776 that explains why the colonies had decided to free themselves from England. On July 4th, Americans celebrate the signing of the **Declaration of Independence**. (p. 150)

desert (dez′ərt) A dry environment where little rain falls. A **desert** gets less than 10 inches of rainfall each year. (p. 78)

designer (di zī′nər) A person who plans how something will look. Book **designers** choose the photographs and illustrations to be used in books. (p. 283)

diary (dī′ə rē) A written record of what someone has seen, done, or thought. In her **diary** Sallie described her life. (p. 213)

domestic trade (də mes′tik trād) Trade within one country. **Domestic trade** may involve buying wheat in Kansas and selling airplanes in Washington. (p. 321)

E

economy (i kon′ə mē) The making and consuming of goods and services. Our country's **economy** needs people to buy and sell products. (p. 277)

editor (ed′i tər) Someone who works with authors and designers in all the steps involved in making a book. The **editor** decided to include a story in the book about Philadelphia. (p. 280)

effect (i fekt′) Something that happens as a result of a cause. The **effect** of the sunburn was that Jane's skin hurt. (p. 290)

elect (i lekt′) To choose by voting. George Washington was **elected** the first president of the United States in 1789. (p. 156)

pronunciation key

a **at**; ā **ape**; ä **far**; âr **care**; e **end**; ē **me**; i **it**; ī **ice**; îr **pierce**; o **hot**; ō **old**; ô **fork**; oi **oil**; ou **out**; u **up**; ū **use**; ü **rule**, ů **pull**; ûr **turn**; hw **white**; ng **song**; th **thin**; <u>th</u> **this**; zh measure; ə **about, taken, pencil, lemon, circus**

R25

employer (em ploi′ər) Someone who hires and pays other people to work. The **employer** had seven people working in the office. (p. 275)

encyclopedia (en si klə pē′dē ə) A book or set of books with facts about people, places, things, and past events. Catherine looked in the **encyclopedia** for information about Senegal. (p. 190)

endangered (en dān′jerd) Plants or animals that are in danger of dying out. The black rhinoceros is one of many **endangered** animals. (p. 30)

environment (en vi′rən mənt) All the air, water, land, and the living things surrounding people. People are working to save the **environment** and its many resources. (p. 48)

equator (i kwā′tər) An imaginary line around the middle of Earth. The **equator** divides Earth into the Northern Hemisphere and Southern Hemisphere. (p. G4)

export (ek′spôrt) To sell and ship goods to another place or country. Canada **exports** fish to the United States. (p. 321)

F

factory (fak′tə rē) A place where things are manufactured. Many of the products we use are made in **factories**. (p. 312)

fertilizer (fûr′tə li zər) Chemicals used to help plants grow. The farmer uses **fertilizers** for the crops. (p. 301)

fiction (fik′shən) Made-up stories of people, places, and events. *Alice in Wonderland* is Jill's favorite **fiction** book. (p. 190)

Fiesta (fē es′tə) An event in San Antonio, Texas that celebrates Texas' independence from Mexico. **Fiesta** means "festival" in Spanish. (p. 130)

flow chart (flō′ chärt) A chart that shows the order of steps that are followed to make a final product. The scientist used a **flow chart** to show how the rocket would be built. (p. 306)

fuel (fū′əl) Something that is burned to provide heat, light, or power. Most cars use gasoline for **fuel**. (p. 247)

G

geography (jē og′rə fē) The study of Earth's surface, bodies of water, climate, and natural resources. It is also about how people change the land around them. Knowing **geography** helps people learn about the land and water in their community. (p. 36)

goods (gùdz) The things for sale that people make or grow. Many **goods** are made in factories. (p. 274)

governor (guv′ər nər) An elected leader of a state's government. The **governor** chooses people to help run state government. (p. 186)

Great Migration (grāt′ mi grā′shən) In the early to mid 1900s, the journey of thousands of African Americans from the South to build new lives in the cities of the North. During the **Great Migration** many people traveled to large cities in the North by train. (p. 224)

grid map (grid map) A map with a set of crisscrossing lines used to find places on the map. The tour book has a **grid map** of Mexico City. (p. G11)

guide words (gīd wûrdz) The words that appear at the top of the page in many reference books. They tell the first and last subjects that appear on each page. Richard used the **guide words** in the dictionary to find the word he wanted to define. (p. 190)

H

harvest (här′vist) Ripe crops that are gathered. The **harvest** was loaded onto trucks at the end of the summer. (p. 301)

hemisphere (hem′i sfêr) Half of a sphere or globe. The United States is located in the Northern **Hemisphere**. (p. 58)

high-tech (hī′ tek′) The use of the latest technology to make electronic and other goods. Computers are **high-tech** products. (p. 294)

history (his′tə rē) The story of what happened in the past. At Jamestown Settlement, people learn about the **history** of the Powhatan and the English. (p. 70)

hurricane (hur′i kān) A storm with very strong winds and heavy rain. Many houses were destroyed in the **hurricane**. (p. 11)

I

immigrant (im′i grənt) Someone who comes from one country or place to live in another. Many **immigrants** to the United States came through Ellis Island. (p. 218)

import (im′pôrt) To buy goods from another place or country. Russia **imports** wheat from the United States. (p. 321)

independence (in di pen′dəns) Freedom from others. Texas won its **independence** from Mexico in 1836. (p. 126)

index (in′deks) An alphabetical list that shows where information can be found. Peter looked at the **index** on the grid map to find the Washington Monument. (p. 176)

interest (in′trist) Money paid for the use of borrowing money. Joe paid **interest** on his loan from the bank. (p. 276)

intermediate directions (in tər mē′dē it di rek′shənz) A direction halfway between two cardinal directions. **Intermediate directions** are helpful in showing the relationship between two different places on a map. (p. 50)

international trade (in tər nash′ə nəl trād) The import and export of goods between countries. **International trade** is important to many countries around the world. (p. 322)

island (ī′lənd) Land surrounded on all sides by water. The boat captain saw birds flying over the **island**. (p. 10)

J

journalist (jûr′nə list) A writer for a newspaper, magazine, or television news program. The President explained his ideas to the **journalist**. (p. 293)

K

kiva (kē′və) A special room used for religious ceremonies by some Native Americans. The Pueblo people held the ceremony in a **kiva**. (p. 84)

L

landform (land′fôrm) One of the shapes of Earth's surface. Pioneers saw many different types of **landforms** while traveling on the Oregon Trail. (p. 38)

---

pronunciation key

a at; ā ape; ä far; âr care; e end; ē me; i it; ī ice; îr pierce; o hot; ō old; ô fork; oi oil; ou out; u up; ū use; ü rule; ů pull; ûr turn; hw white; ng song; th thin; <u>th</u> this; zh measure; ə about, taken, pencil, lemon, circus

landform map (land'fôrm map) A map that shows the different kinds of land on Earth. Mountains and hills can be seen on a **landform map**. (p. G10)

legacy (leg'ə sē) A part of our past that we value in our lives today. Celebrating Thanksgiving is a **legacy** people share from long ago. (p. 14)

line graph (līn graf) A graph that uses the rising or falling of a line to show how something changes over time. The **line graph** shows the total number of cars manufactured in the United States between 1920 and 1960. (p. 134)

living history museum (liv'ing his'tə rē mū zē'əm) A place that shows what the past was like by having people dress, talk, and do things as people did long ago. At the **living history museum**, people can eat food like Native Americans did long ago. (p. 108)

local government (lō'kəl guv'ərn mənt) The people who run a city or community. **Local governments** are often led by a mayor. (p. 186)

locator (lō'kāt tər) A small map included on a bigger, or main, map. Jeff used the **locator** to find California. (p. G9)

manufacturing (man yə fak'chər ing) The business of making things. People who work in **manufacturing** make many different products like cars, clothes, foods, and books. (p. 312)

map key (map kē) Something that tells what the symbols on a map stand for. Jane used the **map key** to help find the airport on the map. (p. G7)

mayor (mā'ər) A person who is the head of a city government. The **mayor** makes sure that local laws are obeyed. (p. 179)

memorial (mə môr'ē əl) Anything, such as a monument or holiday, that is set aside to remember a person or event. The Jefferson **Memorial** in Washington, D.C. honors Thomas Jefferson. (p. 172)

mesa (mā'sə) A landform that looks like a high, flat table. Native Americans grew crops on the **mesa**. (p. 80)

migration (mī grā'shən) The movement of people or animals from one place or country to another. Each year people go to the park to watch the **migration** of birds to the south. (p. 224)

mill (mil) A place where people use machines to turn natural resources into finished products. Steel and paper are products made in a **mill**. (p. 317)

mineral (min'ər əl) Natural substance found in the earth that is not a plant or animal. Iron and diamonds are examples of **minerals**. (p. 47)

mission (mish'ən) Communities set up by Roman Catholic priests to teach their religion to others. The Alamo was established as a **mission** in 1718. (p. 123)

missionary (mish'ə ner ē) A person sent by a church to spread its religion into a different country. Spanish **missionaries** taught Native Americans to speak and write in Spanish. (p. 123)

museum (mū zē'əm) A place where people can look at objects of art, science, or history. The students saw artifacts of colonial life at the **museum**. (p. 89)

national park (nash'ə nəl pärk) Land set aside by a government for all people to enjoy. The family was not allowed to build a house in the **national park**. (p. 28)

natural resource (nach′ər əl rē′sôrs) Something found in nature that people use. Water and soil are examples of **natural resources**. (p. 46)

nonfiction (non fik′shən) Information about real people, places, and events. A book about the life of George Washington would be located in the **nonfiction** section of the library. (p. 190)

nonrenewable resource (non ri nü′ə bəl rē′sôrs) Things found in nature that cannot be replaced, such as minerals. People are taking care to save **nonrenewable resources**. (p. 308)

North Pole (nôrth pōl) The place farthest north on Earth. Very few people live on the **North Pole**. (p. G4)

oath (ōth) A serious promise made in public. New immigrants take an **oath** of loyalty to our country when becoming citizens. (p. 235)

ocean (ō′shən) A very large body of salt water. People are finding new ways to work together to help fight pollution in **oceans** around the world. (p. G5)

oral history (ôr′əl his′tə rē) Recorded interviews with people who can tell firsthand what life was like in the past. The students listened to **oral histories** to learn more about San Antonio. (p. 219)

P

peninsula (pə nin′sə lə) Land that has water on all sides but one. Paracas is a community located on a **peninsula**. (p. 53)

pioneer (pī ə nîr′) A person who is among the first to explore an area not known to them. **Pioneers** traveled for many months on the Oregon Trail. (p. 210)

plain (plān) A large area of flat land. Long ago, many buffalo lived on the **plains** of our country. (p. 38)

plateau (pla tō′) A large area of high, flat land that is raised above surrounding land. The hikers climbed up the **plateau** and pitched their tents. (p. 38)

Pledge of Allegiance (plej uv əlē′jəns) An oath promising to be loyal and to support the government of the United States. In saying the **Pledge of Allegiance**, people are promising to be loyal to the United States. (p. 192)

pollution (pə lü′shən) Anything, such as a harmful chemical, that spoils land, water, or air. At the town meeting, people made laws to help fight **pollution**. (p. 11)

pony express (pō′nē ek spres′) A team of daring horseback riders who swiftly rode across the western United States to deliver mail. The **pony express** delivered mail from 1860 to 1861. (p. 251)

port (pôrt) A place, such as a harbor, where ships load and unload their goods. Francis liked to watch the boats being unloaded at the **port**. (p. 10)

prairie (prâr′ē) Flat or rolling land covered with tall grasses. The rich soil of the **prairie** makes it good for growing corn and other crops. (p. 210)

President (prez′i dənt) The leader of the United States government. People vote for **President** every four years. (p. 157)

pronunciation key

a at; ā ape; ä far; âr care; e end; ē me; i it; ī ice; îr pierce; o hot; ō old; ô fork; oi oil; ou out; u up; ū use; ü rule, ü pull; ûr turn; hw white; ng song; th thin; <u>th</u> this; zh measure; ə about, taken, pencil, lemon, circus

private property (prī′vit prop′ər tē) Land that is owned by people or companies. The mall was built on **private property**. (p. 310)

process (pros′es) To change a product into a different form so that it can be sold. Corn and other grains are **processed** to make breakfast cereals. (p. 305)

producer (prə dü′sər) Someone who makes goods or services. Farmers and car makers are two examples of **producers**. (p. 283)

product map (prod′ukt map) A map that shows the places where goods are made and crops are grown. Tanya used a **product map** to find different products that are grown in Texas. (p. 302)

public property (pub′lik prop′ər tē) Land that has been set aside for all people to use. Many parks are built on **public property**. (p. 310)

publishing (pub′lish ing) The making and selling of books, magazines, CD-ROMs, musical scores, or other informational material. This book was made by a **publishing** company. (p. 280)

R

recycling (rē sī′kling) Using something over again. Karen carried the bottles and cans to the bin for **recycling**. (p. 48)

reference (ref′ər əns) Type of book or other kind of stored information that contains facts on many different subjects. Susan looked at books in the **reference** section of the library for information on gardening. (p. 190)

renewable resource (ri nü′ə bəl rē′sôrs) Things found in nature that can be replaced. Water is a **renewable resource**. (p. 308)

research (ri sûrch′) To look for information. To do their class report, students **researched** facts at the library. (p. 190)

robot (rō′bot) Machine that does jobs instead of people. **Robots** are often used to make cars and other products. (p. 314)

rural (rùr′əl) A community of farms or open country where distances are far between one place and another. Many fishing villages are located in **rural** communities. (p. 19)

S

satellite (sat′ə līt) A spacecraft that is used to connect radio, telephone, and television communications. Many of the TV programs we watch are sent by **satellites**. (p. 254)

scale (skāl) A ruler on a map that measures distance. It helps you to find out the larger, real distance on Earth. The pilot used a **scale** to measure the distance between two cities on a map. (p. 22)

services (sûr′vis əz) Work that helps others by providing something they need or want. Restaurants provide a **service** by making food for customers. (p. 274)

slavery (slā′və rē) The practice of one person owning another. President Abraham Lincoln wanted to end **slavery**. (p. 107)

South Pole (south pōl) The place farthest south on Earth. Explorers and scientists travel to the **South Pole**. (p. G4)

suburb (sub′ûrb) A community located near a city. People who live in **suburbs** often work in nearby cities. (p. 18)

Supreme Court (sə prēm′ kôrt) A part of the American government that makes sure laws follow the Constitution. There are nine judges on the **Supreme Court**. (p. 157)

symbol (sim′bəl) Anything that stands for something else. The Statue of Liberty is a **symbol** of freedom for many people. (p. G6)

T

tax (taks) Money people pay to support the government. The colonists did not want to pay **taxes** to England. (p. 150)

technology (tek nol′ə jē) The use of skills, ideas, and tools to meet people's needs. Computers are an example of a **technology** that some people use every day. (p. 81)

telegraph (tel′i graf) To send messages long distances over wires, using special codes. The ambassador sent a **telegraph** from the United States to Japan. (p. 252)

time line (tīm līn) A strip marked off evenly in periods of time that shows events in the same order as they happened. The **time line** shows important events in the history of Washington, D.C. (p. 112)

town meeting (toun mē′ting) A yearly gathering of town people to discuss and vote on community laws, rules, and other issues. At the **town meeting**, students introduced their plans for building a new park. (p. 187)

trade (trād) The buying and selling of goods and services. Different countries around the world **trade** many kinds of products with each other. (p. 320)

transportation (trans pər tā′shən) The moving of people or goods from one place to another. Buses and trains are important types of **transportation**. (p. 19)

transportation map (trans pər tā′shən map) A map that shows the routes people can use to travel from place to place. Gary used a **transportation map** to locate the subway stops in the city. (p. 248)

U

urban (ûr′bən) A community that includes the city and its surrounding areas. Many people in **urban** communities live in tall apartment buildings. (p. 17)

V

volunteer (vol ən tîr′) Someone who does a job by choice, without pay. Communities need **volunteers** to deliver food to people who can't leave their homes. (p. 130)

W

wildlife (wīld′līf) The animals that live in an area. Birds and fish are two types of **wildlife**. (p. 54)

---

pronunciation key

a **at**; ā **ape**; ä **far**; âr **care**; e **end**; ē **me**; i **it**; ī **ice**; îr **pierce**; o **hot**; ō **old**; ô **fork**; oi **oil**; ou **out**; u **up**; ū **use**; ü **rule**; ù **pull**; ûr **turn**; hw **white**; ng **song**; th **thin**; <u>th</u> **this**; zh **measure**; ə **about, taken, pencil, lemon, circus**

index

This Index lists many topics that appear in the book, along with the pages on which they are found. Page numbers after an *m* refer you to a map. Page numbers after a *p* indicate photographs, artwork, or charts.

R35

CREDITS

Cover design by: Pentagram

Maps: Geosystems

Charts and Graphs: MMSD

Illustrations: Mike Adams: pp 246, 260, 304; Hal Brooks: pp 149; Genevieve Claire: pp 11, 28, 39, 54, 83, 100, 130, 158, 174, 195, 212, 244, 252, 276, 303; Renee Daily: pp 73, 74; Michael Hampshire: pp 116-117, 124-125; Jim Hays: pp 164-165, 208-209; Robert Korta: pp 68-69, 82, 83, 84-85, 86, 240-241; Kelly Maddox: pp 42, 71; Karen Minot: pp 322; Paul Mirocha: pp 55; Hima Pamoedjo: pp 16-19, 22, 50; Rebecca Perry: pp 314, G7, G8, G11; Rodica Prato: pp 106, 112-113; James Ransome: pp 286; Margaret Sanfilipo: pp R19-R22; Rob Schuster: pp 6, 34, 68, 97, 117, 145, 165, 184, 209, 241, 272, 298; Nina Wallace: pp 306, 307, 310; David Wenzel: pp 96-97, 144-145; Lane Yerkes: pp 216-217, 235, 289

PHOTOGRAPHY CREDITS: All photographs are by the Macmillan/ McGraw-Hill School Division (MMSD) except as noted below:

Cover and title page: Henry Francis DuPont Winterthur Museum, Washington at Verplanks, painting by John Trumbull, oil on canvas, detail, 1790/courtesy, Winterthur Museum. iii: t. George Jones/Photo Researchers; b. Lawrence Migdale. iv: b. Laurence Parent; t. Richard T. Nowitz; m. Anne Nielson for MMSD. v: l. Richard T. Nowitz; r. Anne Nielson for MMSD. vi: b.m. Anne Nielson for MMSD; b. Jeff Greenberg/The Picture Cube; t. Chermayeff & Geismar/Metaform. vii: b. Deters/Monkmeyer; m. Gary Buss/FPG International; t. Chermayeff & Geismar/Metaform. G2: t.r. Mark Wagner/Tony Stone Images; b.l. Joseph Muench. G3: t.r. Greg Mellis; m.l. Nicholas DeVore III/Photographers/Aspen; b.r. Thomas Nebbia. G2-G3: Elizabeth Wolf. G6: J.A. Kraulis/MasterFile. **Chapter 1** 2: b.l. Bob Torrez/Tony Stone; m.r. Richard Palsey/Stock Boston; t. Liz Hymans/Tony Stone; r. Lawrence Migdale; m.l. Tim Davis/Photo Researchers. 3: b. J. Sohm/The Image Works; r. Wolfgang Kaehler. 45: Daniel R. Westergren. 6: Jim Schwabel/New England Stock Photo. 7: l. Jack Hoehn/Profiles West; r. Barry Durand/Odyssey; m. Bonnie Sue Rauch/Photo Researchers. 8: Robert Mihovil. 9: Jim Levin for MMSD. 10: Robert Mihovil. 11: b.r. The Rosenberg Library. 12: b. Joe Viesti/Viesti Associates; t. Robert Mihovil. 13: Chuck O'Rear/Westlight. 14: b. Thomas T. Taber/Madison Public Library. 14-15: m. George Jones/Photo Researchers. 14: frame Jim Levin for MMSD. 15: t.r. Matt Bradley/West Stock; b.l. Sobel/Klonsky, The Image Bank; m.r. Robert Mihovil. 16: postcard borders Jim Levin for MMSD; b. Fulton County Historical Society; t. John Neubauer/West Stock, Inc.; m. Louis Beneze/Liaison International. 17: t. David Noble/FPG; b. Bob Krist/Black Star. 18: t. Tim Heneghan/West Stock; b. Louis Bencze/Liaison International. 19: t. Darryl Jones, Fulton County Historical Society; b. Joseph Nettis/Photo Researchers. 21: Bryan Peterson/West Stock. 24: Howard Breitrose for MMSD. 25: J. P. Courau/D. Donne Bryant Stock Photo. 26: t.l. Robert Frerck/Odyssey; b.r. Cameramann Int'l., Ltd. 27: Howard Breitrose for MMSD. 28: r. Howard Breitrose for MMSD; l. Jim Levin for MMSD. 29: Bob Thomason/Leo de Wys Inc., NY. 30: W. Hille/Leo de Wys Inc., NY. 31: t. courtesy Hollia Kemp; b. courtesy Elisabeth Turbow; m. courtesy Ned Marsen. **Chapter 2** 35: l. Uniphoto; m. Wolfgang Kaehler; r. Gabe Palmer/The Stock Market. 36: Uniphoto. 37: m. courtesy Francis Akinsulie; t. Mulvehill/The Image Works; b. Joe Sohm/The Image Works. 38: l. Luis Garcia; r. David Hiser/Photographers Aspen. 39: r. Bryan & Cherry Alexander; l. Chuck Carlton/Black Star. 41: l. Barry L. Runk/Grant Heilman; b.m.r. Trevor Wood/The Image Bank; t.r. William H. Mullins/Photo Researchers; b.r. Harold Sund/The Image Bank; t.m.r. James Randkley/Tony Stone International. 43: Terry E. Eiler/Stock Boston; l. inset Jim Levin for MMSD. 44: l. Pierre Fabre. 44-45: m. Creda Axton. 45: m.r., b.l. Pierre Fabre; t. Bettmann Archives. 46: Peter Cole/Bruce Coleman, Inc. 47: t. Hans Wendler/The Image Bank; m.r. Dwight Kuhn/Bruce Coleman, Inc.; b.l. Gordon M. Kurzweil/Uniphoto Picture Agency; b.r. D.D. Morrison/The Picture Cube. 48: l. Peter Beck/The Stock Market; r. courtesy Tara Church. 49: b. Ken Kerbs for MMSD; t. Jim Levin for MMSD. 52: Alejandro Balaguer. 53: George Holton/Photo Researchers. 54: r. Alejandro Balaguer; l. Brian Parker/Tom Stack Associates. 56: Alejandro Balaguer. 57: Michael McDermott. 60: J.P.Meyers/Academy of Natural Sciences- Vireo. 63: Monica Stevenson for MMSD. 64: m. John Running; b. Laurence Parent; t.l. Tom Bean; t.r. Anne Nielson for MMSD. 65: t.r. Richard T. Nowitz; m.r. Anne Nielson for MMSD; b.l. Robert Llewellyn. 66: b.l. Michael Schwarz. 66-67: © Michael Philip Manheim. 67: t. Dorothy Littell Greco/Stock Boston; b. Cotton Coulson. **Chapter 3** 70: Richard Welch. 72: t.l. National Museum of the American Indian; b.l. David Heald/National Museum of the American Indian; b.r. Joslyn Art Museum. 74: Monty Roessel/TBS, Inc. 75: Richard A. Cooke III/Neah Bay Museum. 76-77: Chris Roberts. 77: b.r. Michael Crummett; b.l. John Running; t. Edwin L. Wisherd/National Geographic Society. 78: David Muench. 79: b. David Muench; t. David Carriere/Tony Stone International. 80: b.l. Todd Powell/Profiles West; b.r. Rod Planck/Tony Stone International; t.l. Ann Trulove/Unicorn Stock Photos. 81: George H.H. Huey. 87: David Hiser/Photographers Aspen; bkgnd. Jim Levin for MMSD. 88: Steve Rudolph. 89: Jerry Jacka Photography. 90: l. David Hiser/Photographers Aspen; r. The Image Bank. 91: courtesy Steve Rudolph. **Chapter 4** 98: Bruce Roberts. 99: Fil Hunter. 100: The Granger Collection. 101: Llewellyn. 102: The Bettmann Archives. 103: b.r. Superstock;l. Archive Photos; t.r. The Granger Collection. 104: b. The Granger Collection. 105: r. Don Henley & Savage/Dominion Photosource; b.l. The Granger Collection. 107: The Bettmann Archives. 108: Jamestown Yorktown Foundation. 109: t. Jamestown Yorktown Foundation; b.l. Robert Llewellyn; b.r. Richard T. Nowitz/Photo Researchers. 110: b.r. Fil Hunter/Time Life Books, Inc.; t.l. Fil Hunter for MMSD. 111: Robert Llewellyn. **Chapter 5** 118: Al Rendon. 119: t.r. Scott Berner/The Picture Cube; t.l. Bullaty-Lomeo/The Image Bank; b. Al Rendon. 120: Scott Berner/The Picture Cube. 121: t.r. Priscilla Connell/PhotoNats; b.l. The Institute of Texas Cultures, San Antonio, TX. courtesy: Vic Fritze. 122: Steve Vidler/Leo de Wys, Inc. 123: t. Richard Reynolds Photography; b. Gil Cohen/National Park Service. 126: Masahiro Sano/The Stock Market. 127: D. Donne Bryant. 128: Bob Daemmrich. 129: b.l. Ron Thomas/FPG; b.r. Sullivan/Texastock; t. courtesy Barbara Shupp. 130: Al Rendon. 131: t. courtesy Barbara Shupp; b. Jim Levin for MMSD. 132: S.A.L.E. Inc., San Antonio TX. 133: courtesy Vernon Mullins, The Children's East Community Garden, San Antonio. 139: Monica Stevenson for MMSD. 140: t.r. Santi Visalli/The Image Bank; b.r. Richard T. Nowitz; l. Anne Nielson for MMSD. 141: b.l. Anne Nielson for MMSD; r. Jeff Hunter/The Image Bank. 142: t.l. Stanley Tretick; b.l. Library of Congress. 142-143: bkgnd: Tony Stone Images. 143: t. The Bettmann Archive; b. Dennis Brack/Black Star. **Chapter 6** 146: The Bettmann Archives. 147: r. Cigna Museum & Art Collection; l. North Wind Picture Archives. 148: Joseph Boggs Beale/Modern Galleries Philadelphia, PA. 150-151: Superstock. 152-153: m. Doug Armand/Tony Stone Worldwide. 152: b.l. NASA. 153: t.l. North Wind Pictures; b. Archive Photos; m.r. Martin Rogers/Stock Boston. 154: FPG International. 155: b.l. Archive Photos; m., t. The Granger Collection. 156: t.r. National Geographic Photographer George F. Mobley/courtesy U.S. Capitol Historical Society; b.l. Superstock. 157: r. Ken Kerbs for MMSD; t. Superstock. 158: r. Ted Spiegel. 159: Harold M. Lambert. 160-161: The Granger Collection. (on page credit). 162: The Granger Collection. **Chapter 7** 166: c. White House Historical Association. Photo by National Geographic Society. 167: Photri. 168: The Granger Collection. 169: North Wind. 170: Mike Yamashita/Woodfin Camp & Associates. 171: courtesy: Ms. Bernadette Senn. 172: David Ball/The Picture Cube. 173: t. Tony Stone Images; b.l. Uniphoto Picture Agency; m. Andre Jenny/Stock South. 174: b.l. Richard T. Nowitz; r. Jim Pickerell/Stock Boston. 175: Dirick Halstead/Gamma-Liaison. 178: Nik Wheeler. 179: courtesy Dorothy Padilla. 180: b. Thierry Prat/Sygma; t. Superstock. 181: b. M & E Bernheim/Woodfin Camp. **Chapter 8** 185: b. William Whitehurst/The Stock Market; t.l. Richard Hutchings/Photo Researchers; t.r. Uniphoto; t.m. Andre Jenny/Stock South. 186: B. Howe/Photri. 187: Kevin A. Byron/ The Sanford News. 188: t. Jim Brown/Gilles Lavigne/Gino Romano; b., m. Jim Brown/Gilles Lavigne. 189: t. courtesy Wendy Wehmeyer; b. courtesy Adam Pierce. 192-193: Mark Pokemper/Tony Stone Worldwide. 193: t.r. courtesy Alberta Reid; b.r. Zigy Kaluzny/Tony Stone Images. 194: t. Ben Brink/The Oregonian; b. Ross Hamilton/The Oregonian. 195: Oakland City Council, courtesy John Russo. 196: b.r. UPI/Bettmann. 197: r. Tony La Gruth/New England Stock Photography; l. Dimaggio Kalish/The Stock Market. 198: Russ Kinne/Comstock. 199: t. courtesy Suzanne Hee; m. courtesy Debbie Macon; b. courtesy Joel Rosch. 203: Robert Milazzo for MMSD. 204: t.m., t.l. Chermayeff & Geismar/Metaform; b. Jeff Greenberg/The Picture Cube; r. Andrea Pistolesi/The Image Bank; m. Anne Nielson for MMSD. 205: l. Anne Nielson for MMSD; r. Southern Stock/NASA, FL. 206: l. David Hiser/Photographers/Aspen. 206-207: bkgnd David Hiser. 207: David Hiser. **Chapter 9** 210: USDI Bureau of Land Management. 211: Oregon Historical Society. 212: The Corcoran Gallery of Art, gift of Mr and Mrs. Lansell K. Christie. 213: b.r. St. Louis Mercantile Library; m. Clackmas County Historical Society - Oregon City, Oregon; t. National Geographic Society. 214: b. Oregon Historical Society; t. The Granger Collection. 215: t. John Elk III/Stock Boston; b. Phyllis Picardi/Stock Boston. 218: Uniphoto. 219: t. Culver Pictures; b.l., b.r. Audrey Buchter. 220: b. The Jacob A. Riis Collection/Museum of the City of New York; t. Brown Brothers. 221: t. Brown Brothers; b. Lewis W. Hine/George Eastman House. 222: Nancy A. Potter/Bruce Coleman, Inc. 223: Superstock. 224: Florida State Archives. 225: Abraham Gardner/Photri. 226: t. National Geographic Society/Dr. Louis Fargo; b. National Geographic Society/Willard Price. 227: courtesy Donna Van Der Zee, photo by James Van Der Zee. 228: t. Discovery Channel/Spike Mafford; b. The Phillips Collection. 229: Superstock. 230-231: Sam Holland for MMSD. 232: Dolores Stivalet. 233: t. Victor Perez de Lara/Leo de Wys, Inc.; b. Bushnell/Soifer//Tony Stone Images. 234: t.l. Kumar S. Nochur; b.l. Nicolas Jawdosiuk; m.l. E. B. Wilson/Oyeyinka Oyelaran; r. John Ortner/Tony Stone International. 236: r. M. Mantel/SIPA Press; l. courtesy: Dept of Immigration. 237: Keith Soon Kim. **Chapter 10** 242: Jeff Hunter/The Image Bank. 243: Brown Brothers. 244: The Bettman Archive. 245: t., b. Brown Brothers; m. Keith Marvin. 247: Norman Owen Tomalin/Bruce Coleman. 248-249: The Granger Collection. 250: The Bettman Archive. 251: Buffalo Bill Historical Center, Cody, WY. 252: l. Charles Harrington, Cornell University Photo; r. The Bettman Archive. 253: t. Leonard Lessin/Peter Arnold; b.r. Charmet/Science/ Photo Library/Photo Researchers; b.l. Archive Photos. 254: NASA. 255: Lawrence Migdale/ Stock Boston. 256: Archive/Imapress/N'Diaye. 257: John Lamb/Tony Stone. 258: t.l., t.r. Q A Photos; b. Monica Stevenson for MMSD. 259: b. Q A Photos; t. Terminus/Gamma Liaison. 260: m. Eurotunnel Education in collaboration w/ Kent Arts and Libraries. 262-263: Benn Mitchell/ The Image Bank. 263: t.l. Culver Pictures; t.r. Lori Adamski Peek/Tony Stone; b.r. Bob Winsett/Tom Stack and Associates; b.l. Bob Daemmrich/Stock Boston. 267: Monica Stevenson for MMSD. 268: b. Deters/Monkmeyer Press; t.r. Gary Buss/FPG; t.l. National Museum of American Art, Smithsonian Institution, DC Art Resource - Thomas Hart Benton, Wheat 1967, Oil on wood, 20"x21", Gift of Mr./Mrs. James A. Mitchell and Museum purchase. 269: b. Superstock. 270: l. Daniel R. Westergren.; bkgnd Richard T. Nowitz. 271: t. Steven Pumphrey; b. Jerry Jacka. **Chapter 11** 273: t. Orion Press; l. Anthony Boccacio/The Image Bank; r. Doug Milner/Uniphoto; m. Sylvain Grandadam/Photo Researchers. 274: Jim Stratford. 275: l. Jim Stratford; r. Skip Flythe. 276-278: Jim Stratford. 279: Joel Seigelman. 280-281: Robert Milazzo for MMSD. 283: t. Robert Milazzo; b. Blair Seitz/Photo Researchers. 284: t.m. Dena Abergel in A Midsummer Night's Dream; m.l. Steve Joester/FPG International; b.l. photo courtesy of Denice Burnham; b.r. Zack Burris Photography. 284-285: t. Bobbie Kingsley/Photo Researchers, Inc. 285: t.r. photo courtesy of Alfredo Estrada; m. (television screen) Superstock; m. Eccles/Outline; b. photo courtesy of Kim Guyette; b.r. Henry Wolf/The Image Bank. 287: Anne Nielsen. 288-289: t. Currier & Ives/Museum of the City of New York. 288: b. Bob Daemmrich. 289: b.r. Eastcott/Momatiuk/The Image Works; t.r. R.L. Wolverto/Profiles West. 289: b.l. Robert Davis. 292: Ken Strait/The Stock Market. 293: courtesy Tsutomu Yamaguchi. 294: t. Richard Nowitz; b.r. Ronald D. Modra/Sports Illustrated/Time, Inc. 295: Michael S. Yamashita. **Chapter 12** 298: IBM. 299: r. Antonio Ribeiro/Gamma Liaison; m. McAllister of Denver/Uniphoto; l. Romilly Lockyer/The Image Bank. 300: Chester Peterson Jr. for MMSD. 301: b.l., t.r. Chester Peterson, Jr. for MMSD; b.r. John & Diane Harper/New England Stock Photo. 302: First Light (A.G.E. Fotostock). 303: m.l. David Overcash/Bruce Coleman; t.r. Chuck O'Rear/WestLight; b.l. Charlie Ott/Photo Researchers. 305: Michael Rosenfeld/Tony Stone Worldwide. 308: t. Alan Kearney/Viesti Assoc. 308-309: b. Peter Dreyer/The Picture Cube. 309: m.r. courtesy Andrew Romero; t.r. courtesy Dana Romero; b.m. Paul Lau/Gamma-Liaison International; b.r. Richard Treplow/Photo Researchers. 310: David E. Spaw/Midwestock. 311: Ron Sanford/F-Stop Pictures. 312: Steve Dunwell/The Image Bank. 313: t. from the collections of Henry Ford Museum & Greenfield Village; b. Brown Brothers. 314: Andy Sacks. 315: t. Frank Fisher/West Stock; b. John Riley/Southern Stock Photos. 316: l. David Ulmer/ Stock Boston; r. Rob Crandall/Stock Boston. 317: Superstock. 318: H. Armstrong Roberts. 319: Marc Morrison. 320: Peter Vandermark/Stock Boston. 321: b.r. Grant V. Faint/The Image Bank; b.l. Greig Cranna/Stock Boston; t. James Kirby/Photri, Inc. 323: Uniphoto. 325: Paul Lau/Gamma Liaison International. 327: Robert Milazzo for MMSD. **Chapter SS** 330: b.l. Townsend P. Dickinson; bkgnd., t.l., b. Monica Stevenson for MMSD. 331: b.l., bkgnd. Monica Stevenson for MMSD. 332: l. From the Collection of Richard Steele/Courtesy of Ocean County Library; r. Ocean County Cultural & Heritage Commission. 332-333: bkgnd. Monica Stevenson for MMSD. 333: Monica Stevenson for MMSD. 334: b.l. courtesy of South Tom's River Elementary School; t.r. Robert J. Novins Plantarium, Ocean County College. 334-335: t., bkgnd. Monica Stevenson for MMSD. 335: t. Townsend P. Dickinson. 336: t.l. Monica Stevenson for MMSD. 336-337: bkgnd. Monica Stevenson for MMSD. 337: Clare Devine/North Dover Elementary School. 338: b.r. Jeffrey Dunn/Viesti Associates, Inc.; b.m. Eric Schweikardt/The Image Bank; b.l. Andy Levin/Photo Researchers. 338-339: bkgnd. Monica Stevenson for MMSD. 339: t. Monica Stevenson for MMSD. R3: Abraham Gardner/Photri. Endpapers: Bridgeman Art Library.

(continued from page ii)

Acknowledgments

From **Ben Franklin of Old Philadelphia** by Margaret Cousins. Copyright 1952 by Margaret Cousins, renewed 1980. Random House. From **New Letters of Abigail Adams** edited w/an Introduction by Stewart Mitchell. Copyright 1947 by the American Antiquarian Society. Greenwood Press Publishers, a division of Williamhouse-Regency, Inc. From **The Great Migration** by Jacob Lawrence. Copyright 1993 by the Museum of Modern Art, New York, and the Phillips Collection. HarperCollins Publishers. "Harvest" from **Slave Songs of the Georgia Sea Islands.** "Georgia Folk Song", book by Lydia Parrish. Copyright 1942 by Lydia Parrish, renewed 1969 by Maxfield Parish, Jr. Farrar, Straus & Giroux, Inc. Reprinted by permission of Farrar, Straus & Giroux, Inc. From **"No Star Nights"** by Anna Egan Smucker. Text copyright 1989 by Anne Egan Smucker. Illustrations copyright 1989 by Steve Johnson. Alfred A. Knopf. **"It's a Small World"** by Richard M. Sherman and Robert B. Sherman. Copyright 1963 by Wonderland Music Co. Inc.

R40

Communities

ADVENTURES IN TIME AND PLACE

Holiday Section – Contents

Bibliography

STUDENT BOOKS

Aliki. **Christmas Tree Memories.** New York: HarperCollins, 1991.

Adler, David A. **A Picture Book of Abraham Lincoln.** New York: Holiday House, 1989.

Adler, David A. **A Picture Book of George Washington.** New York: Holiday House, 1989.

Bunting, Eve. **Night Tree.** San Diego, CA: Harcourt Brace Jovanovich, Publishers, 1991.

Drucker, Malka. **Grandma's Latkes.** San Diego, CA: Harcourt Brace Jovanovich, 1992.

Gibbons, Gail. **St. Patrick's Day.** New York: Holiday House, 1994.

Greene, Carol. **Holidays Around the World.** Chicago, IL: Children's Press, 1982.

Liestman, Vicki. **Columbus Day.** Minneapolis, MN: Carolrhoda Books, 1991.

Livingston, Myra Cohn, sel. **Poems for Fathers.** New York: Holiday House, 1989.

Livingston, Myra Cohn, sel. **Poems for Mothers.** Holiday House, 1988.

Lowery, Lois. **Earth Day.** Minneapolis, MN: Carolrhoda Books, 1991.

Marzollo, Jean. **Happy Birthday, Martin Luther King.** New York: Scholastic Inc., 1993.

Mills, Claudia. **Phoebe's Parade.** New York: Macmillan Children's Group, 1994.

Palacios, Argentina. **¡Viva México! A Story of Benito Juárez and Cinco de Mayo.** Madison, NJ: Steck-Vaughn, 1993.

Pinkney, Andrea D. **Seven Candles for Kwanzaa.** New York: Dial Books, 1993.

Rattigan, Jama Kim. **Dumpling Soup.** Boston, MA: Little, Brown and Co., 1993.

Scott, Geoffrey. **Memorial Day.** Minneapolis, MN: Carolrhoda Books, 1983.

Waters, Kate, and Slovenz-Low, Madeline. **Lion Dancer: Ernie Wan's Chinese New Year.** New York: Scholastic Inc., 1990.

TEACHER BOOKS

Bauer, Caroline Feller. **Celebrations: Read-Aloud Holiday and Theme Book Programs.** New York: H.W. Wilson Co., 1985.

McLester, Cedric. **Kwanzaa: Everything You Always Wanted to Know but Didn't Know Where to Ask.** New York: Gumbs & Thomas, Publishers, 1985.

Penner, Lucille. **Celebration: The Story of American Holidays.** New York: Macmillan Children's Group, 1994.

Silverthorne, Elizabeth. **Fiesta! Mexico's Great Celebrations.** Brookfield, CT: The Millbrook Press, 1992.

READ ALOUDS

Bauer, Caroline Feller, ed. **Thanksgiving Stories and Poems.** New York: HarperCollins, 1994.

Hopkins, Lee Bennett, ed. **Ring Out, Wild Bells: Poems About Holidays and Seasons.** San Diego, CA: Harcourt Brace, 1992.

Low, Alice, sel. **The Family Read-Aloud Holiday Treasury.** Boston, MA: Little, Brown and Co., 1991.

Most, Bernard. **Happy Holidaysaurus.** San Diego, CA: Harcourt Brace, 1992.

TECHNOLOGY MULTIMEDIA

Cinco De Mayo. Filmstrip/Cassette. Society For Visual Education. Toll Free: 1-800-829-1900.

Holiday Facts & Fun Video Series. (11 programs) No. RB8148. Rainbow Educational Media. Toll Free: 1-800-331-4047.

People Behind the Holidays. CD-ROM. National Geographic. Toll Free: 1-800-368-2728.

FREE OR INEXPENSIVE MATERIALS

For a leaflet about flags in early American history, and information about the flag of today, send to: Dettra Flag Company, Inc; Publication Manager; P.O. Box 408; 120 Montgomery Avenue; Oaks, PA 19456-0408.

Labor Day

Background Information

- Labor Day is celebrated on the first Monday of September. The idea for the holiday came about in 1882, as a way to honor people who worked in plants and factories. The first Labor Day parade, in which ten thousand workers marched, took place in New York City that year.

- The date when Labor Day is celebrated is not connected with a specific historical event. It was chosen to break up the long stretch between Independence Day and Thanksgiving.

- Today Labor Day is a celebration of all people who work—government employees, professionals, factory workers, and homemakers. It is the last big celebration of summer when families plan picnics and long weekend trips. It also marks the end of school vacations and the beginning of fall.

  Read Aloud

Labor Day

First Monday in September
that's when we remember
to honor workers who toil long.
Their efforts make our country strong.
We give a gift they all like best;
We give them all a day of rest!

Marci Ridlon

Labor Day Charades

GROUP

Students can play a version of the game of charades to learn about different occupations.

15 TO 30 MINUTES

CURRICULUM CONNECTION   **Mathematics**

Materials: slips of scrap paper, marker, container, clock with second hand or timer, number cube

1. Write the names of different occupations on slips of paper and place them in a container. They might include hairdresser, barber, carpenter, baker, fisher, painter, police officer, veterinarian, doctor, firefighter, letter carrier, teacher, receptionist, dentist, service station attendant, pilot, or waitress.

2. Divide the class into two teams and teach them the four illustrated charade signs and the rules of the game outlined in Step 3. Decide on an overall amount of time to play the game.

3. Determine which team will play first. Have a player from that team draw a slip from the container. The player has 30 seconds to think about how to perform the charade for his or her teammates and 60 seconds to act it out. If the team guesses the charade correctly in the time limit, it rolls a number cube and receives the number of points rolled. That team continues with other players until the team cannot guess a charade in 60 seconds. The team not playing can keep track of the time. Charades not guessed can be placed back in the container.

4. The team that collects the most points at the end of the allotted time wins. This game can be ongoing.

SOUNDS LIKE   NUMBER OF WORDS

A-L   M-Z

Background Information

- Columbus Day is celebrated on the second Monday in October and commemorates the day Christopher Columbus reached the Americas—October 12, 1492.

- Because of Columbus's discovery, the Europeans colonized the Americas. That makes it one of the most important events in world history and explains why Columbus Day is celebrated in the United States as well as most Spanish-speaking countries and Italy.

- Columbus left Spain on August 3, 1492, with three ships and 90 crew members. The ships were very crowded, with no sleeping areas; the men cooked what they could on portable wood-burning stoves.

- The first Columbus Day was celebrated on October 12, 1792, 300 years after the voyage. The 400th anniversary of the landing was celebrated at the Chicago World's Fair in 1893.

- This day is marked with parades and ceremonies reenacting the landing.

Read Aloud

12 October

From where I stand now
    the world is flat,
    flat out flat,
    no end to that.

Where my eyes go the land moves out.

How is it then
five hundred years ago (about)
Columbus found
that far beyond the flat on flat
the world was round?

Myra Cohn Livingston

Ship's Biscuits

GROUP

30 MINUTES OR LONGER

In celebration of Columbus Day students make and eat ship's biscuits much like those sailors ate centuries ago.

CURRICULUM CONNECTION   **Home Economics**

Materials: mixing bowl, measuring cup, measuring spoon, large spoon, rolling pin, pastry board or mat, plastic cups or round cookie cutters, cookie sheet, oven

Ingredients: 2 cups flour, 1/2 teaspoon salt, 1 tablespoon shortening or cooking oil, 9 tablespoons water

1. Combine the flour, salt, and shortening and gradually add the water. Mix to form a workable dough.

2. Have students take turns rolling the dough on a lightly floured pastry board until it is about 1/8 inch thick.

3. Cut the biscuits from the dough using plastic cups or cookie cutters. Transfer them to an ungreased cookie sheet. Reroll the remaining dough and repeat the procedure. Bake at 350°F for 12–15 minutes.

4. As students eat the biscuits, you may tell them that biscuits such as these were kept in wooden barrels aboard ships and eaten on long voyages when food was scarce. Over time they often acquired bugs called weevils.

Election Day

Use with Chapter 8, Citizenship

Background Information

- Election Day takes place on the first Tuesday after the first Monday in November. It is the date national elections are held and is a legal holiday in most states and in all U.S. territories.

- On this day, all citizens of the United States, 18 years old and over, can take advantage of one of their most important rights—the right to vote.

- National elections for President and Vice-President occur every four years. Voters elect state senators and representatives every two years. On the national level, senators run for office every six years, and members of the House of Representatives run every two years.

- At one time there was no specific date for national elections and each state was allowed to choose its own election day. Because this policy led to many problems, Congress established Election Day in 1845.

Read Aloud

Voice Your Choice!

Voice your choice on Election Day!
Cast your vote and show the way
As citizens we have a say
In how our government works each day.

Dorrie Berkowitz

Classroom Campaigns

GROUP

Groups of students promote candidates for the job of class librarian and hold an election.

CURRICULUM CONNECTIONS Art/Language Arts

30 MINUTES OR LONGER

Materials: paper, chart paper, crayons, markers, shoe box, art knife, optional: real campaign materials

1. Divide the class into two parties. Have each party choose a favorite book character as a candidate for class librarian. In this process they should identify the qualifications of each character including his or her abilities, experience, practical knowledge, and good habits, as well as principles he or she stands for, and so on. Then have each party nominate its candidate by announcing its choice to the opposing party.

2. Allow both parties the same amount of time to work on their campaigns. Provide them with materials to prepare promotional materials such as buttons, posters, signs, fliers, and newspaper articles.

3. After each party presents its campaign, hold an election. The voters can be another class or students who do not wish to participate in the campaign. The ballots can be slips of paper with the name of each candidate and a square next to each name for marking X. The ballot box can be a shoe box with a slot cut in the lid.

Background Information

- Thanksgiving is observed on the fourth Thursday in November, a legal holiday in all states. It is celebrated in Canada on the second Monday in October.

- In 1863 President Lincoln made Thanksgiving the last Thursday in November. In 1939 President Roosevelt moved the day one week earlier. In 1941 Congress made the fourth Thursday in November the legal holiday.

- On Thanksgiving we commemorate the Pilgrims' harvest feast in Plymouth in 1621, the year after they landed. The feast lasted three days. The Pilgrims were joined by the Wampanoag with whom they had become friends. They shared duck, geese, deer, wild turkey, and berries. They had foot races and played Stool Ball, a croquet-like game.

- Thanksgiving is marked by sports events and parades signalling the start of the holiday season.

Read Aloud

Thanksgiving

The year has turned its circle,
The seasons come and go.
The harvest is all gathered in
And chilly north winds blow.

Orchards have shared their treasures,
The fields, their yellow grain,
So open wide the doorway—
Thanksgiving comes again!

Anonymous

Thanksgiving Ball Game

GROUP

Students can play the game Pilgrim and Native American children played after the feast.

30 MINUTES OR LONGER

CURRICULUM CONNECTION   Physical Education

Materials: tennis ball, two tall stools of the same height, wooden bat, yard stick

1. This game can be played outside or in the gym. Divide your class into two teams. Then place two stools 16 yards apart and mark a bowling line 8 yards in front of one stool. Position the batter at that stool, the bowler behind the line, and the bowler's team in the field behind the bowler.

2. To play, the bowler tosses the ball at the stool. The batter, using a hand or a bat, tries to hit the ball away from the stool. If the ball hits the stool the bowler scores a point, the batter is out, and another teammate has a turn to bat. If the batter hits the ball, he or she runs to the opposite stool and taps it with a hand or the bat. The batter then returns to the first stool to play again. For each run, he or she scores a point. As the batter is running to the opposite stool, the bowler and his or her team try to put the batter out by throwing the ball at that stool before the batter reaches it. Any fly ball caught is an immediate out and another teammate becomes the batter.

3. Eight balls thrown make an *over*—one team's turn at bat. Then the game changes direction with the other team batting from the opposite stool. The team with the most points after six overs wins.

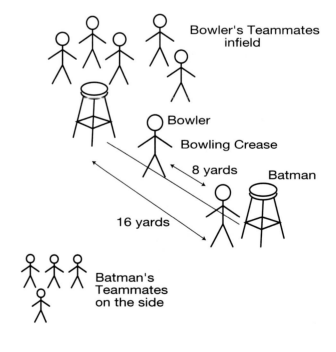

Bowler's Teammates infield

Bowler

Bowling Crease

8 yards

Batman

16 yards

Batman's Teammates on the side

Kwanzaa

Use with Chapter 9, Legacy

- Kwanzaa, celebrated from December 26 to January 1, was created in 1966 by Dr. Maulana Karenga, a professor of African studies.

- *Kwanzaa* means "first fruits of the harvest" in Swahili, an East African language, and includes many African harvest ceremonies.

- Each day of Kwanzaa is dedicated to one of seven principles, or *nguzo saba,* of African culture: *umoja*—unity; *kujichagulia*—self-determination; *ujima*—collective work and responsibility; *ujamaa*—cooperative economics; *nia*—purpose; *kuumba*—creativity; *imani*—faith

- Each evening families discuss the principle of the day and light black, red, or green candles that represent Africa. Some families also exchange gifts.

- On December 31, families and friends get together for a feast called *karamu.* It is a time to honor ancestors, eat traditional foods, play music, and dance.

Read Aloud

from "Kwanzaa Is . . ."

Kwanzaa is "nguzo saba,"
the seven principles that we harbor,
beginning with the unity
that makes us strong and helps us see
in perspective proper light
the other six that we recite.

Cedric McClester

Sweet-Potato Candy

GROUP

30 MINUTES OR LONGER

Students apply the third principle of Kwanzaa as they work together to make a pudding-type dessert they can share.

CURRICULUM CONNECTION Home Economics

Materials: large saucepan, fork, colander, pairing knives, masher, mixing bowl, large spoon, burner, measuring spoons, measuring cup, paper cups, spoons, napkins

Ingredients: 3 cups mashed sweet potatoes, 1/2 cup brown sugar, 1/2 cup white sugar, 2 tablespoons lemon juice, 1 cup miniature marshmallows, 1 tablespoon vanilla, ground cinnamon, colored sprinkles

1. Before you begin, assign students different tasks. Wash and then boil sweet potatoes in a saucepan until tender (to the touch of a fork). Drain the potatoes in a colander and allow them to cool before students peel and mash them. As an alternative, you can use canned sweet potatoes (2 lb, 8 oz) and mash them.

2. Place the mashed sweet potatoes in the saucepan and add lemon juice, sugar, and marshmallows. Cook on medium/low, stirring constantly until thick.

3. Add vanilla and cinnamon and set aside to cool.

4. Serve sweet-potato candy in small paper cups with spoons. Students can add colored sprinkles as a topping.

Background Information

- In the United States New Year's Day is celebrated on January 1; we celebrate New Year's Eve on December 31.

- New Year's Day is celebrated throughout the world, but other cultures may not celebrate on January 1.

- On New Year's Day we celebrate the end of one year and the beginning of a new year. This type of celebration has been observed throughout history. The earliest recorded New Year's Day celebration dates from 2000 B.C. in the ancient city of Mesopotamia.

- One New Year's Day tradition is making resolutions—setting goals—for the coming year.

- In the United States many people attend open-house parties. In large cities New Year's Eve street celebrations are televised. California's Tournament of Roses, a parade of floats covered with flowers, is also televised on New Year's Day.

Read Aloud

Promises

On New Year's Eve the snow came down
And covered every inch of town.
The next day winter sheets of white
Invited us to come and write
Our resolutions in the snow
So everyone in town would know
Of all the things we planned to do
To make the year completely new.

Jane Yolen

Time Capsule

GROUP

Students contribute to a time capsule that can be opened at the end of the school year.

15 TO 30 MINUTES

CURRICULUM CONNECTION Language Arts

Materials: copies of form, box with student lid for a time capsule, tape, pencils

1. Prepare forms students can fill out about themselves. See the illustration for possible items to include on the form. Give one to each student.

2. Have studetns fill out the first two columns and place the forms in the time capsule. Volunteers may wish to label the box and tape it closed.

3. Near the end of the school year, open the time capsule and redistribute the forms to the class. Direct students to fill in the third column. Then have them note any changes in their favorite things.

Martin Luther King, Jr., Day

Use with Chapter 9, Lesson 3

Background Information

- Martin Luther King, Jr., Day is celebrated on the third Monday in January. Congress established the holiday in 1983 to honor Dr. Martin Luther King, Jr., the most important civil rights leader in U.S. history. He is the only American, other than Presidents, to have a legal holiday in his honor.

- In 1955 Dr. King became famous as the leader of the Montgomery, Alabama, bus boycott that began when an African American woman named Rosa Parks refused to give up her seat on a bus to a white person. The boycott lasted for more than a year.

- Dr. King also organized the March on Washington in support of civil rights, where he gave his "I Have a Dream" speech. This march led to the signing of the Civil Rights Act, which made racial discrimination illegal.

- Dr. King was an inspiration to many people because he strived to bring about change peacefully.

- He was assassinated in 1968, at age 39.

Read Aloud

from *Martin Luther King, Jr.*

Dr. King was a man
Who stood on the mountain top
Who stood on the mountain top
Dr. King was a man
Who stood on the mountain top
Because he would not stop
 Free at last
 Free at last

     Useni Eugene Perkins

Dream Books

ON YOUR OWN

30 MINUTES OR LONGER

To celebrate the work of Martin Luther King, Jr., students make dream books.

CURRICULUM CONNECTION Language Arts

Materials: oaktag, scissors, pencils, library books about Martin Luther King, Jr., crayons, markers, stapler

1. Prepare oaktag templates of dream clouds as shown. Also have students read books and articles about Martin Luther King, Jr.

2. Have students place three sheets of paper together and fold them in half. Then have them place the template along the fold and trace it. Students will cut out the dream cloud and staple the pages together along the fold to make a book.

3. On the cover of the book, have students draw a picture of Martin Luther King, Jr., and write a title.

4. On the inside of the cover and on each of the remaining pages, have students write a sentence that tells about the work, dreams, speeches, and achievements of Martin Luther King, Jr. Have them conclude their books with a page about celebrating Martin Luther King, Jr., Day. Encourage students to use the library books and articles.

5. Provide opportunities for students to read each other's books.

Presidents' Day

Background Information

- Presidents' Day is celebrated on the third Monday in February. In some states it is called Washington–Lincoln Day.

- It is a combined holiday that honors George Washington, our nation's first President, and Abraham Lincoln, our nation's sixteenth President. It was Lincoln who wrote the Emancipation Proclamation, which paved the way for freeing enslaved African Americans.

- Official celebrations of Washington's birthday began in 1832. The first formal observance of Lincoln's birthday was held in 1866, the year after he was assassinated. Some states still observe Lincoln's birthday on the Monday before his actual birthday while others observe it on Presidents' Day.

 Read Aloud

I often pause and wonder
At fate's peculiar ways.
For nearly all our famous men
Were born on holidays.

Anonymous

Coin Collecting

GROUP

Students become numismatists as they hunt for Lincoln-head pennies.

30 MINUTES OR LONGER

CURRICULUM CONNECTION Mathematics

Materials: pennies, magnifying glass, tracing paper, envelopes, scissors, pencils, crayons, photo album with transparent covering on pages

1. Show students several Lincoln-head pennies and tell them they are going to hunt for more. Study the pennies to locate the year and the place in which the coins were minted.

2. Assign each student a range of coins to look for at home such as pennies from different decades. Provide students with envelopes to take home to collect their coins. As an alternative to bringing coins to school, students can use tracing paper and a dark crayon to make rubbings of the coins. Suggest that they write the year the coin was minted below the coins as some rubbings can be unclear. Have students bring their coins or rubbings to school on a selected date.

3. Their collections can be organized by decade in the photo album. Students can place the coins or rubbings in order by year. Any missing coins can be located by all members of the class. Return the coins to their owners when the coin collection is complete.

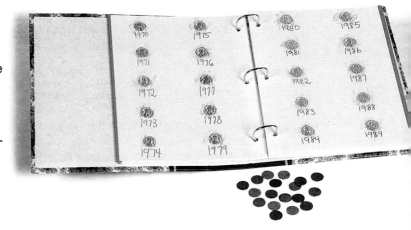

Earth Day

Background Information

- Earth Day is celebrated on April 22 throughout the United States and the world to draw attention to environmental problems. It was first celebrated in 1970.

- On the 10th anniversary of Earth Day, 250,000 people marched in New York City to help focus attention on the environment. On its 20th anniversary, 200 million people from around the world participated in parades, trash cleanups, and other projects to help Earth.

- Although Earth Day is not a legal holiday, it is important to observe because it's a time when everyone can do something to help the environment—such as plant trees, pick up trash, and set up recycling and conservation programs.

Read Aloud

from *Wild!*

Do!—do!—do!
Before the earth is through,
We have to make it green again—
So *do!—do!—do!*

Dennis Lee

Creature Recyclers

GROUP

In honor of Earth Day, groups of students make paper recyclers

30 MINUTES OR LONGER

CURRICULUM CONNECTION Art

Materials: art knife, large paper grocery bags, tempera paints, paintbrushes, construction paper and paper scraps, glue, scissors, markers; optional recycled materials: egg cartons, paper tubes, paper or plastic cups, yarn, ribbon

1. Using an art knife, help each group cut an 8" x 2" opening in the bottom of a grocery bag.

2. Direct the groups to paint their bags and decorate them with cut paper or other accessories to make a monster, a clown, a robot, an animal, or creature recycler of their choice. Tell them that the bottom of the bag will be the top of their creature recycler and the opening cut will be the creature's mouth.

3. Have students fit the decorated bag over the top of an undecorated bag. They may then clean up the classroom by feeding the creature recyclers scraps of reusable paper. In the future when they work on art projects, they can look in the bottom bag for usable scraps.

4. Groups can share their recyclers with students in other classrooms and demonstrate how to feed them pieces of scrap paper. They can also share the benefits of recycling and its impact on the environment.

Background Information

- Memorial Day is celebrated on the last Monday in May. This day honors United States soldiers who have died in wars.

- The idea for the holiday came about after the Civil War when people decorated the graves of Union and Confederate soldiers. At that time it was known as Decoration Day.

- After World War I and World War II, the holiday was extended to include soldiers who died in all wars and its name was changed to Memorial Day. Celebrating Memorial Day after the two world wars helped unite the country and eliminate tensions that existed from the Civil War.

- Soldiers who were killed in combat are honored with parades and wreath-laying ceremonies at commemorative sites and monuments. It is also a tradition for soldiers on American ships to shower the sea with flowers.

Read Aloud

There Is But One May in the Year

There is but one May in the year,
    And sometimes May is wet and cold;
There is but one May in the year
    Before the year grows old.

Yet though it be the chilliest May,
    With least of sun and most of showers,
Its wind and dew, its night and day,
    Bring up the flowers.

Christina G. Rossetti

Memorial Garden

GROUP

Have students honor the memory of loved ones or people who served our country by making flowers for a memorial garden.

30 MINUTES OR LONGER

CURRICULUM CONNECTION   **Art**

Materials: 4 paper lunch bags per student, scissors, tempera paint, paintbrushes, glue, tape, art knife, 6" to 8" deep gift box with a lid, markers

1. To make a tulip, have children measure 5 inches from the bottom of three bags and cut off the tops. Then have them scallop the open end of two of the bags to make petals and fringe the third to form a stamen. Have students apply glue to the bottom of the bag with the stamen and to one of the other bags and then stack them inside the unglued bag.

2. To make a stem have students cut the bottom from another bag and roll the bag lengthwise to form a tube. They can use tape to secure the roll. Leaves can be cut from the tops of the bags, tucked into the edge of the roll and taped. Tape the stem to one half of the base of the tulip. Then further secure it by pasting the two halves of the base together.

3. Have students paint their flowers.

4. Using an art knife, cut an opening in the top of the box. Students may take their flowers home or place them in the memorial garden.

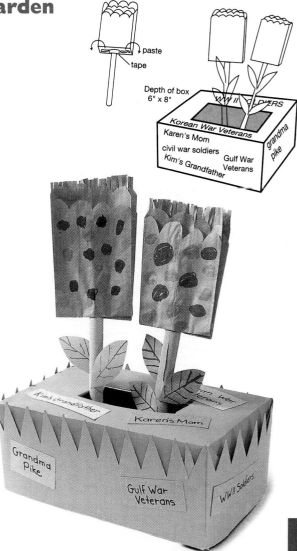

Independence Day

Use with Chapter 6, Lesson 1

Background Information

- Independence Day is our nation's birthday. We celebrate this important event on July 4 because on that day, in 1776, the Declaration of Independence was signed, declaring the colonies' independence from Great Britain.

- Although July 4 is the day we celebrate, it might have been a surprise to the writers and signers of the Declaration of Independence. They assumed we would celebrate on July 2 because that was the date the colonies voted in favor of independence.

- Independence Day was first commemorated in 1777, during the Revolutionary War. It was a noisy holiday celebrated with ringing bells, bonfires, and fireworks.

- Today we celebrate Independence Day with parades, barbecues, and the traditional fireworks.

Read Aloud

Fourth of July Night

Pin wheels whirling round
Spit sparks upon the ground,
And rockets shoot up high
And blossom in the sky—
Blue and yellow, green and red
Flowers falling on my head,
And I don't ever have to go
To bed, to bed, to bed!

Dorothy Aldis

Fireworks and Poems

GROUP

Students write a poem about Independence Day and mount it on a painting of fireworks.

30 MINUTES OR LONGER

CURRICULUM CONNECTIONS Art/Language Arts

Materials: tempera paints, water, paintbrushes, white drawing paper or mural paper, drinking straws, scissors, red or blue markers, large index cards, scrap paper, pencils, glue

1. Cut straws in half and thin different bright colors of tempera paint with water.

2. On individual sheets of drawing paper or collectively on mural paper, have students use a straw painting technique to paint fireworks. Show students how to place drops of paint on the paper with a paintbrush and then, using a straw, blow on the drops in different directions.

3. Have each student use a marker to write a five line poem—a cinquain—on the blank side of an index card. Here are the guidelines for writing a cinquain—**Line 1:** the subject; **Line 2:** two words that describe the subject; **Line 3:** three action words involved with the subject; **Line 4:** four nouns that name feelings or things about the subject; **Line 5:** one or two words to take the place of the subject

4. Have students mount their poems on their paintings.

Independence Day
loud, fun
Watching, listening, eating
picnics, parades, airshows, fireworks
4ᵗʰ of July, holiday

Communities

ADVENTURES IN TIME AND PLACE

FINDING PLACES ON A MODEL OF EARTH

Use the picture to complete the riddles below. For help, you can look back at pages G4–G11 in your textbook.

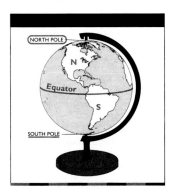

1. Look at my picture above. I am a small model of Earth.

   What am I? **a globe**

2. I am the farthest place north on Earth. What am I?
   Circle my name on the globe above.

3. I am the farthest place south on Earth. What am I?
   Underline my name on the globe.

4. I am an imaginary line circling Earth.
   I am halfway between the North Pole and the South Pole.
   Draw me on the globe. Then label me.

5. I live on the northern half of Earth.
   Put an **N** on the part of Earth where I live.

6. I live on the southern half of Earth.
   Put an **S** on that part of Earth.

WHERE IN THE WORLD?

Dana took a trip around the world. Connect the numbers on the map to see the route she took. Then complete the activities below. For help, you can look back at pages G4–G11 in your textbook.

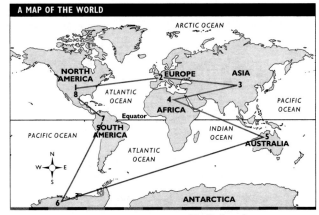

1. Where did Dana begin and end her trip? **North America**

2. Write the name of the continent Dana visited at each stop.

   Stop 2: **Europe**   Stop 5: **Australia**

   Stop 3: **Asia**   Stop 6: **Antarctica**

   Stop 4: **Africa**   Stop 7: **South America**

3. Write the name of the ocean Dana flew over between stops.

   Between Stop 1 and Stop 2: **Atlantic Ocean**

   Between Stop 4 and Stop 5: **Indian Ocean**

   Between Stop 6 and Stop 7: **Pacific Ocean**

USING A MAP AND MAP KEY

Suppose you are visiting a friend who lives in the community shown on the map below. Use the map and the map key to complete the activities. For help, look at pages G4–G11 in your textbook.

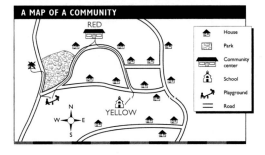

1. Your friend lives next to the park. What symbol shows the park?
   Circle your answer.

2. Your friend's house is west of the park. Put an **X** on the house.

3. You and your friend walk to the playground. What symbol shows the playground? Circle your answer.

4. Next you and your friend decide to visit the community center. Find the community center on the map. Color it red.

5. Now your friend wants to show you the school. Find the school on the map. Color it yellow.

6. Draw a line along the road to show the route you and your friend took on your walk through the neighborhood. For help, read the questions again.

USING A LANDFORM MAP

Use the map on this page to complete the activities below. For help, you can look back at pages G4–G11 in your textbook.

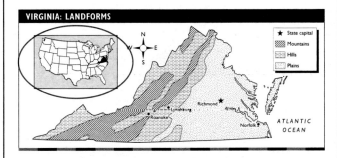

1. Look at the map title. What does the map show?

   the landforms of Virginia

2. Circle the locator map. What does it show?

   where Virginia is located in the United States

3. Look at the map key. Which pattern shows mountains? Circle your answer.

4. What other landforms are shown on the map?

   plains and hills

5. Locate Virginia's state capital. On what kind of landform is it located?

   plains

6. Find the city of Lynchburg, west of the state capital. On what kind of

   landform is Lynchburg located? **hills**

FINDING PLACES ON A GRID

The map below shows Central Park in New York City. Look at the map. Then circle the correct answer to each question. For help, you can look back at pages G4–G11 in your textbook.

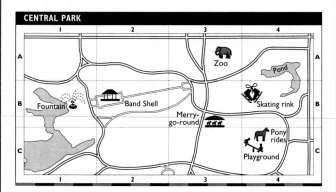

CENTRAL PARK

1. Marcia and her friends wanted to visit the zoo. In which square is the zoo located?

   (A3)   A2   B3   C4

2. After visiting the zoo, Marcia and her friends went to the playground. In which square is the playground located?

   B3   A4   (C4)   B2

3. Marcia wanted to show her friends something in square B3. What did she want to show them?

   a fountain   (a merry-go-round)   a skating rink

4. Marcia and her friends went to square B1. What did they see there?

   a pond   a band shell   (a fountain)

LOOKING AT A COMMUNITY

The pictures show some things that make up a community. Write the word or words from the box that describe each picture. For help, you can look back at pages 8–13 in your book.

| people | neighborhood | people helping |
| stores | people having fun | people working together |

people _____   **neighborhood** _____

stores _____   **people having fun** _____

people helping _____   **people working together** _____

DIFFERENT KINDS OF COMMUNITIES

Read what each person says. Then draw a line to the picture that shows the person's community. For help, you can look back at pages 16–21 in your book.

I live in a farming community. There are few stores nearby, but there is a lot of open land. People need cars to get around.

I live in a very large city. Many people live in apartment buildings. My city has many stores, restaurants, and tall office buildings.

I live in a community near a large city. Most people here live in houses near each other. There are business areas where people work.

urban community

suburban community

rural community

Write a sentence that describes your community. _____

Answers will vary.

USING A MAP SCALE

Use the map and the map scale to answer the questions. For help, you can look back at pages 22–23 in your book.

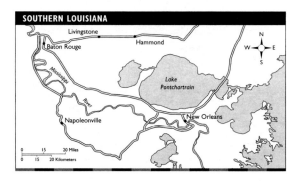

SOUTHERN LOUISIANA

1. Ed's family is going to drive from New Orleans to Baton Rouge. About how far will they travel?
   about 80 miles

2. Cathy's family is driving from New Orleans to Napoleonville. About how far will they travel?
   about 60 miles

3. Whose trip is longer, Ed's or Cathy's?
   Ed's trip is longer.

4. How does the map scale help you know this?
   It helps you measure and
   compare distances.

5. Cathy wants to see the Mississippi River while she is in Napoleonville. About how far will she have to travel?
   about 10 miles

6. Rob lives in Baton Rouge. He wants to take a driving trip. But he does not want to travel more than 40 miles from home. Which city on the map can he visit?
   Livingstone

7. About how far away is this city from Baton Rouge?
   about 35 miles

THINKING ABOUT MEXICO CITY

Use this picture of El Zócalo to help you complete the activities below. For help, you can look back at pages 24–29 in your book.

Adiós.   Buenos días.

1. List two ways Mexico City is different from most urban communities in the United States.

   Possible answers: It is the oldest city in North America, and

   Spanish is the main language.

   Circle the word or words that best describe the reason for these differences. **Answers will vary.**

       size   age   culture

2. List two ways Mexico City is like many urban communities in the United States.

   Possible answers: It is a very large city; many people live

   there; it is an exciting, active place to live; it has a rich past;

   it mixes old and new.

3. List two ways Cuajimalpa, Mexico, and Bothell, Washington, are alike.

   They are both suburban communities, and both communities

   are growing as new people move in.

USING NEW WORDS

Choose a word or words from the box to complete each sentence. For help, you can refer to the lessons in Chapter 1 of your book.

port	suburb	transportation	culture
rural	hurricane	national park	citizen
urban	pollution	community	island

1. A storm with very strong winds and heavy rains is a <u>hurricane</u>.

2. A member of a community or a country is a <u>citizen</u>.

3. Anything that spoils land, water, or air is called <u>pollution</u>.

4. A place made up of several neighborhoods where people live, work, and have fun together is a <u>community</u>.

5. A place where ships load and unload goods is called a <u>port</u>.

6. Land surrounded on all sides by water is called an <u>island</u>.

7. A place of farms and open country is <u>rural</u>.

8. A community that includes a city and its surrounding areas is called an <u>urban</u> community.

9. Moving people and products from place to place is called <u>transportation</u>.

10. Land set aside by a government for all people to enjoy is a <u>national park</u>.

11. A community located near a city is a <u>suburb</u>.

12. The way of life of a group of people is its <u>culture</u>.

LOOKING AT OUR COUNTRY'S GEOGRAPHY

Use the map to complete the activities on this page. For help, you can look back at pages 36–43 in your book.

LANDFORMS OF THE UNITED STATES

1. What two large bodies of water border the United States?

   Pacific Ocean, Atlantic Ocean

2. What large landform extends from the western part of the United States north into Canada?

   Rocky Mountains

3. Find this landform on the map. Color it brown.

4. What body of water lets boats travel from the middle of the United States south to the Gulf of Mexico?

   Mississippi River

5. Find this body of water on the map. Trace it in blue.

LOOKING AT OUR NATURAL RESOURCES

Read the poem. Then complete the activities below. For help, you can look back at pages 46–49 in your book.

Rain
The rain is raining all around.
It falls on field and tree,
It rains on the umbrellas here,
And on the ships at sea.
—Robert Louis Stevenson

1. Name the natural resource mentioned in the poem. <u>rain or water</u>

2. Give two reasons this natural resource is important.

   Possible answers: Plants need water to grow; people and

   animals need water to live; boats travel on water.

3. The poem names one natural resource. In the chart below, three other natural resources are listed. Tell how each resource is used.

NATURAL RESOURCES	USE
trees	**Many things are made from trees, such as paper.**
air	**People and animals need air to breathe.**
soil	**Plants and trees grow in the soil.**

USING INTERMEDIATE DIRECTIONS

Use the map to answer the questions. Draw a circle around your answer. For help, you can look back at pages 50–51 in your book.

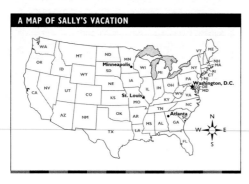

A MAP OF SALLY'S VACATION

1. Sally's family is taking a vacation. First they are going from St. Louis, Missouri, to Atlanta, Georgia. In what direction will they be going?

    NE   (SE)   SW   NW

2. Next Sally's family is going from Atlanta to Washington, D.C. What direction will they take?

    (NE)   SE   SW   NW

3. From Washington, D.C., Sally's family will travel to Minneapolis, Minnesota. In what direction will they be traveling?

    NE   SE   SW   (NW)

4. From Minneapolis, Sally's family will fly home to St. Louis. In what direction will they be flying?

    NE   (SE)   SW   NW

FINDING FACTS ABOUT PARACAS

Use the pictures to complete the activities below. For help, you can look back at pages 52–56 in your book.

Color

1. Color the picture that shows what Paracas is like.

2. Put an **X** next to each sentence that is true about Paracas.

    _X_ **a.** Paracas is a rural ocean community in Peru.

    _X_ **b.** Almost everyone in Paracas makes a living from fishing.

    _____ **c.** There are many tall buildings in Paracas.

    _X_ **d.** The children in Paracas play soccer on the beach.

    _____ **e.** Forests are an important natural resource in Paracas.

    _X_ **f.** People come from all over the world to see the wildlife in Paracas.

    _____ **g.** Farming is an important part of life in Paracas.

HEMISPHERE DETECTIVE

Be a hemisphere detective. Use the maps to answer the questions. For help, you can look back at pages 58–59 in your book.

1. I am on a continent. It is completely in the Western Hemisphere. It is also completely in the Northern Hemisphere. Where am I? Color the continent red. **North America**

2. I am on a different continent now. Most of this continent is in the Northern Hemisphere and the Eastern Hemisphere. Some of it is in every hemisphere. Where am I? Color the continent green. **Asia**

3. I am now on a continent that is in the Eastern Hemisphere. Some of it is also in the Southern Hemisphere and in the Northern Hemisphere. Where am I now? Color the continent yellow. **Africa**

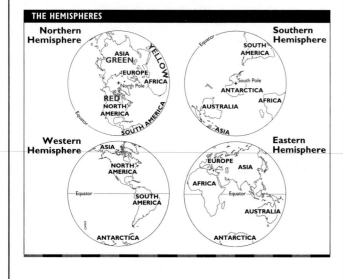

THE HEMISPHERES

THINKING ABOUT NEW WORDS

Write each word or pair of words under its meaning. For help, you can refer to the lessons in Chapter 2 of your book.

coast	environment	landform	wildlife
plain	natural resource	geography	minerals
climate	peninsula	recycling	plateau

1. land surrounded by water on three sides

    peninsula

2. a large area of flat land

    plain

3. the study of Earth's surface, the bodies of water that cover it, and how Earth is important to people's lives

    geography

4. animals that live naturally in an area

    wildlife

5. things found in the earth that are not plants or animals

    minerals

6. the shape of the surface of the land

    landform

7. the weather of a place over a long period of time

    climate

8. land next to an ocean

    coast

9. the air, water, land, and living things around us

    environment

10. something found in nature that people use

    natural resource

11. high, flat land that is raised above surrounding land

    plateau

12. using something over again

    recycling

LOCATING NATIVE AMERICAN CULTURES

Use the map and pages 70–75 in your book to complete the chart. Name each cultural area and one culture group that lives in each area. The first one has been done for you.

NATIVE AMERICAN CULTURAL AREAS

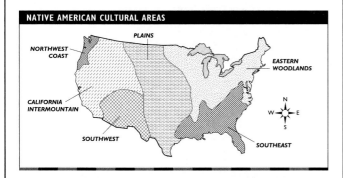

MAP KEY	CULTURAL AREA AND GROUP
	Plains—Blackfoot, **Crow**, Lakota, Cheyenne, Comanche, Coahuiltecan
	California-Intermountain—Pomo, Ute
	Southeast—Seminole, Chickasaw, Timucua, Caddo, Cherokee, Creek
	Northwest Coast—Chinook, Makah
	Eastern Woodlands—Wampanoag, Menominee, Iroquois, Delaware, Illinois, Powhatan
	Southwest—Navajo, Hopi, Zuni, Anasazi, Apache

LOOKING AT WHERE THE ANASAZI LIVED

Draw a line from the first question in each group to the picture that answers it. Then write the answer to the second question. For help, you can look back at pages 78–81 in your book.

1. Which picture shows a landform the Anasazi used for their homes?

   What are two other landforms the Anasazi used for their homes?

   cliffs and canyons

   _____

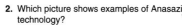

2. Which picture shows examples of Anasazi technology?

   What did the Anasazi use these things for?

   Pointed sticks were for digging

   ditches, and stone axes were

   for clearing land.

3. Which picture shows examples of how the Anasazi used the resources of the desert to make things?

   What natural resources did the Anasazi use to make these things?

   plants and clay

   _____

TALKING WITH AN ANASAZI

Suppose you could talk to Little Rabbit at Mesa Verde. Below are some questions you might ask. Think about how he might answer your questions. Write his answers on the lines in complete sentences. For help, you can look back at pages 82–87 in your book.

Question: What kind of house do you live in? How would you describe it?

Answer: My house is called a cliff house. It has many rooms and is built in the side of a mesa.

Question: What jobs do men and women have in your community?

Answer: The men hunt for food, farm, and weave baskets.

The women take care of the children, work in the fields, make pottery, weave baskets, and cook.

Question: How do children help in your community?

Answer: The children help by working in the fields. They also help their parents with many other tasks.

Question: What do you use the kiva for?

Answer: The kiva is used for religious ceremonies and meetings.

Question: I understand you are having a ceremonial dance tomorrow. Where will it be held? What is it for?

Answer: The dance will be held in the field. We are dancing to give thanks for the ripe food from the fields.

TOURING MESA VERDE NATIONAL PARK

Use the map of Mesa Verde National Park to complete the questions and activities below. For help, you can look back at pages 88–91 in your book.

1. Where is the best place to start your tour of Mesa Verde National Park? Circle that place on the map. Why is this a good place to start?

   You can get an idea of what Anasazi life was like from the museum's artifacts.

2. What sites would you like to see at Mesa Verde National Park? Draw a line on the map to show your route. **Answers will vary.**

3. What are two important lessons we can learn from the Anasazi?

   Possible answer: We can learn to work well together in our communities, and we can also learn to respect nature and think about the results of our actions.

4. What can we learn by studying the past?

   We can learn how people lived in communities and about our own communities today.

MAKING DECISIONS

Read about the choices Sara must make. Circle the answer to each question. For help, you can look back at pages 92–93 in your book.

1. Sara's goal is to visit the sites in Mesa Verde National Park. It is a warm and sunny day, and she will be hiking from one site to another. She will also have to do some climbing to see the cliff houses. Sara wants to be comfortable and safe. What should she wear?

Give a reason for your answer.

Possible answer: Blue jeans and a T-shirt are comfortable for

walking and climbing in warm weather, and hiking boots will

keep Sara from slipping.

2. Sara wants to remember what she sees at Mesa Verde National Park. But she doesn't want to carry too many things. What would be best for her to take along?

Give a reason for your answer.

Possible answer: The pocket camera would be easy to carry

and still allow Sara to keep track of what she sees.

USING NEW WORDS

Use the words in the box to complete the sentences below. For help, you can look back at the lessons in Chapter 3 of your book.

history	mesa	technology
desert	cliff	museum
artifact	kiva	canyon

Maria and Luis decide to go to a ___museum___ to learn about the Anasazi people. There they can look at objects of Anasazi art and science. They can also learn about Anasazi ___history___, the story of the people's past.

The museum has a model of an Anasazi community. In the middle of the model is a landform called a ___mesa___, which looks like a high, flat table. A model of an Anasazi house is built into the side of a steep rock face called a ___cliff___. The rock face is part of a deep river valley with steep sides called a ___canyon___. The Anasazi house has a special room called a ___kiva___ that was used for religious purposes. Maria and Luis also learn from the model that the Anasazi lived in a dry environment called a ___desert___. Very little rain fell there.

The museum also has an Anasazi digging stick. It is an ___artifact___ left behind by the Anasazi people. The digging stick is an example of ___technology___ because the Anasazi used it to serve their needs.

THE GEOGRAPHY OF JAMESTOWN

Look at the map of Jamestown. Then follow the directions. For help, you can look back at pages 98–101 of your book.

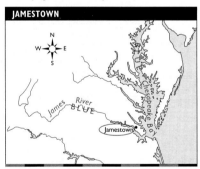

1. Find the part of the map that shows Jamestown. Draw a circle around that part.

   Who was living in this area when the English arrived? **the Powhatan**

2. Find the James River. Trace it in blue. Then label it. What is one way the first people in this area used the river?

   They used the river for fishing.

3. Find Chesapeake Bay on the map. Color it blue. Then label it. What did Chesapeake Bay provide the English settlers?

   It provided them with a good port for their boats and

   protection from attack.

   What did Chesapeake Bay provide the Powhatan?

   It provided them with resources for fishing.

4. Why was the land around Jamestown a good environment for both the Powhatan and the English? **It was good for farming.**

THINKING ABOUT JAMESTOWN

Next to each event write the year it took place. Then answer the questions. For help, look back at pages 102–107 in your book.

1607 — **The Powhatan and the English First Meet**

Where did this meeting take place?
in Jamestown

Who was the leader of the Powhatan?
Powhatan

How long ago was the meeting?
almost 400 years ago

1609 — **Colonists Face "Starving Time"**

What happened in Jamestown during this period?
There was little food for the colonists, and
they were starving and dying from diseases.

1612 — **Colonists Grow New Kind of Tobacco**

Why was this event important for Jamestown?
The tobacco was sold for a lot of money,
which made England and Jamestown richer.

1614 — **John Rolfe Marries Pocahontas**

Why was this marriage important?
It led to a long time of peace between the
Powhatan and the English.

WRITING ABOUT JAMESTOWN

Write a guide for people visiting Jamestown Settlement and the Powhatan village. Use the questions and pictures below to help you. Write your answers in complete sentences. For help, you can look back at pages 108–111 in your book.

> • Why would people want to visit Jamestown Settlement?
> • What would visitors see at the English village?
> • What would visitors see docked in the James River?
> • What would visitors see in the Powhatan village?

Possible answer:

At Jamestown Settlement you can

see what life was like long ago. In

the English village you can see

houses built from plaster and grass.

You can see people dressed in

clothes from long ago, using tools

from that time. You can also see

three boats docked in the James River.

They are copies of the boats colonists

sailed on years ago.

   In the Powhatan village you can see how

Native Americans ground corn and how

they cooked their meals. You can also

make rope like the Powhatan did long ago.

JAMESTOWN'S EARLY HISTORY

Use the time line on this page to answer the questions below. For help, you can look back at pages 112–113 in your book.

Native Americans are living in an area later called Virginia	Colonists arrive at James River to start a new colony	Many colonists die during the "starving time"	John Rolfe grows a new kind of tobacco	Pocahontas marries John Rolfe
1600	1607	1609	1612	1614

1. How many years does the time line cover? **14 years**

2. In what year did colonists arrive at the James River? **1607**

3. What happened at Jamestown five years after it was founded?
   John Rolfe grew a new tobacco.

4. What important event took place in 1614?
   Pocahontas and John Rolfe were married.

5. How many years ago was the "starving time"?
   the difference between 1609 and the current year

Complete the time line below. Show some important events in the recent past. Be sure to include the year you are in now.

USING NEW WORDS

Use the code to figure out the words. Then write the number of each word next to its meaning. For help, you can look back at the lessons in Chapter 4.

Code

a = z	g = t	l = o	q = j	v = e
b = y	h = s	m = n	r = i	w = d
c = x	i = r	n = m	s = h	x = c
d = w	j = q	o = l	t = g	y = b
e = v	k = p	p = k	u = f	z = a
f = u				

1. xlolmb
   colony

2. orermt srhglib nfhvfn
   living history museum

3. yzb
   bay

4. hozevib
   slavery

5. xlolmrhg
   colonist

6. xlzhgzo kozrm
   coastal plain

___3___ a. a body of water partly surrounded by land

___6___ b. flat land along a coast

___1___ c. a place that is ruled by another country

___5___ d. someone who lives in a colony

___4___ e. the practice of one person owning another

___2___ f. a place where people dress, talk, and do things as they did long ago

---

THINKING ABOUT SAN ANTONIO

Use the map of San Antonio to help you complete the following activities. For help, you can refer to pages 118–121 of your book.

1. Find the San Antonio River. Trace it in blue. Then label it.

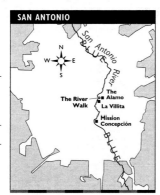

2. Which Native American group lived along this river?
   the Payaya

   What did their name for the river mean in English?
   Refreshing Waters

3. What did the people of San Antonio build along the river in the 1920s?
   the River Walk

   What was the original hope for it? **It was hoped the River Walk**
   would help business and protect the beauty of the river.

4. Until the 1950s what was much of the land around the river used for?
   It was used for farming.

   Why was the land especially good for what it was used for?
   The river made the soil moist and full of minerals.

5. How is the river important to the people of San Antonio today?
   The River Walk provides jobs and a place for the community to
   gather.

WRITING ABOUT THE SPANISH MISSIONS

Use the space provided to answer the questions in each box. Write your answers in complete sentences. For help, look back at pages 122–127 in your book.

> • What were the missions?
> • Who set them up?
> • Why were they set up?

The missions were communities. Roman Catholic priests from

Mexico set up the missions to teach their religion to others.

_____

> • What did the missions offer Native Americans?
> • What did Native Americans have to do in return?

The missions offered Native Americans food and a safe place to

live. The Native Americans had to work for their food. They also

had to learn about the Catholic religion.

_____

> • How did the way of life of many Native Americans change because of the missions?

Over time many Native Americans like the Coahuiltecan lost their

own culture. They began to speak Spanish. They became Catholic.

_____

SAN ANTONIO CELEBRATES ITS PAST

Draw a line from the first question in each group to the picture that answers it. Write the answers to the other questions. For help, you can look back at pages 128–132 in your book.

1. Which picture shows one of San Antonio's old missions?

   How are the missions used today?

   Some are museums, and

   some are churches.

2. Which picture shows San Antonio's biggest celebration?

   What is this celebration called?

   Fiesta

   What special day does it include?

   San Jacinto Day

   What does that day celebrate?

   Texas's freedom from

   Mexico

3. Which picture shows a popular game played in San Antonio? Where did this game come from?

   Mexico

USING GRAPHS

Study the graphs below. Then answer each question. For help, you can look back at pages 134–135 in your book.

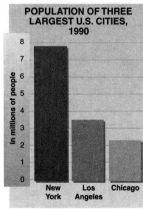

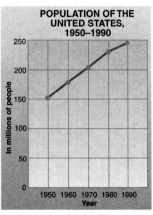

Source: *The World Almanac and Book of Facts, 1995*

Source: *The World Almanac and Book of Facts, 1995*

1. What are graphs such as the one above used for?

   to compare things

   _____

2. About how many people lived in New York City in 1990?

   about 7,800,000 people

3. Which city on the graph had the smallest population in 1990?

   Chicago

4. What are graphs such as the one above used for?

   to show how something

   changes over time

5. What was the population of the United States in 1990?

   249 million

6. How did the population of the United States change from 1950 to 1990?

   It got larger.

FINDING AND USING NEW WORDS

Follow the directions to find each hidden word. Then write the word.

1. Cross out the letters c, p, and b.

   p c f b i c e b c s p b b t p c c a   fiesta

2. Cross out the letters b, w, and u.

   w m b i b u b s s w u i b o b n w b a w u r y   missionary

3. Cross out the letters z, r, and g.

   c r g a z z c g r t z r g u g r s   cactus

4. Cross out the letters k, s, and m.

   i k s n m d s k e p s m e n k d m e n s c s e m   independence

5. Cross out the letters y, d, and x.

   d y m x i y d s y s d x i d o x n   mission

6. Cross out the letters w, h, and m.

   w h v o m w l h u n m h t e m w e r h   volunteer

Write each hidden word next to its meaning. For help, you can look back at the lessons in Chapter 5 of your book.

7. a priest who sets up a mission   missionary

8. a Spanish word that means "festival"   fiesta

9. a type of plant with sharp spines that grows in a dry environment   cactus

10. freedom from others   independence

11. a community set up by Roman Catholic priests to teach their religion to others   mission

12. someone who does something by choice and without pay   volunteer

WRITING ABOUT BENJAMIN FRANKLIN

Use the space provided to answer the questions in each box. Write your answers as sentences in a paragraph. Your paragraphs will be a summary of important facts about Benjamin Franklin. For help, you can look back at pages 146–151 in your textbook.

Benjamin Franklin

- Where did Benjamin Franklin grow up?
- Where did he move when he was 17?
- Why was this an important place?
- What popular book did Benjamin Franklin begin writing a few years after he moved?
- What are two ways Benjamin Franklin helped his community?

Benjamin Franklin grew up in Boston, Massachusetts. When he was 17 he moved to Philadelphia, the biggest, busiest city in all the colonies. A few years later he began writing *Poor Richard's Almanac*. He helped his community by setting up the first lending library and inventing a stove that helped people heat their homes better.

- How did Benjamin Franklin help America in 1776?
- What statement did he and other leaders adopt on July 4, 1776?
- Why was this statement important?

In 1776 Benjamin Franklin met with other leaders to work together to win the war against England. On July 4, 1776, they adopted the Declaration of Independence, which explained why the colonies should be free.

OUR PLAN OF GOVERNMENT

Use the pictures on the right to complete the activities on this page. For help, you can look back at pages 154–159 in your textbook.

1. **a.** Draw a line to the picture that shows where our plan of government is described.

   b. What are the three branches of government named in the plan?

   President, Congress,

   and Supreme Court

   _____

George Washington

United States Constitution

2. **a.** Draw a line to the picture of the person who suggested three branches of government.

   b. How did this person help us know what happened at the meeting in which the Constitution was written?

   He took careful notes.

   _____

3. **a.** Draw a line to the picture of the person who became our country's first President.

   b. How is the President chosen?

   The President is elected.

   c. What is the President's job?

   to see that our country's

   laws are carried out

James Madison

COMPARING AND CONTRASTING

Think about how Benjamin Franklin and George Washington were alike and different. Underline the answer to each question. For help, you can look back at pages 160–161 in your textbook.

Benjamin Franklin

George Washington

1. Where was Benjamin Franklin's home?
   - **a.** Philadelphia
   - **b.** Virginia
   - **c.** New York

2. What did Franklin want the colonies to become?
   - **a.** part of England
   - **b.** an independent country
   - **c.** a state

3. What did Benjamin Franklin do in 1776?
   - **a.** led America's whole army
   - **b.** took part in adopting the Declaration of Independence
   - **c.** wrote the Declaration of Independence

4. What did Franklin do in 1787?
   - **a.** stayed home
   - **b.** helped write the Constitution
   - **c.** took notes at the convention

5. Where was George Washington's home?
   - **a.** Philadelphia
   - **b.** Virginia
   - **c.** New York

6. What did Washington want the colonies to become?
   - **a.** part of England
   - **b.** an independent country
   - **c.** a state

7. What did George Washington do in 1776?
   - **a.** led America's whole army
   - **b.** took part in adopting the Declaration of Independence
   - **c.** wrote the Declaration of Independence

8. What did Washington do in 1787?
   - **a.** stayed home
   - **b.** helped write the Constitution
   - **c.** took notes at the convention

USING NEW WORDS

Finish each sentence by matching a word or term in the box with its meaning. For help, look at the lessons in Chapter 6 of your textbook.

tax	American Revolution	Bill of Rights
elect	Declaration of Independence	Constitution
almanac	Supreme Court	compromise
Congress	President	

1. A book that comes out every year is an almanac _____.

2. Money that people pay to support the government is a tax _____.

3. The fighting that began in 1775 between the colonists and the English is called the American Revolution _____.

4. The statement about why the colonies should be free is called the Declaration of Independence _____.

5. The laws and plan for how the government of our country works is called the Constitution _____.

6. To choose by voting is to elect _____.

7. The settlement of an argument by each side agreeing to give up some of its demands is a compromise _____.

8. The part of the government made up of the Senate and the House of Representatives is the Congress _____.

9. The leader of our country is the President _____.

10. The part of government that makes sure our laws are fair is the Supreme Court _____.

11. The list of our country's most important rights and freedoms is the Bill of Rights _____.

DECIDING ON OUR NATION'S CAPITAL

Answer the following questions by using the map and pages 166–169 in your book.

1. What does the map show?

   <u>the 13 original states in 1790</u>

2. Look closely at the map. Circle the name of the city that is the capital of our country.

3. Why did the leaders of the United States have trouble deciding where to build the capital city?

   <u>Leaders from the South</u>

   <u>wanted the capital to be in</u>

   <u>the South, and leaders from</u>

   <u>the North wanted the capital</u>

   <u>to be in the North.</u>

THE ORIGINAL STATES, 1790

4. How is the location of our country's capital a compromise?

   <u>It is in the middle of the 13 original states.</u>

5. What do you think it was like to live in the capital during the time of John Adams?

   <u>Answers will vary but should indicate that Washington, D.C.,</u>

   <u>was still being built in the late 1790s and 1800.</u>

A VISIT TO WASHINGTON, D.C.

Look at these pictures of memorials in Washington, D.C. Write a fact about each one in the space below. For help, you can look back at pages 170–175 in your book.

Vietnam Veterans Memorial

Fact: <u>The names of the American soldiers who died in the Vietnam War are printed on this memorial.</u>

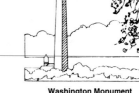

Lincoln Memorial

Fact: <u>This memorial was built to honor President Abraham Lincoln.</u>

Jefferson Memorial

Fact: <u>This memorial was built to honor the man who wrote the Declaration of Independence.</u>

Washington Monument

Fact: <u>This monument is the tallest stone structure in the world and is named after our first President.</u>

FINDING PLACES ON A GRID MAP

Complete the index for this grid map of Washington, D.C. Write each place name in the index box. Next to the name write the place's location on the map. The first one has been done for you. For help, you can look back at pages 176–177 in your textbook.

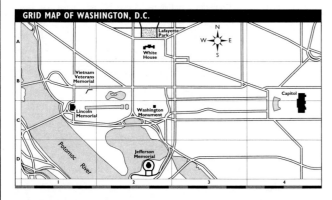

GRID MAP OF WASHINGTON, D.C.

INDEX

PLACE	LOCATION ON MAP
Capitol	B4–C4
Jefferson Memorial	D2
Lafayette Park	A2
Lincoln Memorial	C1
Vietnam Veterans Memorial	B1
Washington Monument	C2
White House	A2

COMPARING CAPITALS

Read each clue. Then circle the picture of the city each clue tells about. If a clue tells about both cities, circle both pictures. For help, you can look back at pages 178–181 in your textbook.

Washington, D.C.   **Dakar**

1. This city is the capital of its country.

2. This city is located on a peninsula that is nearly surrounded by the Atlantic Ocean.

3. This city is part of a program called Sister Cities.

4. This city is located on the western coast of its country.

5. This city is a main seaport.

6. This city has a building called the Capitol, where Congress meets.

7. This city is home for its country's President.

8. This city has a building called the White House, where the country's President lives.

THINKING ABOUT NEW WORDS

Put an **X** next to each statement that correctly uses the word in dark print. For help, you can look back at the lessons in Chapter 7 of your textbook.

1. ambassador

_____ **a.** An ambassador is a person who is the head of a city government.

___X___ **b.** An ambassador is a person who is sent to another country to represent his or her country.

_____ **c.** An ambassador goes to another country to join the parliament of that country.

2. capital

___X___ **a.** A capital is the place where the government of a country or state is located.

___X___ **b.** Washington, D.C., is the capital of the United States.

_____ **c.** A capital is a reminder of a person or event.

3. mayor

___X___ **a.** A mayor is the head of a city government.

_____ **b.** A mayor is the leader of a country.

_____ **c.** George Washington was the mayor of Washington, D.C.

4. memorial

___X___ **a.** A memorial is a reminder of a person or event.

_____ **b.** A memorial is the place where the government of a country or state is located.

___X___ **c.** The Jefferson Memorial is located in Washington, D.C.

STATE AND LOCAL GOVERNMENT

Look at the pictures and read the questions. Draw a line under each correct answer. For help, look back at pages 186–189 in your textbook.

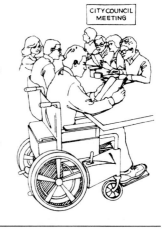

CITY COUNCIL MEETING

1. What group of people is having a meeting?

   a. <u>members of a city council</u>

   b. members of a town meeting

2. Which kind of government is the group a part of?

   a. <u>local government</u>

   b. state government

3. How is this group chosen?

   a. may be chosen by the mayor

   b. <u>may be elected</u>

4. What job does this group have?

   a. makes sure laws are obeyed

   b. <u>makes laws for the city</u>

5. Who is this person?

   a. a mayor

   b. <u>a governor</u>

6. What kind of government is this person a part of?

   a. local government

   b. <u>state government</u>

7. What does the governor do?

   a. <u>helps make state laws</u>

   b. chooses mayors for the cities

GOVERNOR'S OFFICE

USING A LIBRARY

The students of Shapleigh, Maine, want to make a guide to the wildlife they see in their park. Follow the directions to show how they can complete their guide. For help, you can look back at pages 190–191 in your textbook.

REFERENCE   FICTION   NONFICTION

1. The students want to include the birds they see in their park. Circle the sign in the picture that tells where they would find this information.

2. The students want to include a book called *A Field Guide to the Birds* by Roger Tory Peterson. Where in the nonfiction section would they look? Circle your answer.

   (in the animal section)   in the gardening section

3. The students want to include information about robins. Which book would help them? Circle your answer.

   dictionary   (encyclopedia)

Put an **X** on the sign in the picture that names the section where they would find this book.

4. Suppose the students looked up the word *robin* in the encyclopedia. The guide words at the top of the page they turned to were *river* and *rope*. Circle the words that tell where they would find the topic they wanted.

   before this page   (on this page)   after this page

5. Some students want to include made-up stories about animals. Draw a line under the sign in the picture that names the section where they would find these stories.

BEING A GOOD CITIZEN

On the lines, list three ways that you can be a good citizen in your community. Then circle one of the ways. Make a poster in the space below that shows you being a good citizen in the way you circled. For help, you can look back at pages 192–197 in your textbook.

Answers will vary but should include examples of how to take

part in government, ways to volunteer to help others, and ways

to improve community life.

Be a Good Citizen

T23

USING NEW WORDS

Use the code to figure out the words. Then write the number of each word next to its meaning. For help, you can look back at the lessons in Chapter 8 of your textbook.

Code				
a = b	g = n	l = x	q = s	v = i
b = d	h = p	m = z	r = q	w = g
c = f	i = r	n = y	s = o	x = e
d = h	j = t	o = w	t = m	y = c
e = j	k = v	p = u	u = k	z = a
f = l				

1. f s y z f w s k x i g t x g j
   local government

2. H f x b w x s c Z f f x w v z g y x
   Pledge of Allegiance

3. w s k x i g s i
   governor

4. j s o g t x x j v g w
   town meeting

5. y v j n y s p g y v f
   city council

  3 **a.** the head of each state's government

  1 **b.** the government in each city or community

  5 **c.** a group of elected people who make the laws for a city

  4 **d.** a type of local government in which people come together to decide on the laws and rules that are important to their community

  2 **e.** words people say promising to be loyal to our country

---

TRAVELING WEST

Use the map below to complete the activities on this page. For help, you can look back at pages 210–215 in your textbook.

THE OREGON TRAIL

Present-day state borders are shown

1. The map shows one of the trails that many pioneers took west. What is the name of this trail?

   the Oregon Trail

2. Circle the city on the map where the trail began. Why was this a good place to begin the trail?

   It had many shops that
   sold supplies and animals
   for the long journey.

3. According to the map, which large mountain range did the pioneers have to cross?

   the Rocky Mountains

   Label this range on the map.

4. How did groups of pioneers travel along this trail?

   in wagon trains

   What were some of the hardships they encountered?

   They crossed rivers and
   mountains. They faced
   snow, rain, and mud. Many
   died. Some also fought
   with Native Americans.

5. Why did so many pioneers make this dangerous journey?

   They wanted to build better
   lives in new communities.

PLANNING A CAMPING TRIP

Larry and his family are planning a camping trip. Look at the pictures of the things Larry would like to take. Then use the lines below to classify the things that Larry really needs to take and what he doesn't really need to take. For help, you can look back at pages 216–217 in your textbook.

Larry Really Needs	**Larry Doesn't Really Need**
camping stove	kite
compass	ball and bat
flashlight	skateboard
hiking boots	soccer ball
water	radio
food	magazines
tent	
lamp	
bug spray	

Name two other groups you can use to classify some of the things Larry wants to take.

things for cooking   things to play with

IMMIGRANTS IN THE EARLY 1900S

Use the pictures below to complete the activities on this page. For help, you can look back at pages 218–223 in your textbook.

Statue of Liberty   Ellis Island

1. What symbol of our country is shown in the picture?

   the Statue of Liberty

   What does this symbol stand for?

   Our country welcomes
   many immigrants.

2. What were two reasons immigrants came to our country?

   for freedom, for jobs

3. Circle the building that shows where many immigrants were taken.

4. What happened to immigrants when they got to this building?

   Officers decided who could
   stay in the United States.

5. What are two things that immigrants have brought to our country?

   different languages, different
   religions (and other parts of
   their different cultures)

6. What have many immigrants done for our country?

   They have made our
   country rich and strong.

ON THE ROAD TO FREEDOM

Use the pictures on the right to complete the activities on this page. For help, you can look back at pages 224–229 in your textbook.

1. **a.** Draw a line to the picture of the man who was President during the Civil War.

   b. Who fought against each other in this war?

   the Northern and Southern parts of

   the United States

   c. What did this President want to do during the Civil War?

   end slavery

Martin Luther King, Jr.

2. **a.** Draw a line to the picture of a painter.

   b. What event were his paintings about?

   the Great Migration

   c. Why did this event take place?

   African Americans hoped to build

   better lives in the North.

Abraham Lincoln

3. **a.** Draw a line to the picture of a famous leader in the 1950s and 1960s.

   b. What did this man spend his life doing?

   He worked to make sure all people

   were treated fairly.

Jacob Lawrence

TALKING WITH DELORES STIVALET

Suppose you had a chance to interview Delores Stivalet, the girl described in Lesson 4. You might ask her questions similar to the ones below. Write Delores's answers in the space provided. For help, you can look back at pages 232–236 in your textbook.

Question: You and your family are immigrants to the United States. What country and city are you from?

Delores: We are from Veracruz, Mexico.

Question: Why did your family decide to move to the United States?

Delores: My father felt that there were better schools and

more jobs in the United States.

Question: You are now living in San Diego. How is San Diego like Veracruz?

Delores: They both have busy ports and beautiful beaches.

The climate is warm in both places.

Question: What is the main difference between the two cities?

Delores: In Veracruz people speak Spanish. Here they speak

mostly English. My family and I must learn to speak

English.

Question: What do you miss about your old home?

Delores: Sometimes I miss my old friends. But I have new

friends here.

Question: What do you hope will happen someday?

Delores: My family and I hope to become citizens of the

United States.

USING NEW WORDS

Write the word or term from the box below that best matches each description. For help, you can look back at the lessons in Chapter 9 of your textbook.

oath	pioneer	oral history
diary	migration	immigrant
prairie	Civil War	Great Migration

1. flat or rolling land covered with tall grasses — **prairie**

2. a person who is among the first to explore and settle an area that is not known to him or her — **pioneer**

3. a written record of what someone has done or thought each day — **diary**

4. someone who comes to live in a new country — **immigrant**

5. telling stories about what life was like in the past — **oral history**

6. the movement of people from one part of a country or area to another — **migration**

7. the movement north by thousands of African Americans beginning around 1915 — **Great Migration**

8. the war in which the Northern and Southern parts of the United States fought each other — **Civil War**

9. a statement or promise in which a person swears that what he or she says is true — **oath**

IMPROVEMENTS IN TRANSPORTATION

Look at each picture. Name the improvement in transportation it shows. Then answer the questions. For help, you can look back at pages 242–247 in your textbook.

Improvement: steam-powered boat

Who built it? Robert Fulton

How did it improve transportation?

It allowed boats to travel

against the water's current.

Improvement: Model T automobile

Who built it? Henry Ford

How did it improve transportation?

It made cars affordable. Now

many people could travel to

different places on their own in

less time.

Name two other important improvements in transportation.

steam-powered railroad engine   airplane

On the lines that follow, explain how these improvements have helped bring people closer together.

Possible answer: Both the steam railroad and the airplane

shortened travel time and made it easier to transport people and

goods from one place to another.

READING A TRANSPORTATION MAP

Use the map to complete the activities. For help, you can look back at pages 248–249 in your textbook.

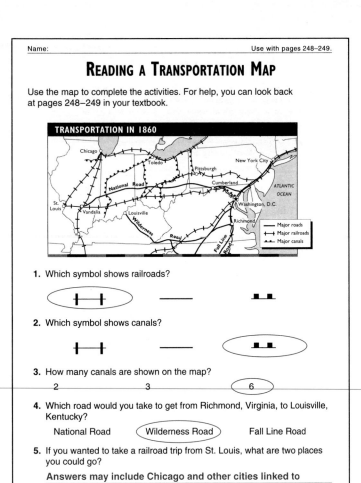

TRANSPORTATION IN 1860

1. Which symbol shows railroads?

   (⊕ ┨┠ ⊕)   ———   •▪•

2. Which symbol shows canals?

   ┨┠   ———   (• ▪ •)

3. How many canals are shown on the map?

   2   3   (6)

4. Which road would you take to get from Richmond, Virginia, to Louisville, Kentucky?

   National Road   (Wilderness Road)   Fall Line Road

5. If you wanted to take a railroad trip from St. Louis, what are two places you could go?

   Answers may include Chicago and other cities linked to

   St. Louis by rail.

THINKING ABOUT COMMUNICATION

Use the terms from the box to complete the chart below. Some information has been filled in for you. For help, look at pages 250–255 in your textbook.

telegraph	wireless telegraph	computers	telephone
television	pony express	satellites	

TYPES OF COMMUNICATION

DESCRIPTION	KIND OF COMMUNICATION	DATE INVENTED
A team of horseback riders delivers mail from one place to another across the West.	pony express	1860
Special codes are used to send words long distances over wires.	telegraph	1861
People can now speak to each other directly over wires from faraway places.	telephone	1876
Signals are sent without using wires. This leads to the invention of the radio.	wireless telegraph	1895
Pictures and sounds are sent through space.	television	1936
Spacecraft make it possible for people to communicate in seconds across oceans.	satellites	1962
People send and receive written information and pictures every day.	computers	1990s

---

TWO COUNTRIES AND A TUNNEL

Look at the picture. Then answer the questions. For help, you can look back at pages 256–261 in your textbook.

1. What event does the boy's newspaper tell about? the completion of the English Channel Tunnel

2. In which year did this event take place? 1994

3. Which two countries took part in this event? England and France

4. What did this event do for the first time? It connected France and England by railroad.

5. Why was this tunnel built? to make it easier to travel between England and France

6. How did this tunnel bring the people in these two countries closer together?

   Now the people of England and France can do business with

   and visit each other more easily. Goods can be trucked from

   one country to the other without having to be loaded onto and

   unloaded from a boat or plane.

LEARNING NEW WORDS

Use the Morse code to figure out each word below. Then write the word on the long line. For help, look at the lessons in Chapter 10 of your textbook.

Morse Code

a = •—	g = ——•	l = •—••	q = ——•—	v = •••—
b = —•••	h = ••••	m = ——	r = •—•	w = •——
c = —•—•	i = ••	n = —•	s = •••	x = —••—
d = —••	j = •———	o = ———	t = —	y = —•——
e = •	k = —•—	p = •——•	u = ••—	z = ——••
f = ••—•				

1. — • •—•• • — ——• •—• •— •—• •••• telegraph

2. —•—• ——— —— —— •• — •—• •— — • communicate

3. ••—• ••— • •—•• fuel

4. •——• ——— —• —•— • —••— •—•• •—• • ••• ••• pony   express

5. —•—• •••• •— —• —• • •—•• channel

6. ••• •— — • •—•• •—•• •• — • satellite

Write the number of each word from the list above next to its meaning.

3   **a.** something that is burned to produce power

5   **b.** a narrow waterway between two larger bodies of water

1   **c.** a machine that used special codes to send words long distances over wires

6   **d.** a spacecraft that connects radio, telephone, and television communication

2   **e.** to pass along feelings, thoughts, or information to each other

4   **f.** a team of horseback riders who rode across the western United States to deliver mail from one place to another

THINKING ABOUT JOBS AND MONEY

The picture shows Mr. Bowan's kite store in a small town. Put an **X** next to each sentence that tells something true about Mr. Bowan and his store. Then answer the question. For help, you can look back at pages 274–278 in your textbook.

__X__ **1.** Mr. Bowan makes a living by selling kites.

__X__ **2.** The kites sold in the store are goods.

__X__ **3.** The person buying a kite is a consumer.

__X__ **4.** Mr. Bowan offers a service by selling and putting together kites.

_____ **5.** The people who work for Mr. Bowan are his employers.

__X__ **6.** Mr. Bowan's store is part of the economy of his town.

You are a consumer. Name two kinds of goods that you buy.

Possible answers: food, clothes, toys, books

WHAT KIND OF JOB?

Each picture shows a person doing a job. Label each picture with a job from the box. Then answer the question at the bottom of the page. For help, you can look back at pages 280–287 in your textbook.

| builder | veterinarian | dancer |
| teacher | | police officer |

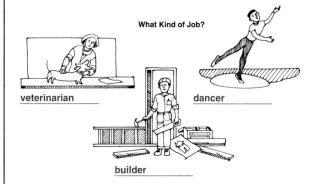

police officer _____   teacher _____

What Kind of Job?

veterinarian _____   dancer _____

builder _____

What are some of the jobs of people you know in your community?

Answers should identify typical jobs in a community.

THINKING ABOUT CAUSE AND EFFECT

Read the sentences below. Draw a circle around the sentence or sentence part that states the cause. Underline the sentence or sentence part that states the effect. For help, you can look back at pages 290–291 in your textbook.

1. Ms. Kim works hard to make textbooks interesting. As a result, children like to read and learn from her books.

2. Ms. Kim's textbooks are interesting to read because she does research to find interesting topics for the books she plans.

3. Since it takes many steps to make a textbook, many people are needed to work on it.

4. Authors and editors use computers to make changes in the books they are working on. As a result, they can make many more changes in a small amount of time.

5. Designers choose pictures and designs that children will like so the book is exciting and fun to look at.

How can understanding cause and effect connections be helpful?

Answers will vary but should reflect the idea that understanding cause and effect connections helps us understand why things happen and helps us make better decisions.

A VISIT TO JAPAN

Use the pictures on the right to complete the activities on this page. For help, you can look back at pages 292–295 in your textbook.

1. a. Draw a line to the picture that shows the country called "the land of the rising sun."

b. What is the real name for this country?

Japan

c. What is this country's capital?

Tokyo

2. a. Draw a line to the picture that shows a high-tech product made in Japan.

b. List two other high-tech products made here.

computers, cars,

televisions

3. a. Draw a line to the picture that shows an example of Japan's culture.

b. What is this event called?

No **theater**

c. List two more examples of Japanese culture that were pictured in your textbook.

pottery making and

baseball

Tokyo

T27

USING NEW WORDS

Match each word in the box to its meaning. For help, you can look back at the lessons in Chapter 11 of your textbook.

editor	services	designer	consumer
goods	economy	journalist	publishing
interest	employer	producer	high-tech

1. a person who writes for a newspaper, magazine, or television news program

   journalist

2. jobs that help other people by providing things they need or want

   services

3. someone who hires and pays other people to work

   employer

4. payment for lending money

   interest

5. a person who buys goods and services

   consumer

6. the making and consuming of goods and services

   economy

7. things that people make or grow

   goods

8. a person who makes sure each page of a book looks good

   designer

9. a maker of goods and services

   producer

10. making books, magazines, CD-ROMs, and other things people can read

    publishing

11. a person who helps with all the steps involved in making a book

    editor

12. the use of the latest technology to make electronics and other goods

    high-tech

ON THE FARM

Suppose you could interview Jon Lofgreen. You might ask him questions like the ones below. Write Mr. Lofgreen's answers in the space provided. For help, look back at pages 300–305 in your textbook.

Question: What farm products do you produce?

Mr. Lofgreen: We grow wheat and alfalfa. We also graze four hundred cattle on our land.

Question: What is most of your farmland used for?

Mr. Lofgreen: Most of the land is used for growing wheat.

Question: When do you plant your wheat crop and when do you harvest it?

Mr. Lofgreen: We plant the wheat toward the end of September. The harvest is gathered at the end of June.

Question: What happens to the wheat in the winter and spring?

Mr. Lofgreen: The wheat freezes in the winter, but the plants still produce seeds. In the spring the plants thaw and turn from dark green to light green to golden.

Question: What happens to the wheat after it is harvested?

Mr. Lofgreen: The wheat is put into holding tanks. Then trucks haul it to storage tanks. Finally it is sold to companies that grind the wheat into flour.

Question: How do you depend on technology to run your farm?

Mr. Lofgreen: I can look at my computer and know in a second what wheat is selling for. I also use my computer to decide when and where to sell my crops.

READING A FLOW CHART

A flow chart shows a sequence of steps. Study the flow chart on this page. Then answer the questions. For help, you can look back at pages 306–307 in your textbook.

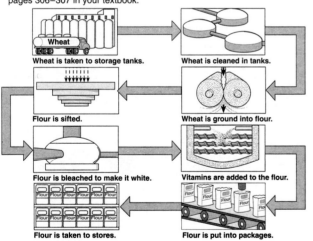

Wheat is taken to storage tanks.

Wheat is cleaned in tanks.

Flour is sifted.

Wheat is ground into flour.

Flour is bleached to make it white.

Vitamins are added to the flour.

Flour is taken to stores.

Flour is put into packages.

1. What is the first step in the flow chart?

   Wheat is taken to storage tanks.

2. Which of these steps comes first? Circle your answer.

   Wheat is ground into flour.   (Wheat is cleaned.)

3. What happens to the flour right after it is sifted?

   It is bleached to make it white.

4. What happens to the flour just before it is put into packages?

   Vitamins are added to the flour.

THINKING ABOUT MINERAL RESOURCES

Look at the picture. Then answer the questions that follow. For help, you can look back at pages 308–311 in your textbook.

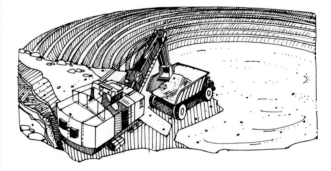

1. What does the picture show? an open pit mine

2. What mineral resource is being mined in the picture? copper

3. What are two things we make with copper? wire and jewelry

4. Is copper a renewable or nonrenewable resource? Explain your answer.

   Copper is a nonrenewable resource, because it cannot be replaced once it is used.

5. List three other mineral resources that people remove from the land.

   Answers may include iron, gold, silver, limestone, coal, and oil.

6. Why is it important to use all natural resources carefully?

   We must use them carefully to be sure they will be here for a long time.

THINKING ABOUT MANUFACTURING

Name the product in each picture. Tell how it is manufactured. Then answer the questions below. For help, you can look back at pages 312–318 in your textbook.

Product: **automobile**

How is it manufactured?
assembly line
_____

Product: **house**

How is it manufactured?
It is built one at a time by people
using tools and machines.

Name another product. Then tell how it is manufactured.
Answers will vary but may include cakes, which may be made by
hand in a local bakery, and steel, which is made in a mill.

Why do you think manufacturing is one of the most important types of businesses in our country?
Millions of people work in manufacturing. They make thousands of
different products. Manufacturing also creates jobs for people who
may sell the products in the United States or ship them to other
countries.

EXPORTS AND IMPORTS

Look at the pictures and follow the directions. For help, you can look back at pages 320–323 in your textbook.

Name a country to which the United States exports these products.
Canada

Name two products we import from this country.
fish and aluminum
_____

Name two countries to which the United States exports this product.
Russia and Japan
_____

Name a state in which this product is grown.
Kansas
_____

Name two countries from which the United States imports this product.
Philippines and India

Name a country from which the United States imports this product.
Colombia

MATCHING WORDS AND THEIR MEANINGS

Write the letter of each word or term next to its meaning. For help, you can look back at the lessons in Chapter 12 of your textbook.

a. mill	**f.** renewable resource	**k.** product map	**p.** harvest
b. robot	**g.** private property	**l.** manufacturing	**q.** fertilizer
c. import	**h.** nonrenewable resource	**m.** assembly line	**r.** process
d. trade	**i.** international trade	**n.** domestic trade	**s.** factory
e. export	**j.** public property	**o.** agriculture	

o 1. the business of growing crops and raising animals

p 2. crops that are gathered when ripe

q 3. chemicals that are used to help plants grow

k 4. a map that shows the places where goods are made or grown

r 5. to change something into a different form

f 6. a resource that can be replaced by nature, if used carefully

l 7. the business of making things

j 8. land that has been set aside for all people to use

h 9. a resource that cannot be replaced

n 10. trade within a country

s 11. a place where things are manufactured

m 12. a line of workers and machines all working together to make a final product

g 13. land that is owned by people or companies

b 14. a machine made to do a task

e 15. to sell goods to another country

d 16. the buying and selling of goods and services

a 17. a place where people use machines to make natural resources into finished products

c 18. to buy goods from another country

i 19. importing and exporting with other countries

THE GEOGRAPHY OF YOUR COMMUNITY

Write the name of your community and the name of your state. Then complete the activities. A reference book, such as an almanac, may help you.

My Community: _____   **My State:** _____

1. What is the population of your community? _____

   Is your community a city, a suburb, or a town? _____

2. How would you describe where in your state your community is located?
   _____
   _____

3. What are the important landforms in your area? _____
   _____
   _____

4. What are the important bodies of water? _____
   _____
   _____

5. How would you describe the climate in your area? _____
   _____
   _____

6. List one or more natural resources in your area.
   _____   _____
   _____   _____

7. List one or more facts that make your community special.
   _____

A Song About the Environment

Make up a song about helping the environment in your community. Write words to a tune you already know. Here's a cleanup song written to the tune of "The Farmer in the Dell." You can use the same tune if you wish.

Don't Litter

Don't throw your litter here.
Don't throw your litter there.
Just put your trash where it belongs,
And do your share!

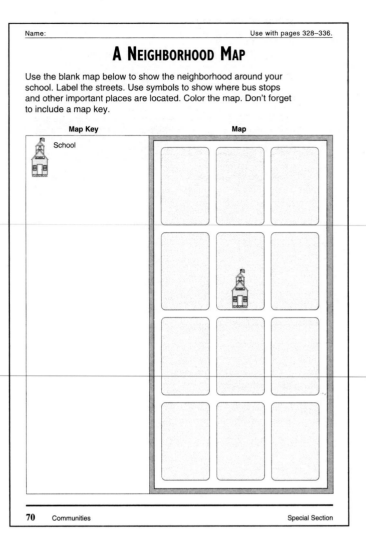

Title _____

To the tune of _____

By _____

_____
_____
_____
_____
_____
_____
_____
_____
_____

A Neighborhood Map

Use the blank map below to show the neighborhood around your school. Label the streets. Use symbols to show where bus stops and other important places are located. Color the map. Don't forget to include a map key.

Map Key

🏫 School

Map

A Community Game

Make a Community Facts game. Play it with a friend.

What to Do

1. Write a question about your community on each card below.
2. Write the answer to each question in the answer box.
3. Cut out the cards.

How to Play

1. Exchange cards with a partner.
2. Take turns reading questions and giving answers.
3. You get ten points for each right answer. The person with the most points wins!

Questions About Your Community

Answer Box

Question 1: _____

1. _____

Question 2: _____

2. _____

Question 3: _____

3. _____

Question 4: _____

4. _____

CREDITS

COVER: Pentagram

PHOTOGRAPHY CREDITS: All photographs are by the Macmillan/McGraw-Hill School Division (MMSD) and Doug David for MMSD, Scott Harvey for MMSD, Ken Karp for MMSD, David Mager for MMSD, Anne Nielson for MMSD, and Monica Stevenson for MMSD.

ART CREDIT: Bulletin Boards: Andrea Maginnis